Microsoft® Office

Word 2003

COMPREHENSIVE

Microsoft® Office

Word 2003

COMPREHENSIVE

ROBERT T.
GRAUER
UNIVERSITY OF MIAMI

MARYANN
BARBER
UNIVERSITY OF MIAMI

PEARSON

Prentice
Hall

**Upper Saddle River,
New Jersey 07458**

Library of Congress Cataloging-in-Publication Data

Grauer, Robert T.
  Microsoft Office Word 2003 / Robert T. Grauer, Maryann Barber.
    p. cm. -- (The exploring Office series)
  Includes index.
  ISBN 0-13-143490-X
  1. Microsoft Word. 2. Word processing.   I. Barber, Maryann M. II. Title. III. Series.
Z52.5.M52G748 2004
005.52--dc22   2003068917

Executive Acquisitions Editor: Jodi McPherson
VP/ Publisher: Natalie E. Anderson
Senior Project Manager, Editorial: Eileen Clark
Editorial Assistants: Brian Hoehl, Alana Meyers, and Sandy Bernales
Media Project Manager: Cathleen Profitko
Marketing Manager: Emily Williams Knight
Marketing Assistant: Lisa Taylor
Project Manager, Production: Lynne Breitfeller
Production Editor: Greg Hubit
Associate Director, Manufacturing: Vincent Scelta
Manufacturing Buyer: Lynne Breitfeller
Design Manager: Maria Lange
Interior Design: Michael J. Fruhbeis
Cover Design: Michael J. Fruhbeis
Cover Printer: Phoenix Color
Composition and Project Management: The GTS Companies
Printer/Binder: Banta Menasha

10 9 8 7 6 5 4
ISBN 0-13-143490-X spiral
ISBN 0-13-145192-8 adhesive

To Marion —
my wife, my lover, and my best friend

Robert Grauer

To Frank —
I love you

To Holly —
for being my friend

Maryann Barber

What does this logo mean?

It means this courseware has been approved by the Microsoft® Office Specialist Program to be among the finest available for learning **Microsoft Word 2003**. It also means that upon completion of this courseware, you may be prepared to take an exam for Microsoft Office Specialist qualification.

What is a Microsoft Office Specialist?

A Microsoft Office Specialist is an individual who has passed exams for certifying his or her skills in one or more of the Microsoft Office desktop applications such as Microsoft Word, Microsoft Excel, Microsoft PowerPoint, Microsoft Outlook, Microsoft Access, or Microsoft Project. The Microsoft Office Specialist Program typically offers certification exams at the "Specialist" and "Expert" skill levels.* The Microsoft Office Specialist Program is the only program approved by Microsoft for testing proficiency in Microsoft Office desktop applications and Microsoft Project. This testing program can be a valuable asset in any job search or career advancement.

More Information:

To learn more about becoming a Microsoft Office Specialist, visit www.microsoft.com/officespecialist

To learn about other Microsoft Office Specialist approved courseware from Pearson Education visit www.prenhall.com

---

*The availability of Microsoft Office Specialist certification exams varies by application, application version, and language. Visit www.microsoft.com/officespecialist for exam availability.

Microsoft, the Microsoft Office Logo, PowerPoint, and Outlook are trademarks or registered trademarks of Microsoft Corporation in the United States and/or other countries, and the Microsoft Office Specialist Logo is used under license from owner.

Contents

MICROSOFT® OFFICE WORD 2003

one

Microsoft Word: What Will Word Processing Do for Me?   1

two

Gaining Proficiency: Editing and Formatting   49

three

Enhancing a Document: The Web and Other Resources   103

four

Advanced Features: Outlines, Tables, Styles, and Sections   153

five

Desktop Publishing: Creating a Newsletter and Other Documents   209

six

Introduction to HTML: Creating a Home Page and a Web Site   257

seven

The Expert User: Workgroups, Forms, Master Documents, and Macros 295

MICROSOFT® WINDOWS® XP

Getting Started with Microsoft® Windows® XP

Getting Started with VBA: Extending Microsoft Office 2003   1

Preface

Continuing a tradition of excellence, Prentice Hall is proud to announce the new *Exploring Microsoft Office 2003* series by Robert T. Grauer and Maryann Barber. The hands-on approach and conceptual framework of this comprehensive series helps students master all aspects of the Microsoft Office 2003 software, while providing the background necessary to transfer and use these skills in their personal and professional lives.

The entire series has been revised to include the new features found in the Office 2003 Suite, which contains Word 2003, Excel 2003, Access 2003, PowerPoint 2003, Publisher 2003, FrontPage 2003, and Outlook 2003.

In addition, this edition includes fully revised end-of-chapter material that provides an extensive review of concepts and techniques discussed in the chapter. Each chapter now begins with an *introductory case study* to provide an effective overview of what the reader will be able to accomplish, with additional *mini cases* at the end of each chapter for practice and review. The conceptual content within each chapter has been modified as appropriate and numerous end-of-chapter exercises have been added.

The new *visual design* introduces the concept of *perfect pages*, whereby every step in every hands-on exercise, as well as every end-of-chapter exercise, begins at the top of its own page and has its own screen shot. This clean design allows for easy navigation throughout the text.

Continuing the success of the website provided for previous editions of this series, Exploring Office 2003 offers expanded resources that include online, interactive study guides, data file downloads, technology updates, additional case studies and exercises, and other helpful information. Start out at www.prenhall.com/grauer to explore these resources!

Organization of the Exploring Office 2003 Series

The new Exploring Microsoft Office 2003 series includes five combined Office 2003 texts from which to choose:

- *Volume I* is Microsoft Office Specialist certified in each of the core applications in the Office suite (Word, Excel, Access, and PowerPoint). Five additional modules (*Essential Computing Concepts, Getting Started with Windows XP, The Internet and the World Wide Web, Getting Started with Outlook,* and *Integrated Case Studies*) are also included. *Volume I Enhanced Edition* adds 18 new chapter-opening case studies, two new integrated case studies, 30 additional end-of-chapter problems, and 20 new mini cases to the existing Volume I.

- *Volume II* picks up where Volume I leaves off, covering the advanced topics for the individual applications. A *Getting Started with VBA* module has been added.

- The *Plus Edition* extends the coverage of Access and Excel to six and seven chapters, respectively (as opposed to four chapters each in Volume I). It also maintains the same level of coverage for PowerPoint and Word as in Volume I so that both applications are Microsoft Office Specialist certified. The Plus Edition includes a new module on XML but does not contain the Essential Computing Concepts or Internet modules.

- The *Brief Microsoft Office 2003* edition provides less coverage of the core applications than Volume I (a total of 10 chapters as opposed to 18). It also includes the *Getting Started with Windows XP* and *Getting Started with Outlook* modules.

- *Getting Started with Office 2003* contains the first chapter from each application (Word, Excel, Access, and PowerPoint), plus three additional modules: *Getting Started with Windows XP, The Internet and the World Wide Web,* and *Essential Computing Concepts.*

Individual texts for Word 2003, Excel 2003, Access 2003, and PowerPoint 2003 provide complete coverage of the application and are Microsoft Office Specialist certified. For shorter courses, we have created brief versions of the Exploring texts that give students a four-chapter introduction to each application. Each of these volumes is Microsoft Office Specialist certified at the Specialist level.

This series has been approved by Microsoft to be used in preparation for Microsoft Office Specialist exams.

The Microsoft Office Specialist program is globally recognized as the standard for demonstrating desktop skills with the Microsoft Office suite of business productivity applications (Microsoft Word, Microsoft Excel, Microsoft PowerPoint, Microsoft Access, and Microsoft Outlook). With a Microsoft Office Specialist certification, thousands of people have demonstrated increased productivity and have proved their ability to utilize the advanced functionality of these Microsoft applications.

By encouraging individuals to develop advanced skills with Microsoft's leading business desktop software, the Microsoft Office Specialist program helps fill the demand for qualified, knowledgeable people in the modern workplace. At the same time, Microsoft Office Specialist helps satisfy an organization's need for a qualitative assessment of employee skills.

Instructor and Student Resources

The **Instructor's CD** that accompanies the Exploring Office series contains:

- Student data files
- Solutions to all exercises and problems
- PowerPoint lectures
- Instructor's manuals in Word format that enable the instructor to annotate portions of the instructor manuals for distribution to the class
- Instructors may also use our *test creation software,* TestGen and QuizMaster. TestGen is a test generator program that lets you view and easily edit test-bank questions, create tests, and print in a variety of formats suitable to your teaching situation. Exams can be easily uploaded into WebCT, BlackBoard, and CourseCompass. QuizMaster allows students to take the tests created with TestGen on a local area network.

Prentice Hall's Companion Website at www.prenhall.com/grauer offers expanded IT resources and downloadable supplements. This site also includes an online study guide for students containing true/false and multiple choice questions and practice projects.

WebCT www.prenhall.com/webct

Gold level customer support available exclusively to adopters of Prentice Hall courses is provided free-of-charge upon adoption and provides you with priority assistance, training discounts, and dedicated technical support.

Blackboard www.prenhall.com/blackboard

Prentice Hall's abundant online content, combined with Blackboard's popular tools and interface, result in robust Web-based courses that are easy to implement, manage, and use—taking your courses to new heights in student interaction and learning.

CourseCompass www.coursecompass.com

CourseCompass is a dynamic, interactive online course management tool powered by Blackboard. This exciting product allows you to teach with marketing-leading Pearson Education content in an easy-to-use, customizable format.

Training and Assessment www2.phgenit.com/support

Prentice Hall offers Performance Based Training and Assessment in one product, Train&Assess IT. The Training component offers computer-based training that a student can use to preview, learn, and review Microsoft Office application skills. Web or CD-ROM delivered, Train IT offers interactive multimedia, computer-based training to augment classroom learning. Built-in prescriptive testing suggests a study path based not only on student test results but also on the specific textbook chosen for the course.

The Assessment component offers computer-based testing that shares the same user interface as Train IT and is used to evaluate a student's knowledge about specific topics in Word, Excel, Access, PowerPoint, Windows, Outlook, and the Internet. It does this in a task-oriented, performance-based environment to demonstrate proficiency as well as comprehension on the topics by the students. More extensive than the testing in Train IT, Assess IT offers more administrative features for the instructor and additional questions for the student.

Assess IT also allows professors to test students out of a course, place students in appropriate courses, and evaluate skill sets.

New! Each chapter now begins with an introductory case study to provide an effective overview of what students will accomplish by completing the chapter.

CHAPTER

1

Getting Started with Microsoft® Windows® XP

OBJECTIVES

After reading this chapter you will:

1. Describe the Windows desktop.
2. Use the Help and Support Center to obtain information.
3. Describe the My Computer and My Documents folders.
4. Differentiate between a program file and a data file.
5. Download a file from the Exploring Office Web site.
6. Copy and/or move a file from one folder to another.
7. Delete a file, and then recover it from the Recycle Bin.
8. Create and arrange shortcuts on the desktop.
9. Use the Search Companion.
10. Use the My Pictures and My Music folders.
11. Use Windows Messenger for instant messaging.

hands-on exercises

1. WELCOME TO WINDOWS XP
   Input: None
   Output: None

2. DOWNLOAD PRACTICE FILES
   Input: Data files from the Web
   Output: Welcome to Windows XP (a Word document)

3. WINDOWS EXPLORER
   Input: Data files from exercise 2
   Output: Screen Capture within a Word document

4. INCREASING PRODUCTIVITY
   Input: Data files from exercise 3
   Output: None

5. FUN WITH WINDOWS XP
   Input: None
   Output: None

CASE STUDY
UNFORESEEN CIRCUMSTANCES

Steve and his wife Shelly have poured their life savings into the dream of owning their own business, a "nanny" service agency. They have spent the last two years building their business and have created a sophisticated database with numerous entries for both families and nannies. The database is the key to their operation. Now that it is up and running, Steve and Shelly are finally at a point where they could hire someone to manage the operation on a part-time basis so that they could take some time off together.

Unfortunately, their process for selecting a person they could trust with their business was not as thorough as it should have been. Nancy, their new employee, assured them that all was well, and the couple left for an extended weekend. The place was in shambles on their return. Nancy could not handle the responsibility, and when Steve gave her two weeks' notice, neither he nor his wife thought that the unimaginable would happen. On her last day in the office Nancy "lost" all of the names in the database—the data was completely gone!

Nancy claimed that a "virus" knocked out the database, but after spending nearly $1,500 with a computer consultant, Steve was told that it had been cleverly deleted from the hard drive and could not be recovered. Of course, the consultant asked Steve and Shelly about their backup strategy, which they sheepishly admitted did not exist. They had never experienced any problems in the past, and simply assumed that their data was safe. Fortunately, they do have hard copy of the data in the form of various reports that were printed throughout the time they were in business. They have no choice but to manually reenter the data.

Your assignment is to read the chapter, paying special attention to the information on file management. Think about how Steve and Shelly could have avoided the disaster if a backup strategy had been in place, then summarize your thoughts in a brief note to your instructor. Describe the elements of a basic backup strategy. Give several other examples of unforeseen circumstances that can cause data to be lost.

1

New! A listing of the input and output files for each hands-on exercise within the chapter. Students will stay on track with what is to be accomplished.

PERFECT PAGES

hands-on exercise

1   Welcome to Windows XP

Objective   To log on to Windows XP and customize the desktop; to open the My Computer folder; to move and size a window; to format a floppy disk and access the Help and Support Center. Use Figure 7 as a guide.

Step 1:   Log On to Windows XP

■ Turn on the computer and all of the peripheral devices. The floppy drive should be empty prior to starting your machine.

■ Windows XP will load automatically, and you should see a login screen similar to Figure 7a. (It does not matter which version of Windows XP you are using.) The number and names of the potential users and their associated icons will be different on your system.

■ Click the icon for the user account you want to access. You may be prompted for a password, depending on the security options in effect.

Bob

Jessica

Window

To begin, click your user nam...

Click icon for user account to be accessed

Turn off Home Computer

(a) Log On to Windows XP (step 1)

FIGURE 7   Hands-on Exercise 1

USER ACCOUNTS

The available user names are cr... Windows XP, but you can add or d... click Control Panel, switch to the Ca... the desired task, such as creating... then supply the necessary informati... user accounts in a school setting.

10   GETTING STARTED WITH MICROSOFT WINDOWS XP

Each step in the hands-on exercises begins at the top of the page to ensure that students can easily navigate through the text.

Step 2:   Choose the Theme and Start Menu

■ Check with your instructor to see if you are able to modify the desktop and other settings at your school or university. If your network administrator has disabled these commands, skip this step and go to step 3.

■ Point to a blank area on the desktop, click the **right mouse button** to display a context-sensitive menu, then click the **Properties command** to open the Display Properties dialog box. Click the **Themes tab** and select the **Windows XP theme** if it is not already selected. Click **OK**.

■ We prefer to work without any wallpaper (background picture) on the desktop. **Right click** the desktop, click **Properties**, then click the **Desktop tab** in the Display Properties dialog box. Click **None** as shown in Figure 7b, then click **OK**. The background disappears.

■ The Start menu is modified independently of the theme. **Right click** a blank area of the taskbar, click the **Properties command** to display the Taskbar and Start Menu Properties dialog box, then click the **Start Menu tab**.

■ Click the **Start Menu option button**. Click **OK**.

Click Desktop tab

Click right mouse button to display shortcut menu

Click None

Right click blank area on taskbar

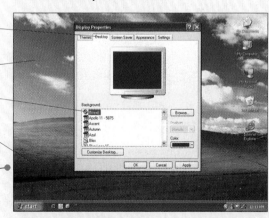

(b) Choose the Theme and Start Menu (step 2)

FIGURE 7   Hands-on Exercise 1 *(continued)*

IMPLEMENT A SCREEN SAVER

A screen saver is a delightful way to personalize your computer and a good way to practice with basic commands in Windows XP. Right click a blank area of the desktop, click the Properties command to open the Display Properties dialog box, then click the Screen Saver tab. Click the down arrow in the Screen Saver list box, choose the desired screen saver, then set the option to wait an appropriate amount of time before the screen saver appears. Click OK to accept the settings and close the dialog box.

New! Larger screen shots with clear callouts.

Boxed tips provide students with additional information.

GETTING STARTED WITH MICROSOFT WINDOWS XP   11

MINI CASES AND PRACTICE EXERCISES

MINI CASES

The Financial Consultant

A friend of yours is in the process of buying a home and has asked you to compare the payments and total interest on a 15- and 30-year loan at varying interest rates. You have decided to analyze the loans in Excel, and then incorporate the results into a memo written in Microsoft Word. As of now, the principal is $150,000, but it is very likely that your friend will change his mind several times, and so you want to use the linking and embedding capability within Windows to dynamically link the worksheet to the word processing document. Your memo should include a letterhead that takes advantage of the formatting capabilities within Word; a graphic logo would be a nice touch.

Fun with the If Statement

Open the *Chapter 4 Mini Case—Fun with the If Statement* workbook in the Exploring Excel folder, then follow the directions in the worksheet to view a hidden message. The message is displayed by various If statements scattered throughout the worksheet, but the worksheet is protected so that you cannot see these formulas. (Use help to see how to protect a worksheet.) We made it easy for you, however, because you can unprotect the worksheet since a password is not required. Once the worksheet is unprotected, pull down the Format menu, click the Cells command, click the Protection tab, and clear the Hidden check box. Prove to your professor that you have done this successfully, by changing the text of our message. Print the completed worksheet to show both displayed values and cell formulas.

The Lottery

Many states raise money through lotteries that advertise prizes of several million dollars. In reality, however, the actual value of the prize is considerably less than the advertised value, although the winners almost certainly do not care. One state, for example, recently offered a twenty million dollar prize that was to be distributed in twenty annual payments of one million dollars each. How much was the prize actually worth, assuming a long-term interest rate of five percent? Use the PV (Present Value) function to determine the answer. What is the effect on the answer if payments to the recipient are made at the beginning of each year, rather than at the end of each year?

A Penny a Day

What if you had a rich u[...]
salary each day for the m[...]
prised at how quickly th[...]
use the Goal Seek comm[...]
(if any) will your uncle p[...]
uncle pay you on the 31s[...]

The Rule of 72

Delaying your IRA for on[...]
on when you begin. Tha[...]
a calculator, using the "R[...]
long it takes money to [...]
money earning 8% annu[...]
money doubles again in [...]
your IRA at age 21, rathe[...]
initial contribution. Use[...]
lose, assuming an 8% ra[...]
determine the exact amo[...]

PRACTICE WITH EXCEL

1. **Theme Park Admissions:** A partially completed version of the worksheet in Figure 3.13 is available in the Exploring Excel folder as *Chapter 3 Practice 1*. Follow the directions in parts (a) and (b) to compute the totals and format the worksheet, then create each of the charts listed below.

   a. Use the AutoSum command to enter the formulas to compute the total number of admissions for each region and each quarter.

   b. Select the entire worksheet (cells A1 through F8), then use the AutoFormat command to format the worksheet. You do not have to accept the entire design, nor do you have to use the design we selected. You can also modify the design after it has been applied to the worksheet by changing the font size of selected cells and/or changing boldface and italics.

   c. Create a column chart showing the total number of admissions in each quarter as shown in Figure 3.13. Add the graphic shown in the figure for emphasis.

   d. Create a pie chart that shows the percentage of the total number of admissions in each region. Create this chart in its own chart sheet with an appropriate name.

   e. Create a stacked column chart that shows the total number of admissions for each region and the contribution of each quarter within each region. Create this chart in its own chart sheet with an appropriate name.

   f. Create a stacked column chart showing the total number of admissions for each quarter and the contribution of each region within each quarter. Create this chart in its own chart sheet with an appropriate name.

   g. Change the color of each of the worksheet tabs.

   h. Print the entire workbook, consisting of the worksheet in Figure 3.13 plus the three additional sheets that you create. Use portrait orientation for the Sales Data worksheet and landscape orientation for the other worksheets. Create a custom header for each worksheet that includes your name, your course, and your instructor's name. Create a custom footer for each worksheet that includes the name of the worksheet. Submit the completed assignment to your instructor.

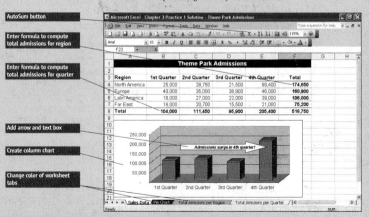

FIGURE 3.13   Theme Park Admissions (exercise 1)

INTEGRATED CASE STUDIES

New!

Each case study contains multiple exercises that use Microsoft Office applications in conjunction with one another.

CASE STUDY 1

Integrated Case Study:
The Totally Fit Wellness Center

OBJECTIVES

1. Use the core applications in Office 2003 individually or in conjunction with one another.
2. Link an Excel chart to a Word document and a PowerPoint presentation.
3. Import an Excel worksheet into an Access database.
4. Create Access tables, queries, reports, and forms.
5. Use an Access table as the basis for a mail merge.
6. Use Word to create a Web page for the organization.

integrated exercises

1. Totally Fit Revenue Workbook and Chart (Excel)
2. Report to the President (Word and Excel)
3. Presentation to the President (PowerPoint and Excel)
4. Last-minute Change (Word, Excel, and PowerPoint)
5. Importing Data (Access and Excel)
6. A Relational Database (Access)
7. Access Objects: Forms, Queries, and Reports (Access)
8. An Access Switchboard (Access)
9. Mail Merge (Word and Access)
10. Worksheet References (Excel)
11. Presentation to the Board (PowerPoint and Excel)
12. Letter to the Board (Word and Excel)
13. Create a Home Page (Word)
14. Submission Checklist (Word)

This document provides a series of 13 exercises in Microsoft Office that relate to the Totally Fit Wellness Center, a health center such as might exist at your school or university. Each exercise describes a specific task for the organization to accomplish and typically requires the use of multiple applications within Microsoft Office for solution. Many of the exercises are cumulative in nature. You may, for example, be asked to create an Excel chart in one exercise, and then incorporate that chart into a Word memo and a PowerPoint presentation in subsequent exercises. Other exercises will ask you to create or modify an Access database, to exchange data between Excel and Access, and to create a Web page for the Wellness Center. Collectively, you will gain considerable expertise in the core applications of Microsoft Office 2003, and especially in how they work together to accomplish complex tasks.

All of the exercises are based on material from the core application chapters in *Exploring Office 2003 Volume I*. Specific chapter references are deliberately not provided so that the case study is as realistic as possible. Think of this assignment as your first day on the job; you were hired by the Wellness Center because you are proficient in Microsoft Office. This is your chance to show what you know.

Your assignment is to follow the directions of your instructor with respect to which of the exercises you are to complete within the case description. You should begin by downloading the practice files from our Web site at www.prenhall.com/grauer. Go to the site, click the book icon for Office 2003, and then click the Students Download tab. Scroll until you can select the link to Integrated Case Studies, and then download the file to your desktop. Double click the file icon and follow the onscreen instructions to install the practice files on your computer. The files you need will be in the Totally Fit folder within the Exploring Integrated Cases folder.

integrated exercises

4. **Last-minute Change (Word, Excel, and PowerPoint):** It was just discovered that the revenue from a few new memberships was not included in the original workbook. Your task is to correct all of the documents that reflect this information. Open the completed *Totally Fit Revenue Solution* workbook from exercise 1.

   a. Click in cell E3 and change the revenue for the Bronze Plan in the fourth quarter to $2,750. Click in cell E4 and change the value of this cell to $5,700. The row and column totals change automatically in the worksheet as do the associated charts. Save the workbook. Exit Excel.

   b. Open the *Report to the President Solution* document from the second exercise. The worksheet and chart should be updated automatically to reflect the corrected revenue data. (The total revenue is now $95,900.) If either the worksheet or the chart is not updated, right click the object to display a context-sensitive menu and click the Update Link command. If the chart is still not updated, right click the object, click the Linked Worksheet (or Chart) Object command, then click the Links command to display the Links dialog box where you can check the source (folder) of the linked objects.

   c. Click at the beginning of the opening paragraph in the memo and enter the new text, which is shown in bold italic in Figure 4. Save and print the completed report. Exit Word.

   d. Start PowerPoint. Open the *Presentation to the President Solution* that you created earlier. PowerPoint detects that a change has been made in the underlying workbook and prompts you to update. Click the button to update the links.

   e. Change to the Slide Sorter view. Press and hold the Shift key as you select the slides containing the Excel worksheet and chart. Pull down the File menu, click the Print command, and print the selection (these two slides) as audience handouts, two slides per page. (Be sure to check the box to frame the slides.)

   f. Save the presentation. Exit PowerPoint.

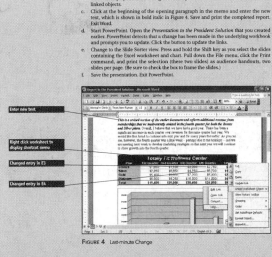

FIGURE 4 Last-minute Change

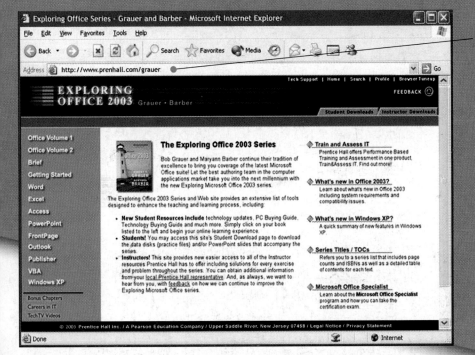

Companion Web site

New!

Updated and enhanced Companion Web site. Find everything you need— student practice files, PowerPoint lectures, online study guides, and instructor support (solutions)!

www.prenhall.com/grauer

Acknowledgments

We want to thank the many individuals who have helped to bring this project to fruition. Jodi McPherson, executive acquisitions editor at Prentice Hall, has provided new leadership in extending the series to Office 2003. Cathi Profitko did an absolutely incredible job on our Web site. Shelly Martin was the creative force behind the chapter-opening case studies. Emily Knight coordinated the marketing and continues to inspire us with suggestions for improving the series. Greg Hubit has been masterful as the external production editor for every book in the series from its inception. Eileen Clark coordinated the myriad details of production and the certification process. Lynne Breitfeller was the project manager and manufacturing buyer. Lori Johnson was the project manager at The GTS Companies and in charge of composition. Chuck Cox did his usual fine work as copyeditor. Melissa Edwards was the supplements editor. Cindy Stevens, Tom McKenzie, and Michael Olmstead wrote the instructor manuals. Michael Fruhbeis developed the innovative and attractive design. We also want to acknowledge our reviewers who, through their comments and constructive criticism, greatly improved the series.

Gregg Asher, Minnesota State University
Lynne Band, Middlesex Community College
Don Belle, Central Piedmont Community College
Stuart P. Brian, Holy Family College
Carl M. Briggs, Indiana University School of Business
Kimberly Chambers, Scottsdale Community College
Jill Chapnick, Florida International University
Alok Charturvedi, Purdue University
Jerry Chin, Southwest Missouri State University
Charles Cole, East Stroudsburg University
Dean Combellick, Scottsdale Community College
Cody Copeland, Johnson County Community College
Larry S. Corman, Fort Lewis College
Janis Cox, Tri-County Technical College
Douglas Cross, Clackamas Community College
Martin Crossland, Southwest Missouri State University
Bill Daley, University of Oregon
Paul E. Daurelle, Western Piedmont Community College
Shawna DePlonty, Sault College of Applied Arts and Technology
Carolyn DiLeo, Westchester Community College
Judy Dolan, Palomar College
David Douglas, University of Arkansas
Carlotta Eaton, Radford University
Cheryl J. Fetterman, Cape Fear Community College
Judith M. Fitspatrick, Gulf Coast Community College
James Franck, College of St. Scholastica
Raymond Frost, Central Connecticut State University
Susan Fry, Boise State University
Midge Gerber, Southwestern Oklahoma State University
James Gips, Boston College
Vernon Griffin, Austin Community College
Ranette Halverson, Midwestern State University
Michael Hassett, Fort Hays State University
Mike Hearn, Community College of Philadelphia
Wanda D. Heller, Seminole Community College

Bonnie Homan, San Francisco State University
Ernie Ivey, Polk Community College
Walter Johnson, Community College of Philadelphia
Mike Kelly, Community College of Rhode Island
Jane King, Everett Community College
Rose M. Laird, Northern Virginia Community College
David Langley, University of Oregon
John Lesson, University of Central Florida
Maurie Lockley, University of North Carolina at Greensboro
Daniela Marghitu, Auburn University
David B. Meinert, Southwest Missouri State University
Alan Moltz, Naugatuck Valley Technical Community College
Kim Montney, Kellogg Community College
Bill Morse, DeVry Institute of Technology
Kevin Pauli, University of Nebraska
Mary McKenry Percival, University of Miami
Marguerite Nedreberg, Youngstown State University
Dr. Francisca Norales, Tennessee State University
Jim Pruitt, Central Washington University
Delores Pusins, Hillsborough Community College
Gale E. Rand, College Misericordia
Judith Rice, Santa Fe Community College
David Rinehard, Lansing Community College
Marilyn Salas, Scottsdale Community College
Herach Safarian, College of the Canyons
John Shepherd, Duquesne University
Barbara Sherman, Buffalo State College
Robert Spear, Prince George's Community College
Michael Stewardson, San Jacinto College—North
Helen Stoloff, Hudson Valley Community College
Margaret Thomas, Ohio University
Mike Thomas, Indiana University School of Business
Suzanne Tomlinson, Iowa State University
Karen Tracey, Central Connecticut State University
Antonio Vargas, El Paso Community College
Sally Visci, Lorain County Community College
David Weiner, University of San Francisco
Connie Wells, Georgia State University
Wallace John Whistance-Smith, Ryerson Polytechnic University
Jack Zeller, Kirkwood Community College

A final word of thanks to the unnamed students at the University of Miami who make it all worthwhile. Most of all, thanks to you, our readers, for choosing this book. Please feel free to contact us with any comments and suggestions.

Robert T. Grauer   Maryann Barber
rgrauer@miami.edu   mbarber@miami.edu
www.prenhall.com/grauer

Microsoft® Office

Word 2003

COMPREHENSIVE

Microsoft® Word:
What Will Word Processing Do for Me?

CASE STUDY
THE STUDENT SENATOR

Jim Johnson is a well-known and well-liked freshman who is majoring in political science at your university. As one of his best friends and "political" advisors, you often engage in discussions about his political aspirations, particularly as they relate to the university. Jim has recently decided to run for student senator, and he has asked you to help him write the personal statement section of the application. The objective of the personal statement is to explain why an individual wants to become a student senator and to describe the skills and experience he or she would bring to the position.

Jim is a bright guy with great ideas and lofty goals, and has most of what it takes to succeed; he just needs a bit of help when it comes to expressing himself on paper. His request reminds you of the time in high school when you wrote several of his speeches, before and after he became student body president. It seems that ever since, Jim has expected you to polish his writing, whether it applies to politics or not. Although you know Jim well enough to write the statement for him, you think it high time that he do his own writing and thus you offer to edit his personal statement instead of simply writing it for him. Moreover, you have just discovered the Track Changes command in Microsoft Word and will do the editing electronically.

Your assignment is to read the chapter, paying special attention to Hands-on Exercises 2 and 3 that describe how to modify an existing document, and how to use the spell check, grammar check, and thesaurus in Microsoft Word. You will then open the document, *Chapter 1 Case Study—The Student Senator*, which is Jim's first attempt at writing his own personal statement. Pull down the Tools menu and toggle the Track Changes command on to record your changes, and then modify the document as you see fit to create the best personal statement for Jim to submit. Basic formatting is also important. Print a copy of the corrected document for your instructor to prove that you've solved the problem, and completed the case.

Have you ever produced what you thought was the perfect term paper only to discover that you omitted a sentence or misspelled a word, or that the paper was three pages too short or one page too long? Wouldn't it be nice to make the necessary changes, and then be able to reprint the entire paper with the touch of a key? Welcome to the world of word processing, where you are no longer stuck with having to retype anything. Instead, you retrieve your work from disk, display it on the monitor and revise it as necessary, then print it at any time, in draft or final form.

This chapter provides a broad-based introduction to word processing in general and Microsoft Word in particular. All word processors adhere to certain basic concepts that must be understood if you are to use the programs effectively. The next several pages introduce ideas that are applicable to any word processor (and which you may already know). We follow the conceptual material with a hands-on exercise that enables you to apply what you have learned.

The Insertion Point

The ***insertion point*** is a flashing vertical line that marks the place where text will be entered. The insertion point is always at the beginning of a new document, but it can be moved anywhere within an existing document. If, for example, you wanted to add text to the end of a document, you would move the insertion point to the end of the document, then begin typing.

Word Wrap

A newcomer to word processing has one major transition to make from a typewriter, and it is an absolutely critical adjustment. Whereas a typist returns the carriage at the end of every line, just the opposite is true of a word processor. One types continually *without* pressing the Enter key at the end of a line because the word processor automatically wraps text from one line to the next. This concept is known as ***word wrap*** and is illustrated in Figure 1.1.

The word *primitive* does not fit on the current line in Figure 1.1a, and is automatically shifted to the next line, *without* the user having to press the Enter key. The user continues to enter the document, with additional words being wrapped to subsequent lines as necessary. The only time you use the Enter key is at the end of a paragraph, or when you want the insertion point to move to the next line and the end of the current line doesn't reach the right margin.

Word wrap is closely associated with another concept, that of hard and soft returns. A ***hard return*** is created by the user when he or she presses the Enter key at the end of a paragraph; a ***soft return*** is created by the word processor as it wraps text from one line to the next. The locations of the soft returns change automatically as a document is edited (e.g., as text is inserted or deleted, or as margins or fonts are changed). The locations of the hard returns can be changed only by the user, who must intentionally insert or delete each hard return.

There are two hard returns in Figure 1.1b, one at the end of each paragraph. There are also six soft returns in the first paragraph (one at the end of every line except the last) and three soft returns in the second paragraph. Now suppose the margins in the document are made smaller (that is, the line is made longer) as shown in Figure 1.1c. The number of soft returns drops to four and two (in the first and second paragraphs, respectively) as more text fits on a line and fewer lines are needed. The revised document still contains the two original hard returns, one at the end of each paragraph.

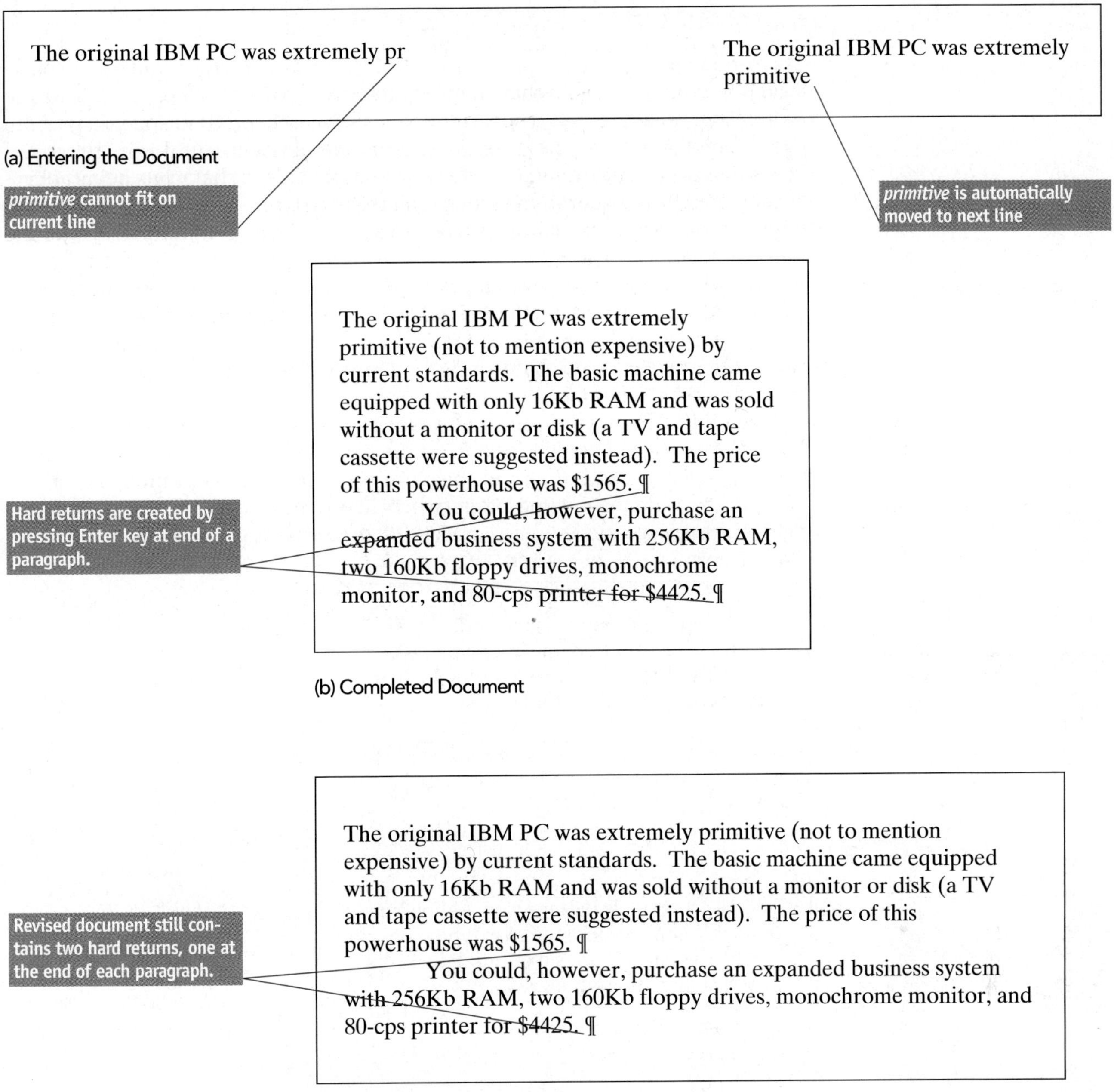

The original IBM PC was extremely pr

The original IBM PC was extremely primitive

(a) Entering the Document

primitive cannot fit on current line

primitive is automatically moved to next line

The original IBM PC was extremely primitive (not to mention expensive) by current standards. The basic machine came equipped with only 16Kb RAM and was sold without a monitor or disk (a TV and tape cassette were suggested instead). The price of this powerhouse was $1565. ¶
You could, however, purchase an expanded business system with 256Kb RAM, two 160Kb floppy drives, monochrome monitor, and 80-cps printer for $4425. ¶

Hard returns are created by pressing Enter key at end of a paragraph.

(b) Completed Document

The original IBM PC was extremely primitive (not to mention expensive) by current standards. The basic machine came equipped with only 16Kb RAM and was sold without a monitor or disk (a TV and tape cassette were suggested instead). The price of this powerhouse was $1565. ¶
You could, however, purchase an expanded business system with 256Kb RAM, two 160Kb floppy drives, monochrome monitor, and 80-cps printer for $4425. ¶

Revised document still contains two hard returns, one at the end of each paragraph.

(c) Completed Document

FIGURE 1.1 Word Wrap

Toggle Switches

Suppose you sat down at the keyboard and typed an entire sentence without pressing the Shift key; the sentence would be in all lowercase letters. Then you pressed the Caps Lock key and retyped the sentence, again without pressing the Shift key. This time the sentence would be in all uppercase letters. You could repeat the process as often as you like. Each time you pressed the Caps Lock key, the sentence would switch from lowercase to uppercase and vice versa.

The point of this exercise is to introduce the concept of a ***toggle switch***, a device that causes the computer to alternate between two states. The Caps Lock key is an example of a toggle switch. Each time you press it, newly typed text will change from uppercase to lowercase and back again. We will see several other examples of toggle switches as we proceed in our discussion of word processing.

Insert versus Overtype

Microsoft Word is always in one of two modes, **insert** or **overtype**, and uses a toggle switch (the Ins key) to alternate between the two. Press the Ins key once and you switch from insert to overtype. Press the Ins key a second time and you go from overtype back to insert. Text that is entered into a document during the insert mode moves existing text to the right to accommodate the characters being added. Text entered from the overtype mode replaces (overtypes) existing text. Regardless of which mode you are in, text is always entered or replaced immediately to the right of the insertion point.

The insert mode is best when you enter text for the first time, but either mode can be used to make corrections. The insert mode is the better choice when the correction requires you to add new text; the overtype mode is easier when you are substituting one or more character(s) for another. The difference between the two is illustrated in Figure 1.2.

Figure 1.2a displays the text as it was originally entered, with two misspellings. The letters *se* have been omitted from the word *insert,* and an *x* has been erroneously typed instead of an *r* in the word *overtype.* The insert mode is used in Figure 1.2b to add the missing letters, which in turn moves the rest of the line to the right. The overtype mode is used in Figure 1.2c to replace the *x* with an *r.*

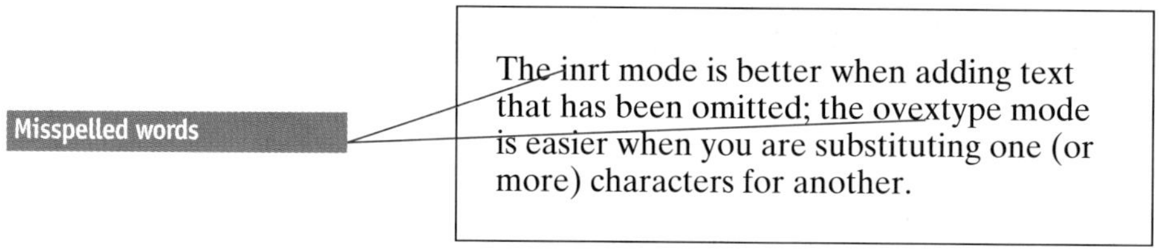

Misspelled words

> The inrt mode is better when adding text that has been omitted; the ovextype mode is easier when you are substituting one (or more) characters for another.

(a) Text to Be Corrected

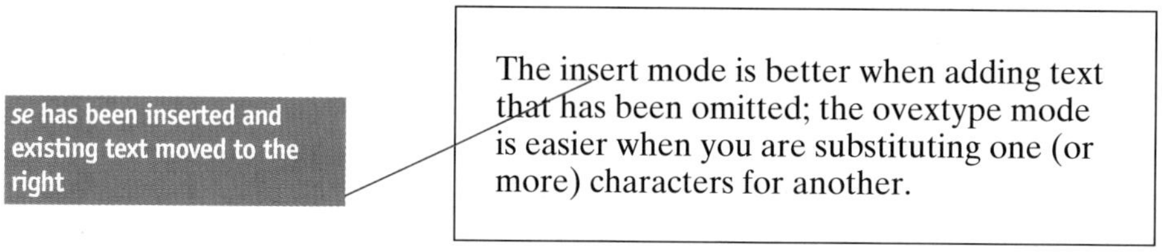

se has been inserted and existing text moved to the right

> The insert mode is better when adding text that has been omitted; the ovextype mode is easier when you are substituting one (or more) characters for another.

(b) Insert Mode

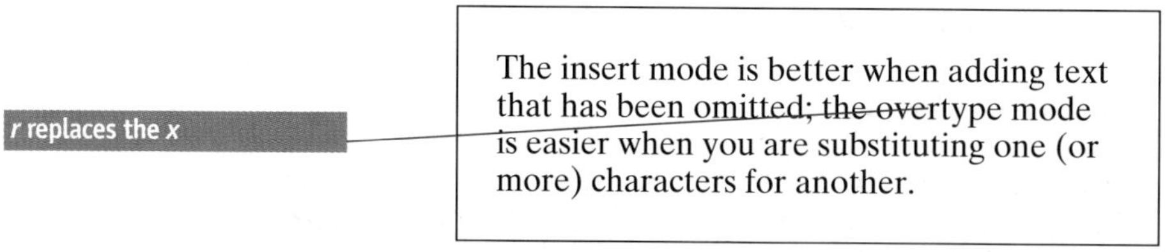

r replaces the x

> The insert mode is better when adding text that has been omitted; the overtype mode is easier when you are substituting one (or more) characters for another.

(c) Overtype Mode

FIGURE 1.2 Insert and Overtype Modes

Deleting Text

The Backspace and Del keys delete one character immediately to the left or right of the insertion point, respectively. The choice between them depends on when you need to erase a character(s). The Backspace key is easier if you want to delete a character (or characters) immediately after typing. The Del key is preferable during subsequent editing.

You can delete several characters at one time by selecting (dragging the mouse over) the characters to be deleted, then pressing the Del key. And finally, you can delete and replace text in one operation by selecting the text to be replaced and then typing the new text in its place.

LEARN TO TYPE

The ultimate limitation of any word processor is the speed at which you enter data; hence the ability to type quickly is invaluable. Learning how to type is easy, especially with the availability of computer-based typing programs. As little as a half hour a day for a couple of weeks will have you up to speed, and if you do any significant amount of writing at all, the investment will pay off many times.

INTRODUCTION TO MICROSOFT WORD

We used Microsoft Word to write this book, as can be inferred from the screen in Figure 1.3. Your screen will be different from ours in many ways. You will not have the same document, nor is it likely that you will customize Word in exactly the same way. You should, however, be able to recognize the basic elements that are found in the Microsoft Word window that is open on the desktop.

There are actually two open windows in Figure 1.3—an application window for Microsoft Word and a document window for the specific document on which you are working. The application window has its own Minimize, Maximize (or Restore), and Close buttons. The document window has only a Close button. However, only one title bar appears at the top of the application window, and it reflects the application (Microsoft Word) as well as the document name (Word Chapter 1). A *menu bar* appears immediately below the title bar. Vertical and horizontal *scroll bars* appear at the right and bottom of the document window.

Microsoft Word is also part of the Microsoft Office suite of applications, and thus shares additional features with Excel, Access, and PowerPoint, that are also part of the Office suite. *Toolbars* provide immediate access to common commands and appear immediately below the menu bar. The toolbars can be displayed or hidden using the Toolbars command in the *View menu*.

The *Standard toolbar* contains buttons corresponding to the most basic commands in Word—for example, opening a file or printing a document. The icon on the button is intended to be indicative of its function (e.g., a printer to indicate the Print command). You can also point to the button to display a *ScreenTip* showing the name of the button. The first several tools and associated keyboard shortcuts (New document, Open, Save, E-mail, and Print) are common to the other applications in Microsoft Office. Thus once you master one application in Microsoft Office, it is that much easier to learn the next.

The *Formatting toolbar* appears under the Standard toolbar and provides access to such common formatting operations as boldface, italics, or underlining. Other tools let you change the font or font size, highlight text, or change its color. Additional buttons enable you to change the alignment and line spacing in a paragraph, add bullets or numbering, and/or box selected text.

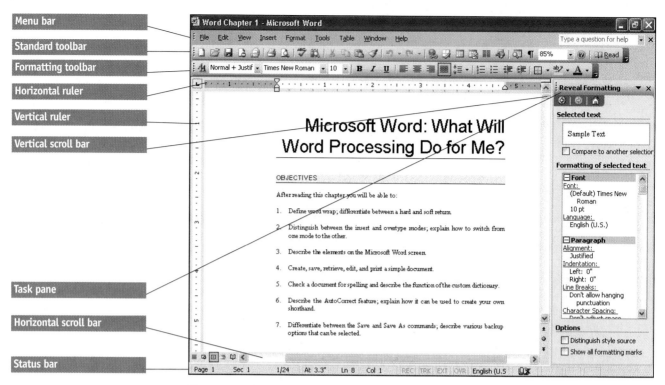

Menu bar

Standard toolbar

Formatting toolbar

Horizontal ruler

Vertical ruler

Vertical scroll bar

Task pane

Horizontal scroll bar

Status bar

FIGURE 1.3 Microsoft Word

The toolbars may appear overwhelming at first, but there is absolutely no need to memorize what the individual buttons do. That will come with time. We suggest, however, that you will have a better appreciation for the various buttons if you consider them in groups, according to their general function, as shown in Figure 1.4a. Note, too, that many of the commands in the pull-down menus are displayed with an image that corresponds to a button on a toolbar.

The ***horizontal ruler*** is displayed underneath the toolbars and enables you to change margins, tabs, and/or indents for all or part of a document. A ***vertical ruler*** shows the vertical position of text on the page and can be used to change the top or bottom margins.

The ***status bar*** at the bottom of the document window displays the location of the insertion point (or information about the command being executed). The status bar also shows the status (settings) of various indicators—for example, OVR to show that Word is in the overtype, as opposed to the insert, mode.

The ***task pane*** at the right of the document window provides access to several basic tasks. Different task panes are displayed at different times, depending on what you want to accomplish. The Home task pane, for example, appears automatically when Word is started initially. It contains links to the last several documents that were opened to facilitate returning to an earlier document. It also provides access to a search command to obtain help on a specific topic.

The task pane can be opened explicitly at any time via the View menu by the user, who may then select a specific task pane by clicking the down arrow in the task pane itself. The Reveal Formatting task pane in Figure 1.3, for example, shows the formatting in effect at the insertion point. It describes the font (typeface) as well as the paragraph. Other task panes include Help, Clip Art, Mail Merge, and Research. You can click the Close button to close the task pane at any time. The task pane may then reopen automatically if it is required by a subsequent command, and/or the user can reopen it at any time.

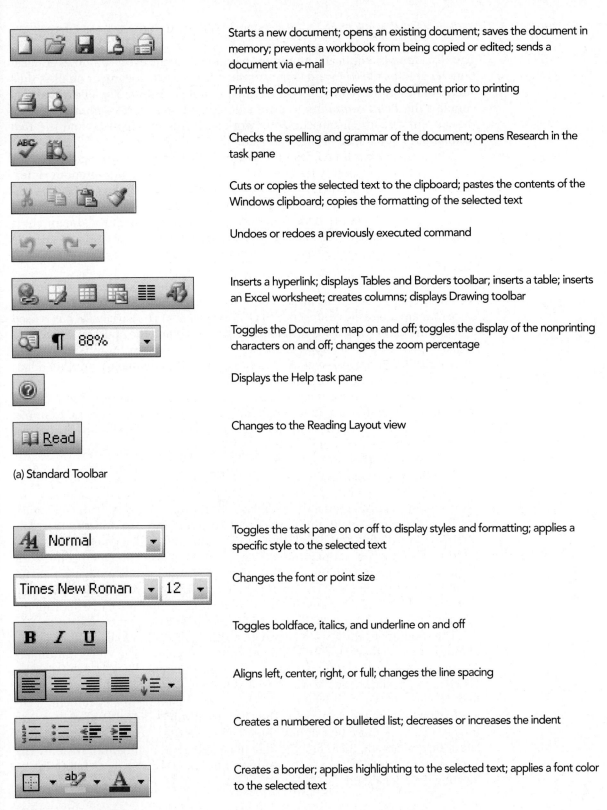

Starts a new document; opens an existing document; saves the document in memory; prevents a workbook from being copied or edited; sends a document via e-mail

Prints the document; previews the document prior to printing

Checks the spelling and grammar of the document; opens Research in the task pane

Cuts or copies the selected text to the clipboard; pastes the contents of the Windows clipboard; copies the formatting of the selected text

Undoes or redoes a previously executed command

Inserts a hyperlink; displays Tables and Borders toolbar; inserts a table; inserts an Excel worksheet; creates columns; displays Drawing toolbar

Toggles the Document map on and off; toggles the display of the nonprinting characters on and off; changes the zoom percentage

Displays the Help task pane

Changes to the Reading Layout view

(a) Standard Toolbar

Toggles the task pane on or off to display styles and formatting; applies a specific style to the selected text

Changes the font or point size

Toggles boldface, italics, and underline on and off

Aligns left, center, right, or full; changes the line spacing

Creates a numbered or bulleted list; decreases or increases the indent

Creates a border; applies highlighting to the selected text; applies a font color to the selected text

(b) Formatting Toolbar

FIGURE 1.4   Toolbars

The File Menu

The **File Menu** is a critically important menu in virtually every Windows application. It contains the Save and Open commands to save a document on disk, then subsequently retrieve (open) that document at a later time. The File Menu also contains the **Print command** to print a document, the **Close command** to close the current document but continue working in the application, and the **Exit command** to quit the application altogether.

The **Save command** copies the document that you are working on (i.e., the document that is currently in memory) to disk. The command functions differently the first time it is executed for a new document, in that it displays the Save As dialog box as shown in Figure 1.5a. The dialog box requires you to specify the name of the document, the drive (and an optional folder) in which the document is stored, and its file type. All subsequent executions of the command will save the document under the assigned name, each time replacing the previously saved version with the new version.

The **file name** (e.g., My First Document) can contain up to 255 characters including spaces, commas, and/or periods. (Periods are discouraged, however, since they are too easily confused with DOS extensions.) The Save In list box is used to select the drive (which is not visible in Figure 1.5a) and the optional folder (e.g., Exploring Word). The **file type** defaults to a Word document. You can, however, choose a different format such as a Web page (HTML document), an XML document, or even a WordPerfect document.

The **Places bar** provides a shortcut to any of the listed folders without having to search through the Save In (or Look In) list box. The desktop icon, for example, saves a file directly to the desktop. My Recent Documents provides links to the last several documents that were opened. My Network Places takes your folders that are contained on other computers to which you have network access.

The **Open command** is the opposite of the Save command as it brings a copy of an existing document into memory, enabling you to work with that document. The Open command displays the Open dialog box in which you specify the file name, the drive (and optionally the folder) that contains the file, and the file type. Microsoft Word will then list all files of that type on the designated drive (and folder), enabling you to open the file you want. The Save and Open commands work in conjunction with one another. The Save As dialog box in Figure 1.5a, for example, saves the file My First Document in the Exploring Word folder. The Open dialog box in Figure 1.5b loads that file into memory so that you can work with the file, after which you can save the revised file for use at a later time.

The toolbars in the Save As and Open dialog boxes have several buttons in common that facilitate the execution of either command. The Views button lets you display the files in either dialog box in several different views. The Details view (in Figure 1.5a) shows the file size as well as the date and time a file was last modified. The Preview view (in Figure 1.5b) shows the beginning of a document, without having to open the document. The List view displays only the file names, and thus lets you see more files at one time. The Properties view shows information about the document, including the date of creation and number of revisions. The Tools button provides access to common file operations such as renaming or deleting the selected file.

Learning by Doing

Every chapter contains a series of hands-on exercises that enable you to apply what you learn at the computer. The exercises in this chapter are linked to one another in that you create a simple document in exercise 1, then open and edit that document in exercise 2. The ability to save and open a document is critical, and you do not want to spend an inordinate amount of time entering text unless you are confident in your ability to retrieve it later.

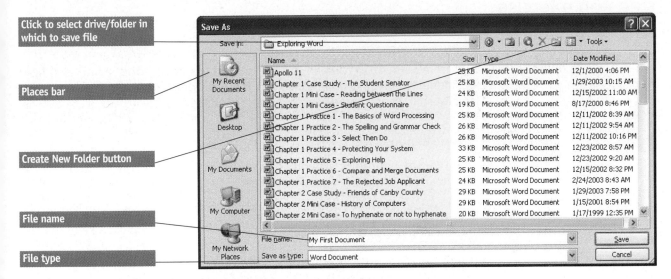

Click to select drive/folder in which to save file

Places bar

Create New Folder button

File name

File type

(a) Save As Dialog Box (Details view)

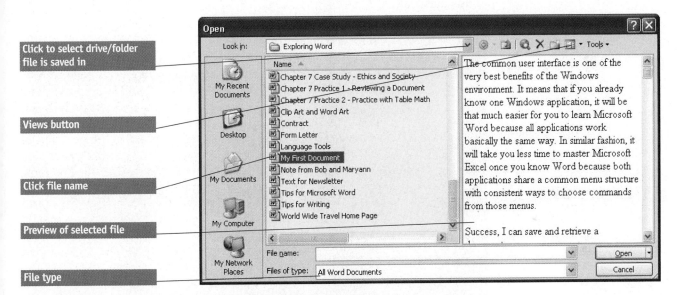

Click to select drive/folder file is saved in

Views button

Click file name

Preview of selected file

File type

(b) Open Dialog Box (Preview view)

FIGURE 1.5   The Save and Open Commands

FILE MANAGEMENT AT YOUR FINGERTIPS

Use the toolbar in the Open and/or Save As dialog boxes to perform basic file management tasks within an Office application. You can select any existing file, then delete it or rename it. You can create a new folder, which is very useful when you begin to work with a large number of documents. Use the Views button to change the way the files are listed within the dialog box.

1 My First Document

Objective To start Microsoft Word in order to create, save, and print a simple document; to execute commands via the toolbar or from pull-down menus. Use Figure 1.6 as a guide in doing the exercise.

Step 1: **Log onto Windows XP**

- Turn on the computer and all of its peripherals. The floppy drive should be empty prior to starting your machine.

- Your system will take a minute or so to get started, after which you should see a logon screen similar to Figure 1.6a. Do not be concerned if the appearance of your desktop is different from ours.

- Click the icon for the user account you want to access. You may be prompted for a password, depending on the security options in effect.

- You should be familiar with basic file management and very comfortable moving and copying files from one folder to another. If not, you may want to review this material.

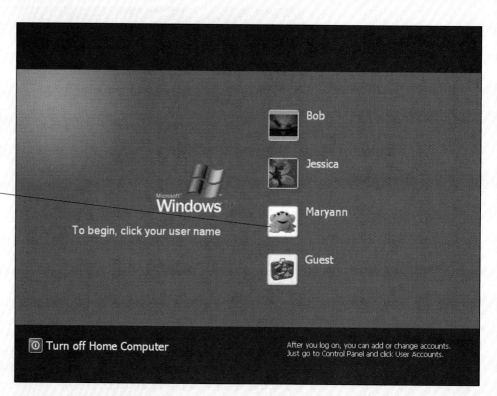

(a) Log onto Windows XP (step 1)

FIGURE 1.6 Hands-on Exercise 1

USER ACCOUNTS

The available user names are created automatically during the installation of Windows XP, but you can add or delete users at any time. Click the Start button, click Control Panel, switch to the Category view, and select User Accounts. Choose the desired task, such as creating a new account or changing an existing account. Do not expect, however, to be able to modify accounts in a school setting.

Step 2: **Obtain the Practice Files**

- Start Internet Explorer and go to **www.prenhall.com/grauer**. Click the book for **Office 2003**, which takes you to the Office 2003 home page. Click the **Student Downloads tab** (near the top of the window) to go to the Student Downloads page as shown in Figure 1.6b.
- Select the appropriate file to download:
  - ❏ Choose **Exploring Word** (or **Word Volume I**) if you are using a stand-alone Word text, as opposed to an Office text with multiple applications.
  - ❏ Choose **Office 2003 Volume I** (for regular or **Enhanced Edition**), **Office 2003 Plus**, or **Office 2003 Brief** if you have an Office text.
- Click the link to download the file. You will see the File Download box asking what you want to do. Click the **Save button**. The Save As dialog box appears.
- Click the **down arrow** in the Save In list box and select the drive and folder where you want to save the file. Click **Save**.
- Start Windows Explorer, select the drive and folder where you saved the file, then double click the file and follow the onscreen instructions.

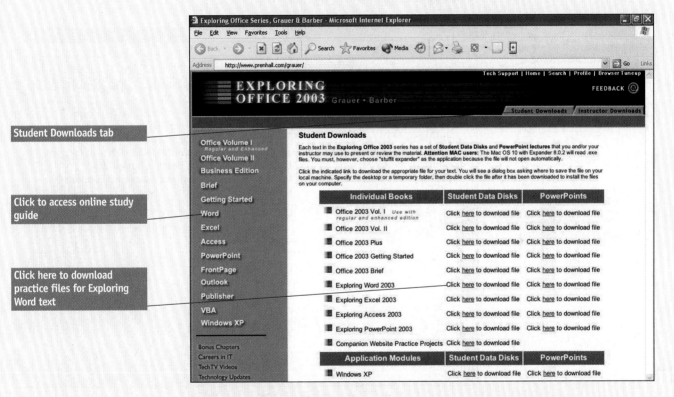

(b) Obtain the Practice Files (step 2)

FIGURE 1.6 Hands-on Exercise 1 (*continued*)

EXPLORE OUR WEB SITE

The Exploring Office Series Web site offers an online study guide (multiple-choice, true/false, and matching questions) for each individual textbook to help you review the material in each chapter. You can take practice quizzes by yourself and/or e-mail the results to your instructor. These online study guides are available via the tabs in the left navigation bar. You can return to the Student Downloads page at any time by clicking the tab toward the top of the window and/or you can click the link to Home to return to the home page for the Office 2003 Series. And finally, you can click the Feedback button at the top of the screen to send a message directly to Bob Grauer.

Step 3: Create a Document

- Click the **Start button** to display the Start menu. Click (or point to) the **All Programs button**, click **Microsoft Office**, then click **Microsoft Word 2003** to start the program.

- You should see a blank document within the Word application window. Close the task pane if it is open.

- Create the document in Figure 1.6c. Type continually from one line to the next; do *not* press the Enter key at the end of each line because Word will automatically wrap text from one line to the next.

- Press the **Enter key** at the end of the paragraph.

- You may see a red or green wavy line to indicate spelling or grammatical errors, respectively. Both features are discussed later in the chapter.

- Point to the red wavy line (if any), click the **right mouse button** to display a list of suggested corrections, then click (select) the appropriate substitution.

- Ignore the green wavy line (if any).

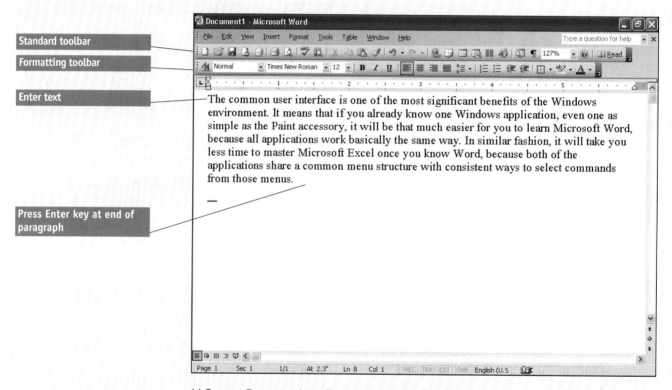

Standard toolbar

Formatting toolbar

Enter text

The common user interface is one of the most significant benefits of the Windows environment. It means that if you already know one Windows application, even one as simple as the Paint accessory, it will be that much easier for you to learn Microsoft Word, because all applications work basically the same way. In similar fashion, it will take you less time to master Microsoft Excel once you know Word, because both of the applications share a common menu structure with consistent ways to select commands from those menus.

Press Enter key at end of paragraph

(c) Create a Document (step 3)

FIGURE 1.6 Hands-on Exercise 1 *(continued)*

SEPARATE THE TOOLBARS

You may see the Standard and Formatting toolbars displayed on one row to save space within the application window. If so, we suggest that you separate the toolbars, so that you see all of the buttons on each. Click the Toolbar Options down arrow that appears at the end of any visible toolbar to display toolbar options, then click the option to show the buttons on two rows. Click the down arrow a second time to show the buttons on one row if you want to return to the other configuration.

Step 4: Save the Document

- Pull down the **File menu** and click **Save** (or click the **Save button** on the Standard toolbar). You should see the Save As dialog box in Figure 1.6d.

- If necessary, click the **drop-down arrow** on the View button and select the **Details view**. To save the file:
  - ❑ Click the **drop-down arrow** on the Save In list box.
  - ❑ Click the appropriate drive, e.g., drive C or drive A.
  - ❑ Double click the **Exploring Word folder** to make it the active folder.
  - ❑ If necessary, click and drag over the default entry in the File name text box. Type **My First Document** as the name of your document.
  - ❑ Click **Save** or press the **Enter key**. The title bar changes to reflect the new document name (My First Document).

- Add your name at the end of the document, then click the **Save button** on the Standard toolbar to save the document with the revision.

- This time the Save As dialog box does not appear, since Word already knows the name of the document.

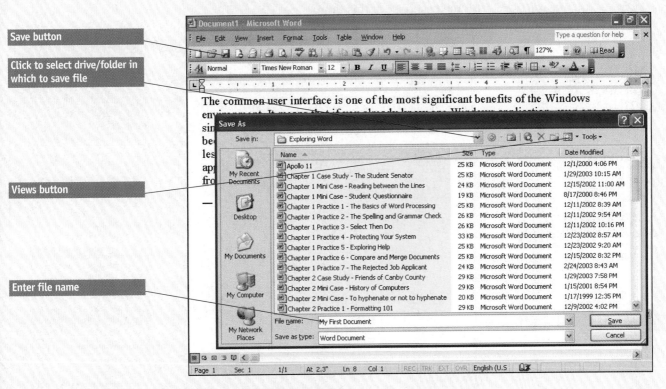

(d) Save the Document (step 4)

FIGURE 1.6 Hands-on Exercise 1 *(continued)*

THE WORD COUNT TOOLBAR

How close are you to completing the 5,000-word paper that your professor assigned? Pull down the Tools menu and click the Word Count command to display a dialog box that shows the number of pages, words, paragraphs, and characters in your document. There is also a command button to display the Word Count toolbar so that it remains on the screen throughout the session. Click the Recount button on the toolbar at any time to see the current statistics for your document.

Step 5: Help with Word

- The best time to obtain help is when you don't need it. Try either of the following:
  - ❏ Pull down the **Help menu** and click the command to **Show the Office Assistant**. Click the **Assistant**, then enter the question, **"How do I get help?"** in the Assistant's balloon and click **Search**, or
  - ❏ Type the question directly in the **Ask a Question box** in the upper right of the Word window and press **Enter**.

- Regardless of the technique you choose, Word will display a message indicating that it is searching the Office Web site for new information.

- You should see a task pane with the results of the search as shown in Figure 1.6e. Click the link that is most appropriate (e.g., About getting help while you work).

- A new window opens containing the detailed help information. Click the **Print button** in the Help window, then click the **Print command button** to print the topic for your instructor.

- Close the Help window. Close the task pane. Pull down the **Help menu** and hide the Office Assistant. Exit Word if you do not want to continue with the next exercise at this time.

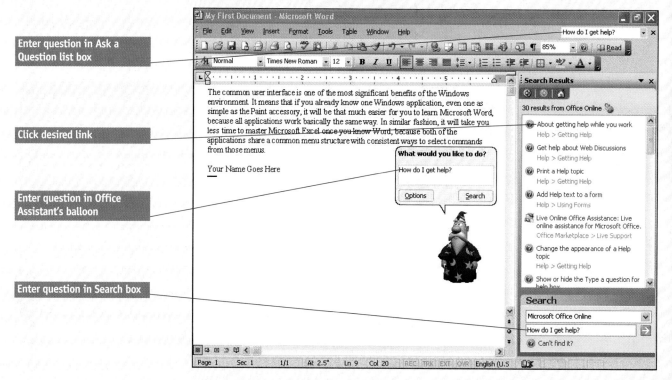

Enter question in Ask a Question list box

Click desired link

Enter question in Office Assistant's balloon

Enter question in Search box

(e) Help with Word (step 5)

FIGURE 1.6   Hands-on Exercise 1 *(continued)*

TIP OF THE DAY

Pull down the Help menu, click the command to show the Office Assistant, click the Office Assistant when it appears, then click the Options button to display the Office Assistant dialog box. Click the Options tab, check the box to Show the Tip of the Day at Startup, and then click OK. The next time you start Word, you will be greeted by the Assistant, who will offer you the tip of the day.

We trust that you completed the hands-on exercise without difficulty, and that you were able to create, save, and print the document in the exercise. There is, however, considerable flexibility in the way you do the exercise in that you can display different toolbars and menus, and/or execute commands in a variety of ways. This section describes various ways in which you can customize Microsoft Word, and in so doing, will help you to troubleshoot future exercises.

Figure 1.7 displays two different views of the same document. Your screen may not match either figure, and indeed, there is no requirement that it should. You should, however, be aware of different options so that you can develop preferences of your own. Consider:

- Figure 1.7a uses short menus (note the double arrow at the bottom of the menu to display additional commands) and a shared row for the Standard and Formatting toolbars. Figure 1.7b displays the full menu and displays the toolbars on separate rows. We prefer the latter settings, which are set through the Customize command in the Tools menu.

- Figure 1.7a shows the Office Assistant (but drags it out of the way), whereas Figure 1.7b hides it. We find the Assistant distracting, and display it only when necessary by pressing the F1 key. You can also use the appropriate option in the Help menu to hide or show the Assistant, and/or you can right click the Assistant to hide it.

- Figure 1.7a shows the document with the task pane open, whereas the task pane is closed in Figure 1.7b. The task pane serves a variety of functions such as opening a document, inserting clip art, creating a mail merge, or displaying the formatting properties of selected text.

- Figure 1.7a displays the document in the *Normal view* whereas Figure 1.7b uses the *Print Layout view*. The Normal view is simpler, but the Print Layout view more closely resembles the printed page as it displays top and bottom margins, headers and footers, graphic elements in their exact position, a vertical ruler, and other elements not seen in the Normal view.

- Figure 1.7a displays the ¶ and other nonprinting symbols, whereas they are hidden in Figure 1.7b. We prefer the cleaner screen without the symbols, but on occasion display the symbols if there is a problem in formatting a document. The *Show/Hide ¶ button* toggles the symbols on or off.

- Figure 1.7b displays an additional toolbar, the Drawing toolbar, at the bottom of the screen. Microsoft Word has more than 20 toolbars that are suppressed or displayed through the Toolbars command in the View menu. Note, too, that you can change the position of any visible toolbar by dragging its move handle (the parallel lines) at the left of the toolbar.

THE READING LAYOUT VIEW

Microsoft Word 2003 introduces the Reading Layout view, which hides the Standard and Formatting toolbars to increase the readability of a document. The pages in a document are presented to fill the screen and do not correspond to the pages as they would appear in the printed version. The Reading Layout view has its own toolbar, which includes buttons to change the font size, display the actual page layout (as it would appear on the printed page), and a Close button to return to the previous view. The Standard toolbar contains a Read button to switch to the Reading Layout. (Word documents sent as e-mail attachments are automatically opened in the Reading Layout View.)

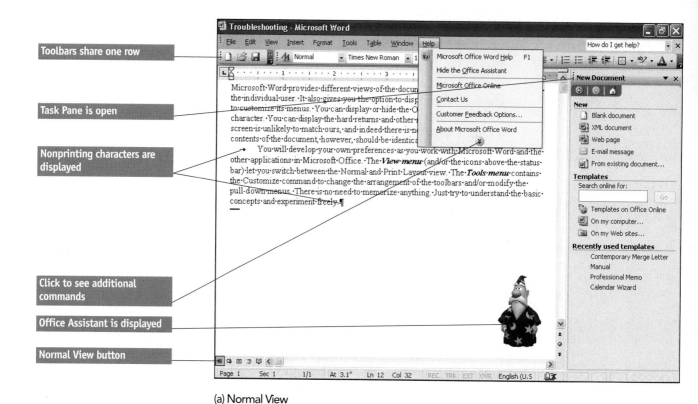

Toolbars share one row

Task Pane is open

Nonprinting characters are displayed

Click to see additional commands

Office Assistant is displayed

Normal View button

(a) Normal View

Toolbars displayed on two rows

Show/Hide button

Top margin is displayed

Vertical ruler

Print Layout View button

Drawing toolbar

(b) Print Layout View

FIGURE 1.7   Troubleshooting

INTRODUCTION TO FORMATTING

The most important task in creating a document is to focus on its content. Once the document is written, however, you can improve its appearance through *formatting*, which is accomplished through the concept of *select then do*. This means that you select a block of text, and then you execute the appropriate formatting command. (The select then do concept also applies to editing commands.) Text can be selected in several ways, the most basic of which is to click and drag over the desired characters. The text continues to be selected until you click elsewhere in the document.

Formatting commands can be executed in three ways: through the Format menu, via a keyboard shortcut, or by clicking the appropriate button on the Formatting toolbar. Click the Bold or Italic buttons, for example, to change the selected text to **bold**, or *italic*, respectively. The selected text is affected by any subsequent operation. Thus you can select the text, click the Bold button, then click the Italic button to create ***bold italic***. Each command functions as a toggle switch. Click the button once to enable the effect, and then click the button a second time to cancel the effect. Each button also has a corresponding keyboard shortcut, Ctrl+B and Ctrl+I, respectively.

The Formatting toolbar also contains the Font and Font Size list boxes to change to a different font (typeface) and/or change the type size. You can also change the color of text and/or highlight text using the appropriate tool. Formatting should be done in moderation, however, or else it will lose its effectiveness.

Some formatting commands apply to the paragraph as a whole, even if the entire paragraph is not selected. You can, for example, click anywhere within a paragraph, then use the center, left-align, right-align, or justify buttons to change the alignment of the entire paragraph. The line spacing and border tools work the same way; that is, click anywhere within a paragraph, and the selected line spacing and border is applied to the entire paragraph. Figure 1.8 displays a document to illustrate different formatting options.

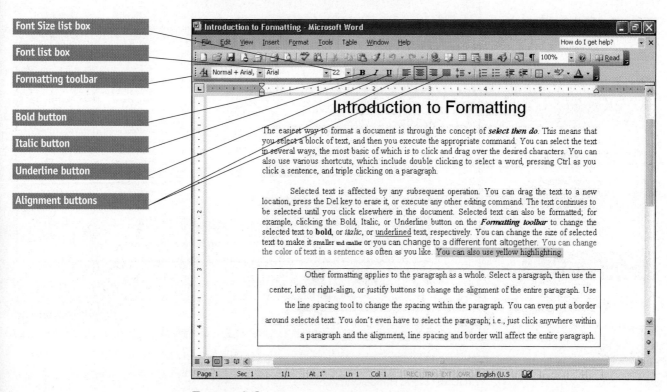

FIGURE 1.8 Introduction to Formatting

2   Modify an Existing Document

Objective   To open an existing document, revise it, and save the revision; to apply basic formatting. Use Figure 1.9 as a guide in doing the exercise.

Step 1:   **Open an Existing Document**

■ Start Word. If necessary, pull down the **View menu** and click the **Task Pane command** to display the task pane.

■ Click the **Home icon** in the task pane to display the most recently opened documents. Click the link to **My First Document** if it is available. (The task pane closes automatically when the document opens.)

■ If you do not see the file, click the link to **More** documents to display the Open dialog box as shown in Figure 1.9a. (You can also click the **Open button** on the Standard toolbar or pull down the **File menu** and click the **Open command**.)

■ If necessary, click the **drop-down arrow** on the Views button and change to the Details view. Click and drag the vertical border between columns to increase (decrease) the size of a column.

■ Click the **drop-down arrow** on the Look In list box. Select (click) the drive that contains the Exploring Word folder. Double click the folder to open it.

■ Click the **down arrow** on the vertical scroll bar until you can select **My First Document** from the previous exercise.

■ Double click the document (or click the **Open button** within the dialog box). Your document should appear on the screen.

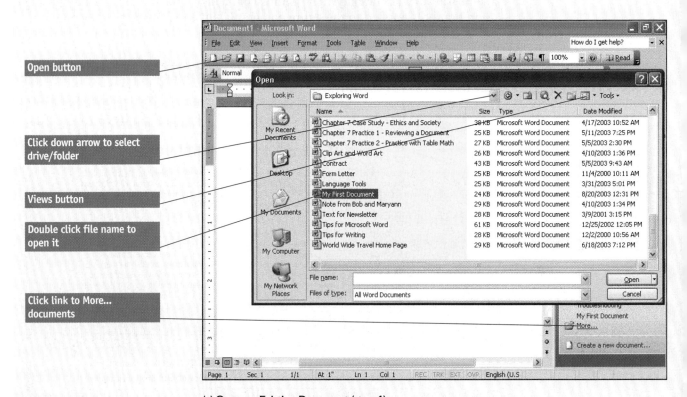

(a) Open an Existing Document (step 1)

FIGURE 1.9   Hands-on Exercise 2

Step 2: **Troubleshooting**

- Modify the settings within Word so that the document on your screen matches Figure 1.9b.
  - ❏ To separate the Standard and Formatting toolbars, pull down the **Tools menu**, click **Customize**, click the **Options tab**, then check the box that indicates the Standard and Formatting toolbars should be displayed on two rows. Click the **Close button**.
  - ❏ To display the complete menus, pull down the **Tools menu**, click **Customize**, click the **Options tab**, then check the box to always show full menus. Click the **Close button**.
  - ❏ To change to the Normal view, pull down the **View menu** and click **Normal** (or click the **Normal View button** at the bottom of the window).
  - ❏ To change the amount of text on the screen, click the **drop-down arrow** on the **Zoom box** on the Standard toolbar and select **Page Width**.

- Click the **Show/Hide ¶ button** to display or hide the hard returns as you see fit.

- There may still be subtle differences between your screen and ours, depending on the resolution of your monitor. These variations, if any, need not concern you as long as you are able to complete the exercise.

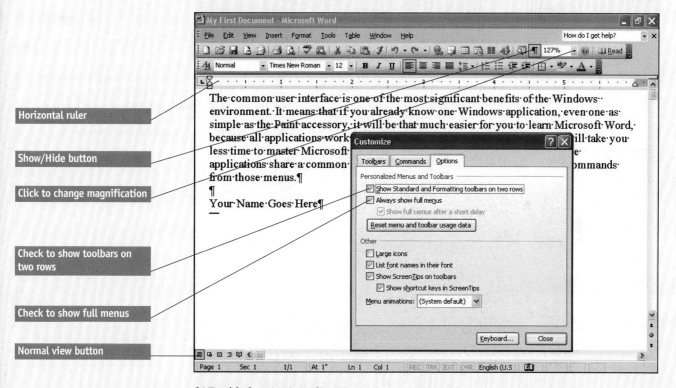

(b) Troubleshooting (step 2)

FIGURE 1.9   Hands-on Exercise 2 *(continued)*

ABOUT MICROSOFT WORD

Pull down the Help menu and click About Microsoft Word to display the specific release number and other licensing information including the Product ID. This help screen also contains two very useful command buttons, System Information and Technical support. The first button displays information about the hardware installed on your system, including the amount of memory and available space on the hard drive.

Step 3: Modify the Document

- Press **Ctrl+End** to move to the end of the document. Press the **up arrow key** once or twice until the insertion point is on a blank line above your name. If necessary, press the **Enter key** once (or twice) to add additional blank line(s).

- Add the sentence, **Success, I can save and retrieve a document!**, as shown in Figure 1.9c.

- Make the following additional modifications to practice editing:
  - ❏ Change the phrase *most significant* to **very best**.
  - ❏ Change *Paint accessory* to **game of Solitaire**.
  - ❏ Change the word *select* to **choose**.

- Use the **Ins key** to switch between insert and overtype modes as necessary. (You can also double click the **OVR indicator** on the status bar to toggle between the insert and overtype modes.)

- Pull down the **File menu** and click **Save**, or click the **Save button** to save the document. (You should do this frequently during every session.)

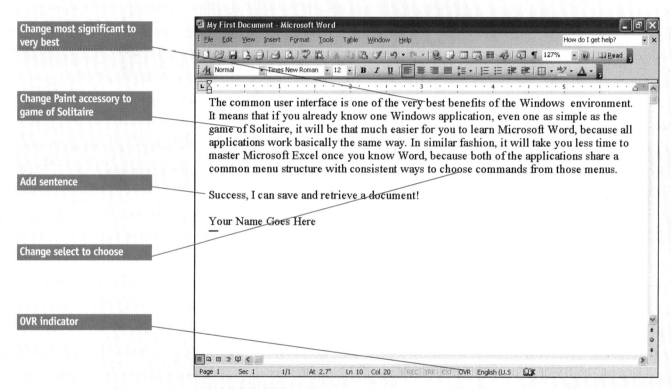

(c) Modify the Document (step 3)

FIGURE 1.9   Hands-on Exercise 2 (*continued*)

MOVING WITHIN A DOCUMENT

Press Ctrl+Home and Ctrl+End to move to the beginning and end of a document, respectively. You can also press the Home or End key to move to the beginning or end of a line. These shortcuts work not just in Word, but in any other Office application, and are worth remembering as they allow your hands to remain on the keyboard as you type.

Step 4: The Undo and Redo Commands

- Press and hold the left mouse button as you drag the mouse over the phrase, **even one as simple as the game of Solitaire**, as shown in Figure 1.9d.

- Press the **Del key** to delete the selected text from the document. Pull down the **Edit menu** and click the **Undo command** (or click the **Undo button** on the Standard toolbar) to reverse (undo) the last command. The deleted text should be returned to your document.

- Pull down the **Edit menu** a second time and click the **Redo command** (or click the **Redo button**) to repeat the Delete command.

- Try this simple experiment. Click the **Undo button** repeatedly to undo the commands one at a time, until you have effectively canceled the entire session. Now click the **Redo command** repeatedly, one command at a time, until you have put the entire document back together.

- Click the **Save button** on the Standard toolbar to save the revised document a final time.

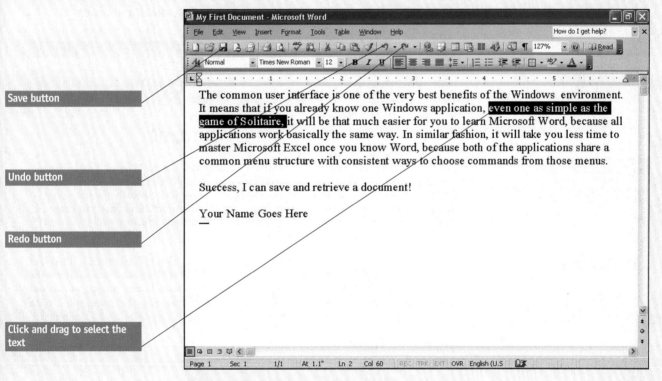

(d) The Undo and Redo Commands (step 4)

FIGURE 1.9   Hands-on Exercise 2 (*continued*)

THE UNDO AND REDO COMMANDS

Click the drop-down arrow next to the Undo button to display a list of your previous actions, then click the action you want to undo, which also undoes all of the preceding commands. Undoing the fifth command in the list, for example, will also undo the preceding four commands. The Redo command works in reverse and cancels the last Undo command.

Step 5: **Format the Document**

- Click and drag to select the phrase **common user interface** in the first paragraph.

- Click the **Bold button** on the Formatting toolbar (or press **Ctrl+B**) to change to bold. Click the **Italic button** (or press **Ctrl+I**) to change to italic.

- Press **Ctrl+Home** to move to the beginning of the document. Press the **Enter key** twice to add two blank lines at the top of the document. Enter **My First Document** on the first blank line as the title of the document.

- Click and drag to select the title. Click the down arrow on the **Font size box** and choose **24**. Click the **Center button** to center the title.

- Click at the end of the second paragraph to add the text shown in Figure 1.9e.

- Click and drag to select the various words and phrases in the second paragraph, and then implement the indicated formatting by clicking the appropriate button on the Formatting toolbar. (You can click the **Undo command** any time the result is not what you intended it to be.)

- Click anywhere in the second paragraph and click the **Align Right button** to change the alignment (see boxed tip below). Save the document.

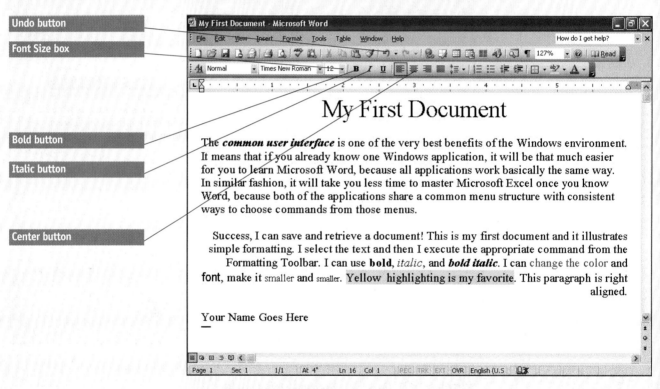

(e) Format the Document (step 5)

FIGURE 1.9 Hands-on Exercise 2 (*continued*)

FORMATTING AT THE PARAGRAPH LEVEL

Line spacing, alignment, and justification take place at the paragraph level and affect the entire paragraph even if the paragraph is not selected. In other words, you can execute these commands by clicking anywhere within the paragraph, then clicking the appropriate button on the Formatting toolbar. Formatting at the character level, however (font, type size, style or color), affects only the selected text.

Step 6: Print the Document

- Click the **Print button** on the Standard toolbar to print the completed document and submit it to your instructor. The document should print immediately, without displaying the Print dialog box.

- Pull down the **File menu** and click the **Print command** to display the Print dialog box shown in Figure 1.9f. The dialog box enables you to select additional options prior to printing:

  ❑ The Printer Name lets you select a printer, which becomes important if you have more than one printer available to you—for example, a high-speed black-and-white network printer and an inkjet color printer.

  ❑ The Print range gives you the option to print the entire document, the current page, or selected pages in a multipage document. Our document has only one page, so the option is not relevant here, but it becomes important as you create more complex documents.

  ❑ The Number of copies lets you print more than one copy at a time.

- Click **OK** to print the document a second time to keep a copy for yourself.

- Pull down the **File menu** and close the document. Exit Word if you do not want to proceed with the next exercise at this time.

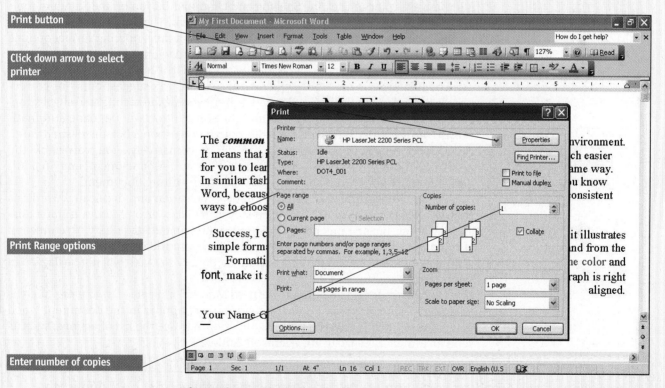

Print button

Click down arrow to select printer

Print Range options

Enter number of copies

(f) Print the Document (step 6)

FIGURE 1.9 Hands-on Exercise 2 (*continued*)

DOCUMENT PROPERTIES

Prove to your instructor how hard you have worked by printing various statistics about your document, including the number of revisions and the total editing time. Pull down the File menu, click the Print command to display the Print dialog box, click the drop-down arrow in the Print What list box, select Document properties, and click OK. You can view the information (without printing) by pulling down the File menu, clicking the Properties command, and then selecting the Statistics tab.

There is simply no excuse to misspell a word, since the ***spell check*** is an integral part of Microsoft Word. (The spell check is also available for every other application in the Microsoft Office.) Spelling errors make your work look sloppy and discourage the reader before he or she has read what you had to say. They can cost you a job, a grade, a lucrative contract, or an award you deserve.

The spell check can be set to automatically check a document as text is entered, or it can be called explicitly by clicking the Spelling and Grammar button on the Standard toolbar. The spell check compares each word in a document to the entries in a built-in dictionary, then flags any word that is in the document, but not in the built-in dictionary, as an error.

The dictionary included with Microsoft Office is limited to standard English and omits many proper names, acronyms, abbreviations, or specialized terms. You can, however, add such words to a ***custom dictionary*** so that they will not be flagged in the future. The spell check will inform you of repeated words and irregular capitalization. It cannot, however, flag properly spelled words that are used improperly, and thus cannot tell you that *Two be or knot to be* is not the answer.

The capabilities of the spell check are illustrated in conjunction with Figure 1.10a. Microsoft Word will indicate the errors as you type by underlining them in red. Alternatively, you can click the Spelling and Grammar button on the Standard toolbar at any time to move through the entire document. The spell check will then go through the document and return the errors one at a time, offering several options for each mistake. You can change the misspelled word to one of the alternatives suggested by Word, leave the word as is, or add the word to a custom dictionary.

The first error is the word *embarassing*, with Word's suggestion(s) for correction displayed in the list box in Figure 1.10b. To accept the highlighted suggestion, click the Change command button, and the substitution will be made automatically in the document. To accept an alternative suggestion, click the desired word, then click the Change command button. Alternatively, you can click the AutoCorrect button to correct the mistake in the current document, and, in addition, automatically correct the same mistake in any future document.

The spell check detects both irregular capitalization and duplicated words, as shown in Figures 1.10c and 1.10d, respectively. The last error, *Marder,* is not a misspelling per se, but a proper noun not found in the standard dictionary. No correction is required, and the appropriate action is to ignore the word (taking no further action)—or better yet, add it to the custom dictionary so that it will not be flagged in future sessions.

The purple dotted line under "Bernard Marder" indicates a ***smart tag***, such as a person's name. A Smart Tag Actions button will appear in the document when you point to the underlined text; click the button to see the list of actions, such as send an e-mail message using Microsoft Outlook.

A spell check will catch embarassing mistakes, iRregular capitalization, and duplicate words words. It will recognize many first names as smart tags, but last names are often flagged as a misspelling; e.g., Bernard Marder. The latter can be added to a custom dictionary so that it will not be flagged in the future. The spell check will not notice properly spelled words that are used incorrectly; for example, too bee or knot to be is not the answer.

(a) The Text

FIGURE **1.10** The Spell Check

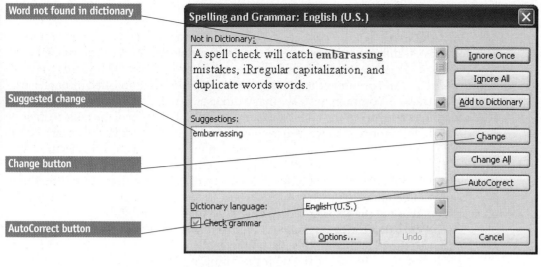

Word not found in dictionary

Suggested change

Change button

AutoCorrect button

(b) Ordinary Misspelling

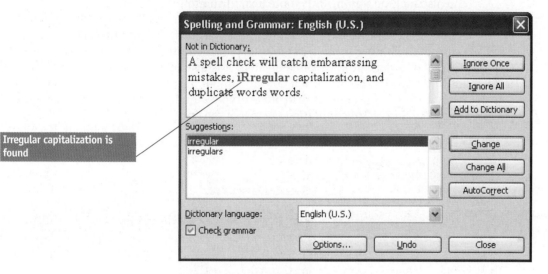

Irregular capitalization is found

(c) Irregular Capitalization

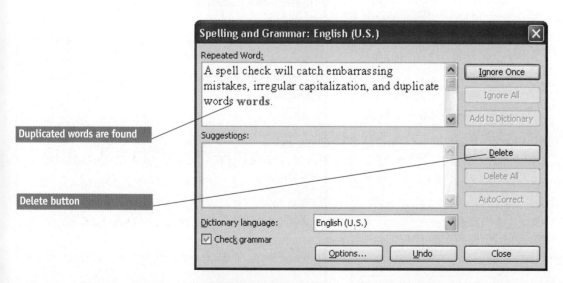

Duplicated words are found

Delete button

(d) Duplicated Word

FIGURE 1.10 The Spell Check (*continued*)

AutoCorrect and AutoText

The **AutoCorrect** feature corrects mistakes as they are made without any effort on your part. It makes you a better typist. If, for example, you typed *teh* instead of *the*, Word would change the spelling without even telling you. Word will also change *adn* to *and*, *i* to *I*, and occurence to occurrence. All of this is accomplished through a predefined table of common mistakes that Word uses to make substitutions whenever it encounters an entry in the table. You can add additional items to the table to include the frequent errors you make. You can also use the feature to define your own shorthand—for example, cis for Computer Information Systems as shown in Figure 1.11a.

The AutoCorrect feature will also correct mistakes in capitalization; for example, it will capitalize the first letter in a sentence, recognize that MIami should be Miami, and capitalize the days of the week. It's even smart enough to correct the accidental use of the Caps Lock key, and it will toggle the key off!

The **AutoText** feature is similar in concept to AutoCorrect in that both substitute a predefined item for a specific character string. The difference is that the substitution occurs automatically with the AutoCorrect entry, whereas you have to take deliberate action for the AutoText substitution to take place. AutoText entries can also include significantly more text, formatting, and even clip art.

Microsoft Word includes a host of predefined AutoText entries. And as with the AutoCorrect feature, you can define additional entries of your own. (You may, however, not be able to do this in a computer lab environment.) The entry in Figure 1.11b is named "Signature" and once created, it is available to all Word documents. To insert an AutoText entry into a new document, just type the first several letters in the AutoText name (Signature in our example), then press the Enter key when Word displays a ScreenTip containing the text of the entry.

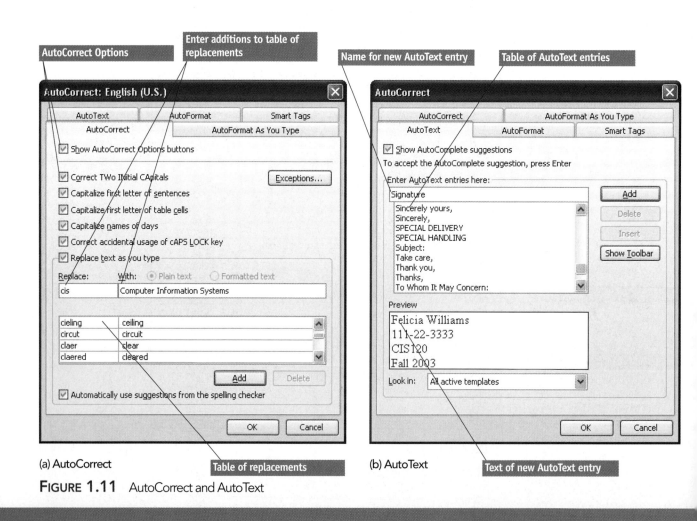

(a) AutoCorrect

(b) AutoText

FIGURE 1.11 AutoCorrect and AutoText

THESAURUS

The ***thesaurus*** helps you to avoid repetition and polish your writing. The thesaurus is called from the Language command in the Tools menu and displays its results in the task pane. You position the cursor at the appropriate word within the document, then invoke the thesaurus and follow your instincts. The thesaurus recognizes multiple meanings and forms of a word (for example, adjective, noun, and verb). You can explore further alternatives by selecting a synonym and looking it up to provide additional choices.

GRAMMAR CHECK

The ***grammar check*** attempts to catch mistakes in punctuation, writing style, and word usage by comparing strings of text within a document to a series of predefined rules. As with the spell check, errors are brought to the screen, where you can accept the suggested correction and make the replacement automatically, or more often, edit the selected text and make your own changes.

You can also ask the grammar check to explain the rule it is attempting to enforce. Unlike the spell check, the grammar check is subjective, and what seems appropriate to you may be objectionable to someone else. Indeed, the grammar check is quite flexible, and can be set to check for different writing styles; that is, you can implement one set of rules to check a business letter and a different set of rules for casual writing.

Many times, however, you will find that the English language is just too complex for the grammar check to detect every error, although it will find many errors. The grammar check missed the error "no perfect" in Figure 1.12 (although it did catch "to" instead of "too"). Suffice it to say, there is no substitute for carefully proofreading every document.

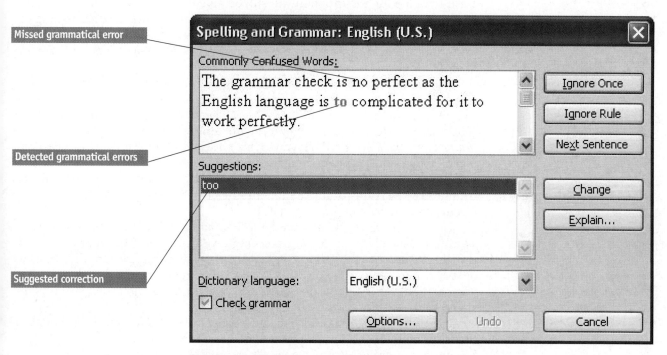

FIGURE 1.12   The Grammar Check

The Save command was used in the first two exercises. The Save As command will be introduced in the next exercise as a very useful alternative. We also introduce you to different backup options. We believe that now, when you are first starting to learn about word processing, is the time to develop good working habits.

You already know that the Save command copies the document currently being edited (the document in memory) to disk. The initial execution of the command requires you to assign a file name and to specify the drive and folder in which the file is to be stored. All subsequent executions of the Save command save the document under the original name, replacing the previously saved version with the new one.

The *Save As command* saves another copy of a document under a different name (and/or a different file type), and is useful when you want to retain a copy of the original document. The Save As command provides you with two copies of a document. The original document is kept on disk under its original name. A copy of the document is saved on disk under a new name and remains in memory. All subsequent editing is done on the new document.

We cannot overemphasize the importance of periodically saving a document, so that if something does go wrong, you won't lose all of your work. Nothing is more frustrating than to lose two hours of effort, due to an unexpected program crash or to a temporary loss of power. Save your work frequently, at least once every 15 minutes. Pull down the File menu and click Save, or click the Save button on the Standard toolbar. Do it!

Backup Options

Microsoft Word offers several different **backup** options, the most important of which is to save **autorecovery information** periodically. If Microsoft Word were to crash (and it will), the program will still be able to recover a previous version of your document when Word is restarted. The only work you will lose is anything you did between the time of the last autorecovery operation and the time of the crash. Set the autorecovery to take place every 10 minutes, and you will never lose more than 10 minutes of work.

You can also set Word to create a backup copy in conjunction with every Save command as shown in Figure 1.13. Assume, for example, that you have created the simple document, *The fox jumped over the fence,* and saved it under the name "Fox". Assume further that you edit the document to read, *The quick brown fox jumped over the fence,* and that you saved it a second time. The second Save command changes the name of the original document from "Fox" to "Backup of Fox", then saves the current contents of memory as "Fox". In other words, the disk now contains two versions of the document: the current version "Fox" and the most recent previous version "Backup of Fox".

The cycle goes on indefinitely, with "Fox" always containing the current version, and "Backup of Fox" the most recent previous version. Thus if you revise and save the document a third time, "Fox" will contain the latest revision while "Backup of Fox" would contain the previous version alluding to the quick brown fox. The original (first) version of the document disappears entirely since only two versions are kept.

The contents of "Fox" and "Backup of Fox" are different, but the existence of the latter enables you to retrieve the previous version if you inadvertently edit beyond repair or accidentally erase the current "Fox" version. Should this occur (and it will), you can always retrieve its predecessor and at least salvage your work prior to the last save operation.

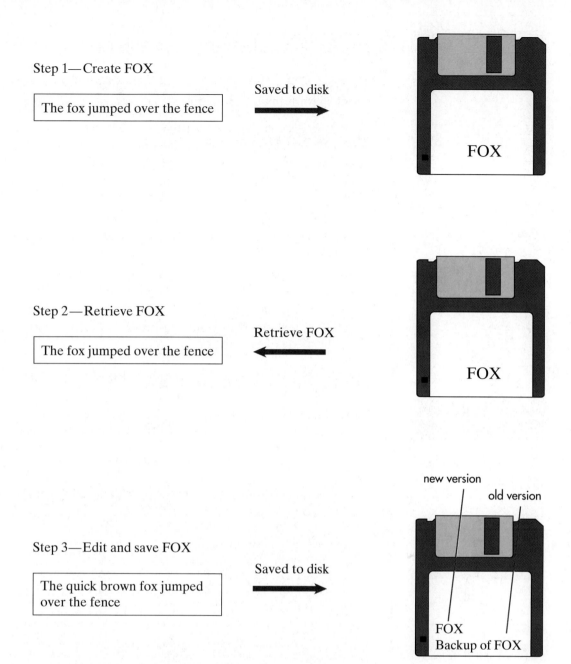

Step 1—Create FOX

The fox jumped over the fence   Saved to disk   FOX

Step 2—Retrieve FOX

The fox jumped over the fence   Retrieve FOX   FOX

new version   old version

Step 3—Edit and save FOX

The quick brown fox jumped over the fence   Saved to disk   FOX
Backup of FOX

FIGURE 1.13   Backup Procedures

BACK UP YOUR WORK

It's not a question of *if* it will happen but *when*. Files are lost, systems crash, and viruses infect a system. That said, we cannot overemphasize the importance of adequate backup and urge you to back up your important files at every opportunity. Exit Word, start Windows Explorer, then copy the document from drive C to a floppy disk. If the document is too large, you can compress the file before you copy it, and/or you can burn a CD. You can also e-mail the document to yourself as an attachment. You can always get another copy of Microsoft Office, but you are the only one with a copy of the term paper due tomorrow.

3   Spell Check, Thesaurus, and Grammar Check

Objective   To check a document for spelling and grammar; to use the thesaurus and practice formatting. Use Figure 1.14 as a guide in the exercise.

Step 1:   **The Save As Command**

■ Start Word. Open the **Language Tools** document in the **Exploring Word folder**. Pull down the **File menu**. Click the **Save As command** to display the dialog box in Figure 1.14a. Click the **Views button** to change to the Details view.

■ Enter **Language Tools Solution** as the name of the new document. (A file name may contain up to 255 characters, and spaces are permitted.) Click the **Save button**.

■ There are now two identical copies of the file on disk—**Language Tools**, which we supplied, and **Language Tools Solution** that you just created.

■ The title bar displays the name of the latter document (Language Tools Solution) as it is the document currently in memory. All subsequent changes will be made to this version.

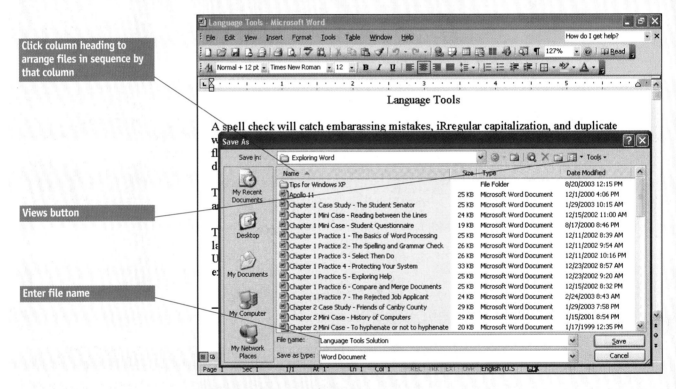

Click column heading to arrange files in sequence by that column

Views button

Enter file name

(a) The Save As Command (step 1)

FIGURE 1.14   Hands-on Exercise 3

CHANGE THE FILE TYPE

Any document created in Microsoft Word is stored in a unique file format that is not understood by other word processors. You can, however, take the document with you by changing its file type although you will lose some or all of the formatting within the document. Pull down the File menu, click the Save As command, click the down arrow in the Save as Type list box and choose a different format such as Rich Text (also known as "rtf") or Plain Text (known as "txt").

Step 2: The Spell Check

- If necessary, press **Ctrl+Home** to move to the beginning of the document. Click the **Spelling and Grammar button** on the Standard toolbar to check the document.

- "Embarassing" is flagged as the first misspelling as shown in Figure 1.14b. Click the **Change button** to accept the suggested spelling.

- "iRregular" is flagged as an example of irregular capitalization. Click the **Change button** to accept the suggested correction.

- Continue checking the document, which displays misspellings and other irregularities one at a time. Click the appropriate command button as each mistake is found.
    - ❏ Click the **Delete button** to remove the duplicated word.
    - ❏ Click the **Ignore Once button** to accept Marder (or click the **Add button** to add Marder to the custom dictionary).

- The last sentence is flagged because of a grammatical error and is discussed in the next step.

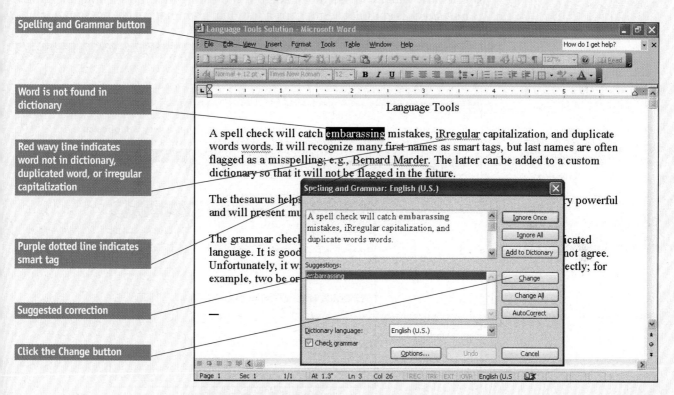

Spelling and Grammar button

Word is not found in dictionary

Red wavy line indicates word not in dictionary, duplicated word, or irregular capitalization

Purple dotted line indicates smart tag

Suggested correction

Click the Change button

(b) The Spell Check (step 2)

FIGURE 1.14 Hands-on Exercise 3 (*continued*)

AUTOMATIC SPELLING AND GRAMMAR CHECKING

Red and green wavy lines may appear throughout a document to indicate spelling and grammatical errors, respectively. Point to any underlined word, then click the right mouse button to display a context-sensitive menu with suggested corrections. To enable (disable) these options, pull down the Tools menu, click the Options command, click the Spelling and Grammar tab, and check (clear) the options to check spelling (or grammar) as you type.

Step 3: The Grammar Check

- The phrase, "verbs and adjectives that does not agree", should be flagged as an error. If this is not the case:
    - ❏ Pull down the **Tools menu**, click **Options**, then click the **Spelling and Grammar tab**.
    - ❏ Check the box to **Check grammar** as you type, then click the button to **Recheck document**. Click **Yes** when told that the spelling and grammar check will be reset, then click **OK** to close the Options dialog box.
    - ❏ Press **Ctrl+Home** to return to the beginning of the document, then click the **Spelling and Grammar button** to recheck the document.

- Word suggests substituting "do" for "does". Click the **Change button** since this is the correct modification.

- The results are not as good in the next sentence, as can be seen in Figure 1.14c. The Grammar Check suggests substituting "are" for "be", which is not what you want. Click in the preview box and make the necessary corrections. Change "two" to "to" and "knot" to "not". Click **Change**.

- Click **OK** when you see the dialog box indicating that the spelling and grammar check is complete. Enter any additional grammatical changes manually.

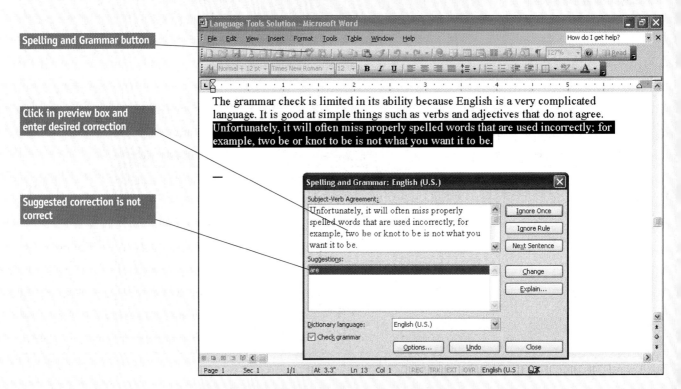

(c) The Grammar Check (step 3)

FIGURE 1.14 Hands-on Exercise 3 (*continued*)

FOREIGN LANGUAGE PROOFING TOOLS

The English version of Microsoft Word supports the spelling, grammar, and thesaurus features in more than 80 foreign languages. Support for Spanish and French is built in at no additional cost, whereas you will have to pay an additional fee for other languages. Just pull down the Tools menu and click the Select Language command to change to a different language. See practice exercise 2 at the end of the chapter.

Step 4: The Thesaurus

- Press **Ctrl+Home** to move to the beginning of the document. Select (double click) the word **"catch"** in the first sentence of the document.

- Pull down the **Tools menu**, click the **Language command** and click **Thesaurus** (or use the **Shift+F7** keyboard shortcut) to open the task pane as shown in Figure 1.14d.

- Scroll until you can click the **+ sign** next to "find (v.)", which is the same form and context for which you are seeking a synonym. The plus sign changes to a minus sign to display the list of potential changes.

- Point to the word **"spot"** and click the **down arrow** that appears to display the context-sensitive menu. Click **Insert** to replace "catch" with "spot" in the document.

- Experiment further with the thesaurus as you see fit. Close the task pane when you are finished.

- Save the document.

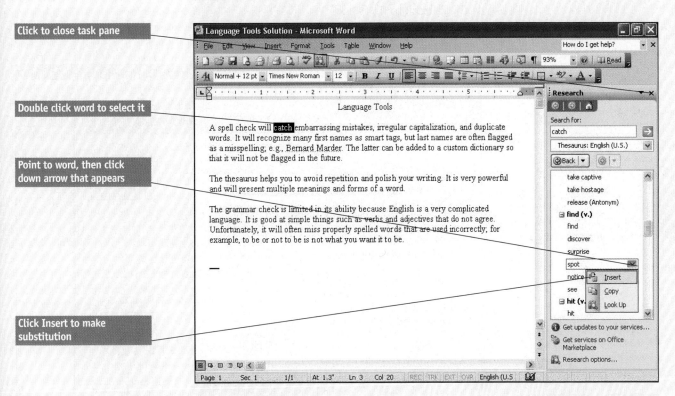

(d) The Thesaurus (step 4)

FIGURE 1.14 Hands-on Exercise 3 *(continued)*

THE RESEARCH PANE—WHAT IS TRISKAIDEKAPHOBIA?

The results of the thesaurus are displayed automatically in the Research task pane, but you can open the research pane at any time and use it to search reference materials. Pull down the Tools menu and click the Research command to display the task pane. Click in the Search for text box, type the word that you want to look up, click the down arrow to select the reference book (e.g., a dictionary, thesaurus, or encyclopedia), then click the green arrow to initiate the search. The results appear directly in the task pane. Close the task pane when you are finished. (The Research pane is a new feature in Microsoft Office Word 2003.)

Step 5: AutoCorrect

- Press **Ctrl+End** to move to the end of the document. Press the **Enter key** twice.

- Type the *misspelled* phrase, **Teh AutoCorrect feature corrects common spelling mistakes**. Word will automatically change "Teh" to "The".

- Press the **Home key** to return to the beginning of the line, where you will notice a blue line under the "T", indicating that an automatic correction has taken place. Point to the blue line, then click the **down arrow** to display the AutoCorrect options.

- Click the command to **Control AutoCorrect options**, which in turn displays the dialog box in Figure 1.14e. Click the **AutoCorrect tab**, then click the **down arrow** on the scroll bar to view the list of corrections. Close the dialog box.

- Add the sentence, **The feature also changes special symbols such as :) to ☺ to indicate I understand my work**.

- You need to restore the first :) rather than have it appear as a smiley face. Thus, point to the first ☺, point to the blue line, then click the down arrow to change the ☺ back to :).

- Save the document.

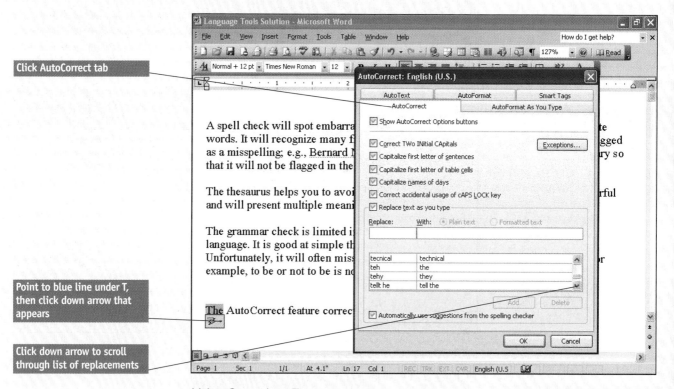

(e) AutoCorrect (step 5)

FIGURE 1.14 Hands-on Exercise 3 *(continued)*

CREATE YOUR OWN SHORTHAND

Use AutoCorrect to expand abbreviations such as "usa" for United States of America. Pull down the Tools menu, click AutoCorrect Options, type the abbreviation in the Replace text box and the expanded entry in the With text box. Click the Add command button, then click OK to exit the dialog box and return to the document. The next time you type usa in a document, it will automatically be expanded to United States of America.

Step 6: **Create an AutoText Entry**

- Press **Ctrl+End** to move to the end of the document. Press the **Enter key** twice. Enter your name and student number.

- Click and drag to select the information you just entered. Pull down the **Insert menu**, select the **AutoText command**, then select **AutoText** to display the AutoCorrect dialog box in Figure 1.14f.

- "Your name" is suggested automatically as the name of the AutoText entry. Click the **Add button**.

- To test the entry, you can delete your name and student number, then use the AutoText feature. Your name and other information should still be highlighted. Press the **Del key** to delete the information.

- Type the first few letters of your name and watch the screen as you do. You should see a ScreenTip containing your name and other information. Press the **Enter key** or the **F3 key** when you see the ScreenTip.

- Save the document.

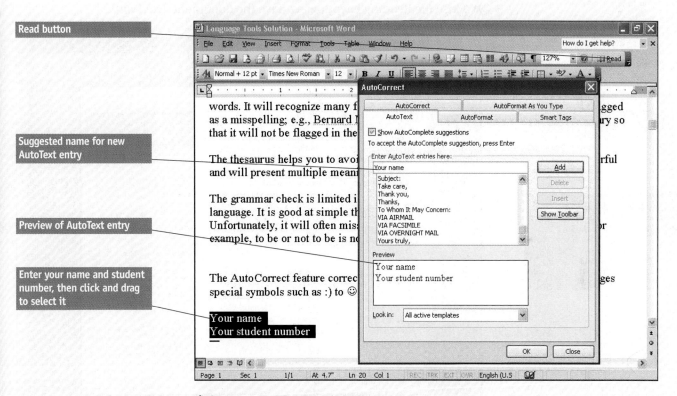

(f) Create an AutoText Entry (step 6)

FIGURE 1.14 Hands-on Exercise 3 (*continued*)

THE AUTOTEXT TOOLBAR

Point to any visible toolbar, click the right mouse button to display a context-sensitive menu, then click AutoText to display the AutoText toolbar. The AutoText toolbar groups the various AutoText entries into categories, making it easier to select the proper entry. Click the down arrow on the All Entries button to display the various categories, click a category, then select the entry you want to insert into the document.

Step 7: **Start Reading**

- Click the **Read button** to change to the Reading Layout view as shown in Figure 1.14g. This view is intended to proofread the final document, but you can still apply formatting through keyboard shortcuts.

- Click and drag to select "spell check", which appears in the first sentence of the document. Press **Ctrl+B**. Press **Ctrl+I**. Click elsewhere in the document to deselect the phrase, which now appears in bold italic.

- Bold face and italicize **"thesaurus", "grammar check",** and **"AutoCorrect feature"** in similar fashion.

- Click at the beginning of the document (immediately to the left of its title). Pull down the **Insert menu** and click the **Comment command**, then type the text of the comment in Figure 1.14g.

- Pull down the **File menu** and click the **Print command** to display the Print dialog box. Check that the Print What box indicates **Document showing markup**. Click **OK** to print the completed document for your instructor.

- Close the Reading Layout view. Save the document. Exit Word.

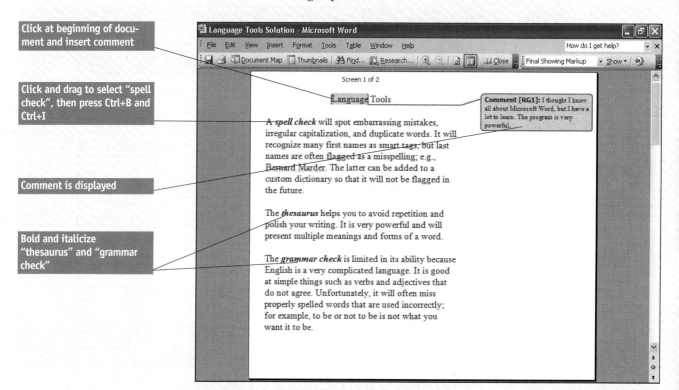

(g) Start Reading (step 7)

FIGURE 1.14 Hands-on Exercise 3 *(continued)*

THE TRACK CHANGES COMMAND

Pull down the Tools menu and click the Track Changes command to record the changes that are made in a document. (Execute the command a second time to turn the recording feature off.) Click the Read button to change the Reading Layout view, and then use the Accept or Reject Change buttons to decide if the revisions should be permanent. This technique is ideal when you are sharing a document with others. The comments of each reviewer are displayed in a different color. See problem 7 at the end of the chapter.

SUMMARY

The chapter provided a broad-based introduction to word processing in general and to Microsoft Word in particular. Help is available from many sources. You can use the Help menu or the Office Assistant as you can in any Office application. You can also go to the Microsoft Web site to obtain more recent, and often more detailed, information.

Microsoft Word is always in one of two modes, insert or overtype; the choice between the two depends on the desired editing. The insertion point marks the place within a document where text is added or replaced. Double clicking the OVR indicator on the status bar is an easy way to switch between the two modes.

The Enter key is pressed at the end of a paragraph, but not at the end of a line because Word automatically wraps text from one line to the next. A hard return is created by the user when he or she presses the Enter key; a soft return is created by Word as it wraps text and begins a new line.

The Save and Open commands work in conjunction with one another. The Save command copies the document in memory to disk under its existing name. The Open command retrieves a previously saved document. The Save As command saves the document in memory under a different name and is useful when you want to retain a copy of the current document prior to all changes.

Many operations in Microsoft Word are accomplished through the concept "select then do." This means that you select a block of text, and then you execute the appropriate editing or formatting command. Formatting commands can be executed in one of three ways: through the Format menu, via a keyboard shortcut, or by clicking the appropriate button on the Formatting toolbar. The selected text is affected by any subsequent operation, and it continues to be selected until you click elsewhere in the document.

A spell check compares the words in a document to those in a standard and/or custom dictionary and offers suggestions to correct the mistakes it finds. It will detect misspellings, duplicated phrases, and/or irregular capitalization, but will not flag properly spelled words that are used incorrectly. Foreign-language proofing tools for French and Spanish are built into the English version of Microsoft Word.

The AutoCorrect feature corrects predefined spelling errors and/or mistakes in capitalization, automatically, as the words are entered. The AutoText feature is similar in concept except that it can contain longer entries that include formatting and clip art. Either feature can be used to create a personal shorthand to expand abbreviations as they are typed.

The thesaurus suggests synonyms and/or antonyms. It can also recognize multiple forms of a word (noun, verb, and adjective) and offer suggestions for each. The grammar check searches for mistakes in punctuation, writing style, and word usage by comparing strings of text within a document to a series of predefined rules.

KEY TERMS

MULTIPLE CHOICE

1. When entering text within a document, the Enter key is normally pressed at the end of every:
   - (a) Line
   - (b) Sentence
   - (c) Paragraph
   - (d) All of the above

2. Which menu contains the commands to save the current document, or to open a previously saved document?
   - (a) The Tools menu
   - (b) The File menu
   - (c) The View menu
   - (d) The Edit menu

3. How do you execute the Print command?
   - (a) Click the Print button on the standard toolbar
   - (b) Pull down the File menu, then click the Print command
   - (c) Use the appropriate keyboard shortcut
   - (d) All of the above

4. The Open command:
   - (a) Brings a document from disk into memory
   - (b) Brings a document from disk into memory, then erases the document on disk
   - (c) Stores the document in memory on disk
   - (d) Stores the document in memory on disk, then erases the document from memory

5. What is the easiest way to change the phrase, *revenues, profits, gross margin,* to read *revenues, profits, and gross margin*?
   - (a) Use the insert mode, position the cursor before the *g* in *gross,* then type the word *and* followed by a space
   - (b) Use the insert mode, position the cursor after the *g* in *gross,* then type the word *and* followed by a space
   - (c) Use the overtype mode, position the cursor before the *g* in *gross,* then type the word *and* followed by a space
   - (d) Use the overtype mode, position the cursor after the *g* in *gross,* then type the word *and* followed by a space

6. The Save command:
   - (a) Brings a document from disk into memory
   - (b) Brings a document from disk into memory, then erases the document on disk
   - (c) Stores the document in memory on disk
   - (d) Stores the document in memory on disk, then erases the document from memory

7. A document has been entered into Word with a given set of margins, which are subsequently changed. What can you say about the number of hard and soft returns before and after the change in margins?
   - (a) The number of hard returns is the same, but the number and/or position of the soft returns is different
   - (b) The number of soft returns is the same, but the number and/or position of the hard returns is different
   - (c) The number and position of both hard and soft returns is unchanged
   - (d) The number and position of both hard and soft returns is different

8. Which of the following is detected by the spell check?
   - (a) Duplicate words
   - (b) Irregular capitalization
   - (c) Both (a) and (b)
   - (d) Neither (a) nor (b)

9. Which of the following is likely to be found in a custom dictionary?
   - (a) Proper names
   - (b) Words related to the user's particular application
   - (c) Acronyms created by the user for his or her application
   - (d) All of the above

10. Ted and Sally both use Word. Both have written a letter to Dr. Joel Stutz and have run a spell check on their respective documents. Ted's program flags *Stutz* as a misspelling, whereas Sally's accepts it as written. Why?
    - (a) The situation is impossible; that is, if they use identical word processing programs, they should get identical results
    - (b) Ted has added *Stutz* to his custom dictionary
    - (c) Sally has added *Stutz* to her custom dictionary
    - (d) All of the above reasons are equally likely as a cause of the problem

... continued

11. The spell check will do all of the following *except*:

(a) Flag properly spelled words used incorrectly

(b) Identify misspelled words

(c) Accept (as correctly spelled) words found in the custom dictionary

(d) Suggest alternatives to misspellings it identifies

12. The AutoCorrect feature will:

(a) Correct errors in capitalization as they occur during typing

(b) Expand user-defined abbreviations as the entries are typed

(c) Both (a) and (b)

(d) Neither (a) nor (b)

13. When does the Save As dialog box appear?

(a) The first time a file is saved using either the Save or Save As commands

(b) Every time a file is saved

(c) Both (a) and (b)

(d) Neither (a) nor (b)

14. Which of the following is true about the thesaurus?

(a) It recognizes different forms of a word; for example, a noun and a verb

(b) It provides antonyms as well as synonyms

(c) Both (a) and (b)

(d) Neither (a) nor (b)

15. The grammar check:

(a) Implements different rules for casual and business writing

(b) Will detect all subtleties in the English language

(c) Is always run in conjunction with a spell check

(d) All of the above

16. What happens if you select a word, then click the Italic button on the Formatting toolbar twice in a row?

(a) The word will be italicized

(b) The word will appear in a regular (nonitalicized) font

(c) The word will have the same appearance as before; clicking the Italic button twice in a row has no effect

(d) Impossible to determine

17. Which of the following applies to the paragraph as a whole—that is, you can apply the command anywhere within the paragraph to format the entire paragraph?

(a) Alignment

(b) Line spacing

(c) Borders

(d) All of the above

18. Which view is new to Microsoft Word 2003?

(a) Reading Layout

(b) Print Preview

(c) Normal

(d) Outline

ANSWERS

1. c	**7.** a	**13.** a
2. b	**8.** c	**14.** c
3. d	**9.** d	**15.** a
4. a	**10.** c	**16.** c
5. a	**11.** a	**17.** d
6. c	**12.** c	**18.** a

PRACTICE WITH WORD

1. **The Basics of Word Processing:** Open the *Chapter 1 Practice 1* document in the Exploring Word folder that is shown in Figure 1.15. Enter your instructor's name and your name in the To and From lines, respectively, then modify the document as described below.

   a. Change the word "worry" to "be concerned" in the first sentence of the second paragraph. Change the word "position" to "location" in the last sentence of the second paragraph.

   b. Delete the word "simply" from the second sentence in the third paragraph. Delete the word "also" in the second line of the last paragraph.

   c. Click at the end of the third paragraph, be sure you are in the insert mode, and add the sentence, "The insert mode adds characters at the insertion point while moving existing text to the right in order to make room for the new text."

   d. Click immediately to the left of the "s" in the word "test" found in the fourth line of the second paragraph. Press the Insert key to turn the OVR indicator on, and change to the overtype mode. Enter an "x", which will replace the "s". Press the Insert key a second time to return to the insert mode.

   e. Delete the two sentences in paragraph three that describe the OVR indicator.

   f. Create a new paragraph between paragraphs three and four, entering the following text: "There are two other keys that function as toggle switches of which you should be aware. The Caps Lock key toggles between upper- and lowercase letters. The Num Lock key alternates between typing numbers and using the arrow keys." As you enter the word "which" in the first sentence, type "whcih" instead. Watch what happens, as the spelling is automatically corrected. Add blank lines as needed.

   g. Select the word "present" in the second line of the first paragraph, then pull down the Tools menu and click the Language command. Click Thesaurus from the submenu. Find an appropriate meaning, click the down arrow next to the desired synonym, and check Insert. Close the task pane.

   h. Save the completed document as *Chapter 1 Practice 1 Solution*. Pull down the File menu, click the Print command, and then click the Options button in the Print dialog box. Check the box to print Document properties. Click OK to close this dialog box, and then click OK to print the document and its properties for your instructor.

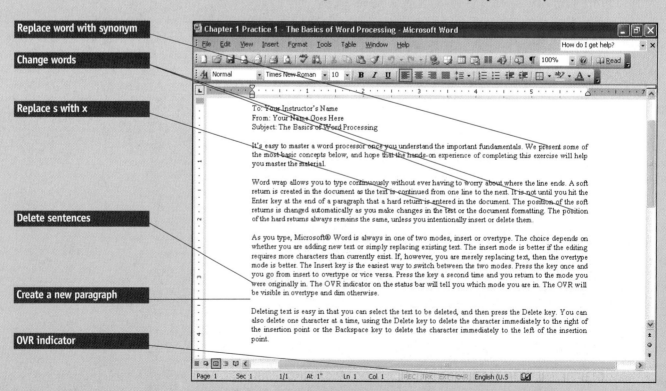

FIGURE 1.15 The Basics of Word Processing (exercise 1)

2. **The Spelling and Grammar Check:** Open the *Chapter 1 Practice 2* document in the Exploring Word folder to display the document in Figure 1.16. Word detects multiple errors in spelling and grammar as denoted by the wavy red and green lines, respectively. Your assignment is to correct the document so that it is error free. Proceed as follows:

   a. Press Ctrl+Home to move to the beginning of the document, then click the Spelling and Grammar button on the Standard toolbar to check the document for errors. Accept, reject, or make the corrections as you see fit. Do not correct the errors that are flagged at the end of the document within the French and Spanish phrases at this time. [English is the default language for spelling and grammar, but you can select other languages as you will see in parts (c) and (d).]

   b. Read the corrected document carefully and make any other necessary corrections (again, ignoring the foreign phrases). You should find several additional errors because the English language is very complicated, and it is virtually impossible to correct every error automatically.

   c. Click and drag to select the French phrases that appear near the end of the document. Pull down the Tools menu, click the Language command, click Set Language, then select French (France). Check this phrase for spelling and grammar. Do you know what the sentences mean?

   d. Click and drag to select the Spanish phrases that appear near the end of the document. Pull down the Tools menu, click the Language command, click Set Language, and then select Spanish (Spain-Modern Sort). Check this phrase for spelling and grammar. Do you know what the sentences mean?

   e. Add your name to the completed document. Save the completed document as *Chapter 1 Practice 2 Solution.*

   f. Pull down the File menu, click the Print command, and then click the Options button in the Print dialog box. Check the box to print Document properties. Click OK to close this dialog box, and then click OK to print the document and its properties for your instructor.

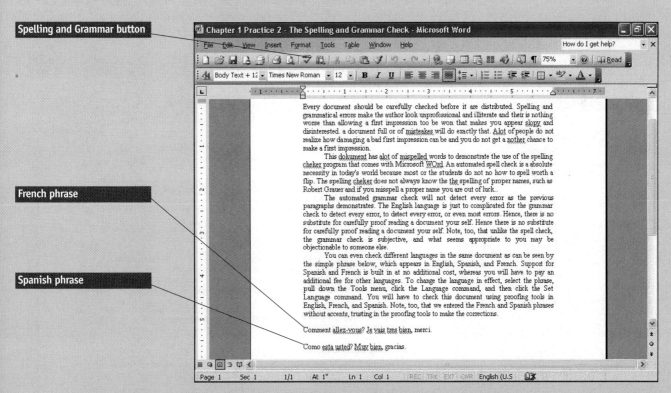

FIGURE 1.16 The Spelling and Grammar Check (exercise 2)

3. **Select Then Do:** Formatting operations are typically implemented in the context of "select then do" as described in the document of Figure 1.17. You select the text that you want to format, then you execute the appropriate formatting command, most easily by clicking the corresponding button on the Formatting toolbar. This assignment will help you to practice basic formatting. Proceed as follows:

a. Open the *Chapter 1 Practice 3* document in the Exploring Word folder. Pull down the Edit menu and click the Select All command to select the entire document. Change the font to Times New Roman.

b. Click and drag to select the title of the document. Change the type size to 18 points. Click the Center button on the Formatting toolbar. Select the text on the second line, type your name, and click the Center button. Change to 14 point type.

c. Click and drag to select the term, "select-then-do" in the first paragraph. Click the Bold button. Click the Italic button. Leave the insertion point in the middle of the selected text and double click the Format Painter. Click and drag to paint the other terms in the document that use the same formatting as shown in Figure 1.17.

d. Apply boldface, underlining, or italic as indicated in the second paragraph.

e. Click and drag to select the word "smaller" in the second paragraph. Change the point size to 10 points. Select the words "and smaller" and change to 8 points.

f. Click the down arrow on the Highlight tool to select yellow, and then highlight the indicated sentence in the first paragraph. Change the color of the tool to complete the highlighting for the last sentence in the second paragraph.

g. Click anywhere in the first paragraph, then click the Justify tool. Click anywhere in the third paragraph and click the Align Right tool.

h. Click anywhere in the last paragraph and click the Justify tool. Now click the down arrow on the line spacing tool and select 1.5. Line spacing and justification take place at the paragraph level; that is, it affects the entire paragraph that contains the insertion point even if the paragraph is not selected.

i. Click the down arrow on the Border tool to select the Outside border. Click anywhere in the last paragraph, then click the Border tool to apply the border to the paragraph.

j. Save the document. Print the completed document for your instructor.

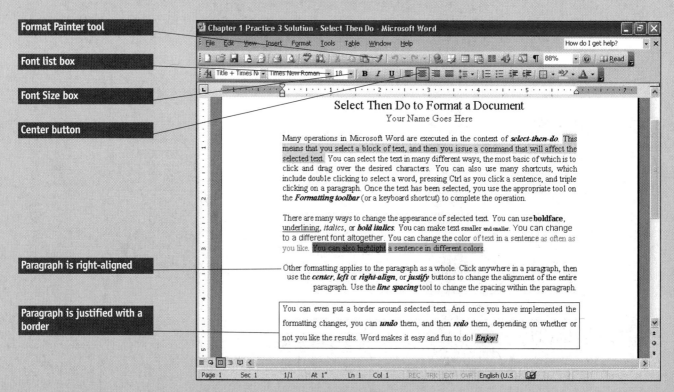

FIGURE 1.17 Select Then Do (exercise 3)

practice exercises

4. **Protecting Your System:** Figure 1.18 displays the first two pages in a document that discusses computer viruses and backup procedures. It's not a question of *if* it will happen, but *when*—hard disks die, files are lost, or viruses may infect a system. You can prepare for the inevitable by creating adequate backup before the problem occurs. The advice in the document is very important, and we suggest you take it to heart. Proceed as follows:

a. Open the partially completed document in *Chapter 1 Practice 4* in the Exploring Word folder. Boldface and italicize the first occurrence of the following terms that are found on the first page: "computer virus" and "antivirus program". Read the information on this page very carefully.

b. Start Internet Explorer and go to www.symantec.com, which is the home page of the company that supplies the Norton antivirus program. Search the Symantec Web site for the information needed to answer the questions on page 2 of the document, which asks several questions about the Norton Antivirus program. Enter your responses directly in the document.

c. Go to www.mcafee.com to obtain information about the McAfee antivirus program. Search the Web site for the information needed to answer the questions on page 2 of the document. Enter your responses directly in the document.

d. Go to the third page in the document, which describes a simple backup strategy. Read the information and use it to answer the indicated questions directly in the document.

e. Press Ctrl+Home to move to the beginning of the document. Pull down the Insert menu, click the Break command, and insert a page break (or use the Ctrl+Enter keyboard shortcut).

f. Pull down the View menu and change to the Print Layout view. Click the down arrow on the Zoom box and select Whole Page. Press Ctrl+Home a second time to move to the newly created title page. Press the Enter key several times, and then enter the title of the document, the subtitle, and your name as shown in Figure 1.18.

g. Print the completed document for your instructor. Read the document carefully before you submit it. Don't make your definition of backup the copy you wish you had made prior to your system crashing.

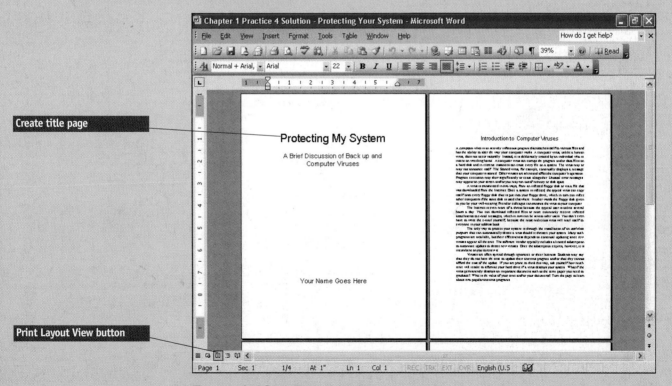

FIGURE 1.18 Protecting Your System (exercise 4)

5. **Exploring Help:** Everything you need to know about Microsoft Word is contained in its help facility. There are several types of help available, but regardless of the type you choose, the best time to look for help is when you don't need it. This exercise helps you to explore the various ways to learn more about Microsoft Word. Open the *Chapter 1 Practice 5* document in the Exploring Word folder and answer each question in the space provided.

a. Pull down the Help menu and click the About command to see which version of Word you are currently using. Why is this information important? What other information is available from the About Microsoft Word window?

b. How do you use the Help task pane in Figure 1.19? What other information (besides the Table of Contents) is available from this task pane?

c. What happens if you click a closed book icon? What happens if you click an open book icon? What happens if you click a topic under an open book?

d. How do you display (hide) the Office Assistant? When does it display a suggestion? Is it useful or just a clever annoyance? Will the same suggestion repeat itself from one session to the next? What steps are necessary to display a tip of the day each time that Microsoft Word is started?

e. What is the Ask a Question list box? When is it available?

f. Where would you prefer the help files to be stored, locally or on the Web? What is the advantage of storing the Help files on the Web? What is the disadvantage?

g. How do you implement a spell check in a foreign language such as French or Spanish? Use any appropriate technique to find the answer. Print the associated help topic(s) for your instructor.

h. Include your name at the top of the document, and then print the completed document for your instructor.

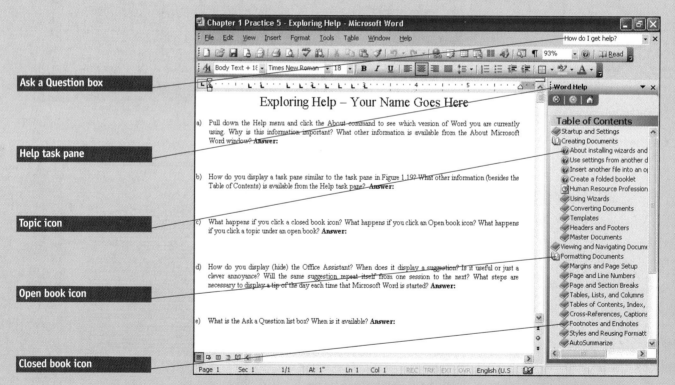

FIGURE 1.19 Exploring Help (exercise 5)

6. **Compare and Merge Documents:** The Compare and Merge Documents command lets you compare two documents in order to see the changes between those documents. You can use the command to see how well you completed the first two hands-on exercises. Proceed as follows:

   a. Open the completed *Chapter 1 Practice 6* document in the Exploring Word folder. This document contains our solution to the first two hands-on exercises followed by a paragraph that describes the Compare and Merge Documents command.

   b. Pull down the Tools menu and click the Compare and Merge Documents command to display the associated dialog box. Select *My First Document* (the document you created in the first hands-on exercise and modified in the second hands-on exercise).

   c. Check the box for Legal Blackline (to display a thin black line in the left margin showing where the changes occur), then click the Compare button. The two documents are merged together as shown in Figure 1.20. The extent of the changes in the first two paragraphs depends on how closely you followed instructions in the hands-on exercises.

   d. Click the Read button on the Standard toolbar to change to the Reading Layout view. Experiment with the Increase (Decrease) Font Size button to make the document easier to read. Accept or reject the changes as you see fit.

   e. Click the Close button to return to the Print Layout view. Pull down the File menu, click the Print command, and then click the Options button in the Print dialog box. Check the box to print Document properties. Click OK to close this dialog box, and then click OK to print the document and its properties for your instructor.

   f. Use the Help command to learn more about merging documents and tracking changes. Summarize your thoughts about these commands in a short note to your instructor.

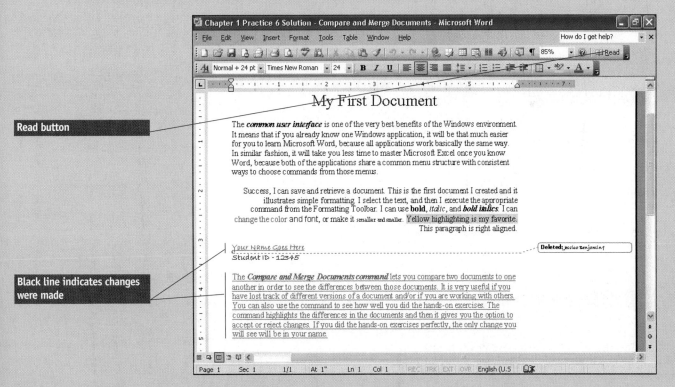

FIGURE 1.20 Compare and Merge Documents (exercise 6)

7. **The Rejected Job Applicant:** The Track Changes command stores the changes to a document electronically, enabling the owner of that document to accept or reject the changes as he or she sees fit. The changes may be entered in different ways; for example, the document can be sent to multiple reviewers requesting their input, in which case the changes of each reviewer are recorded in a different color. The changes may also be entered by a sole author who wants an electronic record of an editing session. Proceed as follows:

a. Open the *Chapter 1 Practice 7* document in the Exploring Word folder. This document was written by a friend of yours who was rejected from every job for which she applied. Your assignment is to edit the letter by eliminating spelling and grammatical errors, and further by making any other changes you see fit.

b. Pull down the Tools menu and toggle the Track Changes command on. The Reviewing toolbar should be displayed automatically. If necessary, click the down arrow in the Display for Review list box and select Final Showing Markup, to display the final version of your document with the indicated corrections as shown in Figure 1.21.

c. Check the document for spelling and grammatical errors, making changes as appropriate. Note that each time you make a change to the document, the nature of the change is recorded in the right margin.

d. Enter additional changes as necessary that were not detected by the tools within Word. Note, for example, that we suggested our friend apply for an entry-level rather than a senior position. We also added a letterhead to the top of the document.

e. Click the Print button to print the document as shown—that is, the final document with the markup (editing) printed in the margin. Click the down arrow on the Display for Review list box to display the Original Showing Markup and print that version. And finally, change to the final version to print the completed document without showing the editing changes. Submit all three versions to your instructor.

f. Save the document. Pull down the Tools menu and toggle the Track Changes command off. Pull down the View menu, click Toolbars, and toggle the display of the Reviewing Toolbar off as well.

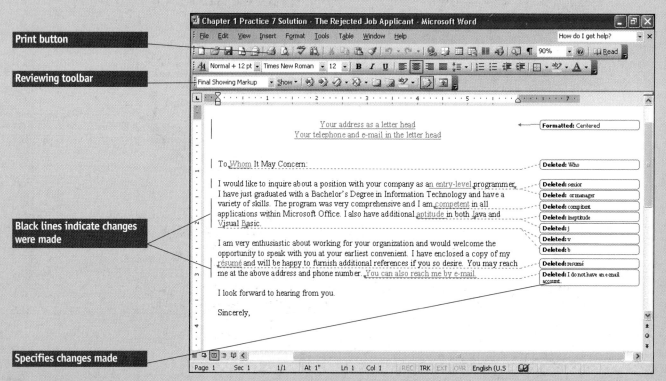

FIGURE 1.21 The Rejected Job Applicant (exercise 7)

MINI CASES

Student Questionnaire

Use the partially completed document in *Chapter 1 Mini Case—Student Questionnaire* as the basis of a document to your instructor describing your background. Click after each question and respond as indicated. If there is time in the class, your instructor can have you exchange assignments with another student, and then have you read the other student's questionnaire to the class. There are many variations on this "ice breaker," but the assignment will let you gain practice with Microsoft Word, while simultaneously learning about your classmates.

Reading Between the Lines

You were recently sent a performance appraisal by a subordinate, followed shortly by a second note with additional information. It seems that John (the individual being evaluated) was standing over your subordinate's shoulder when she wrote the evaluation, and thus her true opinion of the candidate is hidden between the lines of the original document. Open the *Chapter 1 Mini Case—Reading Between the Lines* document and delete the shaded lines within the original letter. Click the Show/Hide button to display the hidden characters, and then delete all of the hard returns (except the last one) to create a single paragraph. Change the font to 12 point Times New Roman, justify the paragraph, and set the line spacing to 2. Add your name to the revised letter and submit it to your instructor.

Acronym Finder

Do you know what the acronym PCMCIA stands for? Some might say it stands for "People Can't Memorize Computer Industry Acronyms," although the real meaning is "Personal Computer Memory Card International Association," which refers to the PC cards that are used with notebook computers. Use your favorite Internet search engine to locate a site that publishes lists of acronyms. Select five computer-related terms and create a short document with the acronym and its meaning. Select a second list of any five acronyms that appeal to you. Print the document and submit it to your instructor.

The Reference Desk

The Reference Desk, at www.refdesk.com, contains a treasure trove of information for the writer. You will find access to several online dictionaries, encyclopedias, and other references. Go to the site and select five links that you think will be of interest to you as a writer. Create a short document that contains the name of the site, its Web address, and a brief description of the information that is found at the site. Print the document and submit it to your instructor.

Planning for Disaster

Do you have a backup strategy? Do you even know what a backup strategy is? You should learn, because sooner or later you will wish you had one. You will erase a file, be unable to read from a floppy disk, or worse yet suffer a hardware failure in which you are unable to access the hard drive. The problem always seems to occur the night before an assignment is due. The ultimate disaster is the disappearance of your computer, by theft or natural disaster (e.g., Hurricane Andrew). Describe in 250 words or less the backup strategy you plan to implement in conjunction with your work in this class.

... continued

A Letter Home

You really like this course and want very much to have your own computer, but you're strapped for cash and have decided to ask your parents for help. Write a one-page letter describing the advantages of having your own system and how it will help you in school. Tell your parents what the system will cost, and that you can save money by buying through the mail. Describe the configuration you intend to buy (don't forget to include the price of software) and then provide prices from at least three different companies. Cut out the advertisements and include them in your letter. Bring your material to class and compare your research with that of your classmates.

A Junior Year Abroad

How lucky can you get? You are spending the second half of your junior year in Paris. The problem is you will have to submit your work in French, and the English version of Microsoft Word won't do. Is there a foreign-language version available? What about the dictionary and thesaurus? How do you enter the accented characters, which occur so frequently? You are leaving in two months, so you'd better get busy. What are your options? *Bon voyage!*

Changing Menus and Toolbars

Microsoft Office enables you to display a series of short menus that contain only basic commands. The additional commands are made visible by clicking the double arrow that appears at the bottom of the menu. New commands are added to the menu as they are used, and conversely, other commands are removed if they are not used. A similar strategy is followed for the Standard and Formatting toolbars that are displayed on a single row, and thus do not show all of the buttons at one time. The intent is to simplify Office for the new user by limiting the number of commands that are visible. The consequence, however, is that the individual is not exposed to new commands, and hence may not use Office to its full potential. Which set of menus do you prefer? How do you switch from one set to the other?

2

Gaining Proficiency:
Editing and Formatting

CASE STUDY
FRIENDS OF CANBY COUNTY

It's that time of year again when auction fever is in the air! Many nonprofit businesses conduct an annual auction to raise funds to support their operation. The *Friends of Canby County* is one such organization, and it seeks to bring citizens together to effectively manage growth and reduce urban sprawl within the county. Other activities include public education and the preparation of policy statements for urban politicians.

Your first task as the new executive director is to inform citizens and local businesses of this year's auction, which is set for April 2nd in the ballroom of the Mountain View Lodge. You also have to procure the actual items that will be auctioned off at this exceedingly popular event. The goal for this year is to net $40,000 at the action, which is $4,000 more than last year.

The former director was helpful and provided copies of letters and other correspondence from last year's gala. Unfortunately, some of her files are not in their final form, and further, several changes in the content of the letter (such as the time and place of the event) have to be made. You also want to add your own touch and create a better-looking document through enhanced formatting. ■

Your assignment is to read the chapter, paying special attention to the character, paragraph, and section level formatting within the document. You are then to open last year's letter, *Chapter 2 Case Study—Friends of Canby County,* and make the necessary changes to achieve a more professional look. You have been asked to improve the letterhead and other formatting. You have also been asked to change the list of auction items to a three-column format so that the entire letter fits on one page and further, to use bullets to highlight the list of forms that are enclosed in the packet, as opposed to listing them in a paragraph. Print the completed letter for your instructor.

UNDO AND REDO COMMANDS

To err is human, but it's easy to recover from a mistake. The **Undo command** is executed by pulling down the Edit menu, by clicking the Undo button on the Standard toolbar, or by using the equivalent keyboard shortcut (Ctrl+Z). Each time the command is executed, it undoes a previous command; for example, executing the undo command three times in a row will undo the last three commands that were executed. You can also click the down arrow next to the Undo button on the Standard toolbar to display a reverse-order list of previous commands. Select (click) the command you want to undo, and you automatically undo all of the preceding commands. Undoing the fifth command in the list, for example, will undo the preceding four commands.

The **Redo command** is the opposite of Undo and reverses the last command that was undone. Clicking the down arrow next to the Redo button on the Standard toolbar will redo (re-execute) all of the previous commands prior to the one you select; for example, redoing the fifth command in the list will redo the preceding four commands. The Undo and Redo commands work in conjunction with one another; that is, every time a command is undone, it can be redone at a later time.

MOVING AND COPYING TEXT

The ability to move and/or copy text is essential in order to develop any degree of proficiency in editing. A move operation removes the text from its current location and places it elsewhere in the same (or even a different) document; a copy operation retains the text in its present location and places a duplicate elsewhere. Either operation can be accomplished using the Windows clipboard and a combination of the **Cut**, **Copy**, and **Paste commands**.

The **Windows clipboard** is a temporary storage area available to any Windows application. Selected text is cut or copied from a document and placed onto the clipboard from where it can be pasted to a new location(s). A move requires that you select the text and execute a Cut command to remove the text from the document and place it on the clipboard. You then move the insertion point to the new location and paste the text from the clipboard into that location. A copy operation necessitates the same steps except that a Copy command is executed rather than a cut, leaving the selected text in its original location as well as placing a copy on the clipboard. (The **Paste Special command** can be used instead of the Paste command to paste the text without the associated formatting.)

The Cut, Copy, and Paste commands are found in the Edit menu, or alternatively, can be executed by clicking the appropriate buttons on the Standard toolbar. The contents of the Windows clipboard are replaced by each subsequent Cut or Copy command, but are unaffected by the Paste command. The contents of the clipboard can be pasted into multiple locations in the same or different documents.

Microsoft Office has its own clipboard that enables you to collect and paste multiple items. The **Office clipboard** differs from the Windows clipboard in that the contents of each successive Copy command are added to the clipboard. Thus, you could copy the first paragraph of a document to the Office clipboard, then copy (add) a bulleted list in the middle of the document to the Office clipboard, and finally copy (add) the last paragraph (three items in all) to the Office clipboard. You could then go to another place in the document or to a different document altogether, and paste the contents of the Office clipboard (three separate items) with a single command. The Office clipboard can hold up to 24 text or graphical elements.

Selected text is copied automatically to the Office clipboard regardless of whether you use the Copy command in the Edit menu, the Copy button on the Standard toolbar, or the Ctrl+C shortcut. The Office clipboard is accessed through the Edit menu and/or the task pane.

FIND, REPLACE, AND GO TO COMMANDS

The Find, Replace, and Go To commands share a common dialog box with different tabs for each command as shown in Figure 2.1. The **Find command** locates one or more occurrences of specific text (e.g., a word or phrase). The **Replace command** goes one step further in that it locates the text, and then enables you to optionally replace (one or more occurrences of) that text with different text. The **Go To command** goes directly to a specific place (e.g., a specific page) in the document.

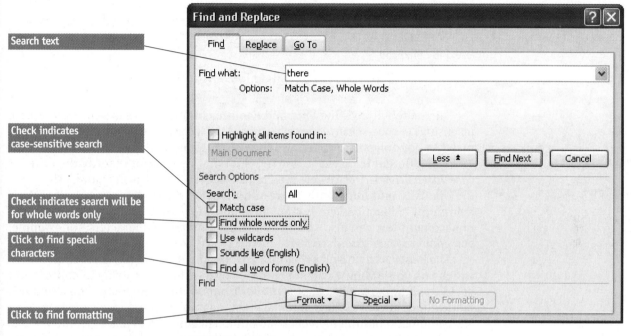

(a) Find Command

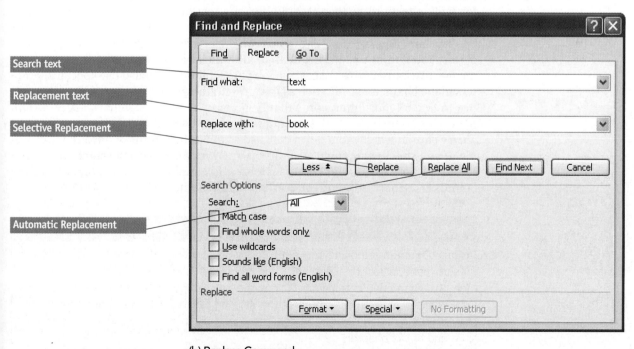

(b) Replace Command

FIGURE 2.1 The Find, Replace, and Go To Commands

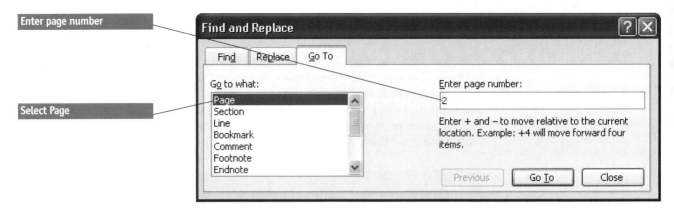

(c) Go To Command

FIGURE 2.1 The Find, Replace, and Go To Commands (*continued*)

The search in both the Find and Replace commands is case sensitive or case insensitive. A *case-sensitive search* (where Match Case is selected as in Figure 2.1a) matches not only the text, but also the use of upper- and lowercase letters. Thus, *There* is different from *there,* and a search on one will not identify the other. A *case-insensitive search* (where Match Case is *not* selected as in Figure 2.1b) is just the opposite and finds both *There* and *there.* A search may also specify *whole words only* to identify *there,* but not *therefore* or *thereby.* And finally, the search and replacement text can also specify different numbers of characters; for example, you could replace *16* with *sixteen.*

The Replace command in Figure 2.1b implements either *selective replacement,* which lets you examine each occurrence of the character string in context and decide whether to replace it, or *automatic replacement,* where the substitution is made automatically. Selective replacement is implemented by clicking the Find Next command button, then clicking (or not clicking) the Replace button to make the substitution. Automatic replacement (through the entire document) is implemented by clicking the Replace All button. This often produces unintended consequences and is not recommended; for example, if you substitute the word *text* for *book,* the word *textbook* would become *texttext,* which is not what you had in mind.

The Find and Replace commands can include formatting and/or special characters. You can, for example, change all italicized text to boldface, or you can change five consecutive spaces to a tab character. You can also use special characters in the character string such as the "any character" (consisting of ^?). For example, to find all four-letter words that begin with "f" and end with "l" (such as *fall, fill,* or *fail*), search for f^?^?l. (The question mark stands for any character, just like a *wild card* in a card game.) You can also search for all forms of a word; for example, if you specify *am,* it will also find *is* and *are.* You can even search for a word based on how it sounds. When searching for *Marion,* for example, check the Sounds Like check box, and the search will find both *Marion* and *Marian.*

INSERT THE DATE AND TIME

Most documents include the date and time they were created. Pull down the Insert menu, select the Date and Time command to display the Date and Time dialog box, then choose a format. Check the box to update the date automatically if you want your document to reflect the date on which it is opened, or clear the box to retain the date on which the document was created. See practice exercise 4 at the end of the chapter.

Scrolling occurs when a document is too large to be seen in its entirety. Figure 2.2a displays a large printed document, only part of which is visible on the screen in Figure 2.2b. In order to see a different portion of the document, you need to scroll, whereby new lines will be brought into view as the old lines disappear.

To: Our Students
From: Bob Grauer and Maryann Barber

Welcome to the wonderful world of word processing. Over the next several chapters we will build a foundation in the basics of Microsoft Word, and then teach you to format specialized documents, create professional looking tables and charts, publish well-designed newsletters, and create Web pages. Before you know it, you will be a word processing and desktop publishing wizard!

The first chapter presented the basics of word processing and showed you how to create a simple document. You learned how to insert, replace, and/or delete text. This chapter will teach you about fonts and special effects (such as **boldfacing** and *italicizing*) and how to use them effectively — how too little is better than too much.

You will go on to experiment with margins, tab stops, line spacing, and justification, learning first to format simple documents and then going on to longer, more complex ones. It is with the latter that we explore headers and footers, page numbering, widows and orphans (yes, we really did mean widows and orphans). It is here that we bring in graphics, working with newspaper-type columns, and the elements of a good page design. And without question, we will introduce the tools that make life so much easier (and your writing so much more impressive) — the Spell Check, Grammar Check, Thesaurus, and Styles.

If you are wondering what all these things are, read on in the text and proceed with the hands-on exercises. We will show you how to create a simple newsletter, and then improve it by adding graphics, fonts, and WordArt. You will create a simple calendar using the Tables feature, and then create more intricate forms that will rival anything you have seen. You will learn how to create a résumé with your beginner's skills, and then make it look like so much more with your intermediate (even advanced) skills. You will learn how to download resources from the Internet and how to create your own Web page. Last, but not least, run a mail merge to produce the cover letters that will accompany your résumé as it is mailed to companies across the United States (and even the world).

It is up to you to practice for it is only through working at the computer, that you will learn what you need to know. Experiment and don't be afraid to make mistakes. Practice and practice some more.

Our goal is for you to learn and to enjoy what you are learning. We have great confidence in you, and in our ability to help you discover what you can do. Visit the home page for the <u>Exploring Office series</u>. You can also send us e-mail. You can email Bob Grauer at <u>rgrauer@miami.edu</u>. You can reach Maryann Barber at <u>mbarber@miami.edu</u>. As you read the last sentence, notice that Microsoft Word is Web-enabled and that the Internet and e-mail references appear as hyperlinks in this document. Thus, you can click the address of our home page from within this document and then you can view the page immediately, provided you have an Internet connection. You can also click the e-mail address to open your mail program, provided it has been configured correctly.

We look forward to hearing from you and hope that you will like our textbook. You are about to embark on a wonderful journey toward computer literacy. Be patient and inquisitive.

(a) Printed Document

FIGURE 2.2   Scrolling

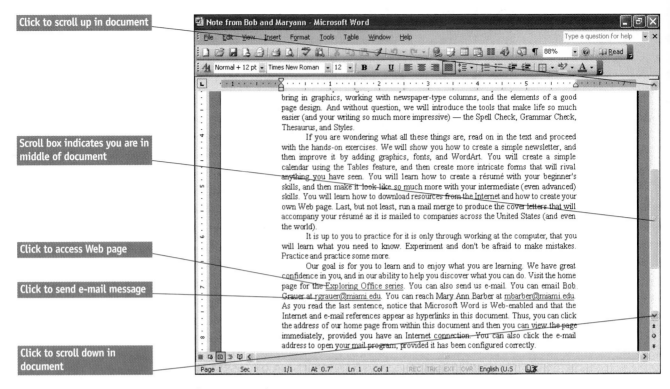

Click to scroll up in document

Scroll box indicates you are in middle of document

Click to access Web page

Click to send e-mail message

Click to scroll down in document

(b) Screen Display

FIGURE 2.2 Scrolling (*continued*)

Scrolling comes about automatically as you reach the bottom of the screen. Entering a new line of text, clicking on the down arrow within the scroll bar, or pressing the down arrow key brings a new line into view at the bottom of the screen and simultaneously removes a line at the top. (The process is reversed at the top of the screen.)

Scrolling can be done with either the mouse or the keyboard. Scrolling with the mouse (e.g., clicking the down arrow in the scroll bar) changes what is displayed on the screen, but does not move the insertion point, so that you must click the mouse after scrolling prior to entering the text at the new location. Scrolling with the keyboard, however (e.g., pressing Ctrl+Home or Ctrl+End to move to the beginning or end of a document, respectively), changes what is displayed on the screen as well as the location of the insertion point, and you can begin typing immediately.

Scrolling occurs most often in a vertical direction as shown in Figure 2.2. It can also occur horizontally, when the length of a line in a document exceeds the number of characters that can be displayed horizontally on the screen.

WRITE NOW, EDIT LATER

You write a sentence, then change it, and change it again, and one hour later you've produced a single paragraph. It happens to every writer—you stare at a blank screen and flashing cursor and are unable to write. The best solution is to brainstorm and write down anything that pops into your head, and to keep on writing. Don't worry about typos or spelling errors because you can fix them later. Above all, resist the temptation to continually edit the few words you've written because overediting will drain the life out of what you are writing. The important thing is to get your ideas on paper.

The *View menu* provides different views of a document. Each view can be displayed at different magnifications, which in turn determine the amount of scrolling necessary to see remote parts of a document.

The *Normal view* is the default view and it provides the fastest way to enter text. The *Print Layout view* more closely resembles the printed document and displays the top and bottom margins, headers and footers, page numbers, graphics, and other features that do not appear in the Normal view. The *Reading Layout view* eliminates unnecessary toolbars, making it easier to read your document. It also enables you to annotate a document with comments and/or highlighting of key sections.

The *Zoom command* displays the document on the screen at different magnifications—for example, 75%, 100%, or 200%. (The Zoom command does not affect the size of the text on the printed page.) A Zoom percentage (magnification) of 100% displays the document in the approximate size of the text on the printed page. You can increase the percentage to 200% to make the characters appear larger. You can also decrease the magnification to 75% to see more of the document at one time.

Word will automatically determine the magnification if you select one of four additional Zoom options—Page Width, Text Width, Whole Page, or Many Pages (Whole Page and Many Pages are available only in the Print Layout view). Figure 2.3, for example, displays a two-page document in Print Layout view. The 40% magnification is determined automatically once you specify the number of pages.

The View menu also provides access to two additional views—the Outline view and the Web Layout view. The Outline view does not display a conventional outline, but rather a structural view of a document that can be collapsed or expanded as necessary. The Web Layout view is used when you are creating a Web page. Both views are discussed in later chapters.

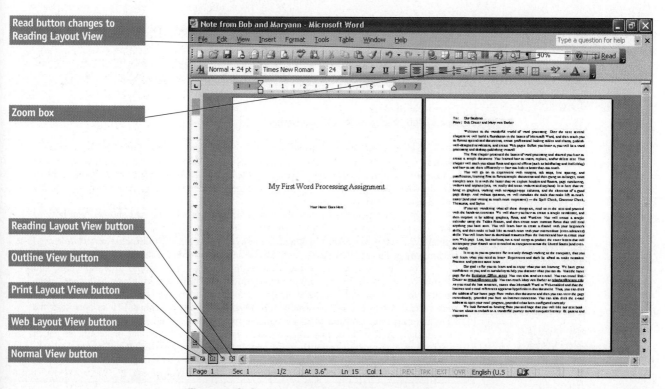

FIGURE 2.3 View Menu and Zoom Command

1   Editing a Document

Objective   To edit an existing document; to use the Find and Replace commands; to move and copy text using the clipboard and the drag-and-drop facility. Use Figure 2.4 as a guide in the exercise.

Step 1:   **The View Menu**

■ Start Word as described in the hands-on exercises from Chapter 1. Pull down the **File menu** and click **Open** (or click the **Open button** on the toolbar).

  ❏ Click the **drop-down arrow** on the Look In list box. Click the appropriate drive, drive C or drive A, depending on the location of your data.

  ❏ Double click the **Exploring Word folder** to make it the active folder (the folder in which you will save the document).

  ❏ Scroll in the Name list box (if necessary) until you can click the **Note from Bob and Maryann** to select this document. Double click the **document icon** or click the **Open command button** to open the file.

■ The document should appear on the screen as shown in Figure 2.4a.

■ Change to the Print Layout view at Page Width magnification:

  ❏ Pull down the **View menu** and click **Print Layout** (or click the **Print Layout View button** above the status bar) as shown in Figure 2.4a.

  ❏ Click the **down arrow** in the Zoom box to change to **Page Width**.

■ Click and drag the mouse to select the phrase **Our Students**, which appears at the beginning of the document. Type your name to replace the selected text.

■ Pull down the **File menu**, click the **Save As command**, then save the document as **Note from Bob and Maryann Solution**. (This creates a second copy of the document.)

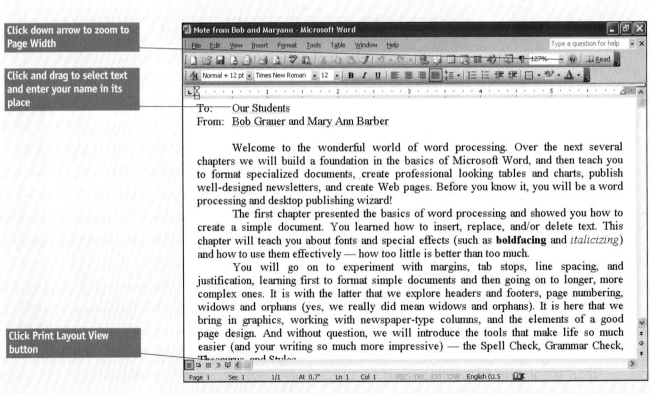

Click down arrow to zoom to Page Width

Click and drag to select text and enter your name in its place

Click Print Layout View button

(a) The View Menu (step 1)

FIGURE 2.4   Hands-on Exercise 1

Step 2: Scrolling

- Click and drag the **scroll box** within the vertical scroll bar to scroll to the end of the document as shown in Figure 2.4b. Click immediately before the period at the end of the last sentence.

- Type a **comma** and a space, then insert the phrase **but most of all**, **enjoy**.

- Drag the **scroll box** to the top of the scroll bar to get back to the beginning of the document.

- Click immediately before the period ending the first sentence, press the **space bar**, then add the phrase **and desktop publishing**.

- Use the keyboard to practice scrolling shortcuts. Press **Ctrl+Home** and **Ctrl+End** to move to the beginning and end of a document, respectively. Press **PgUp** or **PgDn** to scroll one screen in the indicated direction.

- Save the document.

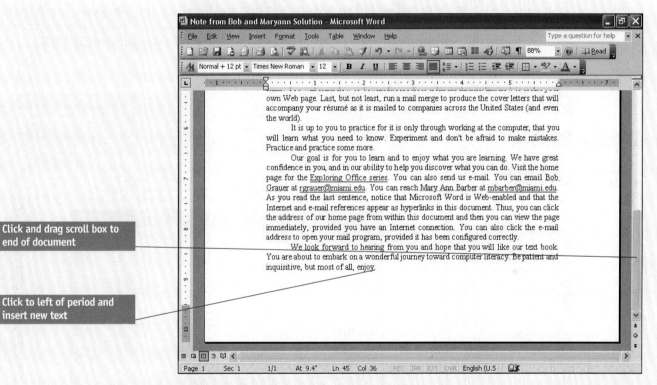

(b) Scrolling (step 2)

FIGURE 2.4 Hands-on Exercise 1 (*continued*)

THE MOUSE AND THE SCROLL BAR

Scroll quickly through a document by clicking above or below the scroll box to scroll up or down an entire screen. Move to the top, bottom, or an approximate position within a document by dragging the scroll box to the corresponding position in the scroll bar; for example, dragging the scroll box to the middle of the bar moves the mouse pointer to the middle of the document. Scrolling with the mouse does not change the location of the insertion point, however, and thus you must click the mouse at the new location prior to entering text at that location.

Step 3: The Replace Command

- Press **Ctrl+Home** to move to the beginning of the document. Pull down the **Edit menu**. Click **Replace** to produce the dialog box of Figure 2.4c. Click the **More button** to display the available options. Clear the check boxes.

- Type **text** in the Find what text box. Press the **Tab key**. Type **book** in the Replace with text box.

- Click the **Find Next button** to find the first occurrence of the word *text*. The dialog box remains on the screen, and the first occurrence of *text* is selected. This is *not* an appropriate substitution.

- Click the **Find Next button** to move to the next occurrence without making the replacement. This time the substitution is appropriate.

- Click **Replace** to make the change and automatically move to the next occurrence, where the substitution is again inappropriate. Click **Find Next** a final time. Word will indicate that it has finished searching the document. Click **OK**.

- Change the Find and Replace strings to **Mary Ann** and **Maryann**, respectively. Click the **Replace All button** to make the substitution globally without confirmation. Word will indicate that two replacements were made. Click **OK**.

- Close the dialog box. Save the document.

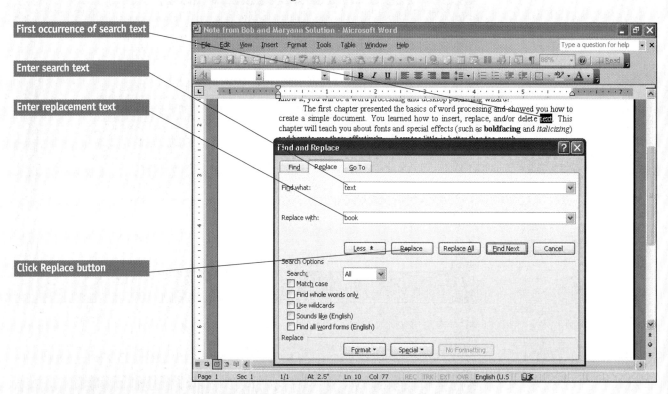

(c) The Replace Command (step 3)

FIGURE 2.4 Hands-on Exercise 1 (*continued*)

SEARCH FOR SPECIAL CHARACTERS

Use the Find and Replace commands to search for special characters such as tabs or paragraph marks. Click the More button in either dialog box, then click the Special command button that appears in the expanded dialog box to search for the additional characters. You could, for example, replace erroneous paragraph marks with a simple space, or replace five consecutive spaces with a Tab character.

Step 4: The Windows Clipboard

- Click and drag to select the sentence asking you to visit our home page, which includes a hyperlink (underlined blue text). Click the **Copy button**.

- Press **Ctrl+End** to move to the end of the document. Pull down the **Edit menu**, click the **Paste Special command** to display the Paste Special dialog box. Select **Unformatted text** and click **OK**.

- The sentence appears at the end of the document, but without the hyperlink formatting. Click the **Undo button** since we do not want the sentence. You have, however, seen the effect of the Paste Special command.

- If necessary, scroll until you see the paragraph beginning **It is up to you**. Select the sentence **Practice and practice some more** by dragging the mouse. (Be sure to include the period.)

- Pull down the **Edit menu** and click the **Copy command** or click the **Copy button**.

- Press **Ctrl+End** to scroll to the end of the document. Press the **space bar**. Pull down the **Edit menu** and click the **Paste command** (or click the **Paste button**).

- Click the **Paste Options button** if it appears as shown in Figure 2.4d to see the available options, then press **Esc** to suppress the context-sensitive menu.

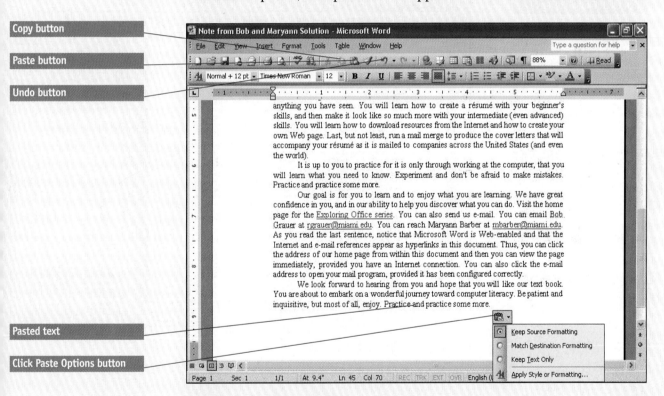

(d) The Windows Clipboard (step 4)

FIGURE 2.4 Hands-on Exercise 1 (*continued*)

PASTE OPTIONS

Text can be copied with or without the associated formatting according to the selected option in the Paste Options button. (The button appears automatically whenever the source and destination paragraphs have different formatting.) The default is to keep the source formatting (the formatting of the copied object). The button disappears as soon as you begin typing.

Step 5: The Office Clipboard

- Pull down the **Edit menu** and click the **Office Clipboard command** to open the clipboard task pane as shown in Figure 2.4e. The contents of your clipboard may differ.

- Delete any items that appear except the one urging you to practice.

- Click and drag to select the three sentences that indicate you can send us e-mail, and that contain our e-mail addresses. Click the **Copy button** to copy these sentences to the Office clipboard, which now contains two icons.

- Press **Ctrl+End** to move to the end of the document, press **Enter** to begin a new paragraph, and press the **Tab key** to indent the paragraph. Click the **Paste All button** on the Office clipboard to paste both items at the end of the document. (You may have to add a space between the two sentences.)

- Close the task pane.

- Save the document.

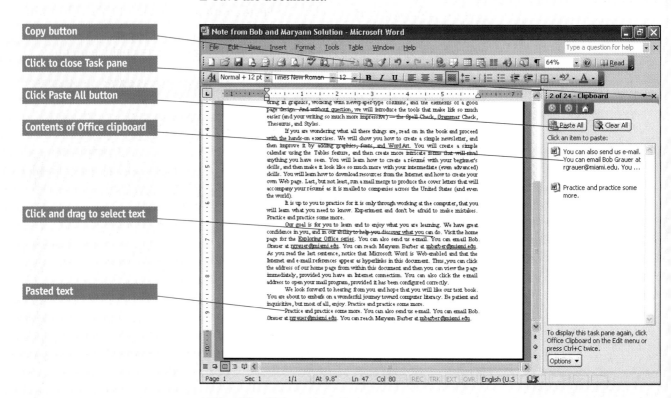

(e) The Office Clipboard (step 5)

FIGURE 2.4 Hands-on Exercise 1 (*continued*)

THE OFFICE CLIPBOARD

The Office clipboard enables you to collect up to 24 text and/or graphical elements from any Office document, and then it lets you paste those elements individually or collectively into an altogether different document. For example, you can cut or copy text from a Word document, data from an Excel worksheet, and a bulleted list from PowerPoint, then you can paste all of those elements into a new Word document. The collected items stay on the Office clipboard until you exit Office. (Press Ctrl+C twice in a row to display the Office clipboard if it is not already visible.)

Step 6: **Undo and Redo Commands**

- Click the **drop-down arrow** next to the Undo button to display the previously executed actions as in Figure 2.4f. The list of actions corresponds to the editing commands you have issued since the start of the exercise.

- Click **Paste** (the first command on the list) to undo the last editing command; the sentence asking you to send us e-mail disappears from the last paragraph.

- Click the **Undo button** a second time and the sentence, Practice and practice some more, disappears.

- Click the remaining steps on the undo list to retrace your steps through the exercise one command at a time. Alternatively, you can scroll to the bottom of the list and click the last command.

- Either way, when the undo list is empty, you will have the document as it existed at the start of the exercise. Click the **drop-down arrow** for the Redo command to display the list of commands you have undone.

- Click each command in sequence (or click the command at the bottom of the list), and you will restore the document.

- Save the document.

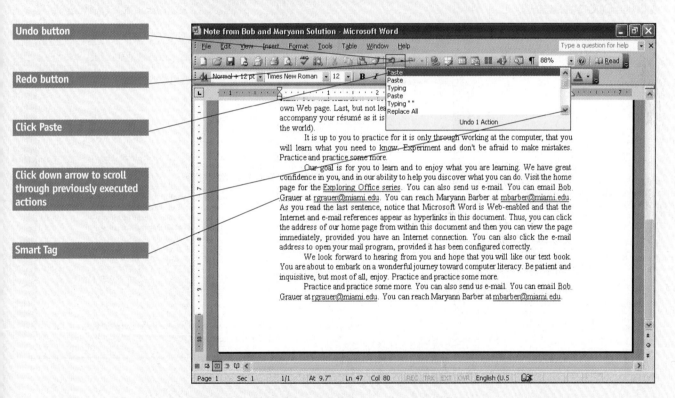

(f) Undo and Redo Commands (step 6)

FIGURE 2.4 Hands-on Exercise 1 (*continued*)

KEYBOARD SHORTCUTS—CUT, COPY AND PASTE

Ctrl+X, Ctrl+C, and Ctrl+V are keyboard shortcuts to cut, copy, and paste, respectively. The "X" is supposed to remind you of a pair of scissors. The shortcuts are easier to remember when you realize that the operative letters, X, C, and V, are next to each other on the keyboard. The shortcuts work in virtually any Windows application. See practice exercise 2 at the end of the chapter.

Step 7: Drag and Drop

- Scroll to the top of the document. Click and drag to select the phrase **format specialized documents** (including the comma and space) as shown in Figure 2.4g, then drag the phrase to its new location immediately before the word *and*. (A dotted vertical bar appears as you drag the text, to indicate its new location.)

- Release the mouse button to complete the move. Click the **drop-down arrow** for the Undo button; click **Move** to undo the move.

- To copy the selected text to the same location (instead of moving it), press and hold the **Ctrl key** as you drag the text to its new location. (A plus sign appears as you drag the text, to indicate it is being copied rather than moved.)

- Practice the drag-and-drop procedure several times until you are confident you can move and copy with precision.

- Click anywhere in the document to deselect the text. Save the document. Print the completed document for your instructor.

- Save the document.

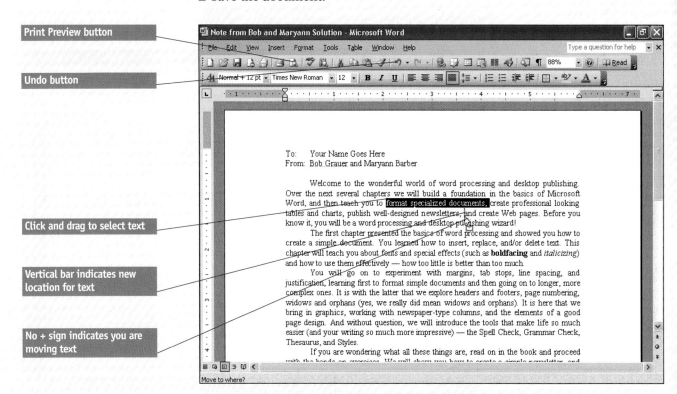

(g) Drag and Drop (step 7)

FIGURE 2.4 Hands-on Exercise 1 (*continued*)

THE PRINT PREVIEW COMMAND

Pull down the File menu and click the Print Preview command or click the Print Preview button on the Standard toolbar to see the document as it will appear when it is printed. The current document should fit on one page; if not, click the Shrink to Fit button on the Print Preview toolbar to automatically reduce the font size and force the document onto one page. Click the Print button to print the document, then close the Print Preview window.

Step 8: E-mail the Completed Document

- Check with your professor before completing this step. Pull down the **File menu**, click the **Send To command**, then choose **Mail Recipient (as Attachment)**.

- Your default e-mail program (e.g., Microsoft Outlook) is started automatically as shown in Figure 2.4h. The subject and attachment are entered automatically.

- Enter your **professor's e-mail address** in the To text box. Press the **Tab key** to move to the CC (courtesy copy) text box and enter your **e-mail address**. (It is always a good idea to send yourself a copy of important e-mail messages.)

- Press the **Tab key** three times to move to the body of the message, then enter a short note to your instructor.

- Click the **Send button** to send the message. The e-mail window closes, and you are back in Microsoft Word.

- Pull down the **File menu** and click the **Close command**. Click **Yes** if prompted to save the changes.

- Exit Word if you do not want to continue with the next exercise at this time.

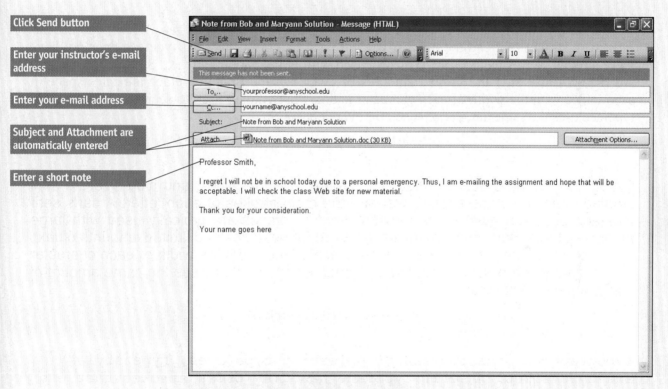

(h) E-mail the Completed Document (step 8)

FIGURE 2.4 Hands-on Exercise 1 (*continued*)

SEND A DOCUMENT FOR REVIEW

Pull down the File menu, click the Send To command, and choose Mail Recipient (for Review), as opposed to Mail Recipient (as Attachment). The result is almost the same except for a minor change in the subject line, which says "please review the attached document". The real difference between the commands occurs after the recipient reviews the document, enters his or her changes electronically, then returns the document to the sender. Word will then compare and merge the two documents (the original and the copy sent for review), giving the author the opportunity to accept or reject the reviewer's comments one at a time.

TYPOGRAPHY

Typography is the process of selecting typefaces, type styles, and type sizes. The importance of these decisions is obvious, for the ultimate success of any document depends greatly on its appearance. Type should reinforce the message without calling attention to itself and should be consistent with the information you want to convey.

A **typeface** or **font** is a complete set of characters (upper- and lowercase letters, numbers, punctuation marks, and special symbols). Figure 2.5 illustrates three typefaces—**Times New Roman**, **Arial**, and **Courier New**—that are accessible from any Windows application.

A definitive characteristic of any typeface is the presence or absence of tiny cross lines that end the main strokes of each letter. A **serif typeface** has these lines. A **sans serif typeface** (*sans* from the French for *without*) does not. Times New Roman and Courier New are examples of a serif typeface. Arial is a sans serif typeface.

Typography is the process of selecting typefaces, type styles, and type sizes. A serif typeface has tiny cross strokes that end the main strokes of each letter. A sans serif typeface does not have these strokes. Serif typefaces are typically used with large amounts of text. Sans serif typefaces are used for headings and limited amounts of text. A proportional typeface allocates space in accordance with the width of each character and is what you are used to seeing. A monospaced typeface uses the same amount of space for every character.

(a) Times New Roman (serif and proportional)

Typography is the process of selecting typefaces, type styles, and type sizes. A serif typeface has tiny cross strokes that end the main strokes of each letter. A sans serif typeface does not have these strokes. Serif typefaces are typically used with large amounts of text. Sans serif typefaces are used for headings and limited amounts of text. A proportional typeface allocates space in accordance with the width of each character and is what you are used to seeing. A monospaced typeface uses the same amount of space for every character.

(b) Arial (sans serif and proportional)

```
Typography is the process of selecting typefaces, type styles,
and type sizes. A serif typeface has tiny cross strokes that end
the main strokes of each letter. A sans serif typeface does not
have these strokes. Serif typefaces are typically used with large
amounts of text. Sans serif typefaces are used for headings and
limited amounts of text. A proportional typeface allocates space
in accordance with the width of each character and is what you
are used to seeing. A monospaced typeface uses the same amount of
space for every character.
```

(c) Courier New (serif and monospaced)

FIGURE 2.5 Typefaces

Serifs help the eye to connect one letter with the next and are generally used with large amounts of text. This book, for example, is set in a serif typeface. A sans serif typeface is more effective with smaller amounts of text and appears in headlines, corporate logos, airport signs, and so on.

A second characteristic of a typeface is whether it is monospaced or proportional. A ***monospaced typeface*** (such as Courier New) uses the same amount of space for every character regardless of its width. A ***proportional typeface*** (such as Times New Roman or Arial) allocates space according to the width of the character. Monospaced fonts are used in tables and financial projections where text must be precisely lined up, one character underneath the other. Proportional typefaces create a more professional appearance and are appropriate for most documents. Any typeface can be set in different ***type styles*** (such as regular, **bold**, *italic*, or ***bold italic***).

Type Size

Type size is a vertical measurement and is specified in points. One ***point*** is equal to $\frac{1}{72}$ of an inch; that is, there are 72 points to the inch. The measurement is made from the top of the tallest letter in a character set (for example, an uppercase T) to the bottom of the lowest letter (for example, a lowercase y). Most documents are set in 10 or 12 point type. Newspaper columns may be set as small as 8 point type, but that is the smallest type size you should consider. Conversely, type sizes of 14 points or higher are ineffective for large amounts of text.

Figure 2.6 shows the same phrase set in varying type sizes. Some typefaces appear larger (smaller) than others even though they may be set in the same point size. The type in Figure 2.6a, for example, looks smaller than the corresponding type in Figure 2.6b even though both are set in the same point size. Note, too, that you can vary the type size of a specific font within a document for emphasis. The eye needs at least two points to distinguish between different type sizes.

Format Font Command

The ***Format Font command*** gives you complete control over the typeface, size, and style of the text in a document. Executing the command before entering text will set the format of the text you type from that point on. You can also use the command to change the font of existing text by selecting the text, then executing the command. Either way, you will see the dialog box in Figure 2.7, in which you specify the font (typeface), style, and point size.

You can choose any of the special effects, such as SMALL CAPS, superscripts, or subscripts. You can also change the underline options (whether or not spaces are to be underlined). You can even change the color of the text on the monitor, but you need a color printer for the printed document. (The ***Character Spacing*** and ***Text Effects*** tabs produce different sets of options in which you control the spacing and appearance of the characters.)

TYPOGRAPHY TIP—USE RESTRAINT

More is not better, especially in the case of too many typefaces and styles, which produce cluttered documents that impress no one. Try to limit yourself to a maximum of two typefaces per document, but choose multiple sizes and/or styles within those typefaces for variation. Use boldface or italic for emphasis (underlining is generally not effective). Use these styles in moderation, because if you emphasize too many elements, the effect is lost.

This is Arial 8 point type

This is Arial 10 point type

This is Arial 12 point type

This is Arial 18 point type

This is Arial 24 point type

This is Arial 30 point type

(a) Sans Serif Typeface

This is Times New Roman 8 point type

This is Times New Roman 10 point type

This is Times New Roman 12 point type

This is Times New Roman 18 point type

This is Times New Roman 24 point type

This is Times New Roman 30 point

(b) Serif Typeface

FIGURE 2.6   Type Size

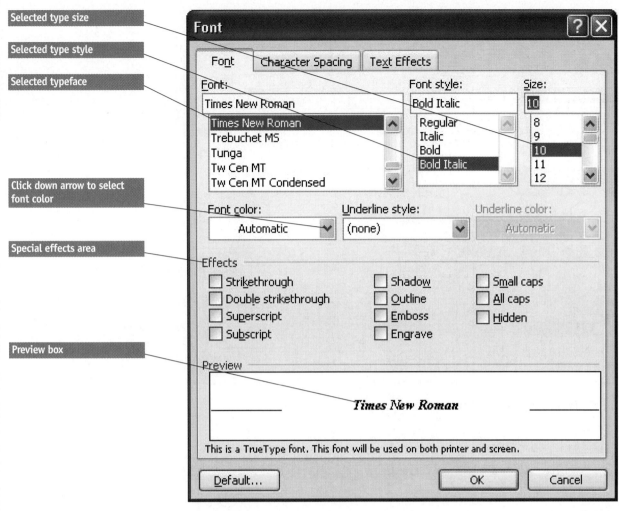

Selected type size

Selected type style

Selected typeface

Click down arrow to select font color

Special effects area

Preview box

FIGURE 2.7   Format Font Command

The Preview box shows the text as it will appear in the document. The message at the bottom of the dialog box indicates that Times New Roman is a TrueType font and that the same font will be used on both the screen and the printer. TrueType fonts ensure that your document is truly WYSIWYG (What You See Is What You Get) because the fonts you see on the monitor will be identical to those in the printed document.

PAGE SETUP COMMAND

The *Page Setup command* in the File menu lets you change margins, paper size, orientation, paper source, and/or layout. All parameters are accessed from the dialog box in Figure 2.8 by clicking the appropriate tab within the dialog box.

The default margins are indicated in Figure 2.8a and are one inch on the top and bottom of the page, and one and a quarter inches on the left and right. You can change any (or all) of these settings by entering a new value in the appropriate text box, either by typing it explicitly or clicking the up/down arrow. All of the settings in the Page Setup command apply to the whole document regardless of the position of the insertion point. (Different settings for any option in the Page Setup dialog box can be established for different parts of a document by creating sections. Sections also affect column formatting, as discussed later in the chapter.)

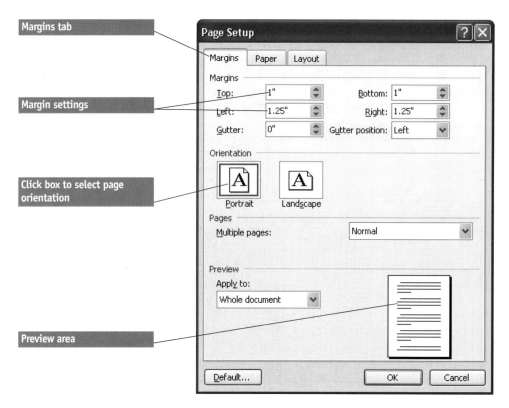

Margins tab

Margin settings

Click box to select page orientation

Preview area

(a) Margins Tab

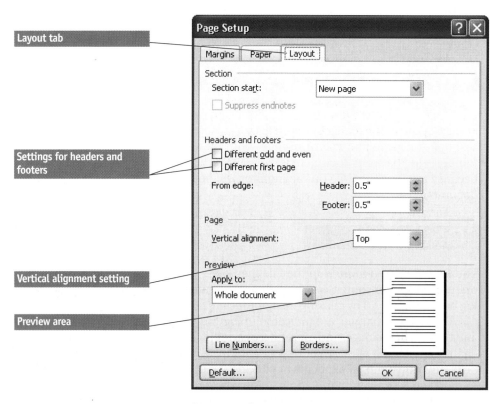

Layout tab

Settings for headers and footers

Vertical alignment setting

Preview area

(b) Layout Tab

FIGURE 2.8   Page Setup Command

The *Margins tab* also enables you to change the orientation of a page as shown in Figure 2.8b. *Portrait orientation* is the default. *Landscape orientation* flips the page 90 degrees so that its dimensions are $11 \times 8\frac{1}{2}$ rather than the other way around. Note, too, the Preview area in both Figures 2.8a and 2.8b, which shows how the document will appear with the selected parameters.

The *Paper tab* (not shown in Figure 2.8) is used to specify which tray should be used on printers with multiple trays, and is helpful when you want to load different types of paper simultaneously. It is also used to specify the paper size. The *Layout tab* in Figure 2.8b is used to specify options for headers and footers (text that appears at the top or bottom of each page in a document), and/or to change the vertical alignment of text on the page. These parameters can also be set at the section level.

Page Breaks

One of the first concepts you learned was that of word wrap, whereby Word inserts a soft return at the end of a line in order to begin a new line. The number and/or location of the soft returns change automatically as you add or delete text within a document. Soft returns are very different from the hard returns inserted by the user, whose number and location remain constant.

In much the same way, Word creates a *soft page break* to go to the top of a new page when text no longer fits on the current page. And just as you can insert a hard return to start a new paragraph, you can insert a *hard page break* to force any part of a document to begin on a new page. A hard page break is inserted into a document using the Break command in the Insert menu or more easily through the Ctrl+Enter keyboard shortcut. (You can prevent the occurrence of awkward page breaks through the Format Paragraph command, which is described in detail later in the chapter.)

AN EXERCISE IN DESIGN

The following exercise has you retrieve an existing document from the set of practice files, then experiment with various typefaces, type styles, and point sizes. The original document uses a monospaced (typewriter style) font, without boldface or italics, and you are asked to improve its appearance. The first step directs you to save the document under a new name so that you can always return to the original if necessary.

There is no right and wrong with respect to design, and you are free to choose any combination of fonts that appeals to you. The exercise takes you through various formatting options but lets you make the final decision. It does, however, ask you to print the final document and submit it to your instructor. Experiment freely and print multiple versions with different designs.

IMPOSE A TIME LIMIT

A word processor is supposed to save time and make you more productive. It will do exactly that, provided you use the word processor for its primary purpose—writing and editing. It is all too easy, however, to lose sight of that objective and spend too much time formatting the document. Concentrate on the content of your document rather than its appearance and remember that the success of a document ultimately depends on its content. Impose a limit on the amount of time you will spend on formatting. End the session when the limit is reached.

2 Character Formatting

Objective   To experiment with character formatting; to change fonts and to use boldface and italic; to copy formatting with the format painter; to insert a page break and see different views of a document. Use Figure 2.9 as a guide in the exercise.

Step 1:   **The Save As Command**

- Start Word. Open the **Tips for Writing** document in the Exploring Word folder.

- Pull down the **File menu**. Click the **Save As command** to save the document as **Tips for Writing Solution**. The new document name appears on the title bar as shown in Figure 2.9a.

- Pull down the **View menu** and click **Normal** (or click the **Normal View button** above the status bar). Click the **down arrow** on the Zoom list box and set the magnification (zoom) to **Page Width**.

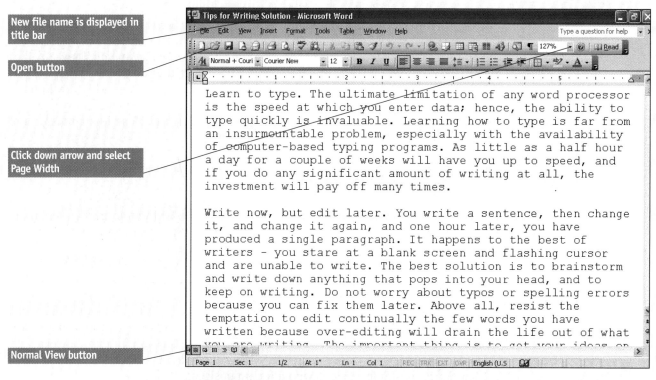

New file name is displayed in title bar

Open button

Click down arrow and select Page Width

Normal View button

(a) The Save As Command (step 1)

FIGURE 2.9   Hands-on Exercise 2

VIEW MULTIPLE DOCUMENTS

You generally work on one document at a time, but what if you wanted to compare or reference text in another document? Open the second document, pull down the Window menu, and click the Arrange all command to display both documents on the screen at one time. Each document appears in its own window, with a minimize, maximize, and close button. Just click in the window for the document you want and continue to edit. You can maximize either document and/or close the document when you are finished.

Step 2: **Change the Font**

■ Pull down the **Edit menu** and click the **Select All command** (or press **Ctrl+A**) to select the entire document as shown in Figure 2.9b.

■ Click the **down arrow** on the Font List box and choose a different font. (Notice how the actual fonts are displayed within the list box.) We selected **Times New Roman**.

■ Click the **down arrow** on the Font Size list box and choose a different type size.

■ Pull down the **Format menu** and select the **Font command** to display the Font dialog box, where you can also change the font and/or font size.

■ Experiment with different fonts and font sizes until you are satisfied. We ended with 12 point Times New Roman.

■ Save the document.

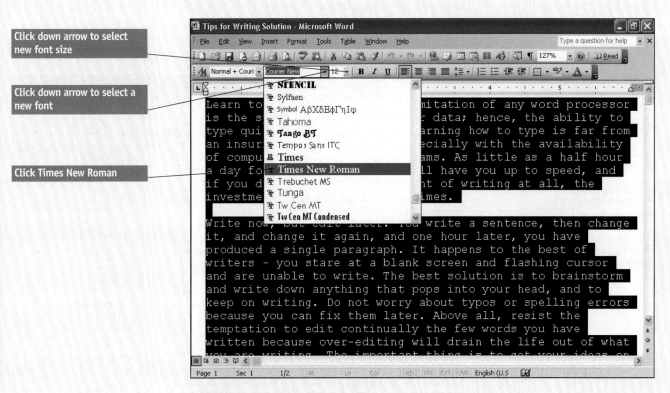

(b) Change the Font (step 2)

FIGURE 2.9 Hands-on Exercise 2 *(continued)*

FIND AND REPLACE FORMATTING

The Replace command enables you to replace formatting as well as text. To replace any text set in bold with the same text in italic, pull down the Edit menu, and click the Replace command. Click the Find what text box, but do *not* enter any text. Click the More button to expand the dialog box. Click the Format command button, click Font, click Bold in the Font Style list, and click OK. Click the Replace with text box and again do *not* enter any text. Click the Format command button, click Font, click Italic in the Font Style list, and click OK. Click the Find Next or Replace All command button to do selective or automatic replacement. Use a similar technique to replace one font with another.

Step 3: **Boldface and Italic**

- Select the sentence **Learn to type** at the beginning of the document.

- Click the **Italic button** on the Formatting toolbar to italicize the selected phrase, which will remain selected after the italic takes effect.

- Click the **Bold button** to boldface the selected text. The text is now in bold italic.

- Pull down the **View menu** and open the task pane. Click the **down arrow** in the task pane and select **Reveal Formatting** as shown in Figure 2.9c.

- Click anywhere in the heading, **Learn to Type**, to display its formatting properties. This type of information can be invaluable if you are unsure of the formatting in effect. Close the task pane.

- Experiment with different styles (bold, italic, underlining, bold italic) until you are satisfied. Each button functions as a toggle switch to turn the selected effect on or off.

- Save the document.

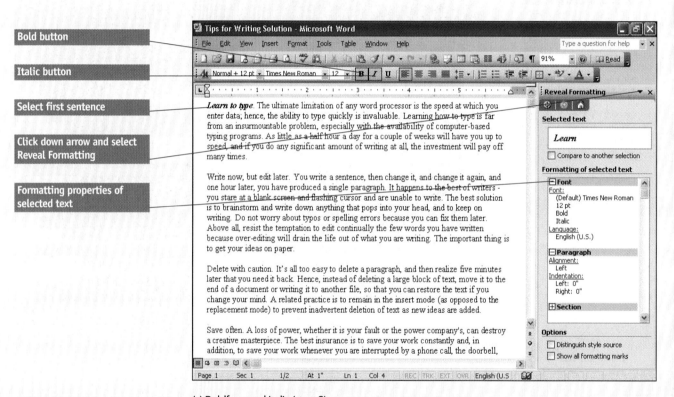

(c) Boldface and Italic (step 3)

FIGURE 2.9 Hands-on Exercise 2 (*continued*)

UNDERLINING TEXT

Underlining is less popular than it was, but Word provides a complete range of underlining options. Select the text to underline, pull down the Format menu, click Font to display the Font dialog box, and click the Font tab if necessary. Click the down arrow on the Underline Style list box to choose the type of underlining you want. You can choose whether to underline the words only (i.e., the underline does not appear in the space between words). You can also choose the type of line you want—solid, dashed, thick, or thin.

Step 4: **The Format Painter**

■ Click anywhere within the sentence Learn to Type. **Double click** the **Format Painter button** on the Standard toolbar. The mouse pointer changes to a paintbrush as shown in Figure 2.9d.

■ Drag the mouse pointer over the next title, **Write now**, **but edit later**, and release the mouse. The formatting from the original sentence (bold italic) has been applied to this sentence as well.

■ Drag the mouse pointer (in the shape of a paintbrush) over the remaining titles (the first sentence in each paragraph) to copy the formatting. You can click the down arrow on the vertical scroll bar to bring more of the document into view.

■ Click the **Format Painter button** after you have painted the title of the last tip to turn the feature off. (Note that clicking the Format Painter button, rather than double clicking it, will paint only one item.)

■ Save the document.

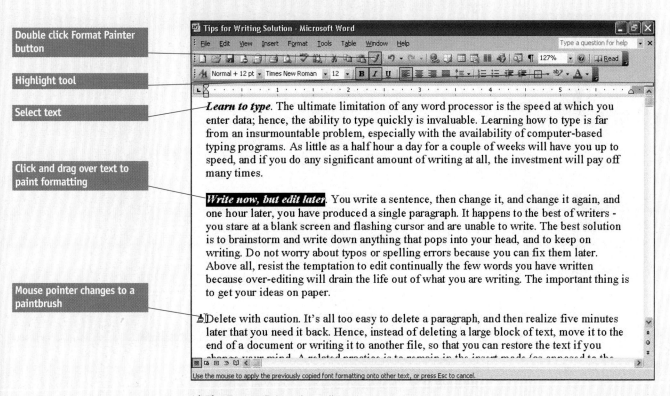

(d) The Format Painter (step 4)

FIGURE 2.9   Hands-on Exercise 2 *(continued)*

HIGHLIGHTING TEXT

You will love the Highlight tool, especially if you are in the habit of highlighting text with a pen. Click the down arrow next to the tool to select a color (yellow is the default) and change the mouse pointer to a pen, then click and drag to highlight the desired text. Continue dragging the mouse to highlight as many selections as you like. Click the Highlight tool a second time to turn off the feature.

Step 5: Change Margins

- Press **Ctrl+End** to move to the end of the document as shown in Figure 2.9e.

- You will see a dotted line indicating a soft page break. (If you do not see the page break, it means that your document fits on one page because you used a different font and/or a smaller point size. We used 12 point Times New Roman.)

- Pull down the **File menu**. Click **Page Setup**. Click the **Margins tab** if necessary. Change the bottom margin to **.75** inch.

- Check that these settings apply to the **Whole Document**. Click **OK**. Save the document.

- The page break disappears because more text fits on the page.

- Save the document.

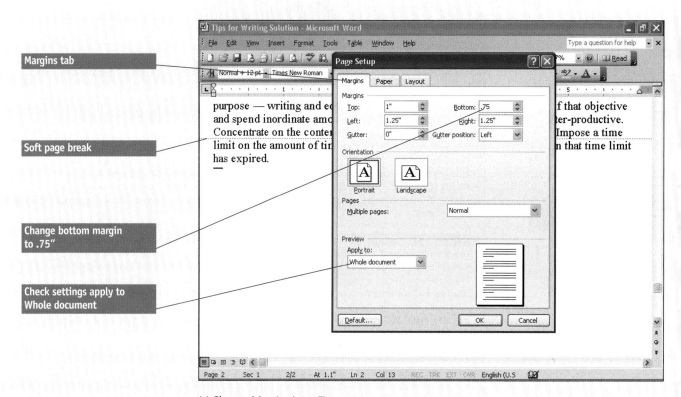

(e) Change Margins (step 5)

FIGURE 2.9 Hands-on Exercise 2 (*continued*)

DIALOG BOX SHORTCUTS

You can use keyboard shortcuts to select options in a dialog box. Press Tab (Shift+Tab) to move forward (backward) from one field or command button to the next. Press Alt plus the underlined letter to move directly to a field or command button. Press Enter to activate the selected command button. Press Esc to exit the dialog box without taking action. Press the space bar to toggle check boxes on or off. Press the down arrow to open a drop-down list box once the list has been accessed, then press the up or down arrow to move between options in a list box. These are uniform shortcuts that apply to any Windows application.

Step 6: Create the Title Page

- Press **Ctrl+Home** to move to the beginning of the document. Press **Enter** three or four times to add a few blank lines.

- Press **Ctrl+Enter** to insert a hard page break. You will see the words "Page Break" in the middle of a dotted line as shown in Figure 2.9f.

- Press the **up arrow key** three times. Enter the title **Tips for Writing**. Select the title, and format it in a larger point size, such as 24 points.

- Press **Enter** to move to a new line. Type your name, and format it in a different point size, such as 14 points.

- Select both the title and your name as shown in the figure. Click the **Center button** on the Formatting toolbar.

- Save the document.

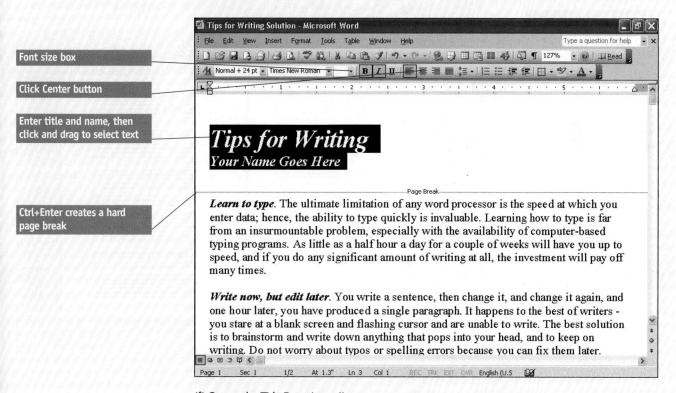

(f) Create the Title Page (step 6)

FIGURE 2.9   Hands-on Exercise 2 (*continued*)

DOUBLE CLICK AND TYPE

Creating a title page is a breeze if you take advantage of the (double) click and type feature. Pull down the View menu and change to the Print Layout view. Double click anywhere on the page, and you can begin typing immediately at that location, without having to type several blank lines, or set tabs. The feature does not work in the Normal view or in a document that has columns. To enable (disable) the feature, pull down the Tools menu, click the Options command, click the Edit tab, then check (clear) the Enable Click and Type check box.

Step 7: **The Completed Document**

- Pull down the **View menu** and click **Print Layout** (or click the **Print Layout button** above the status bar).

- Click the **Zoom arrow** on the Standard toolbar and select **Two Pages**. Release the mouse to view the completed document in Figure 2.9g.

- You may want to add additional blank lines at the top of the title page to move the title further down on the page.

- Save the document. Be sure that the document fits on two pages (the title page and text), then click the **Print button** on the Standard toolbar to print the document for your instructor.

- Exit Word if you do not want to continue with the next exercise at this time.

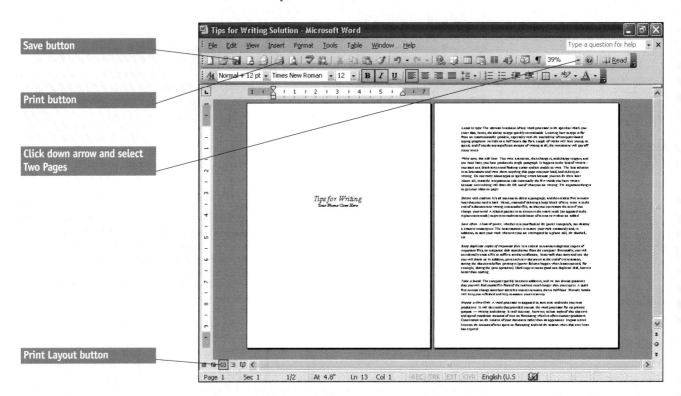

Save button

Print button

Click down arrow and select Two Pages

Print Layout button

(g) The Completed Document (step 7)

FIGURE 2.9 Hands-on Exercise 2 (*continued*)

THE PAGE SETUP COMMAND

The Page Setup command controls the margins of a document, and by extension, it controls the amount of text that fits on a page. Pull down the File menu and click the Page Setup command (or double click a blank area on the ruler) to display the Page Setup dialog box. Click the Margins tab and then adjust the left and right (or top and bottom) margins to fit additional text on a page. Click the down arrow in the Apply to area to select the whole document. Click OK to accept the settings and close the dialog box.

PARAGRAPH FORMATTING

A change in typography is only one way to alter the appearance of a document. You can also change the alignment, indentation, tab stops, or line spacing for any paragraph(s) within the document. You can control the pagination and prevent the occurrence of awkward page breaks by specifying that an entire paragraph has to appear on the same page, or that a one-line paragraph (e.g., a heading) should appear on the same page as the next paragraph. You can include borders or shading for added emphasis around selected paragraphs.

All of these features are implemented at the paragraph level and affect all selected paragraphs. If no paragraphs are selected, the commands affect the entire current paragraph (the paragraph containing the insertion point), regardless of the position of the insertion point when the command is executed.

Alignment

Text can be aligned in four different ways as shown in Figure 2.10. It may be justified (flush left/flush right), left aligned (flush left with a ragged right margin), right aligned (flush right with a ragged left margin), or centered within the margins (ragged left and right).

Left aligned text is perhaps the easiest to read. The first letters of each line align with each other, helping the eye to find the beginning of each line. The lines themselves are of irregular length. There is uniform spacing between words, and the ragged margin on the right adds white space to the text, giving it a lighter and more informal look.

Justified text produces lines of equal length, with the spacing between words adjusted to align at the margins. It may be more difficult to read than text that is left aligned because of the uneven (sometimes excessive) word spacing and/or the greater number of hyphenated words needed to justify the lines.

Text that is centered or right aligned is usually restricted to limited amounts of text where the effect is more important than the ease of reading. Centered text, for example, appears frequently on wedding invitations, poems, or formal announcements. Right aligned text is used with figure captions and short headlines.

Indents

Individual paragraphs can be indented so that they appear to have different margins from the rest of a document. Indentation is established at the paragraph level; thus different indentation can be in effect for different paragraphs. One paragraph may be indented from the left margin only, another from the right margin only, and a third from both the left and right margins. The first line of any paragraph may be indented differently from the rest of the paragraph. And finally, a paragraph may be set with no indentation at all, so that it aligns on the left and right margins.

The indentation of a paragraph is determined by three settings: the *left indent*, the *right indent*, and a *special indent* (if any). There are two types of special indentation, first line and hanging, as will be explained shortly. The left and right indents are set to zero by default, as is the special indent, and produce a paragraph with no indentation at all as shown in Figure 2.11a. Positive values for the left and right indents offset the paragraph from both margins as shown in Figure 2.11b.

The *first line indent* (Figure 2.11c) affects only the first line in the paragraph and is implemented by pressing the Tab key at the beginning of the paragraph. A *hanging indent* (Figure 2.11d) sets the first line of a paragraph at the left indent and indents the remaining lines according to the amount specified. Hanging indents are often used with bulleted or numbered lists.

We, the people of the United States, in order to form a more perfect Union, establish justice, insure domestic tranquillity, provide for the common defense, promote the general welfare, and secure the blessings of liberty to ourselves and our posterity, do ordain and establish this Constitution for the United States of America.

(a) Justified (flush left/flush right)

We, the people of the United States, in order to form a more perfect Union, establish justice, insure domestic tranquillity, provide for the common defense, promote the general welfare, and secure the blessings of liberty to ourselves and our posterity, do ordain and establish this Constitution for the United States of America.

(b) Left Aligned (flush left/ragged right)

We, the people of the United States, in order to form a more perfect Union, establish justice, insure domestic tranquillity, provide for the common defense, promote the general welfare, and secure the blessings of liberty to ourselves and our posterity, do ordain and establish this Constitution for the United States of America.

(c) Right Aligned (ragged left/flush right)

We, the people of the United States, in order to form a more perfect Union, establish justice, insure domestic tranquillity, provide for the common defense, promote the general welfare, and secure the blessings of liberty to ourselves and our posterity, do ordain and establish this Constitution for the United States of America.

(d) Centered (ragged left/ragged right)

FIGURE 2.10 Alignment

The left and right indents are defined as the distance between the text and the left and right margins, respectively. Both parameters are set to zero in this paragraph and so the text aligns on both margins. Different indentation can be applied to different paragraphs in the same document.

(a) No Indents

Positive values for the left and right indents offset a paragraph from the rest of a document and are often used for long quotations. This paragraph has left and right indents of one-half inch each. Different indentation can be applied to different paragraphs in the same document.

(b) Left and Right Indents

A first line indent affects only the first line in the paragraph and is implemented by pressing the Tab key at the beginning of the paragraph. The remainder of the paragraph is aligned at the left margin (or the left indent if it differs from the left margin) as can be seen from this example. Different indentation can be applied to different paragraphs in the same document.

(c) First Line Indent

A hanging indent sets the first line of a paragraph at the left indent and indents the remaining lines according to the amount specified. Hanging indents are often used with bulleted or numbered lists. Different indentation can be applied to different paragraphs in the same document.

(d) Hanging (Special) Indent

FIGURE 2.11 Indents

Tabs

Anyone who has used a typewriter is familiar with the function of the Tab key; that is, press Tab and the insertion point moves to the next **tab stop** (a measured position to align text at a specific place). The Tab key is much more powerful in Word as you can choose from four different types of tab stops (left, center, right, and decimal). You can also specify a **leader character**, typically dots or hyphens, to draw the reader's eye across the page. Tabs are often used to create columns of text within a document.

The default tab stops are set every ½ inch and are left aligned, but you can change the alignment and/or position with the Format Tabs command. Figure 2.12 illustrates a dot leader in combination with a right tab to produce a Table of Contents. The default tab stops have been cleared in Figure 2.12a, in favor of a single right tab at 5.5 inches. The option button for a dot leader has also been checked. The resulting document is shown in Figure 2.12b.

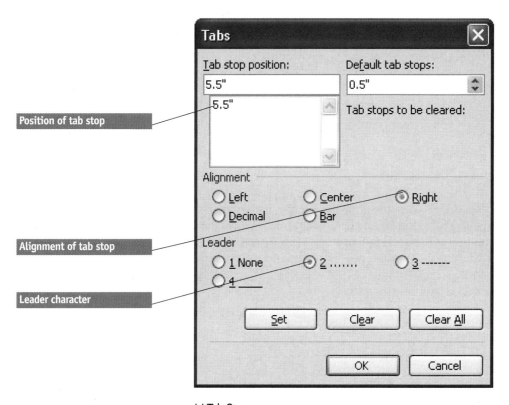

(a) Tab Stops

Right tab with dot leader

(b) Table of Contents

FIGURE 2.12 Tabs

Hyphenation

Hyphenation gives a document a more professional look by eliminating excessive gaps of white space. It is especially useful in narrow columns and/or justified text. Hyphenation is implemented through the Language command in the Tools menu. You can choose to hyphenate a document automatically, in which case the hyphens are inserted as the document is created. (Microsoft Word will automatically rehyphenate the document to adjust for subsequent changes in editing.)

You can also hyphenate a document manually, to have Word prompt you prior to inserting each hyphen. Manual hyphenation does not, however, adjust for changes that affect the line breaks, and so it should be done only after the document is complete. And finally, you can fine-tune the use of hyphenation by preventing a hyphenated word from breaking if it falls at the end of a line. This is done by inserting a *nonbreaking hyphen* (press Ctrl+Shift+Hyphen) when the word is typed initially.

Line Spacing

Line spacing determines the space between the lines in a paragraph. Word provides complete flexibility and enables you to select any multiple of line spacing (single, double, line and a half, and so on). You can also specify line spacing in terms of points (there are 72 points per inch).

Line spacing is set at the paragraph level through the Format Paragraph command, which sets the spacing within a paragraph. The command also enables you to add extra spacing before the first line in a paragraph or after the last line. (Either technique is preferable to the common practice of single spacing the paragraphs within a document, then adding a blank line between paragraphs.)

FORMAT PARAGRAPH COMMAND

The *Format Paragraph command* is used to specify the alignment, indentation, line spacing, and pagination for the selected paragraph(s). As indicated, all of these features are implemented at the paragraph level and affect all selected paragraphs. If no paragraphs are selected, the command affects the entire current paragraph (the paragraph containing the insertion point).

The Format Paragraph command is illustrated in Figure 2.13. The Indents and Spacing tab in Figure 2.13a calls for a hanging indent, line spacing of 1.5 lines, and justified alignment. The preview area within the dialog box enables you to see how the paragraph will appear within the document.

The Line and Page Breaks tab in Figure 2.13b illustrates an entirely different set of parameters in which you control the pagination within a document. The check boxes in Figure 2.13b enable you to prevent the occurrence of awkward soft page breaks that detract from the appearance of a document.

You might, for example, want to prevent widows and orphans, terms used to describe isolated lines that seem out of place. A *widow* refers to the last line of a paragraph appearing by itself at the top of a page. An *orphan* is the first line of a paragraph appearing by itself at the bottom of a page.

You can also impose additional controls by clicking one or more check boxes. Use the Keep Lines Together option to prevent a soft page break from occurring within a paragraph and ensure that the entire paragraph appears on the same page. (The paragraph is moved to the top of the next page if it doesn't fit on the bottom of the current page.) Use the Keep with Next option to prevent a soft page break between the two paragraphs. This option is typically used to keep a heading (a one-line paragraph) with its associated text in the next paragraph.

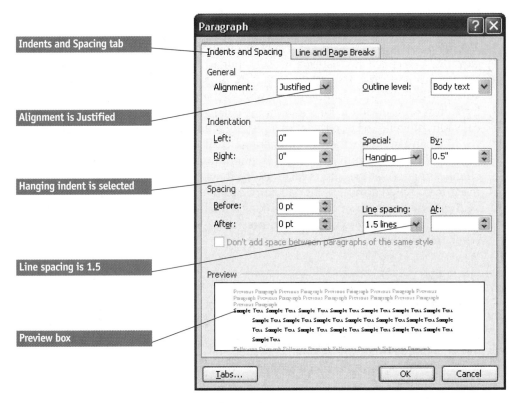

Indents and Spacing tab

Alignment is Justified

Hanging indent is selected

Line spacing is 1.5

Preview box

(a) Indents and Spacing

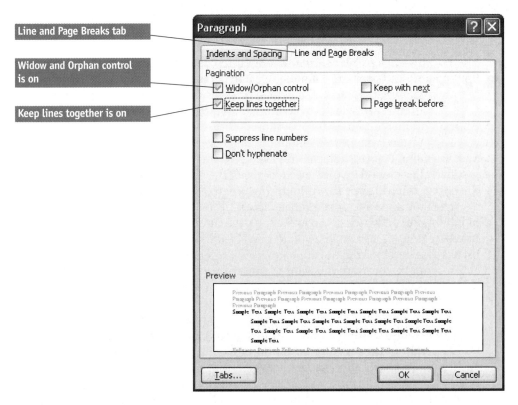

Line and Page Breaks tab

Widow and Orphan control is on

Keep lines together is on

(b) Line and Page Breaks

FIGURE 2.13   Format Paragraph Command

Borders and Shading

The ***Borders and Shading command*** puts the finishing touches on a document and is illustrated in Figure 2.14. The command is applied to selected text within a paragraph, to the entire paragraph if no text is selected, or to the entire page if the Page Border tab is selected. Thus, you can create boxed and/or shaded text as well as place horizontal or vertical lines around different quantities of text.

You can choose from several different line styles in any color (assuming you have a color printer). You can place a uniform border around a paragraph (choose Box), or you can choose a shadow effect with thicker lines at the right and bottom. You can also apply lines to selected sides of a paragraph(s) by selecting a line style, then clicking the desired sides as appropriate.

The Page Border tab enables you to place a decorative border around one or more selected pages. As with a paragraph border, you can place the border around the entire page, or you can select one or more sides. The page border also provides an additional option to use preselected clip art instead of ordinary lines.

Shading is implemented independently of the border. Clear (no shading) is the default. Solid (100%) shading creates a solid box where the text is turned white so you can read it. Shading of 10 or 20 percent is generally most effective to add emphasis to the selected paragraph. The Borders and Shading command is implemented on the paragraph level and affects the entire paragraph (unless text has been selected within the paragraph)—either the current or selected paragraph(s).

The two command buttons at the bottom of the dialog box provide additional options. The Show Toolbar button displays the Tables and Borders toolbar that facilitates both borders and shading. The Horizontal Line button provides access to a variety of attractive designs.

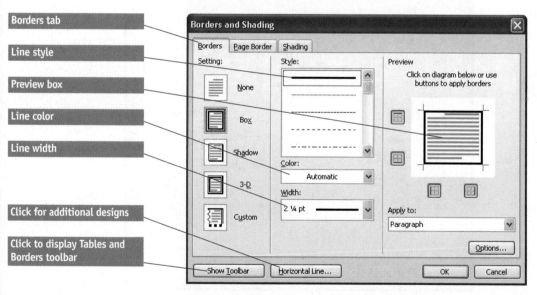

FIGURE 2.14   Paragraph Borders and Shading

FORMATTING AND THE PARAGRAPH MARK

The paragraph mark ¶ at the end of a paragraph does more than just indicate the presence of a hard return. It also stores all of the formatting in effect for the paragraph. Hence in order to preserve the formatting when you move or copy a paragraph, you must include the paragraph mark in the selected text. Click the Show/Hide ¶ button on the toolbar to display the paragraph mark and make sure it has been selected.

COLUMN FORMATTING

Columns add interest to a document and are implemented through the ***Columns command*** in the Format menu as shown in Figure 2.15. You specify the number of columns and, optionally, the space between columns. Microsoft Word does the rest, calculating the width of each column according to the left and right margins on the page and the specified (default) space between columns.

The dialog box in Figure 2.15 implements a design of three equal columns. The 2-inch width of each column is computed automatically based on left and right page margins of 1 inch each and the ¼-inch spacing between columns. The width of each column is determined by subtracting the sum of the margins and the space between the columns (a total of 2½ inches in this example) from the page width of 8½ inches. The result of the subtraction is 6 inches, which is divided by 3, resulting in a column width of 2 inches.

There is, however, one subtlety associated with column formatting, and that is the introduction of the ***section***, which controls elements such as the orientation of a page (landscape or portrait), margins, page numbers, and/or the number of columns. All of the documents in the text thus far have consisted of a single section, and therefore section formatting was not an issue. It becomes important only when you want to vary an element that is formatted at the section level. You could, for example, use section formatting to create a document that has one column on its title page and two columns on the remaining pages. This requires you to divide the document into two sections through insertion of a ***section break***. You then format each section independently and specify the number of columns in each section.

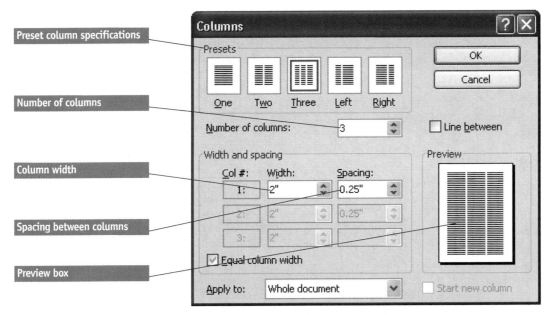

Preset column specifications

Number of columns

Column width

Spacing between columns

Preview box

FIGURE 2.15 The Format Columns Command

THE SECTION VERSUS THE PARAGRAPH

Line spacing, alignment, tabs, and indents are implemented at the paragraph level. Change any of these parameters anywhere within the current (or selected) paragraph(s) and you change *only* those paragraph(s). Margins, page numbering, orientation, and columns are implemented at the section level. Change these parameters anywhere within a section and you change the characteristics of every page within that section.

3   Paragraph Formatting

Objective   To implement line spacing, alignment, and indents; to implement widow and orphan protection; to box and shade a selected paragraph. Use Figure 2.16 as a guide in the exercise.

Step 1:   Select-Then-Do

- Open the **Tips for Writing Solution** document from the previous exercise. If necessary, change to the Print Layout view.

- Click the **drop-down arrow** on the Zoom list box and click **Two Pages** to match the view in Figure 2.16a.

- Select the entire second page as shown in the figure. Point to the selected text and click the **right mouse button** to produce the shortcut menu.

- Click the **Paragraph command** to display the associated dialog box.

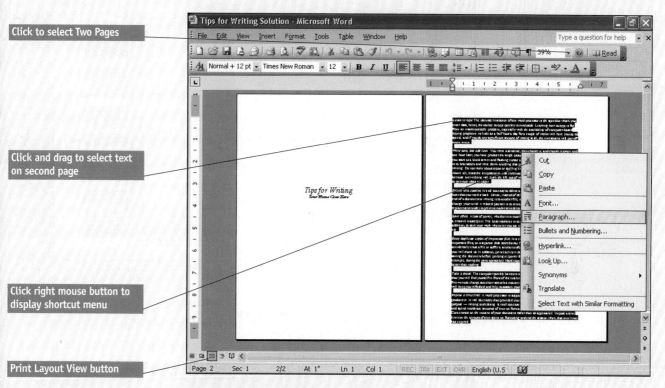

Click to select Two Pages

Click and drag to select text on second page

Click right mouse button to display shortcut menu

Print Layout View button

(a) Select-Then-Do (step 1)

FIGURE 2.16   Hands-on Exercise 3

SELECT TEXT WITH THE F8 (EXTEND) KEY

Move to the beginning of the text you want to select, then press the F8 (extend) key. The letters EXT will appear in the status bar. Use the arrow keys to extend the selection in the indicated direction; for example, press the down arrow key to select the line. You can also type any character—for example, a letter, space, or period—to extend the selection to the first occurrence of that character. Thus, typing a space or period is equivalent to selecting a word or sentence, respectively. Press Esc to cancel the selection mode.

Step 2: Line Spacing, Justification, and Pagination

- If necessary, click the **Indents and Spacing tab** to display the options in Figure 2.16b. Click the **down arrow** on the list box for Line Spacing and select **1.5 lines**. Click the **down arrow** on the Alignment list box and select **Justified**.

- Click the tab for **Line and Page Breaks**. Check the box for **Keep Lines Together**. If necessary, check the box for **Widow/Orphan Control**.

- Click **OK** to accept the settings and close the dialog box.

- Click anywhere in the document to deselect the text and see the effects of the formatting changes that were just specified.

- Save the document.

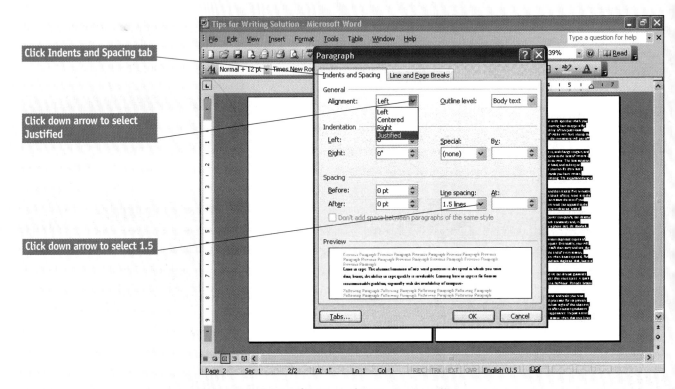

Click Indents and Spacing tab

Click down arrow to select Justified

Click down arrow to select 1.5

(b) Line Spacing, Justification, and Pagination (step 2)

FIGURE 2.16   Hands-on Exercise 3 (*continued*)

REVEAL THE FORMATTING

Open the task pane and click the down arrow in the title bar to select Reveal Formatting to display complete information for the selected text in the document. The properties are displayed by Font, Paragraph, and Section, enabling you to click the plus or minus sign next to each item to view or hide the underlying details. The properties in each area are links to the associated dialog boxes. Click Alignment or Justification, for example, within the Paragraph area to open the associated dialog box, where you can change the indicated property.

Step 3: Indents

■ Select the second paragraph as shown in Figure 2.16c. (The second paragraph will not yet be indented.)

■ Pull down the **Format menu** and click **Paragraph** (or press the **right mouse button** to produce the shortcut menu and click **Paragraph**).

■ If necessary, click the **Indents and Spacing tab** in the Paragraph dialog box.

■ Click the **up arrow** on the Left Indentation text box to set the **Left Indent** to **.5** inch. Set the **Right indent** to **.5** inch.

■ Click **OK**. Your document should match Figure 2.16c.

■ Save the document.

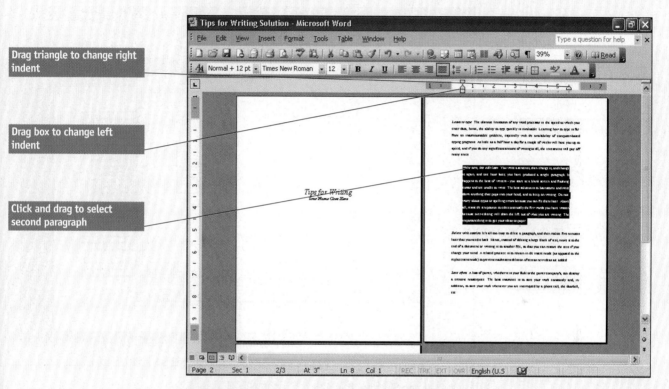

Drag triangle to change right indent

Drag box to change left indent

Click and drag to select second paragraph

(c) Indents (step 3)

FIGURE 2.16 Hands-on Exercise 3 (*continued*)

INDENTS AND THE RULER

Use the ruler to change the special, left, and/or right indents. Select the paragraph (or paragraphs) in which you want to change indents, then drag the appropriate indent markers to the new location(s). If you get a hanging indent when you wanted to change the left indent, it means you dragged the bottom triangle instead of the box. Click the Undo button and try again. (You can always use the Format Paragraph command rather than the ruler if you continue to have difficulty.)

Step 4:   **Borders and Shading**

- Pull down the **Format menu**. Click **Borders and Shading** to produce the dialog box in Figure 2.16d.

- If necessary, click the **Borders tab**. Select a style and width for the border. Click the rectangle labeled **Box** under Setting. You can also experiment with a partial border by clicking in the Preview area to toggle a line on or off.

- Click the **Shading Tab**. Click the **down arrow** on the Style list box. Click **10%**.

- Click **OK** to accept the settings for both Borders and Shading. Click outside the paragraph to deselect it and see the formatting in effect.

- Save the document.

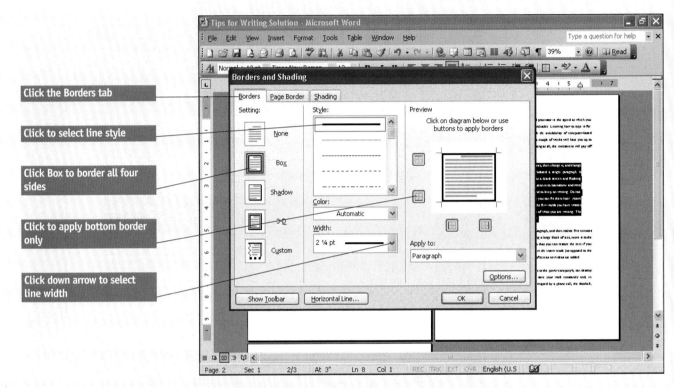

Click the Borders tab

Click to select line style

Click Box to border all four sides

Click to apply bottom border only

Click down arrow to select line width

(d) Borders and Shading (step 4)

FIGURE 2.16   Hands-on Exercise 3 (*continued*)

SELECT NONCONTIGUOUS TEXT

Anyone who has used Microsoft Word prior to Office XP, will be happy to learn that you can select noncontiguous blocks of text, and then apply the same formatting to the selected text with a single command. Click and drag to select the first item, then press and hold the Ctrl key as you continue to drag the mouse over additional blocks of text. All of the selected text is highlighted within the document. Apply the desired formatting, then click anywhere in the document to deselect the text and continue working.

Step 5: **View Many Pages**

- Pull down the **View menu** and click **Zoom** to display the Zoom dialog box. Click the monitor icon under Many Pages, then click and drag to display three pages across. Release the mouse. Click **OK**.

- Your screen should match the one in Figure 2.16e, which displays all three pages of the document.

- The Print Layout view displays both a vertical and a horizontal ruler. The boxed and indented paragraph is clearly shown in the second page.

- The soft page break between pages two and three occurs between tips rather than within a tip; that is, the text of each tip is kept together on the same page.

- Save the document a final time. Print the document at this point in the exercise and submit it to your instructor.

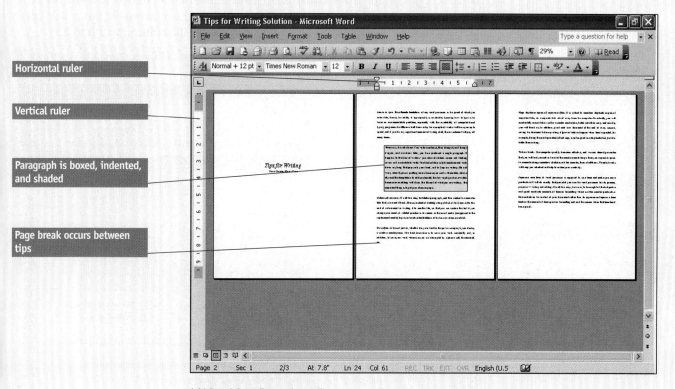

Horizontal ruler

Vertical ruler

Paragraph is boxed, indented, and shaded

Page break occurs between tips

(e) View Many Pages (step 5)

FIGURE 2.16   Hands-on Exercise 3 (*continued*)

THE PAGE BORDER COMMAND

You can apply a border to the title page of your document, to every page except the title page, or to every page including the title page. Click anywhere on the page, pull down the Format menu, click Borders and Shading, and click the Page Border tab. First design the border by selecting a style, color, width, and art (if any). Then choose the page(s) to which you want to apply the border by clicking the drop-down arrow in the Apply to list box. Close the Borders and Shading dialog box.

Step 6: **Change the Column Structure**

- Pull down the **File menu** and click the **Page Setup command** to display the Page Setup dialog box. Click the **Margins tab**, then change the Left and Right margins to **1″** each. Click **OK** to accept the settings and close the dialog box.

- Click the **down arrow** on the Zoom list box and return to **Page Width**. Press the **PgUp** or **PgDn key** to scroll until the second page comes into view.

- Click anywhere in the paragraph, "Write Now but Edit Later". Pull down the **Format menu**, click the **Paragraph command**, click the **Indents and Spacing tab** if necessary, then change the left and right indents to **0**. Click **OK**.

- All paragraphs in the document should have the same indentation as shown in Figure 2.16f. Pull down the **Format menu** and click the **Columns command** to display the Columns dialog box.

- Click the icon for **three columns**. The default spacing between columns is .5″, which leads to a column width of 1.83″. Click in the Spacing list box and change the spacing to **.25″**, which automatically changes the column width to 2″.

- Clear the box for the **Line between** columns. Click **OK**.

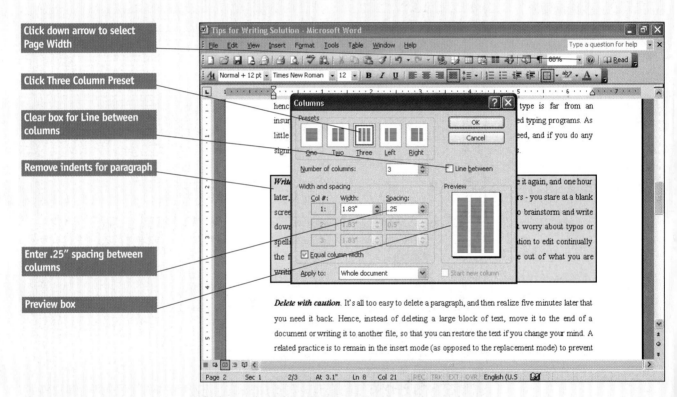

(f) Change the Column Structure (step 6)

FIGURE 2.16   Hands-on Exercise 3 (*continued*)

USE THE RULER TO CHANGE COLUMN WIDTH

Click anywhere within the column whose width you want to change, then point to the ruler and click and drag the right margin (the mouse pointer changes to a double arrow) to change the column width. Changing the width of one column in a document with equal-sized columns changes the width of all other columns so that they remain equal. Changing the width in a document with unequal columns changes only that column.

Step 7: Insert a Section Break

- Pull down the **View menu**, click the **Zoom command**, then click the monitor icon under **Many Pages**. Click and drag over 3 pages, then click **OK**. The document has switched to column formatting.

- Click at the beginning of the second page, immediately to the left of the first paragraph. Pull down the **Insert menu** and click **Break** to display the dialog box in Figure 2.16g.

- Click the **Continuous option button**, then click **OK** to accept the settings and close the dialog box.

- Click anywhere on the title page (before the section break you just inserted). Click the **Columns button**, then click the first column.

- The formatting for the first section of the document (the title page) should change to one column; the title of the document and your name are centered across the entire page.

- Print the document in this format for your instructor. Decide in which format you want to save the document—that is, as it exists now, or as it existed at the end of step 5. Exit Word.

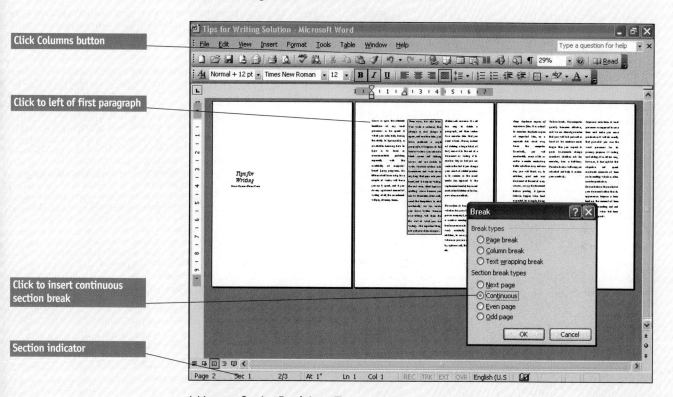

(g) Insert a Section Break (step 7)

FIGURE 2.16   Hands-on Exercise 3 (*continued*)

THE COLUMNS BUTTON

The Columns button on the Standard toolbar is the fastest way to create columns in a document. Click the button, drag the mouse to choose the number of columns, then release the mouse to create the columns. The toolbar lets you change the number of columns, but not the spacing between columns. The toolbar is also limited, in that you cannot create columns of different widths or select a line between the columns.

SUMMARY

Many operations in Word are done within the context of select-then-do; that is, select the text, then execute the necessary command. Text may be selected by dragging the mouse, by using the selection bar to the left of the document, or by using the keyboard. Text is deselected by clicking anywhere within the document.

The Undo command reverses the effect of previous commands. The Undo and Redo commands work in conjunction with one another; that is, every command that is undone can be redone at a later time.

Text is moved or copied through a combination of the Cut, Copy, and Paste commands and/or the drag-and-drop facility. The contents of the Windows clipboard are modified by any subsequent Cut or Copy command, but are unaffected by the Paste command; that is, the same text can be pasted into multiple locations. The Office clipboard retains up to 24 entries that were cut or copied.

The Find and Replace commands locate a designated character string and optionally replace one or more occurrences of that string with a different character string. The search may be case sensitive and/or restricted to whole words. The commands may also be applied to formatting and/or special characters.

Scrolling occurs when a document is too large to be seen in its entirety. Scrolling with the mouse changes what is displayed on the screen, but does not move the insertion point. Scrolling via the keyboard (for example, PgUp and PgDn) changes what is seen on the screen as well as the location of the insertion point.

The Print Layout view displays top and bottom margins, headers and footers, and other elements not seen in the Normal view. The Normal view is faster because Word spends less time formatting the display.

The Format Paragraph command determines the line spacing, alignment, indents, and text flow, all of which are set at the paragraph level. Borders and shading are set at the character or paragraph level. Margins, page size, and orientation are set in the Page Setup command at the section level.

Columns add interest to a document and are implemented through the Columns command in the Format menu and/or through the Columns button on the Standard toolbar. The number of columns is specified at the section level. The insertion of a section break enables you to create a document that contains a varying number of columns; e.g., a single column for the masthead of a newsletter and multiple columns within the body.

KEY TERMS

MULTIPLE CHOICE

1. Which of the following commands does *not* place data onto the clipboard?
   (a) Cut
   (b) Copy
   (c) Paste
   (d) All of the above

2. What happens if you select a block of text, copy it, move to the beginning of the document, paste it, move to the end of the document, and paste the text again?
   (a) The selected text will appear in three places: at the original location, and at the beginning and end of the document
   (b) The selected text will appear in two places: at the beginning and end of the document
   (c) The selected text will appear in just the original location
   (d) The situation is not possible; that is, you cannot paste twice in a row without an intervening cut or copy operation

3. What happens if you select a block of text, cut it, move to the beginning of the document, paste it, move to the end of the document, and paste the text again?
   (a) The selected text will appear in three places: at the original location and at the beginning and end of the document
   (b) The selected text will appear in two places: at the beginning and end of the document
   (c) The selected text will appear in just the original location
   (d) The situation is not possible; that is, you cannot paste twice in a row without an intervening cut or copy operation

4. Which of the following are set at the paragraph level?
   (a) Alignment
   (b) Tabs and indents
   (c) Line spacing
   (d) All of the above

5. How do you change the font for *existing* text within a document?
   (a) Select the text, then choose the new font
   (b) Choose the new font, then select the text
   (c) Either (a) or (b)
   (d) Neither (a) nor (b)

6. The Page Setup command can be used to change:
   (a) The margins in a document
   (b) The orientation of a document
   (c) Both (a) and (b)
   (d) Neither (a) nor (b)

7. Which of the following is a true statement regarding indents?
   (a) Indents are measured from the edge of the page
   (b) The left, right, and first line indents must be set to the same value
   (c) The insertion point can be anywhere in the paragraph when indents are set
   (d) Indents must be set with the Format Paragraph command

8. The default tab stops are set to:
   (a) Left indents every ½ inch
   (b) Left indents every ¼ inch
   (c) Right indents every ½ inch
   (d) Right indents every ¼ inch

9. The spacing in an existing multipage document is changed from single spacing to double spacing throughout the document. What can you say about the number of hard and soft page breaks before and after the formatting change?
   (a) The number of soft page breaks is the same, but the number and/or position of the hard page breaks is different
   (b) The number of hard page breaks is the same, but the number and/or position of the soft page breaks is different
   (c) The number and position of both hard and soft page breaks is the same
   (d) The number and position of both hard and soft page breaks is different

10. Which of the following describes the Arial and Times New Roman fonts?
    (a) Arial is a sans serif font, Times New Roman is a serif font
    (b) Arial is a serif font, Times New Roman is a sans serif font
    (c) Both are serif fonts
    (d) Both are sans serif fonts

... c o n t i n u e d

multiple choice

11. What is the effect of executing two successive Undo commands, one right after the other?

(a) The situation is not possible because the Undo command is not available

(b) The situation is not possible because the Undo command cannot be executed twice in a row

(c) The Undo commands cancel each other out; that is, the document is the same as it was prior to the first Undo command

(d) The last two commands prior to the first Undo command are reversed

12. You are in the middle of a multipage document. How do you scroll to the beginning of the document and simultaneously change the insertion point?

(a) Press Ctrl+Home

(b) Drag the scroll bar to the top of the scroll box

(c) Both (a) and (b)

(d) Neither (a) nor (b)

13. Which of the following substitutions can be accomplished by the Find and Replace command?

(a) All occurrences of the words "Times New Roman" can be replaced with the word "Arial"

(b) All text set in the Times New Roman font can be replaced by the Arial font

(c) Both (a) and (b)

(d) Neither (a) nor (b)

14. Which of the following deselects a selected block of text?

(a) Clicking anywhere outside the selected text

(b) Clicking any alignment button on the toolbar

(c) Clicking the Bold, Italic, or Underline button

(d) All of the above

15. Which point size would be most appropriate for ordinary text?

(a) 4

(b) 10

(c) 20

(d) 72

16. The find and replacement strings must be

(a) The same length

(b) The same case, either upper or lower

(c) The same length and the same case

(d) None of the above

17. Which of the following is a true statement about the Windows and Office clipboards?

(a) Both clipboards can hold only a single item

(b) Both clipboards can hold multiple items

(c) The Windows clipboard can hold only a single item, but the Office clipboard can hold multiple items

(d) The Office clipboard can hold only a single item, but the Windows clipboard can hold multiple items

18. Which of the following is set at the section level?

(a) Columns and margins

(b) Alignment and tabs

(c) Borders and shading

(d) All of the above

ANSWERS

1. c	**7.** c	**13.** c
2. a	**8.** a	**14.** a
3. b	**9.** b	**15.** b
4. d	**10.** a	**16.** d
5. a	**11.** d	**17.** c
6. c	**12.** a	**18.** a

PRACTICE WITH WORD

1. **Formatting 101:** The opening paragraph of the document in Figure 2.17 explains that formatting is implemented at three levels—the section level, the paragraph level, and the character level. The remainder of the document consists of various sentences and paragraphs that describe the formatting specifications you are to implement. The formatting commands can be executed from pull-down menus, from the Formatting toolbar, and/or through the appropriate keyboard shortcut. Open the partially completed *Chapter 2 Practice 1* document in the Exploring Word folder. Proceed as follows to create the finished document in Figure 2.17.

   a. Change the font in the title and first paragraph to Times New Roman. Center the title in 24 point Times New Roman bold. Justify the first paragraph, then boldface the indicated terms.

   b. Click at the end of the first paragraph. Press Enter. Pull down the Insert menu, click the Break command, then click the option button for a continuous section break. Click anywhere in the second section (check the status bar to confirm that you are in the second section). Pull down the Format menu, click the Columns command, and then change to two columns.

   c. Move the insertion point to the beginning of the sentence, "This paragraph is set in 10 point Times New Roman . . . ". Press Ctrl+Shift+Enter to force the paragraph to begin a new column.

   d. Follow the instructions within the document to use the appropriate font (Times New Roman or Arial), style (bold, italic, or bold italic), highlighting, and so on. Apply borders and shading as indicated.

   e. Format each of the paragraphs in the second column according to the specifications that are contained in the individual paragraphs.

   f. Add your name somewhere in the document, then print the completed document for your instructor. Do not be concerned if you do not have a color printer, but indicate this to your instructor in a note at the end of the document. Do you appreciate the difference between formatting at the character, paragraph, or section level?

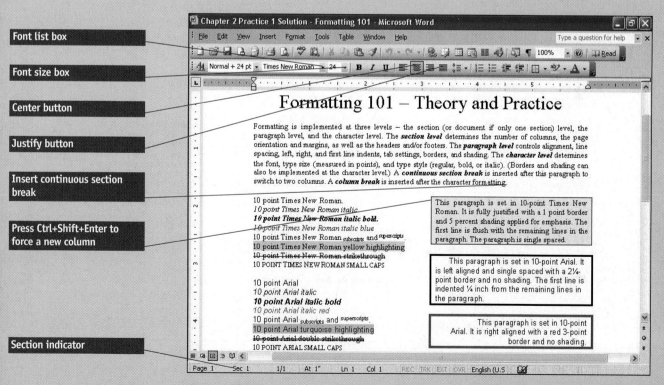

FIGURE 2.17 Formatting 101 (exercise 1)

2. **Keyboard Shortcuts:** Keyboard shortcuts are especially useful if you are a good typist because your hands can remain on the keyboard, as opposed to continually moving to and from the mouse. We never set out to memorize the shortcuts; we just learned them along the way as we continued to use Microsoft Office.

It's much easier than you might think, because the same shortcuts apply to multiple applications. Ctrl+X, Ctrl+C, and Ctrl+V, for example, are the universal Windows shortcuts to cut, copy, and paste the selected text. The "X" is supposed to remind you of a pair of scissors, and the keys are located next to each other to link the commands to one another. Proceed as follows:

a. Start Word. Open the *Chapter 2 Practice 2* document in the Exploring Word folder, a portion of which can be seen in Figure 2.18. Your assignment is to complete the document by entering the indicated shortcuts.

b. Pull down the Tools menu, click the Customize command to display the Customize dialog box, click the Options tab, and then check the box to Show Shortcut Keys in ScreenTips. You can now point to any icon on any toolbar to see the associated shortcut. You can also use Help to identify the various shortcuts in Word. Click in the Ask a Question box, type "keyboard shortcuts", then click the link to keyboard shortcuts from the list of topics that are returned by the search engine.

c. Move to the line below Ctrl+B to enter the shortcut to toggle Italic on and off. (You can point to the Italic button on the Formatting toolbar to display the ScreenTip and the associated shortcut, Ctrl+I.) Enter the remaining shortcuts in similar fashion. Use the Help menu as necessary.

d. Enter your name in the completed document, add the appropriate formatting, and then submit the document to your instructor as proof you did this exercise. Try to learn the shortcuts in groups as they are presented in Figure 2.18. Do you think the shortcuts will help you to use Word more efficiently?

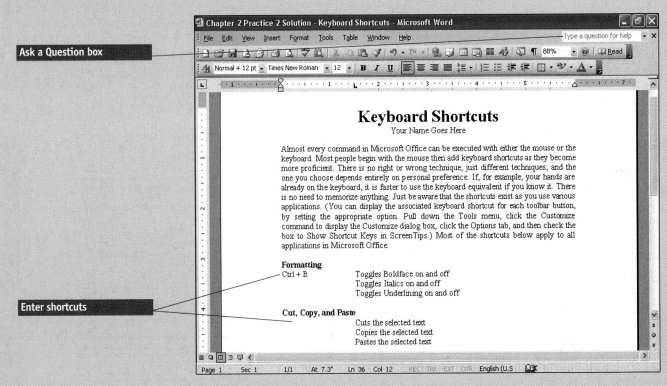

FIGURE 2.18 Keyboard Shortcuts (exercise 2)

3. **Moving Text:** There are two basic ways to move text within a document. You can use a combination of the Cut and Paste commands, or you can simply click and drag text from one location to another. The latter technique tends to be easier if you are moving text a short distance, whereas cutting and pasting is preferable if the locations are far apart within a document. This exercise will give you a chance to practice both techniques.

a. Open the partially completed *Chapter 2 Practice 3* document, where you will find a list of the presidents of the United States together with the years that each man served.

b. The list is out of order, and your assignment is to rearrange the names so that the presidents appear in chronological order. You don't have to be a historian to complete the exercise because you can use the years in office to determine the proper order.

c. Center the first two lines of text. Format the title in 25 point Times New Roman. Use a smaller point size for the second line. Use the Insert Hyperlink command (or click the corresponding button on the Standard toolbar) to insert a link to the White House Web site (www.whitehouse.gov) where you can learn more about the presidents.

d. Display the list of presidents in two columns with a line down the middle as shown in Figure 2.19. You will have to implement a section break because the first two lines (the title and the hyperlink to the White House) are in one-column format, whereas the list of presidents is in two columns. Click immediately before the first president, pull down the Insert menu, click the Break command, and then click the option button for a continuous section break.

e. Click anywhere in the second section (check the status bar to confirm that you are in the second section.) Pull down the Format menu, click the Columns command, and then change to two columns for this section.

f. Press Ctrl+End to move to the end of the document and insert a second continuous section break to balance the text in each column.

g. Add your name to the completed document and submit it to your instructor.

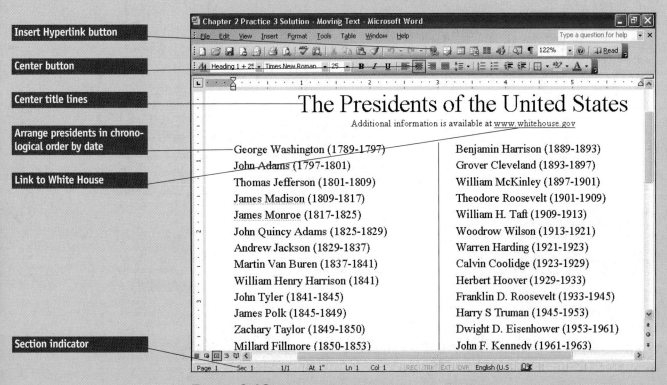

FIGURE 2.19 Moving Text (exercise 3)

4. **Inserting the Date and Time:** The document in Figure 2.20 describes the Insert Date and Time command and shows the various formats in which a date may appear. You need not duplicate our document exactly, but you are asked to insert the date multiple times, as both a fixed value and a field, in multiple formats. Divide your document into sections so that you can display the two sets of dates in adjacent columns. (Use the keyboard shortcut Ctrl+Shift+Enter to force a column break that will take you from the bottom of one column to the top of the next column.)

   a. Start Word and begin a new document. Enter the title of the document as shown in Figure 2.20. Press enter. Type the phrase, "Today's Date – ". Pull down the Insert menu, click the Date and Time command, and select the appropriate format for the date. Check the box to Update Automatically. Click OK.

   b. The date should have been entered as a code (field) because you checked the box to update automatically. Press Alt+F9 to toggle from a displayed date to a code. Press Alt+F9 a second time to show the displayed value.

   c. You can also shade all codes automatically. Pull down the Tools menu, click the Options command, select the View tab, and then click the drop-down arrow in the Field Shading list box. Select Always. Click OK.

   d. Type the first paragraph as shown in Figure 2.20. Insert a continuous section break at the end of the paragraph so that you can display text in two columns. Change to a two-column format. Pull down the Insert menu, click the Date and Time command, and enter the date in the first format shown in the figure. Do not check the box to update automatically. Enter the date four additional times using a different format each time.

   e. Press Ctrl+Shift+Enter to move to the next column, then enter the various dates as fields as shown.

   f. Insert a section break after the last date and change back to a single column. Enter the text of the last paragraph as shown in the figure. Create your document on one day, then open it a day later to be sure that the dates that were entered as fields were updated correctly.

   g. Add your name to the completed document and submit it to your instructor.

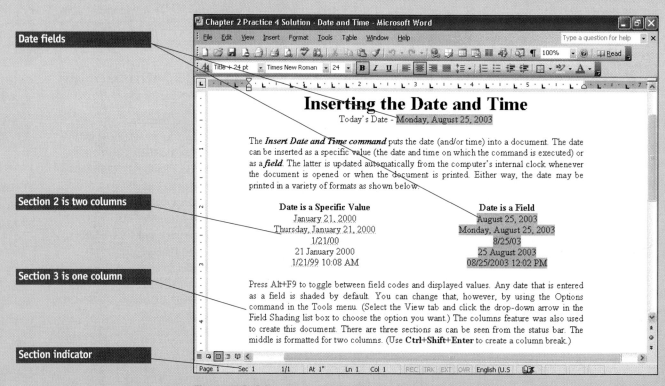

FIGURE 2.20 Inserting the Date and Time (exercise 4)

practice exercises

5. **Tips for Internet Explorer:** You will find a partially completed version of the document in Figure 2.21 in the file *Chapter 2 Practice 5* in the Exploring Word folder. Your assignment is to open that document, then format the various tips in an attractive fashion. You need not follow our formatting exactly, but you are to apply uniform formatting throughout the document. Proceed as follows:

   a. Pull down the View menu, open the task pane, and then click the down arrow to select Reveal Formatting as shown in Figure 2.21. This enables you to see the formatting in effect for every paragraph throughout the exercise.

   b. Format the title of the first tip, "About Internet Explorer". We used 10 point Arial in red. Look closely, however, and you will see that the paragraph formatting includes a specification to keep the heading with the next line to avoid an awkward page break. (Pull down the Format menu, click the Paragraph command to display the Paragraph dialog box, click the Line and Page Breaks tab, and check the box to Keep with next.)

   c. Check that the insertion point is anywhere within the heading. Double click the Format Painter tool on the Standard toolbar (the mouse pointer changes to a paintbrush), then paint the heading of every other tip in the document. The easiest way to do this is to click immediately to the left of each heading throughout the document. Click the Format Painter tool when you are finished to turn off the painting feature.

   d. Return to the top of the document to format the text of the first tip. We used 10 point Times New Roman and justified the paragraph. We also used the Line and Page Breaks command to keep the lines together—that is, so the paragraph does not break from one page to the next. Use the Format Painter to duplicate this formatting for the other tips in the document.

   e. Return to the beginning of the document, locate the tip entitled "Guess the URL", and use the Insert Hyperlink command to create the appropriate hyperlinks within the paragraph. Use the Edit Find (search for "www") command to locate additional instances of hyperlinks that appear in other tips.

   f. Insert a cover page that includes your name and the source of the information, and then print the entire document for your instructor. Read the completed document carefully. Did you learn anything new about Internet Explorer?

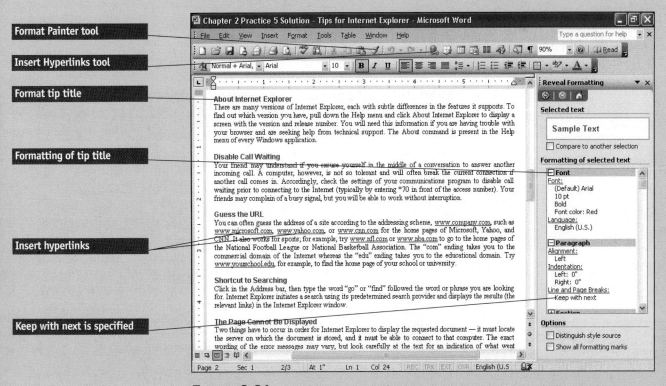

FIGURE 2.21 Tips for Internet Explorer (exercise 5)

practice exercises

6. **Create a Newsletter:** It's not difficult to create an effective newsletter, provided you plan effectively. Use pencil and paper to lay out the overall document before you begin. Decide how many columns you want, what clip art (if any) you will use, and what other elements you want to include. There is no requirement to write meaningful text; that is, all you have to do is write a few short sentences, then copy those sentences to fill the newsletter. You do not have to duplicate our document exactly, but you are required to include the essential elements in Figure 2.22. Proceed as follows:

a. Choose a theme for your newsletter, and then write a short paragraph in support of that theme. Select the paragraph, copy it, and then paste it repeatedly to fill the page. Do not be concerned if you spill onto a second page. Go through the document and periodically add meaningful headings. Format the headings differently from the text.

b. Change the default margins. We used top and bottom margins of .75 inch and left and right margins of .5 inch. Pull down the Format menu, click the Columns command, and then establish the column formatting for the body of your newsletter.

c. Click after the first paragraph and insert clip art in support of your theme. Right click the clip art, click the Format Picture command, then use the Layout (specify square wrapping) and/or the Size tabs as necessary to move and size the clip art.

d. Press Ctrl+Home to move to the beginning of the document. Pull down the Insert menu and select a continuous section break. Press Ctrl+Home to move to the first section, change to a single column, and then create the masthead for your newsletter. We formatted the text in 44 point Arial and used the Format Borders and Shading command (100% shading) to display light text on a solid background. Use a right tab at the right margin on the second line of the masthead, so that your name appears at the extreme right of the masthead.

e. Create a pull quote to emphasize a specific sentence. Select the text, increase the point size, change to italic, center the text, then add a top and bottom border. Use borders and/or shading on other paragraphs as you see fit.

f. Change to the Print Layout view, and then zoom to view the entire page. Add or delete text as necessary, so that your newsletter fills exactly one page.

g. Print the completed newsletter for your instructor as proof you did this exercise.

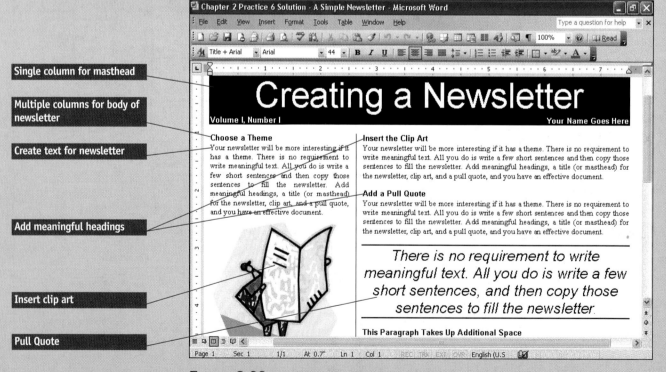

FIGURE 2.22 Create a Newsletter (exercise 6)

7. **Tracking Changes with Tab Stops:** This exercise sets different types of tabs in conjunction with tracking the editing changes during a session. Open the *Chapter 2 Practice 7* document in the Exploring Word folder, which is a partially completed version of the document in Figure 2.23. Pull down the View menu and click the Toolbars command to display the Reviewing toolbar if it is not visible. Click and drag to select the phrase "your name goes here" near the top of the document. Press the Del key, then enter your name instead. The new text will appear in a different color (magenta in our figure), and a description of the change will appear at the right of your document. If this does not occur, double click the TRK indicator on the status bar to toggle track changes on. Complete the document as follows:

a. The tab stops for examples one and two have already been entered into the document by Bob and Maryann, and are indicated in red and green, respectively. You can point to any of the changes in the right margin to see a ScreenTip with the name of the reviewer (Bob or Maryann) and an indication of when the change was made.

b. Click and drag to select the three lines under Example 3 to set the tabs for all three lines at the same time. Click the Tab button (at the left of the ruler) repeatedly until you see the symbol for the left tab. Now click at one inch on the ruler to set a left tab at that position. Click the Tab button until you see the symbol for a right tab, then click at 5.5 inches to set this tab. Pull down the Format menu, click the Tabs command, select the tab at 5.5 inches, and click the option button for a dotted leader. (The leader cannot be set from the ruler.) Click OK. Now press the Tab key to enter tab stops before the chapter and before the page number for all three lines.

c. Click and drag to select the three lines of text under Example 4, then use the ruler to set decimal tabs at the indicated positions. Press the Tab key to enter a tab stop before each of the four numbers in all three lines.

d. Click the Print button to print the document as shown—that is, the final document with the markup (editing) printed in the margin. Click the down arrow in the Display for Review list box to display the Original Showing Markup and print that version. And finally, change to the final version to print the completed document without showing the editing changes. Submit all three versions to your instructor.

e. Click the down arrow next to the Accept Change button on the Reviewing toolbar, then click the command to Accept All Changes in Document. Pull down the Tools menu and toggle the Track Changes command off.

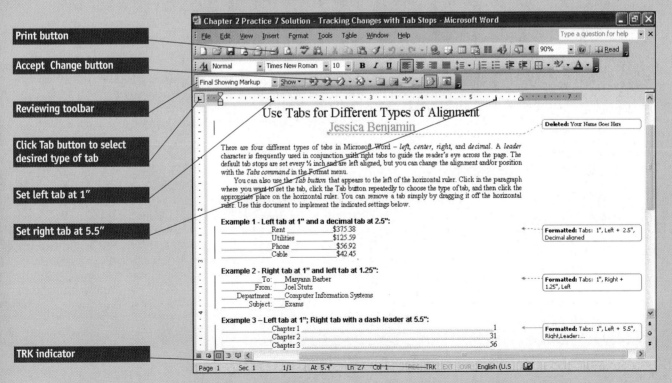

FIGURE 2.23 Tracking Changes with Tab Stops (exercise 7)

Computers Past and Present

The ENIAC was the scientific marvel of its day and the world's first operational electronic computer. It could perform 5,000 additions per second, weighed 30 tons, and took 1,500 square feet of floor space. The price was a modest $486,000 in 1946 dollars. The story of the ENIAC and other influential computers of the author's choosing is found in the file *Chapter 2 Mini Case—History of Computers,* which we forgot to format, so we are asking you to do it for us.

Be sure to use appropriate emphasis for the names of the various computers. Create a title page in front of the document, then submit the completed assignment to your instructor. If you are ambitious, you can enhance this assignment by using your favorite search engine to look for computer museums on the Web. Visit one or two sites, and include this information on a separate page at the end of the document. One last task is to update the description of Today's PC (the last computer in the document).

The Preamble to the Constitution

Use your favorite search engine to locate a Web site that contains the text of the United States Constitution. Click and drag to select the text of the Preamble, use the Ctrl+C keyboard shortcut to copy the text to the Windows clipboard, start Word, and then paste the contents of the clipboard into the document. Format the Preamble in an attractive fashion, add a footnote that points to the Web page where you obtained the text, then add your name to the completed document.

To Hyphenate or Not to Hyphenate

The best way to learn about hyphenation is to experiment with an existing document. Open the *Chapter 2 Mini Case—To Hyphenate or Not to Hyphenate* document that is on the data disk. The document is currently set in 12 point type with hyphenation in effect. Experiment with various formatting changes that will change the soft line breaks to see the effect on the hyphenation within the document. You can change the point size, the number of columns, and/or the right indent. You can also suppress hyphenation altogether, as described within the document. Summarize your findings in a short note to your instructor.

The Invitation

Choose an event and produce the perfect invitation. The possibilities are endless and limited only by your imagination. You can invite people to your wedding or to a fraternity party. Your laser printer and abundance of fancy fonts enable you to do anything a professional printer can do. Special paper will add the finishing touch. Go to it—this assignment is a lot of fun.

One Space after a Period

Touch typing classes typically teach the student to place two spaces after a period. The technique worked well in the days of the typewriter and monospaced fonts, but it creates an artificially large space when used with proportional fonts and a word processor. Select any document that is at least several paragraphs in length and print the document with the current spacing. Use the Find and Replace commands to change to the alternate spacing, then print the document a second time. Which spacing looks better to you? Submit both versions of the document to your instructor with a brief note summarizing your findings.

3

Enhancing a Document: The Web and Other Resources

OBJECTIVES

After reading this chapter you will:

1. Insert clip art and/or a photograph into a document.
2. Display/hide the Picture toolbar; use the crop tool as appropriate.
3. Use the Format Picture command to wrap text around clip art.
4. Use WordArt to insert decorative text into a document.
5. Use the Drawing toolbar to create simple shapes and annotations.
6. Download resources from the Web for inclusion into a Word document.
7. Insert a footnote or endnote.
8. Insert a hyperlink into a document.
9. Save a Word document as a Web page.
10. Use wizards and templates to create a document.
11. Use the Mail Merge Wizard to create a set of form letters.

hands-on exercises

1. CLIP ART AND WORDART
   Input: Clip Art and WordArt
   Output: Clip Art and WordArt Solution

2. MICROSOFT WORD AND THE WORLD WIDE WEB
   Input: Apollo 11
   Output: Apollo 11 Solution (Web page)

3. MAIL MERGE
   Input: Form Letter
   Output: Form Letter Solution (Word document); Names and Addresses (data file)

CASE STUDY
FROM DONUTS TO BAGELS

The donut shop across from campus has been receiving constant and continual feedback from students; namely, that they would like to see a healthier choice of menu options in addition to the scrumptious campus-renowned donuts for which the shop is famous. The owner, Sarah McLean, thought this was a good idea and recently added bagels to the menu to see what kind of response she would get. Sarah was optimistic that since her shop was so close to campus, students would naturally choose it over the two other bagel stores in town that were several blocks away. She hoped that the new menu would boost her business substantially.

Sarah discovered, however, that merely adding bagels to the menu was not enough to get the students through the door. She decided to take an ad in the campus paper that offered a free bagel with the purchase of a cup of tea or coffee. Sarah's fiancé is your instructor, and he in turn has assigned the ad as a design project for your class. The creator of the winning entry gets a dozen free bagels. ■

Your assignment is to read the chapter, paying special attention to the first hands-on exercise that describes how to use clip art and WordArt, and then create a colorful ad that uses both elements. The donut shop is located at 1000 Main Street, its telephone number is (111) 222-3333, and this information must appear within the ad. Size and proportion are important; the size of the ad in the campus newspaper is exactly $4\frac{1}{4} \times 5\frac{3}{4}$. Thus, you are to use the Text Box tool on the Drawing toolbar to draw a box around the completed ad that corresponds to its intended size. Somewhere in the ad include a footnote that contains your name, and then print the completed ad for your instructor for inclusion in a class contest to choose the winning entry. One more thing—the contest is purely hypothetical and there are no free bagels.

This chapter describes how to enhance a document using clip art, photographs, and/or WordArt (decorative text). These objects may be stored locally or downloaded from the Web for inclusion into a document. We start with the document in Figure 3.1, which contains text, clip art, WordArt, and a scroll that was created using the Drawing toolbar. We show you the finished document, describe each of the objects within the document, and then proceed to a hands-on exercise in which you will create the document for yourself.

WordArt

Enhancing a Document

Clip art

Clip art is available from a variety of sources including the Microsoft Clip Organizer that is built into Microsoft Office. The Clip Organizer enables you to select clip art in two different ways, by searching through a predefined collection such as "transportation" or by searching on a keyword such as "automobile". The Clip Organizer also lets you specify the type of object you want—clip art, photographs, movies, or sounds. Once the object has been inserted into a document, it can be moved and sized through various options in the Format Picture command. You can wrap text around a picture, place a border around the picture, or even crop (cut out part of) the picture if necessary.

In addition to clip art, you can use WordArt to create artistic effects to enhance any document. WordArt enables you to create special effects with text. It lets you rotate and/or flip text, display it vertically on the page, shade it, slant it, arch it, or even print it upside down. Best of all, WordArt is intuitively easy to use. In essence you enter text into a dialog box, and then you choose a shape for the text from a dialog box. You can create special effects by choosing one of several different shadows. You can vary the image even further by using any TrueType font on your system. It's fun, it's easy, and you can create some truly dynamite documents.

You can insert clip art and/or WordArt into other Office documents such as PowerPoint presentations or Excel worksheets using the same commands that you will learn in this chapter. Indeed, that is one of the benefits of the Office suite because the same commands are executed from the same menus as you go from one application to another. In addition, every application in the Office suite contains a Standard toolbar and a Formatting toolbar.

The Insert Symbol command enables you to insert special symbols into a document to give it a professional look. You can, for example, use ™ rather than TM, © rather than (C), or ½ and ¼ rather than 1/2 and 1/4. It also enables you to insert accented characters as appropriate in English as in the word résumé, or in a foreign language to create properly accented words and phrases; for example, ¿Cómo está usted? And finally, you can use special symbols such as the logo for Microsoft® Windows 🀫.

AutoShape

This document was created by Your Name

FIGURE 3.1 Enhancing a Document

The Microsoft Clip Organizer

The ***Insert Picture command*** displays a task pane through which you can insert clip art, photographs, sounds, and movies (collectively called clips). The clips can come from a variety of sources. They may be installed locally in the My Collections folder, they may have been installed in conjunction with Microsoft Office in the Office Collections folder, and/or they may have been downloaded from the Web and stored in the Web Collections folder. You can insert a specific clip into a document if you know its location. You can also search for a clip that will enhance the document on which you are working.

The search is made possible by the ***Microsoft Clip Organizer***, which brings order out of potential chaos by cataloging the clips that are available to you. You enter a keyword that describes the clip you are looking for, specify the collections that are to be searched, and indicate the type of clip(s) you are looking for. The results are displayed in the task pane as shown in Figure 3.2, which returns the clips that are described by the keyword "computer". Our example restricted the search to selected collections (those stored locally, thus making it a faster search than one that searches online as well) but requested that all media types be displayed. When you see a clip that you want to use, all you have to do is point to the clip, click the down arrow that appears, and then click the Insert command from the resulting menu.

You can access the Microsoft Clip Organizer (to view the various collections) by clicking the Organize clips link at the bottom of the task pane. You can also access the Clip Organizer outside of Word by clicking the Start button on the task bar, and then clicking All Programs, Microsoft Office, Microsoft Office Tool, and Microsoft Clip Organizer. Once in the Organizer, you can search through the clips in the various collections, reorganize the existing collections, add new collections, and even add new clips (with their associated keywords) to the collections. The other links at the bottom of the task pane in Figure 3.2 provide access to additional clip art online and tips for finding more relevant clips.

Keyword for search

Collections to be searched

Type of clips to be included in results

Search results

Link to Microsoft Clip Organizer

Link to more clips online

FIGURE 3.2 Insert Picture Command

The Insert Symbol Command

The **Insert Symbol command** enables you to enter typographic symbols and/or foreign language characters into a document in place of ordinary typing—for example, ® rather than (R), © rather than (c), ½ and ¼, rather than 1/2 and 1/4, or é rather than e (as used in the word résumé). These special characters give a document a very professional look.

You may have already discovered that some of this formatting can be done automatically through the **AutoCorrect** feature that is built into Word. If, for example, you type the letter "c" enclosed in parentheses, it will automatically be converted to the copyright symbol. Other symbols, such as accented letters like the é in résumé or those in a foreign language (e.g., ¿Cómo está usted?) have to be entered through the Insert Symbol command. (You could also create a macro, based on the Insert Symbol command, to simplify the process.)

The installation of Microsoft Office adds a variety of fonts onto your computer, each of which contains various symbols that can be inserted into a document. Selecting "normal text", however, as was done in Figure 3.3, provides access to the accented characters as well as other common symbols. Other fonts—especially the Wingdings, Webdings, and Symbols fonts—contain special symbols, including the Windows logo. ⊞

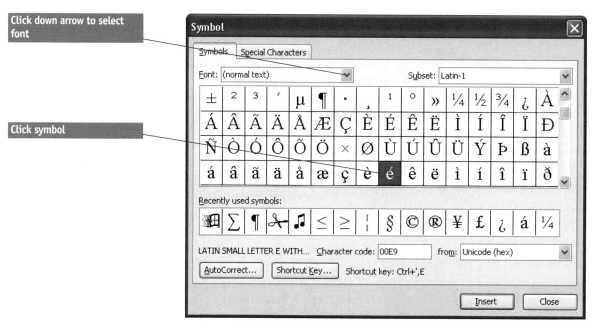

FIGURE 3.3   Insert Symbol Command

USE SYMBOLS AS CLIP ART

The Wingdings, Webdings, and Symbols fonts are among the best-kept secrets in Microsoft Office. Each font contains a variety of symbols that are actually pictures. You can insert any of these symbols into a document as text, select the character and enlarge the point size, change the color, then copy the modified character to create a truly original document. See exercise 5 at the end of the chapter.

Microsoft WordArt

Microsoft WordArt is an application within Microsoft Office that creates decorative text that can be used to add interest to a document. You can use ***WordArt*** in addition to clip art within a document, or in place of clip art if the right image is not available. You can rotate text in any direction, add three-dimensional effects, display the text vertically down the page, slant it, arch it, or even print it upside down. In short, you are limited only by your imagination.

WordArt is intuitively easy to use. In essence you choose a style for the text from among the selections in Figure 3.4a. Then you enter the specific text in a subsequent dialog box, after which the result is displayed as in Figure 3.4b. The finished WordArt is an object that can be moved and sized within a document, just like any other object. It's fun, it's easy, and you can create some truly unique documents.

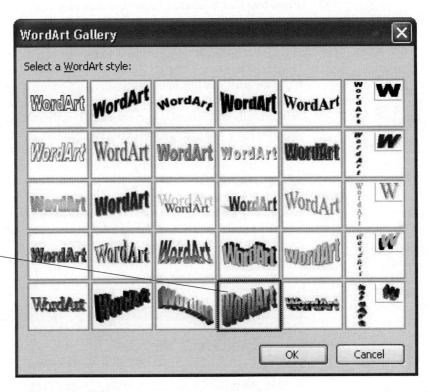

(a) Choose the Style

(b) Completed Entry

FIGURE 3.4 Microsoft WordArt

All clip art is created from basic shapes, such as lines, and other basic tools that are found on the ***Drawing toolbar***. Select the Line tool, for example, then click and drag to create a line. Once the line has been created, you can select it and change its properties (such as thickness, style, or color) by using other tools on the Drawing toolbar. Draw a second line, or a curve, then depending on your ability, you have a piece of original clip art. You do not have to be an artist to use the basic tools to enhance any document.

The ***drawing canvas*** appears automatically whenever you select a tool from the Drawing toolbar and is indicated by a hashed line as shown in Figure 3.5. Each object within the canvas can be selected, at which point it displays its own ***sizing handles***. The blue rectangle is selected in Figure 3.5. You can size an object by clicking and dragging any one of the sizing handles. We don't expect you to create clip art comparable to the images provided with Microsoft Office, but you can use the tools on the Drawing toolbar to modify an existing image and/or create simple shapes of your own.

The Shift key has special significance when used in conjunction with the Line, Rectangle, and Oval tools. Press and hold the Shift key as you drag the Line tool horizontally or vertically to create a perfectly straight line in either direction. Press and hold the Shift key as you drag the Rectangle or Oval tool to create a square or circle, respectively. The AutoShapes button contains a series of selected shapes, such as a callout or banner, and is very useful to create simple drawings. And, as with any other drawing object, you can change the thickness, color, or fill by selecting the object and choosing the appropriate tool.

The Drawing toolbar also provides access to the ***Diagram Gallery***, which enables you to create a variety of charts and diagrams. Click the Insert Diagram or Organization Chart button to display the Diagram Gallery dialog box, choose the type of diagram you want, click OK, then create the diagram within the drawing canvas. (See the end-of-chapter case study on page 152.)

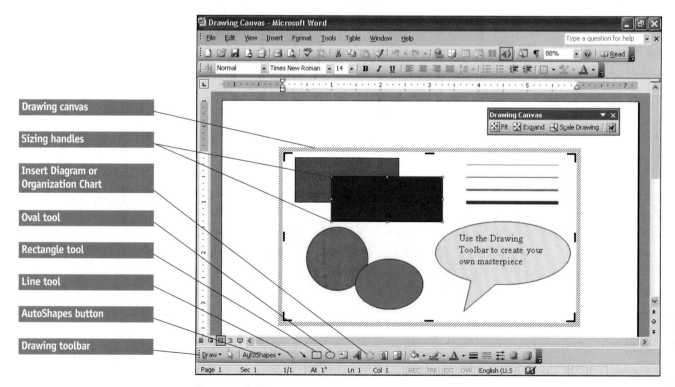

FIGURE 3.5 Drawing Canvas

Clip Art and WordArt

Objective To insert clip art and WordArt into a document; to use the Insert Symbol command to add typographical symbols. Use Figure 3.6 as a guide in completing the exercise.

Step 1: **Insert the Clip Art**

■ Start Word. Open the **Clip Art and WordArt** document in the Exploring Word folder. Save the document as **Clip Art and WordArt Solution**.

■ Check that the insertion point is at the beginning of the document. Pull down the **Insert menu**, click (or point to) **Picture**, then click **Clip Art**.

■ The task pane opens (if it is not already open) and displays the clip art pane as shown in Figure 3.6a.

■ Click in the **Search text box**. Type **computer** to search for any clip art image that is indexed with this keyword, then click the **Go button** or press **Enter**.

■ The images are displayed in the task pane. Point to an image to display a drop-down arrow to its right. Click the arrow to display a context menu.

■ Click **Insert** to insert the image into the document. Do not be concerned about its size or position at this time. Close the task pane.

■ Save the document.

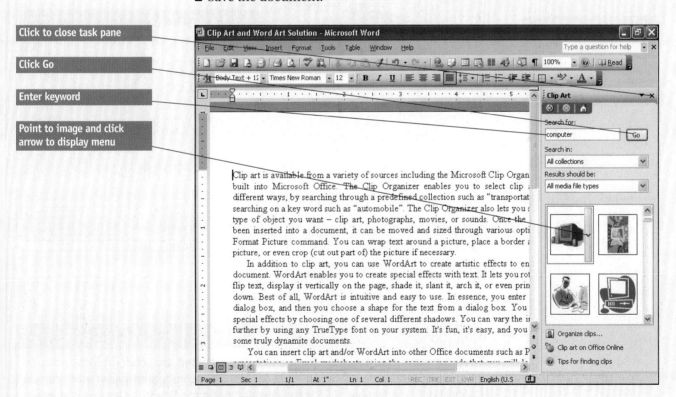

(a) Insert the Clip Art (step 1)

FIGURE 3.6 Hands-on Exercise 1

Step 2: Move and Size the Picture

- Point to the picture, click the **right mouse button** to display the context-sensitive menu, then click the **Format Picture command** to display the Format Picture dialog box in Figure 3.6b.

- You must change the layout in order to move and size the object. Click the **Layout tab**, choose the **Square layout**, then click the option button for **Left alignment**. Click **OK** to close the dialog box.

- To size the picture, click and drag a corner handle (the mouse pointer changes to a double arrow) to change the length and width simultaneously. This keeps the picture in proportion.

- To move the picture, point to any part of the image except a sizing handle (the mouse pointer changes to a four-sided arrow), then click and drag to move the image elsewhere in the document.

- Save the document.

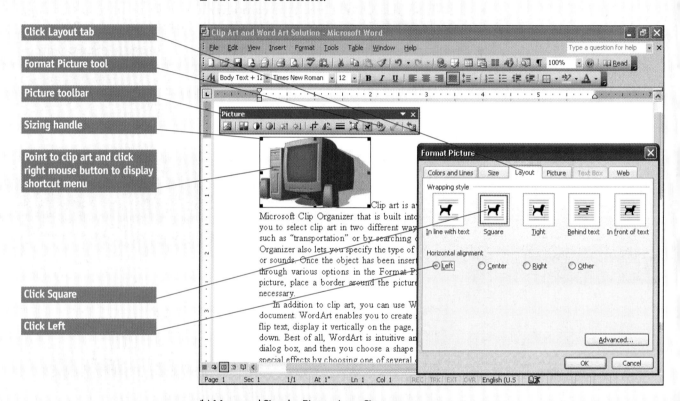

Click Layout tab

Format Picture tool

Picture toolbar

Sizing handle

Point to clip art and click right mouse button to display shortcut menu

Click Square

Click Left

(b) Move and Size the Picture (step 2)

FIGURE 3.6 Hands-on Exercise 1 (*continued*)

THE INSERT PICTURE COMMAND

Pull down the Insert menu, click the Picture command, and click Clip Art to display the Clip Art task pane that enables you to enter the search parameters for an appropriate media object. Click the down arrow in the Search In list box and select all of the collections, including those on the Microsoft Web site. Click the down arrow in the Results list box and choose All media types, then click the Go button to initiate the search. The search may take longer than it did previously since it includes the Web, but you should have a much larger selection of potential clips from which to choose. If necessary, use the drop-down arrow on either search box to limit the search as you see fit.

Step 3: WordArt

- Press **Ctrl+End** to move to the end of the document. Pull down the **Insert menu**, click **Picture**, then click **WordArt** to display the WordArt Gallery dialog box in Figure 3.6c.

- Select the WordArt style you like (you can change it later). Click **OK**. You will see a second dialog box in which you enter the text. Enter **Enhancing a Document**. Click **OK**.

- The WordArt object appears in your document in the style you selected. Point to the WordArt object and click the **right mouse button** to display a shortcut menu. Click **Format WordArt** to display the Format WordArt dialog box.

- Click the **Layout tab**, then select **Square** as the Wrapping style. Click **OK**. It is important to select this wrapping option to facilitate placing the WordArt at the top of the document.

- Save the document.

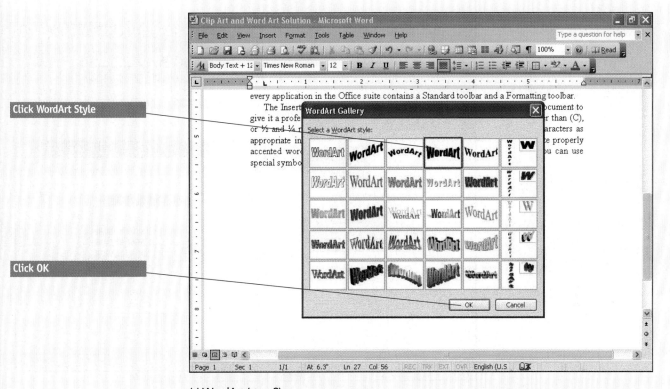

(c) WordArt (step 3)

FIGURE 3.6 Hands-on Exercise 1 (*continued*)

FORMATTING WORDART

The WordArt toolbar offers the easiest way to execute various commands associated with a WordArt object. It is displayed automatically when a WordArt object is selected and is suppressed otherwise. As with any other toolbar, you can point to a button to display a ScreenTip containing the name of the button, which is indicative of its function. The WordArt toolbar contains buttons to display the text vertically, change the style or shape, and/or edit the text.

Step 4: WordArt Continued

- Click and drag the WordArt object to move it the top of the document. (The Format WordArt dialog box is not yet visible.)

- If necessary, click to the left of the word "Clip" in the first sentence and press the **Enter key** two or three times to give yourself more room in which to work at the top of the document.

- Point to the WordArt object, click the **right mouse button** to display a shortcut menu, then click **Format WordArt** to display the Format WordArt dialog box as shown in Figure 3.6d.

- Click the **Colors and Lines tab**, then click the **Fill Color drop-down arrow** to display the available colors. Select a different color (e.g., blue). Click **OK**.

- Move and/or size the WordArt as necessary. Click the **Undo button** if necessary to cancel the action and start again.

- Save the document.

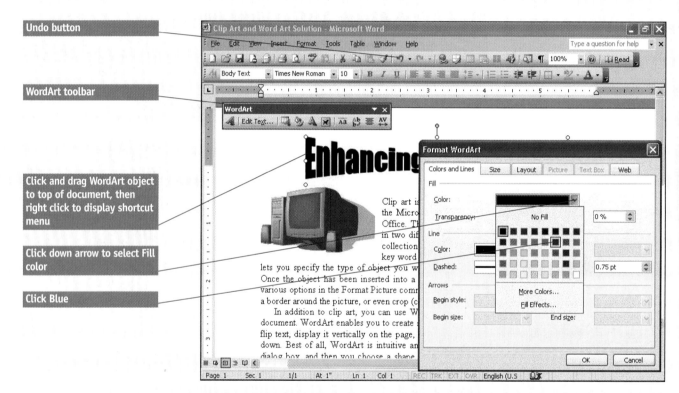

Undo button

WordArt toolbar

Click and drag WordArt object to top of document, then right click to display shortcut menu

Click down arrow to select Fill color

Click Blue

(d) WordArt Continued (step 4)

FIGURE 3.6   Hands-on Exercise 1 (*continued*)

THE THIRD DIMENSION

You can make your WordArt images even more dramatic by adding 3-D effects. You can tilt the text up or down, right or left, increase or decrease the depth, and change the shading. Pull down the View menu, click Toolbars, click Customize, then click the Toolbars tab to display the complete list of available toolbars. Check the box to display the 3-D Settings toolbar. Select the WordArt object, then experiment with various tools and special effects. The results are even better if you have a color printer.

Step 5: The Insert Symbol Command

- Press **Ctrl+End** to move to the end of the document as shown in Figure 3.6e.

- Check that you are positioned at the end of the last sentence. Press the **left arrow key** to move in front of the period.

- Pull down the **Insert menu**, click the **Symbol command**, then choose **Wingdings** from the font list box.

- Click the **Windows logo** (the last character in the last line), click **Insert**, then close the dialog box.

- Click after the word Microsoft in the same sentence, type **(r)**, and try to watch the screen as you enter the text. The (r) will be converted to the ® registered trademark symbol by the AutoCorrect feature.

- Save the document.

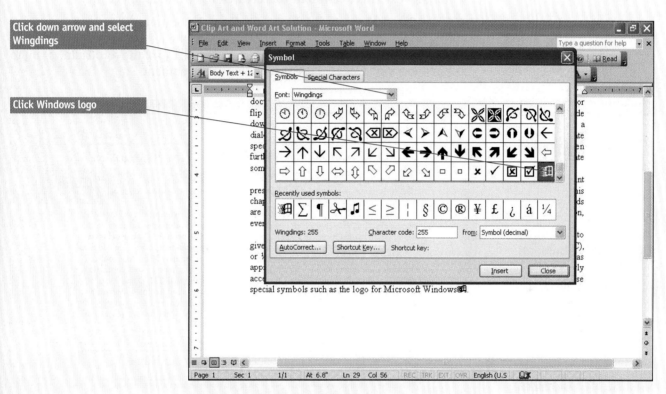

(e) The Insert Symbol Command (step 5)

FIGURE 3.6 Hands-on Exercise 1 (*continued*)

AUTOCORRECT AND AUTOFORMAT

The AutoCorrect feature not only corrects mistakes as you type by substituting one character string for another (e.g., "the" for "teh"), but it will also substitute symbols for typewritten equivalents such as © for (c), provided the entries are included in the table of substitutions. The AutoFormat feature is similar in concept and replaces common fractions such as 1/2 or 1/4 with $^1/_2$ or $^1/_4$. It also converts ordinal numbers such as 1st or 2nd to 1st or 2nd.

Step 6: **Create the AutoShape**

- Pull down the **View menu**, click the **Toolbars command** to display the list of available toolbars, then click **Drawing toolbar**.

- Press the **End key** to move to the end of the line, then press the **Enter key** once or twice to move below the last sentence in the document.

- Click the **down arrow** on the AutoShapes tool to display the menu. Click the **Stars and Banners submenu** and select the **Horizontal Scroll**.

- The mouse pointer changes to a tiny crosshair. Press **Esc** to remove the drawing canvas (we find it easier to work without it), which in turn moves you to the bottom of the page.

- Click and drag to create a scroll, as shown in Figure 3.6f. Release the mouse. Right click in the scroll, click **Add Text**, change the font size to 18 point, then enter the text **This document was created by** (your name). Center the text.

- Click and drag the sizing handle (a circle) at the bottom of the scroll to make it narrow. Click and drag the yellow diamond at the left of the scroll to change the appearance of the scroll. The green dot at the top of the scroll allows you to rotate the scroll. Click off the scroll. Save the document.

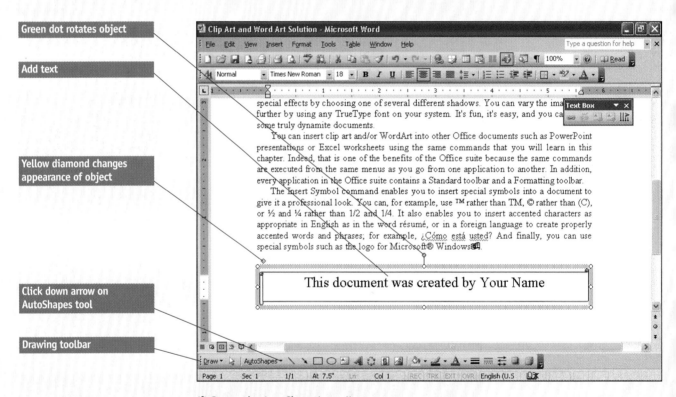

Green dot rotates object

Add text

Yellow diamond changes appearance of object

Click down arrow on AutoShapes tool

Drawing toolbar

(f) Create the AutoShape (step 6)

FIGURE 3.6 Hands-on Exercise 1 (*continued*)

SUPPRESS THE DRAWING CANVAS

The drawing canvas appears by default whenever you create an AutoShape, rectangle, oval, or text box from the Drawing toolbar. You can make the canvas disappear by pressing the Esc key when the canvas appears initially. You can also prevent the canvas from appearing altogether. Pull down the Tools menu, click the Options command, click the General tab, and then clear the box to automatically create the drawing canvas when inserting AutoShapes.

Step 7: **The Completed Document**

- Pull down the **File menu** and click the **Page Setup command** to display the Page Setup dialog box. (You can also double click the ruler below the Formatting toolbar to display the dialog box.)

- Click the **Margins tab** and change the top margin to **1.5 inches** (to accommodate the WordArt at the top of the document). Click **OK**.

- Click the **drop-down arrow** on the Zoom box and select **Whole Page** to preview the completed document as shown in Figure 3.6g. You can change the size and position of the objects from within this view. For example:
  - ❑ Select (click) the clip art to select this object and display its sizing handles.
  - ❑ Select (click) the banner to select it (and deselect the previous selection).
  - ❑ Move and size either object as necessary.

- Print the document and submit it to your instructor as proof that you did the exercise. Save the document. Close the document.

- Exit Word if you do not want to continue with the next exercise at this time.

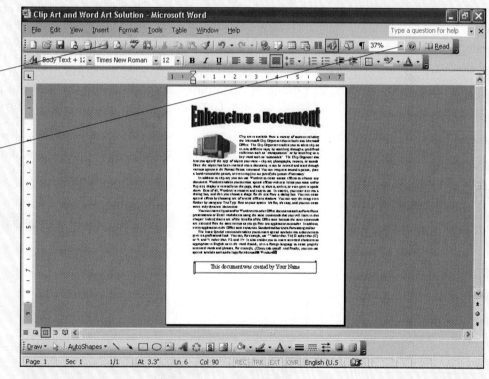

(g) The Completed Document (step 7)

FIGURE 3.6 Hands-on Exercise 1 (*continued*)

ANIMATE TEXT ON SCREEN

Select the desired text, pull down the Format menu, click the Font command to display the Font dialog box, then click the Text Effects tab. Select the desired effect such as "Blinking Background" or "Las Vegas Lights", then click OK to accept the settings and close the dialog box. The selected text should be displayed with the specified effect, which appears on the screen, but not when the document is printed. To cancel the effect, select the text, display the Font dialog box, click the Text Effects tab, select "None" as the effect, then click OK.

The **Internet** is a network of networks that connects computers anywhere in the world. The **World Wide Web** (WWW or simply, the Web) is a very large subset of the Internet, consisting of those computers that store a special type of document known as a **Web page** or **HTML document**. The interesting thing about a Web page is that it contains references called **hyperlinks** to other Web pages, which may in turn be stored on a different computer that is located anywhere in the world. And therein lies the fascination of the Web, in that you simply click on link after link to go effortlessly from one document to the next.

Web pages are developed in a special language called **HyperText Markup Language (HTML)**. Initially, the only way to create a Web page was to learn HTML. Microsoft Office simplifies the process because you can create the document in Word, then simply save it as a Web page. In other words, you start Word in the usual fashion, enter the text of the document with basic formatting, then use the **Save As Web Page command** to convert the document to a Web page. Microsoft Word does the rest and generates the HTML statements for you. (Word 2003 provides a new **Single File Web Page** format that makes the process even easier.) You can continue to enter text and/or change the formatting just as you can with an ordinary document.

Figure 3.7 contains the Web page you will create in the next hands-on exercise. The exercise begins by having you search the Web to locate a suitable photograph for inclusion into the document. You then download the picture to your PC and use the Insert Picture command to insert the photograph into your document. You add formatting, hyperlinks, and footnotes as appropriate, then you save the document as a Web page. The exercise is easy to do, and it will give you an appreciation for the various Web capabilities that are built into Microsoft Office.

Even if you do not place your page on the Web, you can still view it locally on your PC. This is the approach we follow in the next hands-on exercise, which shows you how to save a Word document as a Web page and then see the results of your effort in a Web browser. The Web page is stored on a local drive (e.g., on drive A or

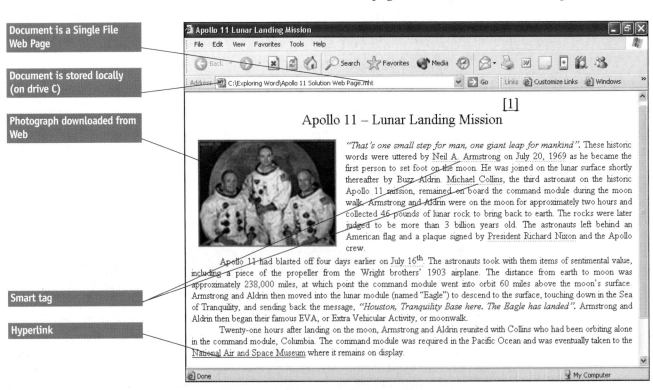

Document is a Single File Web Page

Document is stored locally (on drive C)

Photograph downloaded from Web

Smart tag

Hyperlink

FIGURE 3.7 A Web Document

drive C) rather than on an Internet server, but it can still be viewed through Internet Explorer (or any other browser).

The ability to create links to local documents and to view those pages through a Web browser has created an entirely new way to disseminate information. Organizations of every size are taking advantage of this capability to develop an *Intranet* in which Web pages are placed on a local area network for use within the organizations. The documents on an intranet are available only to individuals with access to the local area network on which the documents are stored.

Copyright Protection

A *copyright* provides legal protection to a written or artistic work, including literary, dramatic, musical, and artistic works such as poetry, novels, movies, songs, and computer software and architecture. It gives the author of a work the exclusive right to the use and duplication of that work. A copyright does not, however, protect facts, ideas, systems, or methods of operation, although it may protect the way these things are expressed.

The owner of the copyright may sell or give up a portion of his or her rights; for example, an author may give distribution rights to a publisher and/or grant movie rights to a studio. *Infringement of a copyright* occurs any time a right reserved by the copyright owner is violated without permission of the owner. Anything on the Internet should be considered copyrighted unless the document specifically says it is in the *public domain*, in which case the author is giving everyone the right to freely reproduce and distribute the material. Does copyright protection prevent you from quoting a document found on the Web in a research paper? Does copyright protection imply that you cannot download an image for inclusion in a term paper? (Facts themselves are not covered by copyright, so you can use statistical data without fear of infringement.)

The answer to what you can use from the Web depends on the amount of the information you reference, as well as the intended use of that information. It is considered *fair use*, and thus not an infringement of copyright, to use a portion of a work for educational, nonprofit purposes, or for the purpose of critical review or commentary. In other words, you can use a quote, downloaded image, or other information from the Web, provided you cite the original work in your footnotes and/or bibliography.

A *footnote* provides additional information about an item, such as its source, and appears at the bottom of the page where the reference occurs. An *endnote* is similar in concept but appears at the end of a document. A horizontal line separates the notes from the rest of the document.

The *Insert Reference command* inserts either a footnote or an endnote into a document, and automatically assigns the next sequential number to that note. The command adjusts for last minute changes, either in your writing or in your professor's requirements. It will, for example, renumber all existing notes to accommodate the addition or deletion of a footnote or endnote. Existing notes are moved (or deleted) within a document by moving (deleting) the reference mark rather than the text of the footnote.

Software piracy (the unauthorized duplication or use of software products such as Microsoft Office) presents a unique problem with respect to copyright protection because of the ease with which it can be done. A program that takes years of development and costs millions of dollars can be copied in a few seconds and results in economic loss to the developer. Software piracy harms everyone in the long run, including you, the end user. It results in higher prices for legitimate licenses, reduced levels of support, and delays in the development of new software. The law imposes stiff penalties for copyright infringement. You may think that this is unduly harsh, but the intent behind the copyright law is to provide economic incentive to an artist or software developer in order that they will invest the necessary resources to create the work. You should honor and respect the copyright process.

2   Microsoft Word and the World Wide Web

Objective   To download a picture from the Internet for use in a Word document; to insert a hyperlink into a Word document; to save a Word document as a Web page. Use Figure 3.8 as a reference.

Step 1:   **Search the Web**

- Start Internet Explorer. It does not matter which page you see initially, as long as you are able to connect to the Internet and start Internet Explorer. Click the **Maximize button** so that Internet Explorer takes the entire screen.

- Click the **Search button** on the Standard Buttons toolbar to display the Search pane in the Explorer bar at the left of the Internet Explorer window.

- Enter **Apollo 11** in the text box, then click the **Go button**. The results of the search are displayed in the left pane as shown in Figure 3.8a. The results you obtain will be different from ours.

- Select (click) the link to Apollo 11 Home. (Enter the URL www.nasm.si.edu/apollo/AS11 manually if your search engine does not display this link.)

- Click the **Close button** to close the Search pane, so that your selected document takes the entire screen.

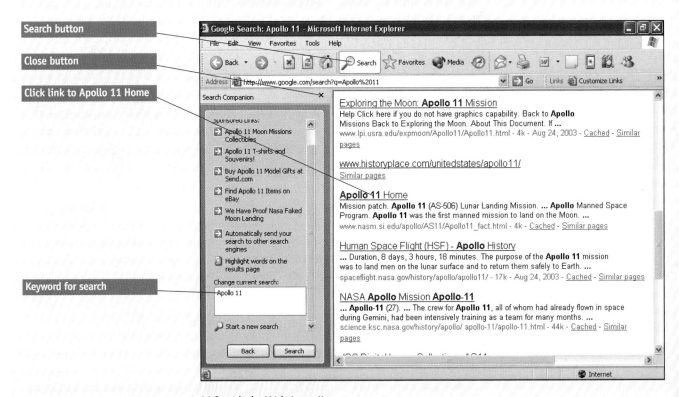

(a) Search the Web (step 1)

FIGURE 3.8   Hands-on Exercise 2

SHORTCUT TO SEARCHING

Click in the Address bar, then type the word "go" or "find" followed by the word or phrase you are looking for. Internet Explorer initiates a search using its predetermined search provider and displays the results (the relevant links) in the Internet Explorer window.

Step 2: Save the Picture

- Click the link to **Apollo 11 Crew** to display the page in Figure 3.8b. Point to the picture of the astronauts, click the **right mouse button** to display a shortcut menu, then click the **Save Picture As command** to display the Save As dialog box.
  - ❏ Click the **drop-down arrow** in the Save In list box to specify the drive and folder in which you want to save the graphic (e.g., in the **Exploring Word folder**).
  - ❏ Internet Explorer supplies the file name and file type for you. You may change the name, but you cannot change the file type.
  - ❏ Click the **Save button** to download the image. Remember the file name and location, as you will need to access the file in the next step.
- The Save As dialog box will close automatically after the picture has been downloaded to your computer.
- Click the **Minimize button** in the Internet Explorer window, since you are temporarily finished using the browser.

Address of Web site

Point to picture and click right mouse button to display shortcut menu

Click Save Picture As command

Click link to Apollo 11 Crew

(b) Save the Picture (step 2)

FIGURE 3.8   Hands-on Exercise 2 (*continued*)

ABOUT INTERNET EXPLORER

There are multiple versions of Internet Explorer, each with subtle differences in the features it supports. To find out which version you have, pull down the Help menu and click About Internet Explorer to display a screen with the version and release number. You will need this information if you have trouble with your browser and seek help from technical support. The About command is present in the Help menu of every Windows application.

Step 3: Insert the Picture

- Start Word and open the **Apollo 11 document** in the **Exploring Word folder**. Save the document as **Apollo 11 Solution** so that you can return to the original document if necessary.

- Pull down the **View menu** to be sure that you are in the **Print Layout view** (or else you will not see the picture after it is inserted into the document). Pull down the **Insert menu**, point to (or click) **Picture command**, then click **From File** to display the Insert Picture dialog box shown in Figure 3.8c.

- Click the **down arrow** on the Look In text box to select the drive and folder where you previously saved the picture. Click the **down arrow** on the Files of type list box and specify **All files**.

- Select (click) **AS11_crew**, which is the file containing the picture that you downloaded earlier. Click the **drop-down arrow** on the **Views button**, then click **Preview** to display the picture prior to inserting. Click **Insert**.

- Save the document.

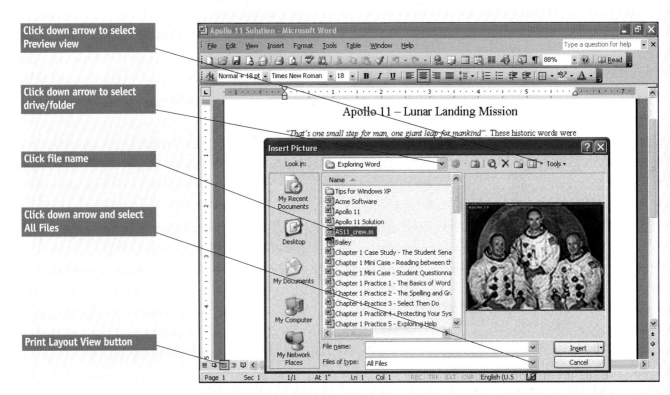

(c) Insert the Picture (step 3)

FIGURE 3.8   Hands-on Exercise 2 (*continued*)

CHANGE THE DEFAULT LOCATION

The default file location is the folder Word uses to open and save a document unless it is otherwise instructed. To change the default location, pull down the Tools menu, click Options, click the File Locations tab, click the desired File type (documents), then click the Modify command button to display the Modify Location dialog box. Click the drop-down arrow in the Look In box to select the new folder (e.g., C:\Exploring Word). Click OK to accept this selection. Click OK to close the Options dialog box. The next time you access the Open or Save commands from the File menu, the Look In text box will reflect the change.

Step 4: Move and Size the Picture

- Point to the picture after it is inserted into the document, click the **right mouse button** to display a shortcut menu, then click the **Format Picture command** to display the Format Picture dialog box.

- Click the **Layout tab** and choose **Square** in the Wrapping style area. Click **OK** to accept the settings and close the Format Picture dialog box.

- Move and/or size the picture so that it approximates the size and position in Figure 3.8d.

- Click the **Undo button** anytime that you are not satisfied with the result. (You can click Redo button to reverse the Undo command.)

- Save the document.

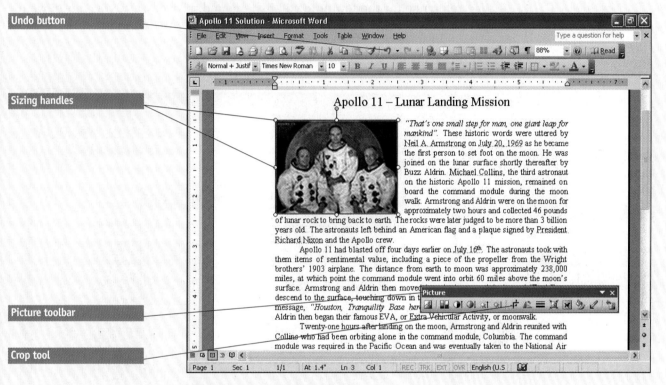

(d) Move and Size the Picture (step 4)

FIGURE 3.8   Hands-on Exercise 2 (*continued*)

CROPPING A PICTURE

The Crop tool is one of the most useful tools when dealing with a photograph as it lets you eliminate (crop) part of a picture. Select (click) the picture to display the Picture toolbar and sizing handles. (If you do not see the Picture toolbar, right click the picture and click the Show Picture Toolbar command.) Click the Crop tool (the ScreenTip will display the name of the tool), then click and drag a sizing handle to crop the part of the picture you want to eliminate. Click the Crop tool a second time to turn the feature off. To restore the picture to its original dimensions, right click the picture, click the Format Picture command, click the Picture tab, and then click the Reset button. Click OK to close the Format Picture dialog box.

Step 5: Insert a Footnote

- Press **Ctrl+Home** to move to the beginning of the document, then click after Lunar Landing Mission in the title of the document. This is where you will insert the footnote.

- Pull down the **Insert menu**. Click **Reference**, then choose **Footnote** to display the Footnote and Endnote dialog box as shown in Figure 3.8e. Check that the option button for **Footnotes** is selected and that the numbering starts at 1. Click **Insert**.

- The insertion point moves to the bottom of the page, where you type the text of the footnote, which should include the Web site from where you downloaded the picture.

- Press **Ctrl+Home** to move to the beginning of the page, where you will see a reference for the footnote you just created. If necessary, you can move (or delete) a footnote by moving (deleting) the reference mark rather than the text of the footnote.

- Save the document.

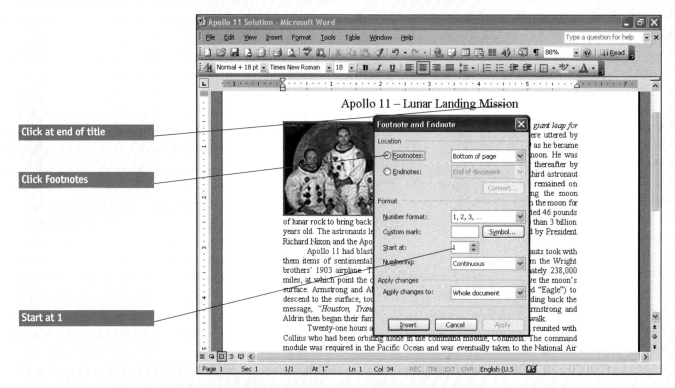

Click at end of title

Click Footnotes

Start at 1

(e) Insert a Footnote (step 5)

FIGURE 3.8 Hands-on Exercise 2 (*continued*)

COPY THE WEB ADDRESS

Use the Copy command to enter a Web address from Internet Explorer into a Word document. Not only do you save time by not having to type the address yourself, but you also ensure that it is entered correctly. Click in the Address bar of Internet Explorer to select the URL, then pull down the Edit menu and click the Copy command (or use the Ctrl+C keyboard shortcut). Switch to the Word document, click at the place in the document where you want to insert the URL, pull down the Edit menu, and click the Paste command (or use the Ctrl+V keyboard shortcut).

Step 6: **Insert a Hyperlink**

- Scroll to the bottom of the document, then click and drag to select the text **National Air and Space Museum**.

- Pull down the **Insert menu** and click the **Hyperlink command** (or click the **Insert Hyperlink button** on the Standard toolbar) to display the Insert Hyperlink dialog box as shown in Figure 3.8f.

- National Air and Space Museum is entered automatically in the Text to display text box. Click **Existing File or Web Page**. Click **Browsed Pages**.

- Click in the **Address** text box to enter the address. Type **http://www.nasm.edu**.

- Click **OK** to accept the settings and close the dialog box. The hyperlink should appear as an underlined entry in the document.

- Save the document.

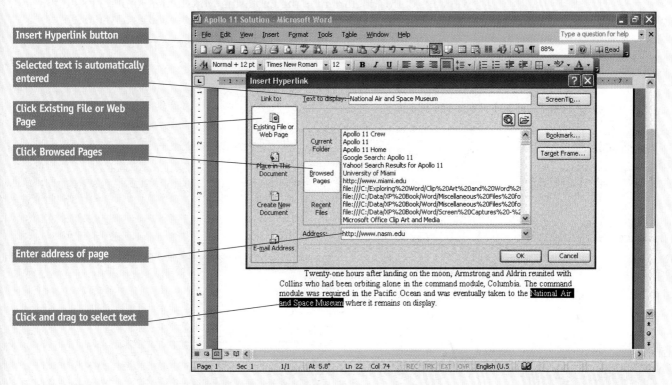

(f) Insert a Hyperlink (step 6)

FIGURE 3.8 Hands-on Exercise 2 (*continued*)

CLICK TO EDIT, CTRL+CLICK TO FOLLOW

Point to a hyperlink within a Word document and you see a ToolTip that says to press and hold the Ctrl key (Ctrl+Click) to follow the link. This is different from what you usually do, because you normally just click a link to follow it. What if, however, you wanted to edit the link? Word modifies the convention so that clicking a link enables you to edit the text of the link. Alternatively, you can right click the hyperlink to display a context-sensitive menu from where you can make the appropriate choice.

Step 7: Create the Web Page

- Pull down the **File menu** and click the **Save As Web Page command** to display the Save As dialog box as shown in Figure 3.8g. Be sure that **Single File Web Page** is specified as the file type.

- Click the **drop-down arrow** in the Save In list box to select the appropriate drive, then open the **Exploring Word folder**.

- Change the name of the Web page to **Apollo 11 Solution Web Page** (to differentiate it from the Word document of the same name). Click the **Change Title button** to display a dialog box in which you can change the title of the Web page to what will appear in the title bar of the Web browser, as in Figure 3.8g. Click **OK**.

- Click the **Save button**. You will see a message indicating that the pictures will be left aligned. Click **Continue**.

- The title bar changes to reflect the name of the Web page. There are now two versions of this document in the Exploring Word folder, Apollo 11 Solution and Apollo 11 Solution Web Page. The latter has been saved as a Web page.

- Click the **Print button** on the Standard toolbar to print this page for your instructor from within Microsoft Word.

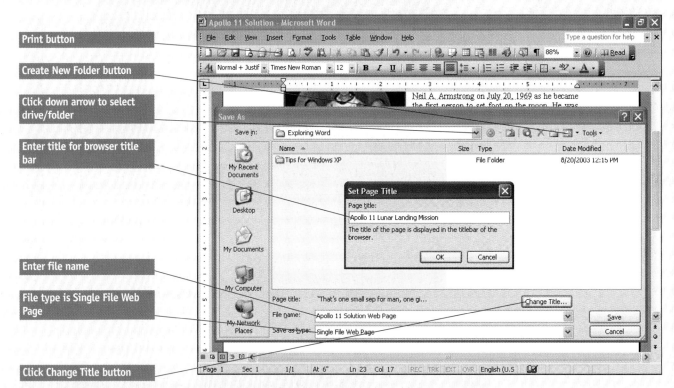

Print button

Create New Folder button

Click down arrow to select drive/folder

Enter title for browser title bar

Enter file name

File type is Single File Web Page

Click Change Title button

(g) Create the Web Page (step 7)

FIGURE 3.8 Hands-on Exercise 2 (*continued*)

CREATE A NEW FOLDER

Do you work with a large number of documents? If so, it may be useful to store those documents in different folders, perhaps one folder for each course you are taking. Pull down the File menu, click the Save As command to display the Save As dialog box, then click the Create New Folder button to display the associated dialog box. Enter the name of the folder, then click OK. Once the folder has been created, use the Look In box to change to that folder the next time you open that document.

Step 8: View the Web Page

- Click the taskbar button for Internet Explorer. Pull down the **File menu** and click the **Open command** to display the Open dialog box. Click the **Browse button**, then select the folder where you saved the Web page. Select the **Apollo 11 Solution Web Page** document, click **Open**, then click **OK.**

- You should see the Web page that was created earlier, as shown in Figure 3.8h. Click the **Print button** on the Internet Explorer toolbar to print this page.

- Click the hyperlink to the **National Air and Space Museum** to display the associated Web page. If you are unable to connect to the site, it is because the site is down, your Internet connection is down, and/or you entered the Web address incorrectly.

- Return to Word. Right click the hyperlink to display a context-sensitive menu, click **Edit Hyperlink**, and make the necessary correction. Save the document.

- Return to Internet Explorer. Click the **Refresh button** to load the corrected page and try the hyperlink a second time. Close Internet Explorer. Exit Word.

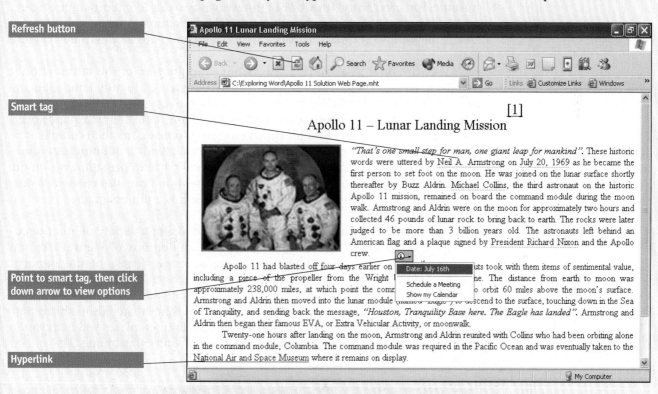

(h) View the Web Page (step 8)

FIGURE 3.8 Hands-on Exercise 2 (*continued*)

SMART TAGS

All applications in Microsoft Office identify specific data types such as a person's name or a date that may exist within a document. The data is identified by a dotted purple line and is known as a smart tag. Point to the smart tag and then click the down arrow in the Smart Tag Actions button to see the list of appropriate actions. The actions for the date in Figure 3.8h are tied to Microsoft Outlook; that is, Word is giving you the opportunity to schedule a meeting for July 16th and/or to display your calendar. The option may not exist in a lab environment.

WIZARDS AND TEMPLATES

We have created some very interesting documents throughout the text, but in every instance we have formatted the document entirely on our own. It is time now to see what is available in terms of "jump starting" the process by borrowing professional designs from others. Accordingly, we discuss the wizards and templates that are built into Microsoft Word.

A *template* is a partially completed document that contains formatting, text, and/or graphics. It may be as simple as a memo or as complex as a résumé or newsletter. Microsoft Word provides a variety of templates for common documents, including a résumé, agenda, and fax cover sheet. You simply open the template, then modify the existing text as necessary, while retaining the formatting in the template. A *wizard* makes the process even easier by asking a series of questions, then creating a customized template based on your answers. A template or wizard creates the initial document for you. It's then up to you to complete the document by entering the appropriate information.

Figure 3.9 illustrates the use of wizards and templates in conjunction with a résumé. You can choose from one of three existing styles (contemporary, elegant, and professional) to which you add personal information. Alternatively, you can select the *Résumé Wizard* to create a customized template, as was done in Figure 3.9a.

After the Résumé Wizard is selected, it prompts you for the information it needs to create a basic résumé. You specify the style in Figure 3.9b, enter the requested information in Figure 3.9c, and choose the categories in Figure 3.9d. The wizard asks additional questions (not shown in Figure 3.9), after which it displays the (partially) completed Résumé based on your responses. You then complete the Résumé by entering the specifics of your employment and/or additional information. As you edit the document, you can copy and paste information within the Résumé, just as you would with a regular document. You can also change the formatting. It takes a little practice, but the end result is a professionally formatted Résumé in a minimum of time.

Microsoft Word contains templates and wizards for a variety of other documents. (Look carefully at the tabs within the dialog box of Figure 3.9a and you can infer that Word will help you to create letters, faxes, memos, reports, legal pleadings, publications, and even Web pages. The Office Web site, www.microsoft.com/office, contains additional templates.) Consider, too, Figure 3.10, which displays four attractive documents that were created using the respective wizards. Realize, however, that while wizards and templates will help you to create professionally designed documents, they are only a beginning. *The content is still up to you.*

THIRTY SECONDS IS ALL YOU HAVE

Thirty seconds is the average amount of time a personnel manager spends skimming your résumé and deciding whether or not to call you for an interview. It doesn't matter how much training you have had or how good you are if your résumé and cover letter fail to project a professional image. Know your audience and use the vocabulary of your targeted field. Be positive and describe your experience from an accomplishment point of view. Maintain a separate list of references and have it available on request. Be sure all information is accurate. Be conscientious about the design of your résumé and proofread the final documents very carefully.

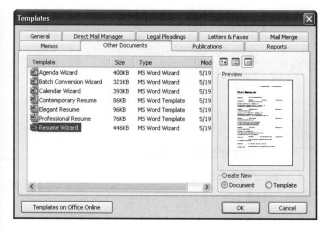

(a) Résumé Wizard

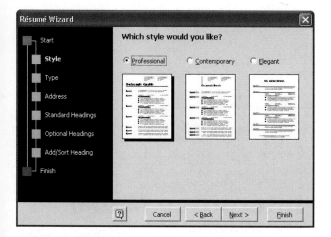

(b) Choose the Style

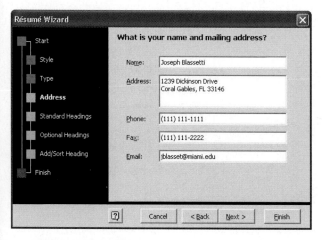

(c) Supply the Information

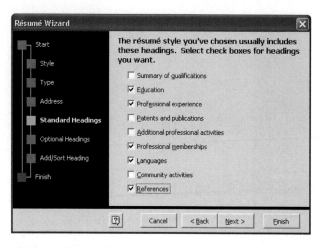

(d) Choose the Headings

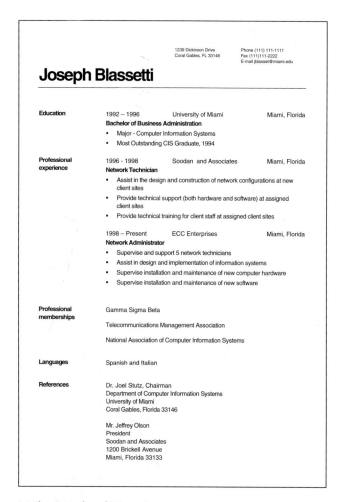

(e) The Completed Résumé

FIGURE 3.9   Creating a Résumé

(a) Calendar

(b) Contemporary Report

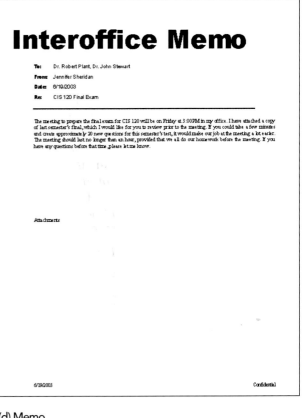

(c) Manual

(d) Memo

FIGURE 3.10 What You Can Do with Wizards

A *mail merge* can create any type of standardized document, but it is used most frequently to create a set of *form letters*. In essence it creates the same letter many times, changing the name, address, and other information as appropriate from letter to letter. You might use a mail merge to look for a job upon graduation, when you send essentially the same cover letter to many different companies. The concept is illustrated in Figure 3.11, in which John Smith has written a letter describing his qualifications, then merges that letter with a set of names and addresses, to produce the individual letters.

The mail merge process uses two files as input, a main document and a data source (or address list). A set of form letters is created as output. The *main document* (e.g., the cover letter in Figure 3.11a) contains standardized text, together with one or more *merge fields* that serve as place holders for the variable data that will be inserted into the individual letters. The address list (the set of names and addresses in Figure 3.11b) contains the information that varies from letter to letter.

The first row in the data source is called the header row and identifies the fields in the remaining rows. Each additional row contains the data to create one letter and is called a data record. Every data record contains the same fields in the same order—for example, Title, FirstName, LastName, and so on. (The fields can also be specified collectively, but for purposes of illustration, we will show the fields individually.)

The main document and the address list work in conjunction with one another, with the merge fields in the main document referencing the corresponding fields in the data source. The first line in the address of Figure 3.11a, for example, contains three entries in angle brackets, <<Title>> <<FirstName>> <<LastName>>. (These entries are not typed explicitly but are entered through special commands, as described in the hands-on exercise that follows shortly.) The merge process examines each record in the data source and substitutes the appropriate field values for the corresponding merge fields as it creates the individual form letters. For example, the first three fields in the first record will produce Mr. Eric Simon. The same fields in the second record will produce Dr. Lauren Howard, and so on.

In similar fashion, the second line in the address of the main document contains the <<Company>> field. The third line contains the <<JobTitle>> field. The fourth line references the <<Address1>> field, and the last line contains the <<City>>, <<State>>, and <<PostalCode>> fields. The salutation repeats the <<Title>> and <<LastName>> fields. The first sentence in the letter uses the <<Company>> field a second time. The mail merge prepares the letters one at a time, with one letter created for every record in the data source until the file of names and addresses is exhausted. The individual form letters are shown in Figure 3.11c. Each letter begins automatically on a new page.

The implementation of a mail merge is accomplished through the *Mail Merge Wizard*, which will open in the task pane and guide you through the various steps in the mail merge process. In essence there are three things you must do:

1. Create and save the main document

2. Create and save the data source

3. Merge the main document and data source to create the individual letters

The same data source can be used to create multiple sets of form letters. You could, for example, create a marketing campaign in which you send an initial letter to the entire list, and then send follow-up letters at periodic intervals to the same mailing list. Alternatively, you could filter the original mailing list to include only a subset of names, such as the individuals who responded to the initial letter. You could also use the wizard to create a different set of documents, such as envelopes and/or e-mail messages. Note, too, that you can sort the addresses to print the documents in a specified sequence, such as zip code to take advantage of bulk mail.

John Doe Computing

1239 Dickinson Drive   •   Coral Gables, FL 33146   •   (305) 666-5555

June 22, 2003

«Title» «FirstName» «LastName»
«JobTitle»
«Company»
«Address1»
«City», «State» «PostalCode»

Dear «Title» «LastName»:

I would like to inquire about a position with «Company» as an entry-level programmer. I have graduated from the University of Miami with a Bachelor's Degree in Computer Information Systems (May 2003) and I am very interested in working for you. I am proficient in all applications in Microsoft Office and also have experience with Visual Basic, C++, and Java. I have had the opportunity to design and implement a few Web applications, both as a part of my educational program, and during my internship with Personalized Computer Designs, Inc.

I am eager to put my skills to work and would like to talk with you at your earliest convenience. I have enclosed a copy of my résumé and will be happy to furnish the names and addresses of my references. You may reach me at the above address and phone number. I look forward to hearing from you.

Sincerely,

John Doe
President

(a) The Form Letter

Title	FirstName	LastName	Company	JobTitle	Address1	City	State	PostalCode
Mr.	Eric	Simon	Arnold and Joyce Computing	President	10000 Sample Road	Coral Springs	FL	33071
Dr.	Lauren	Howard	Unique Systems	President	475 LeJeune Road	Coral Springs	FL	33071
Mr.	Peter	Gryn	Gryn Computing	Director of Human Resources	1000 Federal Highway	Miami	FL	33133
Ms.	Julie	Overby	The Overby Company	President	100 Savona Avenue	Coral Gables	FL	33146

(b) The Data Source

FIGURE 3.11   A Mail Merge

John Doe Computing

1239 Dickinson Drive • Coral Gables, FL 33146 • (305) 666-5555

June 22, 2003

Mr. Eric Simon
Arnold and Joyce Computing
President
10000 Sample Road
Coral Springs, FL 33071

Dear Mr. Simon:

I would like to inquire about a position with your company as an entry-level programmer. I have just graduated from the University of Miami with a Bachelor's Degree in Computer Information Systems (May 2003) and I am very interested in working for you. I am proficient in all applications in Microsoft Office and also have experience with Visual Basic, C++, and Java. I have had the opportunity to design and implement a few Web applications, both as a part of my educational program, and during my internship with Personalized Computer Designs, Inc.

I am eager to put my skills to work and would like to talk with you at your earliest convenience. I have enclosed a copy of my résumé and will be happy to furnish the names and addresses of my references. You may reach me at the above address and phone number. I look forward to hearing from you.

Sincerely,

John Doe
President

John Doe Computing

1239 Dickinson Drive • Coral Gables, FL 33146 • (305) 666-5555

June 22, 2003

Dr. Lauren Howard
Unique Systems
President
475 LeJeune Road
Coral Springs, FL 33071

Dear Dr. Howard:

I would like to inquire about a position with your company as an entry-level programmer. I have just graduated from the University of Miami with a Bachelor's Degree in Computer Information Systems (May 2003) and I am very interested in working for you. I am proficient in all applications in Microsoft Office and also have experience with Visual Basic, C++, and Java. I have had the opportunity to design and implement a few Web applications, both as a part of my educational program, and during my internship with Personalized Computer Designs, Inc.

I am eager to put my skills to work and would like to talk with you at your earliest convenience. I have enclosed a copy of my résumé and will be happy to furnish the names and addresses of my references. You may reach me at the above address and phone number. I look forward to hearing from you.

Sincerely,

John Doe
President

John Doe Computing

1239 Dickinson Drive • Coral Gables, FL 33146 • (305) 666-5555

June 22, 2003

Mr. Peter Gryn
Gryn Computing
Director of Human Resources
1000 Federal Highway
Miami, FL 33133

Dear Mr. Gryn:

I would like to inquire about a position with your company as an entry-level programmer. I have just graduated from the University of Miami with a Bachelor's Degree in Computer Information Systems (May 2003) and I am very interested in working for you. I am proficient in all applications in Microsoft Office and also have experience with Visual Basic, C++, and Java. I have had the opportunity to design and implement a few Web applications, both as a part of my educational program, and during my internship with Personalized Computer Designs, Inc.

I am eager to put my skills to work and would like to talk with you at your earliest convenience. I have enclosed a copy of my résumé and will be happy to furnish the names and addresses of my references. You may reach me at the above address and phone number. I look forward to hearing from you.

Sincerely,

John Doe
President

John Doe Computing

1239 Dickinson Drive • Coral Gables, FL 33146 • (305) 666-5555

June 22, 2003

Ms. Julie Overby
The Overby Company
President
100 Savona Avenue
Coral Gables, FL 33146

Dear Ms. Overby:

I would like to inquire about a position with your company as an entry-level programmer. I have just graduated from the University of Miami with a Bachelor's Degree in Computer Information Systems (May 2003) and I am very interested in working for you. I am proficient in all applications in Microsoft Office and also have experience with Visual Basic, C++, and Java. I have had the opportunity to design and implement a few Web applications, both as a part of my educational program, and during my internship with Personalized Computer Designs, Inc.

I am eager to put my skills to work and would like to talk with you at your earliest convenience. I have enclosed a copy of my résumé and will be happy to furnish the names and addresses of my references. You may reach me at the above address and phone number. I look forward to hearing from you.

Sincerely,

John Doe
President

(c) The Printed Letters

FIGURE 3.11 A Mail Merge (*continued*)

Objective   To create a main document and associated data source; to implement a mail merge and produce a set of form letters; to create a document from a template. Use Figure 3.12 as a guide.

Step 1:   **Open the Form Letter**

- Open the **Form Letter** document in the Exploring Word folder. If necessary, change to the **Print Layout view** and zoom to **Page Width** as shown in Figure 3.12a.

- Modify the letterhead to reflect your name and address. Select **"Your Name Goes Here"**, then type a new entry to replace the selected text. Add your address information to the second line.

- Click immediately to the left of the first paragraph, then press the **Enter key** twice to insert two lines. Press the **up arrow** two times to return to the first line you inserted.

- Pull down the **Insert menu** and click the **Date and Time command** to display the dialog box in Figure 3.12a.

- Select (click) the date format you prefer and, if necessary, check the box to **Update automatically**. Click **OK** to close the dialog box.

- Save the document as **Form Letter Solution** so that you can return to the original document if necessary.

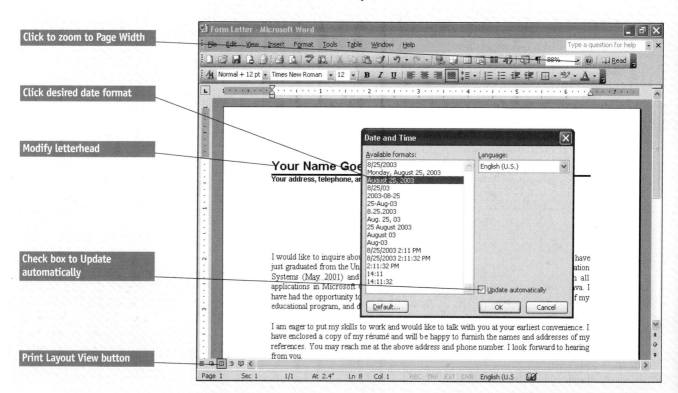

(a) Open the Form Letter (step 1)

FIGURE 3.12   Hands-on Exercise 3

Step 2: The Mail Merge Wizard

- Pull down the **Tools menu**, click **Letters and Mailings**, then click **Mail Merge ...** to open the task pane.

- The option button for **Letters** is selected by default as shown in Figure 3.12b. Click **Next: Starting Document** to begin creating the document.

- The option button to **Use the current document** is selected. (We began the exercise by providing you with the text of the document, as opposed to having you create the entire form letter.)

- Click **Next: Select Recipients** to enter the list of names and addresses.

- Click the option button to **Type a New List**, then click the link to **Create** that appears within the task pane. This brings you to a new screen, where you enter the data for the recipients of your form letter.

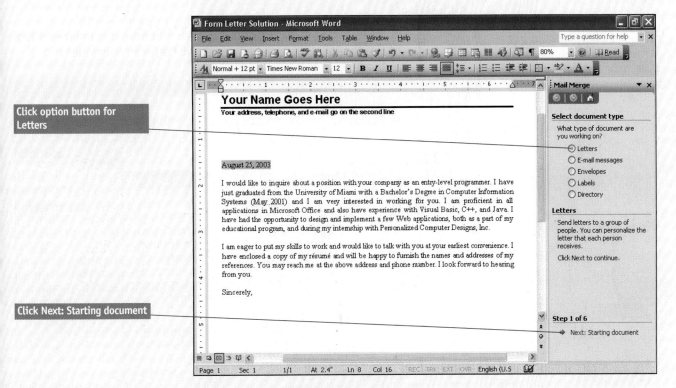

(b) The Mail Merge Wizard (step 2)

FIGURE 3.12   Hands-on Exercise 3 (*continued*)

THE MAIL MERGE WIZARD

The Mail Merge Wizard simplifies the process of creating form letters and other types of merge documents through step-by-step directions that appear automatically in the task pane. The options for the current step appear in the top portion of the task pane and are self-explanatory. Click the link to the next step at the bottom of the pane to move forward in the process, or click the link to the previous step to correct any mistakes you might have made.

Step 3: Select the Recipients

- Enter data for the first record, using your name and address as shown in Figure 3.12c. Type **Mr.** or **Ms.** in the Title field, then press **Tab** to move to the next (FirstName) field and enter your first name.

- Complete the first record by entering your address. You do not need to enter the country, phone number, or e-mail address.

- Click the **New Entry button** to enter the data for the next person. Enter your instructor's name and a hypothetical address. Enter data for one additional person, real or fictitious as you see fit. Click **Close** when you have completed the data entry.

- You will see the Save Address List dialog box, where you will be prompted to save the list of names and addresses. Save the file as **Names and Addresses** in the **Exploring Word folder**. The file type is specified as a Microsoft Office Address list.

- You will see a dialog box showing all of the records you have just entered. Click **OK** to close the dialog box. Click **Next: Write Your Letter** to continue.

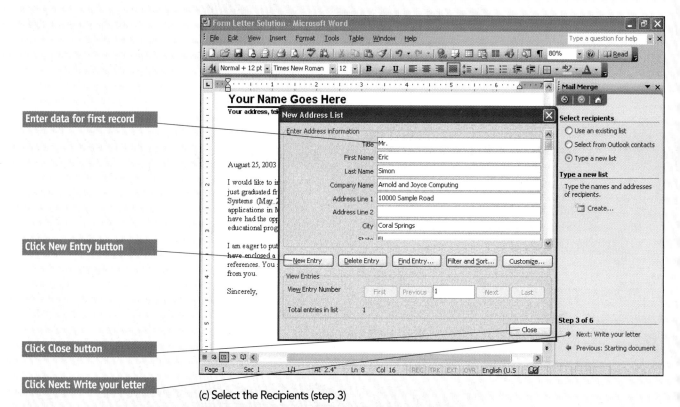

(c) Select the Recipients (step 3)

FIGURE 3.12 Hands-on Exercise 3 (*continued*)

THREE DIFFERENT FILES

A mail merge works with three different files. The main document and data source are input to the mail merge, which creates a set of merged letters as output. You can use the same data source (e.g., a set of names and addresses) with different main documents (a form letter and an envelope) and/or use the same main document with multiple data sources. You typically save, but do not print, the main document(s) and the data source(s). Conversely, you print the set of merged letters, but typically do not save them.

Step 4: Write (Complete) the Letter

- The text of the form letter is already written, but it is still necessary to insert the fields within the form letter.

- Click below the date and press the **Enter key** once or twice. Click the link to the **Address block** to select a single entry that is composed of multiple fields (Street, City, ZipCode, and so on). Click **OK**. The AddressBlock field is inserted into the document as shown in Figure 3.12d.

- Press the **Enter key** twice to leave a blank line after the address block. Click the link to the **Greeting line** to display the Greeting Line dialog box in Figure 3.12d.

- Choose the type of greeting you want. Change the comma that appears after the greeting to a colon since this is a business letter. Click **OK**. The GreetingLine field is inserted into the document and enclosed in angled brackets.

- Press **Enter** to enter a blank line. Save the document. Click **Next: Preview Your Letters** to continue.

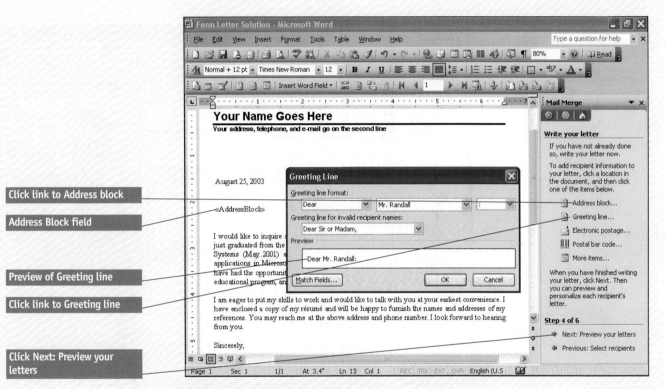

(d) Write (Complete) the Letter (step 4)

FIGURE 3.12 Hands-on Exercise 3 (*continued*)

BLOCKS VERSUS INDIVIDUAL FIELDS

The Mail Merge Wizard simplifies the process of entering field names into a form letter by supplying two predefined entries, AddressBlock and GreetingLine, which contain multiple fields that are typical of the ways in which an address and salutation appear in a conventional letter. You can still insert individual fields by clicking in the document where you want the field to go, then clicking the Insert Merge Fields button on the Mail Merge toolbar. The blocks are easier.

Step 5: View and Print the Letters

- You should see the first form letter as shown. You can click the >> or << button in the task pane (not shown in Figure 3.12e) to move to the next or previous letter, respectively. You can also use the navigation buttons that appear on the Mail Merge toolbar.

- View the records individually to be sure that the form letter is correct and that the data has been entered correctly. Make corrections if necessary.

- Click **Next: Complete the Merge**, then click **Print** to display the dialog box in Figure 3.12e. Click **OK**, then **OK** again, to print the form letters.

- Click the **<<abc>>** button to display the field codes. Pull down the **File menu** and click the **Print command** to display the Print dialog box. Check the option to print the current page. Click **OK**. Submit this page to your instructor as well.

- Pull down the **File menu** and click the **Close command** to close the Form Letter Solution and the associated set of names and addresses.

- Save the documents if you are asked about doing so.

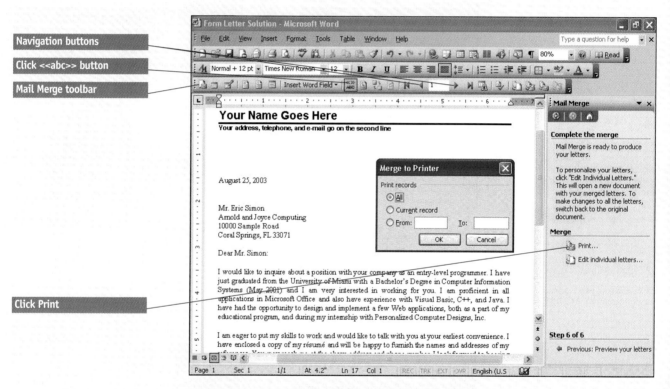

(e) View and Print the Letters (step 5)

FIGURE 3.12 Hands-on Exercise 3 (*continued*)

THE MAIL MERGE TOOLBAR

The Mail Merge toolbar appears throughout the mail merge process and contains various buttons that apply to different steps within the process. Click the <<abc>> button to display field values rather than field codes. Click the button a second time and you switch back to field codes from field values. Click the <<abc>> button to display the field values, then use the navigation buttons to view the different letters. Click the ▶ button, for example, and you move to the next letter. Click the ▶| button to display the form letter for the last record.

Step 6:

Open the Contemporary Merge Letter

- Pull down the **File menu** and click the **New command**. If necessary, pull down the **View menu** and open the **task pane**.

- Click the link to **On my Computer** (under templates) in the task pane to display the Templates dialog box, then click the **Mail Merge tab** to display the Templates dialog box in Figure 3.12f.

- Select (click) the **Contemporary Merge Letter**. Be sure that the **Document option button** is selected. Click **OK** to select this document and begin the merge process.

- You will see a form letter with the AddressBlock and GreetingLine fields already entered.

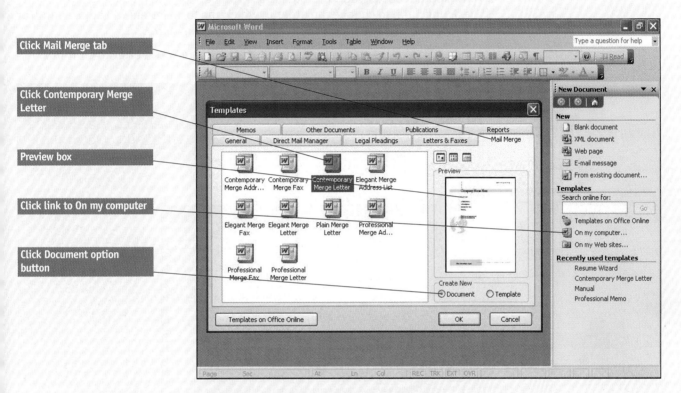

(f) Open the Contemporary Merge Letter (step 6)

FIGURE 3.12 Hands-on Exercise 3 (*continued*)

PAPER MAKES A DIFFERENCE

Most of us take paper for granted, but the right paper can make a significant difference in the effectiveness of the document, especially when you are trying to be noticed. Reports and formal correspondence are usually printed on white paper, but you would be surprised how many different shades of white there are. Other types of documents lend themselves to a specialty paper for additional impact. Consider the use of a specialty paper the next time you have an important project.

Step 7: Select the Recipients

- If necessary, display the **Mail Merge toolbar**.

- The option button to **Use an existing list** is selected. Click the link to **Browse** for the existing list to display the Select Data Source dialog box.

- We will use the same data source that you created earlier. (You could also use the list of Outlook contacts or an Access database as the source of your data.)

- Click the **down arrow** on the Look In box to select the Exploring Word folder. Click the **down arrow** on the File Type list box to select **Microsoft Office Address Lists**. Select the **Names and Addresses** file from step 3. Click **Open**.

- You should see the Mail Merge Recipients dialog box in Figure 3.12g that contains the records you entered earlier. You can use this dialog box to modify existing data, to change the order in which the form letters will appear, and/or to choose which recipients are to receive the form letter.

- Click **OK** to close the dialog box. Click **Next: Write Your Letter** to continue.

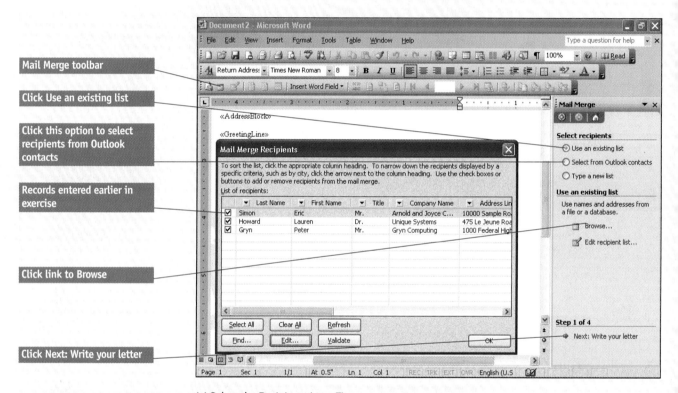

Mail Merge toolbar

Click Use an existing list

Click this option to select recipients from Outlook contacts

Records entered earlier in exercise

Click link to Browse

Click Next: Write your letter

(g) Select the Recipients (step 7)

FIGURE 3.12 Hands-on Exercise 3 (*continued*)

USE OUTLOOK AS THE DATA SOURCE

Think of Microsoft Outlook as a desktop manager, or personal assistant, that keeps track of all types of information for you. You can use Outlook to maintain an address book (contact list), schedule appointments, create a task list, or send and receive e-mail. And since Outlook is an integral part of Microsoft Office, its components are easily linked to other Office applications. You could, for example, use the Outlook address book as the data source for a mail merge in Word. Just start the mail merge in the usual way, then click the option button to select recipients from the Outlook contacts.

Step 8: Write the Form Letter

- The form letter has been created as a template as shown in Figure 3.12h. The AddressBlock and GreetingLine fields have been entered for you.

- Click and drag over **Type Your Letter Here** that appears in the form letter and enter two or three sentences of your own choosing. Our letter indicates that we are seeking to acquire one or more of the consulting firms on the mailing list.

- Continue to personalize the form letter by replacing the text in the original template. Click at the upper right of the letter and enter your return address. Use your name for the company name.

- Replace the signature lines with your name and title. Select the line at the bottom of the page that reads [Click here and type a slogan] and enter a slogan of your own.

- Save the document as **Contemporary Merge Letter Solution** in the Exploring Word folder. Click the link to **Next: Preview your letters**.

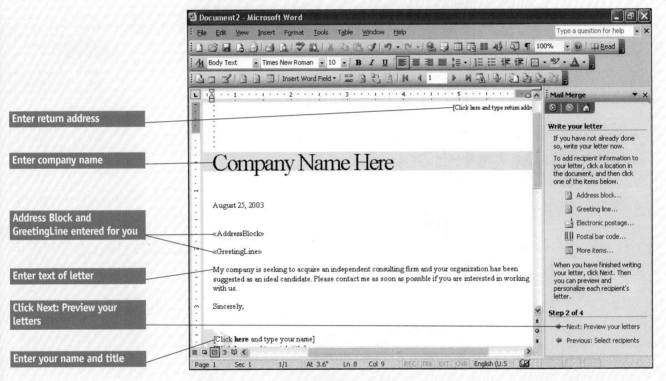

(h) Write the Form Letter (step 8)

FIGURE 3.12 Hands-on Exercise 3 *(continued)*

ENVELOPES AND MAILING LABELS

The set of form letters is only the first step in a true mail merge because you also have to create the envelopes and/or mailing labels to physically mail the letters. Start the Mail Merge Wizard as you normally do, but this time specify labels (or envelopes) instead of a form letter. Follow the instructions provided by the wizard using the same data source as for the form letters. See practice exercise 7 at the end of the chapter.

Step 9: **Complete the Merge**

- You should see the first form letter. The name and address of this recipient are the same as in the set of form letters created earlier. Click **Next: Complete the Merge** to display the screen in Figure 3.12i.

- Use the navigation buttons on the Mail Merge toolbar to view the three form letters. Click the link to **Print . . .** (or click the **Merge to Printer button** on the Mail Merge toolbar).

- Click the option button to print all the letters, then click **OK** to display the Print dialog box. Click **OK** to print the individual form letters.

- Exit Word. Save the form letter and/or the names and addresses document if you are asked about doing so.

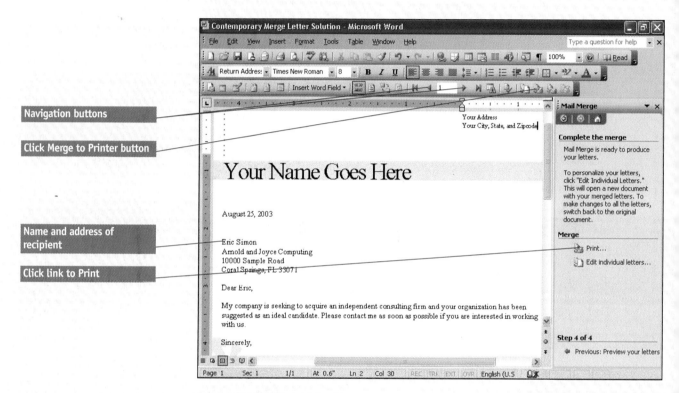

(i) Complete the Merge (step 9)

FIGURE 3.12 Hands-on Exercise 3 (*continued*)

EDIT THE INDIVIDUAL LETTERS

Click the Merge to New Document button (or click the link to Edit individual letters in the task pane) to create a third document (called Letters1 by default) consisting of the individual form letters. There are as many pages in this document as there are records in the address list. You can view and/or edit the individual letters from this document, then print the entire set of merged letters. You need not save this document, however, unless you actually made changes to the individual letters.

SUMMARY

The Insert Picture command displays a task pane in which you enter a keyword that describes the clip you are looking for. The search is made possible by the Microsoft Clip Organizer, which organizes the media files available to you into collections, then enables you to limit the search to specific media types and/or specific collections. The Drawing toolbar enables you to create your own clip art.

Microsoft WordArt is an application within Microsoft Office that creates decorative text that can be used to add interest to a document. WordArt can be used in addition to clip art or in place of clip art if the right image is not available. You can rotate text in any direction, add three-dimensional effects, display the text vertically down the page, or print it upside down.

The Insert Symbol command provides access to special characters, making it easy to place typographic characters into a document. The symbols can be taken from any font and can be displayed in any point size.

Resources (such as clip art or photographs) can be downloaded from the Web for inclusion in a Word document. Web pages are written in a language called HTML (HyperText Markup Language). The Save As Web Page command saves a Word document as a Web page. The new Single File Web Page format saves all of the elements of a Web site, including text and graphics, in a single file.

A copyright provides legal protection to a written or artistic work, giving the author exclusive rights to its use and reproduction, except as governed under the fair use exclusion. Anything on the Internet should be considered copyrighted unless the document specifically says it is in the public domain. The fair use exclusion enables you to use a portion of the work for educational, nonprofit purposes, or for the purpose of critical review or commentary. All such material should be cited through an appropriate footnote or endnote.

Wizards and templates help create professionally designed documents with a minimum of time and effort. A template is a partially completed document that contains formatting and other information. A wizard is an interactive program that creates a customized template based on the answers you supply. The resulting documentation can be modified with respect to content and/or formatting.

A mail merge creates the same letter many times, changing only the variable data, such as the addressee's name and address, from letter to letter. It is performed in conjunction with a main document and a data source, which are stored as separate documents. The mail merge can be used to create a form letter for selected records, and/or print the form letters in a sequence different from the way the records are stored in the data source. The same data source can be used to create multiple sets of form letters.

KEY TERMS

MULTIPLE CHOICE

1. How do you change the size of a selected object so that the height and width change in proportion to one another?

    (a) Click and drag any of the four corner handles in the direction you want to go
    (b) Click and drag the sizing handle on the top border, then click and drag the sizing handle on the left side
    (c) Click and drag the sizing handle on the bottom border, then click and drag the sizing handle on the right side
    (d) All of the above

2. How do you insert a hyperlink into a Word document?

    (a) Pull down the Insert menu and choose the Hyperlink command
    (b) Choose the Insert Hyperlink button on the Standard toolbar
    (c) Both (a) and (b)
    (d) Neither (a) nor (b)

3. How do you search for clip art using the Clip Organizer?

    (a) By entering a keyword that describes the image you want
    (b) By browsing through various collections
    (c) Both (a) and (b)
    (d) Neither (a) nor (b)

4. Which of the following objects can be inserted into a document?

    (a) Clip art
    (b) WordArt
    (c) Photographs
    (d) All of the above

5. Which of the following is true about a mail merge?

    (a) The same form letter can be used with different data sources
    (b) The same data source can be used with different form letters
    (c) Both (a) and (b)
    (d) Neither (a) nor (b)

6. Which of the following best describes the documents that are associated with a mail merge?

    (a) The main document is typically saved, but not necessarily printed
    (b) The names and addresses are typically saved, but not necessarily printed
    (c) The individual form letters are printed, but not necessarily saved
    (d) All of the above

7. Which of the following is true about footnotes or endnotes?

    (a) The addition of a footnote or endnote automatically renumbers the notes that follow
    (b) The deletion of a footnote or endnote automatically renumbers the notes that follow
    (c) Both (a) and (b)
    (d) Neither (a) nor (b)

8. Which of the following is true about the Insert Symbol command?

    (a) It can insert a symbol in different type sizes
    (b) It can access any font installed on the system
    (c) Both (a) and (b)
    (d) Neither (a) nor (b)

9. Which of the following is true regarding objects and the associated toolbars?

    (a) Clicking on a WordArt object displays the WordArt toolbar
    (b) Clicking on a Picture displays the Picture toolbar
    (c) Both (a) and (b)
    (d) Neither (a) nor (b)

10. Which of the following objects can be downloaded from the Web for inclusion into a Word document?

    (a) Clip art
    (b) Photographs
    (c) Sound and video files
    (d) All of the above

... continued

11. What is the significance of the Shift key in conjunction with various tools on the Drawing toolbar?

 (a) It will draw a circle rather than an oval using the Oval tool

 (b) It will draw a square rather than a rectangle using the Rectangle tool

 (c) It will draw a horizontal or vertical line with the Line tool

 (d) All of the above

12. What happens if you enter the text www.intel.com into a document?

 (a) The entry is converted to a hyperlink, and further, the text will be underlined and displayed in a different color

 (b) The associated page will be opened, provided your computer has access to the Internet

 (c) Both (a) and (b)

 (d) Neither (a) nor (b)

13. Which of the following is true about wizards?

 (a) They are accessed from the General Templates link on the task pane

 (b) They always produce a finished document with no further modification necessary

 (c) Both (a) and (b)

 (d) Neither (a) nor (b)

14. Which of the following is true about a Web document that was created from within Microsoft Word?

 (a) It can be viewed locally

 (b) It can be viewed via the Web, provided it is uploaded onto a Web server

 (c) Both (a) and (b)

 (d) Neither (a) nor (b)

15. Microsoft WordArt can be used to:

 (a) Arch text, or print it upside down

 (b) Rotate text, or add three-dimensional effects

 (c) Display text vertically down a page

 (d) All of these answers are correct

16. Which of the following was introduced into Word 2003 to simplify the creation of a Web page from within Microsoft Word?

 (a) The Save as Web Page Command

 (b) Single File Web Page format

 (c) Both (a) and (b)

 (d) Neither (a) nor (b)

17. What provides legal protection to the author for a written or artistic work?

 (a) Public domain

 (b) Copyright

 (c) Fair use

 (d) Footnote

18. How do you insert a date into a document so that the date is automatically updated when the document is retrieved?

 (a) Type the date manually

 (b) Use the Date and Time command in the Insert menu and clear the box to insert the date as a field

 (c) Use the Insert Date and Time command in the Insert menu and check the box to insert the date as a field

 (d) It cannot be done

ANSWERS

1. a	**7.** c	**13.** a
2. c	**8.** c	**14.** c
3. c	**9.** c	**15.** d
4. d	**10.** d	**16.** b
5. c	**11.** d	**17.** b
6. d	**12.** a	**18.** c

PRACTICE WITH WORD

1. **Runner's Paradise:** You have been asked to create a flyer to advertise an upcoming Corporate Run such as the flyer in Figure 3.13. You may create your own flyer, or you can copy our design, but you are required to use a combination of clip art, WordArt, symbols, text boxes, and lines. To create our flyer:

   a. Open a new document. Set the left and right page margins to 1″ and the top and bottom page margins to ½″.

   b. To enter the store locations at the top of the page, set a right tab at the right page margin. Enter the store locations at the left and right margins as shown in the figure.

   c. Change the font to 12 point Comic Sans (orange) and place a 3 point blue bottom border on the line. (Hint: Before you create the bottom line, press the Enter key to move to the next line in the document. Then select the line with the store locations and create the bottom border).

   d. Enter "Annual Corporate Race" in 36 point orange Comic Sans, centered between the margins. Enter the date in 24 point orange Comic Sans, also centered between the margins.

   e. Pull down the Insert menu and click the Symbol command. Select the Wingdings font, select the symbol for 8 o'clock, and then insert it into the document. Add AM, and then format the symbol to 36 point and the AM to 24 point orange Comic Sans.

   f. Insert the clip art of the running shoes. Size the clip art; change the wrapping style to Square, then move the clip art to the left of the date and time.

   g. Use WordArt to create the name of the event, and then format the WordArt. Use the WordArt toolbar to change the shape of the object and/or its color. Move, size, and rotate the object as shown in the figure.

   h. Create a text box for the entry fee information. Change the font, font size, and font color. Change the wrapping style to Square and change the line color to No Line.

   i. Enter the rest of the information at the bottom of the flyer, changing the font, font size, font color, and alignment.

   j. Print the completed flyer and submit it to your instructor.

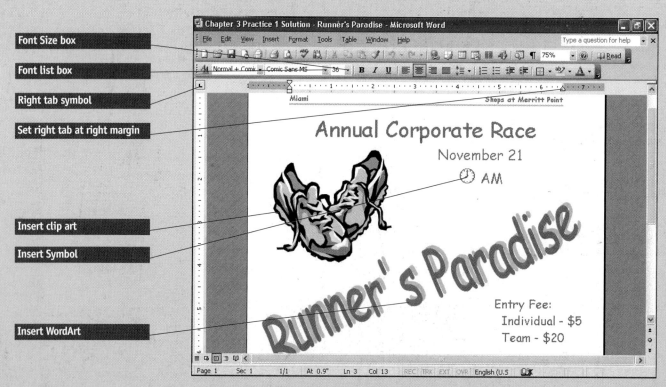

FIGURE 3.13 Runner's Paradise (exercise 1)

2. **Presidential Anecdotes:** Figure 3.14 displays the finished version of a document containing ten presidential anecdotes. The anecdotes were taken from the book *Presidential Anecdotes,* by Paul F. Boller, Jr., published by Penguin Books (New York, NY, 1981). Open the *Chapter 3 Practice 2* document and make the following changes:

a. Add a footnote after Mr. Boller's name, which appears at the end of the second sentence in the first paragraph, citing the information about the book. This, in turn, renumbers all existing footnotes in the document.

b. Switch the order of the paragraphs containing the anecdotes for Lincoln and Jefferson so that the presidents appear in the document in the same order in which they served. The (numbers of the) footnotes for these paragraphs are changed automatically.

c. Click and drag to select the text of all ten anecdotes, pull down the Format menu, and click the Paragraph command to display the Format Paragraph dialog box. Click the Line and Page Breaks tab, and then check the box to keep the lines together (to avoid a page break within the paragraph.) Click the Indents and Spacing tab, and then change the spacing before each paragraph to 12 points. (This has the same visual effect as inserting a blank line before each anecdote, but it provides greater flexibility in that you can change the spacing between paragraphs with a single command.)

d. Convert all of the footnotes to endnotes, as shown in the figure. Which style do you prefer, footnotes or endnotes?

e. Press Ctrl+Home to move to the beginning of the document, pull down the Format menu, click the Drop Cap command, and choose the dropped letter within the paragraph as shown in Figure 3.14.

f. Go to the White House Web site at www.whitehouse.gov and download a picture of any of the 10 presidents to use on a cover page. Press Ctrl+Home to move to the beginning of the document, then press Ctrl+Enter to create a page break. Press Ctrl+Home to return to the beginning of the document (the blank page), press the Enter key several times, and then create a title page such as the one in Figure 3.14. Be sure to cite the source of the picture with an appropriate footnote.

g. Print the completed document for your instructor.

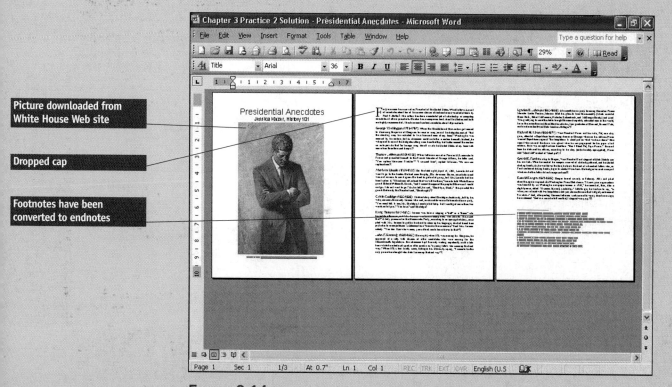

FIGURE 3.14 Presidential Anecdotes (exercise 2)

3. **Create a Home Page:** It's easy to create a home page. Start a new document and enter its text just as you would any other document. Use any and all formatting commands to create a document similar to the one in Figure 3.15. We suggest you use clip art, as opposed to a real picture. Pull down the File menu and use the Save As Web Page command to convert the Word document to a Web document. (Be sure to specify Single File Web Page as the file type.) You do not have to match our page exactly, but you are required to do the following:

   a. Use the Insert Hyperlink command to create a list of 3 to 5 hyperlinks. Be sure to enter accurate Web addresses for each of your sites.

   b. Select all of the links after they have been entered, then click the Bullets button on the Formatting toolbar to create a bulleted list.

   c. Pull down the Format menu, click the Themes command, and then select a professionally chosen design for your Web page.

   d. Save the document a final time, then exit Word. Start Windows Explorer, then go to the folder containing your home page, and double click the file you just created. Internet Explorer will start automatically (because your document was saved as a Web page).

   e. You should see the document that you just created within Internet Explorer as shown in Figure 3.15. Look carefully at the Address bar and note the local address on drive C, as opposed to a Web address. Print the document for your instructor as proof you completed the assignment.

   f. Creating the home page and viewing it locally is easy. Placing the page on the Web where it can be seen by anyone with an Internet connection is not as straightforward. You will need additional information from your instructor about how to obtain an account on a Web server (if that is available at your school), and further how to upload the Web page from your PC to the server.

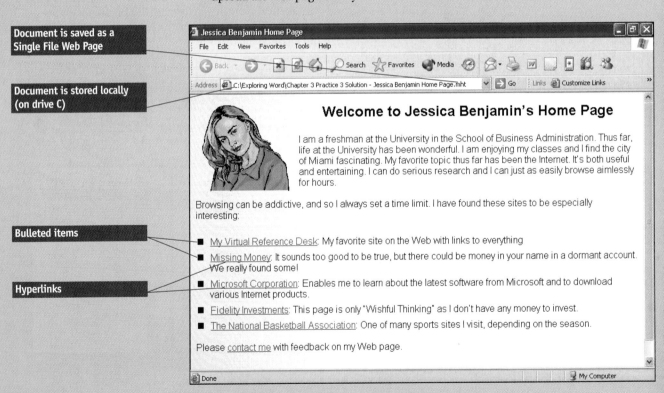

FIGURE 3.15   Create a Home Page (exercise 3)

4. **A Commercial Web Page:** Open the *Chapter 3 Practice 4* document in the Exploring Word folder. Pull down the File menu and click the Save As Web Page command to convert the Word document to a Web page. (Be sure to specify Single File Web Page as the file type.) Click Continue when a message appears that indicates pictures with text wrapping will become left or right aligned.

   a. Review the document and make the basic formatting changes you deem appropriate. Use the Themes command in the Format menu to apply an overall design to the page. Use any theme you like, but the overall document formatting should be similar to the document in Figure 3.16.

   b. Format the title if you have not already done so. Select the text, "Click here to contact us" that appears toward the top of the document. Pull down the Insert menu and click the Hyperlink command (or click the Insert Hyperlink button on the Standard toolbar), then enter your e-mail address.

   c. Go to the last paragraph and insert a hyperlink for the Boeing Company at www.boeing.com. Insert a second link for FlyteComm at www.flytecomm.com, a Web site that lets you track a flight from take-off to landing.

   d. Save the document a final time, then exit Word. Start Windows Explorer, then go to the folder containing your Web page, and double click the file you just created. Internet Explorer will start automatically (because your document was saved as a Web page). You should see your document within Internet Explorer as shown in Figure 3.16. Look carefully at the Address bar and note the local address on drive C, as opposed to a Web address. Print the document for your instructor as proof you completed the assignment.

   e. Creating the home page and viewing it locally is easy. Placing the page on the Web where it can be seen by anyone with an Internet connection is not as straightforward. You will need additional information from your instructor about how to obtain an account on a Web server (if that is available at your school), and further how to upload the Web page from your PC to the server.

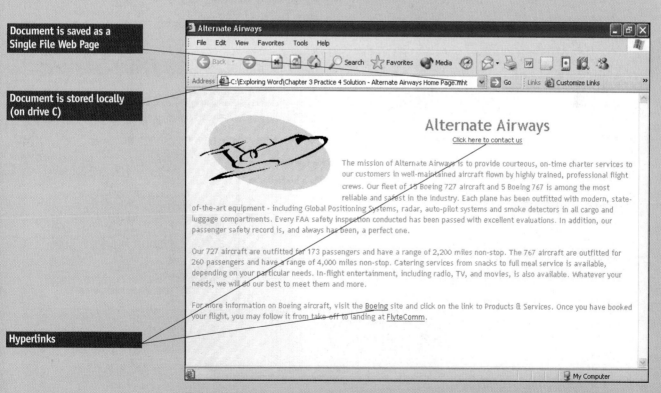

FIGURE 3.16 A Commercial Web Page (exercise 4)

5. **Symbols as Clip Art:** AutoShapes and symbols can be used to create unusual documents such as those shown in Figure 3.17. You do not have to match our documents exactly, but you are to use a combination of AutoShapes and symbols for your documents.

a. Start a new document. Change the page orientation to landscape and set the left and right page margins to 1″. Set a Center tab at 4.5″ and a Right tab at 9″

b. Pull down the Insert menu, click the Symbol command, then select the Webdings font. Find the fork, plate, and knife symbol, and then insert it into the document. Change the font size for the symbol to 30 points, then copy the symbol and paste it as many times as necessary to complete the line.

c. Press the Enter key to move to the next line, and paste the symbol. Press the Tab key twice to move to the right tab, then paste the symbol again. Copy this line nine times. Create the bottom border by copying the first line.

d. Enter the text for the invitation as shown in Figure 3.17 but use your instructor's name instead of Keith Fletcher. Increase the font size to 30 points. Change the Font color for the symbols and text to blue.

e. Start a new document for the Music Festival flyer and change to landscape orientation. Use the AutoShapes menu on the Drawing toolbar to create the banner. Use the Insert Symbol command (Webdings font) to insert the musical note to the left of the title. Copy the symbol and paste it at the end of the title.

f. Change the font size of the title to 50 point, then change the font color to orange. Change the fill color to tan for both the banner and the text box. Change the line color for the text box to No Line.

g. Enter the text for the flyer, centered between the margins. Change the font size and color, as shown in the figure. Create the Explosion AutoShape, size it, and change the fill color to tan. Select the AutoShape and use the Draw menu to change its Order to send it behind the text.

h. Use the Text Box tool on the Drawing toolbar to create a text box, and then insert the musical note inside the text box. Change the font size to 200 point and change the color as shown. Copy it. Move both text boxes as shown.

i. Print both documents for your instructor.

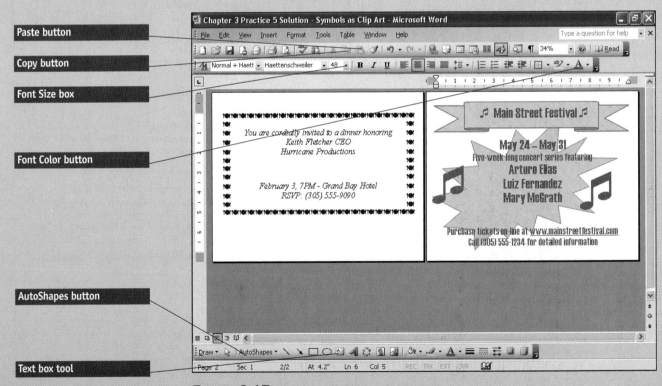

FIGURE 3.17 Symbols as Clip Art (exercise 5)

6. **Mail Merge and Templates:** This exercise combines an existing template with a mail merge to create a document similar to the one in Figure 3.18. You do not have to create the identical document, but you are required to use the indicated features. Proceed as follows:

a. Display the task pane. Click the down arrow on the title bar of the task pane to select New Document. Click the link to the Templates home page.

b. Choose a category (e.g., Marketing and Customer Relations), a subcategory (e.g., Letters to Customers), and a specific document (e.g., Acknowledgement of Order). Microsoft is continually changing the available templates, so you may not find the exact document. It doesn't matter. Choose any document that appeals to you. Click the link to Download now at the top of the document. Close the task pane.

c. The template contains several bracketed entries, which are to be replaced with specific information. The template is intended for a single letter, however, whereas we are using it as the basis for a mail merge. Thus we deleted the bracketed entries to be replaced with mail merge fields in subsequent steps. We also deleted the amount and order number entries within the body of the letter, also to be replaced with mail merge fields. And finally, we specified a uniform two-week delivery time as well as a uniform phone number. Save the document.

d. Pull down the Tools menu, click Letters and Mailings, then click Mail Merge Wizard to start the wizard. Select the Letters option. Click Next. Select the option to use the Current Document. Click Next.

e. Select the option to select the recipients by typing a new list. Click Create to display the New Address List dialog box, then click the Customize button. Delete the Address Line 2, Country, Home Phone, Work Phone, and E-mail address. Click the Add button to add the Amount field; click the button a second time to add the OrderNumber field. Click OK to close the Customize Address List dialog box. Enter data for four recipients. Click the Close button. Save the data source as *Chapter 3 Practice 6 Solution*. Click OK.

f. Complete the form letter by adding an address block, greeting line, amount, and order number fields as shown in Figure 3.18.

g. Complete the remaining steps in the mail merge and then print the individual letters for your instructor. Exit Word. Save the form letter.

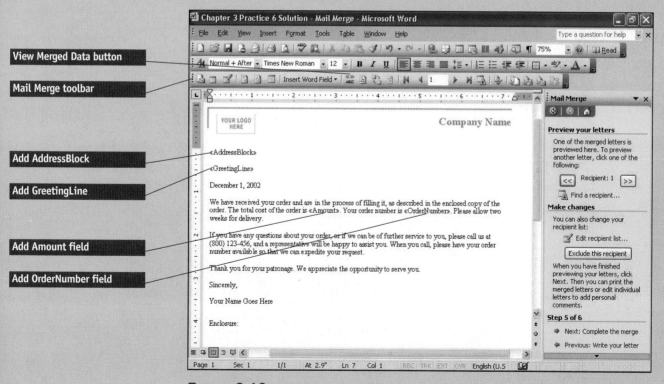

FIGURE 3.18 Mail Merge and Templates (exercise 6)

7. **Mailing Labels:** A mail merge creates the form letters for a mailing. That is only the first step, however, because you also have to create envelopes and/or mailing labels to physically mail the letters. Proceed as follows:

   a. Open a new document. Pull down the Tools menu, click Letters and Mailings, then click Mail Merge Wizard to start the Wizard. Click the Labels option and click Next. Select the option to change document layout. Click Next.

   b. You will see the Label Options dialog box. Select the type of label you want, such as 2160 Mini labels, and click OK. (The type of label you select does not matter since you are going to print the labels.) Click Next.

   c. Click Browse to locate the data source from the previous exercise (the *Chapter 3 Practice 6 Access Solution* database). Click Open. Click the Select All button, then click OK.

   d. Click Next to move to the next step, where you arrange the labels. Click Address Block, click OK, click Postal Bar Code to create the first label, and click OK. Click the button to Update All labels to copy this layout to the other labels.

   e. Click the button to Preview the labels. You should see a screen similar to Figure 3.19. The names and addresses correspond to the data we created in the previous exercise.

   f. Click Next. Do *not* attempt to print the labels unless you actually have mailing labels for the printer. Close the task pane. Save the document as *Chapter 3 Practice 7 solution.*

   g. Press the Print Screen key to capture the screen in Figure 3.19 to the Windows clipboard. Start a new Word document, then click the Paste button to paste the screen into the document. Add a sentence or two that describes the assignment. Include a cover page with your name, then print the completed document for your instructor.

   h. Repeat these steps to create a parallel set of envelopes. Pull down the View menu and click the Zoom command to view all four envelopes in one screen. Capture this screen for your instructor as well. Exit Word.

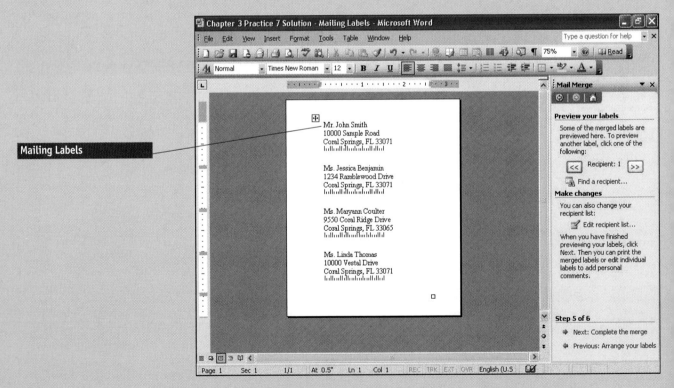

FIGURE 3.19 Mailing Labels (exercise 7)

8. **Create Your Own Stationery:** Figure 3.20 displays an envelope and matching letterhead for use as personal stationery. You do not have to match our design exactly, but you are to create both items and use the same logo for each. Proceed as follows:

a.   Begin with the stationery. Start a new document. Pull down the File menu and click the Page Setup command. Change to one-half-inch margins all around.. Enter your name, address, telephone, and e-mail information at the top of the page. Use a larger font and distinguishing color for your name, then center all of the text at the top of the page. Use the Drawing toolbar or the Borders and Shading command to add a horizontal line below the text.

b.   Pull down the Insert menu, click the Picture command, and locate an appropriate piece of clip art to use as a logo. Right click the image to display a context-sensitive menu, click the Format Picture command, click the Layout tab, and choose Square. Click OK to close the dialog box. Move and size the logo as necessary. Select the clip art, click the Copy button, click Paste, and then drag the copied image to the right side of the page.

c.   Print the completed letterhead for your instructor.

d.   Press Ctrl+Home to move to the beginning of the document. Pull down the Insert menu, click the Break command, and then click Next Page under Section breaks. (This creates a new page as well as a new section. The latter enables you to change the page orientation within a document.) Click OK.

e.   Click on the newly inserted page. Pull down the File menu, click the Page Setup command, click the Margins tab, and select the option for Landscape printing. Click the Paper tab, click the down arrow in the Paper Size list box, and choose Envelope #10 (the standard business envelope). Click OK to accept the settings and close the dialog box.

f.   Click and drag to copy the clip art from the letterhead to the envelope. Complete the envelope by adding your name and return address.

g.   Do not print the envelope in a computer lab at school unless envelopes are available for the printer. You can, however, capture the screen in Figure 3.20 to prove to your instructor that you created the envelope successfully.

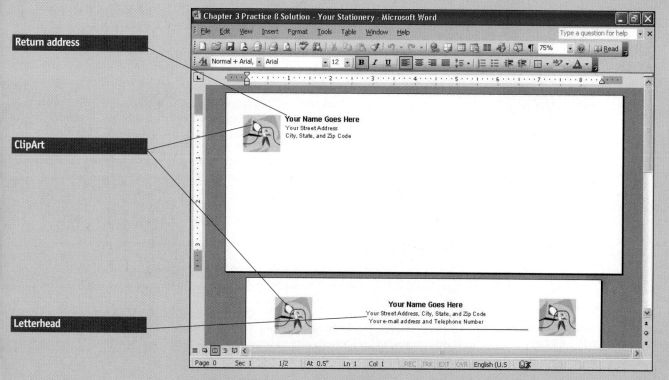

FIGURE 3.20   Create Your Own Stationery (exercise 8)

Organization Charts

All applications in Microsoft Office have access to the Diagram Gallery, which helps you to create an organization chart. All you do is pull down the Insert menu and click the Diagram command to display the Diagram Gallery dialog box from where you can select the Organization chart. The default chart consists of four boxes that are displayed on two levels. The lower level has three subordinates reporting to the single box on the top level. You can modify the chart by adding (removing) boxes at various levels using the Insert Shape button on the Organization Chart toolbar. You can also click in any box to add the appropriate descriptive text. The organization chart is a single object that can be moved and sized within the document, just as any other Windows object.

Your assignment is to open the *Chapter 3 Mini Case—Organization Chart* document, which contains a basic organization chart that we have already created. Your first task is to click the various boxes in the chart to assign a specific person to each box. Copy the completed chart to a second page in the document, then experiment with the Layout and AutoFormat tools on the Organization Chart toolbar to create an alternate version of the initial chart. Print both charts for your instructor.

Travel World

You have been hired as an intern for the Travel World agency and asked to create a flyer to distribute on campus. The only requirement is to include your name and e-mail address as the travel agent. Use any combination of clip art or photographs to make the flyer as attractive as possible. Be sure to spell check the completed flyer, and then print the document for your instructor.

The Calendar Wizard

The Calendar Wizard is one of several wizards that are built into Microsoft Office. Open the Task pane, select New document from the drop-down list box, click the link to the templates on your computer to display the Templates dialog box, then click the Other Documents tab to locate the Calendar Wizard. Create a calendar for the current month using any design and orientation you like. Take advantage of the Office Assistant to add clip art and/or notes to specific dates within the selected month. Include your name somewhere within the calendar and submit it to your instructor.

MLA Guidelines

The Modern Language Association (MLA) guidelines are currently used by over 125 scholarly and literary journals, newsletters, and magazines with circulations over one thousand; by hundreds of smaller periodicals; and by many university and commercial presses. MLA style is commonly followed, not only in the United States, but in Canada and other countries as well. Use your favorite search engine to locate the MLA Web site to download the guidelines for use in a research paper. You may also go to the Microsoft Web site to see if you can locate a template that was created by Microsoft that contains this material.

Leonardo Da Vinci

Use your imagination to create a résumé for Leonardo Da Vinci. The résumé is limited to one page and will be judged for content (yes, you have to do a little research on the Web) as well as appearance. You can intersperse fact and fiction as appropriate; for example, you may want to leave space for a telephone and/or a fax number, but could indicate that these devices have not yet been invented. You can choose a format for the résumé using the Résumé Wizard, or better yet, design your own.

Advanced Features:
Outlines, Tables, Styles, and Sections

CASE STUDY
THE MARTIN COMPANY

A sustainable rate of growth that can continue over time is good business. The Martin Company is committed to the concept of sustainability, be it social or economic, and it provides consulting services to businesses seeking assistance in this area. The company stresses education and offers value-added services, including environmental site audits and environmental consulting, as well as various technical support and training services.

Greg Hubit, the Director of Marketing at Martin, has asked you to review a marketing document that describes the two classes of service currently provided by the company—standard offerings and value-added services. Greg has asked that you make several changes to the document and suggested the use of styles, headers, footers, and bulleted lists where appropriate. He would like you to improve the formatting of the table on the last page, and to delete the empty rows within the table. And finally, Greg would like to see a table of contents on the first page that clearly lists each of the company's services with an appropriate page reference. You think of yourself as proficient in Microsoft Word. This is your chance to show what you can do. ■

Your assignment is to read the chapter, which focuses on several advanced features in Microsoft Word. You will then open *Chapter 4 Case Study—The Martin Company*, and insert a footer on every page that indicates the current page number and the total number of pages (e.g., page 1 of 4). A header that includes your name and the name of the case is required on every page except the title page. The Heading 1, Heading 2, and Body Text styles have been applied throughout the document, but you can modify these styles as you see fit. (The completed document will be printed in color.) Any additional formatting changes are open-ended, and we are confident that you will do a professional job. Print the completed document for your instructor.

This chapter presents a series of advanced features that will be especially useful the next time you have to write a term paper with very specific formatting requirements. We show you how to create a bulleted or numbered list to emphasize important items within a term paper, and how to create an outline for that paper. We introduce the tables feature, which provides an easy way to arrange text, numbers, and/or graphics. We develop the use of styles or sets of formatting instructions that provide a consistent appearance to similar elements in a document. We also discuss several items associated with longer documents, such as page numbers, headers and footers, a table of contents, and an index. We begin with lists.

Bullets and Lists

A list helps you organize information by highlighting important topics. A **bulleted list** emphasizes (and separates) the items. A **numbered list** sequences (and prioritizes) the items and is automatically updated to accommodate additions or deletions. An **outline** (or **outline numbered list**) extends a numbered list to several levels, and it too is updated automatically when topics are added or deleted. Each of these lists is created through the **Bullets and Numbering command** in the Format menu, which displays the Bullets and Numbering dialog box in Figure 4.1.

The tabs within the Bullets and Numbering dialog box are used to choose the type of list and customize its appearance. The Bulleted tab selected in Figure 4.1a enables you to specify one of several predefined symbols for the bullet. Typically, that is all you do, although you can use the Customize button to change the default spacing (of ¼ inch) of the text from the bullet and/or to choose a different symbol for the bullet.

The Numbered tab in Figure 4.1b lets you choose Arabic or Roman numerals, or upper- or lowercase letters, for a numbered list. As with a bulleted list, the Customize button lets you change the default spacing, the numbering style, and/or the punctuation before or after the number or letter. Note, too, the option buttons to restart or continue numbering, which become important if a list appears in multiple places within a document. In other words, each occurrence of a list can start numbering anew, or it can continue from where the previous list left off.

The Outline Numbered tab in Figure 4.1c enables you to create an outline to organize your thoughts. As with the other types of lists, you can choose one of several default styles, and/or modify a style through the Customize command button. You can also specify whether each outline within a document is to restart its numbering, or whether it is to continue numbering from the previous outline.

The List Styles tab (not shown in Figure 4.1) lets you change the style (formatting specifications) associated with a list. You can change the font size, use a picture or symbol for a bullet, add color, and so on. Styles are discussed later in the chapter.

Creating an Outline

Our next exercise explores the Bullets and Numbering command in conjunction with creating an outline for a hypothetical paper on the United States Constitution. The exercise begins by having you create a bulleted list, then asking you to convert it to a numbered list, and finally to an outline. The end result is the type of outline your professor may ask you to create prior to writing a term paper.

As you do the exercise, remember that a conventional outline is created as an outline numbered list within the Bullets and Numbering command. Text for the outline is entered in the Print Layout or Normal view, *not* the Outline view. The latter provides a completely different capability—a condensed view of a document that is used in conjunction with styles and is discussed later in the chapter. We mention this to avoid confusion should you stumble into the Outline view.

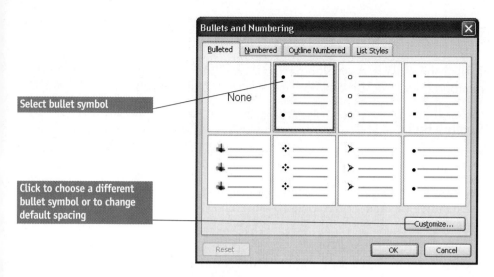

Select bullet symbol

Click to choose a different bullet symbol or to change default spacing

(a) Bulleted List

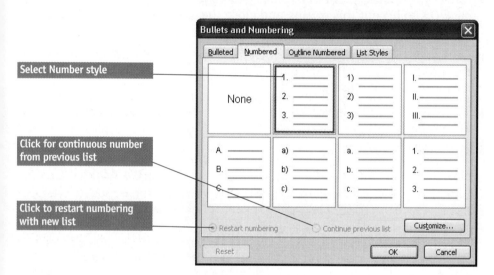

Select Number style

Click for continuous number from previous list

Click to restart numbering with new list

(b) Numbered List

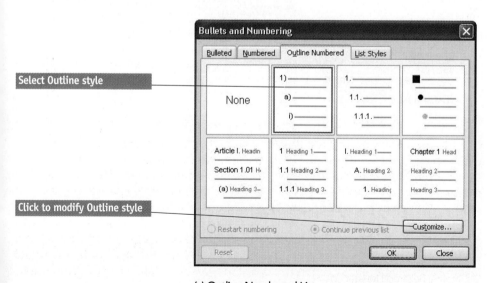

Select Outline style

Click to modify Outline style

(c) Outline Numbered List

FIGURE 4.1 Bullets and Numbering

1   Bullets, Lists, and Outlines

Objective   To use the Bullets and Numbering command to create a bulleted list, a numbered list, and an outline. Use Figure 4.2 as a guide.

Step 1:   **Create a Bulleted List**

- Start Word and begin a new document. Type **Preamble**, the first topic in our list, and press **Enter**.

- Type the three remaining topics, **Article I—Legislative Branch**, **Article II—Executive Branch**, and **Article III—Judicial Branch**. Do not press Enter after the last item.

- Click and drag to select all four topics as shown in Figure 4.2a. Pull down the **Format menu** and click the **Bullets and Numbering command** to display the Bullets and Numbering dialog box.

- If necessary, click the **Bulleted tab**, select the type of bullet you want, then click **OK** to accept this setting and close the dialog box. Bullets have been added to the list.

- Click after the words **Judicial Branch** to deselect the list and also to position the insertion point at the end of the list. Press **Enter** to begin a new line. A bullet appears automatically.

- Type **Amendments**. Press **Enter** to end this line and begin the next, which already has a bullet.

- Press **Enter** a second time to terminate the bulleted list.

- Save the document as **US Constitution** in the **Exploring Word folder**.

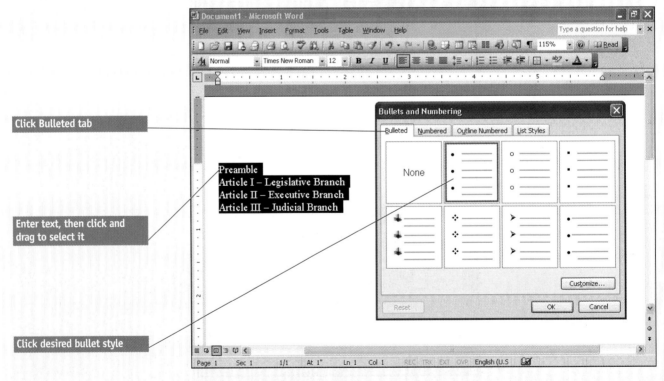

Click Bulleted tab

Enter text, then click and drag to select it

Click desired bullet style

(a) Create a Bulleted List (step 1)

FIGURE 4.2   Hands-on Exercise 1

Step 2: Modify a Numbered List

- Click and drag to select the five items in the bulleted list, then click the **Numbering button** on the Standard toolbar.

- The bulleted list has been converted to a numbered list as shown in Figure 4.2b. (The last two items have not yet been added to the list.)

- Click immediately after the last item in the list and press **Enter** to begin a new line. Word automatically adds the next sequential number to the list.

- Type **History** and press **Enter**. Type **The Constitution Today** as the seventh (and last) item.

- Click in the selection area to the left of the sixth item, **History** (only the text is selected). Now drag the selected text to the beginning of the list, in front of *Preamble*. Release the mouse.

- The list is automatically renumbered. *History* is now the first item, *Preamble* is the second item, and so on.

- Save the document.

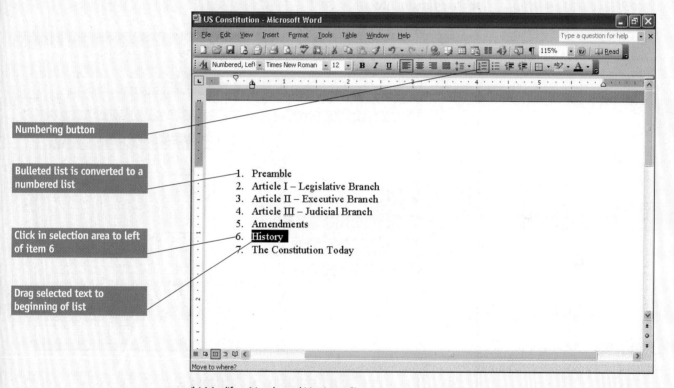

(b) Modify a Numbered List (step 2)

FIGURE 4.2 Hands-on Exercise 1 (*continued*)

THE BULLETS AND NUMBERING BUTTONS

Select the items for which you want to create a list, then click the Numbering or Bullets button on the Formatting toolbar to create a numbered or bulleted list, respectively. The buttons function as toggle switches; that is, click the button once (when the items are selected) and the list formatting is in effect. Click the button a second time and the bullets or numbers disappear. The buttons also enable you to switch from one type of list to another; that is, selecting a bulleted list and clicking the Numbering button changes the list to a numbered list, and vice versa.

Step 3: Convert to an Outline

- Click and drag to select the entire list, then click the **right mouse button** to display a context-sensitive menu.
- Click the **Bullets and Numbering command** to display the Bullets and Numbering dialog box in Figure 4.2c.
- Click the **Outline Numbered tab**, then select the type of outline you want. (Do not be concerned if the selected formatting does not display Roman numerals as we customize the outline later in the exercise.)
- Click **OK** to accept the formatting and close the dialog box. The numbered list has been converted to an outline, although that is difficult to see at this point.
- Click at the end of the third item, **Article I—Legislative Branch**. Press **Enter**. The number 4 is generated automatically for the next item in the list.
- Press the **Tab key** to indent this item and automatically move to the next level of numbering (a lowercase *a*). Type **House of Representatives**.
- Press **Enter**. The next sequential number (a lowercase *b*) is generated automatically. Type **Senate**.
- Save the document.

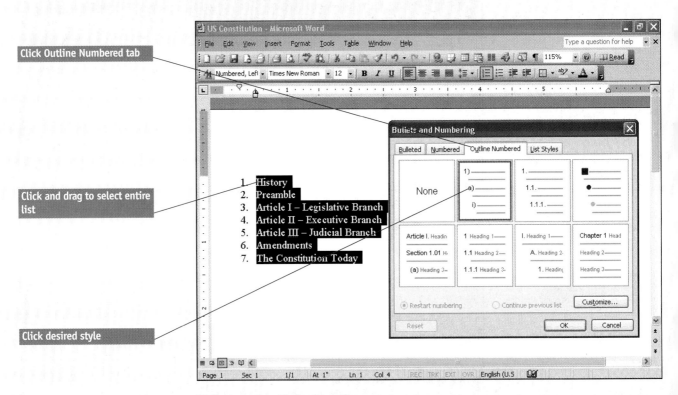

Click Outline Numbered tab

Click and drag to select entire list

Click desired style

(c) Convert to an Outline (step 3)

FIGURE 4.2 Hands-on Exercise 1 (*continued*)

THE TAB AND SHIFT+TAB KEYS

The easiest way to enter text into an outline is to type continually from one line to the next, using the Tab and Shift+Tab keys as necessary. Press the Enter key after completing an item to move to the next item, which is automatically created at the same level, then continue typing if the item is to remain at this level. To change the level, press the Tab key to demote the item (move it to the next lower level), or the Shift+Tab combination to promote the item (move it to the next higher level).

Step 4: **Enter Text into the Outline**

- Your outline should be similar in appearance to Figure 4.2d, except that you have not yet entered most of the text. Click at the end of the line containing House of Representatives.

- Press **Enter** to start a new item (which is at level *b* in the outline). Press **Tab** to indent one level, changing the level to *i*. Type **Length of term**. Press **Enter**. Type **Requirements for office**.

- Click at the end of the line containing the word Senate. Press **Enter** to start a new line (which is at level *c*). Press **Tab** to indent one level, changing the level to an *i*. Type **Length of term**, press **Enter**, type **Requirements for office**, and press **Enter**.

- Press **Shift+Tab** to move up one level. Enter the remaining text as shown in Figure 4.2.d, using the **Tab** and **Shift+Tab** keys to demote and promote the items.

- Save the document.

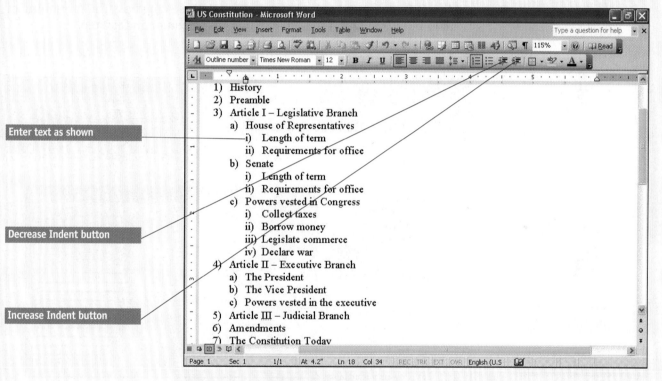

Enter text as shown

Decrease Indent button

Increase Indent button

(d) Enter Text into the Outline (step 4)

FIGURE 4.2   Hands-on Exercise 1 (*continued*)

THE INCREASE AND DECREASE INDENT BUTTONS

The Increase and Decrease Indent buttons on the Standard toolbar are another way to change the level within an outline. Click anywhere within an item, then click the appropriate button to change the level within the outline. Indentation is implemented at the paragraph level, and hence you can click the button without selecting the entire item. You can also click and drag to select multiple item(s), then click the desired button.

Step 5: Customize the Outline

- Select the entire outline, pull down the **Format menu**, then click **Bullets and Numbering** to display the Bullets and Numbering dialog box.

- If necessary, click the **Outline Numbered tab** and click **Customize** to display the Customize dialog box as shown in Figure 4.2e. Level **1** should be selected.
    - Click the **drop-down arrow** in the Number style list box. Select **I, II, III**.
    - Click in the Number format text box, which now contains the Roman numeral I followed by a right parenthesis. Click and drag to select the parenthesis and replace it with a period.
    - Click the **drop-down arrow** in the Number position list box. Click **right** to right-align the Roman numerals that will appear in your outline.

- Click the number **2** in the Level list box. Select **A, B, C** as the Number style. Click in the Number format text box. Replace the right parenthesis with a period.

- Click the number **3** in the Level list box. Select **1, 2, 3** as the Number style. Click in the Number format text box. Replace the right parenthesis with a period.

- Click **OK** to accept these settings and close the dialog box. The formatting of your outline has changed to match the customization in this step.

- Save the document.

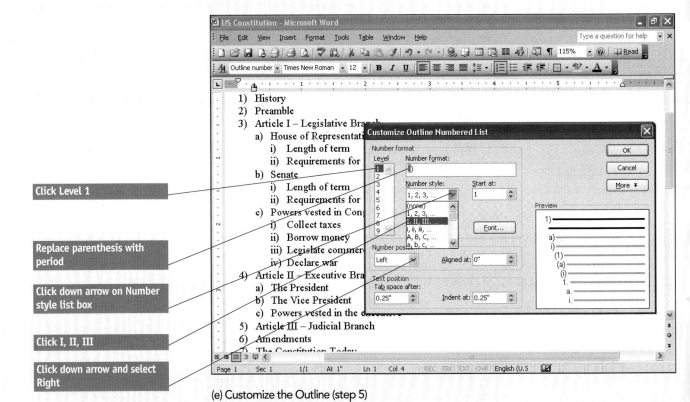

(e) Customize the Outline (step 5)

FIGURE 4.2   Hands-on Exercise 1 (*continued*)

AUTOMATIC CREATION OF A NUMBERED LIST

Word automatically creates a numbered list when you begin a paragraph with a number or letter, followed by a period, tab, or right parenthesis. Press the Enter key at the end of the line and you see the next item in the sequence. To end the list, press the Backspace key once, or press the Enter key twice.

Step 6: The Completed Outline

- Press **Ctrl+Home** to move to the beginning of the outline. The insertion point is after Roman numeral I. Type **The United States Constitution**. Press **Enter**.

- The new text appears as Roman numeral I, and all existing entries have been renumbered appropriately. The insertion point is immediately before the word History. Press **Enter** to create a blank line (for your name).

- The blank line is now Roman numeral II, and History has been moved to Roman numeral III. Move the insertion point to the blank line. Press the **Tab key** so that the blank line becomes item A. This renumbers History as Roman numeral II.

- Enter your name in the outline, then click and drag to select the first two items in the outline as shown in Figure 4.2f.

- Click the **Numbering button** to turn the outline off for the selected text. Click the **Center button** to center the text. Increase the font size to **18 points**.

- Click immediately after your name to deselect the text. Press **Enter** to add a blank line separating your name from the beginning of the outline.

- Save the document. Print the outline for your instructor. Exit Word.

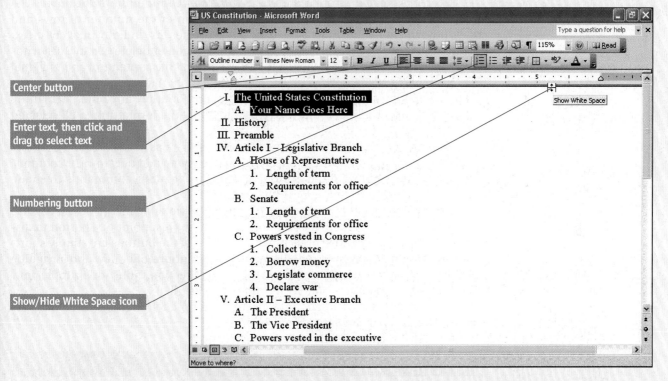

(f) The Completed Outline (step 6)

FIGURE 4.2   Hands-on Exercise 1 (*continued*)

HIDE THE WHITE SPACE

The Print Layout view displays a document as it will be printed, with margins, headers, footnotes, and/or multiple columns. You can, however, gain valuable space on the screen (and show more of your document) by hiding the white space (margins) at the top of every page and the gray space between pages. Scroll until you can see the top or bottom of the page, then click at the top of the page (you will see a Hide/Show White Space icon) to toggle the display of the white space on or off.

TABLES

The ***tables feature*** is one of the most powerful in Word and is the basis for an almost limitless variety of documents. The study schedule in Figure 4.3a, for example, is actually a 12×8 (12 rows and 8 columns) table as can be seen from the underlying structure in Figure 4.3b. The completed table looks quite impressive, but it is very easy to create once you understand how a table works. You can use the tables feature to create almost any type of document. (See the practice exercises at the end of the chapter for other examples.)

The rows and columns in a table intersect to form ***cells***. Each cell is formatted independently of every other cell and may contain text, numbers, and/or graphics. Commands operate on one or more cells. Individual cells can be joined together (merged) to form a larger cell as was done in the first and last rows of Figure 4.3a. Conversely, a single cell can be split into multiple cells. The rows within a table can be different heights, just as each column can be a different width. You can specify the height or width explicitly, or you can let Word determine it for you.

A cell can also contain clip art as shown in the bottom right corner of Figure 4.3a. Just click in the cell where you want the clip art to go, then use the Insert Picture command as you have throughout the text. Use the sizing handles once the clip art has been inserted to move and/or position it within the cell.

A table is created through the ***Insert Table command*** in the ***Table menu***. The command produces a dialog box in which you enter the number of rows and columns. Once the table has been defined, you enter text in individual cells. Text wraps as it is entered within a cell, so that you can add or delete text in a cell without affecting the entries in other cells. You can format the contents of an individual cell the same way you format an ordinary paragraph; that is, you can change the font, use boldface or italic, change the alignment, or apply any other formatting command. You can select multiple cells and apply the formatting to all selected cells at once.

You can also modify the structure of a table after it has been created. The ***Insert*** and ***Delete commands*** in the Table menu enable you to add new rows or columns, or delete existing rows or columns. You can invoke other commands to shade and/or border selected cells or the entire table.

You can work with a table using commands in the Table menu, or you can use the various tools on the Tables and Borders toolbar. (Just point to a button to display a ScreenTip indicative of its function.) Some of the buttons are simply shortcuts for commands within the Table menu. Other buttons offer new and intriguing possibilities, such as the button to Change Text Direction. Note, for example, how we drew an "X" to reserve Sunday morning (for sleeping).

It's easy, and as you might have guessed, it's time for another hands-on exercise in which you create the table in Figure 4.3.

LEFT	CENTER	RIGHT

Many documents call for left, centered, and/or right aligned text on the same line, an effect that is achieved through setting tabs, or more easily through a table. To achieve the effect shown in the heading of this box, create a 1 x 3 table (one row and three columns), type the text in the three cells as needed, then use the buttons on the Formatting toolbar to left align, center, and right align the respective cells. Select the table, pull down the Format menu, click Borders and Shading, then specify None as the Border setting.

Weekly Class and Study Schedule

	Monday	Tuesday	Wednesday	Thursday	Friday	Saturday	Sunday
8:00AM							
9:00AM							
10:00AM							
11:00AM							
12:00PM							
1:00PM							
2:00PM							
3:00PM							
4:00PM							
Notes							

(a) Completed Table

(b) Underlying Structure

FIGURE 4.3 The Tables Feature

2 Tables

Objective To create a table; to change row heights and column widths; to merge cells; to apply borders and shading to selected cells. Use Figure 4.4 as a guide for the exercise.

Step 1: **The Page Setup Command**

- Start Word. Click the **Tables and Borders button** on the Standard toolbar to display the Tables and Borders toolbar as shown in Figure 4.4a.

- The button functions as a toggle switch—click it once and the toolbar is displayed. Click the button a second time and the toolbar is suppressed. Click and drag the title bar on the toolbar to anchor it under the Formatting toolbar.

- Pull down the **File menu** and click the **Page Setup command** to display the dialog box in Figure 4.4a.

- Click the **Margins tab** and click the **Landscape icon**. Change the top and bottom margins to **.75** inch.

- Change the left and right margins to **.5** inch each. Click **OK** to accept the settings and close the dialog box.

- Save the document as **My Study Schedule** in the **Exploring Word folder** that you have used throughout the text.

- Change to the **Print Layout view**. Zoom to **Page Width**. You are now ready to create the table.

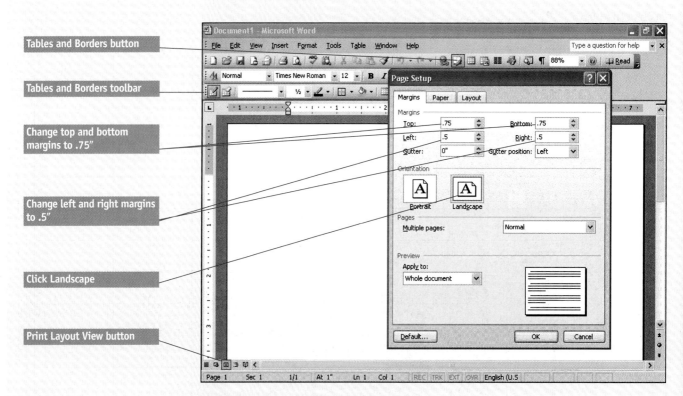

(a) The Page Setup Command (step 1)

FIGURE 4.4 Hands-on Exercise 2

Step 2: Create the Table

- Pull down the **Table menu**, click **Insert**, and click **Table** to display the dialog box in Figure 4.4b. Enter **8** and **12** as the number of columns and rows, respectively. Click **OK** and the table will be inserted into the document.

- Practice selecting various elements from the table, something that you will have to do in subsequent steps:
  - ❏ To select a single cell, click inside the left grid line (the pointer changes to an arrow when you are in the proper position).
  - ❏ To select a row, click outside the table to the left of the first cell in that row.
  - ❏ To select a column, click just above the top of the column (the pointer changes to a small black arrow).
  - ❏ To select adjacent cells, drag the mouse over the cells.
  - ❏ To select the entire table, drag the mouse over the table or click the box that appears at the upper left corner of the table.

- Click outside the table. Save the document.

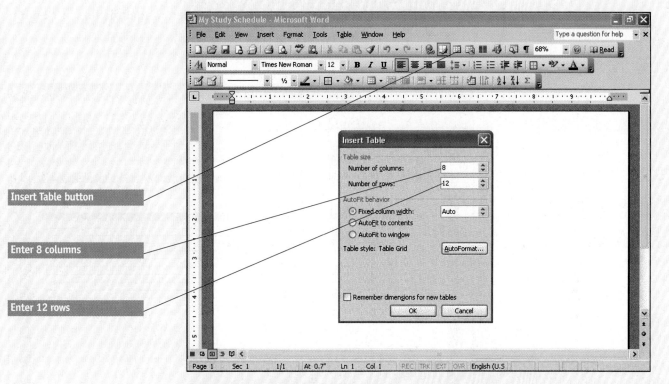

(b) Create the Table (step 2)

FIGURE 4.4   Hands-on Exercise 2 (*continued*)

TABS AND TABLES

The Tab key functions differently in a table than in a regular document. Press the Tab key to move to the next cell in the current row (or to the first cell in the next row if you are at the end of a row). Press Tab when you are in the last cell of a table to add a new blank row to the bottom of the table. Press Shift+Tab to move to the previous cell in the current row (or to the last cell in the previous row). You must press Ctrl+Tab to insert a regular tab character within a cell.

Step 3:   Merge the Cells

- This step merges the cells in the first and last rows of the table. Click outside the table to the left of the first cell in the first row to select the entire first row as shown in Figure 4.4c.

- Pull down the **Table menu** and click **Merge Cells** (or click the **Merge Cells button** on the Tables and Borders toolbar). Click in the second row to deselect the first row, which now consists of a single cell.

- Click in the merged cell. Type **Weekly Class and Study Schedule** and format the text in **24 point Arial bold**. Click the **Center button** on the Formatting toolbar to center the title of the table.

- Click outside the table to the left of the first cell in the last row to select the entire row as shown in Figure 4.4c. Click the **Merge Cells button** on the Tables and Borders toolbar to merge these cells.

- Click outside the cell to deselect it, then click in the cell and type **Notes**. Press the **Enter key** five times. The height of the cell increases to accommodate the blank lines. Click and drag to select the text, then format the text in **12 point Arial bold**.

- Save the document.

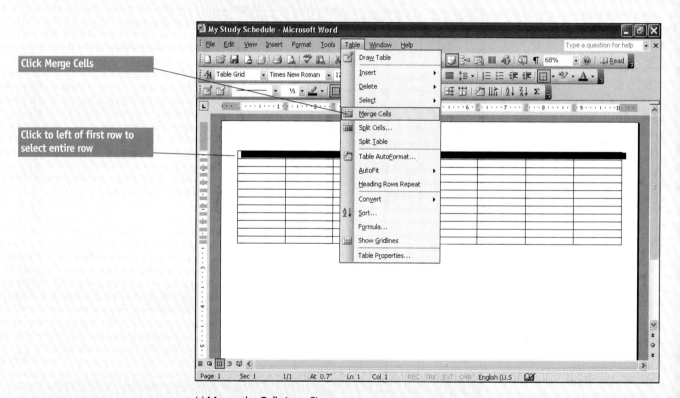

(c) Merge the Cells (step 3)

FIGURE 4.4   Hands-on Exercise 2 (*continued*)

SPLITTING A CELL

Splitting cells is the opposite of merging them. Click in any cell that you want to split, pull down the Table menu, and click the Split Cells command (or click the Split Cells button on the Tables and Borders toolbar) to display the associated dialog box. Enter the number of rows and columns that should appear after the split. Click OK to accept the settings and close the dialog box.

Step 4: Enter the Days and Hours

- Click the second cell in the second row. Type **Monday**. Press the **Tab** (or **right arrow**) **key** to move to the next cell. Type **Tuesday**. Continue until the days of the week have been entered.

- Select the entire row. Use the various tools on the Formatting toolbar to change the text to **10 point Arial Bold**. Click the **Center button** on the Formatting toolbar to center each day within the cell.

- Click the first cell in the third row. Type **8:00AM**. Press the **down arrow key** to move to the first cell in the fourth row. Type **9:00AM**. Continue to enter the hourly periods up to 4:00PM. Format as appropriate.

- Select the cells containing the hours of the day. Pull down the **Table menu**. Click **Table Properties**, then click the **Row tab** to display the Table Properties dialog box in Figure 4.4d.

- Click the **Specify height** check box. Click the **up arrow** until the height is **.5″**. Click the **drop-down arrow** on the Row height list box and select **Exactly**.

- Click the **Cell tab** in the Table Properties dialog box, then click the **Center button**. Click **OK** to accept the settings and close the dialog box. Save the document.

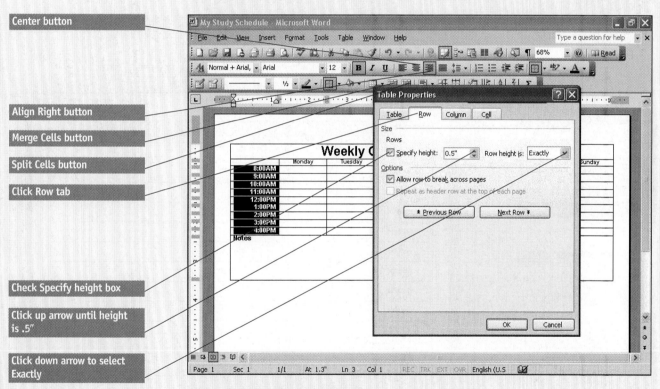

(d) Enter the Days and Hours (step 4)

FIGURE 4.4 Hands-on Exercise 2 (*continued*)

CONVERT TEXT TO A TABLE

The tables feature is outstanding. But what if you are given a lengthy list of items—for example, two items per line separated by a tab that should have been formatted as a table but weren't? All you have to do is convert the existing text to a table. Select the entire list, pull down the Table menu, click the Convert command, and click the Text to Table command. Click the Option button in the Separate text area of the dialog box, and click OK to create the table. (The command also works in reverse; i.e., you can also convert a table to text.)

Step 5: Borders and Shading

- Select (click) the cell containing the title of your table. Click the down arrow on the **Shading Color button** on the Tables and Borders toolbar to display a color palette, then choose a background color. We selected red.

- Click and drag to select the text within the cell. Click the **down arrow** on the **Font Color button** on the Formatting toolbar to display its palette, then choose **white** (that is, we want white letters on a dark background).

- Click and drag to select the first four cells under "Sunday", then click the **Merge Cells button** to merge these cells.

- Click the **down arrow** on the **Line Weight tool** and select **3** pt. Click the **down arrow** on the **Border Color tool** and select the same color you used to shade the first row.

- Click in the upper-left corner of the merged cell, then click and drag to draw a diagonal line as shown in Figure 4.4e. Click and drag to draw a second line to complete the cell.

- Save the document.

Click down arrow on Font Color tool

Click down arrow to select line weight

Click Border Color tool

Click Shading Color tool

Draw diagonal lines

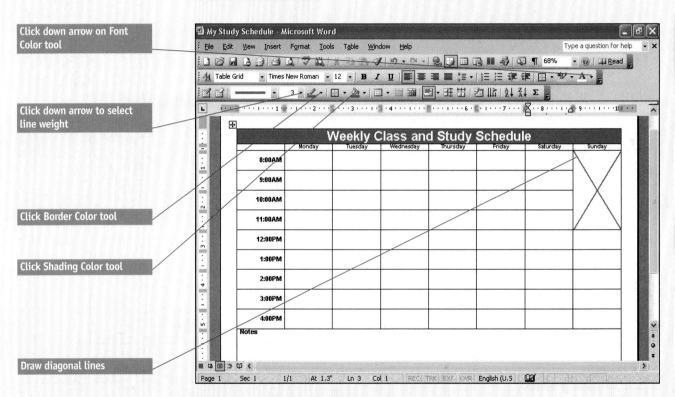

(e) Borders and Shading (step 5)

FIGURE 4.4   Hands-on Exercise 2 (*continued*)

THE AUTOFORMAT COMMAND

The AutoFormat command does not do anything that could not be done through individual formatting commands, but it does provide inspiration by suggesting attractive designs. Click anywhere in the table, pull down the Table menu, and click the Table AutoFormat command to display the associated dialog box. Choose (click) any style, click the Modify button if you want to change any aspect of the formatting, then click the Apply button to format your table in the selected style.

Step 6: Insert the Clip Art

■ Click anywhere in the merged cell in the last row of the table. Pull down the **Insert menu**, click (or point to) **Picture**, then click **Clip Art**. The task pane opens and displays the Search pane as shown in Figure 4.4f.

■ Click in the **Search** text box. Type **books** to search for any clip art image that is indexed with this keyword, then click the **Go button** or press **Enter**.

■ The images are displayed in the task pane. Point to an image to display a drop-down arrow to its right. Click the arrow to display a context menu. Click **Insert** to insert the image into the document.

■ Do not be concerned about the size or position of the image at this time as we adjust the parameters in the next step.

■ Close the task pane. Save the document.

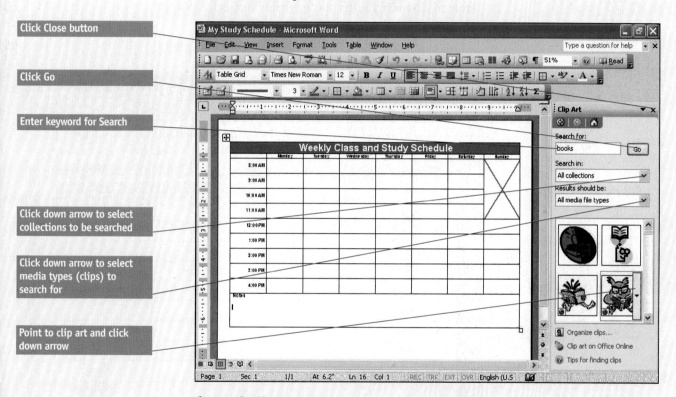

(f) Insert the Clip Art (step 6)

FIGURE 4.4 Hands-on Exercise 2 (*continued*)

SEARCHING FOR CLIP ART

The Clip Art task pane helps you to search for an appropriate media object. Click the down arrow in the Search for list box and choose all collections (including those on the Microsoft Web site). Click the down arrow in the Results should be list box and choose All media file types, then click the Go button to initiate the search. The search may take longer than previously since it includes the Web, but you should have a much larger selection of potential clips from which to choose. If necessary, use the drop-down arrow on either list box to limit the search as you see fit.

Step 7: The Finishing Touches

■ Select the newly inserted clip art to display the Picture toolbar, then click the **Format Picture button** to display the Format Picture dialog box. Click the **Layout tab** and choose the **Square layout**. Click **OK** to close the dialog box.

■ Select (click) the clip art to display its sizing handles as shown in Figure 4.4g. Move and size the image as necessary within its cell.

■ Click anywhere in the first row of the table. Pull down the **Table menu** and click the **Table Properties command** to display the associated dialog box. Change the row height to exactly **.5 inch**. Click **OK**.

■ Click the **down arrow** next to the **Align button** on the Tables and Borders toolbar and select **center alignment** to center the text vertically.

■ Use the **Table Properties command** to change the row height of the second row to **.25 inch**. Center these entries vertically as well.

■ Save the document, then print it for your instructor. Exit Word if you do not want to continue with the next exercise at this time.

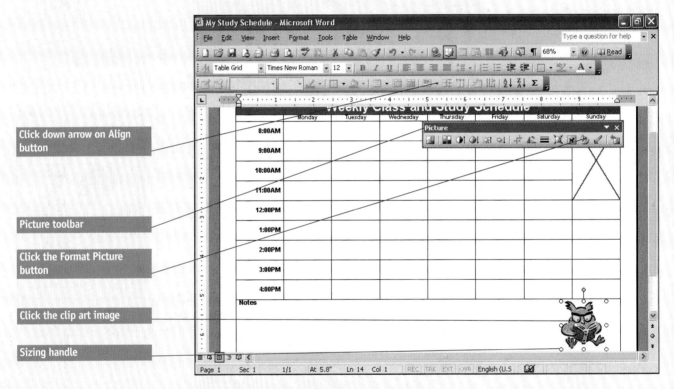

(g) The Finishing Touches (step 7)

FIGURE 4.4 Hands-on Exercise 2 (*continued*)

INSERTING OR DELETING ROWS AND COLUMNS

You can insert or delete rows and columns after a table has been created. To insert a row, click in any cell above or below where the new row should go, pull down the Table menu, click the Insert command, then choose Rows above or below as appropriate. Follow a similar procedure to insert a column, choosing whether you want the new column to go to the left or right of the selected cell.

STYLES

One characteristic of a professional document is the uniform formatting that is applied to similar elements throughout the document. Different elements have different formatting. Headings may be set in one font, color, style, and size, and the text under those headings may be set in a completely different design. The headings may be left aligned, while the text is fully justified. Lists and footnotes can be set in entirely different styles.

One way to achieve uniformity throughout the document is to use the Format Painter to copy the formatting from one occurrence of each element to the next, but this is tedious and inefficient. And if you were to change your mind after copying the formatting throughout a document, you would have to repeat the entire process all over again. A much easier way to achieve uniformity is to store the formatting information as a *style*, then apply that style to multiple occurrences of the same element within the document. Change the style and you automatically change all text defined by that style.

Styles are created on the character or paragraph level. A ***character style*** stores character formatting (font, size, and style) and affects only the selected text. A ***paragraph style*** stores paragraph formatting (such as alignment, line spacing, indents, tabs, text flow, and borders and shading, as well as the font, size, and style of the text in the paragraph). A paragraph style affects the current paragraph or multiple paragraphs if several paragraphs are selected. Styles are created and applied through the ***Styles and Formatting command*** in the Format menu as shown in Figure 4.5.

The document in Figure 4.5a consists of multiple tips for Microsoft Word. Each tip begins with a one-line heading, followed by the associated text. The task pane in the figure displays all of the styles that are in use in the document. The ***Normal style*** contains the default paragraph settings (left aligned, single spacing, and a default font) and is automatically assigned to every paragraph unless a different style is specified. The Clear Formatting style removes all formatting from selected text. It is the ***Heading 1*** and ***Body Text styles***, however, that are of interest to us, as these styles have been applied throughout the document to the associated elements. (The style assignments are done automatically through the AutoFormat command as will be explained shortly.)

The specifications for the Heading 1 and Body Text styles are shown in Figures 4.5b and 4.5c, respectively. The current settings within the Heading 1 style call for 16 point Arial bold type in blue. The text is left justified, and the heading will always appear on the same page as the next paragraph. The Body Text style is in 10 point Times New Roman and is fully justified. The preview box in both figures shows how paragraphs formatted in the style will appear. You can change the specifications of either style using any combination of buttons or associated menu commands. (Clicking the Format button in either dialog box provides access to the various commands in the Format menu.) And as indicated earlier, any changes to the style are automatically reflected in all elements that are defined by that style.

Styles automate the formatting process and provide a consistent appearance to a document. Any type of character or paragraph formatting can be stored within a style, and once a style has been defined, it can be applied to multiple occurrences of the same element within a document to produce identical formatting.

STYLES AND PARAGRAPHS

A paragraph style affects the entire paragraph; that is, you cannot apply a paragraph style to only part of a paragraph. To apply a style to an existing paragraph, place the insertion point anywhere within the paragraph, pull down the Style list box on the Formatting toolbar, then click the name of the style you want.

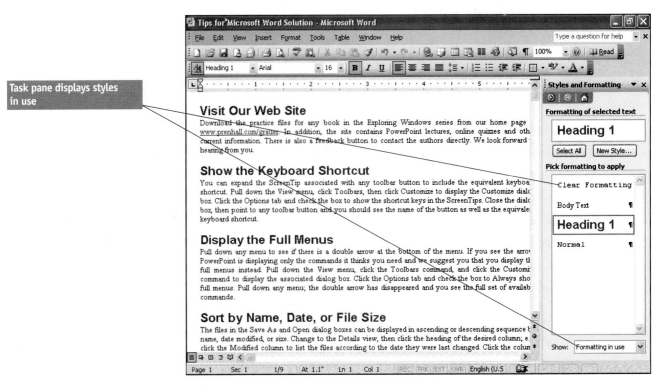

Task pane displays styles in use

(a) The Document

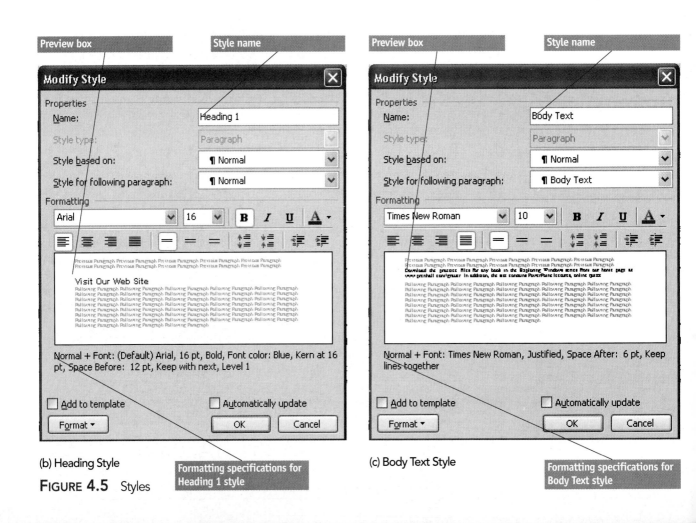

Preview box

Style name

Modify Style

Properties
Name: Heading 1
Style type: Paragraph
Style based on: ¶ Normal
Style for following paragraph: ¶ Normal

Formatting
Arial   16   **B** *I* U **A** ▾

Visit Our Web Site

Normal + Font: (Default) Arial, 16 pt, Bold, Font color: Blue, Kern at 16 pt, Space Before: 12 pt, Keep with next, Level 1

☐ Add to template   ☐ Automatically update
Format ▾   OK   Cancel

(b) Heading Style

Formatting specifications for Heading 1 style

Preview box

Style name

Modify Style

Properties
Name: Body Text
Style type: Paragraph
Style based on: ¶ Normal
Style for following paragraph: ¶ Body Text

Formatting
Times New Roman   10   **B** *I* U **A** ▾

Normal + Font: Times New Roman, Justified, Space After: 6 pt, Keep lines together

☐ Add to template   ☐ Automatically update
Format ▾   OK   Cancel

(c) Body Text Style

Formatting specifications for Body Text style

FIGURE 4.5   Styles

THE OUTLINE VIEW

One additional advantage of styles is that they enable you to view a document in the **Outline view**. The Outline view does not display a conventional outline (such as the multilevel list created earlier in the chapter), but rather a structural view of a document that can be collapsed or expanded as necessary. Consider, for example, Figure 4.6, which displays the Outline view of a document that will be the basis of the next hands-on exercise. The document consists of a series of tips for Microsoft Word 2003. The heading for each tip is formatted according to the Heading 1 style. The text of each tip is formatted according to the Body Text style.

The advantage of the Outline view is that you can collapse or expand portions of a document to provide varying amounts of detail. We have, for example, collapsed almost the entire document in Figure 4.6, displaying the headings while suppressing the body text. We also expanded the text for two tips (Visit Our Web Site and Moving Within a Document) for purposes of illustration.

Now assume that you want to move the latter tip from its present position to immediately below the first tip. Without the Outline view, the text would stretch over two pages, making it difficult to see the text of both tips at the same time. Using the Outline view, however, you can collapse what you don't need to see, then simply click and drag the headings to rearrange the text within the document. The Outline view is very useful with long documents, but it requires the use of styles throughout the document.

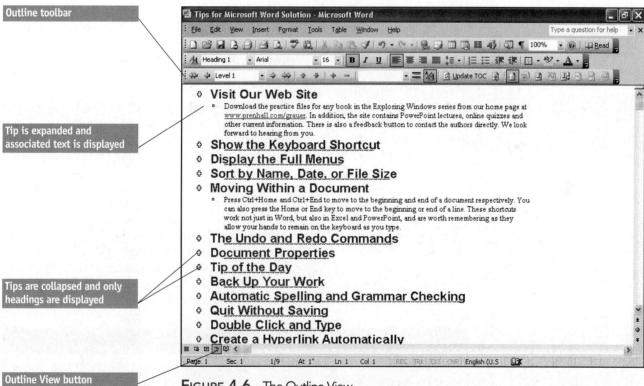

FIGURE 4.6 The Outline View

THE OUTLINE VERSUS THE OUTLINE VIEW

A conventional outline is created as a multilevel list within the Bullets and Numbering command. Text for the outline is entered in the Print Layout or Normal view, *not* the Outline view. The latter provides a condensed view of a document that is used in conjunction with styles.

The AutoFormat Command

Styles are extremely powerful. They enable you to impose uniform formatting within a document, and they let you take advantage of the Outline view. What if, however, you have an existing and/or lengthy document that does not contain any styles (other than the default Normal style, which is applied to every paragraph)? Do you have to manually go through every paragraph in order to apply the appropriate style? Fortunately the answer is no, because the AutoFormat command provides a quick solution.

The ***AutoFormat command*** enables you to format lengthy documents quickly, easily, and in a consistent fashion. In essence the command analyzes a document and formats it for you. Its most important capability is the application of styles to individual paragraphs; that is, the command goes through an entire document, determines how each paragraph is used, then applies an appropriate style to each paragraph. The formatting process assumes that one-line paragraphs are headings and applies the predefined Heading 1 style to those paragraphs. It applies the Body Text style to ordinary paragraphs and can also detect lists and apply a numbered or bulleted style to those lists.

The AutoFormat command will also add special touches to a document if you request those options. It can replace "ordinary quotation marks" with "smart quotation marks" that curl and face each other. It will replace ordinal numbers (1st, 2nd, or 3rd) with the corresponding superscripts (1st, 2nd, or 3rd), or common fractions (1/2 or 1/4) with typographical symbols (½ or ¼).

The AutoFormat command will also replace Internet references (Web addresses and e-mail addresses) with hyperlinks. It will recognize, for example, any entry beginning with http: or www. as a hyperlink and display the entry as underlined blue text (www.microsoft.com). This is not merely a change in formatting, but an actual hyperlink to a document on the Web or corporate Intranet. It also converts entries containing an @ sign, such as rgrauer@miami.edu to a hyperlink as well. (All Word documents are Web enabled. Unlike a Web document, however, you need to press and hold the Ctrl key to follow the link and display the associated page. This is different from what you usually do, because you normally just click a link to follow it. What if, however, you wanted to edit the link? Accordingly, Microsoft Word modifies the convention so that clicking a link enables you to edit the link.)

The various options for the AutoFormat command are controlled through the AutoCorrect Options command in the Tools menu. Once the options have been set, all formatting is done automatically by selecting the AutoFormat command from the Format menu. The changes are not final, however, as the command gives you the opportunity to review each formatting change individually, then accept the change or reject it as appropriate. (You can also format text automatically as it is entered according to the options specified under the AutoFormat As You Type tab.) The next exercise illustrates this powerful command.

AUTOMATIC BORDERS AND LISTS

The AutoFormat As You Type option applies sophisticated formatting as text is entered. It automatically creates a numbered list any time a number is followed by a period, tab, or right parenthesis (press Enter twice in a row to turn off the feature). It will also add a border to a paragraph any time you type three or more hyphens, equal signs, or underscores followed by the Enter key. Pull down the Tools menu, click the AutoCorrect Options command, then click the AutoFormat As You Type tab and select the desired features.

Objective   To use the AutoFormat command to apply styles to an existing document; to modify existing styles; to create a new style. Use Figure 4.7 as a guide for the exercise.

Step 1:   The AutoFormat Command

- Start Word. Open the document **Tips for Microsoft Word** in the **Exploring Word folder**. Save the document as **Tips for Microsoft Word Solution** so that you can return to the original if necessary.

- Press **Ctrl+Home** to move to the beginning of the document. Pull down the **Format menu**. Click **AutoFormat** to display the dialog box in Figure 4.7a.

- Click the **Options command button**. Be sure that every check box is selected to implement the maximum amount of automatic formatting. Click the **OK button** in the AutoCorrect dialog box to close the dialog box.

- If necessary, check the option to **AutoFormat now**, then click the **OK command button** to format the document.

- The status bar indicates the progress of the formatting operation, after which you will see a newly formatted document.

- Save the document.

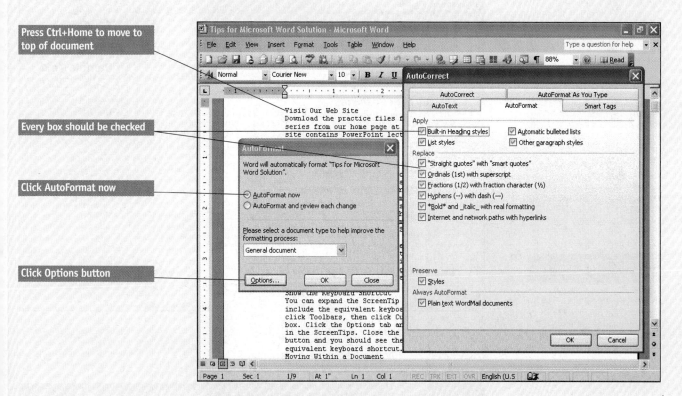

(a) The AutoFormat Command (step 1)

FIGURE 4.7   Hands-on Exercise 3

Step 2: **Formatting Properties**

- Pull down the **Format menu** and click the **Reveal Formatting command** to open the task pane as shown in Figure 4.7b.

- Press **Ctrl+Home** to move to the beginning of the document.

- The task pane displays the formatting properties for the first heading in your document. Heading 1 is specified as the paragraph style within the task pane. The name of the style for the selected text (Heading 1) also appears in the Style list box at the left of the Formatting toolbar.

- Click in the text of the first tip to view the associated formatting properties. This time Body Text is specified as the paragraph style in the task pane. Click the title of any tip and you will see the Heading 1 style in the Style box. Click the text of any tip and you will see the Body Text style in the Style box.

- Click the **down arrow** to the left of the Close button in the task pane and click **Styles and Formatting** to show the styles in your document. If necessary, click the **down arrow** in the Show list box to show **Formatting in use**.

- You should see the Heading 1 and Body Text styles and an option to clear formatting as the styles in your document.

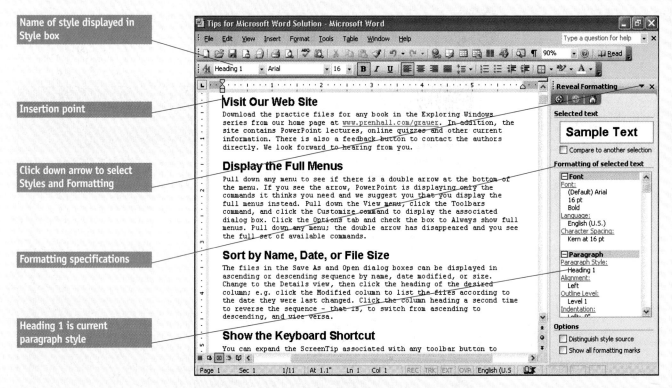

Name of style displayed in Style box

Insertion point

Click down arrow to select Styles and Formatting

Formatting specifications

Heading 1 is current paragraph style

(b) Formatting Properties (step 2)

FIGURE 4.7 Hands-on Exercise 3 (*continued*)

STYLES AND THE AUTOFORMAT COMMAND

The AutoFormat command applies the Heading 1 and Body Text styles to single- and multiple-line paragraphs, respectively. Thus, all you have to do to change the appearance of the headings or paragraphs throughout the document is change the associated style. Change the Heading 1 style, for example, and you automatically change every heading throughout the document. Change the Body Text style and you change every paragraph.

Step 3: **Modify the Body Text Style**

- Point to the **Body Text style** in the task pane, click the **down arrow** that appears to display a context-sensitive menu, and click **Modify** to display the Modify Style dialog box.

- Click the **Justify button** to change the alignment of every Body Text paragraph in the document. Change the font to **Times New Roman**.

- Click the **down arrow** next to the **Format button**, then click **Paragraph** to display the Paragraph dialog box in Figure 4.7c. If necessary, click the **Line and Page Breaks tab**.

- The box for Widow/Orphan control is checked by default. This ensures that any paragraph defined by the Body Text style will not be split to leave a single line at the bottom or top of a page.

- Check the box to **Keep Lines Together**. This is a more stringent requirement and ensures that the entire paragraph is not split. Click **OK** to close the Paragraph dialog box. Click **OK** to close the Modify Style dialog box.

- All of the multiline paragraphs in the document change automatically to reflect the new definition of the Body Text style, which includes full justification, a new font, and ensures that the paragraph is not split across pages. Save the document.

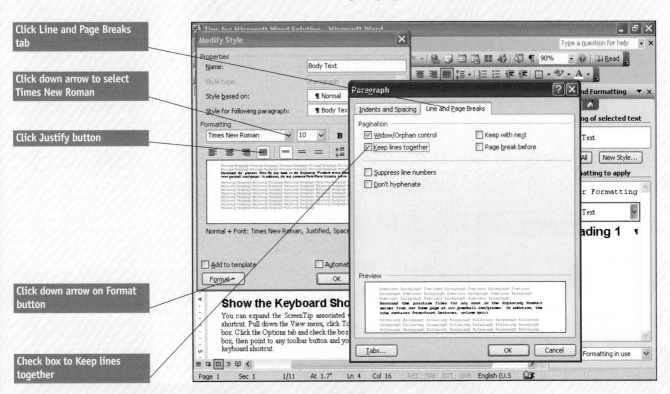

Click Line and Page Breaks tab

Click down arrow to select Times New Roman

Click Justify button

Click down arrow on Format button

Check box to Keep lines together

(c) Modify the Body Text Style (step 3)

FIGURE 4.7   Hands-on Exercise 3 (*continued*)

BE CAREFUL WHERE YOU CLICK

If you click the style name instead of the down arrow, you will apply the style to the selected text instead of modifying it. We know because we made this mistake. Click the Undo button to cancel the command. Click the down arrow next to the style name to display the associated menu, and click the Modify command to display the Modify Style dialog box.

Step 4: **Modify the Heading 1 Style**

- Point to the **Heading 1 style** in the task pane, click the **down arrow** that appears, then click **Modify** to display the Modify Style dialog box.

- Click the **Font Color drop-down arrow** to display the palette in Figure 4.7d. Click **Blue** to change the color of all of the headings in the document. The change will not take effect until you click the OK button to accept the settings and close the dialog box.

- Click the **Format button** toward the bottom of the dialog box, then click **Paragraph** to display the Paragraph dialog box. Click the **Indents and Spacing tab**. Change the **Spacing After** to **0**. Click **OK** to accept the settings and close the Paragraph dialog box.

- Click **OK** to close the Modify Style dialog box. The formatting in your document has changed to reflect the changes in the Heading 1 style.

- Save the document.

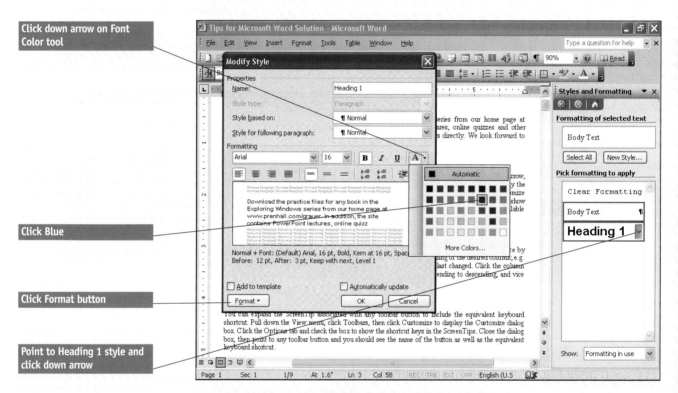

(d) Modify the Heading 1 Style (step 4)

FIGURE 4.7 Hands-on Exercise 3 (*continued*)

SPACE BEFORE AND AFTER

It's common practice to press the Enter key twice at the end of a paragraph (once to end the paragraph, and a second time to insert a blank line before the next paragraph). The same effect can be achieved by setting the spacing before or after the paragraph using the Spacing Before or After list boxes in the Format Paragraph command. The latter technique gives you greater flexibility in that you can specify any amount of spacing (e.g., 6 points) to leave only half a line before or after a paragraph. It also enables you to change the spacing between paragraphs more easily because the spacing information can be stored within the paragraph style.

Step 5: The Outline View

- Close the task pane. Pull down the **View menu** and click **Outline** (or click the **Outline View button** above the status bar) to display the document in Outline view.

- Pull down the **Edit menu** and click **Select All** (or press **Ctrl+A**) to select the entire document. Click the **Collapse button** on the Outlining toolbar to collapse the entire document so that only the headings are visible.

- If necessary, scroll down in the document until you can click in the heading of the tip entitled "Show the Keyboard Shortcut" as shown in Figure 4.7e. Click the **Expand button** on the Outlining toolbar to see the subordinate items under this heading.

- Click and drag to select the tip **Show the Keyboard Shortcut** (title and text). Point to the **plus sign** next to the selected tip (the mouse pointer changes to a double arrow), then click and drag to move the tip toward the top of the document, immediately below the first tip. Release the mouse.

- Save the document.

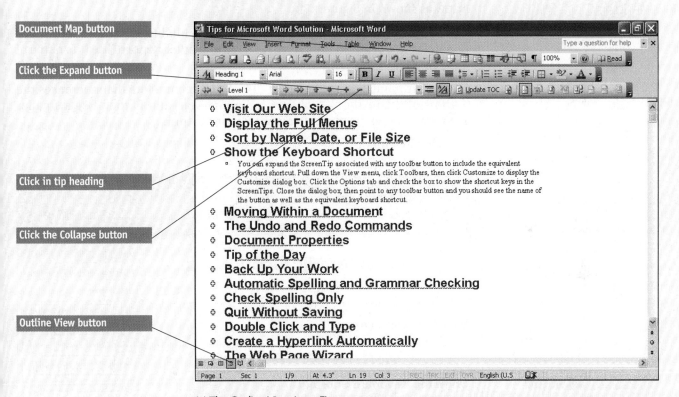

Document Map button

Click the Expand button

Click in tip heading

Click the Collapse button

Outline View button

(e) The Outline View (step 5)

FIGURE 4.7 Hands-on Exercise 3 (*continued*)

THE DOCUMENT MAP

The Document Map helps you to navigate within a large document. Click the Document Map button on the Standard toolbar to divide the screen into two panes. The headings in a document are displayed in the left pane, and the text of the document is visible in the right pane. To go to a specific point in a document, click its heading in the left pane, and the insertion point is moved automatically to that point in the document, which is visible in the right pane. Click the Map button a second time to turn the feature off.

Step 6: **Create a Paragraph Style**

- Pull down the **View menu** and change to the **Normal view**. Pull down the **Format menu** and click **Styles and Formatting** to open the task pane as shown in Figure 4.7f.

- Press **Ctrl+Home** to move the insertion point to the beginning of the document, then press **Ctrl+Enter** to create a page break for a title page.

- Press the **up arrow** to move the insertion point to the left of the page break. Press the **Enter key** twice and press the **up arrow** to move above the page break. Select the two blank lines and click **Clear Formatting** in the task pane. Press the **up arrow**.

- Enter the title of the document, **Tips for Microsoft Word**. Change the text to **24 point Arial Bold** in **blue**. Click the **Center button** on the Formatting toolbar. Press **Enter**.

- The task pane displays the specifications for the text you just entered. You have created a new style, but the style is as yet unnamed. Point to the specification for the title (Arial, 24 pt, Centered) to display a down arrow, then click the arrow as shown in Figure 4.7f.

- Click the **Modify Style command** to display the Modify Style dialog box. Click in the **Name** text box in the Properties area and enter **Report Title** (the name of the new style). Click **OK**.

- Enter your name below the report title. Add a second line that references the authors of the textbook, Robert Grauer and Maryann Barber. Use a smaller point size. Name the associated style **Report Author**.

- Save the document.

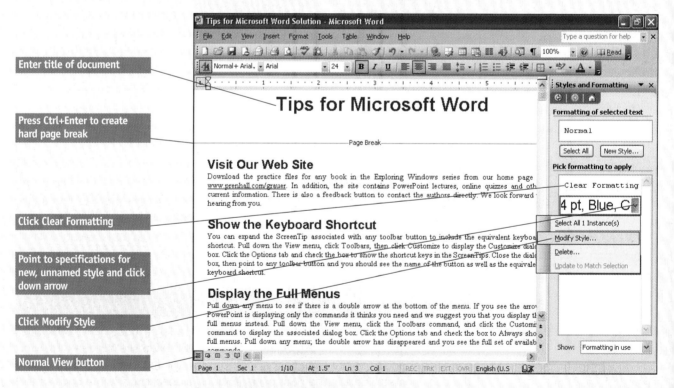

(f) Create a Paragraph Style (step 6)

FIGURE 4.7 Hands-on Exercise 3 (*continued*)

Step 7: **Create a Character Style**

- Click and drag to select the words **ScreenTip** (that appear within the second tip). Click the **Bold** and **Italic buttons** on the Formatting toolbar so that the selected text appears in bold and italics.

- Once again, you have created a style as can be seen in the task pane. Point to the right of the formatting specification in the task pane, click the **down arrow**, then click the **Modify Style command** to display the Modify Style dialog box in Figure 4.7g.

- Click in the **Name** text box in the Properties area and enter **Emphasize** as the name of the style. Click the **down arrow** in the Style type list box and select **Character**. Click **OK**.

- Click and drag to select the words **practice files** that appear in the first tip, click the **down arrow** in the Style list box on the Formatting toolbar, and apply the newly created Emphasize character style to the selected text.

- Save the document. Close the task pane.

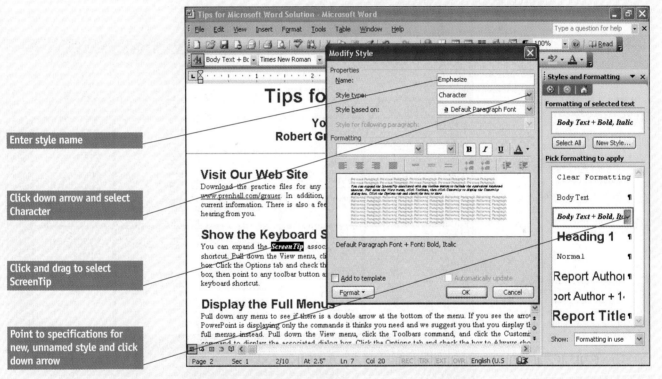

Enter style name

Click down arrow and select Character

Click and drag to select ScreenTip

Point to specifications for new, unnamed style and click down arrow

(g) Create a Character Style (step 7)

FIGURE 4.7 Hands-on Exercise 3 (*continued*)

SHOW THE KEYBOARD SHORTCUT

You can expand the ScreenTip associated with any toolbar button to include the equivalent keyboard shortcut. Pull down the View menu, click Toolbars, then click Customize to display the Customize dialog box. Click the Options tab and check the box to Show the shortcut keys in the ScreenTips. Close the dialog box, then point to any toolbar button, and you should see the name of the button as well as the equivalent keyboard shortcut. There is no need to memorize the shortcuts, but they do save time.

Step 8:   **The Completed Document**

- Change to the **Print Layout view**. Pull down the **View menu** and click the **Zoom command** to display the Zoom dialog box. Click the option button next to **Many Pages**, then click and drag the monitor icon to display **two rows of five pages** (2 × 5) on the same screen. Click **OK**.

- You should see a multipage display similar to Figure 4.7h. The text on the individual pages is too small to read, but you can see the page breaks and overall document flow.

- The various tips should all be justified. Moreover, each tip should fit completely on one page without spilling over to the next page according to the specifications in the Body Text style.

- Click above the title on the first page and press the **Enter key** (if necessary) to position the title further down the page. Conversely, you could press the **Del key** to remove individual lines and move the title up the page.

- Save the document. Print the document only if you do not intend to do the next hands-on exercise. Exit Word if you do not want to continue with the next exercise at this time.

Save button

Press Enter key to add blank lines

Print Layout View button

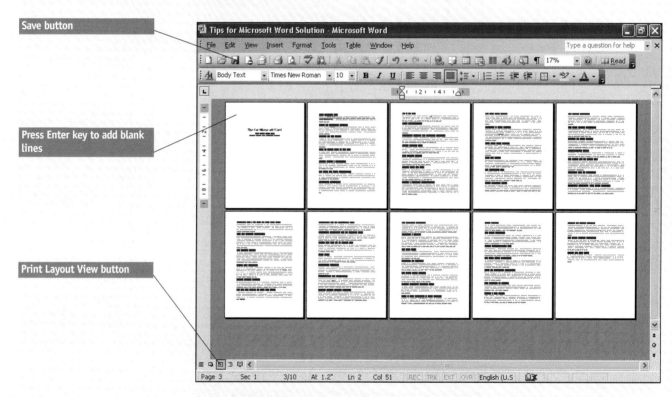

(h) The Completed Document (step 8)

FIGURE **4.7**   Hands-on Exercise 3 (*continued*)

PRINT SELECTED PAGES

Why print an entire document if you want only a few pages? Pull down the File menu and click Print as you usually do, to initiate the printing process. Click the Pages option button, then enter the page numbers and/or page ranges you want; for example, 3, 6-8 will print page three and pages six through eight. You can also print multiple copies by entering the appropriate number in the Number of copies list box.

Long documents, such as term papers or reports, require additional formatting for better organization. These documents typically contain page numbers, headers and/or footers, a table of contents, and an index. Each of these elements is discussed in turn and will be illustrated in a hands-on exercise.

Page Numbers

The *Insert Page Numbers command* is the easiest way to place *page numbers* into a document and is illustrated in Figure 4.8. The page numbers can appear at the top or bottom of a page, and can be left, centered, or right aligned. Word provides additional flexibility in that you can use Roman rather than Arabic numerals, and you need not start at page number one.

The Insert Page Number command is limited, however, in that it does not provide for additional text next to the page number. You can overcome this restriction by creating a header or footer that contains the page number.

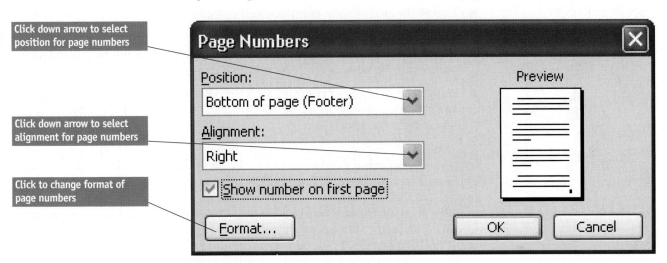

Click down arrow to select position for page numbers

Click down arrow to select alignment for page numbers

Click to change format of page numbers

FIGURE 4.8   Page Numbers

Headers and Footers

Headers and footers give a professional appearance to a document. A *header* consists of one or more lines that are printed at the top of every page. A *footer* is printed at the bottom of the page. A document may contain headers but not footers, footers but not headers, or both headers and footers.

Headers and footers are created from the View menu. (A simple header or footer is also created automatically by the Insert Page Number command, depending on whether the page number is at the top or bottom of a page.) Headers and footers are formatted like any other paragraph and can be centered, left or right aligned. They can be formatted in any typeface or point size and can include special codes to automatically insert the page number, date, and/or time a document is printed.

The advantage of using a header or footer (over typing the text yourself at the top or bottom of every page) is that you type the text only once, after which it appears automatically according to your specifications. In addition, the placement of the headers and footers is adjusted for changes in page breaks caused by the insertion or deletion of text in the body of the document.

Headers and footers can change continually throughout a document. The Page Setup dialog box (in the File menu) enables you to specify a different header or footer for the first page, and/or different headers and footers for the odd and even pages. If, however, you wanted to change the header (or footer) midway through a document, you would need to insert a section break at the point where the new header (or footer) is to begin.

Sections

Formatting in Word occurs on three levels. You are already familiar with formatting at the character and paragraph levels that have been used throughout the text. Formatting at the section level controls headers and footers, page numbering, page size and orientation, margins, and columns. All of the documents in the text so far have consisted of a single *section*, and thus any section formatting applied to the entire document. You can, however, divide a document into sections and format each section independently.

Formatting at the section level gives you the ability to create more sophisticated documents. You can use section formatting to do the following:

- Change the margins within a multipage letter, where the first page (the letterhead) requires a larger top margin than the other pages in the letter.

- Change the orientation from portrait to landscape to accommodate a wide table at the end of the document.

- Change the page numbering to use Roman numerals at the beginning of the document for a table of contents and Arabic numerals thereafter.

- Change the number of columns in a newsletter, which may contain a single column at the top of a page for the masthead, then two or three columns in the body of the newsletter.

In all instances, you determine where one section ends and another begins by using the *Insert menu* to create a *section break*. You also have the option of deciding how the section break will be implemented on the printed page; that is, you can specify that the new section continue on the same page, that it begin on a new page, or that it begin on the next odd or even page even if a blank page has to be inserted.

Word stores the formatting characteristics of each section in the section break at the end of a section. Thus, deleting a section break also deletes the section formatting, causing the text above the break to assume the formatting characteristics of the next section.

Figure 4.9 displays a multipage view of a ten-page document. The document has been divided into two sections, and the insertion point is currently on the fourth page of the document (page four of ten), which is also the first page of the second section. Note the corresponding indications on the status bar and the position of the headers and footers throughout the document.

Figure 4.9 also displays the Header and Footer toolbar, which contains various icons associated with these elements. As indicated, a header or footer may contain text and/or special codes—for example, the word "page" followed by a code for the page number. The latter is inserted into the header by clicking the appropriate button on the Header and Footer toolbar. Remember, headers and footers are implemented at the section level. Thus, changing a header or footer within a document requires the insertion of a section break.

Table of Contents

A *table of contents* lists headings in the order they appear in a document and the page numbers where the entries begin. Word will create the table of contents automatically, provided you have identified each heading in the document with a built-in heading style (Heading 1 through Heading 9). Word will also update the table automatically to accommodate the addition or deletion of headings and/or changes in page numbers brought about through changes in the document.

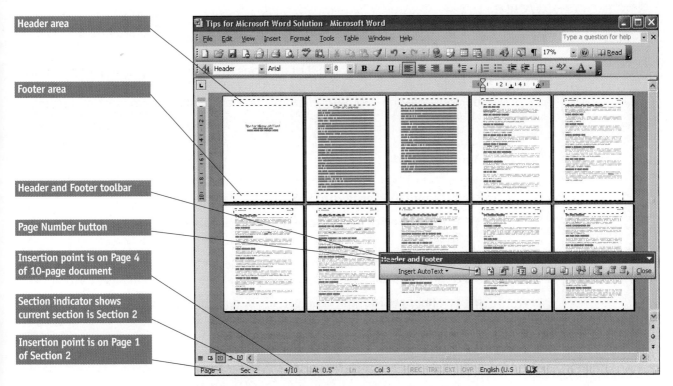

Header area

Footer area

Header and Footer toolbar

Page Number button

Insertion point is on Page 4
of 10-page document

Section indicator shows
current section is Section 2

Insertion point is on Page 1
of Section 2

FIGURE 4.9 Headers and Footers

The table of contents is created through the ***Index and Tables command*** from the Insert menu. You have your choice of several predefined formats and the number of levels within each format; the latter correspond to the heading styles used within the document. You can also choose the ***leader character*** and whether or not to right-align the page numbers.

Creating an Index

An ***index*** is the finishing touch in a long document. Word will create an index automatically, provided that the entries for the index have been previously marked. This, in turn, requires you to go through a document, and one by one, select the terms to be included in the index and mark them accordingly. It's not as tedious as it sounds. You can, for example, select a single occurrence of an entry and tell Word to mark all occurrences of that entry for the index. You can also create cross-references, such as "see also Internet."

After the entries have been specified, you create the index by choosing the appropriate settings in the Index and Tables command. You can choose a variety of styles for the index just as you can for the table of contents. Word will put the index entries in alphabetical order and will enter the appropriate page references. You can also create additional index entries and/or move text within a document, then update the index with the click of a mouse.

The Go To Command

The ***Go To command*** moves the insertion point to the top of a designated page. The command is accessed from the Edit menu by pressing the F5 function key or by double clicking the Page number on the status bar. After the command has been executed, you are presented with a dialog box in which you enter the desired page number. You can also specify a relative page number—for example, P +2 to move forward two pages, or P –1 to move back one page.

Objective To create a header (footer) that includes page numbers; to insert and update a table of contents; to add an index entry; to insert a section break and demonstrate the Go To command; to view multiple pages of a document. Use Figure 4.10 as a guide for the exercise.

Step 1: **Applying a Style**

- Open the **Tips for Microsoft Word Solution document** from the previous exercise. Zoom to **Page Width**. Scroll to the top of the second page.

- Click to the left of the first tip title. Type **Table of Contents**. Press the **Enter key** two times.

- Click anywhere in the phrase "Table of Contents". Click the **down arrow** on the **Styles** list box to pull down the available styles as shown in Figure 4.10a.

- Click **Report Title** (the style you created at the end of the previous exercise). "Table of Contents" is centered in 24 point blue Arial bold according to the definition of Report Title.

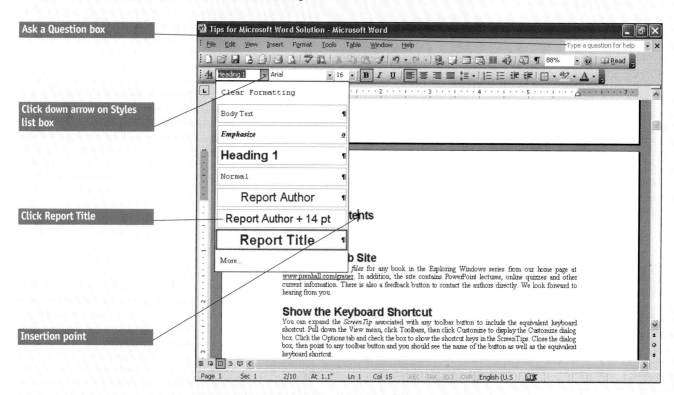

(a) Applying a Style (step 1)

FIGURE 4.10 Hands-on Exercise 4

ASK A QUESTION

Click in the Ask a Question box that appears at the right of the menu bar, enter the text of a question, press Enter, and Word returns a list of potential help topics. Click any topic that appears promising to open the Help window with detailed information. You can ask multiple questions during a session, and then click the down arrow in the list box to return to an earlier question, which will return you to the help topics.

Step 2: Table of Contents

- If necessary, change to the **Print Layout view**. Click the line immediately under the title for the table of contents. Pull down the **View menu**. Click **Zoom** to display the associated dialog box.

- Click the **monitor icon**. Click and drag the **page icons** to display two pages down by five pages across as shown in the figure. Release the mouse.

- Click **OK**. The display changes to show all ten pages in the document.

- Pull down the **Insert menu**. Click **Reference**, then click **Index and Tables**. If necessary, click the **Table of Contents tab** to display the dialog box in Figure 4.10b.

- Check the boxes to **Show Page Numbers** and to **Right Align Page Numbers**.

- Click the **down arrow** on the Formats list box, then click **Distinctive**. Click the **down arrow** in the **Tab Leader list box**. Choose a dot leader. Click **OK**. Word takes a moment to create the table of contents, which will extend to two pages.

- Save the document.

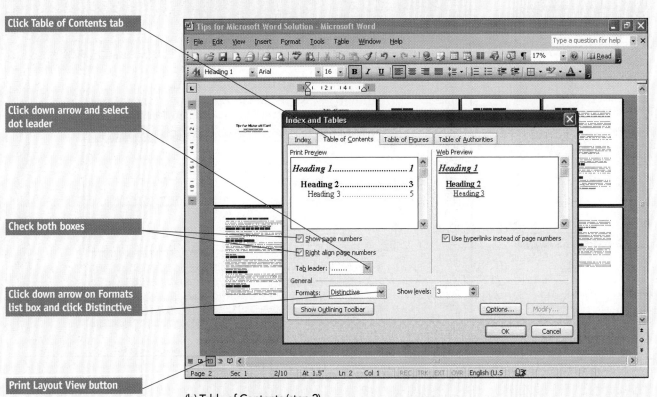

(b) Table of Contents (step 2)

FIGURE 4.10 Hands-on Exercise 4 (*continued*)

AUTOFORMAT AND THE TABLE OF CONTENTS

Word will create a table of contents automatically, provided you use the built-in heading styles to define the items for inclusion. If you have not applied the styles to the document, the AutoFormat command will do it for you. Once the heading styles are in the document, pull down the Insert command, click Reference, then click Index and Tables, then click the Table of Contents tab. Modify options as desired and click OK.

Field Codes and Field Text

- Click the **arrow** on the **Zoom box** on the Standard toolbar. Click **Page Width** in order to read the table of contents as in Figure 4.10c.

- Use the **up arrow key** to scroll to the beginning of the table of contents. Press **Alt+F9**. The table is replaced by an entry similar to {TOC \o "1-3"\h \z \u} to indicate a field code. The exact code depends on the selections you made in step 2.

- Press **Alt+F9** a second time. The field code for the table of contents is replaced by text.

- Pull down the **Edit menu** and click the **Go To command** (or use the **Ctrl+G** keyboard shortcut) to display the dialog box in Figure 4.10c.

- Type **3** and press the **Enter key** to go to page 3, which contains the second page of the table of contents.

- Close the Find and Replace dialog box.

Click down arrow on Zoom box to select Page Width

Scroll to top of Table of Contents

Enter 3

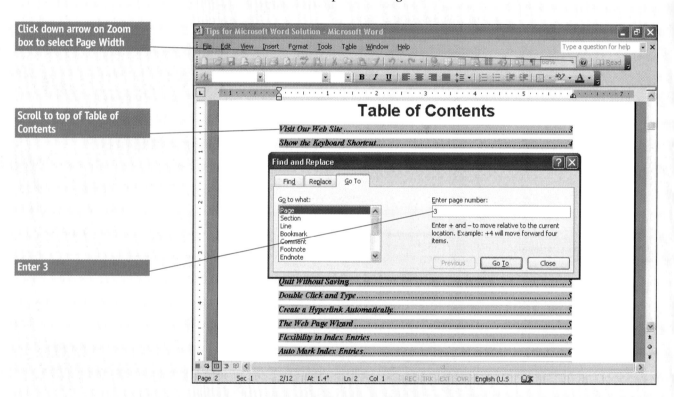

(c) Field Codes and Field Text (step 3)

FIGURE 4.10 Hands-on Exercise 4 (*continued*)

THE GO TO AND GO BACK COMMANDS

The F5 key is the shortcut equivalent of the Go To command and displays a dialog box to move to a specific location (a page or section) within a document. The Shift+F5 combination executes the Go Back command and returns to a previous location of the insertion point; press Shift+F5 repeatedly to cycle through the last three locations of the insertion point.

Step 4: Insert the Page Numbers

- Scroll down page 3 until you are at the end of the table of contents. Click to the left of the first tip heading as shown in Figure 4.10d.
- Pull down the **Insert menu.** Click **Break** to display the Break dialog box. Click the **Next Page button** under Section Break types. Click **OK** to create a section break, simultaneously forcing the first tip to begin on a new page.
- The first tip, Visit Our Web Site, moves to the top of the next page (page 4 in the document). If the status bar already displays Page 1 Section 2, a previous user has changed the default numbering to begin each section on its own page and you can go to step 5. If not, you need to change the page numbering.
- Pull down the **Insert menu** and click **Page Numbers** to display the Page Numbers dialog box. Click the **drop-down arrow** in the Position list box to position the page number at the top of page (in the header).
- Click the **Format command button** to display the Page Number Format dialog box. Click the option button to **Start at** page 1 (i.e., you want the first page in the second section to be numbered as page 1). Click **OK**.
- Click **Close** to close the Page Numbers dialog box. The status bar now displays Page 1 Sec 2. The entry 4/12 indicates that you are physically on the fourth page of a 12-page document.

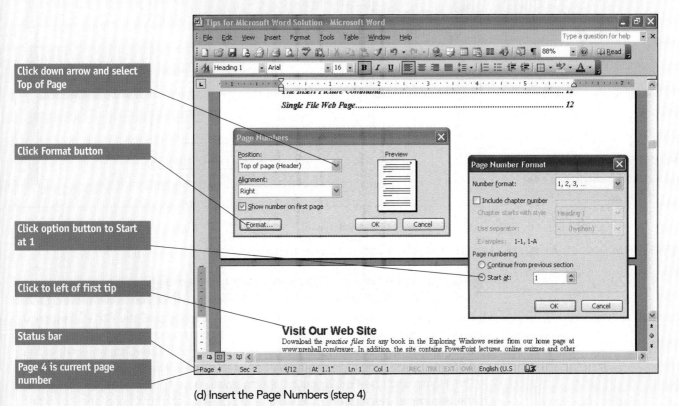

Click down arrow and select Top of Page

Click Format button

Click option button to Start at 1

Click to left of first tip

Status bar

Page 4 is current page number

(d) Insert the Page Numbers (step 4)

FIGURE 4.10   Hands-on Exercise 4 (*continued*)

FORMATTING AT THE SECTION LEVEL

The margins, headers and footers, page numbers, orientation, and the number of columns in a document are implemented at the section level. Thus to change any of these parameters within a document, you must create a new section by inserting a section break. Look closely and you will see that the status bar indicates both the page number and the section number.

Step 5:   **The Page Setup Command**

- Pull down the **File menu** and click the **Page Setup command** (or double click the **ruler**) to display the Page Setup dialog box.

- Click the **Layout tab** to display the options in Figure 4.10e.

- If necessary, clear the box for Different Odd and Even Pages and for Different First Page, as all pages in this section (Section 2) are to have the same header.

- Click **OK** to accept the settings and close the Page Setup dialog box.

- Save the document.

Click Layout tab

Clear both boxes

Double click the page indicator to display the associated dialog box

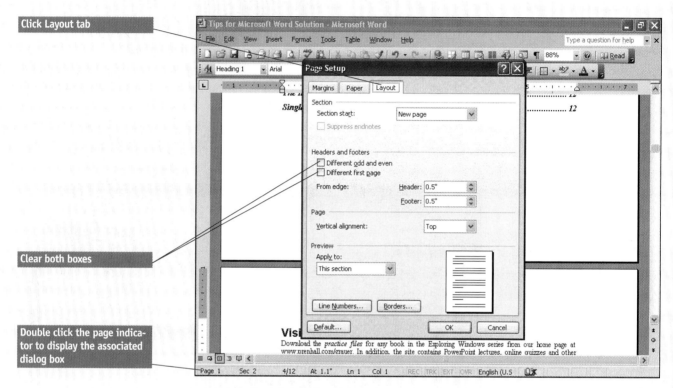

(e) The Page Setup Command (step 5)

FIGURE 4.10   Hands-on Exercise 4 (*continued*)

MOVING WITHIN LONG DOCUMENTS

Double click the page indicator on the status bar (or use the Ctrl+G keyboard shortcut) to display the dialog box for the Go To command from where you can go directly to any page within the document. You can also Ctrl+Click an entry in the table of contents to go directly to the text of that entry. And finally, you can use the Ctrl+Home and Ctrl+End keyboard shortcuts to move to the beginning or end of the document, respectively. The latter are universal shortcuts and apply to other Office documents as well.

Step 6: **Create the Header**

- Pull down the **View menu**. Click **Header and Footer** to produce the screen in Figure 4.10f. The text in the document is faded to indicate that you are editing the header, as opposed to the document.

- The "Link to Previous" indicator is on since Word automatically uses the header from the previous section.

- Click the **Link to Previous button** on the Header and Footer toolbar to toggle the indicator off and to create a different header for this section.

- If necessary, click in the header. Click the **arrow** on the Font list box on the Formatting toolbar. Click **Arial**. Click the **arrow** on the Font Size box. Click **8**. Type **Tips for Microsoft Word**.

- Press the **Tab key** twice. Type **PAGE**. Press the **space bar**. Click the **Insert Page Number button** on the Header and Footer toolbar.

- Click the **Show Previous button** to show the header for Section 1. Delete the page number that appears at the upper right, since we do not want to display page numbers for the table of contents.

- Click the **Close button** on the Header and Footer toolbar. The header is faded, and the document text is available for editing.

Font list box

Font Size box

Enter text for header

Insert Page Number button

Click Link to Previous button

Show Previous button

Close button

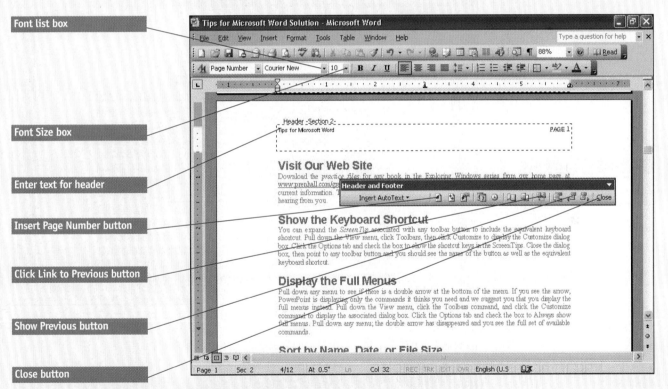

(f) Create the Header (step 6)

FIGURE 4.10 Hands-on Exercise 4 (*continued*)

HEADERS AND FOOTERS

If you do not see a header or footer, it is most likely because you are in the wrong view. Headers and footers are displayed in the Print Layout view but not in the Normal view. [Click the Print Layout button on the status bar to change the view.]

Step 7: **Update the Table of Contents**

- Press **Ctrl+Home** to move to the beginning of the document. The status bar indicates Page 1, Sec 1.

- Click the **Select Browse Object button** on the vertical scroll bar, then click the **Browse by Page** icon.

- If necessary, click the **Next Page button** or **Previous Page button** on the vertical scroll bar (or press **Ctrl+PgDn**) to move to the first page containing the table of contents.

- Click to the left of the first entry in the Table of Contents. Press the **F9 key** to update the table of contents. If necessary, click the **Update Entire Table button** as shown in Figure 4.10g, then click **OK**.

- The pages are renumbered to reflect the actual page numbers in the second section.

- Save the document.

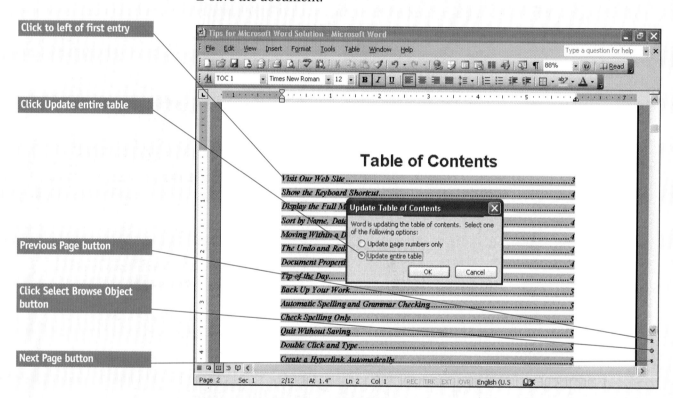

(g) Update the Table of Contents (step 7)

FIGURE **4.10** Hands-on Exercise 4 (*continued*)

SELECT BROWSE OBJECT

Click the Select Browse Object button toward the bottom of the vertical scroll bar to display a palette in which you specify how to browse through a document. Typically you browse from one page to the next, but you can browse by footnote, section, graphic, table, or any of the other objects listed. Once you select the object, click the Next or Previous buttons on the vertical scroll bar (or press Ctrl+PgDn or Ctrl+PgUp) to move to the next or previous occurrence of the selected object.

Step 8: Create an Index Entry

■ Press **Ctrl+Home** to move to the beginning of the document. Pull down the **Edit menu** and click the **Find command**. Search for the first occurrence of the text "Ctrl+Home" within the document, as shown in Figure 4.10h. Close the Find and Replace dialog box.

■ Click the **Show/Hide ¶ button** so you can see the nonprinting characters in the document, which include the index entries that have been previously created by the authors. (The index entries appear in curly brackets and begin with the letters XE.)

■ Check that the text "Ctrl+Home" is selected within the document, then press **Alt+Shift+X** to display the Mark Index Entry dialog box. (Should you forget the shortcut, pull down the **Insert menu**, click **Reference**, click the **Index and Tables command**, click the **Index tab**, then click the **Mark command button**.)

■ Click the **Mark command button** to create the index entry, after which you see the field code, {XE "Ctrl+Home"}, to indicate that the index entry has been created.

■ The Mark Index Entry dialog box stays open so that you can create additional entries by selecting additional text.

■ Click the option button to create a **cross-reference.** Type **keyboard shortcut** in the associated text box. Click **Mark**.

■ Click in the document, click and drag to select the text "Ctrl+End," then click in the dialog box, and the Main entry changes to Ctrl+End automatically. Click the **Mark command button** to create the index entry. Close the Mark Index Entry dialog box.

■ Save the document.

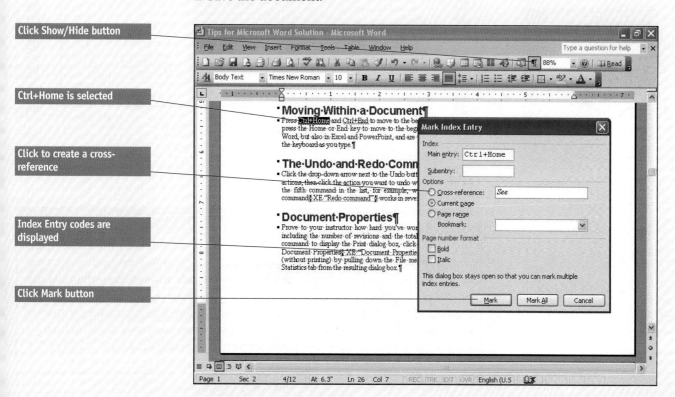

(h) Create an Index Entry (step 8)

FIGURE 4.10 Hands-on Exercise 4 (*continued*)

Step 9: Create the Index

- Press **Ctrl+End** to move to the end of the document, where you will insert the index. Press **Enter** to begin a new line.

- Pull down the **Insert menu**, click **Reference**, then click the **Index and Tables command** to display the Index and Tables dialog box in Figure 4.10i. Click the **Index tab** if necessary.

- Choose the type of index you want. We selected a **classic format** over **two columns**. Click **OK** to create the index.

- Click the **Undo button** if you are not satisfied with the appearance of the index, then repeat the process to create an index with a different style.

- Save the document.

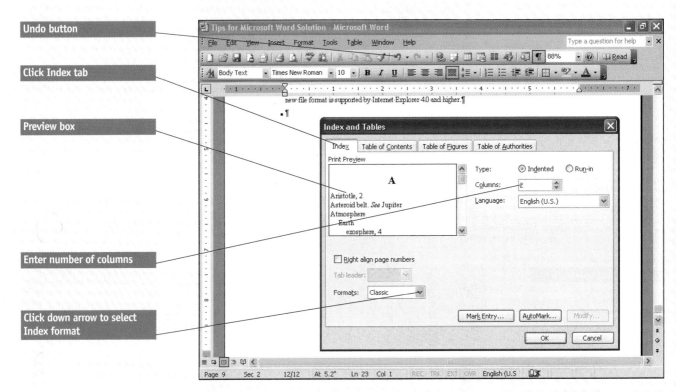

(i) Create the Index (step 9)

FIGURE 4.10 Hands-on Exercise 4 *(continued)*

AUTOMARK INDEX ENTRIES

The AutoMark command will, as the name implies, automatically mark all occurrences of all entries for inclusion in an index. To use the feature, you have to create a separate document that lists the terms you want to reference, then you execute the AutoMark command from the Index and Tables dialog box. The advantage is that it is fast. The disadvantage is that every occurrence of an entry is marked in the index so that a commonly used term may have too many page references. You can, however, delete superfluous entries by manually deleting the field codes. Click the Show/Hide button if you do not see the entries in the document.

Step 10: Complete the Index

- Scroll to the beginning of the index and click to the left of the letter "A." Pull down the **File menu** and click the **Page Setup command** to display the Page Setup dialog box, and click the **Layout tab**.

- Click the **down arrow** in the Section start list box and specify **New page**. Click the **down arrow** in the Apply to list box and specify **This section**. Click **OK**. The index moves to the top of a new page.

- Pull down the **Insert menu** and click the **Page numbers command** to display the Page Numbers dialog box. Click the **Format button** to display the Page Number Format dialog box. Click the option button to **Continue from previous section**. Click **OK**. Click **Close**.

- Pull down the **View menu** and click the **Header and Footer command** to display the Header and Footer toolbar as shown in Figure 4.10j. Click the **Link to Previous button** to toggle the indicator off and create a new header for this section.

- Enter **INDEX** as the text in the header. Close the Header and Footer toolbar to return to the document.

- Save the document.

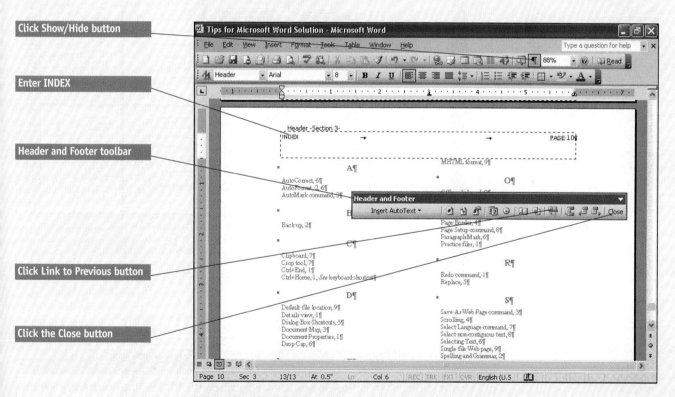

(j) Complete the Index (step 10)

FIGURE 4.10 Hands-on Exercise 4 (*continued*)

CHECK THE INDEX ENTRIES

Every entry in the index should begin with an uppercase letter. If this is not the case, it is because the origin entry within the body of the document was marked improperly. Click the Show/Hide button to display the indexed entries within the document, which appear within brackets; e.g., {XE "Practice Files"}. Change each entry to begin with an uppercase letter as necessary.

Step 11: The Completed Document

- Pull down the **View menu**. Click **Zoom**. Click **Many Pages**. Click the **monitor icon**. Click and drag the **page icon** within the monitor to display two pages down by five pages. Release the mouse. Click **OK**.

- The completed document is shown in Figure 4.10k. The index appears by itself on the last (13th) page of the document.

- Save the document, then print the completed document to prove to your instructor that you have completed the exercise.

- Congratulations on a job well done. You have created a document with page numbers, a table of contents, and an index. Exit Word.

- Read the printed document and highlight five tips you find especially useful. Try to incorporate this information in your daily work.

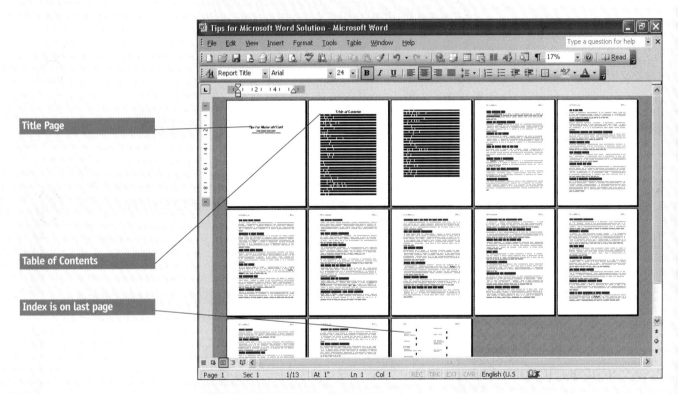

(k) The Completed Document (step 11)

FIGURE 4.10 Hands-on Exercise 4 (*continued*)

UPDATING THE TABLE OF CONTENTS

Use a shortcut menu to update the table of contents. Point to any entry in the table of contents, then press the right mouse button to display a shortcut menu. Click Update Field, click the Update Entire Table command button, and click OK. The table of contents will be adjusted automatically to reflect page number changes as well as the addition or deletion of any items defined by any built-in heading style.

SUMMARY

A list helps to organize information by emphasizing important topics. A bulleted or numbered list can be created by clicking the appropriate button on the Formatting toolbar or by executing the Bullets and Numbering command in the Format menu. An outline extends a numbered list to several levels.

Tables represent a very powerful capability within Word and are created through the Insert Table command in the Table menu or by using the Insert Table button on the Standard toolbar. Each cell in a table is formatted independently and may contain text, numbers, and/or graphics. Individual cells can be joined together to create a larger cell; e.g., the cells in the first row of a table are often merged to create a title for the table. Conversely a single cell can be split into multiple cells. The rows in a table can be different heights and/or each column can be a different width. Tables are the basis for a variety of documents.

A style is a set of formatting instructions that has been saved under a distinct name. Styles are created at the character or paragraph level and provide a consistent appearance to similar elements throughout a document. Any existing styles can be modified to change the formatting of all text defined by that style.

The Outline view displays a condensed view of a document based on styles within the document. Text may be collapsed or expanded as necessary to facilitate moving text within long documents. (The Outline view does not display a conventional outline, which is created from a multilevel list within the Bullets and Numbering command.)

The AutoFormat command analyzes a document and formats it for you. The command goes through an entire document, determines how each paragraph is used, then applies an appropriate style to each paragraph.

Formatting occurs at the character, paragraph, or section level. Section formatting controls margins, columns, page orientation and size, page numbering, and headers and footers. A header consists of one or more lines that are printed at the top of every (designated) page in a document. A footer is text that is printed at the bottom of designated pages. Page numbers may be added to either a header or footer.

A table of contents lists headings in the order they appear in a document with their respective page numbers. It can be created automatically, provided the built-in heading styles were previously applied to the items for inclusion. Word will also create an index automatically, provided that the entries for the index have been previously marked. This, in turn, requires you to go through a document, select the appropriate text, and mark the entries accordingly. The Edit Go To command enables you to move directly to a specific page, section, or bookmark within a document.

KEY TERMS

MULTIPLE CHOICE

1. Which of the following can be stored within a paragraph style?
   (a) Tabs and indents
   (b) Line spacing and alignment
   (c) Shading and borders
   (d) All of the above

2. What is the easiest way to change the alignment of five paragraphs scattered throughout a document, each of which is formatted with the same style?
   (a) Select the paragraphs individually, then click the appropriate alignment button
   (b) Select the paragraphs at the same time, then click the appropriate alignment button on the Formatting toolbar
   (c) Change the format of the existing style, which changes the paragraphs
   (d) Retype the paragraphs according to the new specifications

3. The AutoFormat command does not:
   (a) Apply styles to individual paragraphs
   (b) Apply boldface italics to terms that require additional emphasis
   (c) Replace ordinary quotes with smart quotes
   (d) Substitute typographic symbols for ordinary letters—such as © for (C)

4. Which of the following is used to create a conventional outline?
   (a) The Bullets and Numbering command
   (b) The Outline view
   (c) Both (a) and (b)
   (d) Neither (a) nor (b)

5. In which view do you see headers and/or footers?
   (a) Print Layout view
   (b) Normal view
   (c) Both (a) and (b)
   (d) Neither (a) nor (b)

6. Which of the following numbering schemes can be used with page numbers?
   (a) Roman numerals (I, II, III . . . or i, ii, iii)
   (b) Regular numbers (1, 2, 3, . . .)
   (c) Letters (A, B, C . . . or a, b, c)
   (d) All of the above

7. Which of the following is a true statement regarding headers and footers?
   (a) Every document must have at least one header
   (b) Every document must have at least one footer
   (c) Both (a) and (b)
   (d) Neither (a) nor (b)

8. Which of the following is a *false* statement regarding lists?
   (a) A bulleted list can be changed to a numbered list and vice versa
   (b) The symbol for the bulleted list can be changed to a different character
   (c) The numbers in a numbered list can be changed to letters or roman numerals
   (d) The bullets or numbers cannot be removed

9. Page numbers can be specified in:
   (a) A header but not a footer
   (b) A footer but not a header
   (c) A header or a footer
   (d) Neither a header nor a footer

10. Which of the following is true regarding the formatting within a document?
    (a) Line spacing and alignment are implemented at the section level
    (b) Margins, headers, and footers are implemented at the paragraph level
    (c) Both (a) and (b)
    (d) Neither (a) nor (b)

. . . continued

11. What happens when you press the Tab key from within a table?

    (a) A Tab character is inserted just as it would be for ordinary text

    (b) The insertion point moves to the next column in the same row or the first column in the next row if you are at the end of the row

    (c) Both (a) and (b)

    (d) Neither (a) nor (b)

12. Which of the following is true about pagination in the current document given that the status bar displays "Page 5 Section 3 7/9"?

    (a) The document contains seven pages

    (b) The insertion point is on the seventh page of the document, which is numbered as page 5

    (c) The document cannot contain more than three sections

    (d) All of the above

13. The Edit Go To command enables you to move the insertion point to:

    (a) A specific page

    (b) A relative page forward or backward from the current page

    (c) A specific section

    (d) Any of the above

14. Once a table of contents has been created and inserted into a document:

    (a) Any subsequent page changes arising from the insertion or deletion of text to existing paragraphs must be entered manually

    (b) Any additions to the entries in the table arising due to the insertion of new paragraphs defined by a heading style must be entered manually

    (c) Both (a) and (b)

    (d) Neither (a) nor (b)

15. Which of the following is a *false* statement about the Outline view?

    (a) It can be collapsed to display only headings

    (b) It can be expanded to show the entire document

    (c) It requires the application of styles

    (d) It is used to create a conventional outline

16. What is the best way to create a conventional outline in a Word document?

    (a) Use the Outline view

    (b) Use the Outline Numbered tab within the Bullets and Numbering command

    (c) Use the Outlining toolbar

    (d) All of the above are equally acceptable

17. Which of the following is a predefined Word style that is available in every document?

    (a) Normal

    (b) Heading 1

    (c) Body Text

    (d) All of these answers are correct

18. What happens if you modify the Body Text style in a Word document?

    (a) Only the paragraph where the insertion point is located is changed

    (b) All paragraphs in the document will be changed

    (c) Only those paragraphs formatted with the Body Text style will be changed

    (d) It is not possible to change a Word default style such as Body Text

ANSWERS

1. d	7. d	13. d
2. c	8. d	14. d
3. b	9. c	15. d
4. a	10. d	16. b
5. a	11. b	17. d
6. d	12. b	18. c

PRACTICE WITH WORD

1. **The Résumé:** Microsoft Word includes a Résumé Wizard, but you can achieve an equally good result through the tables feature. Follow the instructions below to create a résumé similar to the document in Figure 4.11.

   a. Start a new document. Pull down the Table menu and click the Insert command to insert a table into your document. Specify that the table should contain two columns and eight rows. Additional rows can be added as needed. Conversely, rows can be deleted at a later time if they are not needed.

   b. Select the two cells in the first row and then merge those two cells. Enter your name in the cell and then center it within the cell. Change the font and font size as shown in Figure 4.11.

   c. Enter your addresses in the next row, entering your campus address, phone, and e-mail address in the cell on the left and your permanent address and phone in the cell on the right. Left align the text in the cell on the left, right align the text in the cell on the right. Be sure to include your e-mail address with your campus address.

   d. Enter the categories in the left cell of each row, being sure to include the following categories: Objective, Education, Honors, Scholarships, Work Experience, and References. Boldface and right align the text in these cells. (Not all of these categories are visible in Figure 4.11.)

   e. Enter the associated information in the right cell of each row. Be sure to include all information that would interest a prospective employer. Left align the text in these cells, using boldface and italic as appropriate.

   f. Select the entire table and remove the borders surrounding the individual cells. (Figure 4.11 displays gridlines, which—unlike borders—do not appear in the printed document.) Print the completed résumé for your instructor.

   g. Open the task pane. Click the down arrow in the title bar of the task pane to select New document. Click the link to Templates on my computer to display the Templates dialog box and then click the Other Documents tab. Print one or more of the suggested résumé templates. How do these designs compare to the résumé based on a table? Summarize your thoughts in a short note to your instructor.

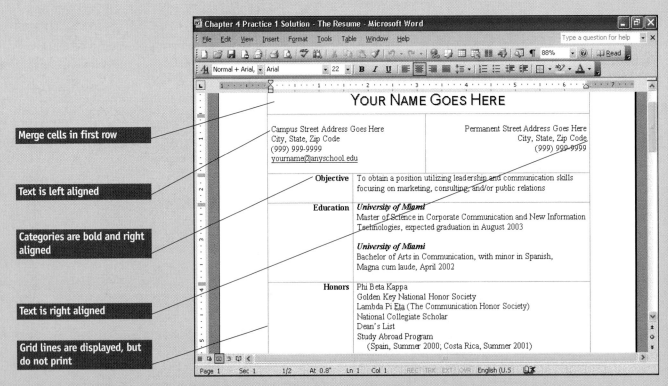

FIGURE 4.11 The Résumé (exercise 1)

2. **The Employment Application:** Use the tables feature to create a real or hypothetical employment application similar to the document in Figure 4.12. You can follow our design, or you can create your own. The Tables and Borders toolbar can be used in place of the Table menu to execute various commands during the exercise. Proceed as follows:

a. Create an 8 × 3 (eight rows and three columns) table to match our design. Select the entire table after it is created initially. Pull down the Format menu, click the Paragraph command, and then click the Indents and Spacing tab. Click the up spin arrow in the Space Before list box to enter six points. This will drop the text in each cell half a line from the top border of the cell, and also determine the spacing between paragraphs within a cell.

b. Merge the cells in the first row to create the title for the application. Enter the text for the first line, press Shift+Enter to create a line break instead of a paragraph break (to minimize the spacing between lines), then enter the text on the second line. Center the text. Select the first cell. Pull down the Format menu, click Borders and Shading, click the Shading tab, and choose Solid as the style. This creates white letters on a dark background.

c. Enter the text in the next several cells as shown in Figure 4.12. Move down in the table until you can select the cell for the highest degree attained. Enter the indicated text, click and drag to select all four degrees, and then pull down the Format menu. Click the Bullets and Numbering command and select the Bulleted tab. Select any bullet style, click the Customize button, click the Character button, select the WingDings font and choose the check box for the style. Click OK.

d. Merge the cells in row 7, then enter the text that asks the applicant to describe his or her computer skills in row 7. Merge the cells in row 8 (these cells are not visible in Figure 4.12) to create a single cell for employment references.

e. Click the down arrow on the zoom box to view the entire document. Change the row heights as necessary so that the completed application fills the entire page.

f. Complete the finished application as though you were applying for a job. Replace the check box next to the highest degree earned (remove the bullet) with the letter X. Submit the completed application to your instructor.

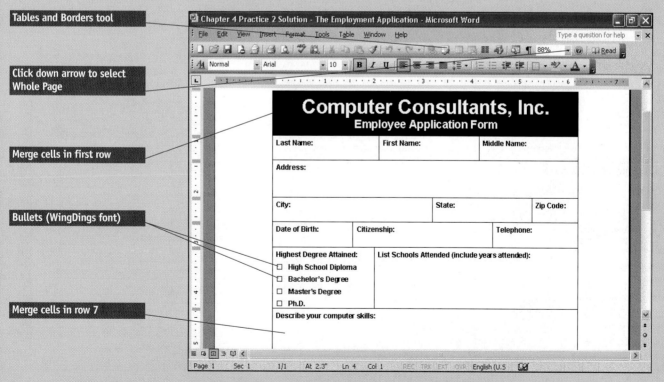

Tables and Borders tool

Click down arrow to select Whole Page

Merge cells in first row

Bullets (WingDings font)

Merge cells in row 7

FIGURE 4.12   The Employment Application (exercise 2)

3. **The Purchase of a PC:** You can purchase a PC from any number of vendors, each of which offers multiple models and typically enable you to upgrade individual components. It is important, therefore, to compare competing systems with respect to their features and cost in a table similar to Figure 4.13. Look closely, however, and you will see that the table is the third page of a three-page document that also contains a cover page as well as a set of tips to consider when selecting a system. Proceed as follows:

a. Open the *Chapter 4, Practice 3* document in the Exploring Word folder that contains a set of tips for purchasing a PC. Press Ctrl+Home to go to the beginning of the document, and then press Ctrl+Enter to insert a page break. Move to the beginning of the document and create a title page for this assignment that contains your name, today's date, and the same clip art image as the table in Figure 4.13.

b. The second page of the document contains various tips that we provide, but it is up to you to complete the formatting. Insert a title at the top of this page, "Tips for Buying a PC". Create a bulleted list for the tips on this page. Use boldface or italic for the title of each tip. Change the margins and/or the font size so that all of this information fits on one page.

c. Press Ctrl+End to move to the end of the document (the bottom of the second page). Pull down the Insert menu, click the Break command, then select Next Page under section break types. A section break is required because we are about to change the page orientation within a document.

d. Move to the third page, pull down the File menu and click the Page Setup command to change to Landscape orientation for the third page. (Look closely at the status bar in Figure 4.13 to see that Page 3 is in Section 2 of the document. The first two pages contain the title page and list of tips, respectively, and are in Section 1.)

e. Create the table in Figure 4.13. You need not follow our design exactly, but you are required to leave space for three competing systems. Insert the home page of each vendor as a hyperlink under the vendor's name. Insert clip art in the upper left of the table to add interest. (Use the Format Picture command to change the layout so that the clip art appears in front of the text.)

f. Print the completed document for your instructor.

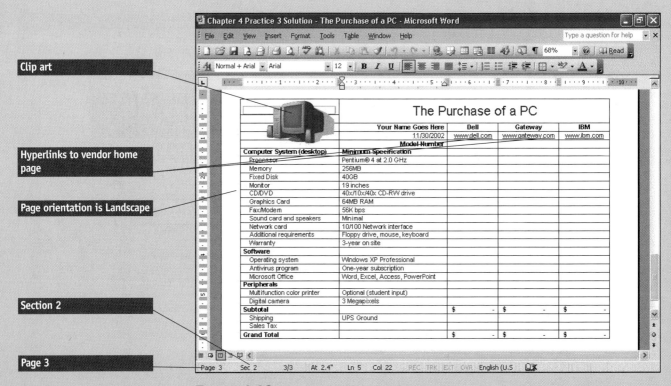

FIGURE 4.13   The Purchase of a PC (exercise 3)

4. **Bring Bailey Home:** Figure 4.14 displays a flyer that is intended to find Bailey, a combination Beagle/Jack Russell Terrier, and bring him home. You do not have to duplicate our document exactly, but you are to use a table as the basis of your document. You can create a document to search for Bailey, or you can use any pet you like. Proceed as follows:

a. Start a new document and insert a table with four rows and ten columns. Click outside the table, immediately to the left of the first cell in the first row to select the entire row. Pull down the Table menu and click the Merge Cells command. Merge the cells in rows 2 and 3 in similar fashion.

b. Click in the first row and enter the text of your message, e.g., "Bring Bailey Home." Select the text and increase the font size. The row height will increase automatically to accommodate the larger text. Center the text.

c. Select (the cell in) the second row. Pull down the Format menu, click the Borders and Shading command, click the Shading tab, then select solid (100% shading) in the Style area. Click OK. This will place a black background in the cell so that the picture you insert in the next step will appear to completely fill the cell.

d. Locate a picture of your pet. (We have provided a picture of Bailey in the Exploring Word folder.) Click in the second row, pull down the Insert menu, and insert the picture. The row height will expand automatically to accommodate the picture. Center the picture and size it appropriately.

e. Click in the third row and enter the appropriate text to describe your pet. Increase the size of the text appropriately and center it within the cell.

f. Enter your name and phone number in the first cell of the fourth row. Pull down the Format menu and click the Text Direction command to change the direction as shown in Figure 4.14. Align the text vertically to the top of the cell. Copy and paste the contents of this cell to the remaining cells in the row. Select the entire row and change the border style to a dashed line.

g. Click the down arrow on the Zoom list box to view the whole page. Use the Table Properties command in the Table menu to change the row heights as necessary so that your document fills the entire page. Adjust the font sizes as necessary.

h. Print the completed document for your instructor.

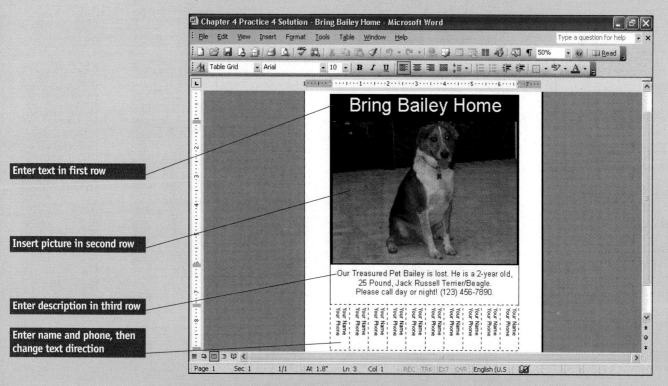

FIGURE 4.14 Bring Bailey Home (exercise 4)

5. **Classic Car for Sale:** The document in Figure 4.15 is a hypothetical flyer to advertise a classic car for sale. The document consists of text at the top of the page, three pictures, and a table with contact information. Use your imagination to create a similar document to sell any automobile. You do not have to match our design exactly, but you are required to include the table at the bottom of the document. Proceed as follows:

a. Start a new document. Center the title of the document as shown in the figure. Use the Borders and Shading command to display the title in light text on a solid background.

b. Write a short paragraph describing your vehicle. Include any extra equipment, a statement of condition, and the current mileage.

c. Use your favorite search engine to locate one or more pictures of the car you wish to sell. Download those photos to your PC.

d. Use the Insert Picture command to insert the photographs one at a time into the document. (If necessary, right click each photo after it has been inserted to display a context-sensitive menu, click the Format Picture command, and then click the Layout tab. Choose the appropriate option to help you position the picture within the text. You might also want to click the Size tab to set the dimensions of your picture more precisely.)

e. Create a 1 × 10 table (one row and ten columns) below the pictures. Enter your name and phone number in the first cell of the table. Pull down the Format menu and click the Text Direction command to change the direction as shown in Figure 4.15. Align the text to the top of the cell.

f. Copy and paste the contents of this cell to the remaining cells in the row. Select the entire row and change the border style to a dashed line.

g. Click the down arrow on the Zoom list box to view the whole page. Use the Table Properties command in the Table menu to change the row heights as necessary so that your document fills the entire page. Add text and photographs as necessary.

h. Print the completed document for your instructor.

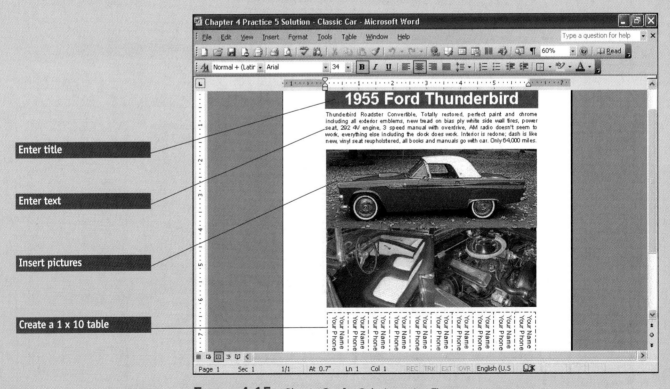

FIGURE 4.15 Classic Car for Sale (exercise 5)

6. **The Workout Schedule:** The table in Figure 4.16 is essentially an exercise in formatting, but it also tests your ability to copy efficiently within a document. You do not have to duplicate our document exactly, but you are required to have the equivalent functionality. Our schedule is for Monday through Friday (we take the weekend off), and it provides three sets for each exercise. You can create the document entirely on your own, or you can follow our suggested procedure.

   a. Start a new document. Pull down the File menu and click the Page Setup command. Change the orientation to landscape. Specify margins of one-half inch all around.

   b. Create a 5 × 17 table (5 rows and 17 columns), which includes the top portion of the table plus the first exercise. Select all but the first two cells in row two (the cells that will contain the days of the week). Pull down the Table menu, click the Table Properties command, click the Column tab, and then reduce the width of these columns to .45 inch. Change the width of the first two columns to 2.25 inches and 1 inch, respectively.

   c. Merge the cells in the first row, and then enter the indicated text. Format the text as you see fit. Insert an appropriate clip art image. (Select the clip art, pull down the Format menu, click Picture to display the Format Picture dialog box, and then click the Layout tab and change the wrapping style to position the clip art within the cell.) Copy the clip art as shown in the figure.

   d. Enter the text in rows 2 and 3 as shown. Use the Borders and Shading command in row 3 to select 100 percent (solid) shading to display white text on a dark background.

   e. Merge the first cell in rows 4 and 5. Type "Pounds" and "Reps" in the second cell in rows 4 and 5, respectively. Shade all but the first cell in row 5.

   f. Click and drag to select all of the cells in rows 4 and 5. Click the Copy button on the Standard toolbar (or use the Ctrl+C keyboard shortcut). Click the Paste button (or use the Ctrl+V keyboard shortcut) to paste the copied cells, effectively creating two additional rows for another exercise. Click the Paste button repeatedly until you have filled the page with space for additional exercises.

   g. Print the completed document for your instructor. Be sure the document fits on a single sheet of paper.

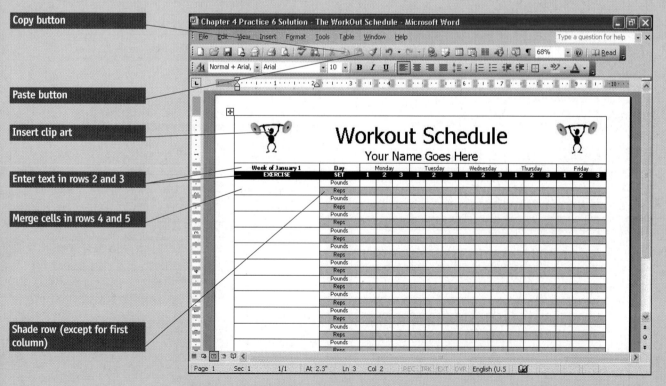

FIGURE 4.16 The Workout Schedule (exercise 6)

7. **Tips for Healthy Living:** The document in Figure 4.17 displays several tips from a document that contains tips for healthier living. The unformatted version of this document can be found in the *Chapter 4 Practice 7* document in the Exploring Word folder. Open that document, then modify it as follows:

a.   Use the AutoFormat command to apply the Heading 1 and Body Text styles throughout the document.

b.   Change the specifications for the Body Text and Heading 1 styles so that your document matches the document in the figure. The Heading 1 style calls for 12 point Arial bold with a blue top border (which requires a color printer). The Body Text style is 12 point Times New Roman, justified, with a ¼ inch left indent.

c.   Create a title page for the document consisting of the title, *Tips for Healthy Living*, the author, *Marion B. Grauer*, and an additional line, indicating that the document was prepared by you.

d.   Create a header for the document consisting of the title, *Tips for Healthy Living*, and a page number. (You can see the header in Figure 4.17.) The header is not to appear on the title page; that is, Page 1 is actually the second page of the document. Look closely at the status bar in Figure 4.17 and you will see that you are on Page 3, but that this is the fourth page of a six-page document.

e.   Click the Document Map button on the Standard toolbar to toggle the left pane on and off. The entries in the left pane correspond to all of the paragraphs in the document that are formatted in a heading style. Click any heading in the left pane and the corresponding text is displayed automatically in the right pane. (The Document Map button functions as a toggle switch.)

f.   Print the completed document for your instructor. Are you ready to follow the advice and adopt a healthier lifestyle?

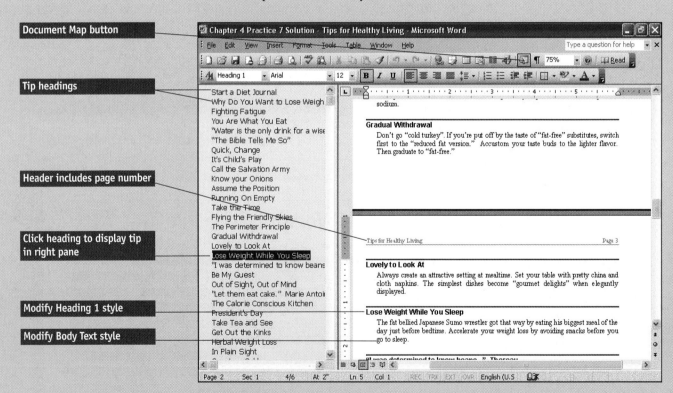

FIGURE 4.17   Tips for Healthy Living (exercise 7)

MINI CASES

Tips for Windows XP

Open the *Chapter 4 Mini Case—Tips for Windows XP* document that can be found in the Exploring Word folder. The tips are not formatted, so we would like you to use the AutoFormat command to create an attractive document. There are lots of tips, so a table of contents is also appropriate. Add a cover page with your name and date, then submit the completed document to your instructor.

Milestones in Communications

We take for granted immediate news of everything that is going on in the world, but it was not always that way. Did you know, for example, that it took five months for Queen Isabella to hear of Columbus' discovery, or that it took two weeks for Europe to learn of Lincoln's assassination? We've done some research on milestones in communications and left the file for you (*Chapter 4 Mini Case—Milestones in Communications*). It runs for two, three, or four pages, depending on the formatting, which we leave to you. We would like you to include a header, and we think you should box the quotations that appear at the end of the document (it's your call as to whether to separate the quotations or group them together). Please be sure to number the completed document and don't forget a title page.

The Term Paper

Go to your most demanding professor and obtain the formatting requirements for the submission of a term paper. Be as precise as possible; for example, ask about margins, type size, and so on. What are the requirements for a title page? Is there a table of contents? Are there footnotes or endnotes, headers or footers? What is the format for the bibliography? Summarize the requirements, then indicate the precise means of implementation within Microsoft Word.

Forms, Forms, and More Forms

Every business uses a multitude of forms. Job applicants submit an employment application, sales personnel process order forms, and customers receive invoices. Even telephone messages have a form of their own. The office manager needs forms for everything, and she has come to you for help. You remember reading something about a tables feature and suggest that as a starting point. She needs more guidance, so you sit down with her and quickly design two forms that meet with her approval. Bring the two forms to class and compare your work with that of your classmates.

Writing Style

Use your favorite search engine to locate documents that describe suggested writing style for research papers. You will find different guidelines for traditional documents versus those that are published on the Web. Can you create a sample document that implements the suggested specifications? Summarize your findings in a brief note to your professor.

Desktop Publishing: Creating a Newsletter and Other Documents

OBJECTIVES

1. Distinguish between formatting at the paragraph level versus the section level.
2. Design and implement a multicolumn newsletter.
3. Define a pull quote and a reverse; implement these techniques in Microsoft Word.
4. Define typography; explain how styles can be used to facilitate changes in design.
5. Insert clip art into a document; use the Format Picture command to move and size a graphic.
6. Describe the importance of a grid in the design of a document.
7. Use the Drawing toolbar to add objects to a Word document.
8. Create a Word document with dynamic links to an Excel worksheet and an Excel chart.

hands-on exercises

1. NEWSPAPER COLUMNS
   Input: Text for Newsletter
   Output: Newsletter Solution

2. COMPLETE THE NEWSLETTER
   Input: Newsletter Solution (from exercise 1)
   Output: Newsletter Solution (additional modifications)

3. OBJECT LINKING AND EMBEDDING
   Input: Acme Software (Excel workbook)
   Output: Acme Software Financial Statement (Word document)

CASE STUDY
NEW FROM THE WILD SIDE

Wild n' Wooly is a theme park that combines education about animal life with fun-filled activities such as roller coasters, water slides, and other attractions. The most unique feature about Wild n' Wooly is that every ride is developed around a specific animal or group. Attractions such as "Lambs and Kittens" or "Where Are the Monkeys?" are aimed at younger children. Other rides such as "An Elephant's Life" or "Lions and Tigers" are for older children and adults. Wild n' Wooly prides itself on the detail and accuracy of all its exhibits.

This summer Wild n' Wooly is introducing a new ride called "The Mouth of the Python" that traverses the entire park and boasts a total ride time of 20 minutes. One enters the mouth of the reptile and is immediately exposed to its habitat, natural history, and feeding techniques. The rider sees many types of pythons as he or she speeds through, or creeps through. It is educational, playful, and engaging, and typical of the wonderful rides throughout the park. Indeed, Wild n' Wooly has just been honored with the first annual Wildlife Federation award for creativity in animal life exhibits. This is incredibly exciting news, and the owners want to share this information with their customers by sending out a newsletter that announces the new ride and their recent award. ■

Your assignment is to read the chapter, paying special attention on how to create an attractive and informative newsletter. You will then apply what you have learned to create a one-page newsletter for the park. The design and content are up to you, but we expect some creative writing to describe the new ride and the recent award. The owners of the park have requested that you include a dominant piece of clip art to add interest to the newsletter. The newsletter should also include the hours of operation as well as your name. Print the completed document for inclusion in a class contest—the winner earns a one-year pass to all attractions at the park.

INTRODUCTION TO DESKTOP PUBLISHING

Desktop publishing evolved through a combination of technologies, including faster computers, laser printers, and sophisticated page composition software to manipulate text and graphics. Desktop publishing was initially considered a separate application, but today's generation of word processors has matured to such a degree that it is difficult to tell where word processing ends and desktop publishing begins. Microsoft Word is, for all practical purposes, a desktop publishing program that can be used to create all types of documents.

The essence of **desktop publishing** is the merger of text with graphics to produce a professional-looking document without reliance on external services. Desktop publishing will save you time and money because you are doing the work yourself rather than sending it out as you did in traditional publishing. That is the good news. The bad news is that desktop publishing is not as easy as it sounds, precisely because you are doing work that was done previously by skilled professionals. Nevertheless, with a little practice, and a basic knowledge of graphic design, you will be able to create effective and attractive documents.

Our chapter begins with the development of a simple newsletter in which we create a multicolumn document, import clip art and other objects, and position those objects within a document. The newsletter also reviews material from earlier chapters on bullets and lists, borders and shading, and section formatting.

THE NEWSLETTER

The newsletter in Figure 5.1 demonstrates the basics of desktop publishing and provides an overview of the chapter. The material is presented conceptually, after which you implement the design in two hands-on exercises. We provide the text and you do the formatting. The first exercise creates a simple newsletter from copy that we provide. The second exercise uses more sophisticated formatting as described by the various techniques mentioned within the newsletter. Many of the terms are new, and we define them briefly in the next few paragraphs.

A **reverse** (light text on a dark background) is a favorite technique of desktop publishers to emphasize a specific element. It is used in the **masthead** (the identifying information) at the top of the newsletter and provides a distinctive look to the publication. The number of the newsletter and the date of publication also appear in the masthead in smaller letters.

A **pull quote** is a phrase or sentence taken from an article to emphasize a key point. It is typically set in larger type, often in a different typeface and/or italics, and may be offset with parallel lines at the top and bottom.

A **dropped-capital letter** is a large capital letter at the beginning of a paragraph. It, too, catches the reader's eye and calls attention to the associated text.

Clip art, used in moderation, will catch the reader's eye and enhance almost any newsletter. It is available from a variety of sources including the Microsoft Media Gallery, which is included in Office XP. Clip art can also be downloaded from the Web, but be sure you are allowed to reprint the image. The banner at the bottom of the newsletter is not a clip art image per se, but was created using various tools on the **Drawing toolbar**.

Borders and shading are effective individually, or in combination with one another, to emphasize important stories within the newsletter. Simple vertical and/or horizontal lines are also effective. The techniques are especially useful in the absence of clip art or other graphics and are a favorite of desktop publishers.

Lists, whether bulleted or numbered, help to organize information by emphasizing important topics. A **bulleted list** emphasizes (and separates) the items. A **numbered list** sequences (and prioritizes) the items and is automatically updated to accommodate additions or deletions.

Creating a Newsletter

Volume I, Number 1   Fall 2003

Desktop publishing is easy, but there are several points to remember. This chapter will take you through the steps in creating a newsletter. The first hands-on exercise creates a simple newsletter with a masthead and three-column design. The second exercise creates a more attractive document by exploring different ways to emphasize the text.

Clip Art and Other Objects
Clip art is available from a variety of sources. You can also use other types of objects such as maps, charts, or organization charts, which are created by other applications, then brought into a document through the Insert Object command. A single dominant graphic is usually more appealing than multiple smaller graphics.

Techniques to Consider
Our finished newsletter contains one or more examples of each of the following desktop publishing techniques. Can you find where each technique is used, and further, explain, how to implement that technique in Microsoft Word?
1. Pull Quotes
2. Reverse
3. Drop Caps
4. Tables
5. Styles
6. Bullets and Numbering
7. Borders and Shading
8. The Drawing Toolbar

Newspaper-Style Columns
The essence of a newsletter is the implementation of columns in which text flows continuously from the bottom of one column to the top of the next. You specify the number of columns, and optionally, the space between columns. Microsoft Word does the rest. It will compute the width of each column based on the number of columns and the margins.

Beginners often specify margins that are too large and implement too much space between the columns. Another way to achieve a more sophisticated look is to avoid the standard two-column design. You can implement columns of varying width and/or insert vertical lines between the columns.

The number of columns will vary in different parts of a document. The masthead is typically a single column, but the body of the newsletter will have two or three. Remember, too, that columns are implemented at the section level and hence, section breaks are required throughout a document.

Typography
Typography is the process of selecting typefaces, type styles, and type sizes, and is a critical element in the success of any document. Type should reinforce the message and should be consistent with the information you want to convey. More is not better, especially in the case of too many typefaces and styles, which produce cluttered documents that impress no one. Try to limit yourself to a maximum of two typefaces per document, but choose multiple sizes and/or styles within those typefaces. Use boldface or italics for emphasis, but do so in moderation, because if you use too many different elements, the effect is lost.

A pull quote adds interest to a document while simultaneously emphasizing a key point. It is implemented by increasing the point size, changing to italics, centering the text, and displaying a top and bottom border on the paragraph.

Use Styles as Appropriate
Styles were covered in the previous chapter, but that does not mean you cannot use them in conjunction with a newsletter. A style stores character and/or paragraph formatting and can be applied to multiple occurrences of the same element within a document. Change the style and you automatically change all text defined by that style. You can also use styles from one edition of your newsletter to the next to insure consistency.

Borders and Shading
Borders and shading are effective individually or in combination with one another. Use a thin rule (one point or less) and light shading (five or ten percent) for best results. The techniques are especially useful in the absence of clip art or other graphics and are a favorite of desktop publishers.

All the News that Fits

FIGURE 5.1 The Newsletter

Typography

Typography is the process of selecting typefaces, type styles, and type sizes. It is a critical, often subtle, element in the success of a document, and its importance cannot be overstated. You would not, for example, use the same design to announce a year-end bonus and a plant closing. Indeed, good typography goes almost unnoticed, whereas poor typography calls attention to itself and detracts from a document. Our discussion reviews basic concepts and terminology that were presented in Chapter 2.

A ***typeface*** (or ***font***) is a complete set of characters (upper- and lowercase letters, numbers, punctuation marks, and special symbols). Typefaces are divided into two general categories, serif and sans serif. A ***serif typeface*** has tiny cross lines at the ends of the characters to help the eye connect one letter with the next. A ***sans serif typeface*** (sans from the French for *without*) does not have these lines. A commonly accepted practice is to use serif typefaces with large amounts of text and sans serif typefaces for smaller amounts. The newsletter in Figure 5.1, for example, uses ***Times New Roman*** (a serif typeface) for the text and ***Arial*** (a sans serif typeface) for the headings.

A second characteristic of a typeface is whether it is monospaced or proportional. A ***monospaced typeface*** (e.g., Courier New) uses the same amount of space for every character regardless of its width. A ***proportional typeface*** (e.g., Times New Roman or Arial) allocates space according to the width of the character. Monospaced fonts are used in tables and financial projections where items must be precisely lined up, one beneath the other. Proportional typefaces create a more professional appearance and are appropriate for most documents.

Any typeface can be set in different styles (such as bold or italic) to create *Times New Roman Italic*, **Arial bold**, or `Courier New Bold Italic`. Other effects are also possible, such as small caps, shadow, and outline, but these should be used with moderation.

Type size is a vertical measurement and is specified in points. One *point* is equal to $\frac{1}{72}$ of an inch. The text in most documents is set in 10 or 12 point type. (The book you are reading is set in 10 point.) Different elements in the same document are often set in different type sizes to provide suitable emphasis. A variation of at least two points, however, is necessary for the difference to be noticeable. The headings in the newsletter, for example, were set in 12 point type, whereas the text of the articles is in 10 point type.

The introduction of ***columns*** into a document poses another concern in that the type size should be consistent with the width of a column. Nine point type, for example, is appropriate in columns that are two inches wide, but much too small in a single-column term paper. In other words, longer lines or wider columns require larger type sizes.

There are no hard and fast rules for the selection of type, only guidelines and common sense. Your objective should be to create a document that is easy to read and visually appealing. You will find that the design that worked so well in one document may not work at all in a different document. Good typography is often the result of trial and error, and we encourage you to experiment freely. All of the techniques and definitions we have discussed can be implemented with commands you already know, as you will see in the hands-on exercise, which follows shortly.

USE MODERATION AND RESTRAINT

More is not better, especially in the case of too many typefaces and styles, which produce cluttered documents that impress no one. Try to limit yourself to a maximum of two typefaces per document, but choose multiple sizes and/or styles within those typefaces. Use boldface or italics for emphasis, but do so in moderation, because if you emphasize too many elements, the effect is lost. A simple design is often the best design.

The Columns Command

The columnar formatting in a newsletter is implemented through the ***Columns command*** as shown in Figure 5.2. Start by selecting one of the preset designs, and Microsoft Word takes care of everything else. It calculates the width of each column based on the number of columns, the left and right margins on the page, and the specified (default) space between columns.

Consider, for example, the dialog box in Figure 5.2, in which a design of three equal columns is selected with a spacing of ¼ inch between columns. The 2-inch width of each column is computed automatically based on left and right margins of 1 inch each and the ¼-inch spacing between columns. The width of each column is computed by subtracting the sum of the margins and the space between the columns (a total of 2½ inches in this example) from the page width of 8½ inches. The result of the subtraction is 6 inches, which is divided by 3, resulting in a column width of 2 inches.

You can change any of the settings in the Columns dialog box, and Word will automatically make the necessary adjustments. The newsletter in Figure 5.1, for example, uses a two-column layout with wide and narrow columns. We prefer this design to columns of uniform width, as we think it adds interest to our document. Note, too, that once columns have been defined, text will flow continuously from the bottom of one column to the top of the next.

Return for a minute to the newsletter in Figure 5.1, and notice that the number of columns varies from one part of the newsletter to another. The masthead is displayed over a single column at the top of the page, whereas the remainder of the newsletter is formatted in two columns of different widths. The number of columns is specified at the section level, and thus a ***section break*** is required whenever the column specification changes. A section break is also required at the end of the last column to balance the text within the columns.

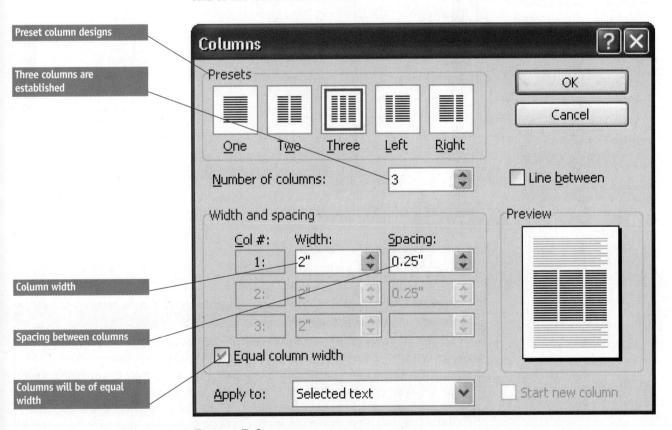

FIGURE 5.2 The Columns Command

1 Newspaper Columns

Objective To create a basic newsletter through the Format Columns command; to use section breaks to change the number of columns. Use Figure 5.3.

Step 1: **The Page Setup Command**

- Start Word. Open the **Text for Newsletter document** in the Exploring Word folder. Save the document as **Newsletter Solution**.
- Pull down the **File menu**. Click **Page Setup** to display the Page Setup dialog box as shown in Figure 5.3a.
- Click in the list box for the Top margin. Type **.75** and press the **Tab key** to move to the list box for the Bottom margin. Enter **.75** and press **Tab** again. Change the left and right margins in similar fashion. Click **OK** to accept these settings.
- Click the **Print Layout View button** above the status bar. Set the magnification (zoom) to **Page Width**.

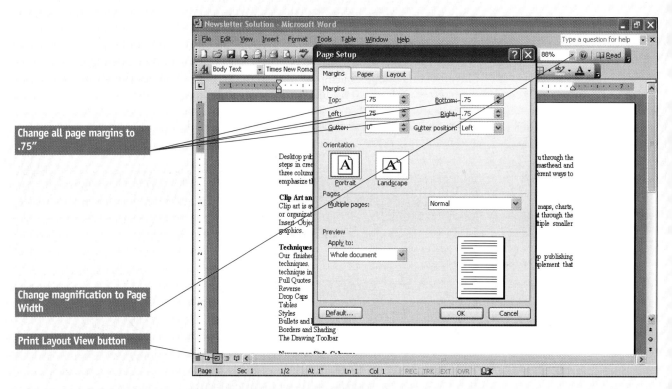

Change all page margins to .75"

Change magnification to Page Width

Print Layout View button

(a) The Page Setup Command (step 1)

FIGURE 5.3 Hands-on Exercise 1

CHANGE THE MEASUREMENT UNITS

We are used to working in inches, but what if you wanted to work in centimeters, points, or picas? (The latter two are common typographical measurements. There are 6 picas to the inch and 12 points in 1 pica. You are unlikely to use either measurement in an academic environment, but very likely to see the terms in a professional environment.) To change the measurement unit, pull down the Tools menu, click the Options command to display the Options dialog box, and click the General tab. Click the down arrow in the Measurement Unit list box to choose the desired unit, then click OK to accept the setting and close the dialog box.

Step 2: Check the Document

- Pull down the **Tools menu**, click **Options**, and click the **Spelling and Grammar tab**. Click the **drop-down arrow** on the Writing style list box and select **Grammar & Style**. Click **OK** to close the Options dialog box.

- Click the **Spelling and Grammar button** on the Standard toolbar to check the document for errors.

- The first error detected by the spelling and grammar check is the omitted hyphen between the words *three* and *column* as shown in Figure 5.3b. (This is a subtle mistake and emphasizes the need to check a document using the tools provided by Word.) Click **Change** to accept the indicated suggestion.

- Continue checking the document, accepting (or rejecting) the suggested corrections as you see fit.

- Save the document.

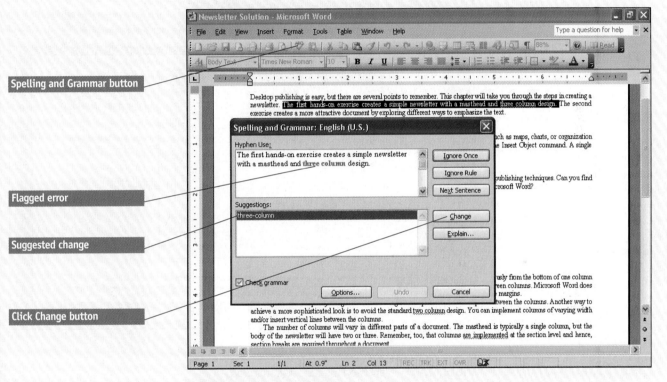

Spelling and Grammar button

Flagged error

Suggested change

Click Change button

(b) Check the Document (step 2)

FIGURE 5.3 Hands-on Exercise 1 (*continued*)

USE THE SPELLING AND GRAMMAR CHECK

Our eyes are less discriminating than we would like to believe, allowing misspellings and simple typos to go unnoticed. To prove the point, count the number of times the letter f appears in this sentence, *"Finished files are the result of years of scientific study combined with the experience of years."* The correct answer is six, but most people find only four or five. Checking your document takes only a few minutes. Do it!

Step 3: Implement Column Formatting

- Pull down the **Format menu**. Click **Columns** to display the dialog box in Figure 5.3c. Click the **Presets icon** for **Two**. The column width for each column and the spacing between columns will be determined automatically from the existing margins.

- If necessary, clear the **Line between box**. Click **OK** to accept the settings and close the Columns dialog box.

- The text of the newsletter should be displayed in two columns. If you do not see the columns, it is probably because you are in the wrong view. Click the **Print Layout View button** above the status bar to change to this view.

- Save the document.

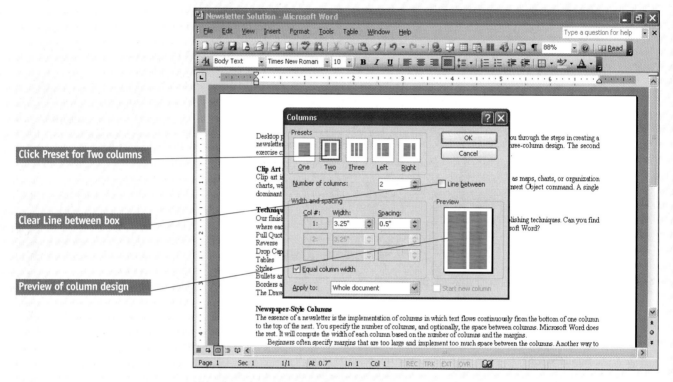

(c) Implement Column Formatting (step 3)

FIGURE 5.3   Hands-on Exercise 1 (*continued*)

PAGE BREAKS, COLUMN BREAKS, AND LINE BREAKS

Force Word to begin the next entry on a new page or column by inserting the proper type of break. Pull down the Insert menu, click the Break command to display the Break dialog box, then choose the option button for a page break or column break, respectively. It's easier, however, to use the appropriate shortcut, Ctrl+Enter or Shift+Ctrl+Enter, for a page or column break, respectively. You can also use Shift+Enter to force a line break, where the next word begins on a new line within the same paragraph. Click the Show/Hide button to display the hidden codes to see how the breaks are implemented.

Step 4: Balance the Columns

- Use the **Zoom box** on the Standard toolbar to zoom to **Whole Page** to see the entire newsletter as shown in Figure 5.3d. Do not be concerned if the columns are of different lengths.

- Press **Ctrl+End** to move the insertion point to the end of the document. Pull down the **Insert menu**. Click **Break** to display the Break dialog box in Figure 5.3d. Select the **Continuous option button** under Section breaks.

- Click **OK** to accept the settings and close the dialog box. The columns should be balanced, although one column may be one line longer than the other.

- Save the document.

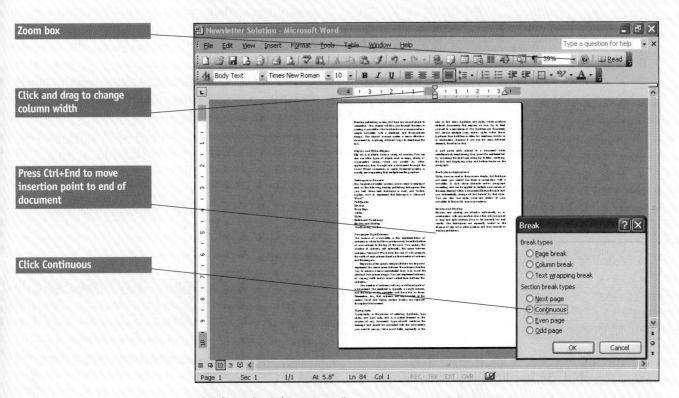

Zoom box

Click and drag to change column width

Press Ctrl+End to move insertion point to end of document

Click Continuous

(d) Balance the Columns (step 4)

FIGURE 5.3 Hands-on Exercise 1 (*continued*)

USE THE RULER TO CHANGE COLUMN WIDTH

Click anywhere within the column whose width you want to change, then point to the ruler and click and drag the right column margin (the mouse pointer changes to a double arrow) to change the column width. Changing the width of one column in a document with equal-sized columns changes the width of all other columns so that they remain equal. Changing the width in a document with unequal columns changes only that column. You can also double click the margin area on the ruler to display the Page Setup dialog box, then click the Margins tab to change the left and right margins, which in turn will change the column width.

Step 5: Create the Masthead

- Use the **Zoom box** on the Standard toolbar to change to **Page Width**. Click the **Show/Hide ¶ button** to display the paragraph and section marks.

- Press **Ctrl+Home** to move the insertion point to the beginning of the document. Pull down the **Insert menu**, click **Break**, select the **Continuous option button**, and click **OK**. You should see a double dotted line indicating a section break as shown in Figure 5.3e.

- Click immediately to the left of the dotted line, which will place the insertion point to the left of the line. Check the status bar to be sure you are in section one.

- Change the format for this section to a single column by clicking the **Columns button** on the Standard toolbar and selecting one column. (Alternatively, you can pull down the **Format menu**, click **Columns**, and choose **One** from the Presets column formats.)

- Type **Creating a Newsletter** and press the **Enter key** twice. Select the newly entered text, click the **Center button** on the Formatting toolbar. Change the font to **48 point Arial Bold**.

- Click underneath the masthead (to the left of the section break). Pull down the **Table menu**, click **Insert** to display a submenu, then click **Table**. Insert a table with one row and two columns as shown in Figure 5.3e.

- Click in the left cell of the table. Type **Volume I, Number 1**. Click in the right cell (or press the **Tab key** to move to this cell and type the current semester (for example, **Fall 2003**). Click the **Align Right button**.

- Save the document.

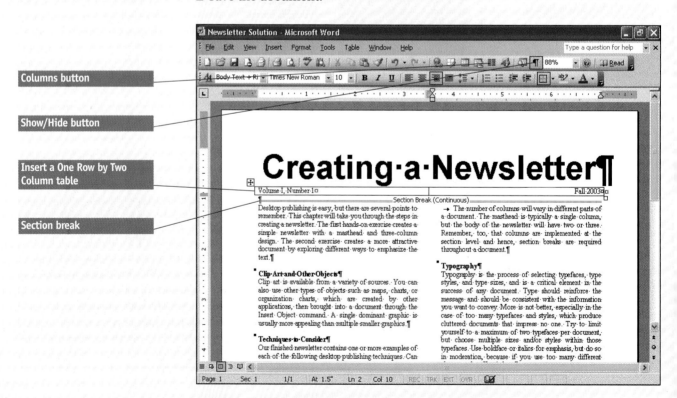

(e) Create the Masthead (step 5)

FIGURE 5.3 Hands-on Exercise 1 (*continued*)

Step 6: Create a Reverse

- Press **Ctrl+Home** to move the insertion point to the beginning of the newsletter. Click anywhere within the title of the newsletter.

- Pull down the **Format menu**, click **Borders and Shading** to display the Borders and Shading dialog box, then click the **Shading tab** in Figure 5.3f.

- Click the **drop-down arrow** in the Style list box (in the Patterns area) and select **Solid (100%)** shading. Click **OK** to accept the setting and close the dialog box. Click elsewhere in the document to see the results.

- The final step is to remove the default border that appears around the table. Click in the selection area to the left of the table to select the entire table.

- Pull down the **Format menu**, click **Borders and Shading**, and if necessary click the **Borders tab**. Click the **None icon** in the Presets area. Click **OK**. Click elsewhere in the document to see the result.

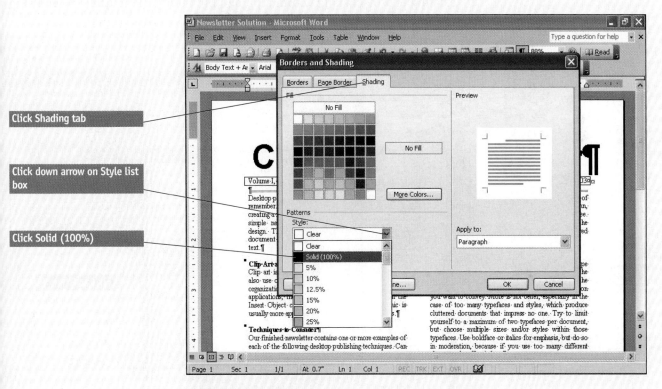

Click Shading tab

Click down arrow on Style list box

Click Solid (100%)

(f) Create a Reverse (step 6)

FIGURE 5.3 Hands-on Exercise 1 (*continued*)

LEFT ALIGNED   CENTERED   RIGHT ALIGNED

Many documents call for left-aligned, centered, and/or right-aligned text on the same line, an effect that is achieved through setting tabs, or more easily through a table. To achieve the effect shown at the top of this box, create a 1 × 3 table (one row and three columns), type the text in the cells, then use the buttons on the Formatting toolbar to left-align, center, and right-align the cells. Select the table, pull down the Format menu, click Borders and Shading, then specify None as the Border setting.

Step 7: Modify the Heading Style

- Two styles have been implemented for you in the newsletter. Click in any text paragraph, and you see the Body Text style name displayed in the Style box on the Formatting toolbar. Click in any heading, and you see the Heading 1 style.

- Pull down the **View menu** and click the **Task Pane command** to open the task pane. Click the **down arrow** within the task pane and choose **Styles and Formatting**.

- Point to the **Heading 1** style, click the **down arrow**, then click the **Modify command** to display the Modify Style dialog box shown in Figure 5.3g.

- Change the font to **Arial** and the font size to **12**. Click **OK** to accept the settings and close the dialog box. All of the headings in the document are changed automatically to reflect the changes in the Heading 1 style.

- Experiment with other styles as you see fit. (You can remove the formatting of existing text by clicking within a paragraph, then clicking **Clear Formatting** within the task pane.)

- Save the newsletter. Close the task pane.

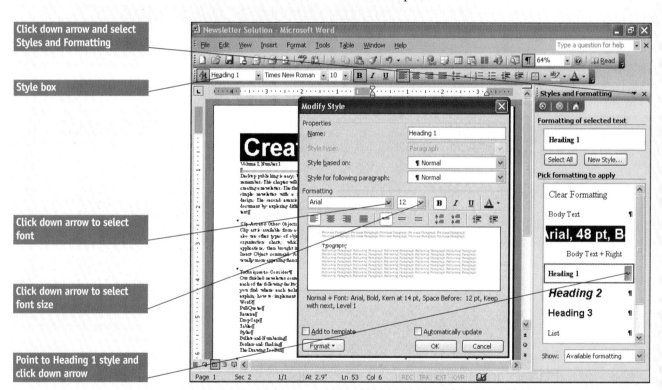

Click down arrow and select Styles and Formatting

Style box

Click down arrow to select font

Click down arrow to select font size

Point to Heading 1 style and click down arrow

(g) Modify the Heading Style (step 7)

FIGURE 5.3 Hands-on Exercise 1 (*continued*)

USE STYLES AS APPROPRIATE

Styles were covered in the previous chapter, but that does not mean you cannot use them in conjunction with a newsletter. A style stores character and/or paragraph formatting and can be applied to multiple occurrences of the same element within a document. Change the style and you automatically change all text defined by that style. Use the same styles from one edition of your newsletter to the next to ensure consistency. Use styles in any document to promote uniformity and increase flexibility.

Step 8: **The Print Preview Command**

- Legend has it that the Print Preview command originated when a Microsoft programmer tired of walking down the hall to pick up a printout of his/her document only to be frustrated when the document did not appear as intended.

- Pull down the **File menu** and click **Print Preview** (or click the **Print Preview button** on the Standard toolbar) to view the newsletter as in Figure 5.3h. This is a basic two-column newsletter with the masthead appearing as a reverse and stretching over a single column.

- Click the **Print button** to print the newsletter at this stage so that you can compare this version with the finished newsletter at the end of the next exercise.

- Click the **Close button** on the Print Preview toolbar to close the Preview view and return to the Page Layout view.

- Save the document. Exit Word if you do not want to continue with the next exercise at this time.

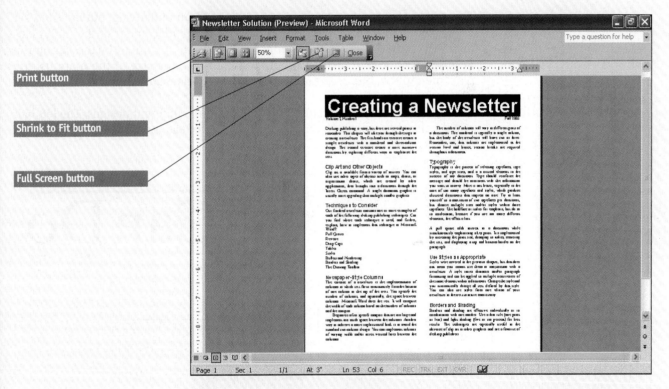

(h) The Print Preview Command (step 8)

FIGURE 5.3 Hands-on Exercise 1 (*continued*)

THE PRINT PREVIEW TOOLBAR

The Print Preview toolbar appears automatically when you switch to this view, and it contains several tools that are helpful prior to printing a document. The Shrink to Fit button is especially useful if a small portion of a document spills over to a second page—click this button, and it uniformly reduces the fonts throughout a document to eliminate the extra page. The down arrow on the Zoom box enables you to change the magnification to see more (less) of the page. The One Page/Multiple Page icons are useful with multipage documents. The View Ruler button toggles the display of the ruler on and off.

We trust you have completed the first hands-on exercise without difficulty and that you were able to duplicate the initial version of the newsletter. That, however, is the easy part of desktop publishing. The more difficult aspect is to develop the design in the first place because the mere availability of a desktop publishing program does not guarantee an effective document, any more than a word processor will turn its author into another Shakespeare. Other skills are necessary, and so we continue with a brief introduction to graphic design.

Much of what we say is subjective, and what works in one situation will not necessarily work in another. Your eye is the best judge of all, and you should follow your own instincts. Experiment freely and realize that successful design is the result of trial and error. Seek inspiration from others by collecting samples of real documents that you find attractive, then use those documents as the basis for your own designs.

The Grid

The design of a document is developed on a **grid**, an underlying, but *invisible,* set of horizontal and vertical lines that determine the placement of the major elements. A grid establishes the overall structure of a document by indicating the number of columns, the space between columns, the size of the margins, the placement of headlines, art, and so on. The grid does *not* appear in the printed document or on the screen.

Figure 5.4 shows the "same" document in three different designs. The left half of each design displays the underlying grid, whereas the right half displays the completed document.

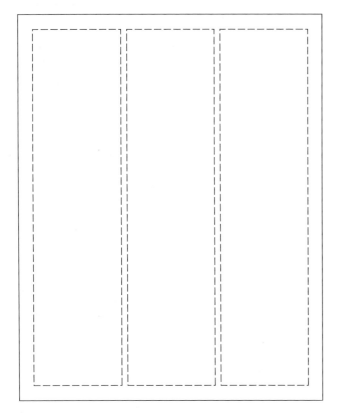

(a) Three-column Grid

FIGURE 5.4 The Grid System of Design

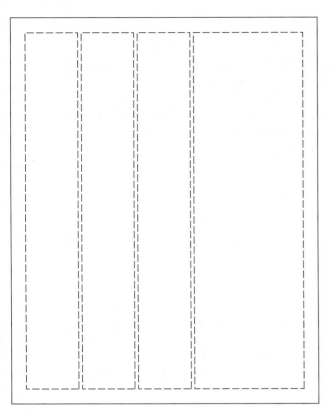

(b) Four-column Grid

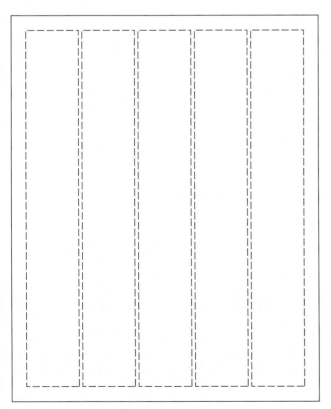

(c) Five-column Grid

FIGURE 5.4 The Grid System of Design (*continued*)

No Can Do

He felt more and more pressure to play the game of not playing. Maybe that's why he stepped in front of that truck.

People wonder why people do things like this, but all you have to do is look around and see all the stress and insanity each person in responsibility is required to put up with. There is no help or end in sight. It seems that managers are managing less and shoveling the workloads on to their underlings. This seems to be the overall response to the absence of raises or benefit packages they feel are their entitlement. Something must be done now!

People wonder why people do things like this, but all you have to do is look around and see all the stress and insanity each person in responsibility is required to put up with. There is no help or end in sight. It seems that managers are managing less and shoveling the workloads on to their underlings. This seems to be the overall response to the absence of raises or benefit packages they feel are their entitlement. Something must be done now!

People wonder why people do things like this, but all you have to do is look around and see all the stress and insanity each person in responsibility is required to put up with. There is no help or end in sight. It seems that managers are managing less. Something must be done now!

People wonder why people do things like this, but all you have to do is look around and see all the stress and insanity each person in responsibility is required to put up with. There is no help or end in sight. It seems that managers are managing less and shoveling the workloads on to their underlings. This seems to be the overall response to the ▼

People wonder why people do things like this, but all you have to do is look around and see all the stress and insanity each person in responsibility is required to put up with. There is no help or end in sight. It seems that managers are managing less and shoveling the workloads on to their underlings. This seems to be the overall response to the absence of raises or benefit packages they feel are their entitlement. Something must be done!

People wonder why people do things like this, but all you have to do is look around and see all the stress and insanity each person in responsibility is required to put up with. There is no help or end in sight. It seems that managers are managing less and shoveling the workloads on to their underlings. This seems to be the overall response to the absence of raises or benefit packages they feel are their entitlement. Something must be done!

He felt more and more pressure to play the game of not playing. Maybe that's why he stepped in front of that truck.

workloads on to their underlings. This seems to be the overall response to the absence of raises or benefit packages they feel are their entitlement. Some-thing must be done now!

People wonder why people do things like this, but all you have to do is look around and see all the stress and insanity each person in responsibility is required to put up with. There is no help or end in sight. It seems that managers are managing less and shoveling the workloads on to their underlings. Something must be done now!

People wonder why people do things like this, but all you have to do ▼

must be done!

People wonder why people do things like this, but all you have to do is look around and see all the stress and insanity each person in responsibility is required to put up with. There is no help or end in sight. It seems that managers are managing less and shoveling the workloads on to their underlings. This seems to be the overall response to the absence of raises or benefit packages they feel are their entitlement. Something must be done!

People wonder why people do things like this, but all you have to do is look around and see all the stress and insanity each person in responsibility is required to put up with. There is no help or end in sight. It seems that managers are managing less and shoveling the workloads on to their underlings. Something must be done now!

People wonder why people do things like this, but all you have to do ▼

A grid may be simple or complex, but it is always distinguished by the number of columns it contains. The three-column grid of Figure 5.4a is one of the most common and utilitarian designs. Figure 5.4b shows a four-column design for the same document, with unequal column widths to provide interest. Figure 5.4c illustrates a five-column grid that is often used with large amounts of text. Many other designs are possible as well. A one-column grid is used for term papers and letters. A two-column, wide-and-narrow format is appropriate for textbooks and manuals. Two- and three-column formats are used for newsletters and magazines.

The simple concept of a grid should make the underlying design of any document obvious, which in turn gives you an immediate understanding of page composition. Moreover, the conscious use of a grid will help you organize your material and result in a more polished and professional-looking publication. It will also help you to achieve consistency from page to page within a document (or from issue to issue of a newsletter). Indeed, much of what goes wrong in desktop publishing stems from failing to follow or use the underlying grid.

Emphasis

Good design makes it easy for the reader to determine what is important. As indicated earlier, *emphasis* can be achieved in several ways, the easiest being variations in type size and/or type style. Headings should be set in type sizes (at least two points) larger than body copy. The use of **boldface** is effective as are *italics,* but both should be done in moderation. (UPPERCASE LETTERS and <u>underlining</u> are alternative techniques that we believe are less effective.)

Boxes and/or shading call attention to selected articles. Horizontal lines are effective to separate one topic from another or to call attention to a pull quote. A reverse can be striking for a small amount of text. Clip art, used in moderation, will catch the reader's eye and enhance almost any newsletter. (Color is also effective, but it is more costly.)

Clip Art

Clip art is available from a variety of sources including the Microsoft Clip Organizer and Microsoft Web site. The Clip Organizer can be accessed in a variety of ways, most easily by clicking the appropriate link at the bottom of the Clip Art task pane. Once clip art has been inserted into a document, it can be moved and sized just like any other Windows object, as will be illustrated in our next hands-on exercise.

The *Format Picture command* provides additional flexibility in the placement of clip art. The Text Wrapping tab, in the Advanced Layout dialog box, determines the way text is positioned around a picture. The Top and Bottom option (no wrapping) is selected in Figure 5.5a, and the resulting document is shown in Figure 5.5b. The sizing handles around the clip art indicate that it is currently selected, enabling you to move and/or resize the clip art using the mouse. (You can also use the Size and Position tabs in the Format Picture dialog box for more precision with either setting.) Changing the size or position of the object, however, does not affect the way in which text wraps around the clip art.

The document in Figure 5.5c illustrates a different wrapping selection in which text is wrapped on both sides. Figure 5.5c also uses an option on the Colors and Lines tab to draw a blue border around the clip art. The document in Figure 5.5d eliminates the border and chooses the tight wrapping style so that the text is positioned as closely as possible to the figure in a free-form design. Choosing among the various documents in Figure 5.5 is one of personal preference. Our point is simply that Word provides multiple options, and it is up to you, the desktop publisher, to choose the design that best suits your requirements.

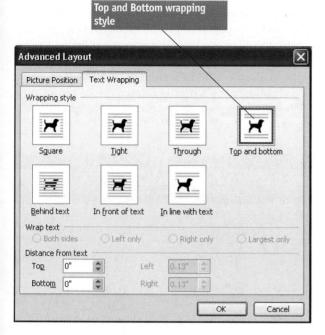

Top and Bottom wrapping style

(a) Advanced Layout Dialog Box

(b) Top and Bottom Wrapping

(c) Square Wrapping (both sides)

(d) Tight Wrapping (both sides)

FIGURE 5.5   The Format Picture Command

THE DRAWING TOOLBAR

Did you ever stop to think how the images in the Clip Organizer were developed? Undoubtedly they were drawn by someone with artistic ability who used basic shapes, such as lines and curves in various combinations, to create the images. The Drawing toolbar in Figure 5.6a contains all of the tools necessary to create original clip art. Select the Line tool for example, then click and drag to create the line. Once the line has been created, you can select it, then change its properties (such as thickness, style, or color) by using other tools on the Drawing toolbar. Draw a second line, or a curve—then, depending on your ability, you have a piece of original clip art.

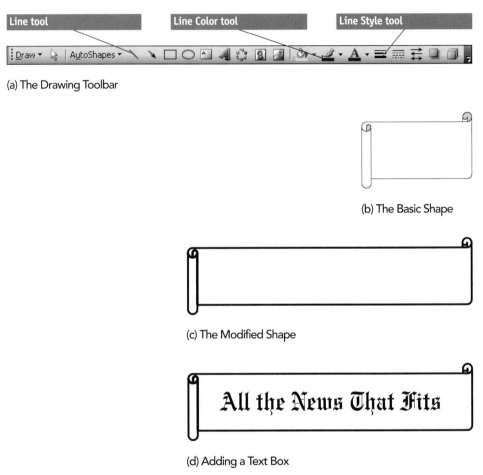

(a) The Drawing Toolbar

(b) The Basic Shape

(c) The Modified Shape

All the News That Fits

(d) Adding a Text Box

FIGURE 5.6   The Drawing Toolbar

We don't expect you to create clip art comparable to the images within the Clip Organizer. You can, however, use the tools on the Drawing toolbar to modify an existing image and/or create simple shapes of your own that can enhance any document. One tool that is especially useful is the AutoShapes button that displays a series of predesigned shapes. Choose a shape (the banner in Figure 5.6b), change its size and color (Figure 5.6c), then use the Textbox tool to add an appropriate message.

The Drawing toolbar is displayed through the Toolbars command in the View menu. The following exercise has you use the toolbar to create the banner and text in Figure 5.6d. It's fun, it's easy; just be flexible and willing to experiment. We think you will be pleased at what you will be able to do.

Objective   To insert clip art into a newsletter; to format a newsletter using styles, borders and shading, pull quotes, and lists. Use Figure 5.7a as a guide in the exercise.

Step 1:   Change the Column Layout

■ Open the **Newsletter Solution** document from the previous exercise. Click in the masthead and change the number of this edition from 1 to **2**. Click the **Show/Hide button** to hide the nonprinting characters.

■ Click anywhere in the body of the newsletter. The status bar should indicate that you are in the second section.

■ Pull down the **Format menu**. Click **Columns** to display the dialog box in Figure 5.7a. Click the **Left Preset icon**.

■ Change the width of the first column to **2.25** and the space between columns to **.25**. Check (click) the **Line Between box**. Click **OK**.

■ Save the newsletter.

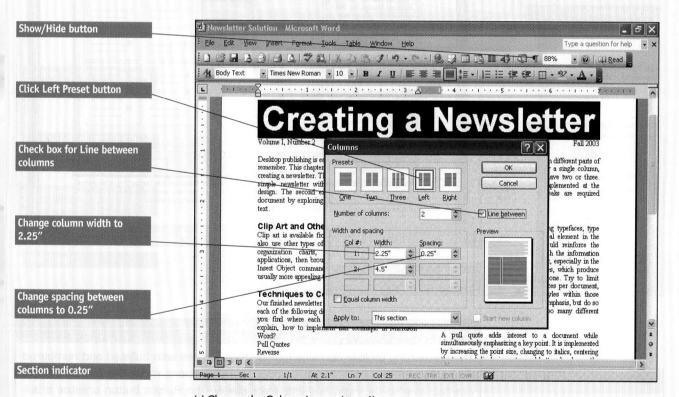

(a) Change the Column Layout (step 1)

FIGURE 5.7   Hands-on Exercise 2

EXPERIMENT WITH THE DESIGN

The number, width, and spacing of the columns in a newsletter is the most important element in its design. Experiment freely and try columns of varying width. Good design is often the result of trial and error. Use the Undo command as necessary to restore the document.

Step 4: Move and Size the Clip Art

- Click the **drop-down arrow** on the Zoom list box and select **Whole Page**.

- Point to the picture, click the **right mouse button** to display a context-sensitive menu, then click the **Format Picture command** to display the Format Picture dialog box as shown in Figure 5.7d.

- Click the **Layout tab**, choose the **Square layout**, then click the option button for left or right alignment. Click **OK** to close the dialog box. You can now move and size the clip art just like any other Windows object.

- To size the clip art, click anywhere within the clip art to select it and display the sizing handles. Drag a corner handle (the mouse pointer changes to a double arrow) to change the length and width of the picture simultaneously and keep the object in proportion.

- To move the clip art, click the object to select it and display the sizing handles. Point to any part of the object except a sizing handle (the mouse pointer changes to a four-sided arrow), then click and drag to move the clip art.

- Save the document.

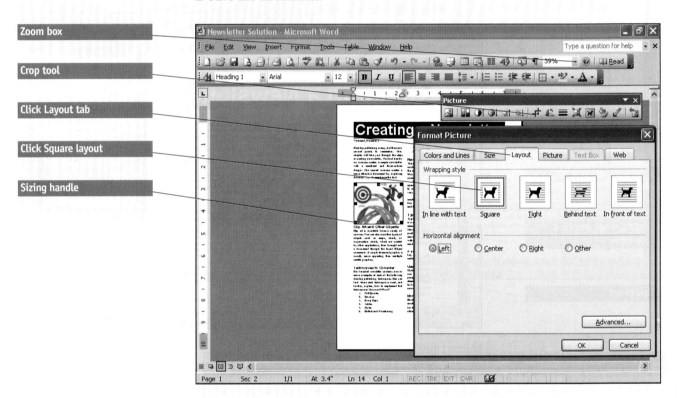

(d) Move and Size the Clip Art (step 4)

FIGURE 5.7   Hands-on Exercise 2 (*continued*)

CROPPING A PICTURE

Select a picture, and Word automatically displays the Picture toolbar, which enables you to modify the picture in subtle ways. The Crop tool enables you to eliminate (crop) part of a picture. Select the picture to display the Picture toolbar and display the sizing handles. Click the Crop tool (the ScreenTip will display the name of the tool), then click and drag a sizing handle to crop the part of the picture you want to eliminate.

Step 5: Borders and Shading

- Change to **Page Width** and click the **Show/Hide ¶ button** to display the paragraph marks. Press **Ctrl+End** to move to the end of the document, then select the heading and associated paragraph for Borders and Shading. (Do not select the ending paragraph mark.)

- Pull down the **Format menu**. Click **Borders and Shading**. If necessary, click the **Borders tab** to display the dialog box in Figure 5.4e. Click the **Box icon** in the Setting area. Click the **drop-down arrow** in the Width list box and select the **1 pt** line style.

- Click the **Shading tab**. Click the **drop-down arrow** in the Style list box (in the Patterns area) and select **5%** shading. Click **OK** to accept the setting.

- Click elsewhere in the document to see the results. The heading and paragraph should be enclosed in a border with light shading.

- Save the document.

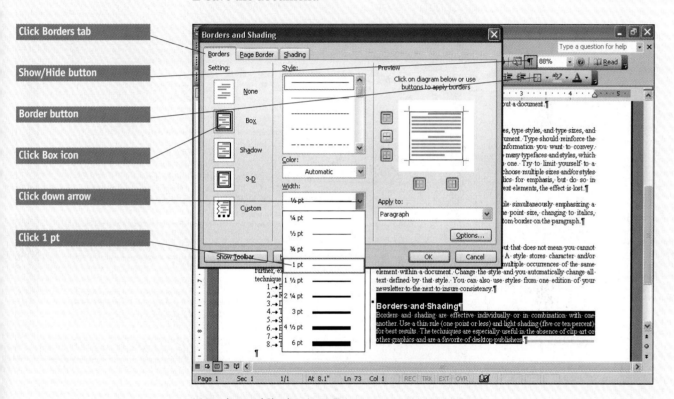

(e) Borders and Shading (step 5)

FIGURE 5.7 Hands-on Exercise 2 (*continued*)

USE THE TOOLBAR

The Border button on the Formatting toolbar changes the style of the border for the selected text. That tool is also accessible from the Tables and Borders toolbar, which contains additional tools to insert or merge cells and/or to change the line style, thickness, or shading within a table. If the toolbar is not visible, point to any visible toolbar, click the right mouse button to show the list of toolbars, then click the Tables and Borders toolbar to display it on your screen.

Step 6: **Create a Pull Quote**

- Scroll to the bottom of the document until you find the paragraph describing a pull quote. Select the entire paragraph and change the text to **14 point Arial italic**.

- Click in the paragraph to deselect the text, then click the **Center button** to center the paragraph.

- Click the **drop-down arrow** on the **Border button** to display the different border styles as shown in Figure 5.7f.

- Click the **Top Border button** to add a top border to the paragraph.

- Click the **Bottom border button** to create a bottom border and complete the pull quote.

- Save the document.

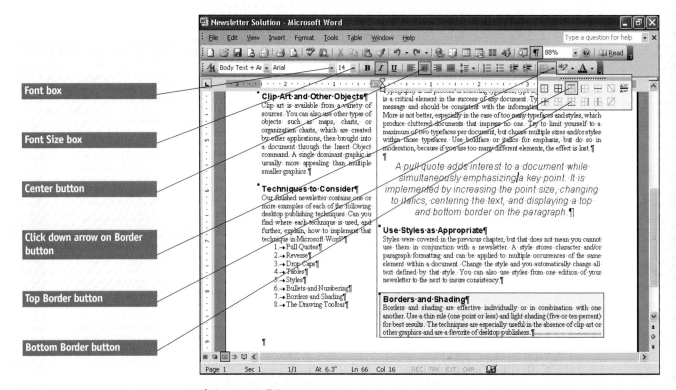

(f) Create a Pull Quote (step 6)

FIGURE 5.7 Hands-on Exercise 2 (*continued*)

EMPHASIZE WHAT'S IMPORTANT

Good design makes it easy for the reader to determine what is important. A pull quote (a phrase or sentence taken from an article) adds interest to a document while simultaneously emphasizing a key point. Boxes and shading are also effective in catching the reader's attention. A simple change in typography, such as increasing the point size, changing the typeface, and/or the use of boldface or italic, calls attention to a heading and visually separates it from the associated text.

Step 7:　Create a Drop Cap

- Scroll to the beginning of the newsletter. Click immediately before the D in *Desktop publishing*.

- Pull down the **Format menu**. Click the **Drop Cap command** to display the dialog box in Figure 5.7g.

- Click the **Position icon** for **Dropped** as shown in the figure. We used the default settings, but you can change the font, size (lines to drop), or distance from the text by clicking the arrow on the appropriate list box.

- Click **OK** to create the Drop Cap dialog box. Click outside the frame around the drop cap.

- Save the newsletter.

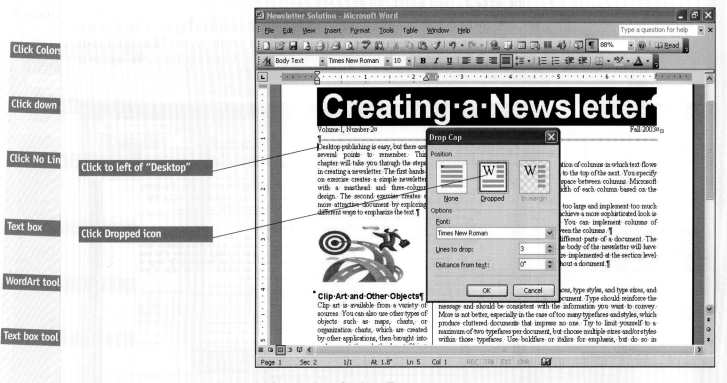

(g) Create a Drop Cap (step 7)

FIGURE 5.7　Hands-on Exercise 2 (*continued*)

MODIFYING A DROP CAP

Select (click) a dropped-capital letter to display a thatched border known as a frame, then click the border or frame to display its sizing handles. You can move and size a frame just as you can any other Windows object; for example, click and drag a corner sizing handle to change the size of the frame (and the drop cap it contains). Experiment with different fonts to increase the effectiveness of the dropped-capital letter, regardless of its size. To delete the frame (and remove the drop cap), press the delete key.

Step 2:   Copy the Worksheet

- Click the **Start button**, click **All Programs**, click **Microsoft Office**, then click **Microsoft Office Excel 2003** to start Excel. The taskbar now contains buttons for both Word and Excel. Click either button to move back and forth between the open applications. End in Excel.

- Pull down the **File menu** and click the **Open command** (or click the **Open button** on the Standard toolbar) to display the Open dialog box.

- Click the **down arrow** on the Look in list box to select the Exploring Word folder that you have used throughout the text. Open the **Acme Software workbook**.

- Click the **Sales Data** worksheet tab. Click and drag to select **cells A1 through F7** as shown in Figure 5.9b.

- Pull down the **Edit menu** and click the **Copy command** (or click the **Copy button** on the Standard toolbar). A moving border appears around the entire worksheet, indicating that it has been copied to the clipboard.

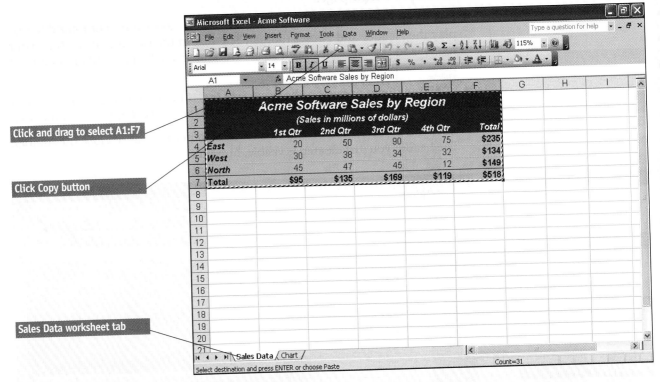

(b) Copy the Worksheet (step 2)

FIGURE 5.9   Hands-on Exercise 3 (*continued*)

THE COMMON USER INTERFACE

The common user interface provides a sense of familiarity from one Office application to the next. Even if you have never used Microsoft Excel, you will recognize many of the elements that are present in Word. The applications share a common menu structure with consistent ways to execute commands from those menus. The Standard and Formatting toolbars are present in both applications. Many keyboard shortcuts are also common; for example: Ctrl+X, Ctrl+C, and Ctrl+V to cut, copy, and paste, respectively.

Step 7: Create a Drop Cap

- Scroll to the beginning of the newsletter. Click immediately before the D in *Desktop publishing*.

- Pull down the **Format menu**. Click the **Drop Cap command** to display the dialog box in Figure 5.7g.

- Click the **Position icon** for **Dropped** as shown in the figure. We used the default settings, but you can change the font, size (lines to drop), or distance from the text by clicking the arrow on the appropriate list box.

- Click **OK** to create the Drop Cap dialog box. Click outside the frame around the drop cap.

- Save the newsletter.

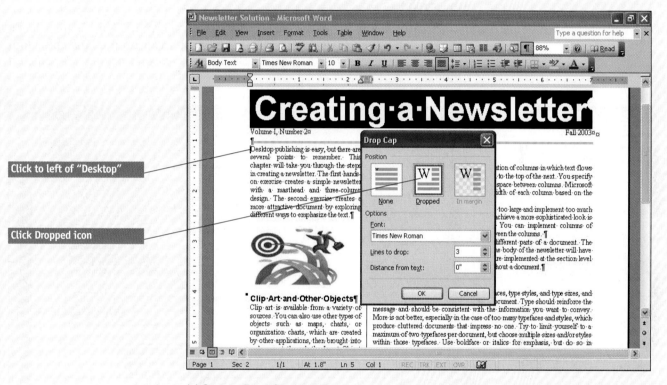

(g) Create a Drop Cap (step 7)

FIGURE 5.7   Hands-on Exercise 2 (*continued*)

MODIFYING A DROP CAP

Select (click) a dropped-capital letter to display a thatched border known as a frame, then click the border or frame to display its sizing handles. You can move and size a frame just as you can any other Windows object; for example, click and drag a corner sizing handle to change the size of the frame (and the drop cap it contains). Experiment with different fonts to increase the effectiveness of the dropped-capital letter, regardless of its size. To delete the frame (and remove the drop cap), press the delete key.

Step 8: Create the AutoShape

- Click the **Show/Hide button** to hide the nonprinting characters. Pull down the **View menu**, click (or point to) the **Toolbars command** to display the list of available toolbars, then click the **Drawing toolbar** to display this toolbar.

- Press **Ctrl+End** to move to the end of the document. Click the **down arrow** on the AutoShapes button to display the AutoShapes menu. Click the **Stars and Banners submenu** and select (click) the **Horizontal scroll**.

- Press **Esc** to remove the drawing canvas. The mouse pointer changes to a tiny crosshair. Click and drag the mouse at the bottom of the newsletter to create the scroll as shown in Figure 5.7h.

- Release the mouse. The scroll is still selected as can be seen by the sizing handles. (You can click and drag the yellow diamond to change the appearance of the scroll.)

- Click the **Line Style tool** to display this menu as shown in Figure 5.7h. Select a thicker line (we chose **3 points**). Click the **down arrow** on the **Line color tool** to display the list of colors (if you have access to a color printer. We selected **blue**).

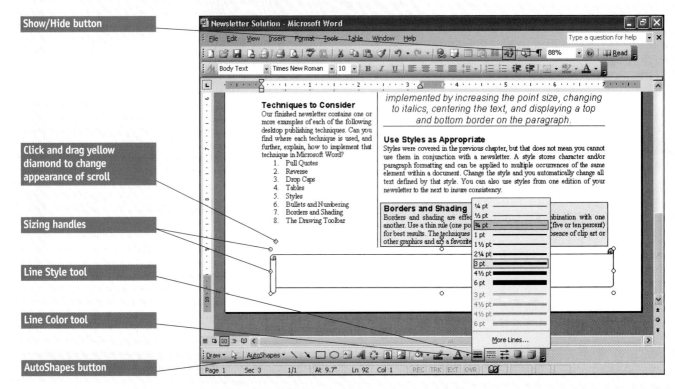

(h) Create the AutoShape (step 8)

FIGURE 5.7 Hands-on Exercise 2 (*continued*)

DISPLAY THE AUTOSHAPES TOOLBAR

Click the down arrow on the AutoShapes button on the Drawing toolbar to display a cascaded menu listing the various types of AutoShapes, then click and drag the move handle at the top of the menu to display the menu as a floating toolbar. Click any item on the AutoShapes toolbar (such as Stars and Banners), then click and drag its move handle to display the various buttons in their own floating toolbar.

Step 9: Create the Text Box

- Click the **Text Box tool**, then click and drag within the banner to create a text box as shown in Figure 5.7i. Type **All the News that Fits** as the text of the banner. Click the **Center button** on the Formatting toolbar.

- Click and drag to select the text, click the **down arrow** on the **Font Size list box**, and select a larger point size (22 or 24 points). If necessary, click and drag the bottom border of the text box, and/or the bottom border of the AutoShape, in order to see all of the text. Click the **down arrow** on the **Font list box** and choose a different font.

- Right click the text box to display a context-sensitive menu, then click the **Format Text Box command** to display the Format Text Box dialog box as shown in Figure 5.7i. Click the **Colors and Lines tab** (if necessary), click the **down arrow** next to Color in the Line section, click **No Line**, then click **OK** to accept the settings and close the dialog box.

- Click anywhere in the document to deselect the text box. Save the document.

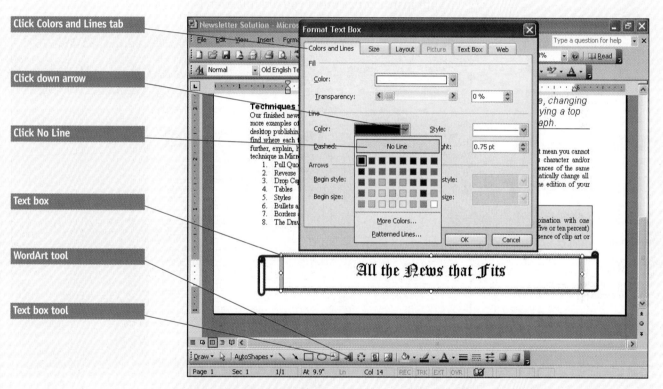

(i) Create the Text Box (step 9)

FIGURE 5.7   Hands-on Exercise 2 (*continued*)

DON'T FORGET WORDART

Microsoft WordArt is another way to create decorative text to add interest to a document. Pull down the Insert menu, click Picture, click WordArt, choose the WordArt style, and click OK. Enter the desired text, then click OK to create the WordArt object. You can click and drag the sizing handles to change the size or proportion of the text. Use any tool on the WordArt toolbar to further change the appearance of the object.

Step 10: **The Completed Newsletter**

- Zoom to **Whole Page** to view the completed newsletter as shown in Figure 5.7j.

- Select the clip art to display the Picture toolbar as shown in Figure 5.7j. Click the **Increase/Decrease Brightness tools** to see the effect on the clip art. Select the brightness level you like best.

- The newsletter should fit on a single page, but if not, there are several techniques that you can use:
  - Pull down the **File menu**, click the **Page Setup command**, click the **Margins tab**, then reduce the top and/or bottom margins to **.5** inch. Be sure to apply this change to the **Whole document** within the Page Setup dialog box.
  - Change the **Heading 1 style** to reduce the point size to **10 points** and/or the space before the heading to **6 points**.
  - Click the **Print Preview button** on the Standard toolbar, then click the **Shrink to Fit button** on the Print Preview toolbar.

- Save the document a final time. Print the completed newsletter and submit it to your instructor as proof you did this exercise.

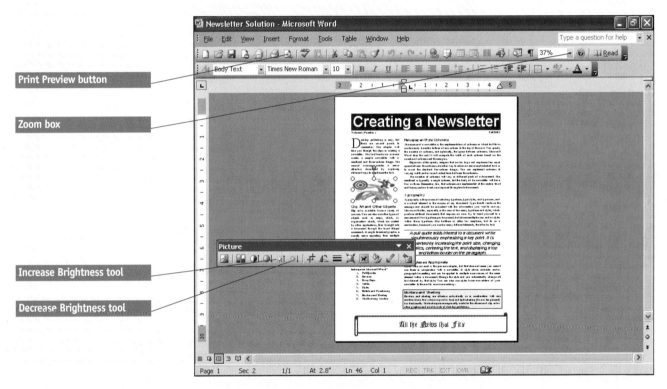

(j) The Completed Newsletter (step 10)

FIGURE 5.7 Hands-on Exercise 2 (*continued*)

A FINAL WORD OF ADVICE

Desktop publishing is not a carefree operation. It is time-consuming to implement, and you will be amazed at the effort required for even a simple document. Computers are supposed to save time, not waste it, and while desktop publishing is clearly justified for some documents, the extensive formatting is not necessary for most documents. And finally, remember that the content of a document is its most important element.

Microsoft Office enables you to create documents that contain data (objects) from multiple applications. The document in Figure 5.8a, for example, was created in Microsoft Word, but it contains objects (a worksheet and a chart) that were developed in *Microsoft Excel*. *Object Linking and Embedding* (*OLE*, pronounced "oh-lay") is the means by which you create the document.

Every Excel chart is based on numerical data that is stored in a worksheet. Figures 5.8b and 5.8c enlarge the worksheet and chart that appear in the document of Figure 5.8a. The worksheet shows the quarterly sales for each of three regions, East, West, and North. There are 12 *data points* (four quarterly values for each of three regions). The data points are grouped into *data series* that appear as rows or columns in the worksheet. (The chart was created through the Chart Wizard that prompts you for information about the source data and the type of chart you want. Any chart can be subsequently modified by choosing appropriate commands from the Chart menu.)

The data in the chart is plotted by rows or by columns, depending on the message you want to convey. Our data is plotted by rows to emphasize the amount of sales in each quarter, as opposed to the sales in each region. Note that when the data is plotted by rows, the first row in the worksheet will appear on the X axis of the chart, and the first column will appear as the legend. Conversely, if you plot the data by columns, the first column appears on the X axis, and the first row appears as a legend.

Look closely at Figures 5.8b and 5.8c to see the correspondence between the worksheet and the chart. The data is plotted by rows. Thus there are three rows of data (three data series), corresponding to the values in the Eastern, Western, and Northern regions, respectively. The entries in the first row appear on the X axis. The entries in the first column appear as a legend to identify the value of each column in the chart. The chart is a *side-by-side column chart* that shows the value of each data point separately. You could also create a *stacked column chart* for each quarter that would put the columns one on top of another. And, as with the stacked-column chart, you have your choice of plotting the data in rows or columns.

After the chart has been created, it is brought into the Word document through Object Linking and Embedding. The essential difference between linking and embedding depends on where the object is stored. An embedded object is physically within the Word document. A *linked object*, however, is stored in its own file, which may in turn be tied to many documents. The same Excel chart, for example, can be linked to a Word document and a PowerPoint presentation or to multiple Word documents and/or to multiple presentations. Any changes to a linked object (the Excel chart) are automatically reflected in all of the documents to which it is linked. An *embedded object*, however, is stored within the Word document and it is no longer tied to its source. Thus, any changes made in the original object or in the embedded object are not reflected in one another.

EMPHASIZE YOUR MESSAGE

A graph exists to deliver a message, and you want that message to be as clear as possible. One way to help put your point across is to choose a title that leads the audience. A neutral title such as *Sales Data* does nothing and requires the audience to reach its own conclusion. A better title might be *Eastern Region Has Record 3rd Quarter* to emphasize the results in the individual sales offices. Conversely, *Western Region Has a Poor Year* conveys an entirely different message. This technique is so simple that we wonder why it isn't used more frequently.

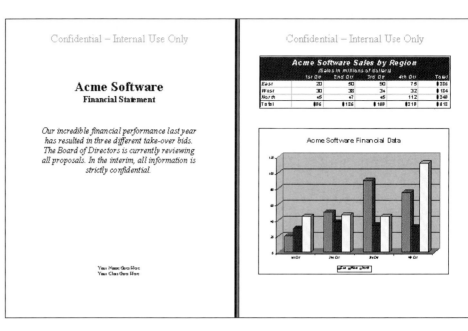

(a) The Word Document

Acme Software Sales by Region					
(Sales in millions of dollars)					
	1st Qtr	2nd Qtr	3rd Qtr	4th Qtr	Total
East	20	50	90	75	$235
West	30	38	34	32	$134
North	45	47	45	112	$249
Total	$95	$135	$169	$219	$618

(b) The Excel Worksheet

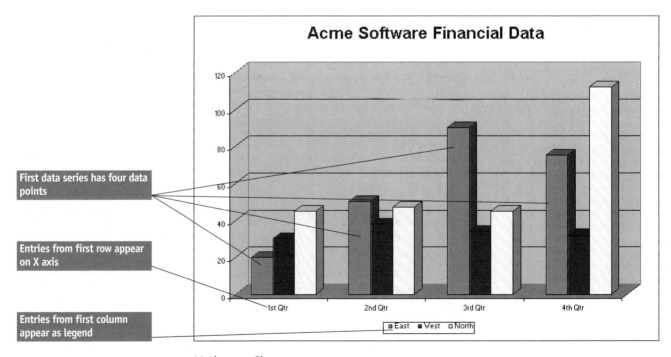

First data series has four data points

Entries from first row appear on X axis

Entries from first column appear as legend

(c) Alternate Chart

FIGURE 5.8 Object Linking and Embedding

3 Object Linking and Embedding

Objective Use object linking to create a Word document that contains an Excel worksheet and an Excel chart. Use Figure 5.9 as a guide in the exercise.

Step 1: **Create the Title Page**

- Start Word. Close the task pane. If necessary, click the **New Blank Document button** on the Standard toolbar to open a new document.

- Press the **Enter key** 6 or 7 times, then enter the title of the document, **Acme Software Financial Statement**, **your name**, and the **course number** with appropriate formatting.

- Save the document as **Confidential Memo** as shown in Figure 5.9a.

- Click the **Print Layout View button** above the status bar, then click the **down arrow** on the Zoom list box and select **Two Pages**. Your document currently takes only a single page.

- Pull down the **View menu** and click the **Header and Footer command** to display the Header and Footer toolbar. The text in the document (its title, your name, and class) is dim since you are working in the header and footer area of the document.

- Click the **down arrow** on the Font Size box and change to **28 points**. Click inside the header and enter **Confidential - Internal Use Only**. Center the text.

- Click the **Close button** on the Header and Footer toolbar to close the toolbar. The header you just created is visible, but dim.

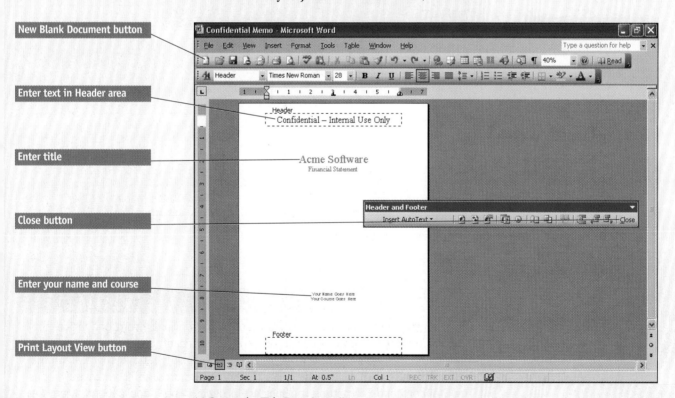

New Blank Document button

Enter text in Header area

Enter title

Close button

Enter your name and course

Print Layout View button

(a) Create the Title Page (step 1)

FIGURE 5.9 Hands-on Exercise 3

Step 2: Copy the Worksheet

- Click the **Start button**, click **All Programs**, click **Microsoft Office**, then click **Microsoft Office Excel 2003** to start Excel. The taskbar now contains buttons for both Word and Excel. Click either button to move back and forth between the open applications. End in Excel.

- Pull down the **File menu** and click the **Open command** (or click the **Open button** on the Standard toolbar) to display the Open dialog box.

- Click the **down arrow** on the Look in list box to select the Exploring Word folder that you have used throughout the text. Open the **Acme Software workbook**.

- Click the **Sales Data** worksheet tab. Click and drag to select **cells A1 through F7** as shown in Figure 5.9b.

- Pull down the **Edit menu** and click the **Copy command** (or click the **Copy button** on the Standard toolbar). A moving border appears around the entire worksheet, indicating that it has been copied to the clipboard.

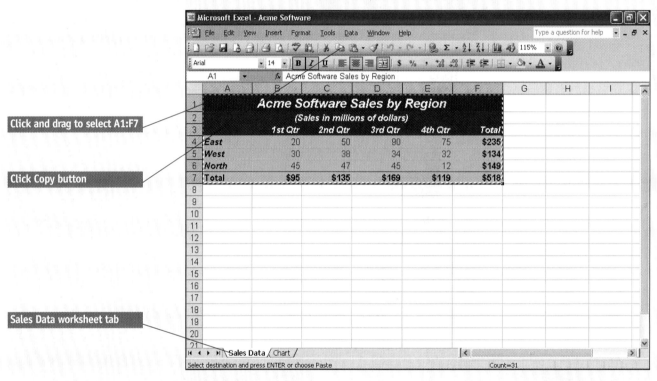

(b) Copy the Worksheet (step 2)

FIGURE 5.9 Hands-on Exercise 3 (*continued*)

THE COMMON USER INTERFACE

The common user interface provides a sense of familiarity from one Office application to the next. Even if you have never used Microsoft Excel, you will recognize many of the elements that are present in Word. The applications share a common menu structure with consistent ways to execute commands from those menus. The Standard and Formatting toolbars are present in both applications. Many keyboard shortcuts are also common; for example: Ctrl+X, Ctrl+C, and Ctrl+V to cut, copy, and paste, respectively.

Step 3: Create the Link

- Click the **Word button** on the taskbar to return to the document as shown in Figure 5.9c. Press **Ctrl+End** to move to the end of the document, which is where you will insert the Excel worksheet.

- Press **Ctrl+Enter** to create a page break, which adds a second page to the document. This page is blank except for the header, which appears automatically.

- Pull down the **Edit menu** and click **Paste Special** to display the dialog box in Figure 5.9c. Select **Microsoft Excel Worksheet Object**. Click the **Paste Link Option button**. Click **OK** to insert the worksheet into the document.

- Do not be concerned about the size or position of the worksheet at this time. Press the **Enter key** twice to create a blank line between the worksheet and the chart, which will be added later.

- Save the document.

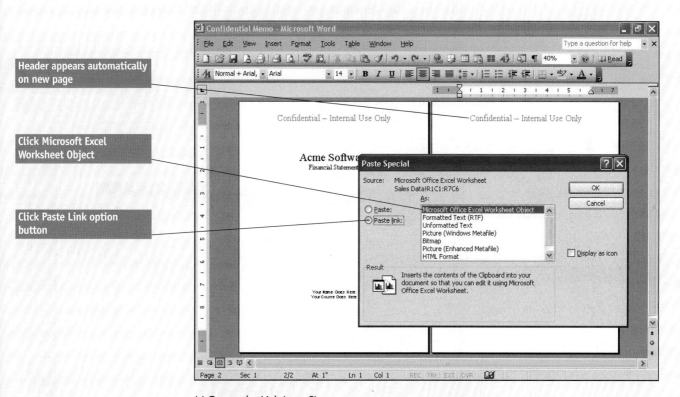

Header appears automatically on new page

Click Microsoft Excel Worksheet Object

Click Paste Link option button

(c) Create the Link (step 3)

FIGURE 5.9 Hands-on Exercise 3 *(continued)*

THE WINDOWS TASKBAR

Multitasking, the ability to run multiple applications at the same time, is one of the primary advantages of the Windows environment. Each button on the taskbar appears automatically when its application or folder is opened and disappears upon closing. (The buttons are resized automatically according to the number of open windows.) You can customize the taskbar by right clicking an empty area to display a shortcut menu, then clicking the Properties command. You can resize the taskbar by pointing to the inside edge and then dragging when you see the double-headed arrow. You can also move the taskbar to the left or right edge, or to the top of the desktop, by dragging a blank area of the taskbar to the desired position.

Step 4: Format the Object

■ Point to the newly inserted worksheet, click the **right mouse button** to display a context-sensitive menu, then click the **Format Object command** to display the dialog box in Figure 5.9d.

■ Click the **Layout tab** and choose **Square**. Click the option button to **Center** the object. Click **OK**. You can now move and size the object.

■ Select (click on) the worksheet to display its sizing handles. Click and drag a corner sizing handle to enlarge the worksheet, keeping it in its original proportions.

■ Click and drag any element except a sizing handle to move the worksheet within the document.

■ Right click the worksheet a second time and click the **Format Object command** to display the associated dialog box. Click the **Colors and Lines tab**, click the **drop-down arrow** next to color in the line area and choose **black**. Click the **Spin button** next to weight and choose **.25**.

■ Click **OK** to accept these settings and close the dialog box. Save the document.

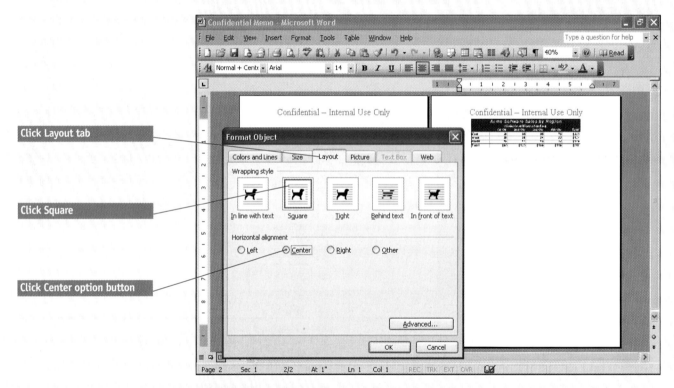

(d) Format the Object (step 4)

FIGURE 5.9 Hands-on Exercise 3 (*continued*)

TO CLICK OR DOUBLE CLICK

An Excel chart that is linked with or embedded into a Word document retains its connection to Microsoft Excel for easy editing. Click the chart to select it within the Word document, then move and size the chart just as any other object. (You can also press the Del key to delete the graph from a document.) Click outside the chart to deselect it, then double click the chart to restart Microsoft Excel (the chart is bordered by a hashed line), at which point you can edit the chart using the tools of the original application.

Step 5: Copy the Chart

■ Click the **Excel button** on the taskbar to return to the worksheet. Click outside the selected area (cells A1 through F7) to deselect the cells.

■ Click the **Chart tab** to select the chart sheet. Point just inside the white border of the chart, then click the left mouse button to select the chart. Be sure you have selected the entire chart as shown in Figure 5.9e.

■ Pull down the **Edit menu** and click **Copy** (or click the **Copy button** on the Standard toolbar). Once again you see the moving border, indicating that the selected object (the chart in this example) has been copied to the clipboard.

■ Click the **Word button** on the taskbar to return to the document.

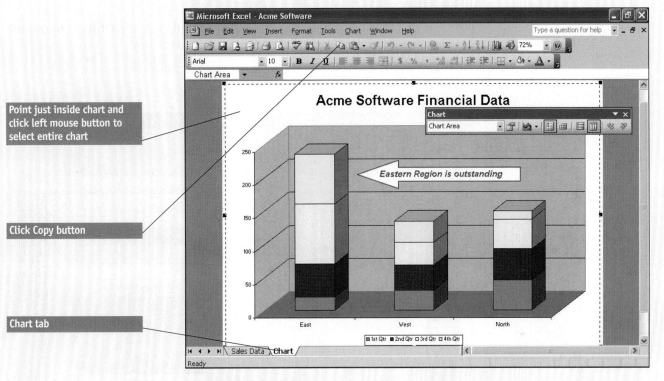

Point just inside chart and click left mouse button to select entire chart

Click Copy button

Chart tab

(e) Copy the Chart (step 5)

FIGURE 5.9 Hands-on Exercise 3 (*continued*)

KEEP IT SIMPLE

Microsoft Excel provides unlimited flexibility with respect to the charts it creates. You can, for example, right click any data series within a graph and click the Format Data Series command to change the color, fill pattern, or shape of a data series. There are other options, such as the 3-D View command that lets you fine-tune the graph by controlling the rotation, elevation, and other parameters. It's fun to experiment, but the best advice is to keep it simple and set a time limit, at which point the project is finished. Use the Undo command at any time to cancel your last action(s).

Step 6:   **Complete the Word Document**

- You should be back in the Word document, where you may need to insert a few blank lines, so that the insertion point is beneath the spreadsheet. Press **Ctrl+End** to move to the end of the document, where you will insert the chart.

- Pull down the **Edit menu**, click the **Paste Special command**, and click the **Paste Link Option button**. If necessary, click **Microsoft Excel Chart Object**.

- Click **OK** to insert the chart into the document. (Do not be concerned if you do not see the entire chart.)

- Select the chart, pull down the **Format menu**, and click the **Object command**.

- Select the **Layout tab** and change the layout to **Square**. **Center** the chart. Click **OK**.

- Pull down the **Format menu** a second time and click the **Object command**. Select the **Color and Lines tab**, and add a **.25″ black line**.

- Move and size the chart as shown in Figure 5.9f. Save the document. Print this version of the document for your instructor.

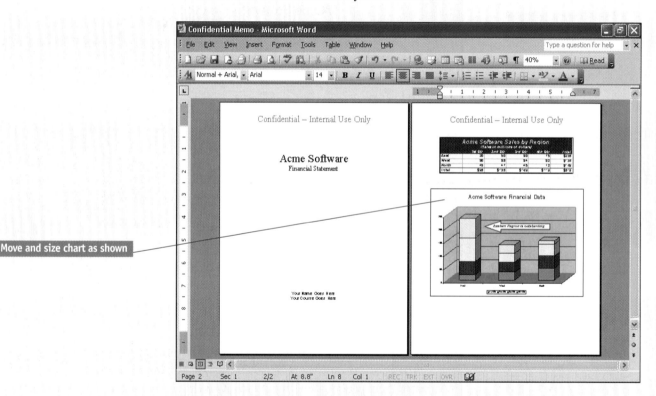

(f) Complete the Word Document (step 6)

FIGURE 5.9   Hands-on Exercise 3 (*continued*)

LINKING VERSUS EMBEDDING

The Paste Special command will link or embed an object, depending on whether the Paste Link or Paste Option button is checked. Linking stores a pointer to the file containing the object together with a reference to the server application, and changes to the object are automatically reflected in all documents that are linked to the object. Embedding stores a copy of the object with a reference to the server application, but changes to the object are not reflected in the document that originally contained the embedded (rather than linked) object.

Step 7: Modify the Chart

- Click the **Excel button** on the taskbar to return to Excel. Click the **Sales Data tab** to return to the worksheet.

- Click in **cell E6**, the cell containing the sales data for the Northern region in the fourth quarter. Type **112**, then press **Enter**. The sales totals for the region and quarter change to $249 and $219, respectively.

- Click the tab for the chart sheet. The chart has changed automatically to reflect the change in the underlying data. The columns for the Eastern and Northern regions are approximately the same size.

- Pull down the **Chart menu** and click the **Chart Type command** to display the Chart Type dialog box. Click the **Standard Types tab**. Select the **Clustered Column Chart with 3D Visual Effect** subtype (the first chart in the second row).

- Click **OK** to accept this chart type and close the dialog box. The chart type changes to side-by-side columns as shown in Figure 5.9g.

- Select the arrow on the chart. Press the **Del key** since the text is no longer applicable. Save the workbook.

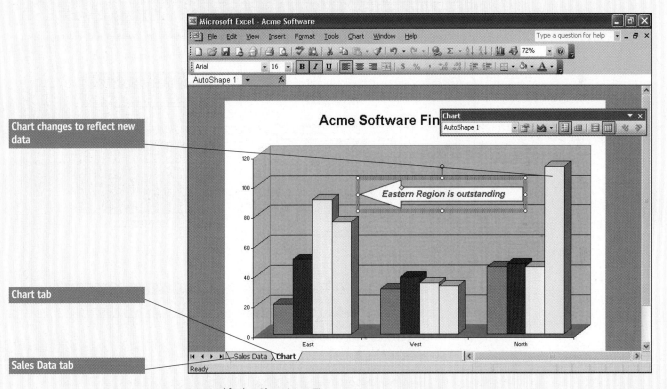

(g) Modify the Chart (step 7)

FIGURE 5.9 Hands-on Exercise 3 (*continued*)

THE DRAWING TOOLBAR

The Drawing toolbar is common to all applications in Microsoft Office. Click the down arrow next to the AutoShapes button to display the various shape menus, then click Block Arrows to display the arrows that are available. Select an arrow. The mouse pointer changes to a tiny crosshair that you click and drag to create the arrow within the document. Right click the arrow, then click the Add Text command to enter text within the arrow. Use the other buttons to change the color or other properties.

Step 8: The Modified Document

- Click the **Word button** on the taskbar to return to the Word document, which should automatically reflect the new chart and associated worksheet. (If this is not the case, right click the chart and click the **Update Link command**. Repeat the process to update the worksheet.)

- Move and/or resize the chart and spreadsheet within the Word document as necessary. Save the document.

- Complete the document by adding text as appropriate as shown in Figure 5.9h. You can use the text in our document that describes a confidential takeover, or make up your own.

- Save the document a final time. Click the **Print button** on the Standard toolbar to print the document for your instructor.

- Exit Word. Congratulations on a job well done.

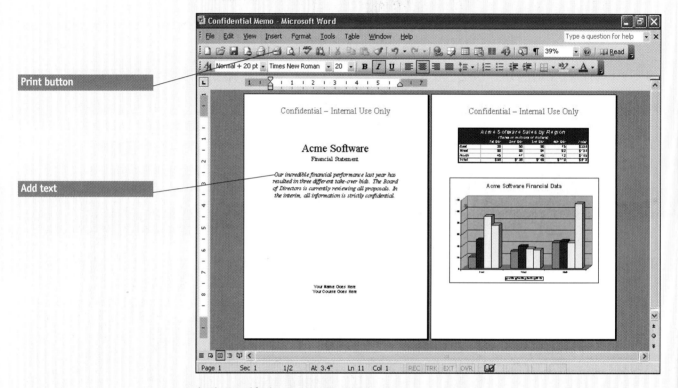

(h) The Modified Document (step 8)

FIGURE 5.9 Hands-on Exercise 3 (*continued*)

ALT+TAB STILL WORKS

Alt+Tab was a treasured shortcut in the original version of Windows that enabled users to switch back and forth between open applications. The shortcut also works in all subsequent versions of Windows. Press and hold the Alt key while you press and release the Tab key repeatedly to cycle through the open applications, whose icons are displayed in a small rectangular window in the middle of the screen. Release the Alt key when you have selected the icon for the application you want.

SUMMARY

The essence of desktop publishing is the merger of text with graphics to produce a professional-looking document. Proficiency in desktop publishing requires knowledge of the associated commands in Microsoft Word, as well as familiarity with the basics of graphic design.

Typography is the process of selecting typefaces, type styles, and type sizes. A typeface (or font) is a complete set of characters (upper- and lowercase letters, numbers, punctuation marks, and special symbols). Type size is a vertical measurement and is specified in points. One point is equal to $\frac{1}{72}$ of an inch.

The design of a document is developed on a grid, an underlying but invisible set of horizontal and vertical lines that determine the placement of the major elements. A newsletter can be divided into any number of newspaper-style columns in which text flows from the bottom of one column to the top of the next. Columns are implemented by clicking the Columns button on the Standard toolbar or by selecting the Columns command from the Format menu. Sections are required if different column arrangements are present in the same document. The Page Layout view is required to see the columns displayed side by side.

Emphasis can be achieved in several ways, the easiest being variations in type size and/or type style. Boxes and/or shading call attention to selected articles in a document. Horizontal lines are effective in separating one topic from another or calling attention to a pull quote (a phrase or sentence taken from an article to emphasize a key point). A reverse (light text on a solid background) is striking for a small amount of text.

Clip art is available from a variety of sources, including the Clip Art task pane, which is accessed through the Insert Picture command. Once clip art has been inserted into a document, it can be moved and sized just like any other Windows object. The Format Picture command provides additional flexibility and precision in the placement of an object. The Drawing toolbar contains various tools that are used to insert and/or modify objects into a Word document.

Graphic design does not have hard and fast rules, only guidelines and common sense. Creating an effective document is an iterative process and reflects the result of trial and error. We encourage you to experiment freely with different designs.

Object linking and embedding enables the creation of a document containing data (objects) from multiple applications. The essential difference between linking and embedding is whether the object is stored within the document (embedding) or stored within its own file (linking). The advantage of linking is that any changes to the linked object are automatically reflected in every document that is linked to that object.

KEY TERMS

MULTIPLE CHOICE

1. Which of the following is a commonly accepted guideline in typography?

   (a) Use a serif typeface for headings and a sans serif typeface for text

   (b) Use a sans serif typeface for headings and a serif typeface for text

   (c) Use a sans serif typeface for both headings and text

   (d) Use a serif typeface for both headings and text

2. According to the guidelines in the chapter, which of the following is most appropriate for the masthead of a newsletter?

   (a) A serif font at 45 points

   (b) A sans serif font at 45 points

   (c) A serif font in 12 point bold italics

   (d) A sans serif font in 12 point bold italics

3. What is the width of each column in a document with two uniform columns, given 1¼-inch margins and ½-inch spacing between the columns?

   (a) 2½ inches

   (b) 2¾ inches

   (c) 3 inches

   (d) Impossible to determine

4. What is the minimum number of sections in a three-column newsletter whose masthead extends across all three columns, with text *balanced* in all three columns?

   (a) One

   (b) Two

   (c) Three

   (d) Four

5. Which of the following describes the Arial and Times New Roman fonts?

   (a) Arial is a sans serif font, Times New Roman is a serif font

   (b) Arial is a serif font, Times New Roman is a sans serif font

   (c) Both are serif fonts

   (d) Both are sans serif fonts

6. How do you balance the columns in a newsletter so that each column contains the same amount of text?

   (a) Check the Balance Columns box in the Format Columns command

   (b) Visually determine where the break should go, then insert a column break at the appropriate place

   (c) Insert a continuous section break at the end of the last column

   (d) All of the above

7. What is the effect of dragging one of the four corner handles on a selected object?

   (a) The length of the object is changed but the width remains constant

   (b) The width of the object is changed but the length remains constant

   (c) The length and width of the object are changed in proportion to one another

   (d) Neither the length nor width of the object is changed

8. Which type size is the most reasonable for columns of text, such as those appearing in the newsletter created in the chapter?

   (a) 6 point

   (b) 10 point

   (c) 14 point

   (d) 18 point

9. A grid is applicable to the design of:

   (a) Documents with one, two, or three columns and moderate clip art

   (b) Documents with four or more columns and no clip art

   (c) Both (a) and (b)

   (d) Neither (a) nor (b)

10. Which of the following can be used to add emphasis to a document?

    (a) Borders and shading

    (b) Pull quotes and reverses

    (c) Both (a) and (b)

    (d) Neither (a) nor (b)

... continued

multiple choice

11. Which of the following is a recommended guideline in the design of a typical newsletter?

    (a) Use at least three different clip art images in every newsletter

    (b) Use at least three different typefaces in a document to maintain interest

    (c) Use the same type size for the heading and text of an article

    (d) None of the above

12. Which of the following is implemented at the section level?

    (a) Columns

    (b) Margins

    (c) Both (a) and (b)

    (d) Neither (a) nor (b)

13. How do you size an object so that it maintains the original proportion between height and width?

    (a) Drag a sizing handle on the left or right side of the object to change its width, then drag a sizing handle on the top or bottom edge to change the height

    (b) Drag a sizing handle on any of the corners

    (c) Both (a) and (b)

    (d) Neither (a) nor (b)

14. A reverse is implemented:

    (a) By selecting 100% shading in the Borders and Shading command

    (b) By changing the Font color to black

    (c) Both (a) and (b)

    (d) Neither (a) nor (b)

15. The Format Picture command enables you to:

    (a) Change the way in which text is wrapped around a figure

    (b) Change the size of a figure

    (c) Place a border around a figure

    (d) All of the above

16. Which of the following should be *avoided* according to the guidelines presented in the chapter?

    (a) Large amounts of white space in the middle of a page

    (b) A reverse (light text on a dark background) in the masthead of a newsletter

    (c) A pull quote in the body of a newsletter

    (d) Mixing a serif and a sans serif font in the same document

17. Which of the following techniques were used to create the pull quote developed in the chapter?

    (a) Placing a horizontal line above and below the selected text

    (b) Using a larger font than the surrounding paragraphs

    (c) Setting the selected text in Italics

    (d) All of the above

18. Which of the following is a recommended guideline in the design of a document?

    (a) Use as many fonts as possible to make the page more interesting

    (b) Use the same type size for the heading and text of an article

    (c) Avoid borders and shading since both techniques tend to be distracting

    (d) None of the above

ANSWERS

1. b	**7.** c	**13.** b
2. b	**8.** b	**14.** a
3. b	**9.** c	**15.** d
4. c	**10.** c	**16.** a
5. a	**11.** d	**17.** d
6. c	**12.** c	**18.** d

PRACTICE WITH WORD

1. **Study Tips:** Create a simple newsletter similar to the document in Figure 5.10. There is no requirement to write meaningful text, but the headings in the newsletter should follow the theme of the document. The intent of this problem is simply to provide practice in graphic design. Proceed as follows:

   a. Choose a topic for your newsletter, such as "Study Tips". Develop an overall design away from the computer; that is, with pencil and paper. Use a grid to indicate the placement of the articles, headings, clip art, and masthead. You may be surprised to find that it is easier to master commands in Word than it is to design the newsletter; do not, however, underestimate the importance of graphic design in the ultimate success of your document.

   b. Use meaningful headings that are consistent with the theme of your newsletter to give the document a sense of realism. The text under each heading can be a single sentence that repeats indefinitely to take up the allotted space. Your eye is the best judge of all, and you may need to decrease the default spacing between columns and/or change the type size to create an appealing document.

   c. Insert clip art to add interest to your document, then write one or two sentences in support of the clip art. Use the clip art within Microsoft Office or any other clip art you have available. You can also download pictures from the Web, but be sure to credit the source. The image you choose should be related to the theme. (A single dominant image is generally preferable to multiple pictures.)

   d. More is not better; that is, do not use too many fonts, styles, sizes, or clip art images just because they are available. Don't crowd the page, and remember white space is a very effective design element. There are no substitutes for simplicity and good taste.

   e. Submit the completed newsletter to your instructor for inclusion in a class contest. Your instructor may want to select the five best designs as semifinalists and let the class vote on the overall winner. You learn by observing good design.

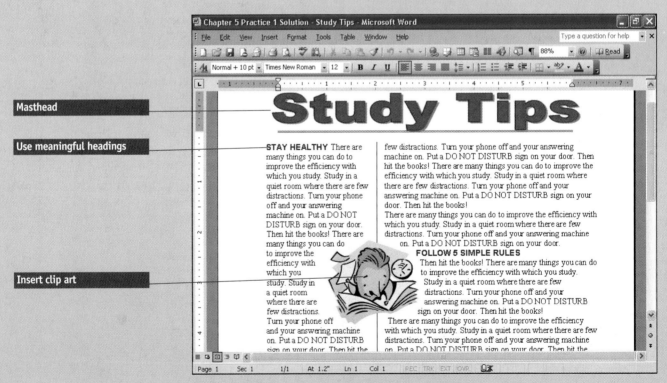

FIGURE 5.10 Study Tips (exercise 1)

practice exercises

2. **A Guide to Smart Shopping:** This problem is more challenging than the previous exercise in that you are asked to consider content as well as design. The objective is to develop a one- (or two-) page document with helpful tips to the novice on buying a computer, as shown in Figure 5.11. We have, however, written the copy for you. Your task is to create an attractive document from our text.

   a. Open and print the *Chapter 5 Practice 2* document in the Exploring Word folder, which takes approximately a page and a half as presently formatted.

   b. Read our text and determine the tips you want to retain and those you want to delete. Add other tips as you see fit. Did you learn anything about buying a computer? The two most important (and least known) tips are to use a major credit card to double the warranty and to insist on 30-day price protection.

   c. Examine the available clip art through the Insert Picture command. There is no requirement, however, to include a graphic; that is, you should use clip art only if you think it will enhance the document.

   d. Use an imaginary grid to develop a rough sketch of the document showing the masthead, the placement of the text, and clip art if any. Do this away from the computer.

   e. Implement your design in Microsoft Word. Try to create a balanced publication, which completely fills the space allotted; that is, your document should take exactly one or two pages (rather than the page and a half in the original document on the data disk). You can adjust the margins, space between columns, and/or type sizes to achieve this result. Inclusion (omission) of a pull quote is another way to change the amount of space that is required.

   f. Complete the final formatting of the document by experimenting with different fonts, styles, and/or point sizes. Set a time limit and stick to it!

   g. Use the AutoSummarize tool to create an executive summary for your document. Pull down the Tools menu and click the AutoSummarize command to display the associated dialog box. Choose the type of summary you want, such as Highlight Key Points, and then click OK. Use the AutoSummary toolbar to change the level of detail and/or use the Highlighting tool to fine-tune the summary. (Select 0% to remove all of the highlighting.)

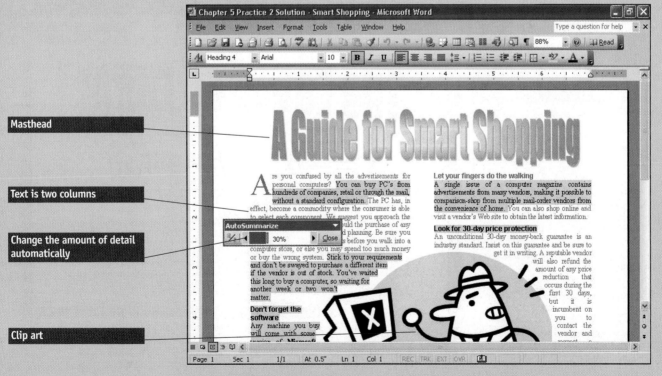

FIGURE 5.11 A Guide to Smart Shopping (exercise 2)

3. **The Equation Editor:** Microsoft Office includes several shared applications, each of which creates an object that can be inserted into a Word document. Microsoft WordArt and the Equation Editor are two such applications, and both are illustrated in Figure 5.12. Proceed as follows:

a. Start a new document. Pull down the Insert menu, click the Picture command, then click the WordArt command to create the title for your document. Move and size the WordArt just as you would any other object, then use the WordArt toolbar to change its shape, fill color, and so on. Use the Format WordArt command to change the wrapping style to square.

b. Click underneath the WordArt object and pull down the Insert menu. Click the Object command, click the Create New tab, select Microsoft Equation 3.0 as the object type, then click OK to start the Equation Editor. The Equation Editor will start and you will see the Drawing Canvas where you create the equation. It will be a trial-and-error process, but you can do it. Do not be intimidated by the Equation toolbar, even if you are not mathematically inclined. You can point to any symbol on the toolbar to see a ToolTip describing the symbol.

c. Type the portion of the equation that does not require any special symbols ($x = -b$). Click the Operator Symbols icon to display a palette of available symbols, and then click the plus or minus sign to insert the symbol.

d. Type the letter b, click the Subscript and Superscript tool, choose superscript, and enter 2 to display b^2. Click to the right of the superscripted 2, and then continue to develop the equation by typing $-4ac$. Select the expression $b^2 - 4ac$. Choose the Fraction and Radical templates tool to select the square root symbol.

e. Complete the equation by selecting the entire entry, then select the Fraction and Radical templates tool once more to select the dividing symbol, then enter the denominator (2a). Click outside the drawing canvas to exit the Equation Editor and return to the Word document. The completed equation is a regular object that can be moved and sized within the document. You can also double click the equation to restart the Equation Editor to modify the equation.

f. Add two or three sentences below the equation and submit the completed document.

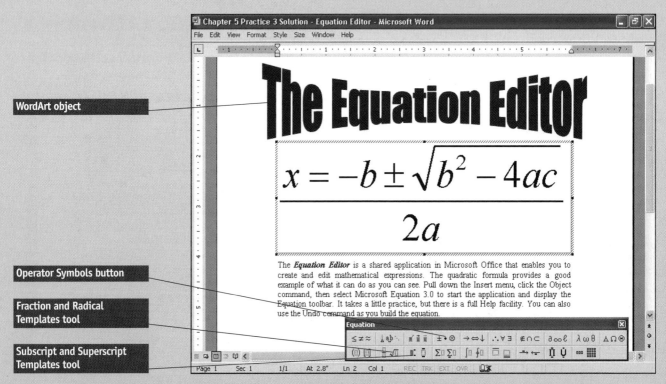

FIGURE 5.12 The Equation Editor (exercise 3)

practice exercises

4. **The Roth IRA:** Retirement is years away, but it is never too soon to start planning. Most corporations include some type of retirement contribution in their benefits package and/or you can supplement that money through an individual retirement account (IRA). The document in Figure 5.13 shows the results of careful planning and a conservative rate of return (starting at 4%). The key to successful saving is to begin as early as possible. Proceed as follows:

a. Open the *Chapter 5 Practice 4* document that contains the text of the memo in Figure 5.13. Create an appropriate letterhead and substitute your name as the addressee. Apply basic formatting to the document. Insert an appropriate piece of clip art at the top of the document.

b. Start Excel. Open the *Chapter 5 Practice 4* workbook that is found in the Exploring Word folder. Change the parameters that appear in the yellow cells at the bottom of the worksheet as you see fit. Experiment with different values, especially the number of years contributing. Our illustration goes out to 45 years, which enables an individual to begin saving at 20, assuming a retirement age of 65. Choose a conservative, but realistic, rate of interest. Anything over 8% should be considered as "irrational exuberance".

c. Save the workbook. Select cells A1 through E11 and then link the worksheet to your Word document. Format the document appropriately. Add your name somewhere in the document and then print it for your instructor.

d. Return to Excel and change one or more of the inputs to the worksheet. Save the modified worksheet, then return to the Word document, which should reflect these changes. Print this version of the document also.

e. Use the PMT function in Excel to compute the monthly payment that is generated by your nest egg. What are the required parameters for the PMT function?

f. Use your favorite search engine to learn more about a Roth IRA. How does this type of account different from an ordinary IRA (Individual Retirement Account)? How do both accounts differ from a 401K plan?

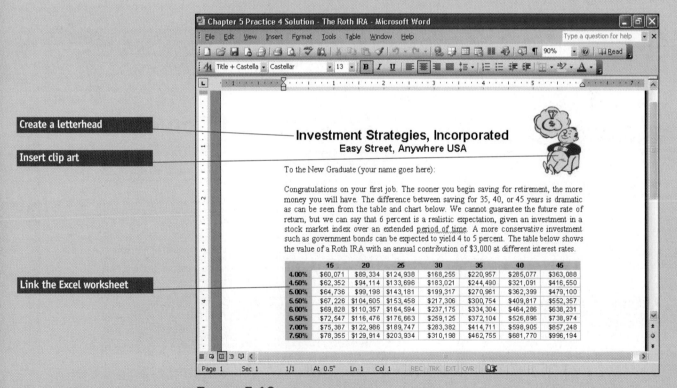

FIGURE 5.13 The Roth IRA (exercise 4)

5. **My Favorite Car:** The document in Figure 5.14 consists of descriptive text, a photograph, and an Excel worksheet to compute a car payment. We have created the spreadsheet for you, but you will have to obtain the other information. Proceed as follows:

a. Choose any vehicle you like, then go to the Web to locate a picture of your vehicle together with descriptive material. *Be sure to credit your source in the completed document.* Start a new Word document. Enter a title for the document and the descriptive information. Do not worry about the precise formatting at this time.

b. You can insert the photograph in conventional fashion, or you can set it in the background as a watermark. Pull down the Format menu, click Background, and then click Printed Watermark to display the associated dialog box. Select the option for Picture Watermark, click the Select Picture button, and insert the picture of your car as shown in Figure 5.14. (If necessary, pull down the View menu and click the Header and Footer command to change the size and/or position of the watermark.)

c. Open the *Chapter 5 Practice 5* workbook that is found in the Exploring Word folder. Enter the information for your vehicle in cells B3, B4, B5, B7, and B8. (The amount to finance is computed automatically based on the price, rebate, and down payment.) The monthly payment will be computed automatically, based on the amount you are borrowing, the interest rate, and the term of your loan. Save the workbook.

d. Click and drag to select cells A1:B9 within the worksheet, return to Word, and use object linking and embedding to link the worksheet to the document. Move and size the various objects as necessary to complete the document. (Right click the picture of the automobile to display a context-sensitive menu, click the Format Object command, click the Layout tab, and choose Square Layout as the wrapping style. Repeat this process for the worksheet.)

e. Return to the Excel workbook, change one or more parameters for the car loan, then return to the Word document. If necessary, right click the worksheet, then click Update Link to see the new payment in the Word document.

f. Add your name somewhere in the document and submit the completed document to your instructor.

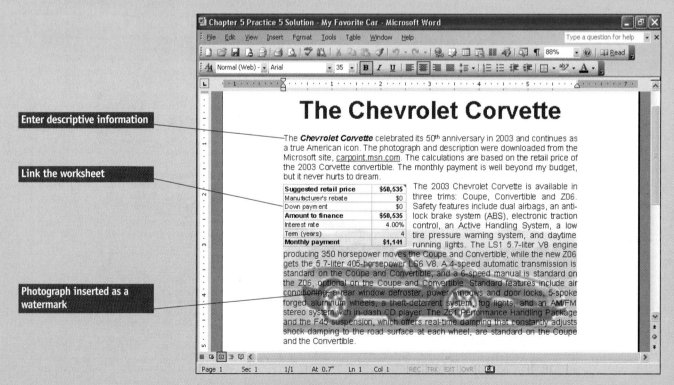

FIGURE 5.14   My Favorite Car (exercise 5)

6. **Exploring Templates:** This chapter described how to create a newsletter and other documents. You don't have to continually reinvent the wheel, however, but can take advantage of several templates that are provided by Microsoft. A template is a partially completed document that specifies the overall design of the document including formatting, but it does not contain specific text. The installation of Microsoft Office stores several templates locally, with additional templates available on the Microsoft Web site. Proceed as follows:

   a. Start Word and close any open document. Pull down the View menu, click the Task Pane command, and then click the down arrow in the task pane to select the New Document task pane. In the Templates section, click the link to On my computer to open the Templates dialog box as shown in Figure 5.15.

   b. Click the Publications tab and change to the Details view. (You may see a different set of templates from those in our figure.) Select the Manual template, and click OK. A new document is started that is based on the selected template. Print the document for your instructor.

   c. Save the document that you just created. What is the default name? How would you save the document under a different name? How many pages are in the document? Is the document easy to modify? Would you create a manual based on this template or would you prefer to create the document from scratch? Close the document.

   d. Repeat the procedure in part (b) to create a thesis or a brochure. Print either or both of these documents according to the requirements of your instructor. Do you think these templates would be useful in creating the actual documents?

   e. Click the link to the Templates on Office Online to see what is available. The contents of the Web site are continually changing, but our experience is that these templates are very useful, especially if you find a template that is similar to a document you need to create. Download at least one template from the Web site and create a document based on that template. Submit the completed document to your instructor. Add a cover sheet to complete the assignment.

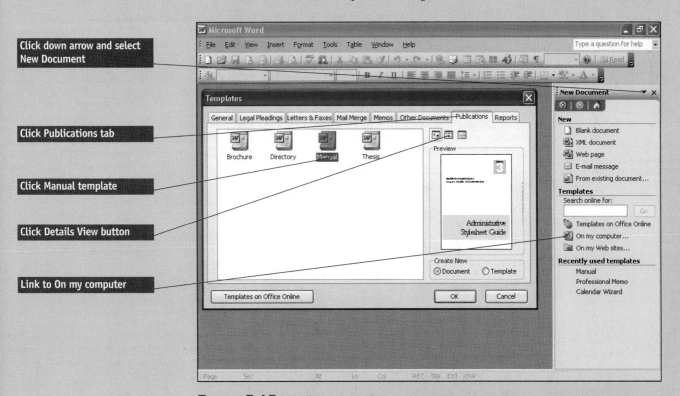

FIGURE 5.15 Exploring Templates (exercise 6)

MINI CASES

Study Session

It's the end of the semester and your instructor has asked you to publicize a review session for CIS100, the computer class you are currently taking. She has even given you the text of the flyer in the form of a poem that includes the place and time. Your assignment is to open the *Chapter 5 Mini Case—Study Session* document in the Exploring Word folder and create the flyer. Use WordArt and a photograph or clip art to complete the document.

Microsoft Office Publisher 2003

Microsoft Word enables you to create virtually any type of document, with full formatting, clip art, and photographs. Microsoft Publisher takes desktop publishing one step further by providing a wide selection of documents and templates from which to choose. It enables you to create a variety of professional-looking publications without reliance on graphic designers or other services. Publisher is ideal for any type of business communication, as it facilitates a uniform look across multiple publications through a series of templates or Master Design Sets. Each set contains the same design (logo and color scheme) for common publications such as newsletters, flyers, postcards, CD/DVD labels, and other publications. Locate a copy of Microsoft Publisher and use it to create two or three documents of different types—for example, a newsletter, brochure, and a flyer from within the same set. How do your results compare to the documents you created in this chapter? Which program do you prefer?

Before and After

The best way to learn about the dos and don'ts of desktop publishing is to study the work of others. Choose a particular type of document—for example, a newsletter, résumé, or advertising flyer—and then collect samples of that document. Choose one sample that is particularly bad and redesign the document. You need not enter the actual text, but you should keep all of the major headings so that the document retains its identity. Add or delete clip art as appropriate. Bring the before and after samples to class and hold a contest to determine the most radical improvement.

Subscribe to a Newsletter

There are literally thousands of regularly published newsletters that are distributed in printed and/or electronic form. Some charge a subscription fee, but many are available just for the asking. Use your favorite search engine to locate a free newsletter in an area of interest to you. Download an issue, then summarize the results of your research in a brief note to your instructor.

Introduction to HTML:
Creating a Home Page and a Web Site

CASE STUDY
REALTOR OF THE YEAR

Benjamin Lee, a successful realtor in South Florida, is seeking to expand his practice by establishing a Web presence to advertise his current listings and to attract new business. Ben is a dedicated professional and a born salesman. He has won the prestigious "Realtor of the Year Award" in South Florida, but is totally inept on the computer. Ben is a long-time family friend and has come to you for help. You agree to meet for a business lunch to learn more about his requirements.

Ben has several objectives for his site. He wants to describe his qualifications and the many services he provides for his clients. He wants to display his current listings and enable individuals who are looking for a home to fill out a form that describes their requirements. Ben also wants a place where individuals seeking to sell a home can describe their property. This information is changing continually as existing listings are sold and new properties become available. It is very important, therefore, that Ben be able to maintain the Web site after it has been created. ■

Your assignment is to read the chapter and focus on the third hands-on exercise that describes how to develop a Web site, as opposed to a single Web page. You will begin by creating a home page that describes Ben's credentials and basic services, and then expand that page into a Web site by adding navigation to other pages (such as Current Listings or Sell Your Home) through links on a vertical or horizontal frame.

The Web site will be developed incrementally, which requires you to create an "Under Construction" page as a placeholder for the various links. This enables Ben to experience the "look and feel" of the site before it is completed. Each page within the site should use the Single File Web Page command, and all of the pages for the site should be stored in a folder named "Realtor of the Year". An appealing and consistent visual design throughout the site is important. (You do not have to upload the finished site to a Web server.)

Sooner or later anyone who cruises the World Wide Web wants to create a home page and/or a Web site of their own. That, in turn, requires an appreciation for *HyperText Markup Language (HTML)*, the language in which all Web pages are written. A Web page consists of text and graphics, together with a set of codes (or tags) that describe how the document is to appear when viewed in a Web browser such as Internet Explorer.

In the early days of the Web, anyone creating a Web document (home page) had to learn each of these codes and enter it explicitly. Today, however, it's much easier as you can create a Web document within any application in Microsoft Office. In essence, you enter the text of a document, apply basic formatting such as boldface or italic, then simply save the file as a Web document. Microsoft Office also provides an FTP (File Transfer Protocol) capability that lets you upload your documents directly onto a Web server.

There are, of course, other commands that you will need to learn, but all commands are executed from within Word, through pull-down menus, toolbars, or keyboard shortcuts. You can create a single document (called a home page), or you can create multiple documents to build a simple Web site. Either way, the document(s) can be viewed locally within a Web browser such as Internet Explorer, and/or they can be placed on a Web server where they can be accessed by anyone with an Internet connection.

Figure 6.1 displays a simple Web page that is similar to the one you will create in the hands-on exercise that follows shortly. Our page has the look and feel of Web pages you see when you access the World Wide Web. It includes different types of formatting, a bulleted list, underlined links, and a heading displayed in a larger font. All of these elements are associated with specific HTML codes that identify the appearance and characteristics of the item. Figure 6.1a displays the document as it would appear when viewed in Internet Explorer. Figure 6.1b shows the underlying HTML codes *(tags)* that are necessary to format the page.

Fortunately, however, it is not necessary to memorize the HTML tags since you can usually determine their meaning from the codes themselves. Nor is it even necessary for you to enter the tags, as Word will create the HTML tags for you based on the formatting in the document. Nevertheless, we think it worthwhile for you to gain an appreciation for HTML by comparing the two views of the document.

HTML codes become less intimidating when you realize that they are enclosed in angle brackets and are used consistently from document to document. Most tags occur in pairs, at the beginning and end of the text to be formatted, with the ending code preceded by a slash, such as <p and </p> to indicate the beginning and end of a paragraph. Links to other pages (which are known as hyperlinks) are enclosed within a pair of anchor tags <a and </a> in which you specify the URL address of the document through the HREF parameter. There are additional codes for boldface, italic, font styles and sizes, and so on.

WHAT IS XML?

Extensible Markup Language, or XML for short, is an industry standard for structuring data. It is very different from HTML and serves an entirely different function. HTML describes how a document should look; for example, <B>John Doe</B> indicates that John Doe should appear in boldface, but it does not tell us anything more. You don't know that "John" is the first name or that "Doe" is the last name. XML on the other hand, is data about data, and it lets you define your own tags; for example, <name><first>John</first><last>Doe</last></name>. The XML codes can be read by any XML-compliant application and processed accordingly. See problem 9 at the end of the chapter.

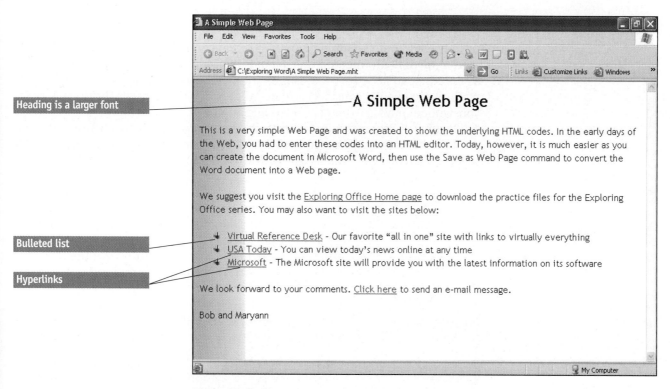

Heading is a larger font

Bulleted list

Hyperlinks

(a) Internet Explorer

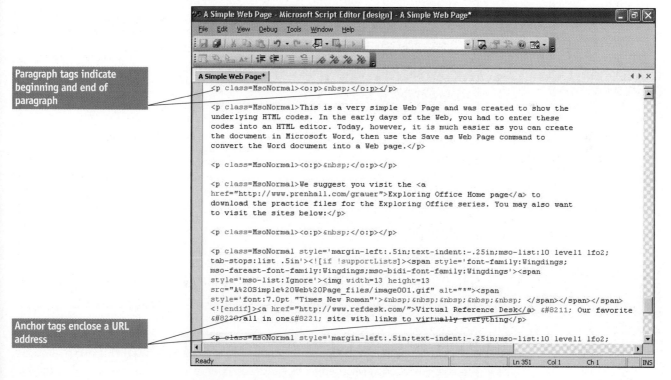

Paragraph tags indicate beginning and end of paragraph

Anchor tags enclose a URL address

(b) HTML Source Code

FIGURE 6.1   Introduction to HTML

Microsoft Word

As indicated, there are different ways to create an HTML document. The original (and more difficult) method was to enter the codes explicitly in a text editor such as the Notepad accessory that is built into Windows. An easier way (and the only method you need to consider) is to use Microsoft Word to create the document for you, without having to enter or reference the HTML codes at all.

Figure 6.2 displays Jessica Benjamin's *home page* in Microsoft Word. You can create a similar page by entering the text and formatting just as you would enter the text of an ordinary document. The only difference is that instead of saving the document in the default format (as a Word document), you use the ***Save As Web Page command*** to specify the HTML format. Microsoft Word does the rest, generating the HTML codes needed to create the document. Microsoft Office 2003 introduces the ***Single File Web Page*** format that stores all of the elements that comprise a page (both text and graphics) in a single file.

Hyperlinks are added through the Insert Hyperlink button on the Standard toolbar or through the corresponding ***Insert Hyperlink command*** in the Insert menu. You can format the elements of the document (the heading, bullets, text, and so on) individually, or you can select a ***theme*** from those provided by Microsoft Word. A theme (or template) is a set of unified design elements and color schemes that will save you time, while making your document more attractive.

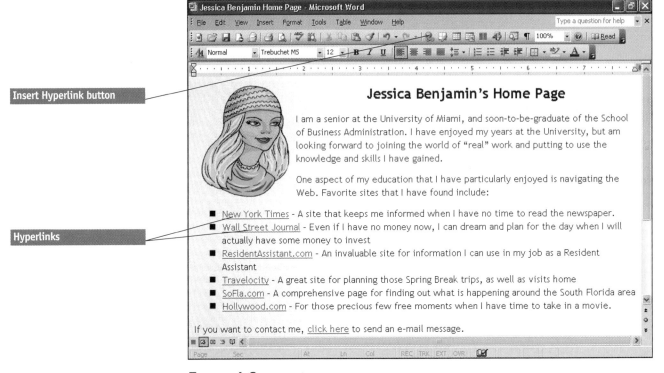

FIGURE 6.2 A Student's Home Page

ROUND-TRIP HTML

Each application in Microsoft Office lets you open a Web document in both Internet Explorer and the application that created the Web page initially. In other words, you can start with a Word document and use the Save As Web Page command to convert the document to a Web page, then view that page in a Web browser. You can then reopen the Web page in Word (the original Office application) with full access to all Word commands, should you want to modify the document.

Introduction to HTML

Objective To use Microsoft Word to create a simple home page with clip art and multiple hyperlinks; to format a Web page by selecting a theme. Use Figure 6.3 as a guide in the exercise.

Step 1: **Enter the Text**

- Start Microsoft Word. Close the task pane. Pull down the **View menu** and click the **Web Layout command**. Enter the text of your home page as shown in Figure 6.3a. Use any text you like and choose an appropriate font and type size. Center and enlarge the title for your page.

- Enter the text for our links (e.g., *New York Times* and the *Wall Street Journal* sites), or choose your own. You do not enter the URL addresses at this time.

- Click and drag to select all of your links, then click the **Bullets button** on the Formatting toolbar to precede each link with a bullet.

- Click the **Spelling and Grammar button** to check the document for spelling.

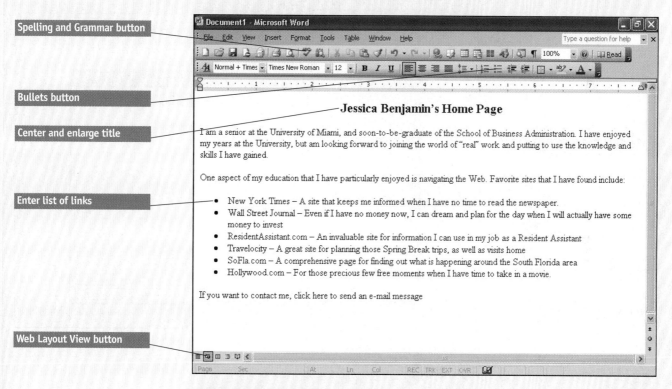

Spelling and Grammar button

Bullets button

Center and enlarge title

Enter list of links

Web Layout View button

(a) Enter the Text (step 1)

FIGURE 6.3 Hands-on Exercise 1

FOREIGN LANGUAGE PROOFING TOOLS

The English version of Microsoft Word supports the spelling, grammar, and the-saurus features in more than 80 foreign languages. Support for Spanish and French is built in at no additional cost, whereas you will have to pay an additional fee for other languages. Pull down the Tools menu, click Language, and click the Set Language command to change to a different language. You can even check multiple languages within the same document.

Step 2: **Save the Document**

- Pull down the **File menu** and click the **Save as Web Page** command to display the Save As dialog box in Figure 6.3b.

- Click the **drop-down arrow** in the Save In list box to select the appropriate drive—drive C or drive A. Click to open the **Exploring Word folder** that contains the documents you have used throughout the text.

- Enter the file name, then be sure to select the **Single File Web Page** format as shown in Figure 6.3b. This enables you to save all of the elements for a Web page in one file.

- Click the **Change Title button** if you want to change the title of the Web page as it will appear in the Title bar of the Web browser. (The default title is the opening text in your document.)

- Click the **Save button**. The title bar reflects the name of the Web page, but the screen does not change in any other way.

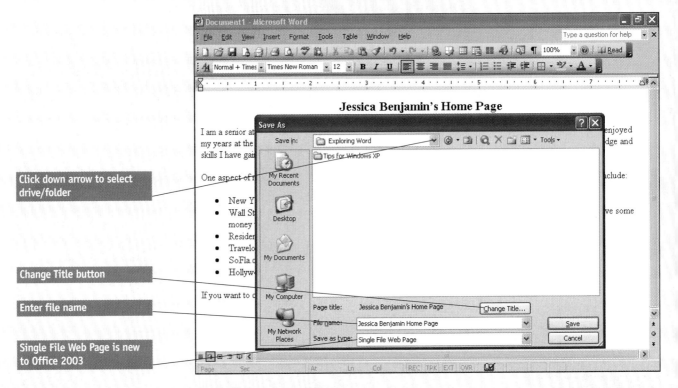

(b) Save the Document (step 2)

FIGURE 6.3 Hands-on Exercise 1 (*continued*)

WHAT'S IN A FILE NAME?

You can choose any meaningful file name for your home page. One common convention is to use "index" (with a lowercase "i") as the file name for the initial page on a Web site to take advantage of the convention of a Web browser, which automatically displays the index document if it exists. Start Internet Explorer, click in the address bar, enter a URL such as www.prenhall.com/grauer, and press Enter. You are taken to the home page of the Grauer Web site, but you do not see the document name; that is, the index.html document is displayed automatically and need not be shown in the URL within the address bar.

Step 3: Insert the Clip Art

- Click to the left of the first sentence in the document. Pull down the **Insert menu**, click (or point to) **Picture**, then click **Clip Art** to display the Insert Clip Art task pane in Figure 6.3c.
- Click in the **Search for** text box and type **woman** to search for all pictures that have been catalogued to describe this attribute. Click the **Go button**. The search begins and the various pictures appear individually within the task pane.
- Point to the image you want in your newsletter, click the **down arrow** that appears, then click **Insert** to insert the clip art.
- The picture should appear in the document. Close the task pane.
- Point to the picture and click the **right mouse button** to display the context-sensitive menu. Click the **Format Picture command** to display the Format Picture dialog box.
- Click the **Layout tab**, choose the **Square layout**, then click the option button for Left or Right alignment. Click **OK** to close the dialog box. Move and size the picture as appropriate. Save the document.

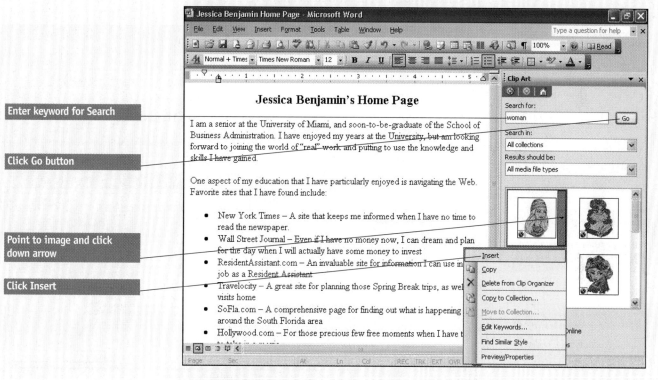

(c) Insert the Clip Art (step 3)

FIGURE 6.3 Hands-on Exercise 1 (*continued*)

SEARCH FOR THE APPROPRIATE CLIP ART OR PHOTOGRAPH

Pull down the Insert menu, click the Picture command, and click Clip Art to display the Clip Art task pane that enables you to enter search parameters for an appropriate media object. Click the down arrow in the Search in list box and select All collections. Click the down arrow in the Results should be list box and choose All media file types, then click the Go button to initiate the search. The search may take a little while as it includes the Web, but you should have a much larger selection of potential clips from which to choose. If necessary, use the drop-down arrow on either search box to limit the search as you see fit.

Step 4: Add the Hyperlinks

- Select **New York Times** (the text for the first hyperlink). Pull down the **Insert menu** and click **Hyperlink** (or click the **Insert Hyperlink button**) to display the Insert Hyperlink dialog box in Figure 6.3d.

- The text to display (New York Times) is already entered because the text was selected prior to executing the Insert Hyperlink command. If necessary, click the icon for **Existing File or Web Page**, then click **Browsed Pages**.

- Click in the second text box and enter the address **www.nytimes.com** (the http is assumed). Click **OK**.

- Add the additional links in similar fashion. The addresses we used in our document are: **www.wsj.com**, **www.residentassistant.com**, **www.travelocity.com**, **www.sofla.com**, and **www.hollywood.com**.

- Click and drag to select the words **click here**, then click the **Insert Hyperlink button** to display the Insert Hyperlink dialog box.

- Click the **E-mail Address icon**, then click in the E-mail Address text box and enter your e-mail address. Click **OK**.

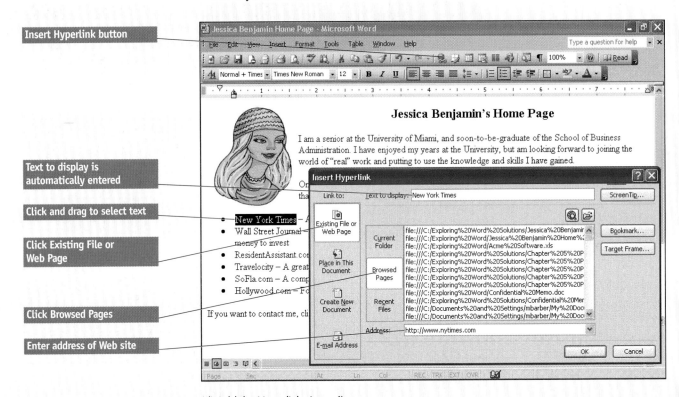

(d) Add the Hyperlinks (step 4)

FIGURE 6.3   Hands-on Exercise 1 (*continued*)

RIGHT CLICK TO SELECT, CTRL+CLICK TO FOLLOW

Point to a hyperlink within a Word document, and you see a ScreenTip that says to press and hold the Ctrl key (Ctrl+Click) to follow the link. This is different from what you usually do, because you typically just click a link to follow it. What if, however, you wanted to edit, copy, or remove the link? Clicking the link has no effect. Thus, you have to right click the link to display a context-sensitive menu from which you can make the appropriate choice—for example, to edit or remove the hyperlink.

Step 5:   Apply a Theme

■ You should see underlined hyperlinks in your document. Pull down the **Format menu** and click the **Theme command** to display the Theme dialog box in Figure 6.3e.

■ Select (click) a theme from the list box on the left, and a sample of the design appears on the right. Only a limited number of the listed themes are installed by default, however, and thus you may be prompted for the Microsoft Office CD, depending on your selection. Click **OK**.

■ You can go from one theme to the next by clicking the new theme. There are approximately 65 themes to choose from, and they are all visually appealing. Every theme offers a professionally designed set of formatting specifications for the various headings, horizontal lines, bullets, and links.

■ Set a time limit, then make your decision as to which theme you will use when your time is up.

■ Save the document.

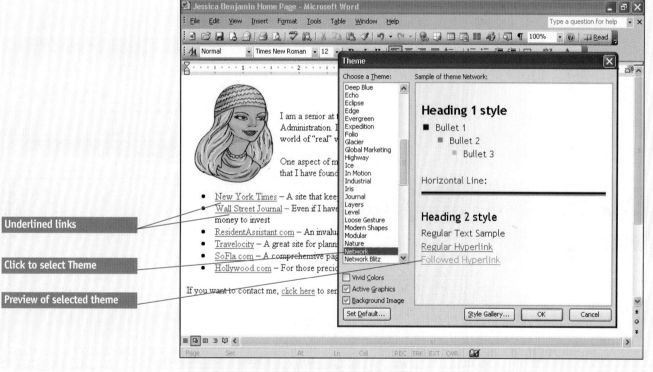

(e) Apply a Theme (step 5)

FIGURE 6.3   Hands-on Exercise 1 (*continued*)

KEEP IT SIMPLE

Too many would-be designers clutter a page unnecessarily by importing a complex background, which tends to obscure the text. The best design is a simple design—either no background or a very simple pattern. We also prefer light backgrounds with dark text (e.g., black or dark blue text on a white background), as opposed to the other way around. Design, however, is subjective, and there is no consensus as to what makes an attractive page. Variety is indeed the spice of life. Look at existing Web pages for inspiration.

Step 6: View the Web Page

- Start your Web browser. Pull down the **File menu** and click the **Open command** to display the Open dialog box in Figure 6.3f.

- Click the **Browse button**, then select the drive folder (e.g., Exploring Word on drive C) where you saved the Web page.

- Select (click) your home page, click **Open**, then click **OK** to open the document. You should see the Web page that was just created except that you are viewing it in your browser rather than in Microsoft Word.

- The Address bar shows the local address (C:\Exploring Word\Jessica Benjamin Home Page.mht) of the document. (You can also open the document from the Address bar, by clicking in the **Address bar**, then typing the address of the document—for example, **c:\Exploring word\Jessica Benjamin Home Page.mht**.)

- Click the **Print button** on the Internet Explorer toolbar to print this page for your instructor.

- Exit Word and Internet Explorer if you do not want to continue with the next exercise at this time.

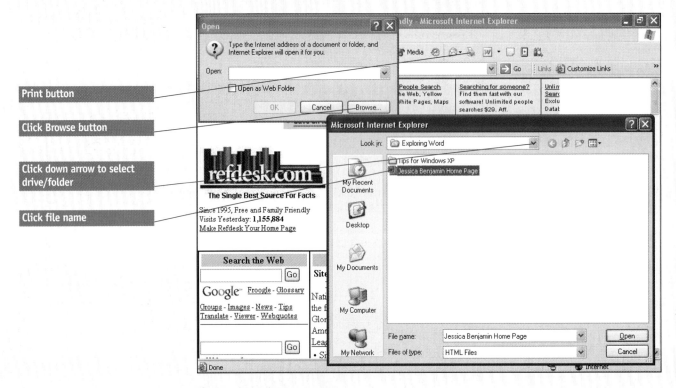

(f) View the Web Page (step 6)

FIGURE 6.3   Hands-on Exercise 1 *(continued)*

SINGLE FILE WEB PAGE

Microsoft Office 2003 introduces the Single File Web Page (MHTML) format that saves all of the elements of a Web page, including text and graphics, in a single file. The new format enables you to upload a single file to a Web server, as opposed to sending multiple files and folders. It also lets you send the entire page as a single e-mail attachment. The new file format is supported by Internet Explorer 4.0 and higher.

Figure 6.4 displays the home page of a hypothetical travel agency. The Address bar displays the name of the document (World Wide Travel Home Page) and indicates that the document is stored in the World Wide Travel folder. (We created a separate folder to hold the home page because we will develop a Web site in the next exercise, and it is easiest to store all of the pages for the site in a single folder.) The extension in the file name (mht) indicates the Single File Web Page format.

The table at the top of the document facilitates the placement of text and/or graphical elements on the page. The cell on the left contains the name of the agency, a hyperlink, a telephone number, and an e-mail address. The latter is also a hyperlink that starts the default e-mail program to create a message to the travel agency. Note, too, that the first hyperlink, "Click here for travel agents", branches to a ***bookmark*** or place within the document, as opposed to a separate Web page. One or more bookmarks are helpful in long documents, as they enable you to move easily from one place to another (within a document) without having to manually scroll through the document. Creating a bookmark and branching to it is a two-step process. You use the Insert menu to create the bookmark, and then you insert a hyperlink to branch to the bookmark that you just created.

The second cell in the table contains the agency logo. You can center the clip art within the cell, and then you can center the table within the document. Microsoft Word is limited when compared to other Web editors, and thus a table makes it easier to position the graphics within a Web page.

Look once again at the Address bar and note that the page is stored on drive C, as opposed to a Web server. Creating the home page and viewing it locally is easy. Placing the page on the Web where it can be seen by anyone with an Internet connection is not as straightforward. You will need additional information from your instructor about how to obtain an account on a Web server (if that is available at your school), and further how to upload the Web page from your PC to the server. The latter is typically accomplished using ***File Transfer Protocol (FTP)***, a program that uploads files from a PC to a Web server.

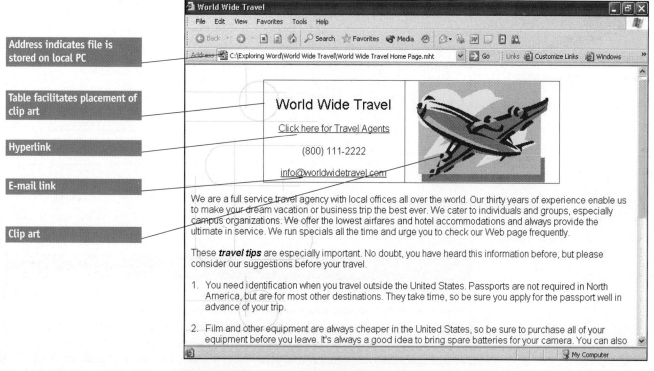

FIGURE 6.4 World Wide Travel Web Page

2 World Wide Travel Home Page

Objective To use a table to facilitate placement of clip art and other elements on a Web page; to insert a bookmark; to create hyperlinks to external Web pages, bookmarks, and e-mail addresses. Use Figure 6.5 as a guide.

Step 1: **Create the World Wide Travel Folder**

- Start Word. Open the **World Wide Travel Home Page document** in the **Exploring Word folder**.

- Pull down the **Format menu**, click the **Theme command**, select a theme (we chose **Capsules**), and click **OK**. The formatting changes as shown in Figure 6.5a.

- Pull down the **File menu** and click the **Save as Web page command** to display the Save as dialog box in Figure 6.5a. Click the **down arrow** in the Save in list box to select the **Exploring Word folder**.

- Click the **Create New Folder button** and enter **World Wide Travel** as the name of the folder. Click **OK** to close the New folder dialog box. Click the **Save button** to save the document. Close the Save As dialog box.

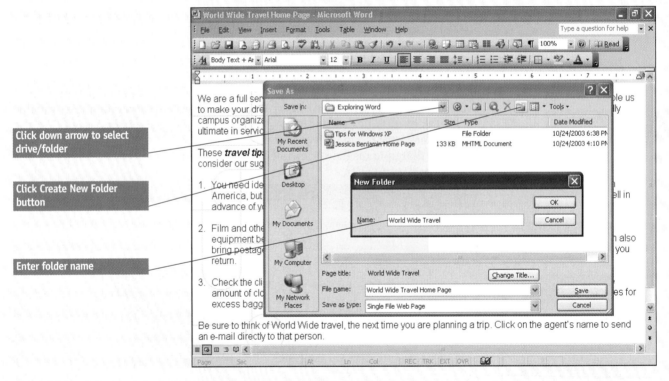

Click down arrow to select drive/folder

Click Create New Folder button

Enter folder name

(a) Create the World Wide Travel Folder (step 1)

FIGURE 6.5 Hands-on Exercise 2

MICROSOFT OFFICE FRONTPAGE 2003

Microsoft Word is an excellent way to begin creating Web documents. It is only a beginning, however, and there are many specialty programs that have significantly more capability. One such product is FrontPage, a product aimed at creating a Web site, as opposed to isolated documents. Search the Web for information on FrontPage, then summarize your findings in a short note to your instructor.

Step 2: Insert the Clip Art

■ Press **Ctrl+Home** to move to the beginning of the document. Press **Enter** to add a blank line, then click the **Insert Table button** to display a table grid.

■ Click and drag to select a **one-by-two grid** (one row and two columns). Release the mouse to create the table. Click in the left cell. Type **World Wide Travel**.

■ Press the **Enter key** twice, type the sentence, **Click here for Travel Agents**, press the **Enter key** twice, and enter the agency's phone number, **(800) 111-2222**.

■ Press **Enter** twice more, type **info@worldwidetravel.com** (or substitute your e-mail address instead), and press **Enter**. A hyperlink is created automatically. Click and drag to select the hyperlink to change the font to Arial.

■ Click in the right pane. Pull down the **Insert menu**, click (or point to) **Picture**, then click **Clip Art** to display the Clip Art task pane in Figure 6.5b.

■ Click in the Search for text box and type **airplane**. Click the **Go button**. Point to the image you want, click the **down arrow**, and then click **Insert** to insert the clip art into the document. Close the task pane.

■ Click the picture to select it, then click and drag the sizing handle on the lower right to make the picture smaller. Click the **Center button** to center the picture.

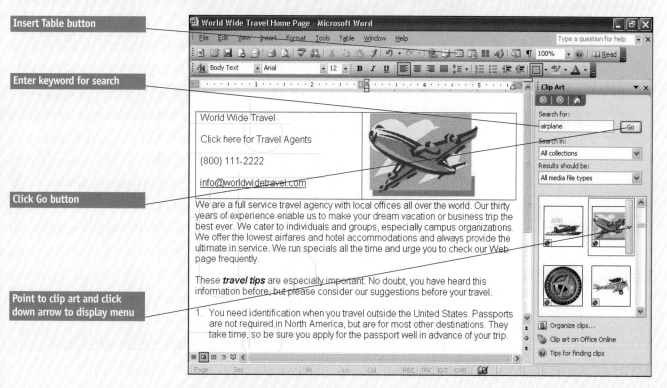

(b) Insert the Clip Art (step 2)

FIGURE 6.5 Hands-on Exercise 2 *(continued)*

WORKING WITH A TABLE—MENUS AND TOOLBARS

Click anywhere within a table and then pull down the Table menu to access the commands to modify the table. You can also display the Tables and Borders toolbar, which contains additional tools to change the line style, thickness, and/or shading within the table. Pull down the View menu, click the Toolbars command, and then click the Tables and Borders toolbar to toggle the toolbar on or off.

Step 3: Insert Hyperlinks and a Bookmark

- Press **Ctrl+End** to go to the end of the document. Click and drag to select the text **Click here for weather report**, then click the **Insert Hyperlink button** to display the Insert Hyperlink text box.

- Click the **Existing File or Web Page button**, then click the **Browsed Pages button**. Enter a Web address such as **http://www.intellicast.com** in the Address list box. Click **OK** to create the link and close the dialog box.

- Click at the end of the document, then enter the bulleted list with your name and your instructor's name as shown in Figure 6.5c. Enter the text **Return to the top of the document** after your instructor's name.

- Click and drag to select your name, then enter a hyperlink to your e-mail address. Enter a hyperlink to your instructor's e-mail address in similar fashion.

- Click at the beginning of the last paragraph. Pull down the **Insert menu** and click **Bookmark** to display the Bookmark dialog box.

- Enter **TravelAgents** (spaces are not allowed) as the name of the bookmark, then click the **Add button** to add the bookmark and close the dialog box.

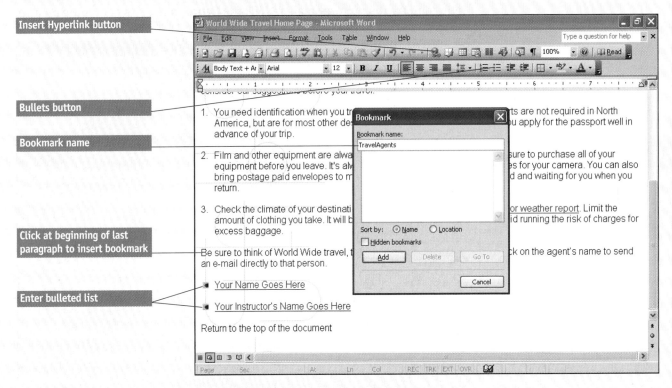

(c) Insert Hyperlinks and a Bookmark (step 3)

FIGURE 6.5 Hands-on Exercise 2 (*continued*)

AUTOMATIC CREATION OF HYPERLINKS

Type any Internet path or e-mail address, and Word will automatically convert the entry to a hyperlink. (If this does not work on your system, pull down the Tools menu, click AutoCorrect Options, then click the AutoFormat as you Type tab. Check the box in the Replace as you Type area for Internet and Network paths, and click OK.) To modify the hyperlink after it is created, right click the link to display a shortcut menu, then click the Edit Hyperlink command to display the associated dialog box in which to make the necessary changes.

Step 4: Link to the Bookmark

- Press **Ctrl+Home** to move to the beginning of the document. Click and drag to select the text **Click here for Travel Agents** as shown in Figure 6.5d. Click the **Insert Hyperlink button** to display the Insert Hyperlink dialog box.

- Click the icon for **Place in This Document**, click the **plus sign** next to Bookmarks to display the existing bookmarks, then click **TravelAgents**. Click **OK** to close the Insert Hyperlink dialog box.

- Click anywhere in the document to deselect the hyperlink you just created. The sentence, Click here for Travel Agents, should appear as underlined text to indicate that it is now a hyperlink.

- Point to the hyperlink, then press **Ctrl+click** to follow the link and position the insertion point at the bookmark you created in the previous step.

- Save the document.

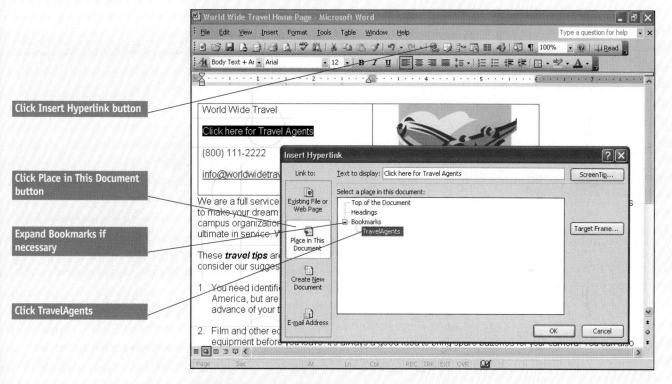

(d) Link to the Bookmark (step 4)

FIGURE 6.5 Hands-on Exercise 2 (*continued*)

THE TOP OF DOCUMENT BOOKMARK

Simplify the navigation within a long page with a link to the top of the document. Press Ctrl+End to move to the bottom of the document (one of several places where you can insert this link), then click the Insert Hyperlink button to display the Insert Hyperlink dialog box. Click the icon for Place in This Document, click Top of the Document from the list of bookmarks (Word creates this bookmark automatically), then click OK. You will see the underlined text, Top of Document, as a hyperlink. (Right click the link after it has been created, click Select Hyperlink, and press Ctrl+C to copy it. Move elsewhere in the document, then press Ctrl+V to paste the link to a second location.)

Step 5: **View the Web Page**

- Open the Web page that you just created in Internet Explorer. You can accomplish this in one of two ways:

- Start **Internet Explorer**. Pull down the **File menu**, click the **Open command**, click the **Browse button**, change to the **World Wide Travel folder** (within the **Exploring Word folder**), then open the **World Wide Travel Home Page**, *or*

- Start **Windows Explorer**. Click the **down arrow** in the Address bar, change to the **World Wide Travel folder** (within the **Exploring Word folder**), then double click the **World Wide Travel Home Page**.

- Either way you should see the home page for the World Wide Travel agency that you just created. The Address bar indicates that you are viewing the page locally, as opposed to viewing it on a Web server.

- Click the **Edit with Microsoft Word button** (or click the **Word button** on the Windows taskbar) to return to the document in Word to apply the finishing touches to your Web page.

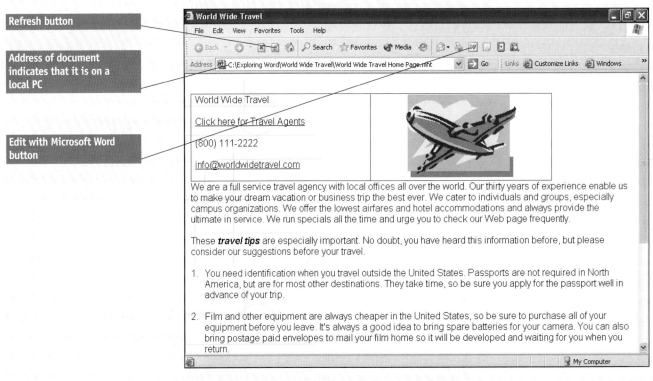

(e) View the Web Page (step 5)

FIGURE 6.5 Hands-on Exercise 2 (*continued*)

HYPERLINKS BEFORE AND AFTER (INTERNET EXPLORER)

Hyperlinks are displayed in different colors, depending on whether (or not) the associated page has been displayed. You can change the default colors, however, to suit your personal preference. Start Internet Explorer, pull down the Tools menu, click the Internet Options command to display the Internet Options dialog box, and click the General tab. Click the Colors button and then click the color box next to the Visited or Unvisited links to display a color palette. Select (click) the desired color, click OK to close the palette, click OK to close the Colors dialog box, then click OK to close the Internet Options dialog box.

Step 6: The Finishing Touches

- You should be back in Word where you can apply the final changes to the document.
- Click and drag to select the **World Wide Travel** in the left cell. Click the **Bold button**. Increase the font size and/or change the font color as appropriate.
- Click and drag to select the four lines of text in the left cell, then click the **Center button** on the Formatting toolbar to center each line within the cell.
- Point to the upper-left corner of the table to display a plus sign, then click the **plus sign** to select the entire table as shown in Figure 6.5f. Pull down the **Table menu**, click the **Table Properties command** to display the associated dialog box, and click the Table tab.
- Click the **Center icon** to center the table itself within the document. Click **OK** to accept the settings and close the dialog box. Click elsewhere in the document to deselect the table. Add and/or delete blank lines as needed.
- Save the document. Click the **Internet Explorer button** on the Windows taskbar to return to the Web browser, then click the **Refresh button** to view the revised version of the page. Return to Word to make additional changes as necessary.
- Close the Word document. Close Internet Explorer.

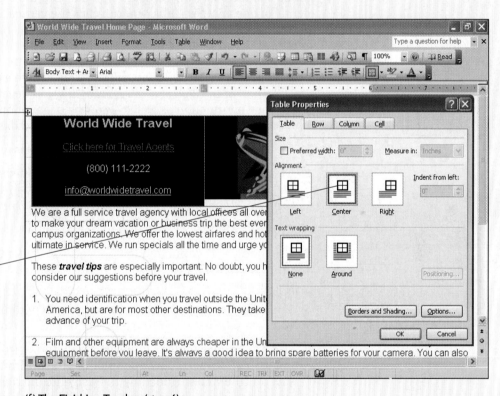

(f) The Finishing Touches (step 6)

FIGURE 6.5 Hands-on Exercise 2 (*continued*)

WHY REFRESH MAY NOT WORK

A Web browser cannot display an MHTML document directly, but must expand it to one or more temporary HTML documents. Thus, if you update a Word document that is saved in MHTML format, then click the Refresh button in Internet Explorer, the browser simply reloads the previous HTML documents. You have to close Internet Explorer, reopen Internet Explorer, and then open the updated MHTML file to create the updated set of HTML documents for the browser.

A **Web site** is composed of multiple pages, which include a home page, navigation page, and other pages as appropriate—for example, a New York Weekend and an Italian Holiday in the case of the travel agency. Two **frames** are typically visible—one displaying the navigation page and another displaying the detailed page (the latter is displayed by clicking the appropriate hyperlink within the navigation page). Vertical frames are the most common means of navigation, but you can also choose horizontal frames and/or open each document in a separate window. Figure 6.6 displays the Web site of our travel agency.

Figure 6.6a shows the home page as it existed at the end of the last exercise, whereas Figure 6.6b displays the home page within a Web site. Figure 6.6c displays a page within the site during development, whereas Figure 6.6d displays the same page after it has been completed. Vertical frames appear in Figures 6.6b, c, and d and divide the browser window in two. The left frame provides the overall navigation for the site via the hyperlinks that are associated with the other pages.

Click the Home Page link in the left pane, and you display information about the agency in the right frame as shown in Figure 6.6b. Click the link to the New York Weekend, however, and you display a page describing a trip to New York. Each frame can have its own vertical scroll bar, and the scroll bars function independently of one another. Thus, you can click the vertical scroll bar in the left pane to view additional links, and/or you can click the scroll bar in the right frame to view additional information on the displayed page. The address bar throughout Figure 6.6 indicates that the Web documents are stored in the World Wide Travel folder on drive C; that is, the site has not yet been uploaded to a Web server.

Creation of the Web site will require that you develop separate documents for the agency information as well as for each destination. It is helpful to outline the procedure for creating the Web site prior to attempting the exercise.

1. Create a new folder to hold all of the documents for the site.

2. Create the home page, and in so doing, establish the visual design that you will follow for every subsequent page. The design should include the font and formatting specifications, a theme (if any), and/or a logo.

3. Create an Under Construction page that follows the design of the home page.

4. Use the Save As command to duplicate the Under Construction page as many times as necessary to create the additional pages on the eventual site. Modify the title of each new Under Construction page to indicate its purpose.

5. Create the navigation page that contains hyperlinks to the various pages that you created. The navigation page should adhere to the visual design.

6. Use the **Frames toolbar** to insert a new frame to the right of the navigation page; this creates a new document with two frames that will eventually be saved as the Web site document. Designate the right frame as the **target frame** (the frame in which the documents will be displayed).

7. Set the home page as the default page when the Web site document is opened (the page that will be displayed in the right frame initially).

8. Save the Web site document.

A well-designed site simplifies the addition of new pages and/or the modification of existing pages. To add a new page, start Word, save the page in the folder that contains the other documents for the site, then modify the navigation page to include a hyperlink to the new page. It's even easier to modify an existing page—all you do is edit the page in Word and save it in the original folder. The navigation does not change.

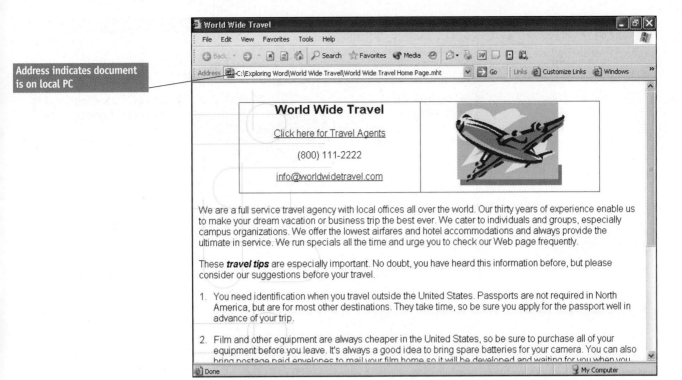

(a) Home Page

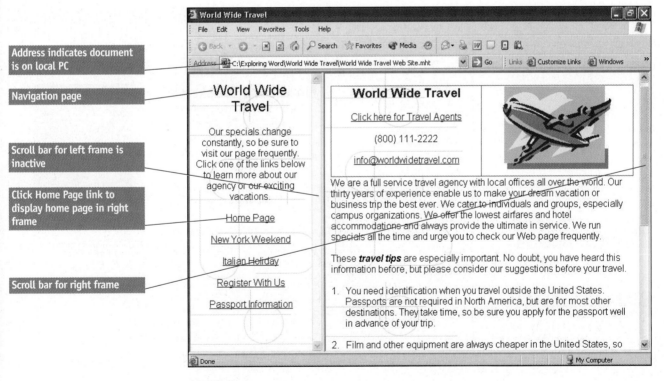

(b) Web Site

FIGURE 6.6 From a Home Page to a Web Site

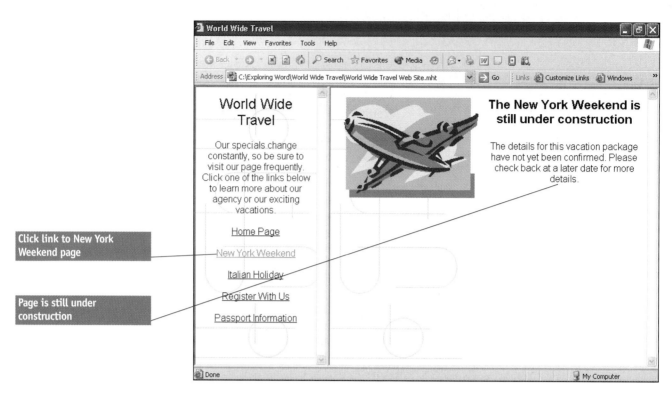

Click link to New York Weekend page

Page is still under construction

(c) Under Construction

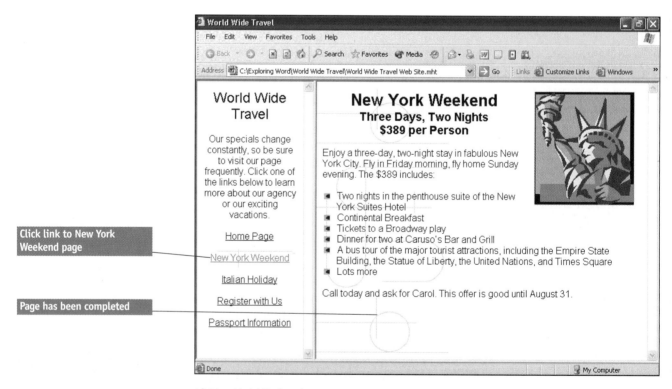

Click link to New York Weekend page

Page has been completed

(d) New York Weekend

FIGURE 6.6 From a Home Page to a Web Site (*continued*)

3   Creating a Web Site

Objective   To create a Web site consisting of multiple Web pages; to add a frame to an existing page. Use Figure 6.7 as a guide in the exercise.

Step 1:   **Create the Under Construction Page**

- Start Word. Create a new document that is similar to the document in Figure 6.7a. Use the same clip art that you selected in the previous exercise.

- Pull down the **Format menu**, click the **Theme command**, and choose the same theme you used for the other pages. (We are using the **Capsules theme**.)

- Pull down the **File menu** and click the **Save as Web Page command**. Save the page as **Under Construction** in the **World Wide Travel folder** (within the Exploring Word folder). Specify **Single File Web Page** as the file format.

- Change the title to reflect the New York Weekend. Pull down the **File menu**, click the **Save As command** a second time, and enter **New York Weekend**. Change the title to reflect the Italian Holiday, then save the page one additional time as **Italian Holiday**. Close the Word document.

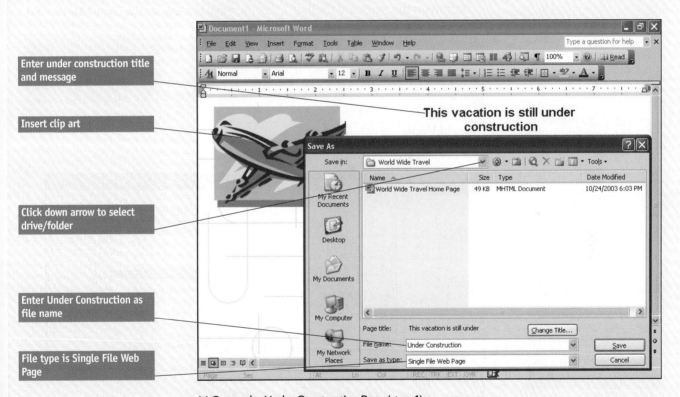

Enter under construction title and message

Insert clip art

Click down arrow to select drive/folder

Enter Under Construction as file name

File type is Single File Web Page

(a) Create the Under Construction Page (step 1)

FIGURE 6.7   Hands-on Exercise 3

UNDER CONSTRUCTION

Use prototyping to let the end user experience the "look and feel" of a site before the site has been finished. The user sees the opening document and a set of links to partially completed documents, which indicates how the eventual site will function. The site is "complete" but incomplete. The user can suggest improvements in the visual design, content, and/or navigation. The developer can then make the necessary adjustments before extensive work has been done.

Step 2: **Create the Navigation Page**

- Click the **New Blank document button** on the Standard toolbar to start a new Word document. Enter the text of the document as shown in Figure 6.7b.

- Pull down the **File menu** and click the **Save as Web Page command**. Save the page as **Navigation** in the **World Wide Travel folder** (within the Exploring Word folder). Be sure to specify **Single File Web Page** as the file format.

- Pull down the **Format menu**, click the **Theme command**, and choose the same theme you used for the other pages in this site. (We are using the **Capsules theme**.)

- Click and drag to select **Home Page** and then click the **Insert Hyperlink button** to display the associated dialog box. Click the **Existing File or Web Page button**, then click the **Current Folder button**.

- Click in the Look in list box and select the **World Wide Travel folder** as shown in Figure 6.7b. Select the **World Wide Travel Home Page** that you created earlier. Click **OK**.

- Add the hyperlinks for **New York Weekend** and **Italian Holiday** in similar fashion. Click and drag to select all of the text in the document, then click the Center button on the Standard toolbar. Click the **Save button** on the Standard toolbar.

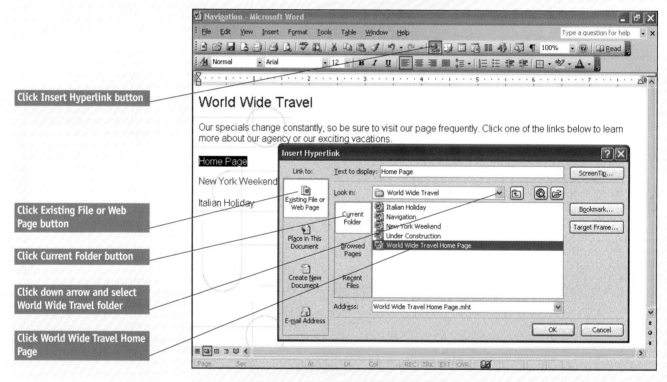

(b) Create the Navigation Page (step 2)

FIGURE 6.7 Hands-on Exercise 3 (*continued*)

THE WORLD WIDE TRAVEL FOLDER

A Web site is composed of multiple documents that are stored in a single folder. Each document is saved in the Single File Web Page (MHTML) format. Every site has a navigation page that contains links to the other documents within the site. The Under Construction page can be duplicated as necessary to create additional (temporary) documents that are used in testing and development.

Step 3: Add a Second Frame

- Pull down the **View menu**, click the **Toolbars command**, and then click the **Frames toolbar**. The command functions as a toggle switch; that is, execute the command a second time and the Frames toolbar is closed.

- Click the **New Frame Right button** to create a second frame to the right of the existing Navigation page as shown in Figure 6.7c. Click and drag the border of the left frame to make that frame narrower.

- Right click any hyperlink to display a context-sensitive menu, then click the **Edit Hyperlink command** to display the Edit Hyperlink dialog box. Click the **Target Frame button** to display the Set Target Frame dialog box.

- Click in the right frame within the dialog box. Frame2 appears in the list box that specifies where you want the page to appear.

- Check the box to **Set as default for all hyperlinks**, so that the associated page for every hyperlink in the left frame is displayed in the right frame.

- Click **OK** to close the Set Target Frame dialog box. Click **OK** to close the Edit Hyperlink dialog box.

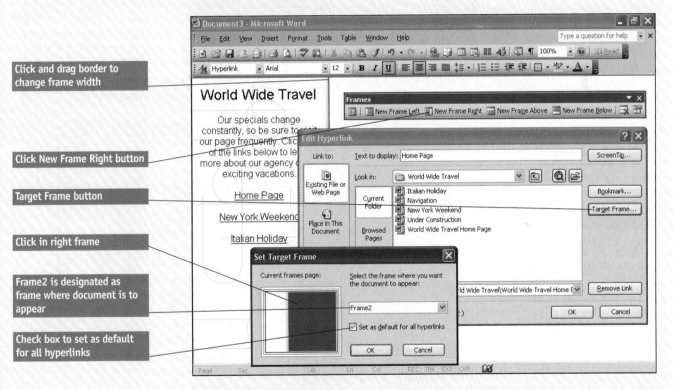

(c) Add a Second Frame (step 3)

FIGURE 6.7 Hands-on Exercise 3 (*continued*)

FIXED VERSUS FLOATING TOOLBARS

A toolbar is either fixed (docked) along an edge of a window or floating within the window. To move a docked toolbar, click and drag the move handle (the vertical dotted line that appears at the left of the toolbar) to a new position. To move a floating toolbar, click and drag its title bar—if you drag a floating toolbar to the edge of the window, it becomes a docked toolbar and vice versa. You can also change the shape of a floating toolbar by dragging any border in the direction you want to go.

Step 4: Set the Default Frame

- Click anywhere in the right frame, then click the **Frame Properties button** on the Frames toolbar to display the Frame Properties dialog box as shown in Figure 6.7d.

- Click in the initial page list box and then click the **Browse button**. Select the **World Wide Travel Home Page** that you created earlier.

- Click the **Borders tab** to view the options that are available. Select the option button to **Show all frame borders**. Set the list box to show scrollbars in browser if needed, and check the box to make the frame resizable in the browser.

- Use the **spin buttons** to experiment with the width of the border. Click the **down arrow** on the Border color list box to choose a different color.

- Click **OK** to accept your choices and close the Frame Properties dialog box. You should see the home page of the travel agency displayed in the right frame.

- Close the Frames toolbar.

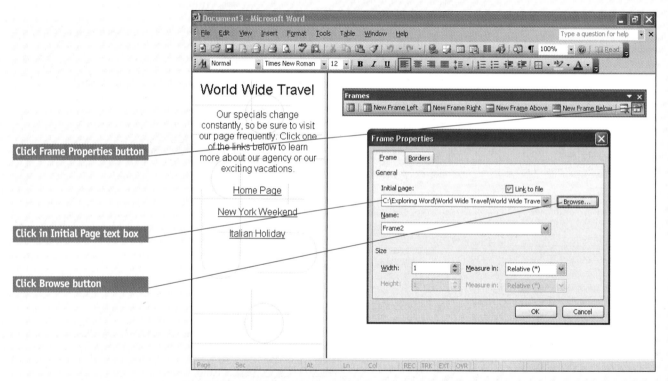

(d) Set the Default Frame (step 4)

FIGURE 6.7   Hands-on Exercise 3 (*continued*)

SET A TIME LIMIT

It's fun to experiment with the visual design of your Web page, but it can also be counterproductive. Try different settings for the width and color of the frame border, set a time limit, and stick to it when your time is up. The more important options are those that affect the *behavior* of the border. We recommend that you show all frame borders, show scrollbars if needed, and make the frame resizable in the browser.

Step 5: **Test the Navigation**

- Click on the **Navigation page**, then point to the New York Weekend. Press **Ctrl+Click** (press the **Ctrl key** while you click the mouse) to display this page in the right frame. Test the link to the Italian Holiday in similar fashion.

- Pull down the **File menu** and click the **Save button**, which in turn displays the Save As dialog box as shown in Figure 6.7e. You should be in the World Wide Travel folder with Single File Web Page selected as the file type. The following documents are already in the folder:
  - ❏ The Navigation document contains the hyperlinks in the left frame
  - ❏ The World Wide Travel Home Page, Italian Holiday, and New York Weekend are the specific pages that will be displayed in the right frame.
  - ❏ The Under Construction page can be used as the basis for additional pages.

- Enter **World Wide Travel Web Site** as the name of the current page. This is a small document that functions as a container to hold the left and right frames.

- Click the **Change Title button** to display the Set Page Title dialog box. Enter **World Wide Travel** as the title. Click **OK** to close this dialog box. Click the **Save button** to save the page. Exit Word.

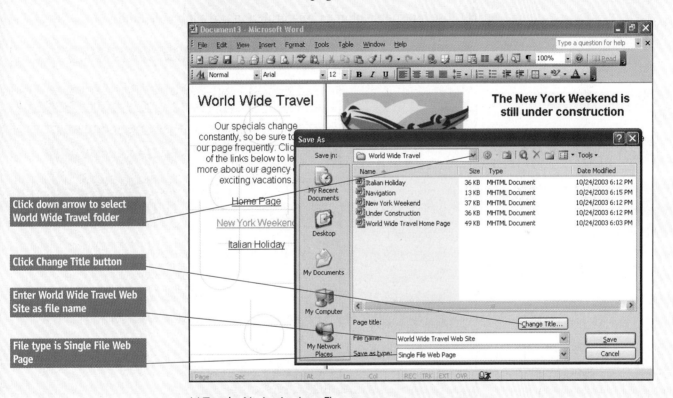

(e) Test the Navigation (step 5)

FIGURE 6.7 Hands-on Exercise 3 *(continued)*

THE WEB TOOLBAR

The Web toolbar appears automatically when you view Web pages within Microsoft Word as you develop a Web site. The buttons on the toolbar are similar to those on the Standard toolbar in Internet Explorer: the Back, Forward, and Favorites buttons, and the Address bar. You can display or hide the toolbar at any time by right clicking any visible toolbar to display the list of available toolbars, then clicking the Web toolbar to toggle the display on or off.

Step 6: View the Completed Site

- Start Internet Explorer. Pull down the **File menu** and click the **Open command** to display the Open dialog box. Click the **Browse button**, locate the **World Wide Travel folder**, then open the **World Wide Travel Web Site document**.

- You should see the Web site in Figure 6.7f. Look closely at the components of the URL in the address bar, reading from right to left:
  - ❏ You are viewing the **World Wide Travel Web Site.mht document** (mht is the extension to indicate the Single File Web Page format).
  - ❏ The document is in the **World Wide Travel folder** that is contained within the Exploring Word folder.
  - ❏ The document is on drive C; that is, you are viewing the site locally, as opposed to seeing it on the Web.

- Test the hyperlinks in the left frame to ensure that they are working correctly.

- Pull down the **File menu**, click the **Print Preview command**, then click the **down arrow** on the Print What list box to select **As laid out on screen**. Click the **Print button** in the Preview window to display the Print dialog box and print the page.

- Close Internet Explorer. Congratulations on a job well done.

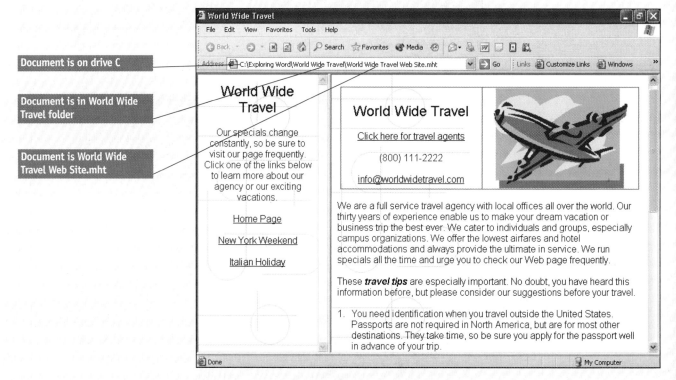

(f) View the Completed Site (step 6)

FIGURE 6.7 Hands-on Exercise 3 (*continued*)

EXPANDING THE SITE

You can expand the site at any time, by creating the additional Web pages, then adding the links to those pages to the navigation frame at the left. You can also add hyperlinks to external Web sites to the navigation frame and open those pages in the right frame within the Web site. See practice exercise 2 at the end of the chapter.

SUMMARY

All Web documents are written in HyperText Markup Language (HTML), a language that consists of codes (or tags) that format a document for display on the World Wide Web. The easiest way to create an HTML document is through Microsoft Word. You start Word in the usual fashion, enter the text of the document with basic formatting, then you use the Save as Web Page command to convert the Word document to its Web equivalent. Microsoft Word does the rest, generating the HTML tags that are needed to create the document. The new Single File Web Page format saves all of the elements of a Web site, including text and graphics, in a single file.

An existing Web page can be modified with respect to its content and/or appearance just like an ordinary Word document; that is, any Word command can be used to create and/or edit a Web page. The Insert Hyperlink command links a document to another page and/or to a bookmark on the same page. The Insert Picture command inserts clip art or a photograph. The Format Theme command applies a professional design to the document.

HTML is not to be confused with XML. HTML describes how a document should look; for example, it might specify that "John Doe" is to appear in bold when viewed in a browser. Extensible Markup Language (XML) is very different as it describes the structure of the data. It might specify that "John" and "Doe" represent an individual's first and last name, respectively, and it makes that information available to virtually any application.

A Web site is composed of multiple pages, which include a home page, navigation page, and other pages as appropriate. Two pages (frames) are typically visible—the navigation page and a detailed page that is displayed by clicking a hyperlink within the navigation page. Vertical frames are the most common means of navigation, but you can also choose horizontal frames and/or open each document in a separate window. All of the pages comprising the site should be stored in the same folder.

The development of a Web site starts with the creation of a home page to provide information about the site and establish the visual design. An Under Construction page is created and duplicated several times for use as the various pages that will comprise the site. A separate navigation page is also created that contains the hyperlinks to the individual pages. The navigation page is then expanded to include a (horizontal or vertical) frame, and the second frame is designated as the target frame. The next step is to specify the default page (the page that will be displayed in the right frame initially) when the Web site document is opened. And finally, you save the document that contains the two frames as the Web site document, the document that is opened to view the site.

After a Web document or Web site has been created, it can be placed on a server or local area network so that other people will be able to access it. This, in turn, requires you to check with your professor or system administrator to obtain the necessary username and password, after which you can use FTP (File Transfer Protocol) to upload your page. Even if your page is not placed on the Web, you can still view it locally on your PC through a Web browser.

KEY TERMS

MULTIPLE CHOICE

1. Which of the following requires you to enter HTML tags explicitly in order to create a Web document?
   - (a) A text editor such as the Notepad accessory
   - (b) Microsoft Word
   - (c) Both (a) and (b)
   - (d) Neither (a) nor (b)

2. What is the easiest way to switch back and forth between Word and Internet Explorer, given that both are open?
   - (a) Click the appropriate button on the Windows taskbar
   - (b) Click the Start button, click Programs, then choose the appropriate program
   - (c) Minimize all applications to display the Windows desktop, then double click the icon for the appropriate application
   - (d) All of the above are equally convenient

3. When should you click the Refresh button on the Internet Explorer toolbar?
   - (a) Whenever you visit a new Web site
   - (b) Whenever you return to a Web site within a session
   - (c) Whenever you view a document on a corporate Intranet
   - (d) Whenever you return to a document that has changed during the session

4. How do you view the HTML tags for a Web document from Internet Explorer?
   - (a) Pull down the View menu and select the Source command
   - (b) Pull down the File menu, click the Save As command, and specify HTML as the file type
   - (c) Click the Web Page Preview button on the Standard toolbar
   - (d) All of the above

5. Internet Explorer can display an HTML page that is stored on:
   - (a) A local area network
   - (b) A Web server
   - (c) Drive A or drive C of a stand-alone PC
   - (d) All of the above

6. How do you save a Word document as a Web page?
   - (a) Pull down the Tools menu and click the Convert to Web Page command
   - (b) Pull down the File menu and click the Save As Web Page command
   - (c) Both (a) and (b)
   - (d) Neither (a) nor (b)

7. Which program transfers files between a PC and a remote computer?
   - (a) Telnet
   - (b) FTP
   - (c) Homer
   - (d) PTF

8. Which of the following requires an Internet connection?
   - (a) Using Internet Explorer to view a document that is stored locally
   - (b) Using Internet Explorer to view the Microsoft home page
   - (c) Both (a) and (b)
   - (d) Neither (a) nor (b)

9. Which of the following requires an Internet connection?
   - (a) The Save as Web Page command
   - (b) The Single File Web Page format
   - (c) Both (a) and (b)
   - (d) Neither (a) nor (b)

10. Which file format is new to Office 2003?
    - (a) HTML
    - (b) XML
    - (c) MHTML
    - (d) All of the above

11. The Insert Hyperlink command can reference:
    - (a) An e-mail address
    - (b) A bookmark
    - (c) A Web page
    - (d) All of the above

... continued

multiple choice

12. The Format Theme command:

    (a) Is required in order to save a Word document as a Web page

    (b) Applies a uniform design to the links and other elements within a document

    (c) Both (a) and (b)

    (d) Neither (a) nor (b)

13. Which of the following features were introduced in Word 2003 to simplify the creation of a Web page?

    (a) The Save as Web Page command

    (b) The Format Theme command

    (c) The Single File Web Page format

    (d) All of the above

14. The Frames toolbar enables you to insert a frame:

    (a) To the left or right of the current frame

    (b) Above or below the current frame

    (c) Both (a) and (b)

    (d) Neither (a) nor (b)

15. Which of the following is true?

    (a) A Web page is saved as an HTTP document

    (b) All of the pages for an entire Web site are typically stored in a single document

    (c) Both (a) and (b)

    (d) Neither (a) nor (b)

16. How do you display the Frames toolbar?

    (a) Pull down the View menu, click the Toolbars command, and toggle the Frames toolbar on

    (b) Right click any visible toolbar, then toggle the Frames toolbar on

    (c) Both (a) and (b)

    (d) Neither (a) nor (b)

17. Which of the following best describes XML?

    (a) It is a replacement for HTML

    (b) It stores the documents for a Web site in a single file

    (c) It describes the structure of data, as opposed to the appearance of data

    (d) All of the above

18. You are viewing a Web page in Internet Explorer in which the hyperlinks are displayed in two different colors. What is the most likely explanation?

    (a) One or more errors must have occurred

    (b) One or more of the hyperlinks was previously accessed

    (c) Some of the hyperlinks are invalid and are shown in the second color

    (d) All of the above

ANSWERS

1. a	**7.** b	**13.** c
2. a	**8.** b	**14.** c
3. d	**9.** d	**15.** d
4. a	**10.** c	**16.** c
5. d	**11.** d	**17.** c
6. b	**12.** b	**18.** b

1. **Milestones in Communications:** The document in Figure 6.8 describes various milestones in the history of communications and is truly informative. Hyperlinks to the various milestones are listed in a table near the top of the document. (Each hyperlink branches to a place within the document, as opposed to branching to an external document.) Proceed as follows:

   a. Open the *Chapter 6 Practice 1* document in the Exploring Word folder. Pull down the Format menu, click the AutoFormat command to display the AutoFormat dialog box, verify that the AutoFormat Now option is selected, and click OK. Modify the Body Text style and/or the Heading 1 style after the document has been formatted in any way that makes sense to you.

   b. Insert a three-by-three table at the top of the document that will contain the hyperlink to each milestone within the document. Enter the title of each milestone as shown in Figure 6.8. Format the text as desired, then create the hyperlinks to the associated text. (You do not have to create bookmarks to each milestone because the associated headings are automatically recognized as places within the document.) Click and drag to select the title—for example, The Pony Express—pull down the Insert menu, click the Hyperlink command, then click the Place in this Document button to select from the listed headings.

   c. You also need to insert a hyperlink at the end of the text for each milestone to return to the top of the document. Scroll down in the document to move to the end of a milestone and type "Top of Document". Click and drag to select this text, pull down the Insert menu, click the Hyperlink command, click the Place in This Document button, and select Top of the Document. Copy this hyperlink to the end of each milestone.

   d. Use the Format Theme command to complete the formatting. Save the document as a Web page in the Single File Web Page format. Exit Word.

   e. Start Windows Explorer, then go to the folder containing your Web page, and double click the file you just created. Internet Explorer will start automatically (because your document was saved as a Web page). Print the document for your instructor as proof you completed the assignment.

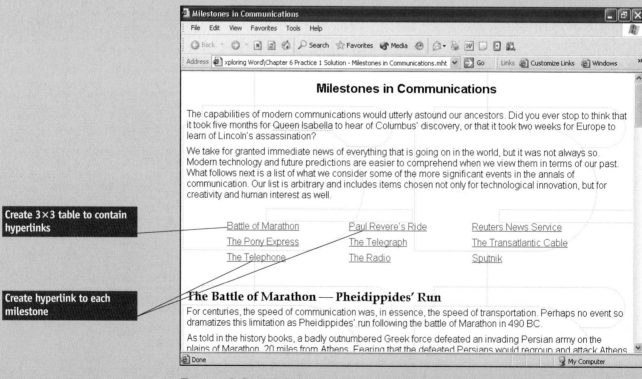

FIGURE 6.8 Milestones in Communications (exercise 1)

practice exercises

2. **Expanding the World Wide Web Site:** This assignment asks you to update the World Wide Travel Web site that was developed in the chapter as shown in Figure 6.9. Look closely and you will see that we added two links in the navigation pane. We have also expanded the content of the existing New York Weekend page. Proceed as follows:

   a. Start Word and open the existing New York Weekend Web document in the World Wide Travel folder. The page is currently under construction and does not contain any specific information. Your task is to create a page describing a weekend holiday similar to the page in Figure 6.9. You do not have to match our page exactly, but you are required to use clip art and a bulleted list. Save the completed page. Close the New York Weekend document.

   b. Start Internet Explorer and open the World Wide Travel Web Site document. Click the link to the New York Weekend, which should display the page that you just created. The modification was easy because the navigation already existed; that is, all you had to do to introduce the new vacation was modify the content of an existing page.

   c. Return to Word and open the existing Under Construction document. Pull down the File menu and click the Save as Web Page command to save the page as Register with Us in the Single File Web Page format. Close the document.

   d. Open the Navigation document that was created earlier. Press Ctrl+End to move to the end of the document, press Enter twice, and then insert a hyperlink to the Register with Us page that you just created. Save the document. Remain in the Navigation document and insert a second hyperlink to Passport Information. This time, however, you will link to an external page (http://travel.state.gov/passport_services), which is an official site of the U.S. government. Save the Navigation document. Exit Word.

   e. Return to Internet Explorer. Click in the Navigation pane and click the Refresh button to see the updated version of this page. (You may have to close Internet Explorer, then reopen it and reload the World Wide Travel Web site if the refresh button does not work.) Click the link to Register with Us to view the page you created previously. Now click the link to Passport Information to view the external site.

   f. Print all of the pages in the completed Web site for your instructor. Add a cover page to complete the assignment.

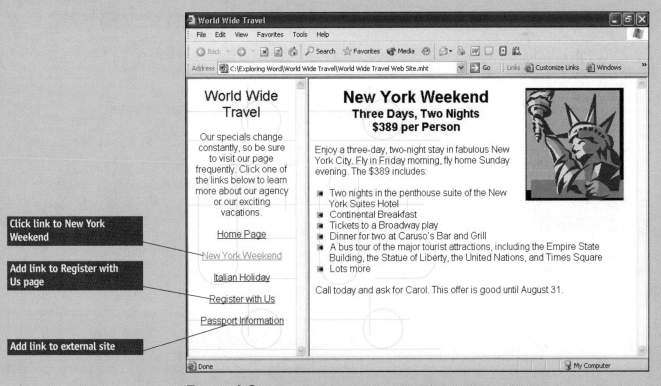

FIGURE 6.9 Expanding the World Wide Web Site (exercise 2)

3. **Realtor of the Year Home Page:** The home page in Figure 6.10 is appropriate for the Realtor of the Year Case study that was presented at the beginning of the chapter. You do not have to duplicate our page exactly, but you are asked to create an attractive page that contains clip art, one or more hyperlinks to an appropriate Web site, and a bulleted list. Proceed as follows:

a. Start Word and create a new document. Use the Insert Table command to create a one-by-two table (one row and two columns) at the top of the document that contains clip art and the identifying information for the agency. Format the text within the table as appropriate.

b. Enter the remaining text for your page. Pull down the Format menu, click the Themes command, and select a professionally chosen design. Make additional formatting changes as necessary.

c. Use the Insert Hyperlink command to enter at least one hyperlink somewhere in the document. (Our link is to the *Miami Herald* at www.herald.com.)

d. Pull down the File menu and click the Save as Web Page command to convert the Word document to a Web document. Save the document in a new folder (Realtor of the Year) within the Exploring Word folder. (The folder will be used in the next exercise as well, when we expand the page to include a Web site.) Choose an appropriate file name such as "Realtor Home Page" and use the Single File Web Page format. Use the Change Title command button to change the title of the page to reflect your name. Close Word.

e. Start Windows Explorer, go to the folder containing your Web page, and double click the file you just created. Internet Explorer will start automatically (because your document was saved as a Web page). You should see your document within Internet Explorer as shown in Figure 6.10. Look carefully at the Address bar and note the local address on drive C, as opposed to a Web address. Print the document for your instructor as proof you completed the assignment.

f. Creating the home page and viewing it locally is easy. Placing the page on the Web where it can be seen by anyone with an Internet connection is not as straightforward. You will need additional information from your instructor about how to obtain an account on a Web server (if that is available at your school), and further how to upload the Web page from your PC to the server.

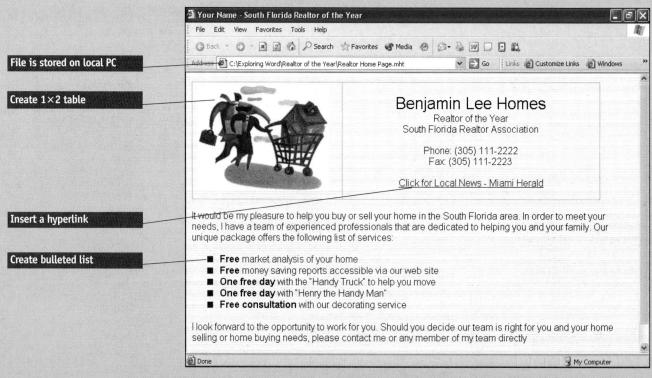

FIGURE 6.10   Realtor of the Year Home Page (exercise 3)

4. **Realtor of the Year Web Site:** This exercise expands the previous problem to create the Web site in Figure 6.11. You do not have to create all of the detailed pages, but you should complete at least one, such as the Current Listing page in Figure 6.11. An "Under Construction" page can be used for the remaining links. Proceed as follows:

   a. Create the Under Construction page. Save the document as a Single File Web Page in the Realtor of the Year folder from the previous exercise. The formatting and theme of your page should be consistent with the design of the Realtor of the Year home page.

   b. The Under Construction page should still be open. Change the text to reflect a new page (current listings). Pull down the File menu, click the Save as Web Page command, and save the page as Current Listings. Change the text and save the page a second time as Sell Your Current Home. Create additional pages corresponding to the links in Figure 6.11. Close all open documents.

   c. Open the Current Listings page that you just created. Complete the page by adding information similar to that in Figure 6.11. (The picture is optional.)

   d. Start a new document and create the navigation page that contains the hyperlinks to the various pages that you just created. Format the navigation page using the same theme as the other pages on your site. Save the page in the Realtor of the Year folder using the Single File Web Page format. Leave the document open.

   e. Display the Frames toolbar. Click the New Frame Right button to insert a frame to the right of the navigation page. Right click any hyperlink in the left frame; click the Edit Hyperlink command, then set the target frame as the frame on the right (frame 2). Click in the right frame, click the Frame Properties button, and set the initial page to the Realtor Home page.

   f. Save the current document as *Realtor of the Year Web Site* document in the Realtor of the Year folder. Change the title of the page.

   g. Start Internet Explorer and open the Realtor of the Year Web Site document that you just created. You should see the Web site in Figure 6.11. Pull down the File menu (from Internet Explorer), click the Print Preview command, then click the down arrow on the Print What list box to select As laid out on screen. Click the Print button from the Preview window to display the Print dialog box and print the page.

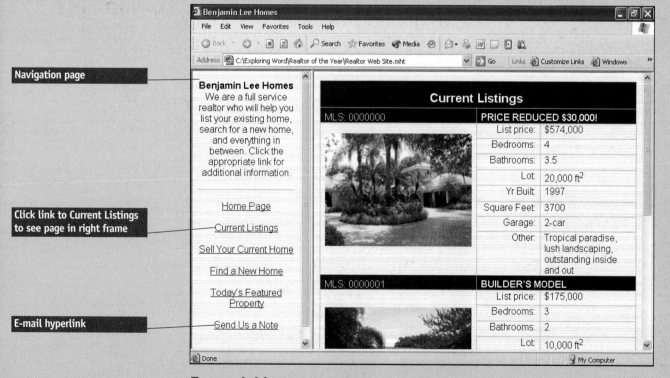

FIGURE 6.11   Realtor of the Year Web Site (exercise 4)

practice exercises

5. **Alternate Airways Home Page:** Open the *Chapter 6 Practice 5* document in the Exploring Word folder and use that document as the basis of the home page in Figure 6.12. Your first task will be to save the existing document as a Web page in its own folder. Proceed as follows:

a. Pull down the File menu, click the Save as Web Page command, and create an Alternate Airways folder within the Exploring Word folder. Enter Alternate Airways Home Page as the file name and specify Single File Web Page as the file type. Use the Change Title button to change the title of the page to reflect the name of the Web site. Click Continue if a message appears that indicates pictures with text wrapping will become left or right justified.

b. Review the document and make the basic formatting changes you deem appropriate. Use the Themes command in the Format menu to apply an overall design to the page. Use any theme you like, but the overall document formatting should be similar to the document in Figure 6.12.

c. Format the title if you have not already done so. Select the text, "Click here to contact us" that appears toward the top of the document. Pull down the Insert menu and click the Hyperlink command (or click the Insert Hyperlink button on the Standard toolbar), click the E-mail Address button, and then enter your e-mail address.

d. Go to the last paragraph and insert hyperlinks for the Boeing Company at www.boeing.com and FlyteComm at www.flytecomm.com. The latter Web site enables you to track a flight from takeoff to landing.

e. Save the document a final time, then exit Word. Start Windows Explorer, then go to the folder containing your Web page, and double click the file you just created. Internet Explorer will start automatically (because your document was saved as a Web page). You should see your document within Internet Explorer as shown in Figure 6.12. Look carefully at the Address bar and note the local address on drive C, as opposed to a Web address.

f. Print the document for your instructor as proof you completed the assignment. Add a cover sheet to complete the assignment.

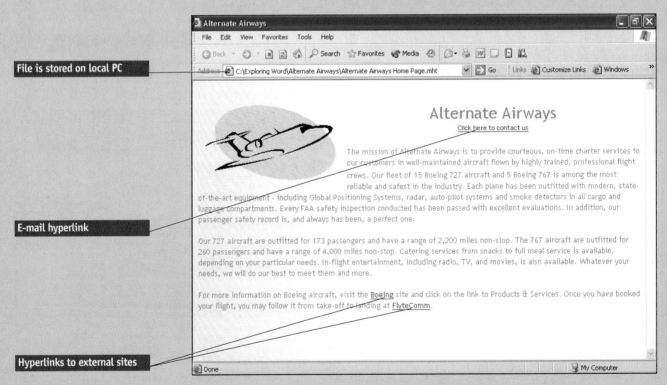

FIGURE 6.12 Alternate Airways Home Page (exercise 5)

290 CHAPTER 6: INTRODUCTION TO HTML

6. **Alternate Airways Web Site:** This exercise expands the previous problem to create the Web site in Figure 6.13, as opposed to a single Web page. You do not have to create the detailed pages for Our Employees and Our Destinations, but you are required to complete the navigation for the site. Proceed as follows:

   a. Create the Under Construction page. Save the document as a Single File Web Page in the Alternate Airways folder from the previous exercise. You do not have to match our design exactly, but the formatting and theme of your page should be consistent with the design of the Alternate Airways home page.

   b. The Under Construction page should still be open. Change the text on the page to reflect Our Employees, pull down the File menu, click the Save As command, and save the page as Our Employees. Save the page a second time as Our Destinations. All three pages should be saved in the Alternate Airways folder. Close all open documents.

   c. Start a new document and create the navigation page that contains the hyperlinks to the various pages that you just created. Format the navigation page using the same theme as the other pages on your site. Save the page in the Alternate Airways folder using the Single File Web Page format.

   d. Display the Frames toolbar. Click the New Frame Right button to insert a frame to the right of the navigation page. Right click any hyperlink in the left frame; click the Edit Hyperlink command, then set the target frame as the frame on the right (frame 2). Click in the right frame, click the Frame Properties button, and set the initial page to the Alternate Airways home page.

   e. Save the current document as Alternate Airways Web Site in the Alternate Airways folder. Use the Change Title button to change the title of the page. Exit Word.

   f. Start Internet Explorer and open the Alternate Airways Web site that you just created. You should see the Web site in Figure 6.13. Test the navigation to be sure that the site is functioning correctly.

   g. Pull down the File menu (from Internet Explorer), click the Print Preview command, then click the down arrow on the Print What list box to select As laid out on screen. Click the Print button from the Preview window to display the Print dialog box and print the page.

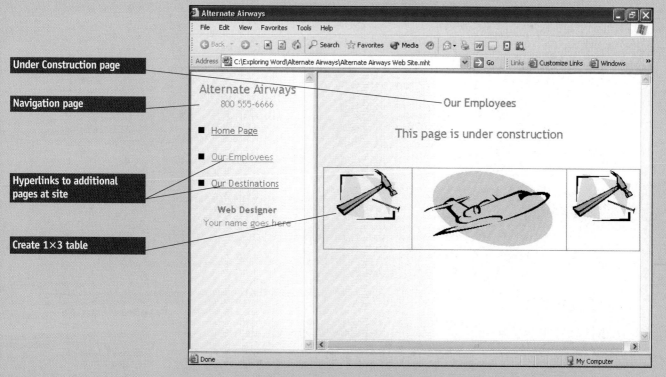

FIGURE 6.13 Alternate Airways Web Site (exercise 6)

7. **University Housing Web Site:** The Web site in Figure 6.14 uses horizontal (as opposed to vertical) navigation. We supply the text of the home page, which is displayed in the lower frame, but it is up to you to develop the site. (You can use an Under Construction page, as opposed to completing the detailed pages for Activities and Programs and Meal Plan.)

   a. Open the *Chapter 6 Practice 7* document in the Exploring Word folder. Review the document and insert bookmarks and associated links as appropriate—for example, to the visitation rules, rules and regulations, and payment options sections within the document. Format the document as you see fit. Use the Themes command in the Format menu to apply an overall design to the page.

   b. Pull down the File menu, click the Save as Web Page command, and create a University Housing folder within the Exploring Word folder. Enter University Housing Home Page as the file name and specify Single File Web Page as the file type.

   c. Start a new document and create the Under Construction page. Save the document as a Single File Web Page in the University Housing folder. The formatting of this page should be consistent with the home page. The Under Construction page should still be open. Change the text on the page to reflect Activities and Programs. Pull down the File menu, click the Save As command, and save the page as Activities and Programs. Save the page a second time as Meal Plan. All three pages should be saved in the University Housing folder. Close all open documents.

   d. Start a new document and create the navigation page that contains the hyperlinks to the various pages that you just created. Format the navigation page using the same theme as the other pages on your site. Use clip art to add interest to the page. Save the page in the University Housing folder.

   e. Display the Frames toolbar. Click the New Frame Below button to insert a frame below the navigation page. Right click any hyperlink in the left frame; click the Edit Hyperlink command, then set the target frame as the bottom frame. Click in the bottom frame and set the initial page to the home page. Save the current document as University Housing Web site in the University Housing folder. Exit Word.

   f. Start Internet Explorer and open the University Housing Web site as shown in Figure 6.14. Print the individual pages for your instructor.

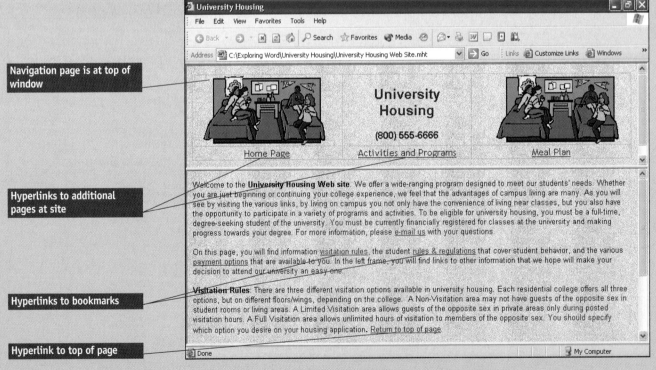

Navigation page is at top of window

Hyperlinks to additional pages at site

Hyperlinks to bookmarks

Hyperlink to top of page

FIGURE 6.14   University Housing Web Site (exercise 7)

8. **Totally Fit Web Site:** The Web site in Figure 6.15 is for a hypothetical fitness center. We supply the text of the home page, which is displayed in the right frame, but it is up to you to develop the site. (You can use an Under Construction page, as opposed to completing the detailed pages for Exercise Tips and Enroll Now.) Proceed as follows:

   a. Open the *Chapter 6 Practice 8* document in the Exploring Word folder. Review the document and insert hyperlinks as appropriate, such as to the American Heart Association, which is referenced in the document. Format the document as you see fit. Use the Themes command in the Format menu to apply an overall design to the page.

   b. Pull down the File menu, click the Save as Web Page command, and create a Totally Fit folder within the Exploring Word folder. Enter Totally Fit Home Page as the file name and specify Single File Web Page as the file type. Close the document.

   c. Start a new document and create the Under Construction page. Save the document as a Single File Web Page in the Totally Fit folder. The formatting of this page should be consistent with the home page. The Under Construction page should still be open. Change the text on the page to reflect exercise tips. Pull down the File menu, click the Save As command, and save the page as Exercise Tips. Change the text on the page, then save the page a second time as Enroll Now. All three pages should be saved in the Totally Fit folder. Close all open documents.

   d. Start a new document and create the navigation page that contains the hyperlinks to the various pages that you just created. Add a (Contact Us) hyperlink to your e-mail address. Format the navigation page using the same theme as the other pages on your site. Save the page as a Web page in the Totally Fit folder.

   e. Display the Frames toolbar. Click the New Frame Right button to insert a frame to the right of the navigation page. Right click any hyperlink in the left frame, click the Edit Hyperlink command, then set the target frame as the frame on the right (frame 2). Click in the right frame, click the Frame Properties button, and set the initial page to the Totally Fit Home page. Save the current document as Totally Fit Web site in the Totally Fit folder. Exit Word.

   f. Start Internet Explorer and open the Totally Fit Web site as shown in Figure 6.15. Print the individual pages for your instructor.

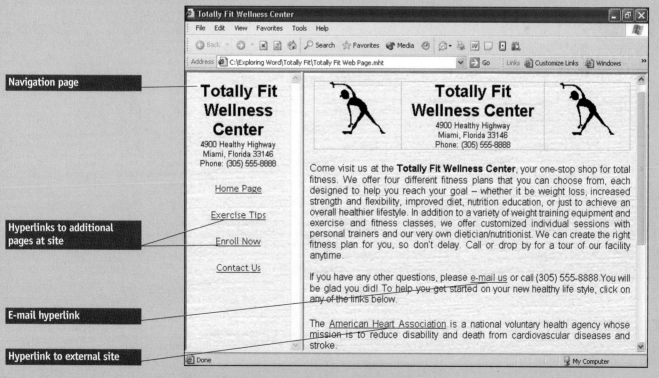

FIGURE 6.15 Totally Fit Web Site (exercise 8)

9. **Word and XML:** This exercise describes how to convert (map) the essential elements of a résumé to an XML document. You can use your own résumé or the sample we provide, but you will have to use the schema (XML definition) that is included on the data disk. Proceed as follows:

a. Open the *Chapter 6 Practice 9* document that contains our sample résumé. Change the name and other information at the top of the document to reflect your name and e-mail address. Pull down the Tools menu, click Templates and Add-Ins to display the associated dialog box, and then click the XML Schema tab. Click the Add Schema button, then navigate to, then open, the Resume.XSD document in the Exploring Word folder. Type Resume as the Alias and clear the Changes affect current user only check box. Click OK. The résumé schema has been added to the Schema library.

b. The Templates and Add-ins dialog box should still be open with the XML Schema tab selected. Be sure that the Resume schema is checked so that this schema is attached to the current document. Click OK. The XML Structure task pane opens automatically as shown in Figure 6.16.

c. Select (click) the Resume element in the list of schema elements that appears in the lower portion of the task pane, then click Apply to Entire Document. XML tags for Resume will appear at the beginning and end of the document. You can now apply the various tags within the Resume schema to different portions of the document. Click and drag to select your name at the top of the résumé, and then apply the Name tag. Apply the FirstName and LastName tags in similar fashion.

d. Map the other elements of your résumé in similar fashion, save the completed résumé, and then print it. The résumé prints as a regular Word document; i.e., you do not see the XML codes that you added.

e. Save the document a second time, but specify XML document as the file type in the Exploring Word folder. Exit Word. Start Windows Explorer and locate the XML document that you just created. It is much smaller than the Word document (approximately 3K). Double click the XML document, which opens automatically in Internet Explorer. Print the XML document.

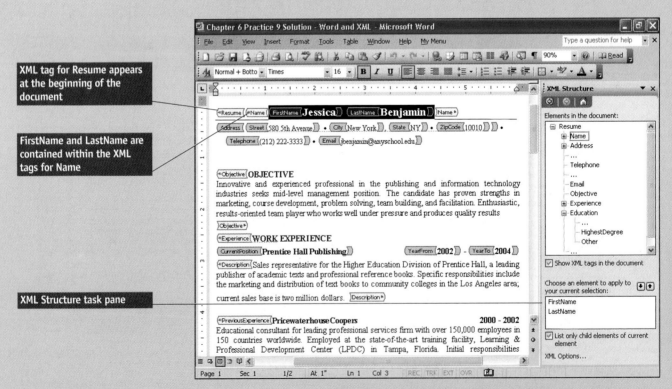

FIGURE 6.16 Word and XML (exercise 9)

The Expert User:
Workgroups, Forms, Master Documents, and Macros

CASE STUDY
A QUESTION OF ETHICS

You would never walk into a music store, put a CD under your arm, and walk out without paying for it. What if, however, you could download the same CD from the Web for free? Are you hurting anyone? Or what if you gave a clerk a $5 bill, but received change for a $50? Would you return the extra money? Would you speak up if it was the person ahead of you on line who received change for the $50, when you clearly saw that they gave the clerk $5? Ethical conflicts occur all the time and result when one person or group benefits at the expense of another.

Your instructor has assigned a class project whereby students are divided into teams to consider questions of ethics and society. Each team is to submit a single document that represents the collective efforts of all the team members. The completed project is to include a brief discussion of ethical principles followed by five examples of ethical conflicts. Every member of the team will receive the same grade, regardless of their level of participation; indeed, this might be an ethical dilemma, in and of itself. ■

Your assignment is to read the chapter and focus on the Track Changes command whereby multiple individuals can enter changes electronically in the same document. You will then open the *Chapter 7 Case Study Ethics and Society* document in the Exploring Word folder and display the Reviewing toolbar if it is not already visible. Click the down arrow on the Display for Review list box and select Final Showing Markup to show the changes that have been entered, but not yet reviewed.

You will notice that several individuals have suggested changes, with each person's recommendations in a different color. Print the document in this format so that the suggested changes appear in the hard copy. Use the Show button on the Reviewing toolbar to match the reviewers with their suggested changes. Print the document in final form after all of the suggested changes have been accepted. Read the document carefully in preparation for a class discussion of the ethical decisions involved.

This chapter introduces several capabilities that will make you a true expert in Microsoft Word. The features go beyond the needs of the typical student and extend to capabilities that you will appreciate in the workplace, as you work with others on a collaborative project. We begin with a discussion of workgroup editing, whereby suggested revisions from one or more individuals can be stored electronically within a document. This enables the original author to review each suggestion individually before it is incorporated into the final version of the document, and further, allows multiple people to work on the same document in collaboration with one another.

The suggested revisions from the various reviewers are displayed in one of two ways, as the "Original Showing Markup" in Figure 7.1a or as the "Final Showing Markup" in Figure 7.1b. The difference is subtle and depends on personal preference with respect to displaying the insertions to, and deletions from, a document. (All revisions fall into one of these two categories: insertions or deletions. Even if you are simply substituting one word for another, you are deleting the original word, then inserting its replacement.)

The *Original Showing Markup* view in Figure 7.1a shows the deleted text within the body of the document (with a line through the deleted text) and displays the inserted text in a balloon to the right of the actual document. The *Final Showing Markup* view in Figure 7.1b is the opposite; that is, it displays the inserted text in the body of the document and shows the deleted text in a balloon. Both views display *revision marks* to the left of any line that has been changed. Comments are optional and are enclosed in balloons at the right of either document. The suggestions of multiple reviewers appear in different colors, with each reviewer assigned a different color.

The review process is straightforward. The initial document is sent for review to one or more individuals, who record their changes by executing the *Track Changes command* in the Tools menu (or by double clicking the TRK indicator in the status bar) to start (or stop) the recording process. The author of the original document receives the corrected document and then uses the *Accept Change* and *Reject Change buttons* on the *Reviewing toolbar* to review the document and implement the suggested changes.

The Versions of a Document

The Save command is one of the most basic in Microsoft Office. Each time you execute the command, the contents in memory are saved to disk under the designated file name, and the previous contents of the file are erased. What if, however, you wanted to retain the previous version of the file in addition to the current version that was just saved? You could use the Save As command to create a second file. It's easier to use the *Versions command* in the File menu because it lets you save multiple versions of a document in a single file.

The existence of multiple versions is transparent in that the latest version is opened automatically when you open the file at the start of a session. You can, however, review previous versions to see the changes that were made. Word displays the date and time each version was saved as well as the name of the person who saved each version.

Word provides two different levels of *password protection* in conjunction with saving a document. You can establish one password to open the document and a different password to modify it. A password can contain any combination of letters, numbers, and symbols, and can be 15 characters long. Passwords are case sensitive.

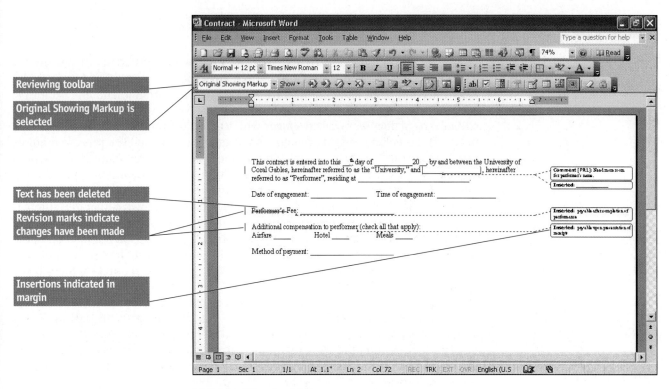

(a) Original Showing Markup

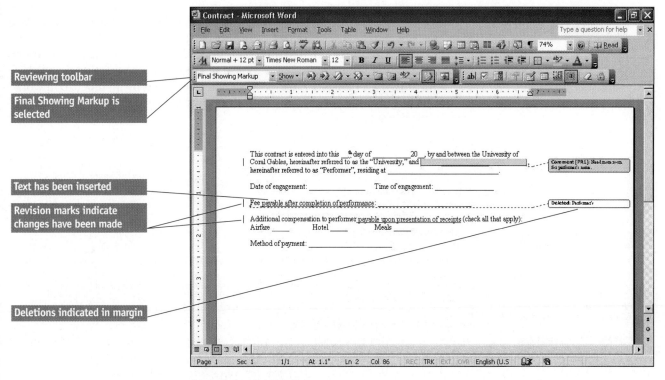

(b) Final Showing Markup

FIGURE 7.1 Workgroup Editing

FORMS

Forms are ubiquitous in the workplace and our society. You complete a form, for example, when you apply for a job or open any type of account. The form may be electronic and completed online, or it may exist as a printed document. All forms, however, are designed for some type of data entry. Microsoft Word lets you create a special type of document called a ***form***, which allows the user to enter data in specific places, but precludes editing the document in any other way. The process requires you to create the form and save it to disk, where it serves as a template for future documents. Then, when you need to enter data for a specific document, you open the original form, enter the data, and save the completed form as a new document.

Figure 7.2 displays a "forms" version of the document shown earlier in Figure 7.1. The form does not contain specific data, but it does contain the text of a document (a contract in this example) that is to be completed by the user. It also contains shaded entries, or ***fields***, that represent the locations where the user enters data that is unique to the individual. To complete the form, the user presses the Tab key to go from one field to the next and enters data as appropriate. Then, when all fields have been entered, the form is printed to produce the finished document (a contract for a specific event). The data that was entered into the various fields appears as regular text.

The form is created as a regular document with the various fields added through tools on the ***Forms toolbar***. Word enables you to create three types of fields—text boxes, check boxes, and drop-down list boxes. A ***text field*** is the most common and is used to enter any type of text. The length of a text field can be set exactly; for example, to two positions for the day in the first line of the document. The length can also be left unspecified, in which case the field will expand to the exact number of positions that are required as the data is entered. A ***check box***, as the name implies, consists of a box, which is checked or not. A ***drop-down list box*** enables the user to choose from one of several existing entries.

After the form is created, it is protected to prevent further modification other than data entry. Our next hands-on exercise has you open an existing document, review the multiple changes to that document as suggested by members of a workgroup, accept the changes as appropriate, then convert the revised document into a form for data entry.

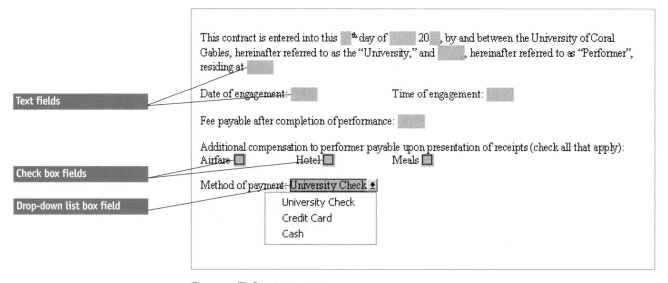

FIGURE 7.2 A Blank Form

1   Workgroups and Forms

Objective   To review the editing comments within a document; to create a form containing text fields, check boxes, and a drop-down list.

Step 1:   **Display the Forms and Reviewing Toolbars**

- Start Word. If Word is already open, pull down the **File menu** and click the **Close command** to close any open documents.

- Point to any visible toolbar, click the **right mouse button**, then click the **Customize command** to display the Customize dialog box as shown in Figure 7.3a.

- If necessary, click the **Toolbars tab** in the Customize dialog box. The boxes for the Standard and Formatting toolbars should be checked.

- Check the boxes to display the **Forms** and **Reviewing toolbars** as shown in Figure 7.3a. Click the **Close button** to close the Customize dialog box.

- Move the Forms toolbar so it is on the same row as the Reviewing toolbar.

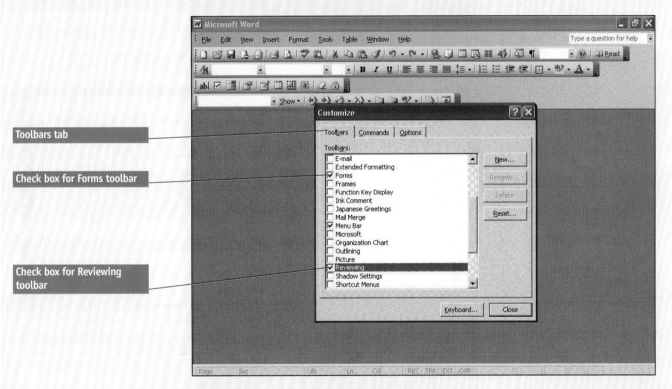

Toolbars tab

Check box for Forms toolbar

Check box for Reviewing toolbar

(a) Display the Forms and Reviewing Toolbars (step 1)

FIGURE 7.3   Hands-on Exercise 1

DOCKED VERSUS FLOATING TOOLBARS

A toolbar is either docked along an edge of a window or floating within the window. To move a docked toolbar, click and drag the move handle (the dotted vertical line that appears at the left of the toolbar) to a new position. To move a floating toolbar, click and drag its title bar—if you drag a floating toolbar to the edge of the window, it becomes a docked toolbar and vice versa. You can also change the shape of a floating toolbar by dragging any border in the direction you want to go.

Step 2: Highlight the Changes

- Open the document called **Contract** in the **Exploring Word folder** as shown in Figure 7.3b. Save the document as **Contract Solution**.

- The **Track Changes** command functions as a toggle switch; that is, execute the command, and the tracking is in effect. Execute the command a second time, and the tracking is off. You can track changes in one of three ways:
  - ❑ Pull down the **Tools menu** and click the **Track Changes command**.
  - ❑ Double click the **TRK indicator** on the status bar.
  - ❑ Click the **Track Changes button** on the Reviewing toolbar.

- Tracking is in effect if the TRK indicator is visible on the status bar.

- Press **Ctrl+Home** to move to the beginning of the document. Press the **Del key** four times to delete the word "The" and the blank space that follows. You will see an indication in the right margin that the text was deleted.

- Move to the end of the address (immediately after the zip code). Press the **space bar** three or four times, then enter the phone number **(305) 111-2222**. The new text is underlined.

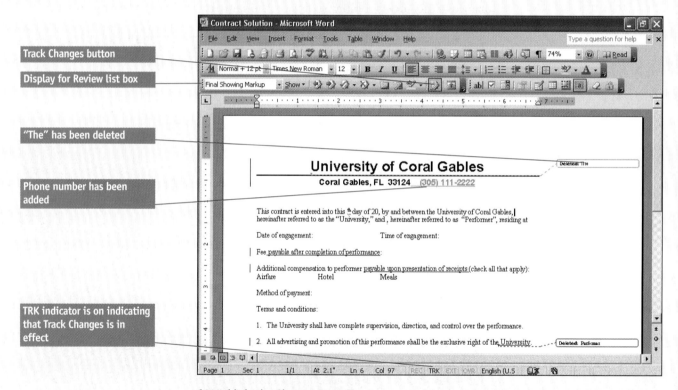

(b) Highlight the Changes (step 2)

FIGURE 7.3   Hands-on Exercise 1 (*continued*)

CHOOSE THE VIEW THAT YOU WANT

Click the down arrow on the Display for Review list box to choose the view you want. The Original Showing Markup view displays the deleted text within the body of the document (with a line through the deleted text) and shows the inserted text in a balloon to the right of the actual document. The Final Showing Markup view is the opposite; it displays the inserted text within the body of the document and displays the deleted text in a balloon at the right. Both views display revision marks to the left of any line that has been changed.

Step 3: Accept or Reject Changes

■ Press **Ctrl+Home** to move to the beginning of the document, then click the **Next button** on the Reviewing toolbar to move to the first change, which is your deletion of the word "the".

■ Click the **Accept Change button** to accept the change. Click the **Next button** to move to the next change, where you will review the next change.

■ You can continue to review changes individually, or you can accept all of the changes as written. Click the **down arrow** on the Accept Change button and click **Accept All Changes in Document** as shown in Figure 7.3c.

■ Save the document.

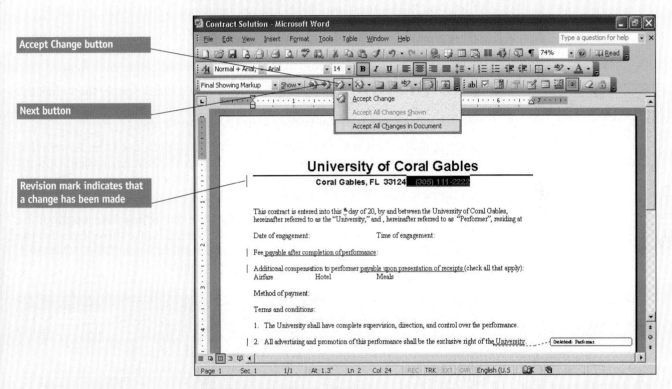

(c) Accept or Reject Changes (step 3)

FIGURE 7.3 Hands-on Exercise 1 (*continued*)

INSERT COMMENTS INTO A DOCUMENT

Add comments to a document to remind yourself (or a reviewer) of action that needs to be taken. Click in the document where you want the comment to appear, then pull down the Insert menu and click the Comment command (or click the Insert Comment button on the Reviewing toolbar) to open the Comments balloon. Enter the text of the comment and click outside the comment area. The word containing the insertion point is highlighted in the color assigned to the reviewer. To delete a comment, right click within the balloon, and then select the Delete Comment command.

Step 4: Create the Text and Check Box Fields

- Click the **Track Changes button** on the Reviewing toolbar to stop tracking changes, which removes the TRK indicator from the status bar. Click the button a second time and tracking is again in effect. (You can also double click the **TRK indicator** on the status bar to toggle tracking on or off.) End with tracking on.

- Move to the first line of text in the contract, then click to the right of the space following the second occurrence of the word "this".

- Click the **Text Form Field button** on the Forms toolbar to create a text field as shown in Figure 7.3d. The field should appear in the document as a shaded entry. Do not worry, however, about the length of this field as we adjust it shortly via the Text Form Field Options dialog box (which is not yet visible).

- Click after the space to the right of the word **of** on the same line and insert a second text field followed by a blank space. Insert the six additional text fields as shown in Figure 7.3d. Add blank spaces as needed before each field.

- Click immediately after the word **Airfare**. Add a blank space, then click the **Check Box Form Field** to create a check box as shown in the figure. Create additional check boxes after the words **Hotel** and **Meals**.

- Click in the first text field (after the word *this*), then click the **Form Field Options button** on the Forms toolbar to display the Text Form Field Options dialog box. Click the **down arrow** in the Type list box and choose **Number**. Enter **2** in the Maximum Length box.

- Click **OK** to accept these settings and close the dialog box. The length of the form field changes automatically to two positions. Change the options for the Year (Number, 2 positions) and Date of Engagement fields (Date, MMMM d, yyyy format) in similar fashion. Save the document.

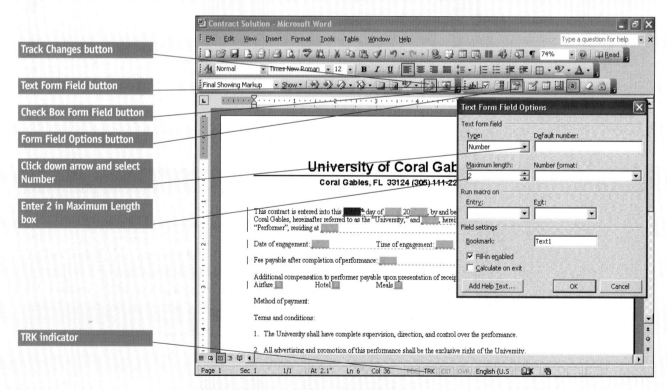

(d) Create the Text and Check Box Fields (step 4)

FIGURE 7.3 Hands-on Exercise 1 (*continued*)

Step 5: Add the Drop-down List Box

- Double click the **TRK indicator** on the status bar to stop tracking changes. (The indicator should be dim after double clicking.)

- Click the **down arrow** on the Accept Changes button on the Reviewing toolbar. Click **Accept All Changes in Document**.

- Click in the document after the words **Method of Payment**, then click the **Drop-down Form Field button** to create a drop-down list box. **Double click** the newly created field to display the dialog box in Figure 7.3e.

- Click in the Drop-down Item text box, type **University Check**, and click the **Add button** to move this entry to the Items in drop-down list box. Type **Credit Card** and click the **Add button**. Type **Cash**, then click the **Add button** to complete the entries for the drop-down list box.

- Click **OK** to accept the settings and close the dialog box.

- Save the document.

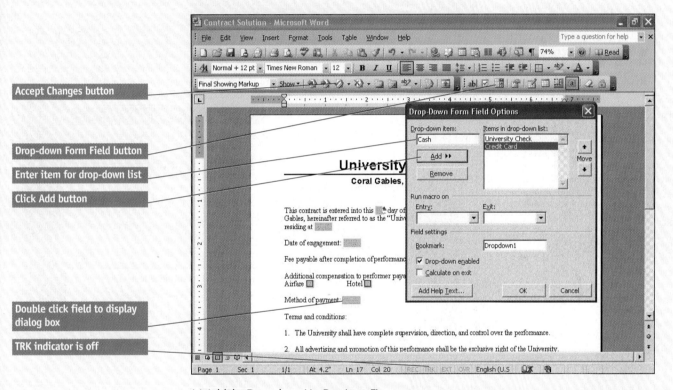

(e) Add the Drop-down List Box (step 5)

FIGURE 7.3 Hands-on Exercise 1 (*continued*)

FIELD CODES VERSUS FIELD RESULTS

All fields are displayed in a document in one of two formats, as a field code or as a field result. A field code appears in braces and indicates instructions to insert variable data when the document is printed; a field result displays the information as it will appear in the printed document. (The field results of a form field are blank until the data is entered into a form.) You can toggle the display between the field code and field result by selecting the field and pressing Shift+F9 during editing. To show (hide) field codes for all fields in the document, press Alt+F9.

Step 6: **Save a New Version**

■ Proofread the document to be sure that it is correct. Once you are satisfied with the finished document, click the **Protect Form button** on the Forms toolbar to prevent further changes to the form. (You can still enter data into the fields on the form, as we will do in the next step.)

■ Pull down the **File menu** and click the **Versions command** to display the Versions dialog box for this document. There is currently one previous version, the one created by Robert Grauer on May 5, 2003.

■ Click the **Save Now button** to display the Save Version dialog box in Figure 7.3f. Enter the text of a comment you want to associate with this version.

■ The author's name will be different on your screen and will reflect the person who registered the version of Microsoft Word you are using.

■ Click **OK** to save the version and close the dialog box.

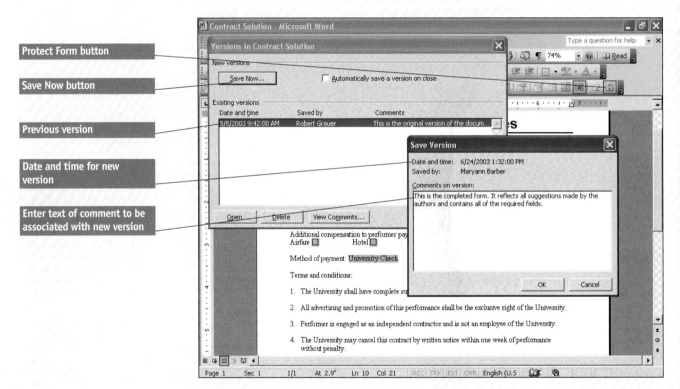

(f) Save a New Version (step 6)

FIGURE 7.3 Hands-on Exercise 1 (*continued*)

SET EDITING AND FORMATTING RESTRICTIONS

You can extend the protection associated with a document to impose a specific set of formatting and/or editing restrictions. Pull down the Tools menu and click the Protect Document command to display the associated task pane, and then implement the specific restrictions you want to impose. You can, for example, restrict the user to a limited number of formatting styles within a document. You can also make the entire document read-only and then select the parts of the document that are exempt (i.e., those parts of the document that can be modified). You can also restrict editing to specific users. See problem 3 at the end of the chapter.

Step 7: Fill In the Form

■ Be sure that the form is protected; that is, that all buttons are dim on the Forms toolbar except for the Protect Form and Form Field Shading buttons. Press **Ctrl+Home** to move to the first field.

■ Enter today's date, press the **Tab key** (to move to the next field), enter today's month, press the **Tab key**, and enter the year.

■ Continue to press the **Tab key** to complete the form. Enter your name as the performer. Enter a fee of **$1,000**.

■ Press the **space bar** on the keyboard to check or clear the various check boxes. Check the boxes for airfare, hotel, and meals.

■ Click the **down arrow** on the Method of Payment list box and choose **University Check**.

■ Your completed form should be similar to our form as shown in Figure 7.3g.

■ You can make changes to the text of the contract by unprotecting the form. Do not, however, click the Protect Form button after data has been entered, or you will lose the data.

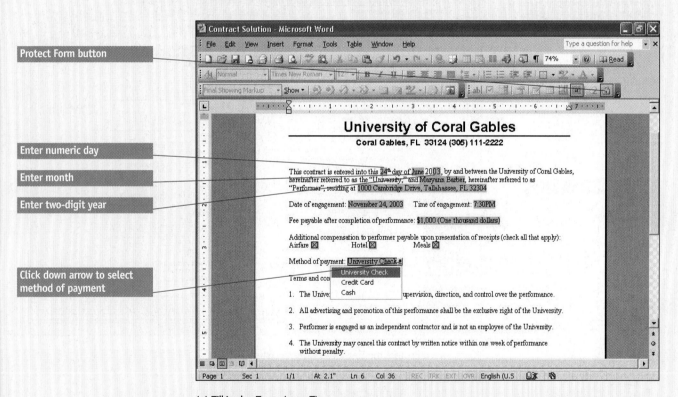

(g) Fill in the Form (step 7)

FIGURE 7.3 Hands-on Exercise 1 (*continued*)

PROTECTING AND UNPROTECTING A FORM

The Protect Form button toggles protection on and off. Click the button once, and the form is protected; data can be entered into the various fields, but the form itself cannot be modified. Click the button a second time, and the form is unprotected and can be fully modified. Be careful, however, about unprotecting a form once data has been entered. That action will not create a problem in and of itself, but protecting a form a second time (after the data was previously entered) will reset all of its fields.

Step 8: Password Protect the Executed Contract

- Pull down the **File menu**, click the **Save As command** to display the Save As dialog box, then type **Executed Contract** as the file name.

- Click the **drop-down arrow** next to the Tools button and click the **Security Options command** to display the Security dialog box in Figure 7.3h.

- Click in the **Password to open** text box and enter **password** (the password is case sensitive) as the password. Click **OK**.

- A Confirm Password dialog box will open, asking you to reenter the password and warning you not to forget the password; once a document is protected by a password, it cannot be opened without that password.

- Reenter the password and click **OK** to establish the password.

- Click **Save** to save the document and close the Save As dialog box. Exit Word if you do not want to continue with the next exercise at this time.

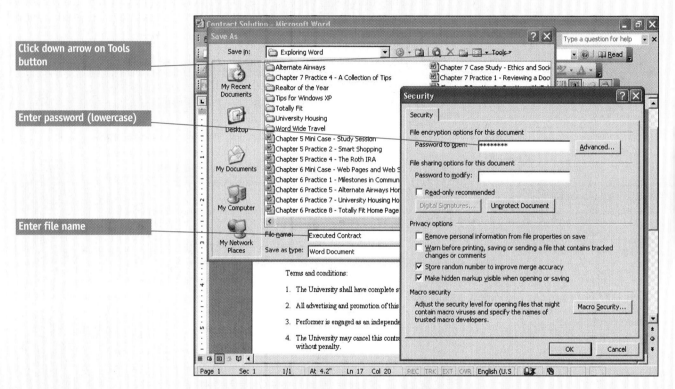

Click down arrow on Tools button

Enter password (lowercase)

Enter file name

(h) Password Protect the Executed Contract (step 8)

FIGURE 7.3   Hands-on Exercise 1 (*continued*)

AUTHENTICATE YOUR DOCUMENTS

What if you sent a contract or other important document to a third party and the document was intercepted and altered en route? Or more likely, what if someone sent a forged document to a third party in your name? You can avoid both situations by using a digital signature to authenticate your correspondence. A digital signature is an electronic stamp of authenticity that confirms the origin and status of an e-mail attachment. You can obtain a digital signature from a variety of sources, then use Word to apply that signature to any document.

Tables were introduced in an earlier chapter and provide an easy way to arrange text, numbers, and/or graphics within a document. This section extends that discussion to include calculations within a table, giving a Word document the power of a simple spreadsheet. We also describe how to *sort* the rows within a table in a different sequence, according to the entries in a specific column of the table.

We begin by reviewing a few basic concepts. The rows and columns in a table intersect to form *cells*, each of which can contain text, numbers, and/or graphics. Text is entered into each cell individually, enabling you to add, delete, or format text in one cell without affecting the text in other cells. The rows within a table can be different heights, and each row may contain a different number of columns.

The commands in the *Tables menu* or the *Tables and Borders toolbar* operate on one or more cells. The Insert and Delete commands add new rows or columns, or delete existing rows or columns, respectively. Other commands shade and/or border selected cells or the entire table. You can also select multiple cells and merge them into a single cell. All of this was presented earlier, and should be familiar.

Figure 7.4 displays a table of expenses that is associated with the performer's contract. The table also illustrates two additional capabilities that are associated with a table. First, you can sort the rows in a table to display the data in different sequences as shown in Figures 7.4a and 7.4b. Both figures display the same 6×4 table (six rows and four columns). The first row in each figure is a header row and contains the field names for each column. The next four rows contain data for a specific expense, while the last row displays the total for all expenses

Figure 7.4a lists the expenses in alphabetical order—airfare, hotel, meals, and performance fee. Figure 7.4b, however, lists the expenses in *descending* (high to low) *sequence* according to the amount. Thus, the performance fee (the largest expense) is listed first, and the meals (the smallest expense) appear last. Note, too, that the sort has been done in such a way as to affect only the four middle rows; that is, the header and total rows have not moved. This is accomplished according to the select-then-do methodology that is used for many operations in Microsoft Word. You select the rows that are to be sorted, then you execute the command (the Sort command in the Tables menu in this example).

Figure 7.4c displays the same table as in Figure 7.4b, albeit in a different format that displays the field codes rather than the field results. The entries consist of formulas that were entered into the table to perform a calculation. The entries are similar to those in a spreadsheet. Thus, the rows in the table are numbered from one to six while the columns are labeled from A to D. The row and column labels do not appear in the table per se, but are used to enter the formulas.

The intersection of a row and column forms a cell. Cell D4, for example, contains the entry to compute the total hotel expense by multiplying the number of days (in cell B4) by the per diem amount (in cell C4). In similar fashion, the entry in cell D5 computes the total expense for meals by multiplying the values in cells B5 and C5, respectively. The formula is not entered (typed) into the cell explicitly, but is created through the Formula command in the Tables menu.

Figure 7.4d is a slight variation of Figure 7.4c in which the field codes for the hotel and meals have been toggled off to display the calculated values, as opposed to the field codes. The cells are shaded, however, to emphasize that these cells contain formulas (fields), as opposed to numerical values. (The shading is controlled by the Options command in the Tools menu. The *field codes* are toggled on and off by selecting the formula and pressing the Shift+F9 key or by right clicking the entry and selecting the Toggle Field Codes command.)

The formula in cell D6 has a different syntax and sums the value of all cells directly above it. You do not need to know the syntax since Word provides a dialog box that supplies the entry for you. It's easy, as you shall see in our next hands-on exercise.

Expense	Number of Days	Per Diem Amount	Amount
Airfare			$349.00
Hotel	2	$129.99	$259.98
Meals	2	$75.00	$150.00
Performance Fee			$1000.00
Total			$1758.98

(a) Expenses (alphabetical order by expense)

Descending order by amount

Expense	Number of Days	Per Diem Amount	Amount
Performance Fee			$1000.00
Airfare			$349.00
Hotel	2	$129.99	$259.98
Meals	2	$75.00	$150.00
Total			$1758.98

(b) Expenses (descending order by amount)

Column labels

Row labels

Field codes

	A	B	C	D
1	Expense	Number of Days	Per Diem Amount	Amount
2	Performance Fee			$1000.00
3	Airfare			$349.00
4	Hotel	2	$129.99	{=b4*c4}
5	Meals	2	$75.00	{=b5*c5}
6	Total			{=SUM(ABOVE)}

(c) Field Codes

Shading indicates a cell formula

	A	B	C	D
1	Expense	Number of Days	Per Diem Amount	Amount
2	Performance Fee			$1000.00
3	Airfare			$349.00
4	Hotel	2	$129.99	$259.98
5	Meals	2	$75.00	$150.00
6	Total			$1758.98

(d) Field Codes (toggles and shading)

FIGURE 7.4 Sorting and Table Math

2   Table Math

Objective   To open a password-protected document and remove the password protection; to create a table containing various cell formulas. Use Figure 7.5.

Step 1:   **Open the Document**

■ Open the **Executed Contract** in the **Exploring Word folder** from the first exercise. You will be prompted for a password as shown in Figure 7.5a.

■ Type **password** (in lowercase) since this was the password that was specified when you saved the document originally.

■ Pull down the **File menu** and click the **Save As command** to display the Save As dialog box. Click the **Tools button**. Click **Security Options**.

■ Click and drag to select the existing password (which appears as a string of eight asterisks). Press the **Del key** to remove the password. Click **OK** to close the Save dialog box.

■ Click the **Save command button** to close the Save As dialog box. The document is no longer password protected.

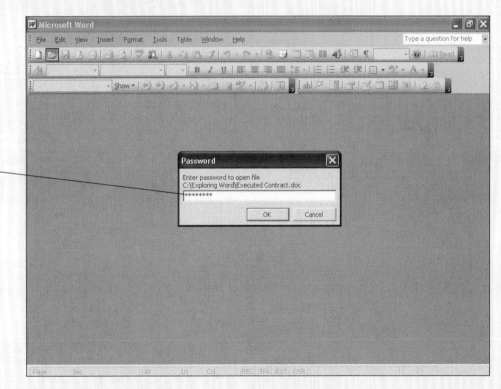

Enter password (lowercase)

(a) Open the Document (step 1)

FIGURE 7.5   Hands-on Exercise 2

CHANGE THE DEFAULT FOLDER

The default folder is the folder where Word saves and retrieves documents unless it is otherwise instructed. To change the default folder, pull down the Tools menu, click Options, click the File Locations tab, click Documents, and click the Modify command button to display the associated dialog box. Enter the name of the new folder (for example, C:\Exploring Word), click OK, then click the Close button.

Step 2: Review the Contract

- You should see the executed contract from the previous exercise. Click the **Protect Form button** on the Forms toolbar to unprotect the document so that its context can be modified.

- Do *not* click the Protect Form button a second time or else the data will disappear. (You can quit the document without saving the changes, as described in the boxed tip below.)

- Point to any toolbar, and click the **right mouse button** to display the list of toolbars shown in Figure 7.5b. Click the **Forms toolbar** to toggle the toolbar off (the check will disappear).

- Right click any visible toolbar a second time, and toggle the Reviewing toolbar off as well.

Protect Form button

Right click an existing toolbar to display shortcut menu

Click Forms to toggle toolbar off (the check will disappear)

Click Reviewing to toggle toolbar off (the check will disappear)

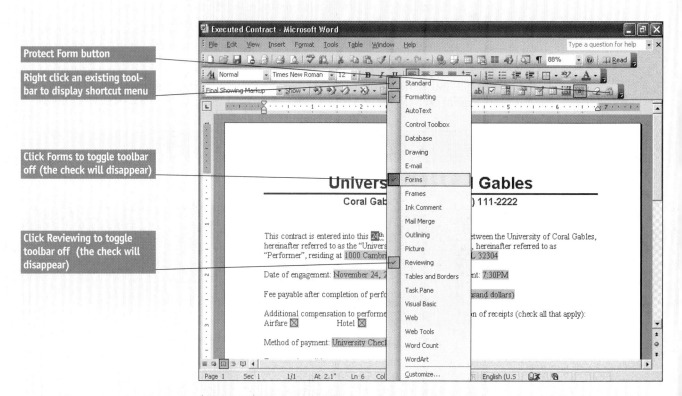

(b) Review the Contract (step 2)

FIGURE 7.5   Hands-on Exercise 2 *(continued)*

QUIT WITHOUT SAVING

There will be times when you do not want to save the changes to a document—for example, when you have edited it beyond recognition and wish you had never started. Pull down the File menu and click the Close command, then click No in response to the message asking whether you want to save the changes to the document. Pull down the File menu and reopen the document (it should appear as the first file in the list of most recently edited documents), then start over from the beginning.

Step 3: Create the Table

- Press **Ctrl+End** to move to the end of the contract, then press **Ctrl+Enter** to create a page break. You should be at the top of page two of the document.

- Press the **Enter key** three times and then enter **Summary of Expenses** in **24 point Arial bold** as shown in Figure 7.5c. Center the text. Press **Enter** twice to add a blank line under the heading.

- Change to **12 point Times New Roman**. Click the **Insert Table button** on the Standard toolbar to display a grid, then drag the mouse across and down the grid to create a 6 × 4 table (six rows and four columns). Release the mouse to create the table.

- Enter data into the table as shown in Figure 7.5c. You can format the entries by selecting multiple cells, then clicking the appropriate tools on the formatting toolbar.

- Save the document.

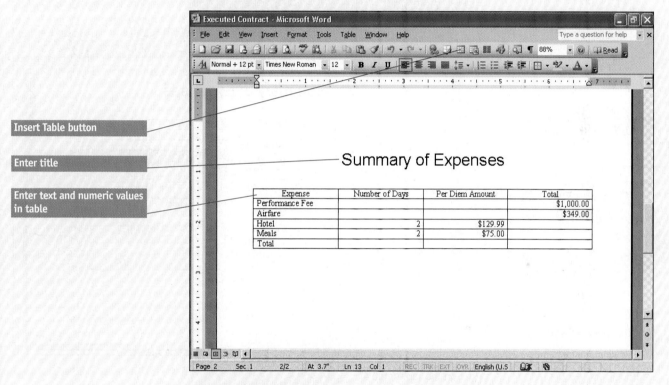

(c) Create the Table (step 3)

FIGURE 7.5   Hands-on Exercise 2 (*continued*)

TABS AND TABLES

The Tab key functions differently in a table than in a regular document. Press the Tab key to move to the next cell in the current row (or to the first cell in the next row if you are at the end of a row). Press Tab when you are in the last cell of a table to add a new blank row to the bottom of the table. Press Shift+Tab to move to the previous cell in the current row (or to the last cell in the previous row). You must press Ctrl+Tab to insert a regular tab character within a cell.

Step 4: Sort the Table

- Click and drag to select the entire table except for the last row. Pull down the **Table menu** and click the **Sort command** to display the Sort dialog box in Figure 7.5d.

- Click the **drop-down arrow** in the Sort by list box and select **Expense** (the column heading for the first column). The **Ascending option button** is selected by default.

- Verify that the option button to include a Header row is selected. Click **OK**. The entries in the table are rearranged alphabetically according to the entry in the Expenses column.

- The Total row remains at the bottom of the table since it was not included in the selected rows for the Sort command.

- Save the document.

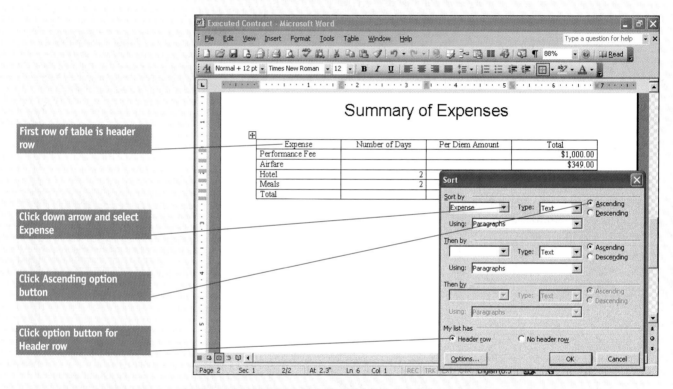

First row of table is header row

Click down arrow and select Expense

Click Ascending option button

Click option button for Header row

(d) Sort the Table (step 4)

FIGURE 7.5 Hands-on Exercise 2 (*continued*)

THE HEADER ROW

The first row in a table is known as the header row and contains the column names (headings) that describe the values in each column of the table. The header row is typically included in the range selected for the sort so that the Sort by list box displays the column names. The header row must remain at the top of the table, however, and thus it is important that the option button that indicates a header row be selected. In similar fashion, the last row typically contains the totals and should remain as the bottom row of the table. Hence it (the total row) is not included in the rows that are selected for sorting.

Step 5: **Enter the Formulas for Row Totals**

- Click in **cell D3** (the cell in the fourth column and third row). Pull down the **Table menu** and click the **Formula command** to display the Formula dialog box.

- Click and drag to select the =SUM(ABOVE) function, which is entered by default. Type **=b3*c3** as shown in Figure 7.5e to compute the total hotel expense. The total is computed by multiplying the number of days (in cell B3) by the per diem amount (in cell C3).

- Click **OK**. You should see $259.98 in cell D3.

- Click in **cell D4** and repeat the procedure to enter the formula **=b4*c4** to compute the total expense for meals. You should see $150.00 (two days at $75.00 per day).

- Save the document.

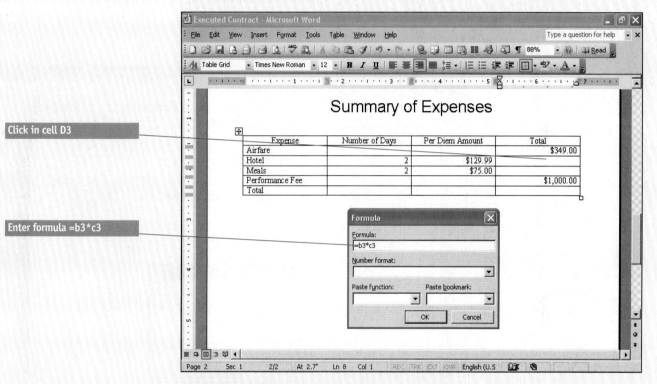

(e) Enter the Formulas for Row Totals (step 5)

FIGURE 7.5 Hands-on Exercise 2 (*continued*)

IT'S NOT EXCEL

Your opinion of table math within Microsoft Word depends on what you know about a spreadsheet. If you have never used Excel, then you will find table math to be very useful, especially when simple calculations are necessary within a Word document. If, on the other hand, you know Excel, you will find table math to be rather limited; for example, you cannot copy a formula from one cell to another, but must enter it explicitly in every cell. Nevertheless, the feature enables simple calculations to be performed entirely within Word, without having to link an Excel worksheet to a Word document.

Step 6: Enter the SUM(ABOVE) Formula

- Click in **cell D6** (the cell in row 6, column 4), which is to contain the total of all expenses. Pull down the **Table menu** and click the **Formula command** to display the Formula dialog box in Figure 7.5f.

- The =SUM(ABOVE) function is entered by default. Click **OK** to accept the formula and close the dialog box. You should see $1,758.98 (the sum of the cells in the last column) displayed in the selected cell.

- Select the formula and press **Shift+F9** to display the code {=SUM(ABOVE)}. Press **Shift+F9** a second time to display the field value ($1,758.98).

- Click in **cell D2** (the cell containing the airfare). Replace $349 with **$549.00** and press the **Tab key** to move out of the cell. The total expenses are *not* yet updated in cell D6.

- Point to **cell D6**, click the **right mouse button** to display a context-sensitive menu, and click the **Update Field command**. Cell D6 displays $1,958.98, the correct total for all expenses.

- Save the document.

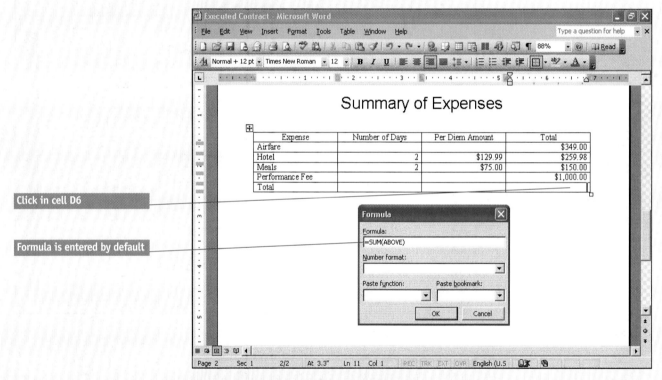

(f) Enter the SUM(ABOVE) Formula (step 6)

FIGURE 7.5   Hands-on Exercise 2 *(continued)*

FORMATTING A CALCULATED VALUE

Word does its best to format a calculation according to the way you want it. You can, however, change the default format while entering the formula by clicking the down arrow on the Number format list box and choosing a different format. You can also enter a format directly in the Number format text box. To display a dollar sign and comma without a decimal point, enter $#,##0 into the text box. You can use trial and error to experiment with other formats.

Step 7: Print the Completed Contract

- Zoom to two pages to preview the completed document. The first page contains the text of the executed contract that was completed in the previous exercise. The second page contains the table of expenses from this contract.

- Pull down the **File menu** and click the **Print command** to display the Print dialog box in Figure 7.5g. Click the **Options command button** to display the second Print dialog box.

- Check the box to include **Field codes** with the document. Click **OK** to close that dialog box, then click **OK** to print the document.

- Repeat the process to print the document a second time, but this time with field values, rather than field codes. Thus, pull down the **File menu**, click the **Print command** to display the Print dialog box, and click the **Options command button** to display a second Print dialog box.

- Clear the box to include **Field codes** with the document. Click **OK** to close that dialog box, then click **OK** to print the document.

- Exit Word if you do not want to continue with the next exercise at this time. Click **Yes** if asked to save the changes.

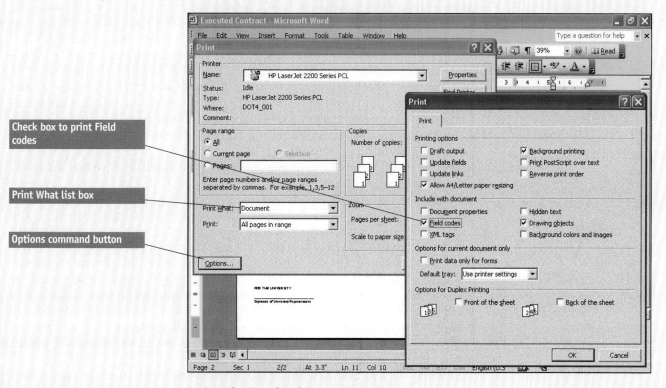

(g) Print the Completed Contract (step 7)

FIGURE 7.5 Hands-on Exercise 2 (continued)

DOCUMENT PROPERTIES

Prove to your instructor how hard you've worked by printing various statistics about your document, including the number of revisions and the total editing time. Pull down the File menu, click the Print command to display the Print dialog box, click the drop-down arrow in the Print What list box, select Document properties, then click OK.

A ***master document*** is composed of multiple ***subdocuments***, each of which is stored as a separate file. The advantage of the master document is that you can work with several smaller documents, as opposed to a single large document. Thus, you edit the subdocuments individually and more efficiently than if they were all part of the same document. You can create a master document to hold the chapters of a book, where each chapter is stored as a subdocument. You can also use a master document to hold multiple documents created by others, such as a group project, where each member of the group is responsible for a section of the document.

Figure 7.6 displays a master document with five subdocuments. The subdocuments are collapsed in Figure 7.6a and expanded in Figure 7.6b. (The ***Outlining toolbar*** contains the Collapse and Expand Subdocuments buttons, as well as other tools associated with master documents.) The collapsed structure in Figure 7.6a enables you to see at a glance the subdocuments that comprise the master document. You can insert additional subdocuments and/or remove existing subdocuments from the master document. Deleting a subdocument from within a master document does *not* delete the subdocument from disk.

The expanded structure in Figure 7.6b enables you to view and/or edit the contents of the subdocuments. Look carefully, however, at the first two subdocuments in Figure 7.6b. A padlock appears to the left of the first line in the first subdocument, whereas it is absent from the second subdocument. These subdocuments are locked and unlocked, respectively. (All subdocuments are locked when collapsed as in Figure 7.6a.)

Changes to the master document can be made at any time. Changes to the subdocuments, however, can be made only when the subdocument is unlocked. Note, too, that you can make changes to a subdocument in one of two ways, either when the subdocument is expanded (and unlocked) within a master document as in Figure 7.6b or by opening the subdocument as an independent document within Microsoft Word. Both techniques work equally well, and we find ourselves alternating between the two.

Regardless of how you edit the subdocuments, the attraction of a master document is the ability to work with multiple subdocuments simultaneously. The subdocuments are created independently of one another, with each subdocument stored in its own file. Then, when all of the subdocuments are finished, the master document is created and the subdocuments are inserted into the master document, from where they are easily accessed. Inserting page numbers into the master document, for example, causes the numbers to run consecutively from one subdocument to the next. You can also create a table of contents or index for the master document that will reflect the entries in all of the subdocuments. And finally, you can print all of the subdocuments from within the master document with a single command.

Alternatively, you can reverse the process by starting with an empty master document and using it as the basis to create the subdocuments. This is ideal for organizing a group project in school or at work, the chapters in a book, or the sections in a report. Start with a new document, enter the topics assigned to each group member. Format each topic in a heading style within the master document, then use the ***Create Subdocument command*** to create subdocuments based on those headings. Saving the master document will automatically save each subdocument in its own file. This is the approach that we will follow in our next hands-on exercise.

The exercise also illustrates the ***Create New Folder command*** that lets you create a new folder on your hard drive (or floppy disk) from within Microsoft Word, as opposed to using Windows Explorer. The new folder can then be used to store the master document and all of its subdocuments in a single location apart from any other documents.

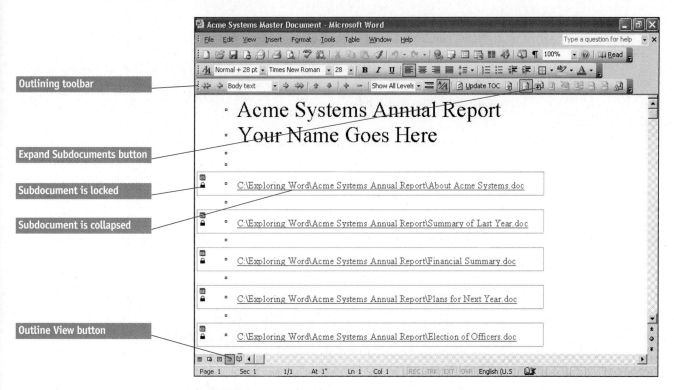

Outlining toolbar

Expand Subdocuments button

Subdocument is locked

Subdocument is collapsed

Outline View button

(a) Collapsed Subdocuments

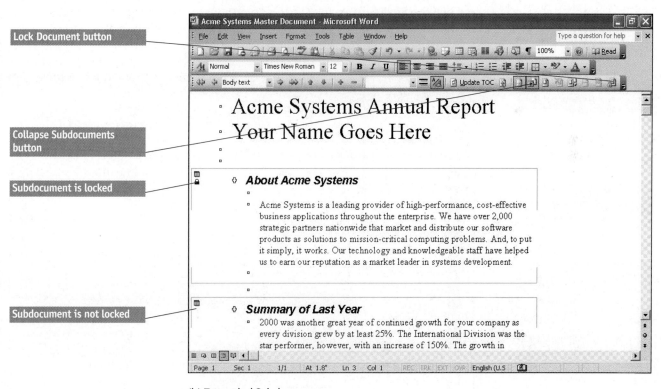

Lock Document button

Collapse Subdocuments button

Subdocument is locked

Subdocument is not locked

(b) Expanded Subdocuments

FIGURE 7.6 A Master Document

Master Documents

Objective To create a master document and various subdocuments; to create a new folder from within the Save As dialog box in Microsoft Word. Use Figure 7.7 as a guide in the exercise.

Step 1: **Create a New Folder**

■ Start Word. If necessary, click the **New Blank Document button** on the Standard toolbar to begin a new document. Enter the text of the document in Figure 7.7a in **12 point Times New Roman**.

■ Press **Ctrl+Home** to move to the beginning of the document. Pull down the **Style list box** on the Formatting toolbar, then select **Heading 2** as the style for the document title.

■ Click the **Save button** to display the Save As dialog box. If necessary, click the **drop-down arrow** on the Save in list box to select the **Exploring Word folder** you have used throughout the text.

■ Click the **Create New Folder button** to display the New Folder dialog box. Type **Acme Systems Annual Report** as the name of the new folder. Click **OK** to create the folder and close the New Folder dialog box.

■ The Save in list box indicates that the Acme Systems Annual Report folder is the current folder. The name of the document, **About Acme Systems**, is entered by default (since this text appears at the beginning of the document).

■ Click the **Save button** to save the document and close the Save As dialog box. The title bar changes to reflect the name of the document (About Acme Systems).

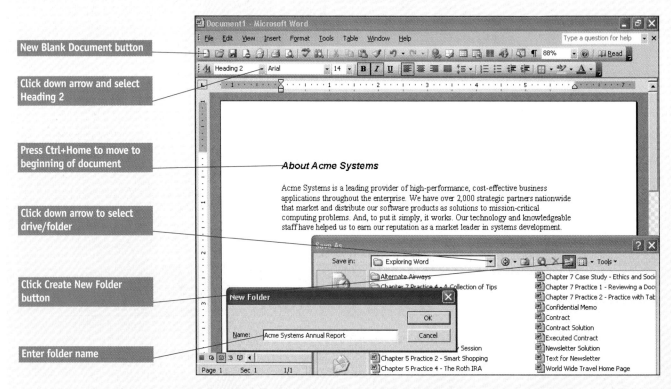

(a) Create a New Folder (step 1)

FIGURE 7.7 Hands-on Exercise 3

Step 2: **Create the Master Document**

- Click the **New Blank Document button** on the Standard toolbar. Enter **Acme Systems Annual Report** as the first line of the document. Enter your name under the title.

- Press the **Enter key** twice to leave a blank line after your name before the first subdocument. Type **Summary of Last Year** in the default typeface and size. Press **Enter**.

- Enter the remaining topics for the subdocuments, **Financial Summary**, **Plans for Next Year**, and **Election of Officers**.

- Change the format of the title and your name to **28 pt Times New Roman**.

- Pull down the **View menu** and click **Outline** to change to the Outline view. Click and drag to select the four headings as shown in Figure 7.7b. Click the **drop-down arrow** on the Style list box and select **Heading 2**.

- Be sure that all four headings are still selected. Click the **Create Subdocument button**. Each heading expands automatically into a subdocument.

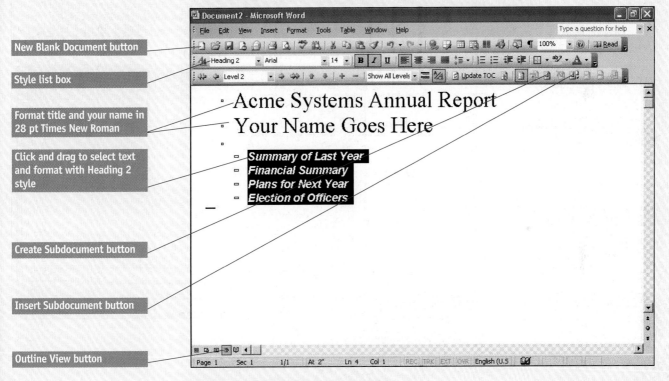

(b) Create the Master Document (step 2)

FIGURE 7.7 Hands-on Exercise 3 (*continued*)

THE CREATE SUBDOCUMENT BUTTON

You can enter subdocuments into a master document in one of two ways, through the Insert Subdocument button if the subdocuments already exist, or through the Create Subdocument button to create the subdocuments from within the master document. Start a new document, enter the title of each subdocument on a line by itself, format them in a heading style, then click the Create Subdocument button to create the subdocuments. Save the master document. The subdocuments are saved automatically as individual files in the same folder.

Step 3: Save the Documents

- Click the **Save button** to display the Save As dialog box in Figure 7.7c. If necessary, click the **drop-down arrow** on the Save in list box to select the **Acme Systems Annual Report folder** that was created in step 1. You should see the About Acme Systems document in this folder.

- Enter **Acme Systems Master Document** in the File name list box, then click the **Save button** within the Save As dialog box to save the master document (which automatically saves the subdocuments in the same folder).

- Press the **Collapse Subdocuments button** to collapse the subdocuments. You will see the name of each subdocument as it appears on disk, with the drive and folder information.

- Press the **Expand Subdocuments button**, and the subdocuments are reopened within the master document.

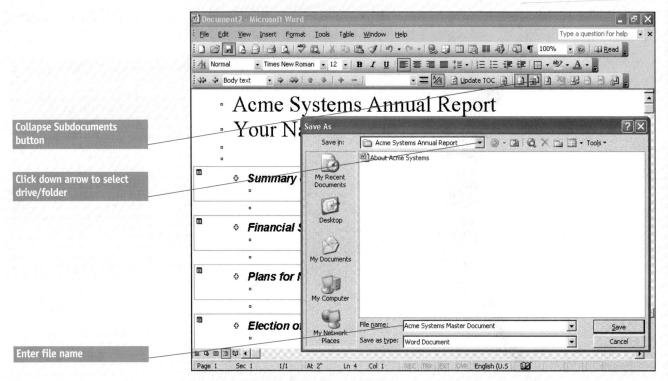

Collapse Subdocuments button

Click down arrow to select drive/folder

Enter file name

(c) Save the Documents (step 3)

FIGURE 7.7 Hands-on Exercise 3 (*continued*)

HELP WITH TOOLBAR BUTTONS

The Outlining toolbar is displayed automatically in the Outline view and suppressed otherwise. As with every toolbar you can point to any button to see a ToolTip with the name of the button. The Outlining toolbar contains buttons that pertain specifically to master documents such as buttons to expand and collapse subdocuments, or insert and remove subdocuments. The Outlining toolbar also contains buttons to promote and demote items, to display or suppress formatting, and/or to collapse and expand the outline.

Insert a Subdocument

- Click below your name, but above the first subdocument. Click the **Insert Subdocument button** to display the Insert Subdocument dialog box in Figure 7.7d. If necessary, click the **drop-down arrow** on the Look in list box to change to the Acme Systems Annual Report folder.

- There are six documents, which include the About Acme Systems document from step 1, the Acme Systems Master document that you just saved, and the four subdocuments that were created automatically in conjunction with the master document.

- Select the **About Acme Systems** document, then click the **Open button** to insert this document into the master document.

- Save the master document.

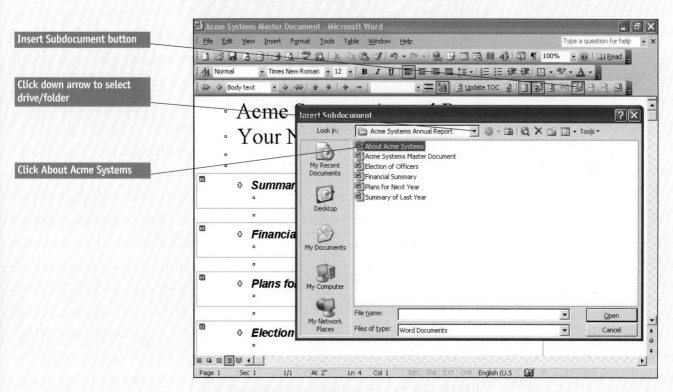

(d) Insert a Subdocument (step 4)

FIGURE 7.7 Hands-on Exercise 3 (*continued*)

CHANGE THE VIEW

The Outline view is used to create and/or modify a master document through insertion, repositioning, or deletion of its subdocuments. You can also modify the text of a subdocument within the Outline view (provided the document is unlocked) and/or implement formatting changes at the character level such as a change in font, type size, or style. More sophisticated formatting, however—such as changes in alignment, indentation, or line spacing—has to be implemented in the Normal or Print Layout views.

Step 5: Modify a Subdocument

- Click within the second subdocument, which will summarize the activities of last year. (The text of the document has not yet been entered.)

- Click the **Lock Document button** on the Outlining toolbar to display the padlock for this document. Click the **Lock Document button** a second time, which unlocks the document.

- Enter the text of the document as shown in Figure 7.7e, then click the **Save button** to save the changes to the master document.

- Be sure the subdocument is unlocked so that the changes you have made will be reflected in the subdocument file as well.

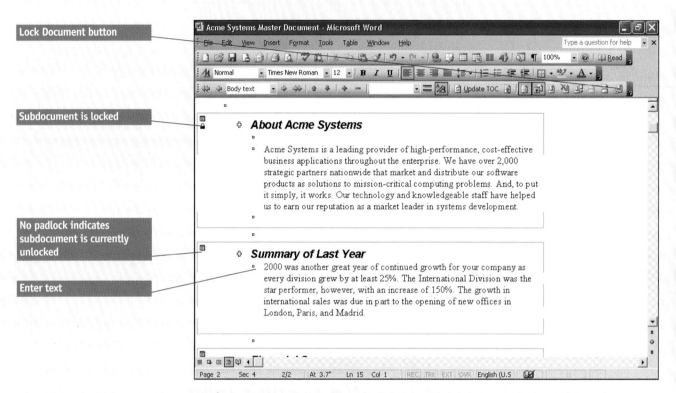

(e) Modify a Subdocument (step 5)

FIGURE 7.7 Hands-on Exercise 3 (*continued*)

OPEN THE SUBDOCUMENT

You can edit the text of a subdocument from within a master document, but it is often more convenient to open the subdocument when the editing is extensive. You can open a subdocument in one of two ways, by double clicking the document icon in the Outline view when the master document is expanded, or by following the hyperlink to the document when the Master Document is collapsed. Either way, the subdocument opens in its own window. Enter the changes into the subdocument, then save the subdocument and close its window to return to the master document, which now reflects the modified subdocument.

Print the Completed Document

■ Click the **Collapse Subdocuments button** to collapse the subdocuments as shown in Figure 7.7f. Click **OK** if asked to save the changes in the master document.

■ Click the **Print button** on the Standard toolbar to print the document. Click **No** when asked whether to open the subdocuments before printing. The entire document appears on a single page. The text of the subdocuments is not printed, only the address of the documents.

■ Click the **Print button** a second time, but click **Yes** when asked whether to open the subdocuments before printing.

■ Submit both versions of the printed document to your instructor as proof that you did this exercise. Exit Word if you do not want to continue with the next exercise at this time.

Print button

Document Map button

Subdocuments are collapsed and locked

(f) Print the Completed Document (step 6)

FIGURE 7.7 Hands-on Exercise 3 (*continued*)

THE DOCUMENT MAP

The Document Map is one of our favorite features when working with large documents. Be sure that the master document is expanded to display the text of the subdocuments, then click the Document Map button on the Standard toolbar to divide the screen into two panes. The headings in a document are displayed in the left pane, and the text of the document is visible in the right pane. To go to a specific point in a document, click its heading in the left pane, and the insertion point is moved automatically to that point in the document, which is visible in the right pane. Click the Document Map button a second time to turn the feature off.

INTRODUCTION TO MACROS

Have you ever pulled down the same menus and clicked the same sequence of commands over and over? Easy as the commands may be to execute, it is still burdensome to continually repeat the same mouse clicks or keystrokes. If you can think of any task that you do repeatedly, whether in one document or in a series of documents, you are a perfect candidate to use macros.

A ***macro*** is a set of instructions (that is, a program) that executes a specific task. It is written in ***Visual Basic for Applications (VBA)***, a programming language that is built into Microsoft Office. Fortunately, however, you don't have to be a programmer to use VBA. Instead, you use the ***macro recorder*** within Word to record your actions, which are then translated automatically into VBA. You get results that are immediately usable, and you can learn a good deal about VBA through observation.

Figure 7.8 illustrates a simple macro to enter your name, date, and class into a Word document. We don't expect you to be able to write the VBA code by yourself, but, as indicated, you don't have to. You just invoke the macro recorder and let it create the VBA statements for you. It is important, however, for you to understand the individual statements so that you can modify them as necessary. Do not be concerned with the precise syntax of every statement, but try instead to get an overall appreciation of what the statements do.

Every macro begins and ends with a Sub and End Sub statement, respectively. These statements identify the macro and convert it to a VBA ***procedure***. The ***Sub statement*** contains the name of the macro, such as NameAndCourse in Figure 7.8. (Spaces are not allowed in a macro name.) The ***End Sub statement*** is always the last statement in a VBA procedure. Sub and End Sub are Visual Basic keywords and appear in blue.

The next several statements begin with an apostrophe, appear in green, and are known as ***comments***. Comments provide information about the procedure, but do not affect its execution. The comments are inserted automatically by the macro recorder and include the name of the macro, the date it was recorded, and the author. Additional comments can be inserted at any time.

Every other statement in the procedure corresponds directly to a command that was executed in Microsoft Word. It doesn't matter how the commands were executed—whether from a pull-down menu, toolbar, or keyboard shortcut, because the end results, the VBA statements that are generated by the commands, are the same. In this example the user began by changing the font and font size,

Macro begins with Sub statement, which contains macro name

Comments are in green, begin with apostrophe, and do not affect execution

Macro ends with End Sub statement

```
Sub NameAndCourse()
'
'  NameAndCourse Macro
'  Macro recorded 6/25/2003 by John Doe
'
    With Selection.Font
        .Name = "Arial"
        .Size = 24
    End With
    Selection.TypeText Text:="John Doe"
    Selection.TypeParagraph
    Selection.TypeText Text:="June 25, 2003"
    Selection.TypeParagraph
    Selection.TypeText Text:="CIS120"
    Selection.TypeParagraph
End Sub
```

FIGURE 7.8 The NameAndCourse Macro

and these commands were converted by the macro recorder to the VBA statements that specify Arial and 24 point, respectively. Next, the user entered his name and pressed the Enter key to begin a new paragraph. Again, the macro recorder converts these actions to the equivalent VBA statements. The user entered the date, pressed the Enter key, entered the class, and pressed the Enter key. Each of these actions resulted in an additional VBA statement.

You do not have to write VBA statements from scratch, but you should understand their function once they have been recorded. You can also edit the statements after they have been recorded. It's easy, for example, to change the procedure to include your name instead of John Doe. All changes to a macro are done through the Visual Basic Editor.

The Visual Basic Editor

Figure 7.9a displays the NameAndCourse macro as it appears within the **Visual Basic Editor (VBE)**. The Visual Basic Editor is a separate application, and it is accessible from any application in Office XP. The left side of the VBE window displays the **Project Explorer**, which is similar in concept and appearance to the Windows Explorer. Macros are stored by default in the Normal template, which is available to all Word documents. The VBA code is stored in the NewMacros module. (A **module** contains one or more procedures.)

The macros for the selected module (NewMacros in Figure 7.9) appear in the **Code window** in the right pane. (Additional macros, if any, are separated from one another by a horizontal line.) The VBA statements are identical to what we described earlier. The difference between Figure 7.8 and 7.9a is that the latter shows the macro within the Visual Basic Editor.

Figure 7.9b displays the TitlePage macro, which is built from the NameAndCourse macro. The new macro (a VBA procedure) is more complicated than its predecessor. "Complicated" is an intimidating word, however, and we prefer to use "powerful" instead. In essence, the TitlePage procedure moves the insertion point to the beginning of a Word document, inserts three blank lines at the beginning of the document, then enters three additional lines that center the student's name, date, and course in 24 point Arial. The last statement creates a page break within the document so that the title appears on a page by itself. The macro recorder created these statements for us, as we executed the corresponding actions from within Word.

Note, too, that the TitlePage macro changed the way in which the date is entered to make the macro more general. The NameAndCourse macro in Figure 7.9a specified a date (June 25, 2003). The TitlePage macro, however, uses the VBA InsertDateTime command to insert the current date. We did not know the syntax of this statement, but we didn't have to. Instead we pulled down the Insert menu from within Word, and chose the Date and Time command. The macro recorder kept track of our actions and created the appropriate VBA statement for us. In similar fashion, the macro recorder kept track of our actions when we moved to the beginning of the document and when we inserted a page break.

A SENSE OF FAMILIARITY

Visual Basic for Applications has the basic capabilities found in any other programming language. If you have programmed before, whether in Pascal, C, or even COBOL, you will find all of the logic structures you are used to. These include the Do While and Do Until statements, the If-Then-Else statement for decision making, nested If statements, a Case statement, and calls to subprograms. See the "Getting Started with VBA" module at the end of the text for additional information.

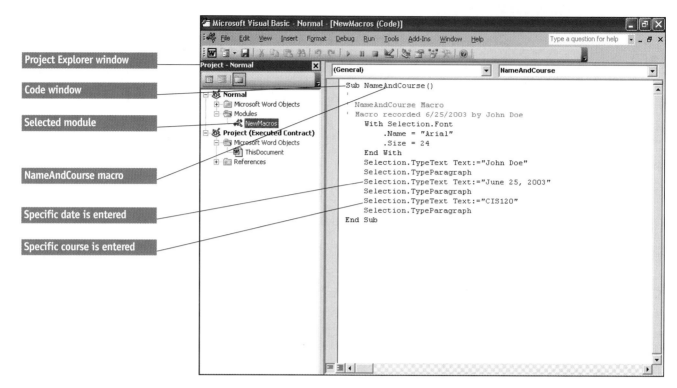

Project Explorer window

Code window

Selected module

NameAndCourse macro

Specific date is entered

Specific course is entered

(a) NameAndCourse Macro

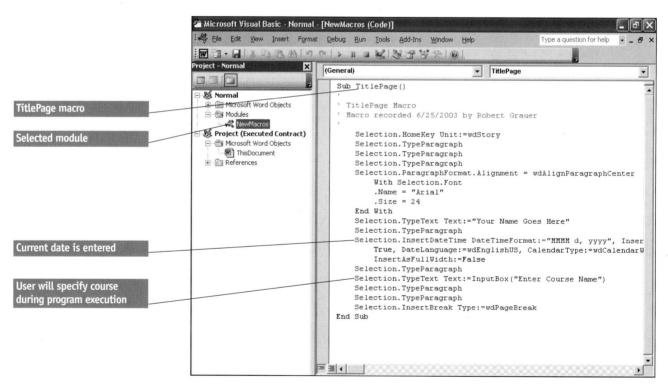

TitlePage macro

Selected module

Current date is entered

User will specify course
during program execution

(b) TitlePage Macro

FIGURE 7.9 The Visual Basic Editor

Objective   To record, run, view, and edit simple macros; to run a macro from an existing Word document via a keyboard shortcut. Use Figure 7.10.

Step 1:   **Create a Macro**

- Start Word. Open a new document if one is not already open.

- Pull down the **Tools menu**, click (or point to) the **Macro command**, then click **Record New Macro** to display the Record Macro dialog box in Figure 7.10a.

- Enter **NameAndCourse** as the name of the macro. (Do not leave any spaces.) If necessary, change the description to include your name. Click **OK**.

- Click **Yes** if asked whether you want to replace the existing macro. (The existing macro may have been created by another student or if you previously attempted the exercise. Either way, you want to replace the existing macro.)

- The mouse pointer changes to include a recording icon, and the Stop Recording toolbar is displayed.

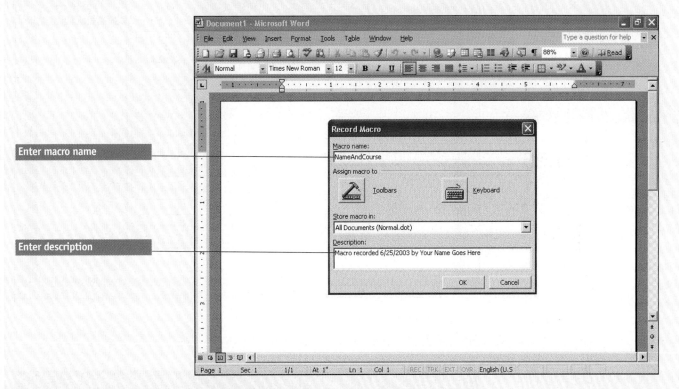

Enter macro name

Enter description

(a) Create a Macro (step 1)

FIGURE 7.10   Hands-on Exercise 4

MACRO NAMES

Macro names are not allowed to contain spaces or punctuation except for the underscore character. To create a macro name containing more than one word, capitalize the first letter of each word and/or use the underscore character—for example, NameAndCourse or Name_And_Course.

Record the Macro

- The first task is to change the font. Pull down the **Format menu** and click the **Font command** to display the Font dialog box in Figure 7.10b. Select **14 point Arial**. Click **OK** to accept the setting and close the dialog box.

- Type your name. Press **Enter**.

- Pull down the **Insert menu** and click the **Date and Time command** to display the Date and Time dialog box. Choose the format of the date that you prefer. Check the box to **Update Automatically**, then click **OK** to accept the settings and close the dialog box.

- Press the **Enter key** to move to the next line.

- Enter the course you are taking this semester. Press the **Enter key** a final time.

- Click the **Stop Recording button** to end the macro.

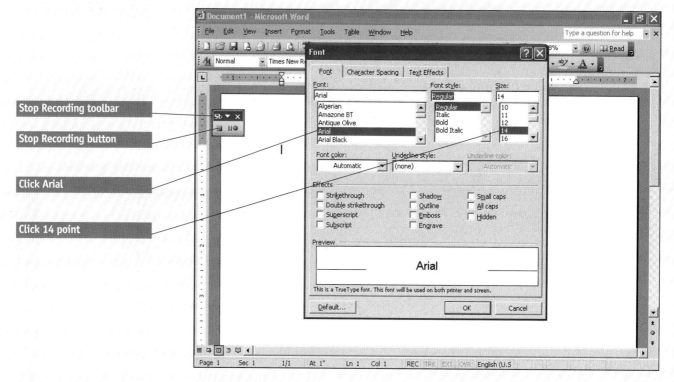

(b) Record the Macro (step 2)

FIGURE 7.10   Hands-on Exercise 4 (*continued*)

THE INSERT DATE COMMAND

A date is inserted into a document in one of two ways—as a field that is updated automatically to reflect the current date or as a specific value (the date and time on which the command is executed). The determination of which way the date is entered depends on whether the Update Automatically check box is checked or cleared, respectively. Be sure to choose the option that reflects your requirements.

Step 3: **Test the Macro**

- Click and drag to select your name, date, and class, then press the **Del key** to erase this information from the document.

- Pull down the **Tools menu**. Click **Macro**, then click the **Macros ... command** to display the Macros dialog box in Figure 7.10c. Select **NameAndCourse** (the macro you just recorded) and click **Run**.

- Your name and class information should appear in the document. The type-face is 14 point Arial, which corresponds to your selection when you recorded the macro initially.

- Do not be dismayed if the macro did not work properly, as we show you how to correct it in the next several steps.

- Press the **Enter key** a few times. Press **Alt+F8** (a keyboard shortcut) to display the Macros dialog box.

- Double click the **NameAndCourse** macro to execute the macro. Your name and class information is entered a second time.

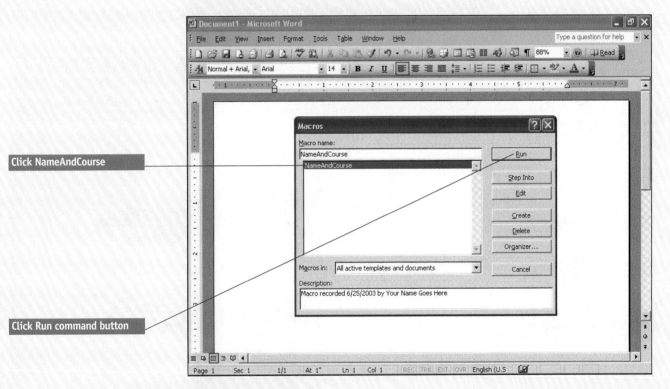

(c) Test the Macro (step 3)

FIGURE 7.10 Hands-on Exercise 4 (*continued*)

KEYBOARD SHORTCUTS

Take advantage of built-in shortcuts to facilitate the creation and testing of a macro. Press Alt+F11 to toggle between the VBA editor and the Word document. Use the Alt+F8 shortcut to display the Macros dialog box, then double click a macro to run it. You can also assign your own keyboard shortcut to a macro, as will be shown later in the exercise.

Step 4: View the Macro

■ Pull down the **Tools menu**, click the **Macro command**, then click **Visual Basic Editor** (or press **Alt+F11**) to open the Visual Basic Editor. Maximize the VBE window. If necessary, pull down the **View menu** and click **Project Explorer** to open the Project window in the left pane. Close the Properties window if it is open.

■ There is currently one project open, Document1, corresponding to the Word document on which you are working. Click the **plus sign** next to the Normal folder to expand that folder. Click the **plus sign** next to the **Modules folder** (within the Normal folder), then click **NewMacros**.

■ Pull down the **View menu**, and click **Code** to open the Code window in the right pane. If necessary, click the **Maximize Button** in the Code window.

■ Your screen should be similar to the one in Figure 7.10d except that it will reflect your name within the macro. The name in the comment statement may be different, however (especially if you are doing the exercise at school), as it corresponds to the person in whose name the program is registered.

■ Select the statements as shown in Figure 7.10d. Press the **Del key** to delete the superfluous statements.

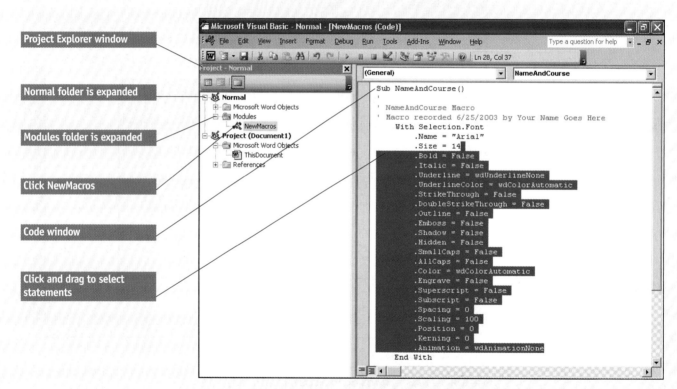

(d) View the Macro (step 4)

FIGURE 7.10 Hands-on Exercise 4 (*continued*)

RED, GREEN, AND BLUE

Visual Basic automatically assigns different colors to different types of statements (or a portion of those statements). Comments appear in green and are nonexecutable (i.e., they do not affect the outcome of a macro). Any statement containing a syntax error appears in red. Keywords such as Sub and End Sub, With and End With, and True and False, appear in blue.

Step 5:   Edit the Macro

- If necessary, change the name in the comment statement to reflect your name. The macro will run identically regardless of the changes in the comments. Changes to the statements within the macro, however, affect its execution.

- Click and drag to select the existing font name, **Arial**, then enter **Times New Roman** as shown in Figure 7.10e. Be sure that the **Times New Roman** appears within quotation marks. Change the font size to **24**.

- Click and drag to select the name of the course, which is "CIS120" in our example. Type **InputBox("Enter Course Name")** to replace the selected text.

- Note that as you type the left parenthesis after the Visual Basic keyword InputBox, a prompt (containing the correct syntax) is displayed on the screen as shown in Figure 7.10e.

- Ignore the prompt and keep typing to complete the entry. Be sure you enter a closing parenthesis.

- Click the **Save button** to save the macro.

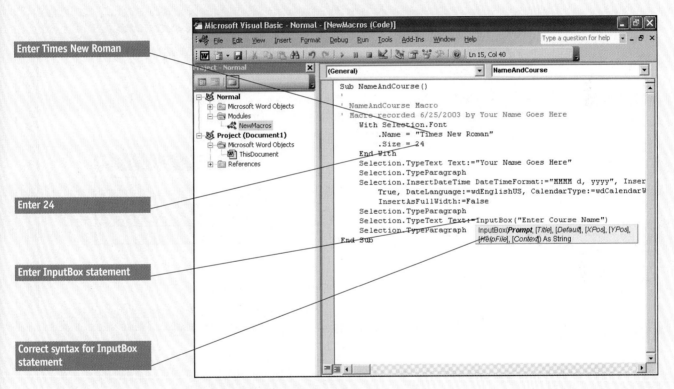

(e) Edit the Macro (step 5)

FIGURE 7.10   Hands-on Exercise 4 (*continued*)

COPY, RENAME, AND DELETE MACRO

You can copy a macro, change its name, then use the duplicate macro as the basis of a new macro. Click and drag to select the entire macro, click the Copy button, click after the End Sub statement, and click the Paste button to copy the macro. Click and drag to select the macro name in the Sub statement, type a new name, and you have a new (duplicate) macro. Make the necessary changes to the new macro. To delete a macro, click and drag to select the entire macro and press the Del key.

Step 6: Test the Revised Macro

- Press **Alt+F11** to toggle back to the Word document (or click the **Word button** on the taskbar). **Delete any text that is in the document**. If necessary, press **Ctrl+Home** to move to the beginning of the Word document.

- Press the **Alt+F8 key** to display the Macros dialog box, then double click the **NameAndCourse macro**. The macro enters your name and date, then displays the input dialog box shown in Figure 7.10f.

- Enter any appropriate course and click **OK** (or press the **Enter key**). You should see your name, today's date, and the course you entered in 24 point Times New Roman type.

- Press **Alt+F11** to return to the Visual Basic Editor if the macro does not work as intended. Correct your macro so that its statements match those in step 5 on the previous page.

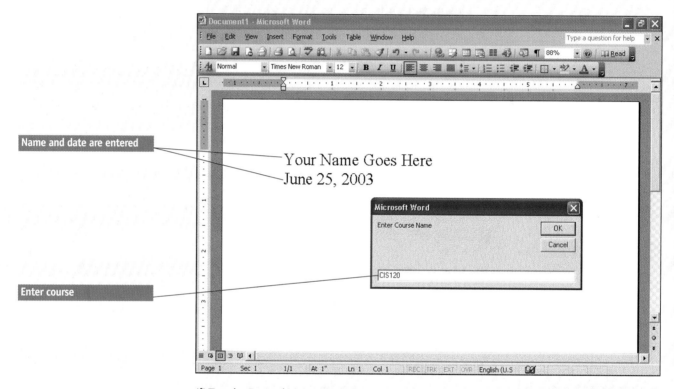

(f) Test the Revised Macro (step 6)

FIGURE 7.10   Hands-on Exercise 4 (*continued*)

HELP FOR VISUAL BASIC

Click within any Visual Basic keyword, then press the F1 key for context-sensitive help. You will see a help screen containing a description of the statement, its syntax, key elements, and several examples. You can print the help screen by clicking the Printer button. (If you do not see the help screens, ask your instructor to install Visual Basic Help.)

Step 7: Record the TitlePage Macro

- If necessary, return to Word and delete the existing text in the document. Pull down the **Tools menu**. Click the **Macro command**, then click **Record New Macro** from the cascaded menu. You will see the Record Macro dialog box as described earlier.

- Enter **TitlePage** as the name of the macro. Do not leave any spaces in the macro name. Click the **Keyboard button** in the Record Macro dialog box to display the Customize Keyboard dialog box in Figure 7.10g. The insertion point is positioned in the Press New Shortcut Key text box.

- Press **Ctrl+T** to enter this keystroke combination as the new shortcut; note, however, that this shortcut is currently assigned to the Hanging Indent command:
  - ❏ Click the **Assign button** if you do not use the Hanging Indent shortcut,
  - ❏ *Or*, choose a different shortcut for the macro (or omit the shortcut altogether) if you are already using Ctrl+T for the Hanging Indent command.

- Close the Customize Keyboard dialog box.

- You are back in your document and can begin recording your macro:
  - ❏ Press **Ctrl+Home** to move to the beginning of the document (even if you are already there).
  - ❏ Press the **Enter key** three times to insert three blank lines.
  - ❏ Click the **Center button** to center the text that will be subsequently typed.
  - ❏ Press the **Enter key** to create an additional blank line.
  - ❏ Press **Ctrl+Enter** to create a page break.

- Click the **Stop Recording button** to end the macro.

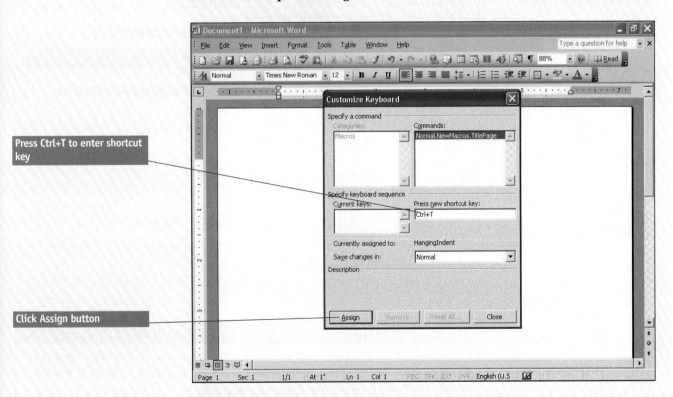

(g) Record the TitlePage Macro (step 7)

FIGURE 7.10 Hands-on Exercise 4 (*continued*)

Step 8: **Complete the TitlePage Macro**

- Press **Alt+F11** to return to the Visual Basic Editor. You should see two macros, NameAndCourse and TitlePage. Click and drag to select the statements in the **NameAndCourse macro** as shown in Figure 7.10h. Do not select the Sub or End Sub statements.

- Click the **Copy button** on the Standard toolbar (or use the **Ctrl+C** shortcut) to copy these statements to the clipboard.

- Move to the TitlePage macro and click at the end of the VBA statement to center a paragraph. Press **Enter** to start a new line. Click the **Paste button** on the Standard toolbar (or use the **Ctrl+V** shortcut) to paste the statements from the NameAndCourse macro into the TitlePage macro.

- You can see the completed macro by looking at Figure 7.10j, the screen in step 10. Click the **Save button** to save your macros.

- Press **Alt+F11** to return to Word. Pull down the File menu and click the **Close command** to close the document you were using to create the macros in this exercise. There is no need to save that document.

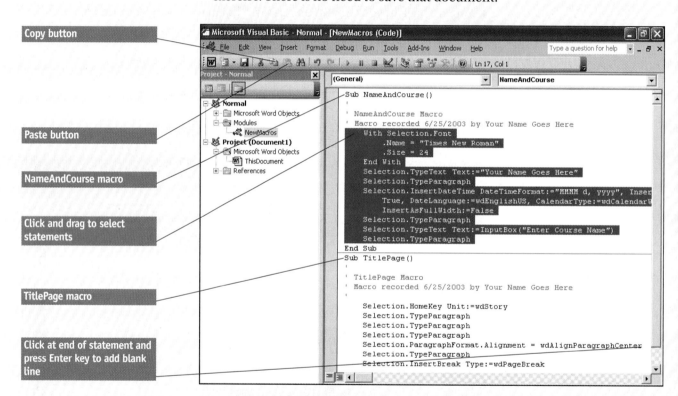

(h) Complete the TitlePage Macro (step 8)

FIGURE 7.10 Hands-on Exercise 4 (*continued*)

THE PAGE BORDER COMMAND

Add interest to a title page with a border. Click anywhere on the page, pull down the Format menu, click the Borders and Shading command, then click the Page Border tab in the Borders and Shading dialog box. You can choose a box, shadow, or 3-D style in similar fashion to placing a border around a paragraph. You can also click the drop-down arrow on the Art list box to create a border consisting of a repeating clip art image.

Step 9   Test the TitlePage Macro

- Open the completed Word document (Executed Contract) from the second hands-on exercise.

- Click anywhere in the document, then press **Ctrl+T** to execute the TitlePage macro.

- You will be prompted for your course. Enter the course you are taking, and the macro will create the title page.

- Pull down the **View menu** and change to the **Print Layout view**. Pull down the **View menu** a second time, click the **Zoom command**, click the option button for **Many Pages**, then click and drag the monitor icon to display three pages. Click **OK**.

- You should see the executed contract with a title page as shown in Figure 7.10i. Print this document for your instructor.

- Save the document.

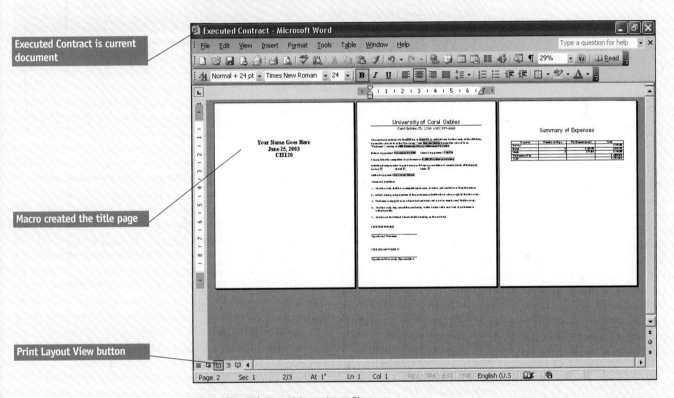

Executed Contract is current document

Macro created the title page

Print Layout View button

(i) Test the TitlePage Macro (step 9)

FIGURE 7.10   Hands-on Exercise 4 (*continued*)

TROUBLESHOOTING

If the shortcut keys do not work, it is probably because they were not defined properly. Pull down the View menu, click Toolbars, click Customize, click the Options tab, then click the Keyboard command button to display the Customize Keyboard dialog box. Drag the scroll box in the Categories list box until you can select the Macros category. Select (click) the macro that is to receive the shortcut and click in the Press New Shortcut Key text box. Enter the desired shortcut, click the Assign button to assign the shortcut, then click the Close button to close the dialog box.

Step 10: Print the Module

- Press **Alt+F11** to return to the Visual Basic Editor.

- Pull down the **File menu**. Click **Print** to display the Print dialog box in Figure 7.10j. Click the option button to print the current module. Click **OK**.

- Submit the listing of the current module, which contains the procedures for both macros, to your instructor as proof you did this exercise.

- Delete all of the macros you have created in this exercise if you are not working on your own machine. Pull down the **File menu**. Click the **Close and Return to Word command**.

- Exit Word. The Title Page macro will be waiting for you the next time you use Microsoft Word, provided you did the exercise on your own computer.

- Congratulations on a job well done.

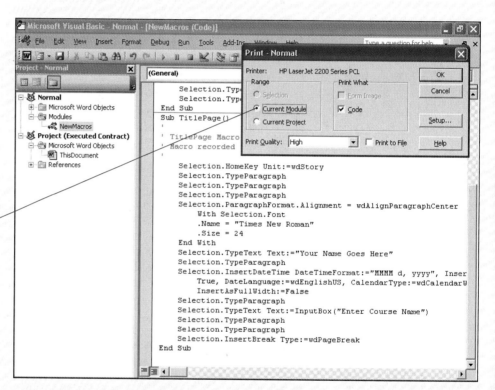

Click Current Module option button

(j) Print the Module (step 10)

FIGURE 7.10   Hands-on Exercise 4 (*continued*)

INVEST IN MACROS

Creating a macro takes time, but that time can be viewed as an investment, because a well-designed macro will simplify the creation of subsequent documents. A macro is recorded once, tested and corrected as necessary, then run (executed) many times. It is stored by default in the Normal template, where it is available to every Word document. Yes, it takes time to create a meaningful macro, but once that's done, it is only a keystroke away.

SUMMARY

Multiple persons within a workgroup can review a document and have their revisions stored electronically within that document. The revisions are displayed in one of two ways, as "Original Showing Markup" or as "Final Showing Markup". The difference is subtle and depends on personal preference with respect to displaying the insertions to, and deletions from, a document. The Original Showing Markup view displays the deleted text within the body of the document (with a line through the deleted text) and shows the inserted text in a balloon to the right of the actual document. The Final Showing Markup view is the opposite; it displays the inserted text within the body of the document and displays the deleted text in a balloon at the right. Both views display revision marks to the left of any line that has been changed.

A form facilitates data entry when the document is made available to multiple individuals via a network. It is created as a regular document with the various fields added through tools on the Forms toolbar. Word enables you to create three types of fields—text boxes, check boxes, and drop-down list boxes. After the form is created, it is protected to prevent further modification other than data entry.

The rows in a table can be sorted to display the data in ascending or descending sequence, according to the values in one or more columns in the table. Sorting is accomplished by selecting the rows within the table that are to be sorted, then executing the Sort command in the Tables menu. Calculations can be performed within a table using the Formula command in the Tables menu.

A master document consists of multiple subdocuments, each of which is stored as a separate file. It is especially useful for very large documents such as a book or dissertation, which can be divided into smaller, more manageable documents. The attraction of a master document is that you can work with multiple subdocuments simultaneously. Changes to the master document can be made at any time. Changes to the subdocuments can be made in one of two ways—either when the subdocument is unlocked within a master document, or by opening the subdocument as an independent document within Microsoft Word.

A macro is a set of instructions that automates a repetitive task. It is, in essence, a program, and its instructions are written in Visual Basic for Applications (VBA), a programming language. A macro is created initially through the macro recorder in Microsoft Word, which records your commands and generates the corresponding VBA statements. Once a macro has been created, it can be edited manually by inserting, deleting, or changing its statements. A macro is run (executed) by the Run command in the Tools menu or more easily through a keyboard shortcut.

KEY TERMS

MULTIPLE CHOICE

1. Which of the following is a true statement regarding password protection?

   (a) All documents are automatically saved with a default password

   (b) The password is case sensitive

   (c) A password cannot be changed once it has been implemented

   (d) All of the above

2. What happens if you double click the TRK indicator on the status bar?

   (a) Tracking changes is in effect

   (b) Tracking changes has been turned off

   (c) Tracking changes has been turned either on or off, depending on its current status

   (d) The situation is impossible; there is no TRK indicator on the status bar

3. Which of the following types of fields *cannot* be inserted into a form?

   (a) Check boxes

   (b) Text fields

   (c) A drop-down list

   (d) Radio buttons

4. Which of the following is true about a protected form?

   (a) Data can be entered into the form

   (b) The text of the form cannot be modified

   (c) Both (a) and (b)

   (d) Neither (a) nor (b)

5. Which of the following describes the function of the Form Field Shading button on the Forms toolbar?

   (a) Clicking the button shades every field in the form

   (b) Clicking the button shades every field in the form and prevents further modification to the form

   (c) Clicking the button removes the shading from every field

   (d) Clicking the button toggles the shading on or off

6. You have created a table containing numerical values and have entered the SUM(ABOVE) function at the bottom of a column. You then delete one of the rows included in the sum. Which of the following is true?

   (a) The row cannot be deleted because it contains a cell that is included in the sum function

   (b) The sum is updated automatically

   (c) The sum cannot be updated unless the Form Protect button is toggled off

   (d) The sum will be updated provided you right click the cell and select the Update field command

7. Which of the following is suitable for use as a master document?

   (a) An in-depth proposal that contains component documents

   (b) A lengthy newsletter with stories submitted by several people

   (c) A book

   (d) All of the above

8. Which of the following is a true statement regarding changes to a master document and its associated subdocuments?

   (a) The master document cannot be changed if subdocuments have been added to it

   (b) Changes can be made to any locked subdocument

   (c) Changes can be made to any unlocked subdocument

   (d) All of the above

9. What happens if you click inside a subdocument, then click the Lock button on the Outlining toolbar?

   (a) The subdocument is locked

   (b) The subdocument is unlocked

   (c) The subdocument is locked or unlocked depending on its status prior to clicking the button

   (d) All editing to the subdocument is disabled

... continued

multiple choice

10. Which of the following describes the storage of a master document and the associated subdocuments?

   (a) Each document is saved as a separate file

   (b) All of the subdocuments must be stored in the same folder

   (c) Both (a) and (b)

   (d) Neither (a) nor (b)

11. Which of the following best describes the recording and execution of a macro?

   (a) A macro is recorded once and executed once

   (b) A macro is recorded once and executed many times

   (c) A macro is recorded many times and executed once

   (d) A macro is recorded many times and executed many times

12. Which of the following is true regarding comments in Visual Basic?

   (a) A comment is not executable; that is, its inclusion or omission does not affect the outcome of a macro

   (b) A comment begins with an apostrophe

   (c) Both (a) and (b)

   (d) Neither (a) nor (b)

13. Which commands are used to copy an existing macro so that it can become the basis of a new macro?

   (a) Copy command

   (b) Paste command

   (c) Both (a) and (b)

   (d) Neither (a) nor (b)

14. What is the default location for a macro created in Microsoft Word?

   (a) In the Normal template, where it is available to every Word document

   (b) In the document in which it was created, where it is available only to that document

   (c) In the Macros folder on your hard drive

   (d) In the Office folder on your hard drive

15. Which of the following correctly matches the shortcut to the associated task?

   (a) Alt+F11 toggles between Word and the Visual Basic Editor

   (b) Alt+F8 displays the Macros dialog box

   (c) Both (a) and (b)

   (d) Neither (a) nor (b)

16. Which of the following is true regarding a document that has been sent for review to four different people on a project team?

   (a) The original author cannot begin to review changes until comments have been received from every reviewer

   (b) The revisions from each reviewer must be accepted or rejected collectively; that is, the changes cannot be reviewed individually

   (c) The document can be printed with or without the suggested changes

   (d) The suggested additions and deletions will appear in blue and red, respectively, for all reviewers

17. Which of the following is true about indented text in a VBA procedure?

   (a) The indented text is always executed first

   (b) The indented text is always executed last

   (c) The indented text is rendered a comment and is never executed

   (d) None of the above

18. Which of the following is *true* regarding VBA statements?

   (a) Comments appear in green, syntax errors appear in red

   (b) Comments appear in red, syntax errors appear in green

   (c) Comments appear in green, VBA keywords appear in red

   (d) Comments appear in blue, VBA keywords appear in green

ANSWERS

1.	b	7.	d	13.	c
2.	c	8.	c	14.	a
3.	d	9.	c	15.	c
4.	c	10.	a	16.	c
5.	d	11.	b	17.	d
6.	d	12.	c	18.	a

PRACTICE WITH WORD

1. **Reviewing a Document:** Figure 7.11 displays a document that has been reviewed by multiple individuals. Your assignment is to go through the document and accept or reject the various changes that have been suggested. Open the *Chapter 7 Practice 1* document in the Exploring Word folder and proceed as follows:

   a. Pull down the Tools menu, click the Options command, then click the Track Changes tab as shown in Figure 7.11. Examine the default options and experiment with the various settings—for example, change the width and/or location of the margin that contains the editing changes.

   b. Track Changes should be on as seen by the TRK indicator on the status bar. The indicator functions as a toggle switch; double click the indicator, and Track Changes is on. Double click the indicator a second time, and the feature is off. (You can also use the Track Changes button on the Reviewing toolbar to toggle Track Changes on and off.) Leave Track Changes on.

   c. Click the down arrow on the Show button and click the Reviewers command to see the names of the reviewers, each of which is displayed in a different color. The revisions in the document are also displayed in different colors, corresponding to the reviewers' names. Press Esc to close the menu.

   d. Click the down arrow on the Display for Review list box and select Final Showing Markup as shown in Figure 7.11. Pull down the File menu, click the Print command to display the Print dialog box, click Document Showing Markup in the Print What list box, then click OK to print the document in this format.

   e. Press Ctrl+Home to move the insertion point to the beginning of the document. Click the Next button to move to the first revision, then click the Accept Change button to accept this change. Click the Next button to move to the next change, then click the Accept Change button a second time. (It would be much easier if Word moved to the next revision automatically, but we could not make that happen.) Click the down arrow next to the Accept Change button, then click the command to Accept All Changes in Document.

   f. Insert a comment indicating that you have completed your review. Pull down the File menu, click the Print command to display the Print dialog box, click Document in the Print What list box, then click OK to print the final document.

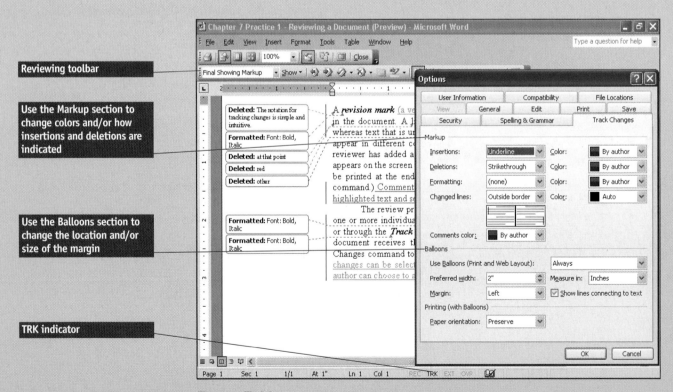

FIGURE 7.11 Reviewing a Document (exercise 1)

2. **Table Math:** The document in Figure 7.12 displays two versions of a table, the original table prior to any modification, and the completed table at the end of the exercise. Open the partially completed *Chapter 7 Practice 2* document in the Exploring Word folder. Select the existing table and copy it. Leave the original table in part (a) as it is, and apply all subsequent commands to the second table in part (b) of the document.

a. Enter your last name in the indicated cell (replacing "Your Name Goes Here"). Click outside the table immediately to the left of the row containing your name to select that row. Pull down the Format menu, click the Borders and Shading command, click the Shading tab, select a color, and click OK.

b. Click and drag to select the first five rows of the table (do not select the Total row). Pull down the Table menu, click the Sort command to display the Sort dialog box, sort by Sales Person, and click the option button to indicate a header row. Click OK to sort the table and display the sales persons in alphabetical order. The shading should travel with the sort.

c. Click in the last column of the second row (the cell that will contain the first person's sales gain). Pull down the Table menu, click the formula command, click in the Formula text box, and replace the existing formula with =c2-b2. Click OK. You should see the result of the calculation.

d. Enter parallel formulas to compute the sales gain for each sales person as well as the total sales gain. You have to enter each formula individually, adjusting the cell references as necessary; the Copy command will not adjust the formulas in each cell.

e. Change Brown's sales for this year to 300, and note that the computed value does not change automatically. Select the computed value. Point to the selection and click the right mouse button, and then click the Update Field command to display the new result.

f. Print the completed document for your instructor to show the displayed values.

g. Print the document a second time to show the cell formulas. Pull down the File menu, click the Print command to display the Print dialog box, click the Options button to display a second Print dialog box, and check the box to print Field Codes. Click OK to close the Print Options dialog box, then click OK a second time to print the document showing the field codes.

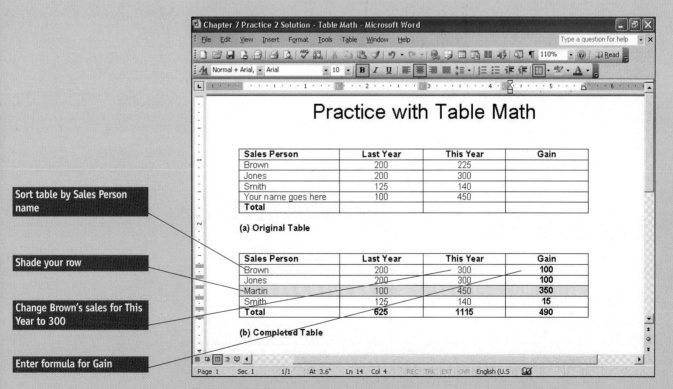

FIGURE 7.12   Table Math (exercise 2)

practice exercises

3. **Tips for Windows XP:** The master document in Figure 7.13 is composed of three subdocuments, each of which contains a series of tips for Windows XP. The documents were created by different individuals. Your assignment is to create the master document.

   a. Start Microsoft Word and create a new document. Pull down the View menu and change to the Outline view. The Outlining toolbar should be displayed automatically. (You cannot create a master document unless you are in the Outline view.)

   b. Enter the title of the document, Tips for Windows XP. Pull down the Insert menu, click the Symbol command, click the Symbols tab, and choose the Wingdings font. Scroll to the end of the displayed characters until you can click the Windows symbol. Insert the symbol. Close the Symbols dialog box. Change the title to 24-point Arial.

   c. Enter the additional text for the master document as shown in Figure 7.13. Format the text appropriately using 12 point Times New Roman for the first paragraph.

   d. Click the Master Document View button on the Outlining toolbar. Click the Insert Subdocument button, then insert the *Tips by Tom* Document from the Tips for Windows XP folder. Insert the two additional documents, *Tips by Dick*, and *Tips by Harry* that are stored in the same folder. (You may have to click the Expand Subdocuments button on the Outlining toolbar to insert a subdocument.)

   e. Protect the document by setting Formatting and/or Editing restrictions. Pull down the Tools menu and click the Protect Document command to display the task pane in Figure 7.13. Check the box to allow only the specified type of editing (no changes in our example), then check the box in the Exceptions area to designate sections of the document that can be edited; e.g., "Your Name Goes Here". Click the button to Start Enforcing Password Protection to display the associated dialog box. Click OK (you do not have to enter a password).

   f. Try to modify the document. You will not be able to change anything except the line containing your name. Enter your name in the indicated area.

   g. Click the Print Preview button, then click Yes if asked if you want to open the subdocuments before continuing with the command. The document will open in the Preview window. Click the Print button to print the completed document.

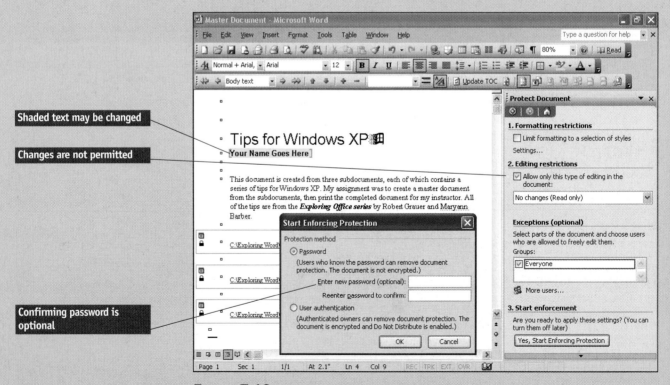

FIGURE 7.13 Tips for Windows XP (exercise 3)

4. **Debugging a Macro:** A "bug" is a mistake in a computer program and hence the term "debugging" refers to the process of finding and correcting programming errors. One of the best techniques for debugging is to execute the statements in a macro one at a time, so that you can see the effect of each statement. You can learn the technique with a working macro, and then apply the method if and when you need to debug another procedure. Complete Hands-on Exercise 4 if you have not already done so. Proceed as follows:

a. Close all open applications. Start Word and open any document. Pull down the Tools menu, click the Macro command, and click the Visual Basic Editor command to start the editor. Click the Close button in the left pane to close the Project window within the Visual Basic Editor. The Code window expands to take the entire Visual Basic Editor window. Pull down the View menu, click the Toolbars command, and display the Debug toolbar.

b. Point to an empty area on the Windows taskbar, then click the right mouse button to display a shortcut menu. Click the Tile Windows Vertically command to tile the open windows (Word and the Visual Basic Editor). Your desktop should be similar to Figure 7.14. It doesn't matter if the document is in the left or right window. If additional windows are open on the desktop, minimize the other windows, and then repeat the command to tile the open windows.

c. Click in the Visual Basic Editor window, then click anywhere within the TitlePage macro. Click the Procedure View button. Click the Step Into button on the Debug toolbar (or press the F8 key) to enter the macro. The Sub statement is highlighted. Press the F8 key a second time to move to the first executable statement (the comments are skipped). The statement is selected (highlighted), but it has not yet been executed. Press the F8 key again to execute this statement and move to the next statement.

d. Continue to press the F8 key to execute the statements in the macro one at a time. You can see the effect of each statement as it is executed in the Word window. Figure 7.14 displays the macro as the last statement (the statement to create a page break after the title has been entered) is about to be executed.

e. Do you think this procedure is useful in finding any bugs that might exist? Summarize the steps in debugging a macro in a short note to your instructor.

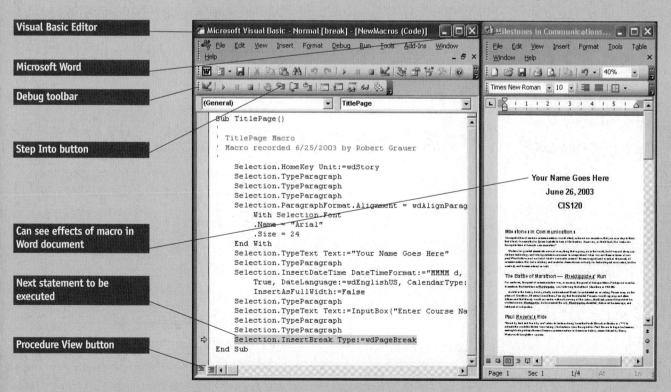

FIGURE 7.14 Debugging a Macro (exercise 4)

practice exercises

5. **Customizing a Toolbar:** The chapter illustrated different ways to execute a macro—from the Tools menu in Word, by pressing Alt+F8 to display the Macros dialog box, and via a keyboard shortcut. You can also add a customized button to a toolbar and/or add a new command to an existing menu. Proceed as follows:

   a. Complete the fourth hands-on exercise in the chapter, which creates the TitlePage macro. Start a new document and test the macro to be sure that it works properly. You should be prompted to enter the name of your course, after which the title page is created.

   b. Pull down the View menu, click Toolbars, click Customize to display the Customize dialog box, and then click the Commands tab. Click the down arrow in the Categories list box until you see the Macros category as shown in Figure 7.15.

   c. Click and drag the TitlePage macro from the Commands area to an existing toolbar (e.g., to the extreme left of the Formatting toolbar as shown in Figure 7.15), then release the mouse to drop the macro onto the toolbar. The icon on the mouse pointer will change from an "X" to a plus sign when you are able to drop the macro onto the toolbar. (You can delete the macro from the toolbar by dragging it off the toolbar.)

   d. You will see the name of the macro and/or a button icon (e.g., a smiley face), according to the options in effect. Click the macro button after it has been added to the toolbar, then click the Modify Selection button within the Customize dialog box. Select the desired option such as the default style (image only), text only, or image and text. (You can also choose the Change Button Image command to select a different button icon to diplay on the toolbar.) Close the Customize dialog box.

   e. Delete the title page from the existing document, then click the newly added toolbar button to test the button. Once again you are prompted for the course you are taking, after which the title page is created.

   f. Prove to your instructor that you have modified the toolbar successfully by capturing a screen similar to Figure 7.15. Press the Print Screen key to capture the screen to the clipboard, start a new Word document, then click the Paste button to paste the screen into your document. Print this document for your instructor.

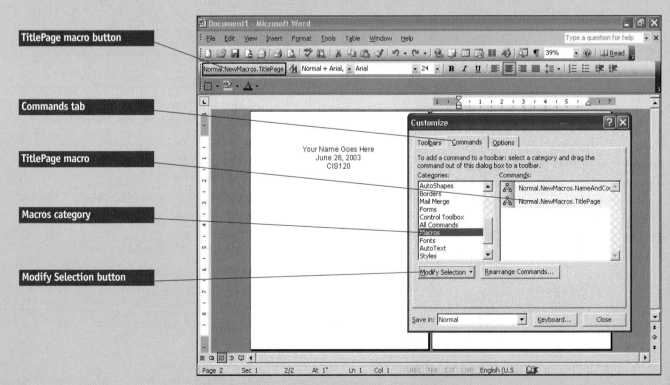

FIGURE 7.15 Customizing a Toolbar (exercise 5)

6. **Enhancing a Macro**: The macro recorder jump starts the creation of a macro (VBA procedure) by translating commands that are executed within Microsoft Word to the equivalent VBA statements. You can then open the VBA editor and edit the resulting code. Some changes are intuitive and do not require knowledge of VBA per se; for example, changing the font or point size. VBA is a language unto itself, however, that lets you enhance the functionality of any macro by adding statements as necessary as shown in Figure 7.16. Proceed as follows:

   a. Start Word and open a new document. Pull down the Tools menu, click the Macro command, click Record New Macro, and enter CreateTable as the name of the macro you are about to create. Click OK.

   b. Pull down the Table menu, click the Insert command, click Table, and then insert a two-by-five table (two rows and five columns) into the current document. Click the Stop Recording button.

   c. Open the VBA editor. Click the Full Module View button and display the macro you just created as shown in Figure 7.16. Note, however, that your procedure will contain additional statements (With . . . End With) that are not essential to the creation of the table. Delete these statements so that your procedure matches ours.

   d. Click and drag to select the entire CreateTable macro, including the Sub and End Sub statements. Click the Copy button, click beneath the End Sub statement, and then click the Paste button to duplicate the macro. Rename the duplicate procedure CreateBetterTable.

   e. Insert the indicated comments at the beginning of the CreateBetterTable procedure, then add the four VBA statements in Figure 7.16. The Dim statements define the variables intRows and intColumns, and the InputBox statements obtain these values from the user. Now replace the number 2 that appears in the ActiveDocument statement with the variable IntRows. Replace the number 5 with the variable IntColumns.

   f. Return to the original Word document and close the document without saving it. Start a new document. Pull down the Tools menu, click the Macro command, click Macros . . . and run the CreateBetterTable macro. You should be prompted for the number of rows and columns, respectively, after which the table should be created in your document.

   g. Return to the VBA editor and print the procedures you created in this exercise. Refer to the VBA primer at the end of the text for additional information on VBA.

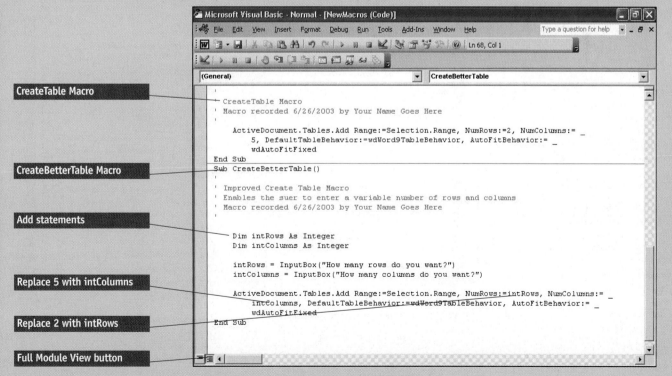

FIGURE 7.16 Enhancing a Macro (exercise 6)

7. **Create a Custom Menu:** You can create a custom menu that contains commands from any existing menu and/or additional commands corresponding to various macros that you have created. Proceed as follows:

a. Pull down the View menu, click Toolbars, click Customize to display the Customize dialog box, click the Commands tab, and then scroll until you can select New menu from the Categories list box at the left. Click and drag the New menu command to the right of the menu bar, then release the mouse to create a new menu.

b. Select the newly created menu on the menu bar, click the Modify Selection button in the Customize dialog box, then change the name of the menu to "&My Menu". The ampersand will not appear in the menu name, but the letter "M" will be underlined, enabling you to pull down the menu using the Alt+M keyboard shortcut. (This is the same shortcut used to pull down other menus; e.g., Alt+F and Alt+E pull down the File and Edit menus, respectively.)

c. You are now ready to add commands to the menu. Select the Macros category in the Category area, and then drag an existing macro to the menu you just created. Repeat this process to add additional commands (corresponding to the macros you created in earlier exercises) to the menu. You can create a custom menu, even if you do not have any macros, by selecting commands from other categories. Test your menu to be sure that all of its commands work properly.

d. Prove to your instructor that you have created the menu successfully by capturing the screen in Figure 7.17. Complete the menu as described above, pull down the menu to display the commands, and then press the Print Screen key to capture the screen to the Windows clipboard. Start a new Word document and press the enter key three times. Click the Paste button to paste the screen into your document. Press Ctrl+Home to return to the beginning of the document. Enter a title for the assignment followed by your name. Print the completed document to submit to your instructor.

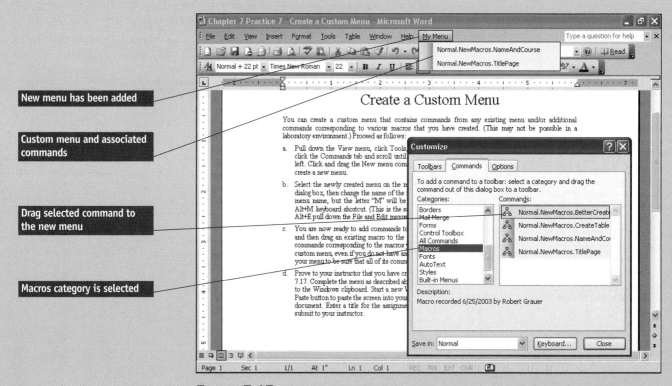

FIGURE 7.17 Create a Custom Menu (exercise 7)

Toolbars for Microsoft® Office Word 2003

TOOLBARS

Standard

Formatting

3-D Settings

AutoText

Control

Database

Diagram

Drawing

Drawing Canvas

E-mail

Extended Formatting

Forms

Frames

Function Key Display

Ink Comment

Japanese Greeting

Mail Merge

Microsoft

Organization Chart

Outlining

Picture

Reviewing

Shadow Settings

Shortcut Menus

Tables and Borders

Visual Basic

Web

Web Tools

Word Count

WordArt

OVERVIEW

Microsoft Word has 30 predefined toolbars that provide access to commonly used commands. The toolbars are displayed in Figure A.1 and are listed here for convenience. They are: the Standard, Formatting, 3-D Settings, AutoText, Control, Database, Diagram, Drawing, Drawing Canvas, E-mail, Extended Formatting, Forms, Frames, Function Key Display, Ink Comment, Japanese Greeting, Mail Merge, Microsoft, Organization Chart, Outlining, Picture, Reviewing, Shadow Settings, Shortcut Menus, Tables and Borders, Visual Basic, Web, Web Tools, Word Count, and WordArt toolbars. The Standard and Formatting toolbars are displayed by default and appear on the same row immediately below the menu bar. The other predefined toolbars are automatically displayed (hidden) at the discretion of the user, and in some cases are displayed automatically when their corresponding features are in use (e.g., the Picture toolbar and the WordArt toolbar).

The buttons on the toolbars are intended to be indicative of their function. Clicking the Printer button, for example, (the sixth button from the left on the Standard toolbar) executes the Print command. If you are unsure of the purpose of any toolbar button, point to it, and a ScreenTip will appear that displays its name.

You can display multiple toolbars at one time, move them to new locations on the screen, customize their appearance, or suppress their display.

■ To separate the Standard and Formatting toolbars and simultaneously display all of the buttons for each toolbar, pull down the Tools menu, click the Customize command, click the Options tab, then check the box to show the toolbars on two rows. Alternatively, the toolbars appear on the same row with only a limited number of buttons visible on each toolbar, and hence you may need to click the double arrow at the end of the toolbar to view additional buttons. Additional buttons will be added to either toolbar as you use the associated feature, and conversely, buttons will be removed from the toolbar if the feature is not used.

■ To display or hide a toolbar, pull down the View menu and click the Toolbars command. Select (deselect) the toolbar that you want to display (hide). The selected toolbar will be displayed in the same position as when last displayed. You may also point to any toolbar and click with the right mouse button to bring up a shortcut menu, after which you can select the toolbar to be displayed (hidden). If the toolbar to be displayed is not listed, click the Customize command, click the Toolbars tab, check the box for the toolbar to be displayed, and then click the Close button.

- To change the size of the buttons, suppress the display of the ScreenTips, or display the associated shortcut key (if available), pull down the View menu, click Toolbars, and click Customize to display the Customize dialog box. If necessary, click the Options tab, then select (deselect) the appropriate check box. Alternatively, you can right click on any toolbar, click the Customize command from the context-sensitive menu, then select (deselect) the appropriate check box from within the Options tab in the Customize dialog box.

- Toolbars are either docked (along the edge of the window) or floating (in their own window). A toolbar moved to the edge of the window will dock along that edge. A toolbar moved anywhere else in the window will float in its own window. Docked toolbars are one tool wide (high), whereas floating toolbars can be resized by clicking and dragging a border or corner as you would with any window.
  - To move a docked toolbar, click anywhere in the background area and drag the toolbar to its new location. You can also click and drag the move handle (the single vertical line) at the left of the toolbar.
  - To move a floating toolbar, drag its title bar to its new location.

- To customize one or more toolbars, display the toolbar on the screen. Then pull down the View menu, click Toolbars, and click Customize to display the Customize dialog box. Alternatively, you can click on any toolbar with the right mouse button and select Customize from the shortcut menu.
  - To move a button, drag the button to its new location on that toolbar or any other displayed toolbar.
  - To copy a button, press the Ctrl key as you drag the button to its new location on that toolbar or any other displayed toolbar.
  - To delete a button, drag the button off the toolbar and release the mouse button.
  - To add a button, click the Commands tab in the Customize dialog box, select the category (from the Categories list box) that contains the button you want to add, then drag the button to the desired location on the toolbar.
  - To restore a predefined toolbar to its default appearance, pull down the View menu, click Toolbars, click Customize, click the Toolbars tab, select (highlight) the desired toolbar, and click the Reset command button.

- Buttons can also be moved, copied, or deleted without displaying the Customize dialog box.
  - To move a button, press the Alt key as you drag the button to the new location.
  - To copy a button, press the Alt and Ctrl keys as you drag the button to the new location.
  - To delete a button, press the Alt key as you drag the button off the toolbar.

- To create your own toolbar, pull down the View menu, click Toolbars, click Customize, click the Toolbars tab, then click the New command button. Alternatively, you can click on any toolbar with the right mouse button, select Customize from the shortcut menu, click the Toolbars tab, and then click the New command button.
  - Enter a name for the toolbar in the dialog box that follows. The name can be any length and can contain spaces.
  - The new toolbar will appear on the screen. Initially it will be big enough to hold only one button. Add, move, and delete buttons following the same procedures as outlined above. The toolbar will automatically size itself as new buttons are added and deleted.
  - To delete a custom toolbar, pull down the View menu, click Toolbars, click Customize, and click the Toolbars tab. *Verify that the custom toolbar to be deleted is the only one selected (highlighted).* Click the Delete command button. Click Yes to confirm the deletion. (Note that a predefined toolbar cannot be deleted.)

Standard

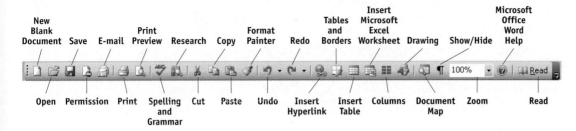

New Blank Document · Save · E-mail · Print Preview · Research · Copy · Format Painter · Redo · Tables and Borders · Insert Microsoft Excel Worksheet · Drawing · Show/Hide · Microsoft Office Word Help

Open · Permission · Print · Spelling and Grammar · Cut · Paste · Undo · Insert Hyperlink · Insert Table · Columns · Document Map · Zoom · Read

Formatting

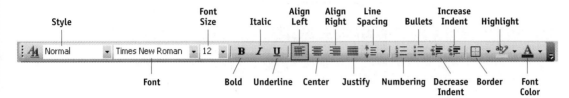

Style · Font Size · Italic · Align Left · Align Right · Line Spacing · Bullets · Increase Indent · Highlight

Font · Bold · Underline · Center · Justify · Numbering · Decrease Indent · Border · Font Color

3-D Settings

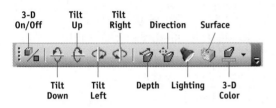

3-D On/Off · Tilt Up · Tilt Right · Direction · Surface

Tilt Down · Tilt Left · Depth · Lighting · 3-D Color

AutoText

AutoText · Create AutoText

All Entries Menu

Control Toolbox

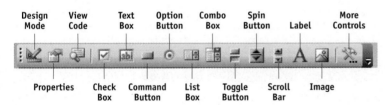

Design Mode · View Code · Text Box · Option Button · Combo Box · Spin Button · Label · More Controls

Properties · Check Box · Command Button · List Box · Toggle Button · Scroll Bar · Image

Database

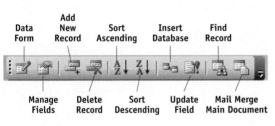

Data Form · Add New Record · Sort Ascending · Insert Database · Find Record

Manage Fields · Delete Record · Sort Descending · Update Field · Mail Merge Main Document

Diagram

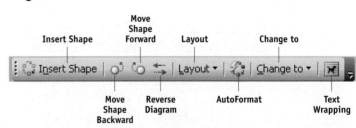

Insert Shape · Move Shape Forward · Layout · Change to

Move Shape Backward · Reverse Diagram · AutoFormat · Text Wrapping

Drawing Canvas

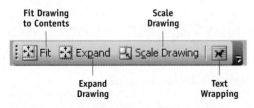

Fit Drawing to Contents · Scale Drawing

Expand Drawing · Text Wrapping

FIGURE A.1 Toolbars

Drawing

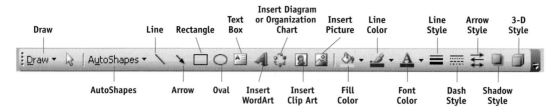

E-mail

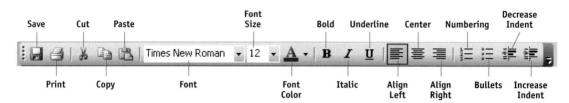

Extended Formatting

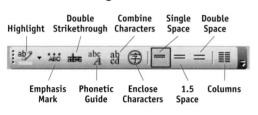

Forms

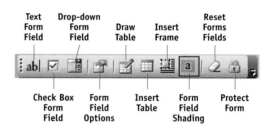

Frames

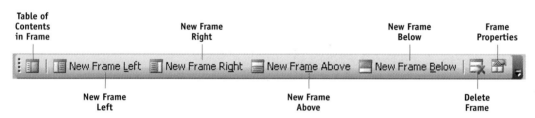

Function Key Display

Japanese Greeting

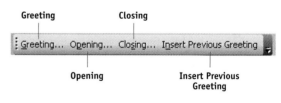

Mail Merge

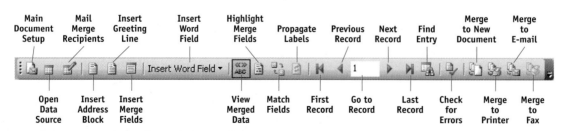

FIGURE A.1 Toolbars (continued)

Microsoft

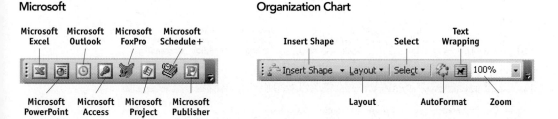

Microsoft Excel
Microsoft Outlook
Microsoft FoxPro
Microsoft Schedule+

Microsoft PowerPoint
Microsoft Access
Microsoft Project
Microsoft Publisher

Organization Chart

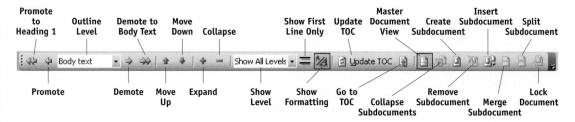

Insert Shape
Select
Text Wrapping

Layout
AutoFormat
Zoom

Outlining

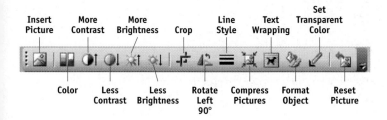

Promote to Heading 1
Outline Level
Demote to Body Text
Move Down
Collapse
Show First Line Only
Update TOC
Master Document View
Create Subdocument
Insert Subdocument
Split Subdocument

Promote
Demote
Move Up
Expand
Show Level
Show Formatting
Go to TOC
Collapse Subdocuments
Remove Subdocument
Merge Subdocument
Lock Document

Picture

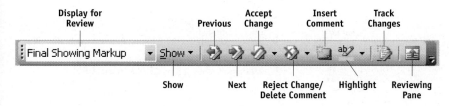

Insert Picture
More Contrast
More Brightness
Crop
Line Style
Text Wrapping
Set Transparent Color

Color
Less Contrast
Less Brightness
Rotate Left 90°
Compress Pictures
Format Object
Reset Picture

Reviewing

Display for Review
Previous
Accept Change
Insert Comment
Track Changes

Final Showing Markup

Show
Next
Reject Change/ Delete Comment
Highlight
Reviewing Pane

Shadow Settings

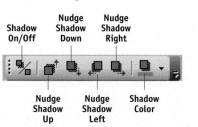

Shadow On/Off
Nudge Shadow Down
Nudge Shadow Right

Nudge Shadow Up
Nudge Shadow Left
Shadow Color

Shortcut Menus

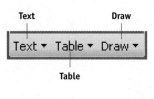

Text
Draw

Text ▼ Table ▼ Draw ▼

Table

FIGURE A.1   Toolbars (continued)

Tables and Borders

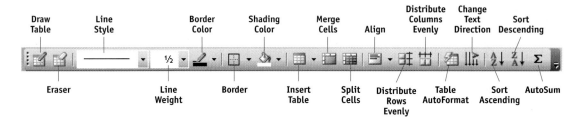

Visual Basic

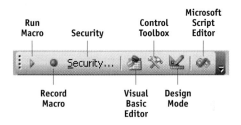

Web

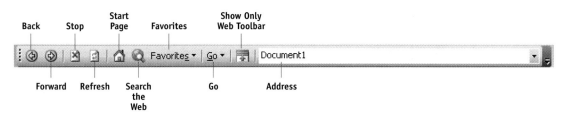

Web Tools

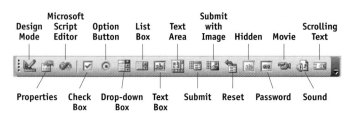

Word Count

WordArt

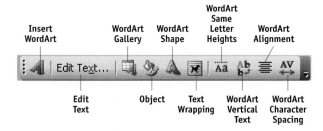

FIGURE A.1   Toolbars (continued)

1

Getting Started with Microsoft® Windows® XP

CASE STUDY
UNFORESEEN CIRCUMSTANCES

Steve and his wife Shelly have poured their life savings into the dream of owning their own business, a "nanny" service agency. They have spent the last two years building their business and have created a sophisticated database with numerous entries for both families and nannies. The database is the key to their operation. Now that it is up and running, Steve and Shelly are finally at a point where they could hire someone to manage the operation on a part-time basis so that they could take some time off together.

Unfortunately, their process for selecting a person they could trust with their business was not as thorough as it should have been. Nancy, their new employee, assured them that all was well, and the couple left for an extended weekend. The place was in shambles on their return. Nancy could not handle the responsibility, and when Steve gave her two weeks' notice, neither he nor his wife thought that the unimaginable would happen. On her last day in the office Nancy "lost" all of the names in the database—the data was completely gone!

Nancy claimed that a "virus" knocked out the database, but after spending nearly $1,500 with a computer consultant, Steve was told that it had been cleverly deleted from the hard drive and could not be recovered. Of course, the consultant asked Steve and Shelly about their backup strategy, which they sheepishly admitted did not exist. They had never experienced any problems in the past, and simply assumed that their data was safe. Fortunately, they do have hard copy of the data in the form of various reports that were printed throughout the time they were in business. They have no choice but to manually reenter the data. ■

Your assignment is to read the chapter, paying special attention to the information on file management. Think about how Steve and Shelly could have avoided the disaster if a backup strategy had been in place, then summarize your thoughts in a brief note to your instructor. Describe the elements of a basic backup strategy. Give several other examples of unforeseen circumstances that can cause data to be lost.

Windows® XP is the newest and most powerful version of the Windows operating system. It has a slightly different look than earlier versions, but it maintains the conventions of its various predecessors. You have seen the Windows interface many times, but do you really understand it? Can you move and copy files with confidence? Do you know how to back up the Excel spreadsheets, Access databases, and other documents that you work so hard to create? If not, now is the time to learn.

We begin with an introduction to the desktop, the graphical user interface that lets you work in intuitive fashion by pointing at icons and clicking the mouse. We identify the basic components of a window and describe how to execute commands and supply information through different elements in a dialog box. We stress the importance of disk and file management, but begin with basic definitions of a file and a folder. We also introduce Windows Explorer and show you how to move or copy a file from one folder to another. We discuss other basic operations, such as renaming and deleting a file. We also describe how to recover a deleted file (if necessary) from the Recycle Bin.

Windows XP is available in different versions. Windows *XP Home Edition* is intended for entertainment and home use. It includes a media player, new support for digital photography, and an instant messenger. Windows *XP Professional Edition* has all of the features of the Home Edition plus additional security to encrypt files and protect data. It includes support for high-performance multiprocessor systems. It also lets you connect to your computer from a remote station.

The login screen in Figure 1 is displayed when the computer is turned on initially and/or when you are switching from one user account to another. Several individuals can share the same computer. Each user, however, retains his or her individual desktop settings, individual lists of favorite and recently visited Web sites, as well as other customized Windows settings. Multiple users can be logged on simultaneously, each with his or her programs in memory, through a feature known as *fast user switching*.

Multiple users can be logged on

Accounts can be password-protected

FIGURE 1 Windows XP Login

Windows XP, as well as all previous versions of Windows, creates a working environment for your computer that parallels the working environment at home or in an office. You work at a desk. Windows operations take place on the *desktop*. There are physical objects on a desk such as folders, a dictionary, a calculator, or a phone. The computer equivalents of those objects appear as icons (pictorial symbols) on the desktop. Each object on a real desk has attributes (properties) such as size, weight, and color. In similar fashion, Windows assigns properties to every object on its desktop. And just as you can move the objects on a real desk, you can rearrange the objects on the Windows desktop.

Windows XP has a new interface, but you can retain the look and feel of earlier versions as shown in Figure 2. The desktop in Figure 2a uses the default *Windows XP theme* (the wallpaper has been suppressed), whereas Figure 2b displays the "same" desktop using the *Windows Classic theme*. The icons on either desktop are used to access specific programs or other functions.

The *Start button*, as its name suggests, is where you begin; it works identically on both desktops. Click the Start button to see a menu of programs and other functions. The Windows XP *Start menu* in Figure 2a is divided into two columns. The column on the left displays the most recently used programs for easy access, whereas the column on the right contains a standard set of entries. It also shows the name of the individual who is logged into the computer. The *Classic Start menu* in Figure 2b contains only a single column. (Note the indication of the Windows XP Professional operating system that appears at the left of the menu.)

Do not be concerned if your desktop is different from ours. Your real desk is arranged differently from those of your friends, just as your Windows desktop will also be different. Moreover, you are likely to work on different systems—at school, at work, or at home; what is important is that you recognize the common functionality that is present on all desktops.

Look now at Figure 2c, which displays an entirely different desktop, one with four open windows that is similar to a desk in the middle of a working day. Each window in Figure 2c displays a program or a folder that is currently in use. The ability to run several programs at the same time is known as *multitasking*, and it is a major benefit of the Windows environment. Multitasking enables you to run a word processor in one window, create a spreadsheet in a second window, surf the Internet in a third window, play a game in a fourth window, and so on. You can work in a program as long as you want, then change to a different program by clicking its window.

The *taskbar* at the bottom of the desktop contains a button for each open window, and it enables you to switch back and forth between the open windows by clicking the appropriate button. A *notification area* appears at the right end of the taskbar. It displays the time and other shortcuts. It may also provide information on the status of such ongoing activities as a printer or Internet connection.

The desktop in Figure 2d is identical to the desktop in Figure 2c except that it is displayed in the Windows Classic theme. The open windows are the same, as are the contents of the taskbar and notification area. The choice between the XP theme or Windows Classic (or other) theme is one of personal preference.

Moving and Sizing a Window

A window can be sized or moved on the desktop through appropriate actions with the mouse. To *size a window*, point to any border (the mouse pointer changes to a double arrow), then drag the border in the direction you want to go—inward to shrink the window or outward to enlarge it. You can also drag a corner (instead of a border) to change both dimensions at the same time. To *move a window* while retaining its current size, click and drag the title bar to a new position on the desktop.

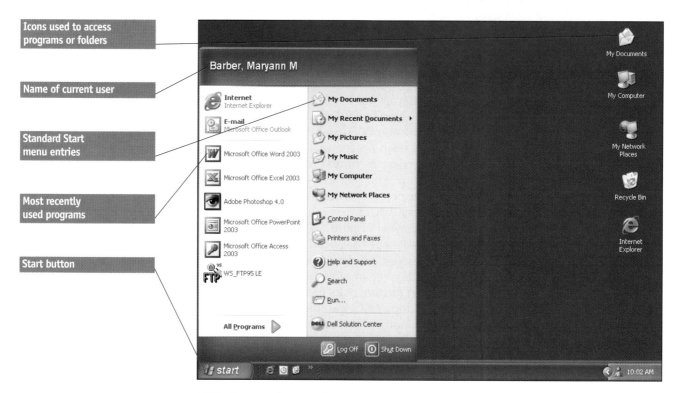

Icons used to access programs or folders

Name of current user

Standard Start menu entries

Most recently used programs

Start button

(a) Windows XP Theme and Start Menu

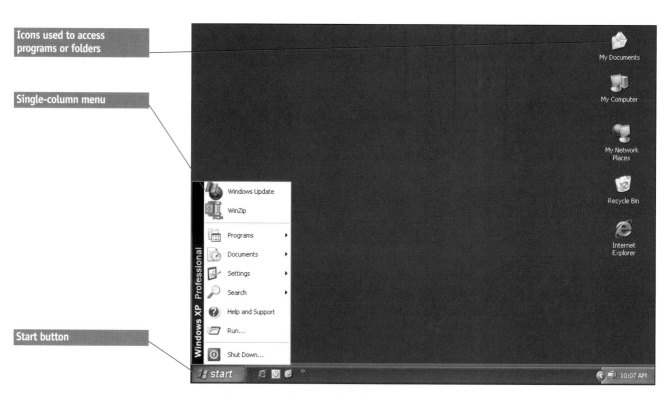

Icons used to access programs or folders

Single-column menu

Start button

(b) Windows Classic Theme and Start Menu

FIGURE 2   The Desktop and Start Menu

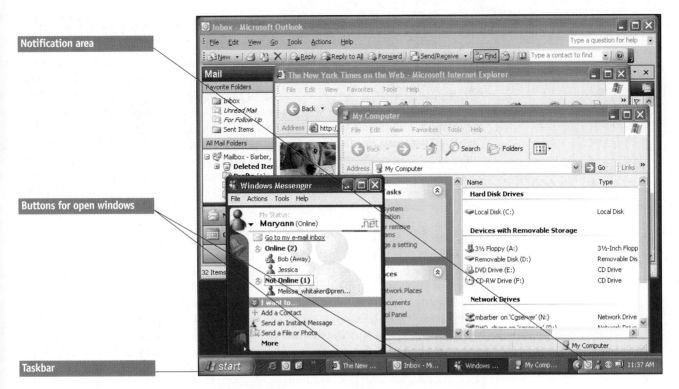

Notification area

Buttons for open windows

Taskbar

(c) Windows XP Theme

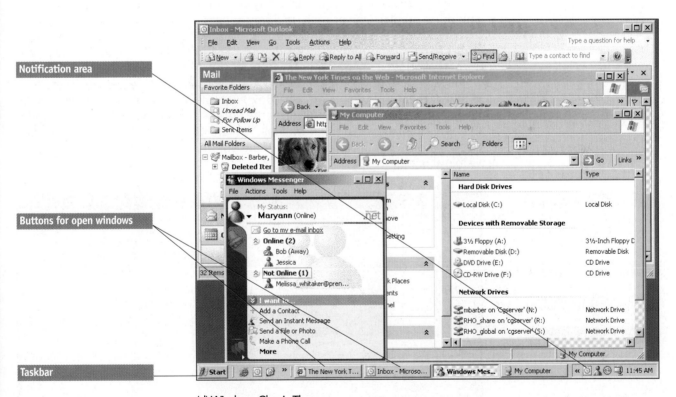

Notification area

Buttons for open windows

Taskbar

(d) Windows Classic Theme

FIGURE 2   The Desktop and Start Menu (*continued*)

All Windows applications share a common user interface and possess a consistent command structure. This means that every Windows application works essentially the same way, which provides a sense of familiarity from one application to the next. In other words, once you learn the basic concepts and techniques in one application, you can apply that knowledge to every other application.

The *My Computer folder* in Figure 3 is used to illustrate basic technology. This folder is present on every system, and its contents depend on the hardware of the specific computer. Our system, for example, has one local disk, a floppy drive, a removable disk (an Iomega Zip® drive), a DVD drive, and a CD-RW (recordable) drive. Our intent at this time, however, is to focus on the elements that are common to every window. A *task pane* (also called a task panel) is displayed at the left of the window to provide easy access to various commands that you might want to access from this folder.

The *title bar* appears at the top of every window and displays the name of the folder or application. The icon at the extreme left of the title bar identifies the window and also provides access to a control menu with operations relevant to the window, such as moving it or sizing it. Three buttons appear at the right of the title bar. The *Minimize button* shrinks the window to a button on the taskbar, but leaves the window in memory. The *Maximize button* enlarges the window so that it takes up the entire desktop. The *Restore button* (not shown in Figure 3) appears instead of the Maximize button after a window has been maximized, and restores the window to its previous size. The *Close button* closes the window and removes it from memory and the desktop.

The *menu bar* appears immediately below the title bar and provides access to pull-down menus. One or more *toolbars* appear below the menu bar and let you execute a command by clicking a button, as opposed to pulling down a menu. The *status bar* at the bottom of the window displays information about the window as a whole or about a selected object within a window.

A vertical (or horizontal) *scroll bar* appears at the right (or bottom) border of a window when its contents are not completely visible and provides access to the unseen areas. The vertical scroll bar at the right of the task panel in Figure 3 implies that there are additional tasks available that are not currently visible. A horizontal scroll bar does not appear since all of the objects in the My Computer folder are visible at one time.

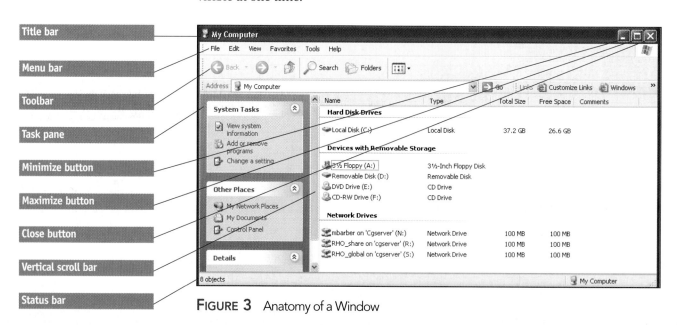

FIGURE 3 Anatomy of a Window

Pull-down Menus

The menu bar provides access to ***pull-down menus*** that enable you to execute commands within an application (program). A pull-down menu is accessed by clicking the menu name or by pressing the Alt key plus the underlined letter in the menu name; for example, press Alt+V to pull down the View menu. (You may have to press the Alt key to see the underlines.) Figure 4 displays three pull-down menus that are associated with the My Computer folder.

Commands within a menu are executed by clicking the command or by typing the underlined letter. Alternatively, you can bypass the menu entirely if you know the equivalent shortcuts shown to the right of the command in the menu (e.g., Ctrl+X, Ctrl+C, or Ctrl+V to cut, copy, or paste as shown within the Edit menu). A dimmed command (e.g., the Paste command in the Edit menu) means the command is not currently executable, and that some additional action has to be taken for the command to become available.

An ellipsis (. . .) following a command indicates that additional information is required to execute the command; for example, selection of the Format command in the File menu requires the user to specify additional information about the formatting process. This information is entered into a dialog box (discussed in the next section), which appears immediately after the command has been selected.

A check next to a command indicates a toggle switch, whereby the command is either on or off. There is a check next to the Status Bar command in the View menu of Figure 4, which means the command is in effect (and thus the status bar will be displayed). Click the Status Bar command and the check disappears, which suppresses the display of the status bar. Click the command a second time and the check reappears, as does the status bar in the associated window.

A bullet next to an item, such as Icons in the View menu, indicates a selection from a set of mutually exclusive choices. Click a different option within the group—such as Thumbnails—and the bullet will move from the previous selection (Icons) to the new selection (Thumbnails).

An arrowhead after a command (e.g., the Arrange Icons by command in the View menu) indicates that a submenu (also known as a cascaded menu) will be displayed with additional menu options.

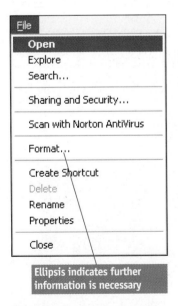

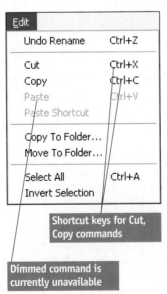

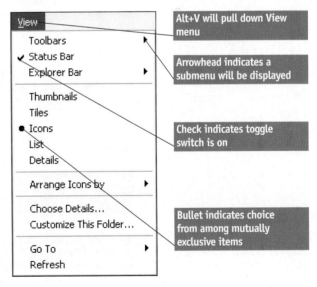

FIGURE 4 Pull-down Menus

Dialog Boxes

A *dialog box* appears when additional information is necessary to execute a command. Click the Print command in Internet Explorer, for example, and you are presented with the Print dialog box in Figure 5, requesting information about precisely what to print and how. The information is entered into the dialog box in different ways, depending on the type of information that is required. The tabs at the top of the dialog box provide access to different sets of options. The General tab is selected in Figure 5.

Option (radio) buttons indicate mutually exclusive choices, one of which *must* be chosen, such as the page range. In this example you can print all pages, the selection (if it is available), the current page (if there are multiple pages), or a specific set of pages (such as pages 1–4), but you can choose *one and only one* option. Any time you select (click) an option, the previous option is automatically deselected.

A *text box* enters specific information such as the pages that will be printed in conjunction with selecting the radio button for pages. A *spin button* is another way to enter specific information such as the number of copies. Click the up or down arrow to increase or decrease the number of pages, respectively. You can also enter the information explicitly by typing it into a spin box, just as you would a text box.

Check boxes are used instead of option buttons if the choices are not mutually exclusive or if an option is not required. The Collate check box is checked, whereas the Print to file box is not checked. Individual options are selected and cleared by clicking the appropriate check box, which toggles the box on and off. A *list box* (not shown in Figure 5) displays some or all of the available choices, any one of which is selected by clicking the desired item.

The *Help button* (a question mark at the right end of the title bar) provides help for any item in the dialog box. Click the button, then click the item in the dialog box for which you want additional information. The Close button (the X at the extreme right of the title bar) closes the dialog box without executing the command.

All dialog boxes also contain one or more *command buttons*, the function of which is generally apparent from the button's name. The Print button in Figure 5, for example, initiates the printing process. The Cancel button does just the opposite and ignores (cancels) any changes made to the settings, then closes the dialog box without further action.

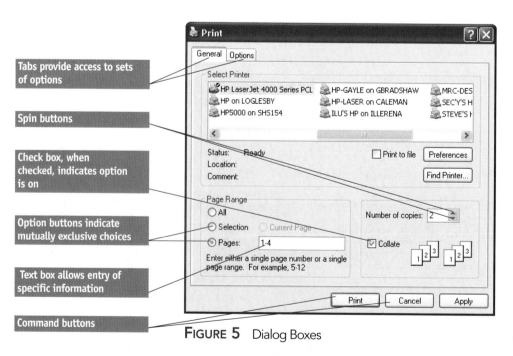

FIGURE 5   Dialog Boxes

HELP AND SUPPORT CENTER

The ***Help and Support Center*** combines such traditional features as a search function and an index of help topics. It also lets you request remote help from other Windows XP users, and/or you can access the Microsoft Knowledge base on the Microsoft Web site. Click the Index button, type the keyword you are searching for, then double click the subtopic to display the associated information in the right pane. The mouse is essential to Windows, and you are undoubtedly familiar with its basic operations such as pointing, clicking, and double clicking. Look closely, however, at the list of subtopics in Figure 6 and you might be surprised at the amount of available information. Suffice it to say, therefore, that you will find the answer to almost every conceivable question if only you will take the trouble to look.

The toolbar at the top of the window contains several buttons that are also found in ***Internet Explorer 6.0***, the Web browser that is built into Windows XP. The Back and Forward buttons enable you to navigate through the various pages that were viewed in the current session. The Favorites button displays a list of previously saved (favorite) help topics from previous sessions. The History button shows all pages that were visited in this session.

The Support button provides access to remote sources for assistance. Click the Support button, then click the link to ask a friend to help, which in turn displays a Remote Assistance screen. You will be asked to sign in to the Messenger service (Windows Messenger is discussed in more detail in a later section). Your friend has to be running Windows XP for this feature to work, but once you are connected, he or she will be able to view your computer screen. You can then chat in real time about the problem and proposed solution. And, if you give permission, your friend can use his or her mouse and keyboard to work on your computer. Be careful! It is one thing to let your friend see your screen. It is quite a leap of faith, however, to give him or her control of your machine.

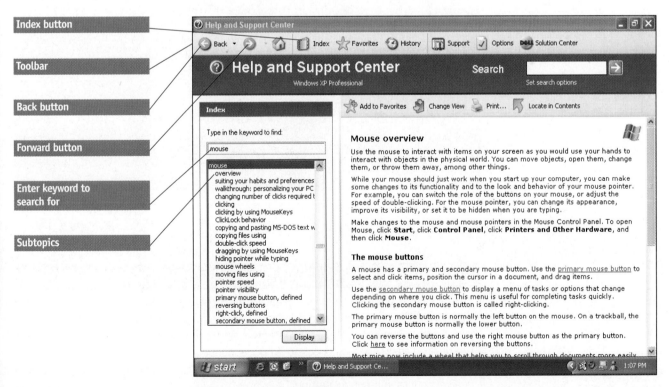

FIGURE 6   Help and Support Center

Welcome to Windows XP

Objective To log on to Windows XP and customize the desktop; to open the My Computer folder; to move and size a window; to format a floppy disk and access the Help and Support Center. Use Figure 7 as a guide.

Step 1: **Log On to Windows XP**

- Turn on the computer and all of the peripheral devices. The floppy drive should be empty prior to starting your machine.

- Windows XP will load automatically, and you should see a login screen similar to Figure 7a. (It does not matter which version of Windows XP you are using.) The number and names of the potential users and their associated icons will be different on your system.

- Click the icon for the user account you want to access. You may be prompted for a password, depending on the security options in effect.

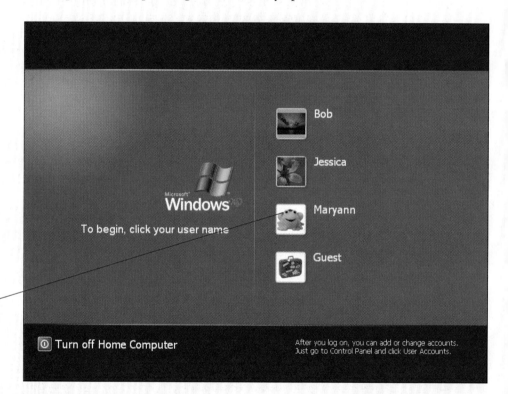

Click icon for user account to be accessed

(a) Log On to Windows XP (step 1)

FIGURE 7 Hands-on Exercise 1

USER ACCOUNTS

The available user names are created automatically during the installation of Windows XP, but you can add or delete users at any time. Click the Start button, click Control Panel, switch to the Category view, and select User Accounts. Choose the desired task, such as creating a new account or changing an existing account, then supply the necessary information. Do not expect, however, to be able to modify user accounts in a school setting.

Step 2: **Choose the Theme and Start Menu**

- Check with your instructor to see if you are able to modify the desktop and other settings at your school or university. If your network administrator has disabled these commands, skip this step and go to step 3.

- Point to a blank area on the desktop, click the **right mouse button** to display a context-sensitive menu, then click the **Properties command** to open the Display Properties dialog box. Click the **Themes tab** and select the **Windows XP theme** if it is not already selected. Click **OK**.

- We prefer to work without any wallpaper (background picture) on the desktop. **Right click** the desktop, click **Properties**, then click the **Desktop tab** in the Display Properties dialog box. Click **None** as shown in Figure 7b, then click **OK**. The background disappears.

- The Start menu is modified independently of the theme. **Right click** a blank area of the taskbar, click the **Properties command** to display the Taskbar and Start Menu Properties dialog box, then click the **Start Menu tab**.

- Click the **Start Menu option button**. Click **OK**.

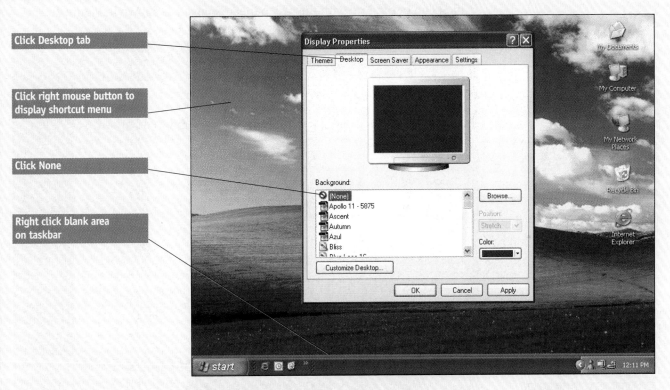

(b) Choose the Theme and Start Menu (step 2)

FIGURE 7   Hands-on Exercise 1 (*continued*)

IMPLEMENT A SCREEN SAVER

A screen saver is a delightful way to personalize your computer and a good way to practice with basic commands in Windows XP. Right click a blank area of the desktop, click the Properties command to open the Display Properties dialog box, then click the Screen Saver tab. Click the down arrow in the Screen Saver list box, choose the desired screen saver, then set the option to wait an appropriate amount of time before the screen saver appears. Click OK to accept the settings and close the dialog box.

Step 3: **Open the My Computer Folder**

- Click the **Start button** to display a two-column Start menu that is characteristic of Windows XP. Click **My Computer** to open the My Computer folder. The contents of your window and/or its size and position on the desktop will be different from ours.

- Pull down the **View menu** as shown in Figure 7c to make or verify the following selections. (You have to pull down the View menu each time you make an additional change.)
  - ❏ The **Status Bar command** should be checked. The Status Bar command functions as a toggle switch. Click the command and the status bar is displayed; click the command a second time and the status bar disappears.
  - ❏ Click the **Tiles command** to change to this view. Selecting the Tiles view automatically deselects the previous view.

- Pull down the **View menu**, then click (or point to) the **Toolbars command** to display a cascaded menu. If necessary, check the commands for the **Standard Buttons** and **Address Bar**, and clear the other commands.

- Click the **Folders button** on the Standard Buttons toolbar to toggle the task panel on or off. End with the task panel displayed as shown in Figure 7c.

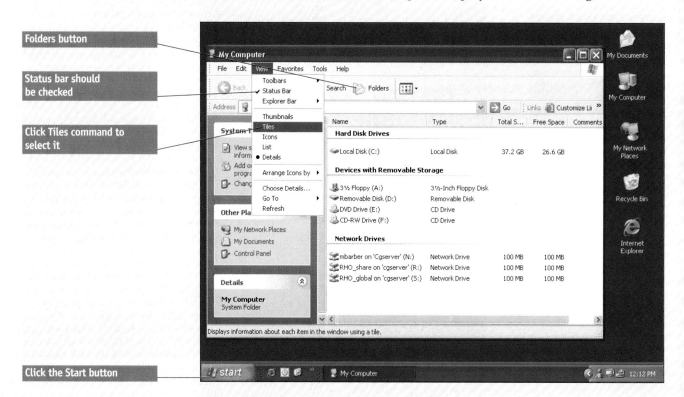

(c) Open the My Computer Folder (step 3)

FIGURE 7   Hands-on Exercise 1 (*continued*)

DESIGNATING THE DEVICES ON A SYSTEM

The first (usually only) floppy drive is always designated as drive A. (A second floppy drive, if it were present, would be drive B.) The first hard (local) disk on a system is always drive C, whether or not there are one or two floppy drives. Additional local drives, if any, such as a zip (removable storage) drive, a network drive, a CD and/or a DVD, are labeled from D on.

Step 4:   Move and Size a Window

■ Move and size the My Computer window on your desktop to match the display in Figure 7d.
  ❏ To change the width or height of the window, click and drag a border (the mouse pointer changes to a double arrow) in the direction you want to go; drag the border inward to shrink the window or outward to enlarge it.
  ❏ To change the width and height at the same time, click and drag a corner rather than a border.
  ❏ To change the position of the window, click and drag the title bar.

■ Click the **Minimize button** to shrink the My Computer window to a button on the taskbar. My Computer is still active in memory although its window is no longer visible. Click the **My Computer button** on the taskbar to reopen the window.

■ Click the **Maximize button** so that the My Computer window expands to fill the entire screen. Click the **Restore button** (which replaces the Maximize button and is not shown in Figure 7d) to return the window to its previous size.

■ Practice these operations until you can move and size a window with confidence.

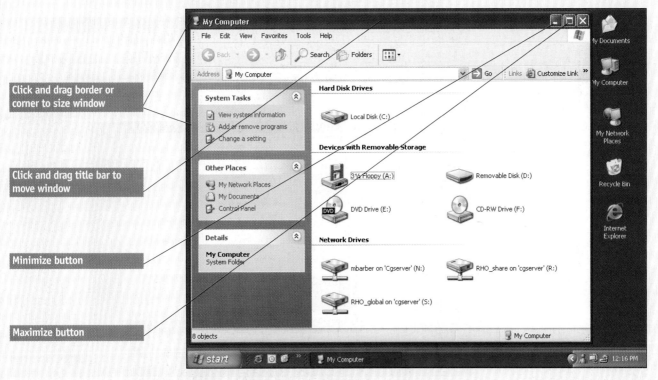

(d) Move and Size a Window (step 4)

FIGURE 7   Hands-on Exercise 1 (*continued*)

MINIMIZING VERSUS CLOSING AN APPLICATION

Minimizing a folder or an application leaves the object open in memory and available at the click of the appropriate button on the taskbar. Closing it, however, removes the object from memory, which also causes it to disappear from the taskbar. The advantage of minimizing an application or folder is that you can return to it immediately with the click of the mouse. The disadvantage is that too many open applications will eventually degrade the performance of a system.

Step 5:   Capture a Screen

- Prove to your instructor that you have sized the window correctly by capturing the desktop that currently appears on your monitor. Press the **Print Screen key** to copy the current screen display to the **clipboard**, an area of memory that is available to every application.

- Nothing appears to have happened, but the screen has in fact been copied to the clipboard and can be pasted into a Word document. Click the **Start button**, click the **All Programs command**, then start **Microsoft Word** and begin a new document.

- Enter the title of your document (I Did My Homework) followed by your name as shown in Figure 7e. Press the **Enter key** two or three times to leave blank lines after your name.

- Pull down the **Edit menu** and click the **Paste command** (or click the **Paste button** on the Standard toolbar) to copy the contents of the clipboard into the Word document.

- Print this document for your instructor. There is no need to save this document. Exit Word.

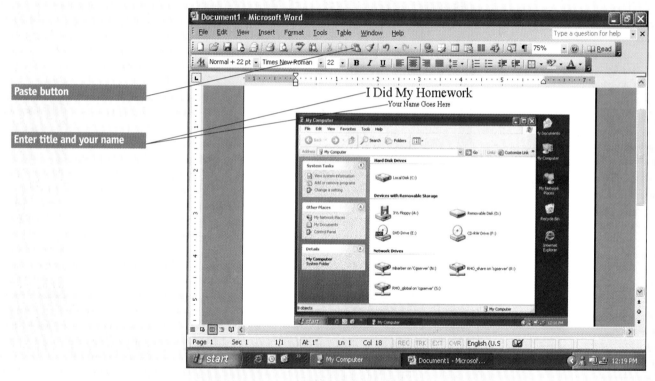

(e) Capture a Screen (step 5)

FIGURE 7   Hands-on Exercise 1 (*continued*)

THE FORMAT PICTURE COMMAND

Use the Format Picture command to facilitate moving and/or sizing an object within a Word document. Right click the picture to display a context-sensitive menu, then click the Format Picture command to display the associated dialog box. Click the Layout tab, choose any layout other than Inline with text, and click OK. You can now click and drag the picture to position it elsewhere within the document.

Step 6: Format a Floppy Disk

- Place a floppy disk into drive A. Select (click) **drive A** in the My Computer window, then pull down the **File menu** and click the **Format command** to display the Format dialog box in Figure 7f.
  - ❏ Set the **Capacity** to match the floppy disk you purchased (1.44MB for a high-density disk and 720KB for a double-density disk. The easiest way to determine the type of disk is to look for the label HD or DD, respectively.).
  - ❏ Click the **Volume label text box** if it's empty, or click and drag over the existing label if there is an entry. Enter a new label (containing up to 11 characters), such as **Bob's Disk**.
  - ❏ You can check the **Quick Format box** if the disk has been previously formatted, as a convenient way to erase the contents of the disk.
- Click the **Start button,** then click **OK**—after you have read the warning message—to begin the formatting operation. The formatting process erases anything that is on the disk, so be sure that you do not need anything on the disk.
- Click **OK** after the formatting is complete. Close the dialog box, then save the formatted disk for the next exercise. Close the My Computer window.

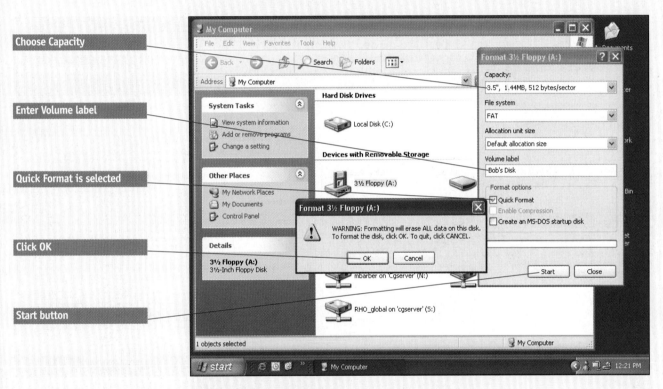

(f) Format a Floppy Disk (step 6)

FIGURE 7 Hands-on Exercise 1 (*continued*)

THE DEMISE OF THE FLOPPY DISK

You may be surprised to discover that your system no longer has a floppy disk drive, but it is only the latest victim in the march of technology. Long-playing records have come and gone. So too have 8-track tapes and the laser disk. The 3½-inch floppy disk has had a long and successful run, but it, too, is slated for obsolescence with Dell's recent announcement that it will no longer include a floppy drive as a standard component in desktop systems. Still, the floppy disk will "live forever" in the Save button that has the floppy disk as its icon.

Step 7: **The Help and Support Center**

- Click the **Start button**, then click the **Help and Support command** to open the Help and Support Center. Click the **Index button** to open the index pane. The insertion point moves automatically to the text box where you enter the search topic.

- Type **help**, which automatically moves you to the available topics within the index. Double click **central location for Help** to display the information in the right pane as shown in Figure 7g.

- Toggle the display of the subtopics on and off by clicking the plus and minus sign, respectively. Click the **plus sign** next to Remote Assistance, for example, and the topic opens. Click the **minus sign** next to Tours and articles, and the topic closes.

- Right click anywhere within the right pane to display the context-sensitive menu shown in Figure 7g. Click the **Print command** to print this information for your instructor.

- Close the Help and Support window.

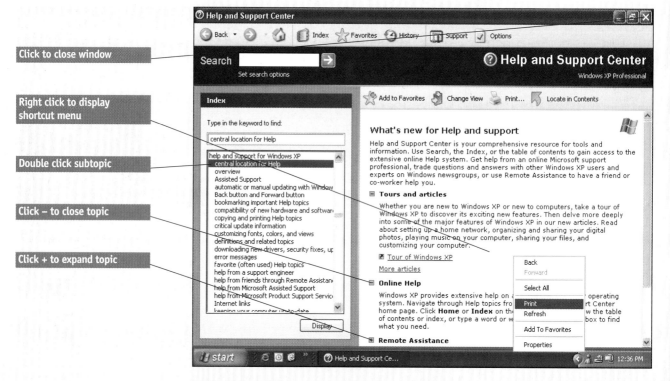

(g) The Help and Support Center (step 7)

FIGURE 7 Hands-on Exercise 1 (*continued*)

THE FAVORITES BUTTON

Do you find yourself continually searching for the same information? If so, you can make life a little easier by adding the page to a list of favorite help topics. Start the Help and Support Center, use the Index button to display the desired information in the right pane, and then click the Add to Favorites button to add the topic to your list of favorites. You can return to the topic at any time by clicking the Favorites button at the top of the Help and Support window, then double clicking the bookmark.

Step 8: Log (or Turn) Off the Computer

- It is very important that you log off properly, as opposed to just turning off the power. This enables Windows to close all of its system files and to save any changes that were made during the session.

- Click the **Start button** to display the Start menu in Figure 7h, then click the **Log Off button** at the bottom of the menu. You will see a dialog box asking whether you want to log off or switch users.
  - ❏ Switching users leaves your session active. All of your applications remain open, but control of the computer is given to another user. You can subsequently log back on (after the new user logs off) and take up exactly where you left off.
  - ❏ Logging off ends your session, but leaves the computer running at full power. This is the typical option you would select in a laboratory setting at school.

- To turn the computer off, you have to log off as just described, then select the **Turn Computer Off command** from the login screen. Welcome to Windows XP!

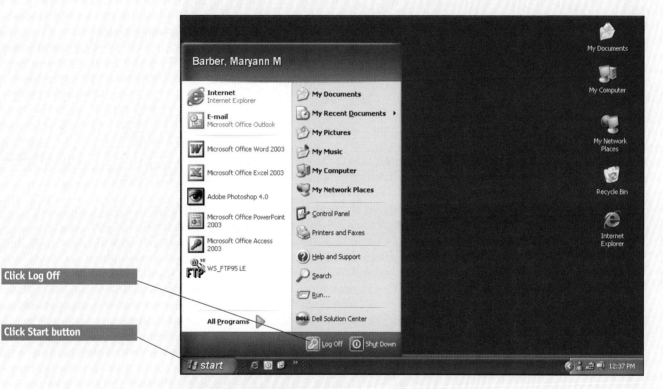

Click Log Off

Click Start button

(h) Log (or Turn) Off Computer (step 8)

FIGURE 7 Hands-on Exercise 1 (*continued*)

THE TASK MANAGER

The Start button is the normal way to exit Windows. Occasionally, however, an application may "hang"—in which case you want to close the problem application but continue with your session. Press Ctrl+Alt+Del to display the Windows Task Manager dialog box, then click the Applications tab. Select the problem application (it will most likely say "not responding"), and click the End Task button. This capability is often disabled in a school setting.

A *file* is a set of instructions or data that has been given a name and stored on disk. There are two basic types of files, ***program files*** and ***data files***. Microsoft Word and Microsoft Excel are examples of program files. The documents and workbooks that are created by these programs are data files. A program file is executable because it contains instructions that tell the computer what to do. A data file is not executable and can be used only in conjunction with a specific program. In other words, you execute program files to create and/or edit the associated data files.

Every file has a ***filename*** that identifies it to the operating system. The filename can contain up to 255 characters and may include spaces and other punctuation. (Filenames cannot contain the following characters: \, /, :, *, ?, ", <, >, and |.) We find it easier, however, to restrict the characters in a filename to letters, numbers, and spaces, as opposed to having to remember the special characters that are not permitted.

Files are kept in ***folders*** to better organize the thousands of files on a typical system. A Windows folder is similar to an ordinary manila folder that holds one or more documents. To continue the analogy, an office worker stores his or her documents in manila folders within a filing cabinet. Windows stores its files in electronic folders that are located on a disk, CD-ROM, or other device.

Many folders are created automatically by Windows XP, such as the My Computer or My Documents folders that are present on every system. Other folders are created whenever new software is installed. Additional folders are created by the user to hold the documents he or she creates. You might, for example, create a folder for your word processing documents and a second folder for your spreadsheets. You could also create a folder to hold all of your work for a specific class, which in turn might contain a combination of word processing documents and spreadsheets. The choice is entirely up to you, and you can use any system that makes sense to you. A folder can contain program files, data files, or even other folders.

Figure 8 displays the contents of a hypothetical folder with nine documents. Figure 8a displays the folder in ***Tiles view***. Figure 8b displays the same folder in ***Details view***, which also shows the date the file was created or last modified. Both views display a file icon next to each file to indicate the ***file type*** or application that was used to create the file. *Introduction to E-mail*, for example, is a PowerPoint presentation. *Basic Financial Functions* is an Excel workbook.

The two figures have more similarities than differences, such as the name of the folder (*Homework*), which appears in the title bar next to the icon of an open folder. The Minimize, Restore, and Close buttons are found at the right of the title bar. A menu bar with six pull-down menus appears below the title bar. The Standard Buttons toolbar is below the menu, and the Address bar (indicating the drive and folder) appears below the toolbar. Both folders also contain a task pane that provides easy access to common tasks for the folder or selected object.

Look closely and you will see that the task panes are significantly different. This is because there are no documents selected in Figure 8a, whereas the *Milestones in Communications* document is selected (highlighted) in Figure 8b. Thus, the File and Folder Tasks area in Figure 8a pertains to folders in general, whereas the available tasks in Figure 8b are pertinent to the selected document. The Details areas in the two task panes are also consistent with the selected objects and display information about the Homework folder and selected document, respectively. A status bar appears at the bottom of both windows and displays the contents of the selected object.

The last difference between the task panes reflects the user's preference to open or close the Other Places area. Click the upward chevron in Figure 8a to suppress the display and gain space in the task pane, or click the downward chevron in Figure 8b to display the specific links to other places. The task pane is new to Windows XP and did not appear in previous versions of Windows.

Folder name

Task pane

Click ≈ chevron to
suppress display

Status bar

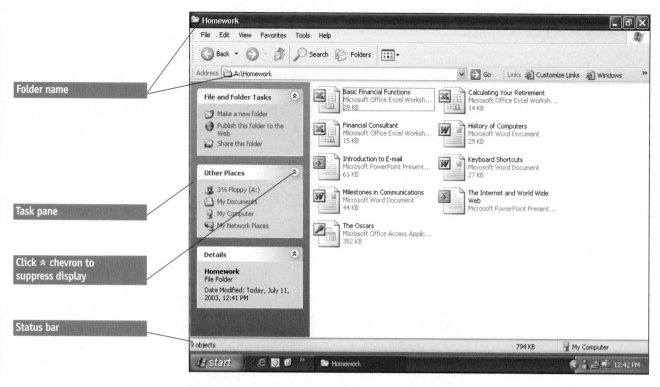

(a) Tiles View

Folder name

Selected file

Task pane

Click ≈ chevron to
display information

Status bar

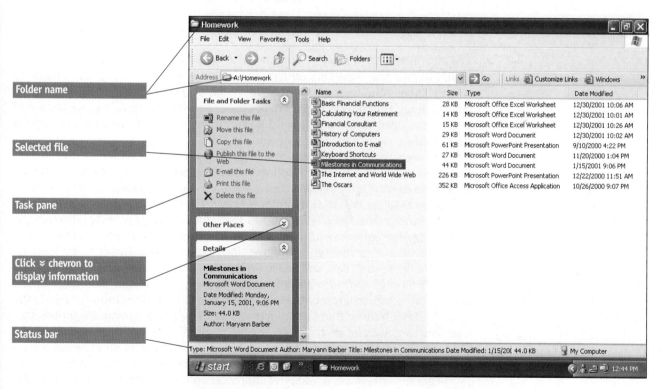

(b) Details View

FIGURE 8   Files and Folders

THE EXPLORING OFFICE PRACTICE FILES

There is only one way to master disk and file management and that is to practice at the computer. To do so requires that you have a series of files with which to work. We have created these files for you, and we use the files in the next two hands-on exercises. Your instructor will make the practice files available to you in different ways:

- The files can be downloaded from our Web site at www.prenhall.com/grauer. Software and other files that are downloaded from the Internet are typically compressed (made smaller) to reduce the amount of time it takes to transmit the file. In essence, you will download a single *compressed file* and then uncompress the file into multiple files onto a local drive as described in the next hands-on exercise.

- The files may be on a network drive at your school or university, in which case you can copy the files from the network drive to a floppy disk.

- There may be an actual "data disk" in the computer lab. Go to the lab with a floppy disk, then use the Copy Disk command (on the File menu of My Computer when drive A is selected) to duplicate the data disk and create a copy for yourself.

It doesn't matter how you obtain the practice files, only that you are able to do so. Indeed, you may want to try different techniques to gain additional practice with Windows XP. Note, too, that Windows XP provides a *firewall* to protect your computer from unauthorized access while it is connected to the Internet. (See exercise 2 at the end of the chapter.)

CONNECTING TO THE INTERNET

The easiest way to obtain the practice files is to download the files from the Web, which requires an Internet connection. There are two basic ways to connect to the Internet—from a local area network (LAN) or by dialing in. It's much easier if you connect from a LAN (typically at school or work) since the installation and setup have been done for you, and all you have to do is follow the instructions provided by your professor. If you connect from home, you will need a modem, a cable modem, or a DSL modem, and an Internet Service Provider (or ISP).

A *modem* is the hardware interface between your computer and the telephone system. In essence, you instruct the modem, via the appropriate software, to connect to your ISP, which in turn lets you access the Internet. A cable modem provides high-speed access (20 to 30 times that of an ordinary modem) through the same type of cable as used for cable TV. A DSL modem also provides high-speed access through a special type of phone line that lets you connect to the Internet while simultaneously carrying on a conversation.

An *Internet Service Provider* is a company or organization that maintains a computer with permanent access to the Internet. America Online (AOL) is the largest ISP with more than 30 million subscribers, and it provides a proprietary interface as well as Internet access. The Microsoft Network (MSN) is a direct competitor to AOL. Alternatively, you can choose from a host of other vendors who provide Internet access without the proprietary interface of AOL or MSN.

Regardless of which vendor you choose as an ISP, be sure you understand the fee structure. The monthly fee may entitle you to a set number of hours per month (after which you pay an additional fee), or it may give you unlimited access. The terms vary widely, and you should shop around for the best possible deal. Price is not the only consideration, however. Reliability of service is also important. Be sure that the equipment of your provider is adequate so that you can obtain access whenever you want.

2 Download the Practice Files

Objective To download a file from the Web and practice basic file commands. The exercise requires a formatted floppy disk and access to the Internet. Use Figure 9 as a guide.

Step 1: Start Internet Explorer

- Click the **Start button**, click the **All Programs command**, and then click **Internet Explorer** to start the program. If necessary, click the **Maximize button** so that Internet Explorer takes the entire desktop.

- Click anywhere within the **Address bar**, which automatically selects the current address (so that whatever you type replaces the current address). Enter **www.prenhall.com/grauer** (the http:// is assumed). Press **Enter**.

- You should see the Exploring Office Series home page as shown in Figure 9a. Click the book for **Office 2003**, which takes you to the Office 2003 home page.

- Click the **Student Downloads tab** (at the top of the window) to go to the Student Download page.

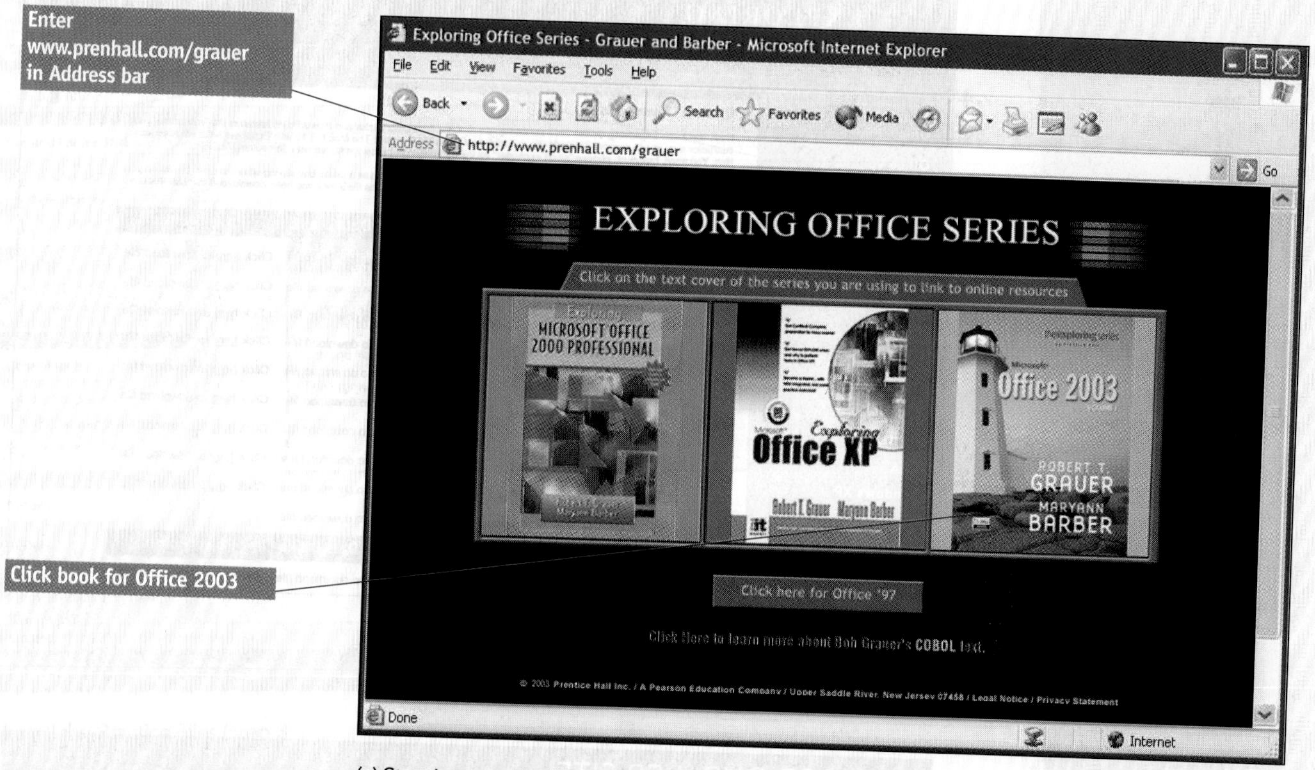

Step 3: Ins...

- C...

- C...
  M...

- C...
  ...

Click to select D

Click Up button

Drive A has bee

Click and drag A
Windows Explore
Information fold
pane

Enter
www.prenhall.com/grauer
in Address bar

Click to select Details view

Double click XPData file

Click book for Office 2003

Click OK

(a) Start Internet Explorer (step 1)

FIGURE 9 Hands-on Exercise 2

A NEW INTERNET EXPLORER

The installation of Windows XP automatically installs a new version of Internet Explorer. Pull down the Help menu and click the About Internet Explorer command to display the current release (version 6.0). Click OK to close the About Internet Explorer window.

Step 9: Complete the Exercise

- Prove to your instructor that you have completed the exercise correctly by capturing the screen on your monitor. Press the **Print Screen key**. Nothing appears to have happened, but the screen has been copied to the clipboard.

- Click the **Start button**, click the **All Programs command**, then start Microsoft Word and begin a new document. Enter the title of your document, followed by your name as shown in Figure 11i. Press the **Enter key** two or three times.

- Pull down the **Edit menu** and click the **Paste command** (or click the **Paste button** on the Standard toolbar) to copy the contents of the clipboard into the Word document.

- Print this document for your instructor. There is no need to save this document. Exit Word.

- Delete the **Windows Information folder** from the My Documents folder as a courtesy to the next student. Close Windows Explorer.

- Log off if you do not want to continue the next exercise at this time. (Click the **Start button**, click **Log Off**, then click **Log Off** a second time to end your session.)

Student Downloads tab

Click here for online study guide

Click here to download practice files

Click

Point right short

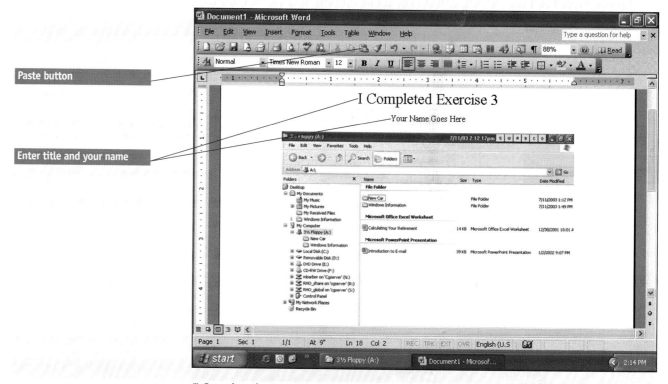

Paste button

Enter title and your name

(i) Complete the Exercise (step 9)

FIGURE 11   Hands-on Exercise 3 (*continued*)

SWITCHING USERS VERSUS LOGGING OFF

Windows XP gives you the choice of switching users or logging off. Switching users leaves all of your applications open, but it relinquishes control of the computer to another user. This lets you subsequently log back on (after the new user logs off) and take up exactly where you were. Logging off, on the other hand, closes all of your applications and ends the session, but it leaves the computer running at full power and available for someone else to log on.

Step 2: **Move the Files**

- If necessary, change to the **Details view** and click the **plus sign** next to drive A to expand the drive as shown in Figure 11b. Note the following:
  - ❏ The left pane shows that drive A is selected. The right pane displays the contents of drive A (the selected object in the left pane). The folders are shown first and appear in alphabetical order. If not, press the **F5 (Refresh) key** to refresh the screen.
  - ❏ There is a minus sign next to the icon for drive A in the left pane, indicating that it has been expanded and that its folders are visible. Thus, the folder names also appear under drive A in the left pane.

- Click and drag the **About Windows Explorer** document in the right pane to the **Windows Information folder** in the left pane, to move the file into that folder.

- Click and drag the **Tips for Windows XP** and the **Welcome to Windows XP** documents to move these documents to the **Windows Information folder**.

- Click the **Windows Information folder** in the left pane to select the folder and display its contents in the right pane. You should see the three files that were just moved.

- Click the **Up button** to return to drive A.

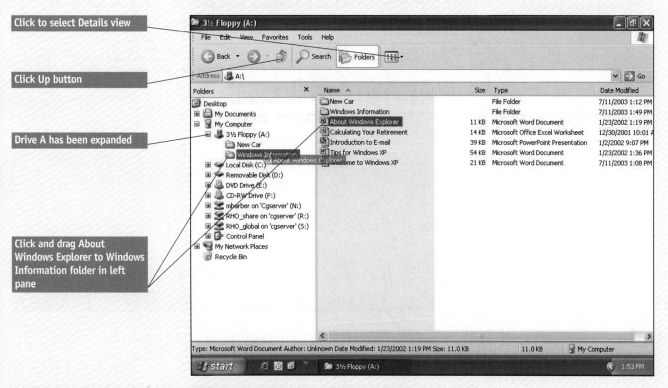

(b) Move the Files (step 2)

FIGURE 11   Hands-on Exercise 3 (*continued*)

SELECT MULTIPLE FILES

Selecting (clicking) one file automatically deselects the previously selected file. You can, however, select multiple files by clicking the first file, then pressing and holding the Ctrl key as you click each additional file. Use the Shift key to select multiple files that are adjacent to one another by clicking the icon of the first file, then pressing and holding the Shift key as you click the icon of the last file.

Step 3: Copy a Folder

- Point to the **Windows Information folder** in the right pane, then **right click and drag** this folder to the **My Documents folder** (on drive C) in the left pane. Release the mouse to display a context-sensitive menu.

- Click the **Copy Here command** as shown in Figure 11c.
  - ❑ You may see a Copy files message box as the individual files within the Windows Information folder are copied to the My Documents folder.
  - ❑ If you see the Confirm Folder Replace dialog box, it means that you (or another student) already copied these files to the My Documents folder. Click the **Yes to All button** so that your files replace the previous versions in the My Documents folder.

- Click the **My Documents folder** in the left pane. Pull down the **View menu** and click the **Refresh command** (or press the **F5 key**) so that the hierarchy shows the newly copied folder. (Please remember to delete the Windows Information folder from drive C at the end of the exercise.)

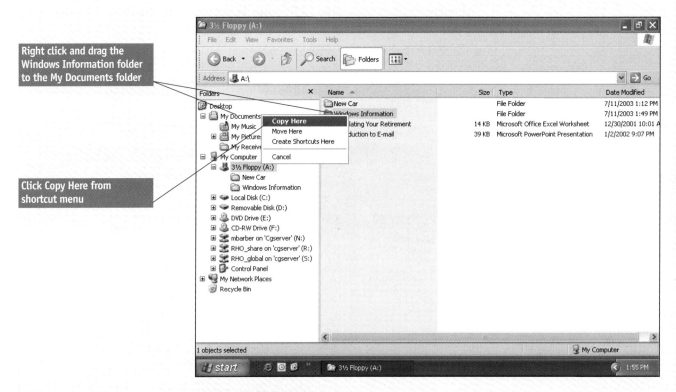

Right click and drag the Windows Information folder to the My Documents folder

Click Copy Here from shortcut menu

(c) Copy a Folder (step 3)

FIGURE 11   Hands-on Exercise 3 (*continued*)

RIGHT CLICK AND DRAG

The result of dragging a file with the left mouse button depends on whether the source and destination folders are on the same or different drives. Dragging a file to a folder on a different drive copies the file, whereas dragging the file to a folder on the same drive moves the file. If you find this hard to remember, and most people do, click and drag with the right mouse button to display a context-sensitive menu asking whether you want to copy or move the file. This simple tip can save you from making a careless (and potentially serious) error. Use it!

Step 4: **Modify a Document**

- Click the **Windows Information folder** within the My Documents folder to make it the active folder and to display its contents in the right pane. Change to the **Details view**.

- Double click the **About Windows Explorer** document to start Word and open the document. Do not be concerned if the size and/or position of the Microsoft Word window are different from ours. Read the document.

- If necessary, click inside the document window, then press **Ctrl+End** to move to the end of the document. Add the text shown in Figure 11d.

- Pull down the **File menu** and click **Save** to save the modified file (or click the **Save button** on the Standard toolbar). Pull down the **File menu** and click **Exit** to exit from Microsoft Word.

- Pull down the **View menu** and click the **Refresh command** (or press the **F5 key**) to update the contents of the right pane. The date and time associated with the About Windows Explorer document (on drive C) have been changed to indicate that the file has been modified.

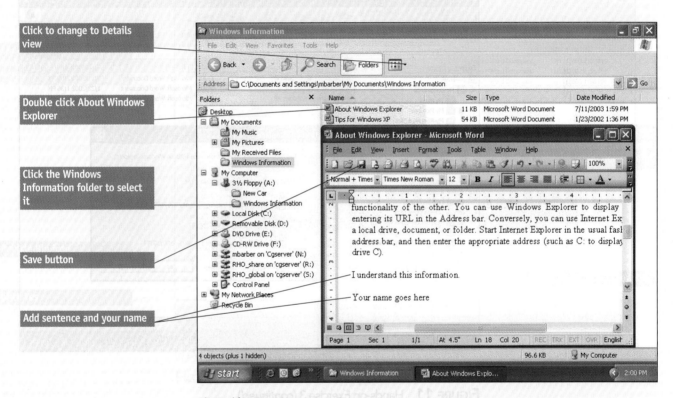

(d) Modify a Document (step 4)

FIGURE 11 Hands-on Exercise 3 (*continued*)

KEYBOARD SHORTCUTS

Most people begin with the mouse, but add keyboard shortcuts as they become more proficient. Ctrl+B, Ctrl+I, and Ctrl+U are shortcuts to boldface, italicize, and underline, respectively. Ctrl+X (the X is supposed to remind you of a pair of scissors), Ctrl+C, and Ctrl+V correspond to Cut, Copy, and Paste, respectively. Ctrl+Home and Ctrl+End move to the beginning or end of a document. These shortcuts are not unique to Microsoft Word, but are recognized in virtually every Windows application.

Step 9: Complete the Exercise

- Prove to your instructor that you have completed the exercise correctly by capturing the screen on your monitor. Press the **Print Screen key**. Nothing appears to have happened, but the screen has been copied to the clipboard.

- Click the **Start button**, click the **All Programs command**, then start Microsoft Word and begin a new document. Enter the title of your document, followed by your name as shown in Figure 11i. Press the **Enter key** two or three times.

- Pull down the **Edit menu** and click the **Paste command** (or click the **Paste button** on the Standard toolbar) to copy the contents of the clipboard into the Word document.

- Print this document for your instructor. There is no need to save this document. Exit Word.

- Delete the **Windows Information folder** from the My Documents folder as a courtesy to the next student. Close Windows Explorer.

- Log off if you do not want to continue the next exercise at this time. (Click the **Start button**, click **Log Off**, then click **Log Off** a second time to end your session.)

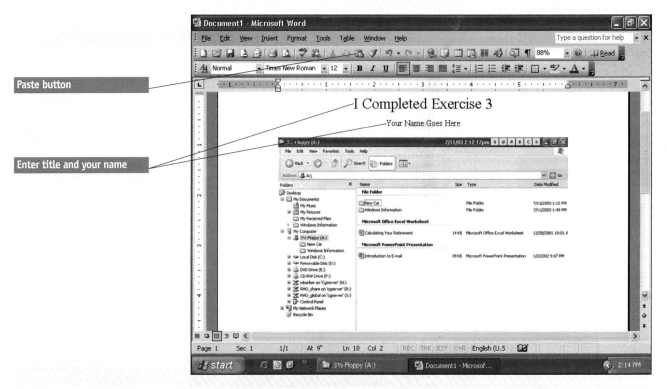

(i) Complete the Exercise (step 9)

FIGURE 11   Hands-on Exercise 3 (*continued*)

SWITCHING USERS VERSUS LOGGING OFF

Windows XP gives you the choice of switching users or logging off. Switching users leaves all of your applications open, but it relinquishes control of the computer to another user. This lets you subsequently log back on (after the new user logs off) and take up exactly where you were. Logging off, on the other hand, closes all of your applications and ends the session, but it leaves the computer running at full power and available for someone else to log on.

INCREASING PRODUCTIVITY

You have learned the basic concepts of disk and file management, but there is so much more. Windows XP has something for everyone. It is easy and intuitive for the novice, but it also contains sophisticated tools for the more knowledgeable user. This section describes three powerful features to increase your productivity. Some or all of these features may be disabled in a school environment, but the information will stand you in good stead on your own computer.

The Control Panel

The ***Control Panel*** affects every aspect of your system. It determines the appearance of your desktop, and it controls the performance of your hardware. You can, for example, change the way your mouse behaves by switching the function of the left and right mouse buttons and/or by replacing the standard mouse pointers with animated icons that move across the screen. You will not have access to the Control Panel in a lab environment, but you will need it at home whenever you install new hardware or software. You should be careful about making changes, and you should understand the nature of the new settings before you accept any of the changes.

The Control Panel in Windows XP organizes its tools by category as shown in Figure 12. Point to any category and you see a Screen Tip that describes the specific tasks within that category. The Appearance and Themes category, for example, lets you select a screen saver or customize the Start menu and taskbar. You can also switch to the Classic view that displays every tool in a single screen, which is consistent with all previous versions of Windows.

The task pane provides access to the ***Windows Update*** function, which connects you to a Web site where you can download new device drivers and other updates to Windows XP. You can also configure your system to install these updates automatically as they become available. Some updates, especially those having to do with Internet security, are absolutely critical.

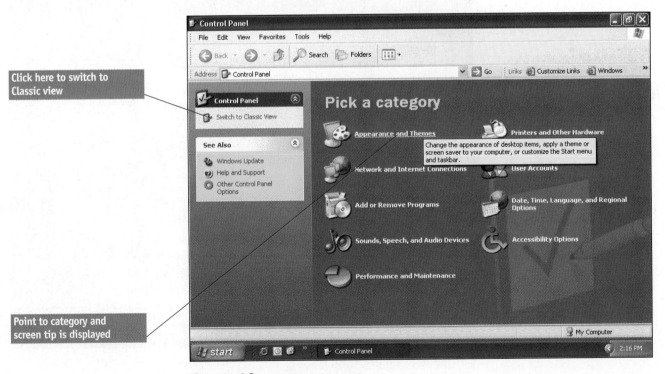

Click here to switch to Classic view

Point to category and screen tip is displayed

FIGURE 12   The Control Panel

Shortcuts

A **shortcut** is a link to any object on your computer, such as a program, file, folder, disk drive, or Web page. Shortcuts can appear anywhere, but are most often placed on the desktop or on the Start menu. The desktop in Figure 13 contains a variety of shortcuts, each of which contains a jump arrow to indicate a shortcut icon. Double click the shortcut to Election of Officers, for example, and you start Word and open this document. In similar fashion, you can double click the shortcut for a Web page (Exploring Windows Series), folder, or disk drive (drive A) to open the object and display its contents.

Creating a shortcut is a two-step process. First, you use Windows Explorer to locate the object such as a file, folder, or disk drive. Then you select the object, use the right mouse button to drag the object to the desktop, and then click the Create Shortcut command from the context-sensitive menu. A shortcut icon will appear on the desktop with the phrase "shortcut to" as part of the name. You can create as many shortcuts as you like, and you can place them anywhere on the desktop or in individual folders. You can also right click a shortcut icon after it has been created to change its name. Deleting the icon deletes the shortcut and not the object.

Windows XP also provides a set of predefined shortcuts through a series of desktop icons that are shown at the left border of the desktop in Figure 13. Double click the My Computer icon, for example, and you open the My Computer folder. These desktop icons were displayed by default in earlier versions of Windows, but not in Windows XP. They were added through the Control Panel as you will see in our next exercise.

Additional shortcuts are found in the **Quick Launch toolbar** that appears to the right of the Start button. Click any icon and you open the indicated program. And finally, Windows XP will automatically add to the Start menu shortcuts to your most frequently used programs. Desktop shortcuts are a powerful technique that will increase your productivity by taking you directly to a specified document or other object.

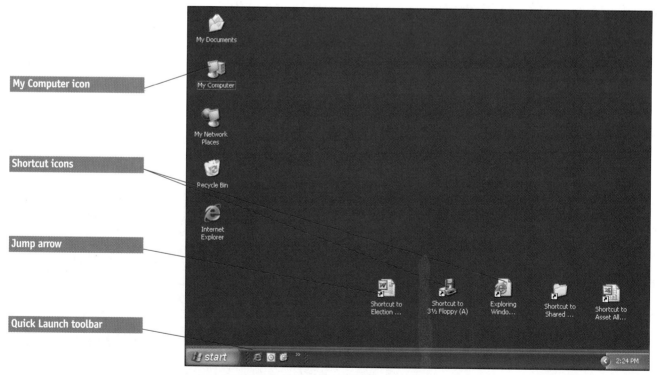

FIGURE 13 Desktop with Shortcuts

The Search Companion

Sooner or later you will create a file, and then forget where (in which folder) you saved it. Or you may create a document and forget its name, but remember a key word or phrase in the document. Or you may want to locate all files of a certain file type—for example, all of the sound files on your system. The **Search Companion** can help you to solve each of these problems and is illustrated in Figure 14.

The Search Companion is accessed from within any folder by clicking the Search button on the Standard Buttons toolbar to open the search pane at the left of the folder. You are presented with an initial search menu (not shown in Figure 14) that asks what you want to search for. You can search your local machine for media files (pictures, music, or video), documents (such as spreadsheets or Word documents), or any file or folder. You can also search the Help and Support Center or the Internet.

Once you choose the type of information, you are presented with a secondary search pane as shown in Figure 14. You can search according to a variety of criteria, each of which will help to narrow the search. In this example we are looking for any document on drive C that has "Windows" as part of its filename and further, contains the name "Maryann" somewhere within the document. The search is case sensitive. This example illustrates two important capabilities, namely that you can search on the document name (or part of its name) and/or its content.

Additional criteria can be entered by expanding the chevrons for date and size. You can, for example, restrict your search to all documents that were modified within the last week, the past month, or the last year. You can also restrict your search to documents of a certain size. Click the Search button after all of the criteria have been specified to initiate the search. The results of the search (the documents that satisfy the search criteria) are displayed in the right pane. You can refine the search if it is unsuccessful and/or you can open any document in which you are interested. The Search Companion also has an indexing service to make subsequent searches faster.

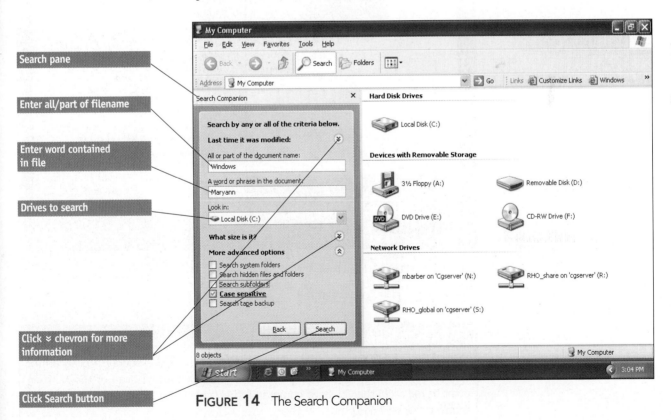

Search pane

Enter all/part of filename

Enter word contained in file

Drives to search

Click ≫ chevron for more information

Click Search button

FIGURE 14 The Search Companion

4 Increasing Productivity

Objective To create and use shortcuts; to locate documents using the Search Companion; to customize your system using the Control Panel; to obtain a passport account. The exercise requires an Internet connection. Use Figure 15 as a guide.

Step 1: **Display the Desktop Icons**

■ Log on to Windows XP. Point to a blank area on the desktop, click the **right mouse button** to display a context-sensitive menu, then click the **Properties command** to open the Display Properties dialog box in Figure 15a.

■ Click the **Desktop tab** and then click the **Customize Desktop button** to display the Desktop Items dialog box.

■ Check the boxes to display all four desktop icons. Click **OK** to accept these settings and close the dialog box, then click **OK** a second time to close the Display Properties dialog box.

■ The desktop icons should appear on the left side of your desktop. Double click any icon to execute the indicated program or open the associated folder.

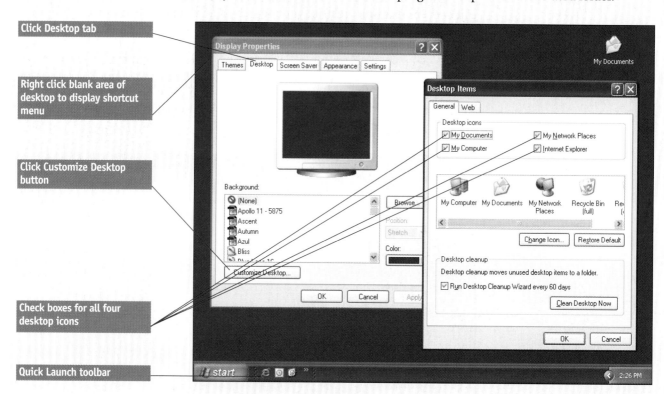

(a) Display the Desktop Icons (step 1)

FIGURE 15 Hands-on Exercise 4

THE QUICK LAUNCH TOOLBAR

The Quick Launch toolbar is a customizable toolbar that executes a program or displays the desktop with a single click. Right click a blank area of the taskbar, point to (or click) the Toolbars command, then check the Quick Launch toolbar to toggle its display on or off.

Step 2: **Create a Web Shortcut**

- Start Internet Explorer. You can double click the newly created icon at the left of the desktop, or you can single click its icon in the Quick Launch toolbar. Click the **Restore button** so that Internet Explorer is not maximized, that is, so that you can see a portion of the desktop.

- Click in the Address bar and enter the address **www.microsoft.com/windowsxp** to display the home page of Windows XP. Now that you see the page, you can create a shortcut to that page.

- Click the **Internet Explorer icon** in the Address bar to select the entire address, point to the Internet Explorer icon, then click and drag the icon to the desktop (you will see a jump arrow as you drag the text). Release the mouse to create the shortcut in Figure 15b.

- Prove to yourself that the shortcut works. Close Internet Explorer, and then double click the shortcut you created. Internet Explorer will open, and you should see the desired Web page. Close (or minimize) Internet Explorer since you do not need it for the remainder of the exercise.

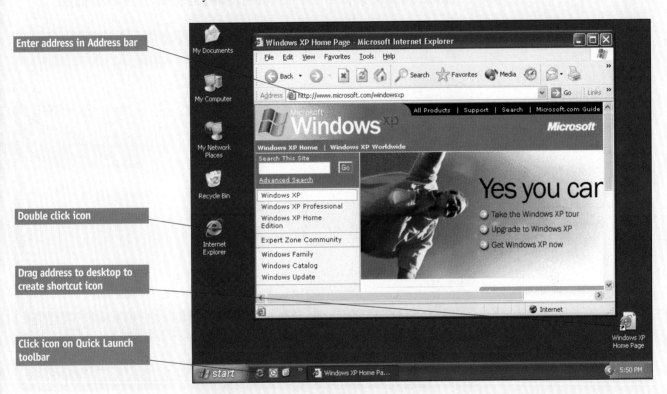

(b) Create a Web Shortcut (step 2)

FIGURE 15 Hands-on Exercise 4 (*continued*)

WORKING WITH SHORTCUTS

You can work with a shortcut icon just as you can with any other icon. To move a shortcut, drag its icon to a different location on the desktop. To rename a shortcut, right click its icon, click the Rename command, type the new name, then press the enter key. To delete a shortcut, right click its icon, click the Delete command, and click Yes in response to the confirming prompt. Deleting a shortcut deletes just the shortcut and not the object to which the shortcut refers.

Step 3: Create Additional Shortcuts

■ Double click the **My Computer icon** to open this folder. Place the floppy disk from hands-on exercise 3 into the floppy drive. Double click the icon for **drive A** to display the contents of the floppy disk as shown in Figure 15c.

■ The contents of the Address bar have changed to A:\ to indicate the contents of the floppy disk. You should see two folders and two files.

■ Move and size the window so that you see a portion of the desktop. Right click and drag the icon for the **Windows Information folder** to the desktop, then release the mouse. Click the **Create Shortcuts Here command** to create the shortcut.

■ Look for the jump arrow to be sure you have created a shortcut (as opposed to moving or copying the folder). If you made a mistake, right click a blank area of the desktop, then click the **Undo command** to reverse the unintended move or copy operation.

■ Right click and drag the icon for the **PowerPoint presentation** to the desktop, release the mouse, and then click the **Create Shortcuts Here command**.

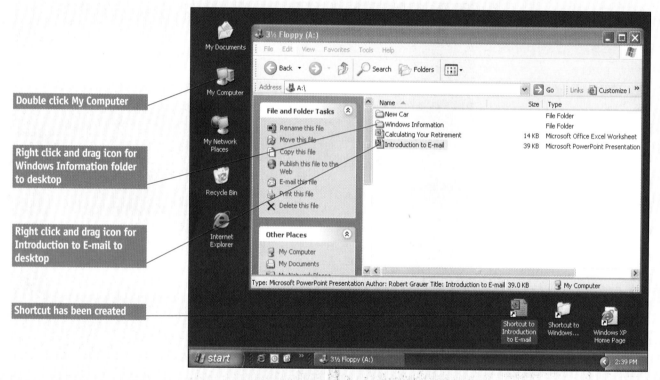

Double click My Computer

Right click and drag icon for Windows Information folder to desktop

Right click and drag icon for Introduction to E-mail to desktop

Shortcut has been created

(c) Create Additional Shortcuts (step 3)

FIGURE 15 Hands-on Exercise 4 (*continued*)

THE ARRANGE ICONS COMMAND

The most basic way to arrange the icons on your desktop is to click and drag an icon from one place to another. It may be convenient, however, to have Windows arrange the icons for you. Right click a blank area of the desktop, click (or point to) the Arrange Icons by command, then click Auto Arrange. All existing shortcuts, as well as any new shortcuts, will be automatically aligned along the left edge of the desktop. Execute the Auto Arrange command a second time to cancel the command, and enable yourself to manually arrange the icons.

Step 4: Search for a Document

- Maximize the My Computer window. Click the **Search button** on the Standard Buttons toolbar to display the Search pane. The button functions as a toggle switch. Click the button and the Search pane appears. Click the button a second time and the task pane replaces the Search Companion.

- The initial screen (not shown in Figure 15d) in the Search Companion asks what you are searching for. Click **Documents (word processing, spreadsheet, etc.)**.

- You may be prompted to enter when the document was last modified. Click the option button that says **Don't Remember**, then click **Use advanced search options**. You should see the screen in Figure 15d.

- Enter the indicated search criteria. You do not know the document name and thus you leave this text box blank. The other criteria indicate that you are looking for any document that contains "interest rate" that is located on drive A, or in any subfolder on drive A.

- Click the **Search button** to initiate the search. You will see a Search dialog box to indicate the progress of the search, after which you will see the relevant documents.

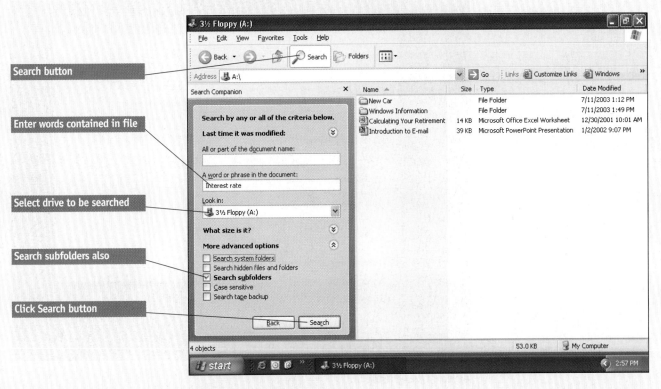

(d) Search for a Document (step 4)

FIGURE 15 Hands-on Exercise 4 (*continued*)

YOU DON'T NEED THE COMPLETE FILENAME

You can enter only a portion of the filename, and the Search Companion will still find the file(s). If, for example, you're searching for the file "Marketing Homework," you can enter the first several letters such as "Marketing" and Windows will return all files whose name begins with the letters you've entered—for example, "Marketing Homework" and "Marketing Term Paper."

Step 5: Search Results

- The search should return two files that satisfy the search criteria as shown in Figure 15e. Click the **Views button** and select **Tiles view** if you want to match our figure. If you do not see the same files, it is for one of two reasons:
  - ❏ You did not specify the correct search criteria. Click the **Back button** and reenter the search parameters as described in step 4. Repeat the search.
  - ❏ Your floppy disk is different from ours. Be sure to use the floppy disk as it existed at the end of the previous hands-on exercise.

- Click the **Restore button** so that you again see a portion of the desktop. Right click and drag the **Calculating Your Retirement** workbook to the desktop to create a shortcut on the desktop.

- Close the Search Results window, close the My Documents window, then double click the newly created shortcut to open the workbook.

- Retirement is a long way off, but you may want to experiment with our worksheet. It is never too early to start saving.

- Exit Excel when you are finished.

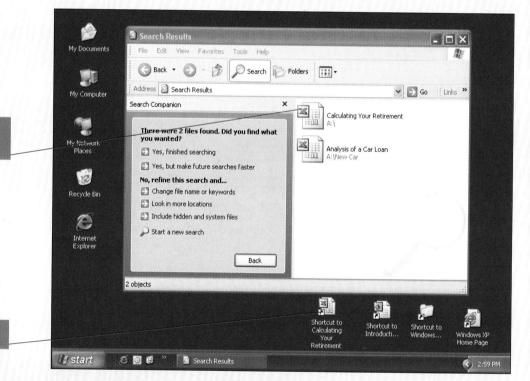

(e) Search Results (step 5)

FIGURE 15   Hands-on Exercise 4 (*continued*)

SHORTCUT WIZARD

Shortcuts can be created in many ways, including the use of a wizard. Right click a blank area of the desktop, click (or point) to the New command, then choose Shortcut to start the wizard. Enter the Web address in the indicated text box (or click the Browse button to locate a local file). Click Next, then enter the name for the shortcut as it is to appear on the desktop. Click the Finish button to exit the wizard. The new shortcut should appear on the desktop.

Step 6: **Open the Control Panel Folder**

- Click the **Start button**, then click **Control Panel** to open the Control Panel folder. Click the command to **Switch to Classic View** that appears in the task pane to display the individual icons as shown in Figure 15f. Maximize the window.

- Double click the **Taskbar and Start Menu icon** to display the associated dialog box. Click the **Taskbar tab**, then check the box to **Auto-hide the taskbar.** Your other settings should match those in Figure 15f. Click **OK** to accept the settings and close the dialog box.

- The taskbar (temporarily) disappears from your desktop. Now point to the bottom edge of the desktop, and the taskbar reappears. The advantage of hiding the taskbar in this way is that you have the maximum amount of room in which to work; that is, you see the taskbar only when you want to.

- Double click the **Fonts folder** to open this folder and display the fonts that are installed on your computer. Change to the **Details view**.

- Double click the icon of any font other than the standard fonts (Arial, Times New Roman, and Courier New) to open a new window that displays the font. Click the **Print button**. Close the Font window.

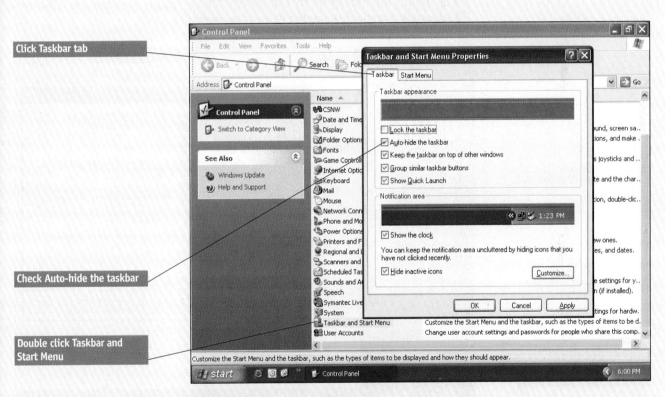

(f) Open the Control Panel Folder (step 6)

FIGURE 15 Hands-on Exercise 4 (*continued*)

MODIFY THE START MENU

Click and drag a shortcut icon to the Start button to place the shortcut on the Start menu. It does not appear that anything has happened, but the shortcut will appear at the top of the Start menu. Click the Start button to display the Start menu, then press the Esc key to exit the menu without executing a command. You can delete any item from the menu by right clicking the item and clicking the Unpin from the Start menu command.

Step 7: **Obtain a .NET Passport**

■ Click the **Back button** to return to the Control Panel, then double click the **User Accounts icon** in the Control Panel folder. Maximize the User Accounts window so that it takes the entire desktop.

■ Click the icon corresponding to the account that is currently logged to display a screen similar to Figure 15g. Click the command to **Set up my account to use a .NET passport**. You will see the first step in the Passport Wizard.

■ Click the link to **View the privacy statement**. This starts Internet Explorer and goes to the .NET Passport site on the Web. Print the privacy agreement. It runs nine pages, but it contains a lot of useful information.

■ Close Internet Explorer after you have printed the agreement. You are back in the Passport Wizard. Click **Next** to continue.

■ Follow the instructions on the next several screens. You will be asked to enter your e-mail address and to supply a password. Click **Finish** when you have reached the last screen.

■ You will receive an e-mail message after you have registered successfully. You will need your passport in our next exercise when we explore Windows Messenger and the associated instant messaging service.

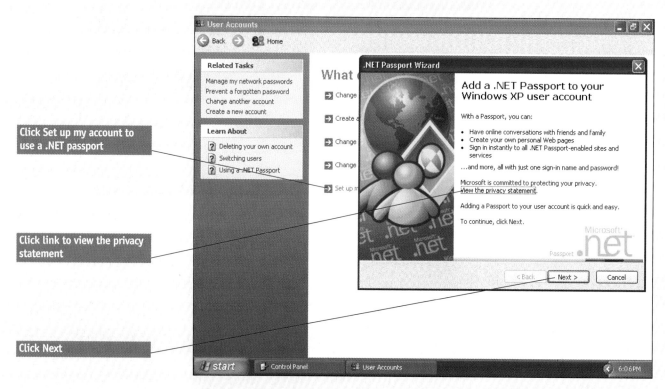

(g) Obtain a .NET Passport (step 7)

FIGURE 15 Hands-on Exercise 4 (*continued*)

UPDATING YOUR PASSPORT

You can modify the information in your passport profile at any time. Open the Control Panel, click User Accounts, select your account, then click the command to Change Your .NET passport. You can change your password, change the question that will remind you about your password should you forget it, and/or change the information that you authorize the passport service to share with others.

Step 8: Windows Update

- Close the User Accounts window to return to the Control Panel folder. Click the link to **Windows Update** to display a screen similar to Figure 15h.

- Click the command to **Scan for updates**. (This command is not visible in our figure.) This command will take several seconds as Windows determines which (if any) updates it recommends. Our system indicates that there are no critical updates but that additional updates are available.

- Click the link(s) to review the available updates. You do not have to install the vast majority of available updates. It is essential, however, that you install any updates deemed critical. One critical update appeared shortly after the release of Windows XP and closed a hole in the operating system that enabled hackers to break into some XP machines.

- Click the link to **View installation history** to see which updates were previously installed. Print this page for your instructor.

- Close the Update window. Log off the computer if you do not want to continue with the next exercise at this time.

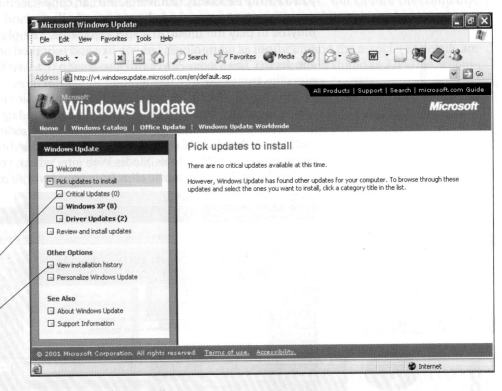

Click link to view critical updates

Click View installation history

(h) Windows Update (step 8)

FIGURE 15 Hands-on Exercise 4 (*continued*)

THE SHOW DESKTOP BUTTON

The Show Desktop button or command minimizes every open window and returns you immediately to the desktop. You can get to this command in different ways, most easily by clicking the Show Desktop icon on the Quick Launch toolbar. The button functions as a toggle switch. Click it once and all windows are minimized. Click it a second time and the open windows are restored to their position on the desktop.

SUMMARY

Windows XP is the newest and most powerful version of the Windows operating system. It has a slightly different look than earlier versions, but it maintains the conventions of its predecessors. All Windows operations take place on the desktop. Every window contains the same basic elements, which include a title bar, a Minimize button, a Maximize or Restore button, and a Close button. All windows may be moved and sized. The taskbar contains a button for each open program and enables you to switch back and forth between those programs by clicking the appropriate button. You can obtain information about every aspect of Windows through the Help and Support Center.

A file is a set of data or set of instructions that has been given a name and stored on disk. There are two basic types of files, program files and data files. A program file is an executable file, whereas a data file can be used only in conjunction with a specific program. Every file has a filename and a file type.

Files are stored in folders to better organize the hundreds (or thousands) of files on a disk. A folder may contain program files, data files, and/or other folders. Windows automatically creates a set of personal folders for every user. These include the My Documents folder and the My Pictures folder and My Music folder within the My Documents folder. Windows also provides a Shared Documents folder that can be accessed by every user. The My Computer folder is accessible by all users and displays the devices on a system.

Windows Explorer facilitates every aspect of disk and file management. It presents a hierarchical view of your system that displays all devices and, optionally, the folders on each device. Any device may be expanded or collapsed to display or hide its folders.

Windows XP contains several tools to help you enjoy your system. The Windows Media Player combines the functions of a radio, CD player, DVD player, and an information database into a single program. Windows Messenger is an instant messaging system in which you chat with friends and colleagues over the Internet.

The Control Panel affects every aspect of your system. It determines the appearance of your desktop and it controls the performance of your hardware. A shortcut is a link to any object on your computer, such as a program, file, folder, disk drive, or Web page. The Search Companion enables you to search for a file according to several different criteria.

KEY TERMS

Step 8: Windows Update

- Close the User Accounts window to return to the Control Panel folder. Click the link to **Windows Update** to display a screen similar to Figure 15h.

- Click the command to **Scan for updates**. (This command is not visible in our figure.) This command will take several seconds as Windows determines which (if any) updates it recommends. Our system indicates that there are no critical updates but that additional updates are available.

- Click the link(s) to review the available updates. You do not have to install the vast majority of available updates. It is essential, however, that you install any updates deemed critical. One critical update appeared shortly after the release of Windows XP and closed a hole in the operating system that enabled hackers to break into some XP machines.

- Click the link to **View installation history** to see which updates were previously installed. Print this page for your instructor.

- Close the Update window. Log off the computer if you do not want to continue with the next exercise at this time.

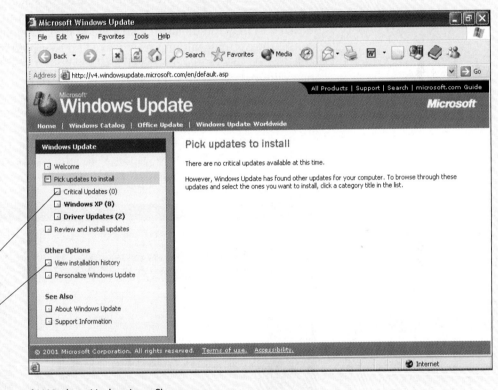

(h) Windows Update (step 8)

FIGURE 15   Hands-on Exercise 4 (*continued*)

THE SHOW DESKTOP BUTTON

The Show Desktop button or command minimizes every open window and returns you immediately to the desktop. You can get to this command in different ways, most easily by clicking the Show Desktop icon on the Quick Launch toolbar. The button functions as a toggle switch. Click it once and all windows are minimized. Click it a second time and the open windows are restored to their position on the desktop.

The "XP" in Windows XP is for the experience that Microsoft promises individuals who adopt its operating system. Windows XP makes it easy to enjoy music and video, work with **digital photographs**, and chat with your friends. This section describes these capabilities and then moves to a hands-on exercise in which you practice at the computer. All of the features are available on your own machine, but some may be disabled in a laboratory setting. It's not that your professor does not want you to have fun, but listening to music or engaging in instant messaging with your friends is not practical in a school environment. Nevertheless, the hands-on exercise that follows enables you to practice your skills in disk and file management as you work with multiple files and folders.

Windows Media Player

The **Windows Media Player** combines the functions of a radio, a CD, or DVD player, and an information database into a single program. It lets you listen to radio stations anywhere in the world, play a CD, or watch a DVD movie (provided you have the necessary hardware). You can copy selections from a CD to your computer, organize your music by artist and album, and then create a customized **playlist** to play the music in a specified order. The playlist may include as many songs from as many albums as you like and is limited only by the size of your storage device. The Media Player will also search the Web for audio or video files and play clips from a favorite movie.

The buttons at the left of the Media Player enable you to switch from one function to the next. The Radio Tuner button is active in Figure 16, and the BBC station is selected. Think of that—you are able to listen to radio stations from around the world with the click of a button. The Media Guide button connects you to the home page of the Windows Media Web site, where you can search the Web for media files and/or play movie clips from your favorite movies.

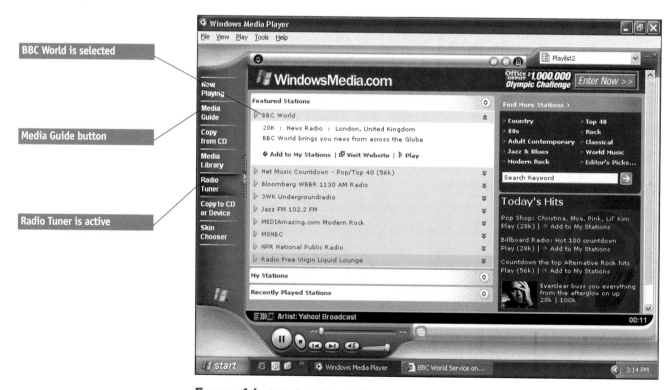

FIGURE 16 Windows Media Player

Digital Photography

Windows XP helps you to organize your pictures and share them with others. The best place to store photographs is in the My Pictures folder or in a subfolder within this folder as shown in Figure 17. The complete path to the folder appears in the Address bar and is best read from right to left. Thus, you are looking at pictures in the Romance Folder, which is in the My Pictures folder, which in turn is stored in a My Documents folder. Remember that each user has his or her unique My Documents folder, so the path must be further qualified. Hence, you are looking at the My Documents folder, within a folder for Jessica (one of several users), within the Documents and Settings folder on drive C. The latter folder maintains the settings for all of the users that are registered on this system.

The pictures in Figure 17 are shown in the **_Thumbnails view_**, which displays a miniature image of each picture in the right pane. (Other views are also available and are accessed from the View menu or Views button.) The Picture Tasks area in the upper right lists the functions that are unique to photographs. You can view the pictures as a slide show, which is the equivalent of a PowerPoint presentation without having to create the presentation. You can print any picture, use it as the background on your desktop, or copy multiple pictures to a CD, provided you have the necessary hardware. You can also order prints online. You choose the company; select print sizes and quantities, supply the billing and shipping information, and your photographs are sent to you.

One photo is selected (BenWendy) in Figure 17, and the associated details are shown in the Details area of the task pane. The picture is stored as a JPG file, a common format for photographs. It was created on January 21, 2002.

The File and Folder Tasks area is collapsed in our figure, but you can expand the area to gain access to the normal file operations (move, copy, and delete). You can also e-mail the photograph from this panel. Remember, too, that you can click the Folders button on the Standard Buttons toolbar to switch to the hierarchical view of your system, which is better suited to disk and file management.

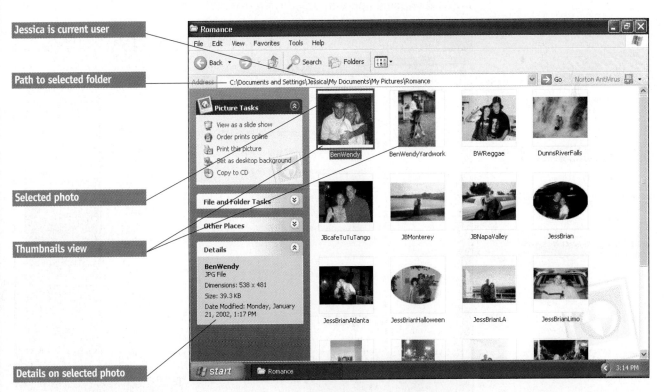

FIGURE 17 Working with Pictures

Windows Messenger

Windows Messenger is an instant messaging system in which you chat with friends and colleagues over the Internet. (It is based on the same technology as the "buddies list" that was made popular by America Online.) You need an Internet connection, a list of contacts, and a **Microsoft passport** that is based on your e-mail address. The passport is a free Microsoft service that enables you to access any passport-enabled Internet site with a single user name and associated password. (Step 7 in the previous hands-on exercise described how to obtain a passport.)

You can initiate a conversation at any time by monitoring the contacts list to see who is online and starting a chat session. Up to four people can participate in the same conversation. It is easy, fun, and addictive. You know the instant someone signs on, and you can begin chatting immediately. The bad news, however, is that it is all too easy to chat incessantly when you have real work to do. Hence you may want to change your status to indicate that you are busy and unable to participate in a conversation.

Figure 18 displays a conversation between Maryann and Bob. The session began when Maryann viewed her contact list, noticed that Bob was online, and started a conversation. Each person enters his or her message at the bottom of the conversation window, and then clicks the Send button. Additional messages can be sent without waiting for a response. Emoticons can be added to any message for effect. Note, too, the references to the file transfer that appear within the conversation, which are the result of Maryann clicking the command to send a file or photo, then attaching the desired file.

Windows Messenger is more than just a vehicle for chatting. If you have speakers and a microphone, you can place phone calls from your computer without paying a long distance charge. The most intriguing feature, however, is the ability to ask for remote assistance, whereby you can invite one of your contacts to view your desktop as you are working in order to ask for help. It is as if your friend were in the room looking over your shoulder. He or she will see everything that you do and can respond immediately with suggestions.

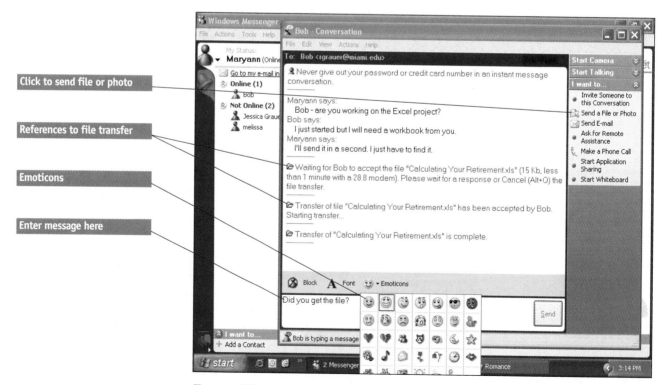

FIGURE 18 Windows Messenger

5   Fun with Windows XP

Objective   To use Windows Media Player, work with photographs, and experiment with Windows Messenger. Check with your professor regarding the availability of the resources required for this exercise. Use Figure 19.

Step 1:   Open the Shared Music Folder

- Start Windows Explorer. Click the **Folders button** to display the tree structure. You need to locate some music to demonstrate the Media Player.

- The typical XP installation includes some files within the Shared Documents folder. Expand the My Computer folder to show the **Shared Documents folder**, expand the **Shared Music folder**, and then open the **Sample Music folder** as shown in Figure 19a.

- Point to any file (it does not matter if you have a different selection of music) to display the ScreenTip describing the music. Double click the file to start the Media Player and play the selected music.

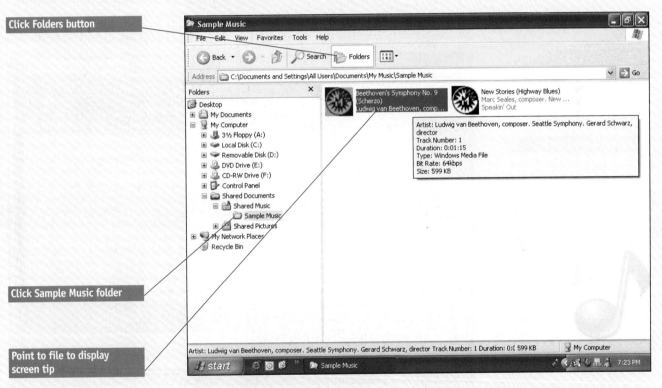

(a) Open the Shared Music Folder (step 1)

FIGURE 19   Hands-on Exercise 5

SHARED FOLDERS VERSUS PERSONAL FOLDERS

Windows XP automatically creates a unique My Documents folder for every user, which in turn contains a unique My Pictures folder and My Music folder within the My Documents folder. These folders are private and cannot be accessed by other users. Windows also provides a Shared Documents folder that is accessible to every user on a system.

Step 2: **Listen to the Music**

- You should hear the music when the Windows Media Player opens in its own window as shown in Figure 19b. The controls at the bottom of the window are similar to those on any CD player.
    - ❏ You can click the **Pause button**, then click the **Play button** to restart the music at that point.
    - ❏ You can click the **Stop button** to stop playing altogether.
    - ❏ You can also drag the slider to begin playing at a different place.

- You can also adjust the volume as shown in Figure 19b. Double click the **Volume Control icon** in the notification area at the right of the taskbar to display the Volume Control dialog box. Close this window.

- Click the **Radio Tuner button** at the side of the Media Player window. The system pauses as it tunes into the available radio stations.

- Select a radio station (e.g., **BBC World**) when you see the list of available stations, then click the **Play button** after you choose a station.

- You will see a message at the bottom of the window indicating that your computer is connecting to the media, after which you will hear the radio station.

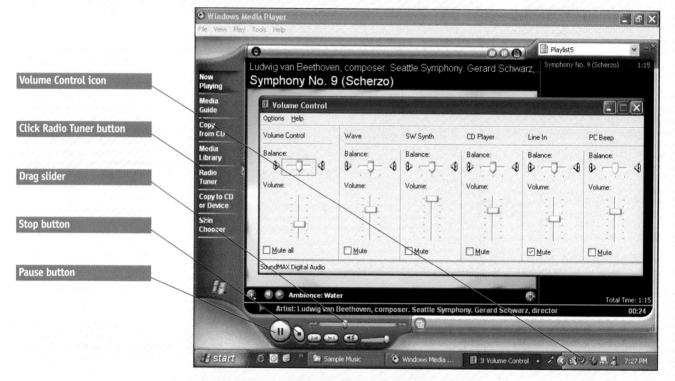

(b) Listen to the Music (step 2)

FIGURE 19   Hands-on Exercise 5 *(continued)*

OTHER MEDIA PLAYERS

If you double click a music (MP3) file, and a program other than Windows Media starts to play, it is because your system has another media player as its default program. You can still use the Windows Media Player, but you will have to start the program explicitly from the Start menu. Once the Media Player is open, pull down the File menu and click the Open command, then select the music file you want to play.

Step 3: Create a Playlist

- Click the **Media Library button** at the side of the Media player to display the media files that are currently on your computer.
  - ❑ The left pane displays a tree structure of your media library. Thus, you click the plus or minus sign to collapse or expand the indicated folder.
  - ❑ The right pane displays the contents of the selected object (the My Music playlist) in Figure 19c.

- Do not be concerned if your media library is different from ours. Click the **New playlist button**, enter **My Music** as the name of the new list, and click **OK**.

- Click the newly created playlist in the left pane to display its contents in the left pane. The playlist is currently empty.

- Start **Windows Explorer**. Open the **My Music Folder** within the My Documents folder. If necessary, click the **Restore button** to move and size Windows Explorer so that you can copy documents to the Media library.

- Click and drag one or more selections from the My Music folder to the right pane of the Media library to create the playlist. Close Windows Explorer.

- Click the **down arrow** in the list box at the upper right of the Media Gallery and select the My Music playlist to play the songs you have selected.

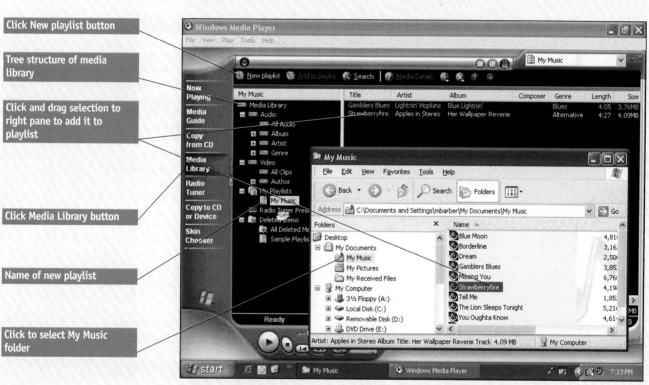

(c) Create a Playlist (step 3)

FIGURE 19 Hands-on Exercise 5 (*continued*)

THE MEDIA GUIDE

Click the Media Guide button at the left of the Media Player to display the home page of the Windows Media Site. You can also get there by starting Internet Explorer and entering windowsmedia.com in the Address bar. Either way, you will be connected to the Internet and can search the Web for media files and/or play clips from your favorite movie.

Step 4: **Create a Pictures Folder**

- You can use your own pictures, or if you don't have any, you can use the sample pictures provided with Windows XP. Start (or maximize) Windows Explorer. Open the **My Pictures folder** within the **My Documents folder**.

- Do not be concerned if the content of your folder is different from ours. Our folder already contains various subfolders with different types of pictures in each folder.

- Click the **Views button** and change to the **Thumbnails view**. This view is especially useful when viewing folders that contain photographs because (up to four) images are displayed on the folder icon.

- Right click anywhere in the right pane to display a context-sensitive menu as shown in Figure 19d. Click **New**, and then click **Folder** as the type of object to create.

- The icon for a new folder will appear with the name of the folder (New Folder) highlighted. Enter a more appropriate name (we chose **Romance** because our pictures are those of a happy couple), and press **Enter**.

- Copy your pictures from another folder, a CD, or floppy disk to the newly created folder.

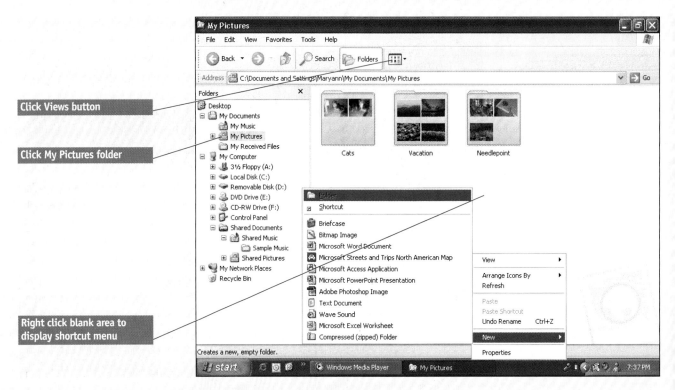

(d) Create a Pictures Folder (step 4)

FIGURE 19 Hands-on Exercise 5 (*continued*)

DESIGN GALLERY LIVE

The Microsoft Design Gallery is an excellent source of photographs and other media. Start Internet Explorer and go to the Design Gallery at dgl.microsoft.com. Enter the desired topic in the Search for text box, indicate that you want to search everywhere, and specify that the results should be photos. Download one or more of the photos that are returned by the search and use those pictures to complete this exercise.

Step 5: Display Your Pictures

- Double click the newly created folder to display its contents. Click the **Folders button** to display the Windows Explorer task pane, as opposed to the hierarchy structure. Click the **Views button** and change to the **Filmstrip view** as shown in Figure 19e.

- Click the **Next Image** or (**Previous Image**) **button** to move from one picture to the next within the folder. If necessary, click the buttons to rotate pictures clockwise or counterclockwise so that the pictures are displayed properly within the window.

- Click the command to **View as a slide show**, then display your pictures one at a time on your monitor. This is a very easy way to enjoy your photographs. Press the **Esc key** to stop.

- Choose any picture, then click the command to **Print this picture** that appears in the left pane. Submit this picture to your instructor.

- Choose a different picture and then click the command to **Set as desktop background**. Minimize Windows Explorer.

(e) Display Your Pictures (step 5)

FIGURE 19 Hands-on Exercise 5 *(continued)*

CHANGE THE VIEW

Click the down arrow next to the Views button on the Standard toolbar to change the way files are displayed within a folder. The Details view provides the most information and includes the filename, file type, file size, and the date that the file was created or last modified. (Additional attributes are also possible.) Other views are more visual. The Thumbnails view displays a miniature image of the file and is best used with clip art, photographs, or presentations. The Filmstrip view is used with photographs only.

Step 6: Customize the Desktop

■ Your desktop should once again be visible, depending on which (if any) applications are open. If you do not see the desktop, right click a blank area of the taskbar, then click the **Show Desktop command**.

■ You should see the picture you selected earlier as the background for your desktop. The picture is attractive (you chose it), but it may be distracting.

■ To remove the picture, **right click** the background of the desktop and click the **Properties command** to display the Display Properties dialog box in Figure 19f.

■ Click the **Desktop tab**, then click **None** in the Background list box. Click **OK** to accept this setting and close the dialog box. The picture disappears.

■ Regardless of whether you keep the background, you can use your pictures as a screen saver. Redisplay the Display Properties dialog box. Click the **Screen Saver tab** in the Display Properties box, then choose **My Picture Slideshow** from the screen saver list box.

■ Wait a few seconds and the picture within the dialog box will change, just as it will on your desktop. Click **OK** to accept the screen saver and close the Display Properties dialog box.

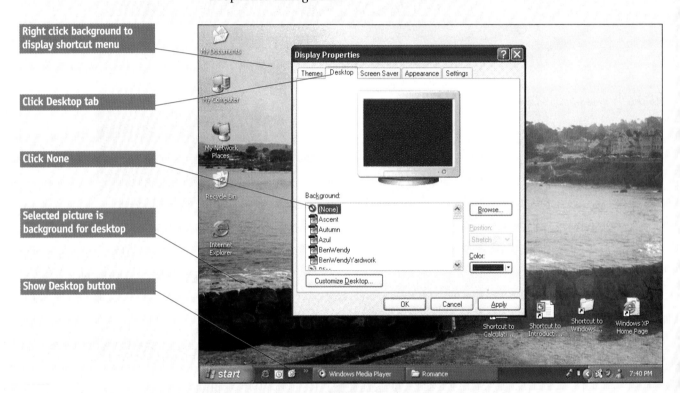

Right click background to display shortcut menu

Click Desktop tab

Click None

Selected picture is background for desktop

Show Desktop button

(f) Customize the Desktop (step 6)

FIGURE 19 Hands-on Exercise 5 (*continued*)

CHANGE THE RESOLUTION

The resolution of a monitor refers to the number of pixels (picture elements or dots) that are displayed at one time. The higher the resolution, the more pixels are displayed, and hence you see more of a document at one time. You can change the resolution at any time. Right click the desktop, click the Properties command to show the Display Properties dialog box, then click the Settings tab. Drag the slider bar to the new resolution, then click OK.

Step 7: Start Windows Messenger

- You need a passport to use Windows Messenger. Double click the **Windows Messenger icon** in the notification area of the taskbar to sign in.

- Maximize the Messenger window. You will see a list of your existing contacts with an indication of whether they are online.

- Add one or more contacts. Pull down the **Tools menu**, click the command to **Add a Contact**, then follow the onscreen instructions. (The contact does not have to have Windows XP to use instant messaging.)

- Double click any contact that is online to initiate a conversation and open a conversation window as shown in Figure 19g.

- Type a message at the bottom of the conversation window, then click the **Send button** to send the message. The text of your message will appear immediately on your contact's screen. Your friend's messages will appear on your screen.

- Continue the conversation by entering additional text. You can press the **Enter key** (instead of clicking the **Send button**) to send the message. You can also use **Shift + enter** to create a line break in your text.

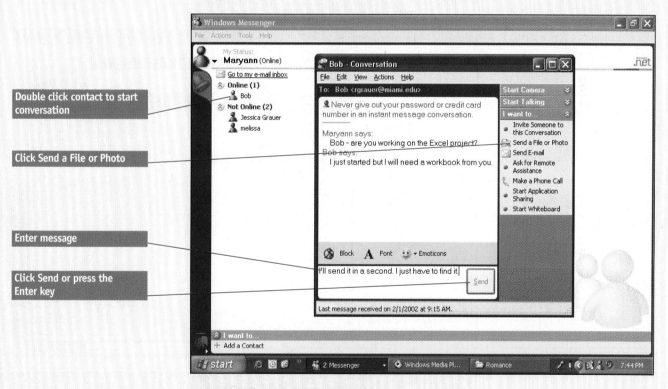

(g) Start Windows Messenger (step 7)

FIGURE 19 Hands-on Exercise 5 (*continued*)

CHANGE YOUR STATUS

Anyone on your contact list knows immediately when you log on; thus, the larger your contact list, the more likely you are to be engaged in idle chitchat when you have real work to do. You can avoid unwanted conversations without being rude by changing your status. Click the down arrow next to your name in the Messenger window and choose a different icon. You can appear offline or simply indicate that you are busy. Either way you will be more likely to get your work done.

Step 8: **Attach a File**

■ Click the command to **Send a File or Photo**, which displays the Send a File dialog box in Figure 19h. It does not matter which file you choose, since the purpose of this step is to demonstrate the file transfer capability.

■ A series of three file transfer messages will appear on your screen. Windows Messenger waits for your friend to accept the file transfer, then it indicates the transfer has begun, and finally, that the transfer was successful.

■ Click the command to **Invite someone to this conversation** if you have another contact online. You will see a second dialog box in which you select the contact.

■ There are now three people in the conversation. (Up to four people can participate in one conversation.) Your friends' responses will appear on your screen as soon as they are entered.

■ Send your goodbye to end the conversation, then close the conversation window to end the chat session. You are still online and can participate in future conversations.

■ Close Windows Messenger. You will be notified if anyone wants to contact you.

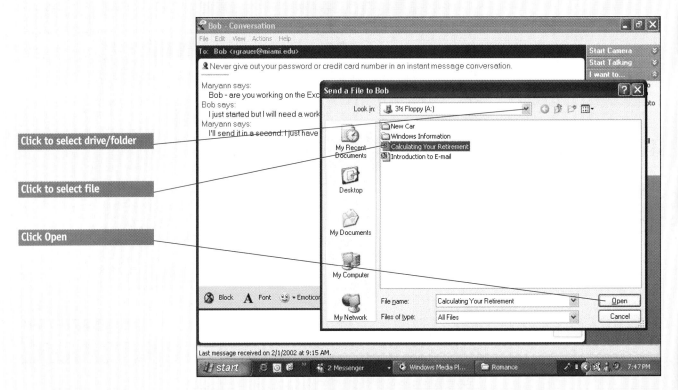

(h) Attach a File (step 8)

FIGURE 19   Hands-on Exercise 5 *(continued)*

E-MAIL VERSUS INSTANT MESSAGING

E-mail and instant messaging are both Internet communication services, but there are significant differences. E-mail does not require both participants to be online at the same time. E-mail messages are also permanent and do not disappear when you exit your e-mail program. Instant messaging, however, requires both participants to be online. Its conversations are not permanent and disappear when you end the session.

SUMMARY

Windows XP is the newest and most powerful version of the Windows operating system. It has a slightly different look than earlier versions, but it maintains the conventions of its predecessors. All Windows operations take place on the desktop. Every window contains the same basic elements, which include a title bar, a Minimize button, a Maximize or Restore button, and a Close button. All windows may be moved and sized. The taskbar contains a button for each open program and enables you to switch back and forth between those programs by clicking the appropriate button. You can obtain information about every aspect of Windows through the Help and Support Center.

A file is a set of data or set of instructions that has been given a name and stored on disk. There are two basic types of files, program files and data files. A program file is an executable file, whereas a data file can be used only in conjunction with a specific program. Every file has a filename and a file type.

Files are stored in folders to better organize the hundreds (or thousands) of files on a disk. A folder may contain program files, data files, and/or other folders. Windows automatically creates a set of personal folders for every user. These include the My Documents folder and the My Pictures folder and My Music folder within the My Documents folder. Windows also provides a Shared Documents folder that can be accessed by every user. The My Computer folder is accessible by all users and displays the devices on a system.

Windows Explorer facilitates every aspect of disk and file management. It presents a hierarchical view of your system that displays all devices and, optionally, the folders on each device. Any device may be expanded or collapsed to display or hide its folders.

Windows XP contains several tools to help you enjoy your system. The Windows Media Player combines the functions of a radio, CD player, DVD player, and an information database into a single program. Windows Messenger is an instant messaging system in which you chat with friends and colleagues over the Internet.

The Control Panel affects every aspect of your system. It determines the appearance of your desktop and it controls the performance of your hardware. A shortcut is a link to any object on your computer, such as a program, file, folder, disk drive, or Web page. The Search Companion enables you to search for a file according to several different criteria.

KEY TERMS

1. **Two Different Views:** The document in Figure 20 is an effective way to show your instructor that you understand the My Computer folder, the various views available, the task pane, and the hierarchy structure. It also demonstrates that you can capture a screen for inclusion in a Word document. Proceed as follows:

   a. Open the My Computer folder, click the Views button, and switch to the Tiles view. Click the Folders button to display the task pane. Size the window as necessary so that you will be able to fit two folders onto a one-page document as shown in Figure 20.

   b. Press and hold the Alt key as you press the Print Screen key to copy the My Computer window to the Windows clipboard. (The Print Screen key captures the entire screen. Using the Alt key, however, copies just the current window.) Click the Start menu, click Programs, and then click Microsoft Word to start the program. Maximize the window.

   c. Enter the title of the document, press Enter, and type your name. Press the Enter key twice in a row to leave a blank line.

   d. Pull down the Edit menu. Click the Paste command to copy the contents of the clipboard to the document. Press the Enter key to add a figure caption, then press the Enter key two additional times.

   e. Click the taskbar to return to the My Computer folder. Change to the Details view. Click the Folders button to display the hierarchy structure, as opposed to the task pane. Expand My Computer in the left pane, but collapse all of the individual devices. Press Alt+Print Screen to capture the My Computer folder in this configuration.

   f. Click the taskbar to return to your Word document. Press Ctrl+V to paste the contents of the clipboard into your document. Enter an appropriate caption below the figure. Save the completed document and print it for your instructor.

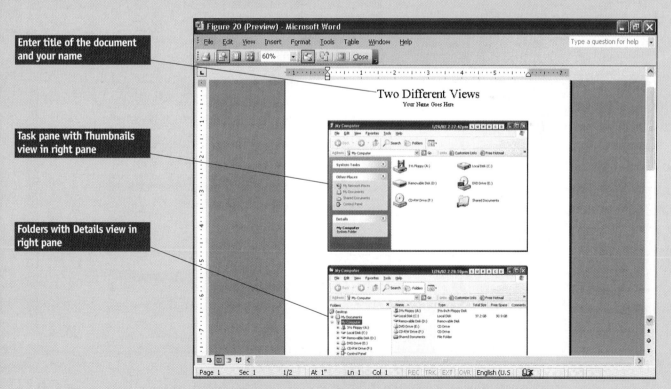

Enter title of the document and your name

Task pane with Thumbnails view in right pane

Folders with Details view in right pane

FIGURE 20 Two Different Views (exercise 1)

2. **Network Connections:** The document in Figure 21 displays the network connections on our system as well as the status of one of those connections. Your assignment is to create the equivalent document for your computer. Proceed as follows:

   a. Open the Control Panel, switch to the Classic view, then double click the Network Connections icon to display the Network Connections folder. (You can also get to this folder from My Computer, by clicking the link to My Network Places, and then clicking Network Connections from within the Network Tasks area.)

   b. Maximize the Network Connections folder so that it takes the entire desktop. Change to the Tiles view. Click the Folders button to display the task pane. Select (click) a connection, then click the link to View status of the connection, to display the associated dialog box.

   c. Press the Print Screen key to print this screen. Start Microsoft Word and open a new document. Press the Enter key several times, then click the Paste button to copy the contents of the clipboard into your document.

   d. Press Ctrl+Home to return to the beginning of the Word document, where you can enter the title of the document and your name. Compose a paragraph similar to the one in our figure that describes the network connections on your computer. Print this document for your instructor.

   e. Experiment with the first two network tasks that are displayed in the task pane. How difficult is it to set up a new connection? How do you set a firewall to protect your system from unauthorized access when connected to the Internet? How do you establish a home or small office network?

   f. Use the Help and Support Center to obtain additional information. Print one or two Help screens for your instructor.

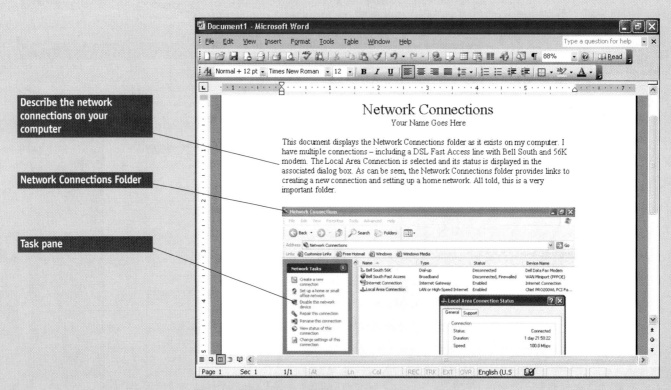

FIGURE 21 Network Connections (exercise 2)

practice exercises

3. **Create Your Own Folders:** Folders are the key to the Windows storage system. Folders can be created at any time and in any way that makes sense to you. The My Courses folder in Figure 22, for example, contains five folders, one folder for each class you are taking. In similar fashion, the Correspondence folder in this figure contains two additional folders according to the type of correspondence. Proceed as follows:

   a. Place the floppy disk from hands-on exercise 3 into drive A. Start Windows Explorer. Click the Folders button to display the hierarchy structure in the left pane. Change to the Details view.

   b. Create a Correspondence folder on drive A. Create a Business folder and a Personal folder within the Correspondence folder.

   c. Create a My Courses folder on drive A. Create a separate folder for each course you are taking within the My Courses folder. The names of your folders will be different from ours.

   d. Pull down the View menu, click the Arrange Icons by command, and click the command to Show in Groups. Click the Date Modified column header to group the files and folders by date. The dates you see will be different from the dates in our figure.

   e. The Show in Groups command functions as a toggle switch. Execute the command, and the files are displayed in groups; execute the command a second time, and the groups disappear. (You can change the grouping by clicking the desired column heading.)

   f. Use the technique described in problems 1 and 2 to capture the screen in Figure 22 and incorporate it into a document. Add a short paragraph that describes the folders you have created, then submit the document to your instructor.

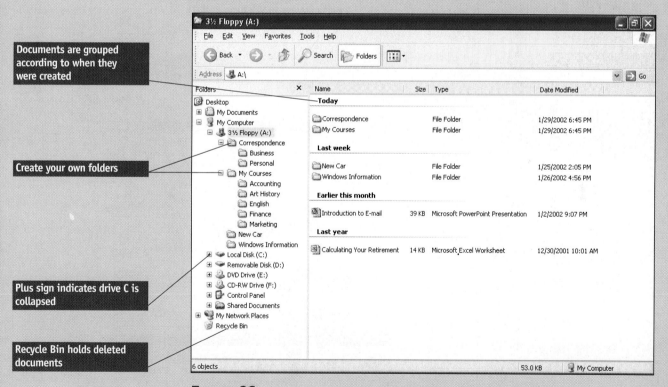

FIGURE 22 Create Your Own Folders (exercise 3)

4. **What's New in Windows XP:** Anyone, whether an experienced user or a computer novice, can benefit from a quick overview of new features in Windows XP. Click the Start button, click Help and Support, and then click the link to What's New in Windows XP. Click the second link in the task pane (taking a tour or tutorial), select the Windows XP tour, and choose the desired format. We chose the animated tour with animation, music, and voice narration.

   a. Relax and enjoy the show as shown in Figure 23. The task bar at the bottom of the figure contains three buttons to restart the show, exit, or toggle the music on and off. Exit the tutorial when you are finished. You are back in the Help and Support window, where you can take a tour of the Windows Media Player. Try it. Click the Close button at the upper right of any screen or press Escape to exit the tour. Write a short note to your instructor with comments about either tour.

   b. Return to the Help and Support Center and find the topic, "What's New in Home Networking." Print two or three subtopics that describe how to create a home network. Does the task seem less intimidating after you have read the information?

   c. Locate one or more topics on new features in digital media such as burning a CD or Windows Movie Maker. Print this information for your instructor.

   d. Return once again to the Help and Support Center to explore some of the other resources that describe new features in Windows XP. Locate the link to Windows News Groups, and then visit one of these newsgroups online. Locate a topic of interest and print several messages within a threaded discussion. Do you think newsgroups will be useful to you in the future?

   e. You can also download a PowerPoint presentation by the authors that describes new features in Windows XP. Go to www.prenhall.com/grauer, click the text for Office XP, then click the link to What's New in Windows XP, from where you can download the presentation.

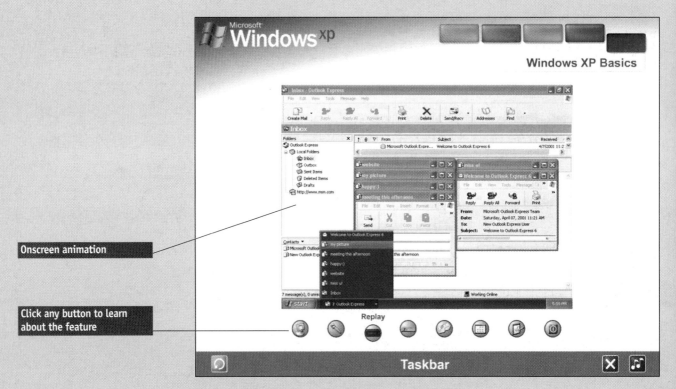

FIGURE 23   What's New in Windows XP (exercise 4)

5. **Keyboard Shortcuts:** Almost every command in Windows can be executed in different ways, using either the mouse or the keyboard. Most people start with the mouse and add keyboard shortcuts as they become more proficient. There is no right or wrong technique, just different techniques, and the one you choose depends entirely on personal preference. If, for example, your hands are already on the keyboard, it is faster to use the keyboard equivalent if you know it.

   There is absolutely no need to memorize these shortcuts, nor should you even try. A few, however, have special appeal and everyone has favorites. You are probably familiar with general Windows shortcuts such as Ctrl+X, Ctrl+C, and Ctrl+V to cut, copy, and paste, respectively. (The X is supposed to remind you of a pair of scissors.) Ctrl+Z is less well known and corresponds to the Undo command. You can find additional shortcuts through the Help command.

   a. Use the Help and Support Center to display the information in Figure 24, which shows the available shortcuts within a dialog box. Two of these, Tab and Shift+Tab, move forward and backward, respectively, from one option to the next within the dialog box. The next time you are in a physician's office or a dentist's office, watch the assistant as he or she labors over the keyboard to enter information. That person will typically type information into a text box, then switch to the mouse to select the next entry, return to the keyboard, and so on. Tell that person about Tab and Shift+Tab; he or she will be forever grateful.

   b. The Help and Support Center organizes the shortcuts by category. Select the Natural keyboard category (not visible in Figure 24), then note what you can do with the ⊞ key. Press the ⊞ key at any time, and you display the Start menu. Press ⊞+M and you minimize all open windows. There are several other, equally good shortcuts in this category.

   c. Select your five favorite shortcuts in any category, and submit them to your instructor. Compare your selections to those of your classmates. Do you prefer the mouse or your newly discovered shortcuts?

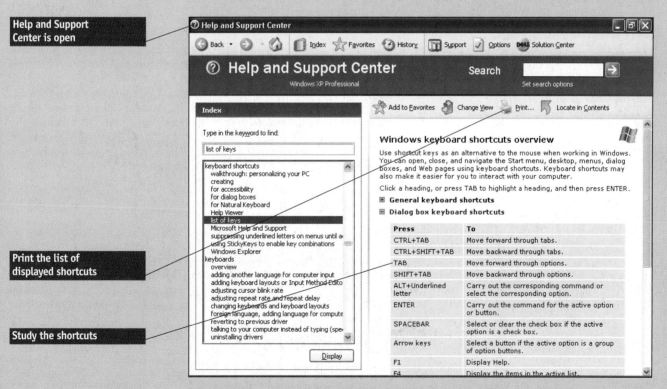

FIGURE 24 Keyboard Shortcuts (exercise 5)

MINI CASES

Planning for Disaster

Do you have a backup strategy? Do you even know what a backup strategy is? You had better learn, because sooner or later you will wish you had one. You will erase a file, be unable to read from a floppy disk, or worse yet, suffer a hardware failure in which you are unable to access the hard drive. The problem always seems to occur the night before an assignment is due. The ultimate disaster is the disappearance of your computer, by theft or natural disaster. Describe, in 250 words or less, the backup strategy you plan to implement in conjunction with your work in this class.

Tips for Windows XP

Print the *Tips for Windows XP* document that was downloaded as one of the practice files in the hands-on exercises. This document contains many of the boxed tips that appeared throughout the chapter. Read the document as a review and select five of your favorite tips. Create a new document for your instructor consisting of the five tips you selected. Add a cover page titled, "My Favorite Tips." Include your name, your professor's name, and a reference to the Grauer/Barber text from where the tips were taken.

File Compression

You've learned your lesson and have come to appreciate the importance of backing up all of your data files. The problem is that you work with large documents that exceed the 1.44MB capacity of a floppy disk. Accordingly, you might want to consider the acquisition of a file compression program to facilitate copying large documents to a floppy disk in order to transport your documents to and from school, home, or work. You can download an evaluation copy of the popular WinZip program at www.winzip.com. Investigate the subject of file compression and submit a summary of your findings to your instructor.

The Threat of Virus Infection

A computer virus is an actively infectious program that attaches itself to other programs and alters the way a computer works. Some viruses do nothing more than display an annoying message at an inopportune time. Most, however, are more harmful, and in the worst case, erase all files on the disk. Use your favorite search engine to research the subject of computer viruses to answer the following questions. When is a computer subject to infection by a virus? What precautions does your school or university take against the threat of virus infection in its computer lab? What precautions, if any, do you take at home? Can you feel confident that your machine will not be infected if you faithfully use a state-of-the-art anti-virus program that was purchased in June 2002?

Your First Consultant's Job

Go to a real installation such as a doctor's or attorney's office, the company where you work, or the computer lab at school. Determine the backup procedures that are in effect, then write a one-page report indicating whether the policy is adequate and, if necessary, offering suggestions for improvement. Your report should be addressed to the individual in charge of the business, and it should cover all aspects of the backup strategy; that is, which files are backed up and how often, and what software is used for the backup operation. Use appropriate emphasis (for example, bold italics) to identify any potential problems. This is a professional document (it is your first consultant's job), and its appearance should be perfect in every way.

Getting Started with VBA:
Extending Microsoft Office 2003

CASE STUDY
ON-THE-JOB TRAINING

Your first job is going exceedingly well. The work is very challenging and your new manager, Phyllis Simon, is impressed with the Excel workbooks that you have developed thus far. Phyllis has asked you to take it to the next level by incorporating VBA procedures into future projects. You have some knowledge of Excel macros and have already used the macro recorder to record basic macros. You are able to make inferences about the resulting code, but you will need additional proficiency in VBA to become a true expert in Excel.

The good news is that you work for a company that believes in continuing education and promotes from within. Phyllis has assigned you to a new interdepartmental team responsible for creating high-level Excel applications that will be enhanced through VBA. Moreover, you have been selected to attend a week-long seminar to learn VBA so that you can become a valued member of the team. The seminar will be held in San Diego, California, where there is a strong temptation to study sand and surf rather than VBA. Thus, Phyllis expects you to complete a series of VBA procedures upon your return—just to be sure that you were not tempted to skip class and dip your toes in the water. ■

Your assignment is to read the VBA primer at the end of the text and focus on the first three hands-on exercises that develop the syntax for basic VBA statements—MsgBox, InputBox, decision making through If/Else and Case statements, and iteration through the For . . . Next and Do Until statements. You will then open the partially completed *VBA Case Study—On-the-Job Training*, start the VBA editor, and then complete the tasks presented in the procedures in Module1. (The requirements for each procedure appear as comments within the procedure.) Add a command button for each macro to the Excel workbook, and then print the worksheet and a copy of the completed module for your instructor. Last, but not least, create a suitable event procedure for closing the workbook.

INTRODUCTION TO VBA

Visual Basic for Applications (VBA) is a powerful programming language that is accessible from all major applications in Microsoft Office XP. You do not have to know VBA to use Office effectively, but even a basic understanding will help you to create more powerful documents. Indeed, you may already have been exposed to VBA through the creation of simple macros in Word or Excel. A ***macro*** is a set of instructions (i.e., a program) that simplifies the execution of repetitive tasks. It is created through the ***macro recorder*** that captures commands as they are executed, then converts those commands into a VBA program. (The macro recorder is present in Word, Excel, and PowerPoint, but not in Access.) You can create and execute macros without ever looking at the underlying VBA, but you gain an appreciation for the language when you do.

The macro recorder is limited, however, in that it captures only commands, mouse clicks, and/or keystrokes. As you will see, VBA is much more than just recorded keystrokes. It is a language unto itself, and thus, it contains all of the statements you would expect to find in any programming language. This lets you enhance the functionality of any macro by adding extra statements as necessary—for example, an InputBox function to accept data from the user, followed by an If . . . Then . . . Else statement to take different actions based on the information supplied by the user.

This supplement presents the rudiments of VBA and is suitable for use with any Office application. We begin by describing the VBA editor and how to create, edit, and run simple procedures. The examples are completely general and demonstrate the basic capabilities of VBA that are found in any programming language. We illustrate the MsgBox statement to display output to the user and the InputBox function to accept input from the user. We describe the For . . . Next statement to implement a loop and the If . . . Then . . . Else and Case statements for decision making. We also describe several debugging techniques to help you correct the errors that invariably occur. The last two exercises introduce the concept of event-driven programming, in which a procedure is executed in response to an action taken by the user. The material here is application-specific in conjunction with Excel and Access, but it can be easily extended to Word or PowerPoint.

One last point before we begin is that this supplement assumes no previous knowledge on the part of the reader. It is suitable for someone who has never been exposed to a programming language or written an Office macro. If, on the other hand, you have a background in programming or macros, you will readily appreciate the power inherent in VBA. VBA is an incredibly rich language that can be daunting to the novice. Stick with us, however, and we will show you that it is a flexible and powerful tool with consistent rules that can be easily understood and applied. You will be pleased at what you will be able to accomplish.

VBA is a programming language, and like any other programming language its programs (or procedures, as they are called) are made up of individual statements. Each ***statement*** accomplishes a specific task such as displaying a message to the user or accepting input from the user. Statements are grouped into ***procedures***, and procedures, in turn, are grouped into ***modules***. Every VBA procedure is classified as either public or private. A ***private procedure*** is accessible only from within the module in which it is contained. A ***public procedure***, on the other hand, can be accessed from any module.

The statement, however, is the basic unit of the language. Our approach throughout this supplement will be to present individual statements, then to develop simple procedures using those statements in a hands-on exercise. As you read the discussion, you will see that every statement has a precise ***syntax*** that describes how the statement is to be used. The syntax also determines the ***arguments*** (or parameters) associated with that statement, and whether those arguments are required or optional.

THE MSGBOX STATEMENT

The ***MsgBox statement*** displays information to the user. It is one of the most basic statements in VBA, but we use it to illustrate several concepts in VBA programming. Figure 1a contains a simple procedure called MsgBoxExamples, consisting of four individual MsgBox statements. All procedures begin with a ***procedure header*** and end with the ***End Sub statement***.

The MsgBox statement has one required argument, which is the message (or prompt) that is displayed to the user. All other arguments are optional, but if they are used, they must be entered in a specified sequence. The simplest form of the MsgBox statement is shown in example 1, which specifies a single argument that contains the text (or prompt) to be displayed. The resulting message box is shown in Figure 1b. The message is displayed to the user, who responds accordingly, in this case by clicking the OK button.

Example 2 extends the MsgBox statement to include a second parameter that displays an icon within the resulting dialog box as shown in Figure 1c. The type of icon is determined by a VBA ***intrinsic*** (or predefined) ***constant*** such as vbExclamation, which displays an exclamation point in a yellow triangle. VBA has many such constants that enable you to simplify your code, while at the same time achieving some impressive results.

Example 3 uses a different intrinsic constant, vbInformation, to display a different icon. It also extends the MsgBox statement to include a third parameter that is displayed on the title bar of the resulting dialog box. Look closely, for example, at Figures 1c and 1d, whose title bars contain "Microsoft Excel" and "Grauer/Barber", respectively. The first is the default entry (given that we are executing the procedure from within Microsoft Excel). You can, however, give your procedures a customized look by displaying your own text in the title bar.

Procedure header

```
Public Sub MsgBoxExamples()
'This procedure was written by John Doe on 6/10/2003

    MsgBox "Example 1 - VBA is not difficult"
    MsgBox "Example 2 - VBA is not difficult", vbExclamation
    MsgBox "Example 3 - VBA is not difficult", vbInformation, "Grauer/Barber"
    MsgBox "Example 4 - VBA is not difficult", , "Your name goes here"
```

End Sub statement

```
End Sub
```

(a) VBA Code

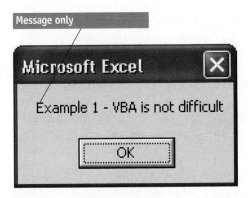

(b) Example 1—One Argument

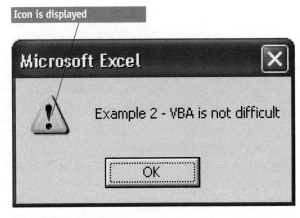

(c) Example 2—Two Arguments

FIGURE 1 The MsgBox Statement

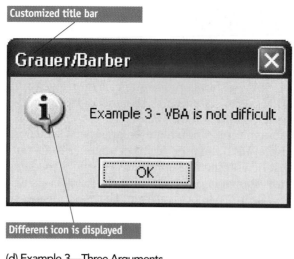

(d) Example 3—Three Arguments

(e) Example 4—Omitted Parameter

FIGURE 1   The MsgBox Statement (*continued*)

Example 4 omits the second parameter (the icon), but includes the third parameter (the entry for the title bar). The parameters are positional, however, and thus the MsgBox statement contains two commas after the message to indicate that the second parameter has been omitted.

THE INPUTBOX FUNCTION

The MsgBox statement displays a prompt to the user, but what if you want the user to respond to the prompt by entering a value such as his or her name? This is accomplished using the ***InputBox function***. Note the subtle change in terminology in that we refer to the InputBox *function*, but the MsgBox *statement*. That is because a function returns a value, in this case the user's name, which is subsequently used in the procedure. In other words, the InputBox function asks the user for information, then it stores that information (the value returned by the user) for use in the procedure.

Figure 2 displays a procedure that prompts the user for a first and last name, after which it displays the information using the MsgBox statement. (The Dim statement at the beginning of the procedure is explained shortly.) Let's look at the first InputBox function, and the associated dialog box in Figure 2b. The InputBox function displays a prompt on the screen, the user enters a value ("Bob" in this example), and that value is stored in the variable that appears to the left of the equal sign (strFirstName). The concept of a variable is critical to every programming language. Simply stated, a ***variable*** is a named storage location that contains data that can be modified during program execution.

The MsgBox statement then uses the value of strFirstName to greet the user by name as shown in Figure 2c. This statement also introduces the ampersand to ***concatenate*** (join together) two different character strings, the literal "Good morning", followed by the value within the variable strFirstName.

The second InputBox function prompts the user for his or her last name. In addition, it uses a second argument to customize the contents of the title bar (VBA Primer in this example) as can be seen in Figure 2d. Finally, the MsgBox statement in Figure 2e displays both the first and last name through concatenation of multiple strings. This statement also uses the ***underscore*** to continue a statement from one line to the next.

VBA is not difficult, and you can use the MsgBox statement and InputBox function in conjunction with one another as the basis for several meaningful procedures. You will get a chance to practice in the hands-on exercise that follows shortly.

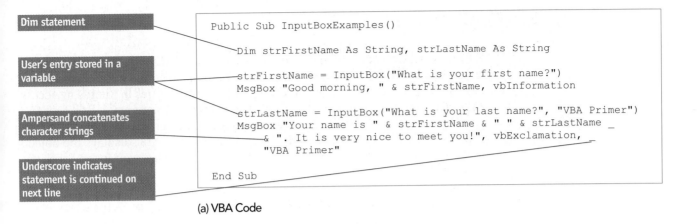

Dim statement	

```
Public Sub InputBoxExamples()

    Dim strFirstName As String, strLastName As String

    strFirstName = InputBox("What is your first name?")
    MsgBox "Good morning, " & strFirstName, vbInformation

    strLastName = InputBox("What is your last name?", "VBA Primer")
    MsgBox "Your name is " & strFirstName & " " & strLastName _
        & ". It is very nice to meet you!", vbExclamation, _
        "VBA Primer"

End Sub
```

Dim statement

User's entry stored in a variable

Ampersand concatenates character strings

Underscore indicates statement is continued on next line

(a) VBA Code

(b) InputBox

(c) Concatenation

(d) Input Box Includes Argument for Title Bar

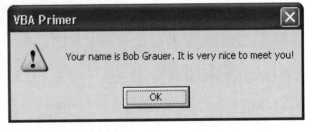

(e) Concatenation and Continuation

FIGURE 2   The InputBox Function

Declaring Variables

Every variable must be declared (defined) before it can be used. This is accomplished through the **Dim** (short for Dimension) **statement** that appears at the beginning of a procedure. The Dim statement indicates the name of the variable and its type (for example, whether it will hold characters or numbers), which in turn reserves the appropriate amount of memory for that variable.

A variable name must begin with a letter and cannot exceed 255 characters. It can contain letters, numbers, and various special characters such as an underscore, but it cannot contain a space or the special symbols !, @, &, $, or #. Variable names typically begin with a prefix to indicate the type of data that is stored within the variable such as "str" for a character string or "int" for integers. The use of a prefix is optional with respect to the rules of VBA, but it is followed almost universally.

Step 9: **Ask for Assistance**

- Your contacts do not require Windows XP to converse with you using Windows Messenger. Windows XP is required, however, to use the remote assistance feature.

- Click the **Start button**, then click the **Help and Support command** to display the home page of the Help and Support Center. Click the **Support button**, then click the command to **Ask a friend to help**.

- A Remote Assistance screen will open in the right pane. Click the command to **Invite someone to help**, which will display your contact list as shown in Figure 19i. You can choose any contact who is online, or you can enter the e-mail address of someone else.

- You will see a dialog box indicating that an invitation has been sent. Once your friend accepts the invitation, he or she will be able to see your screen. A chat window will open up in which you can discuss the problem you are having. Close the session when you are finished.

- Pull down the **File menu** and click the command to **Sign out**. The Windows Messenger icon in the notification will indicate that you have signed out.

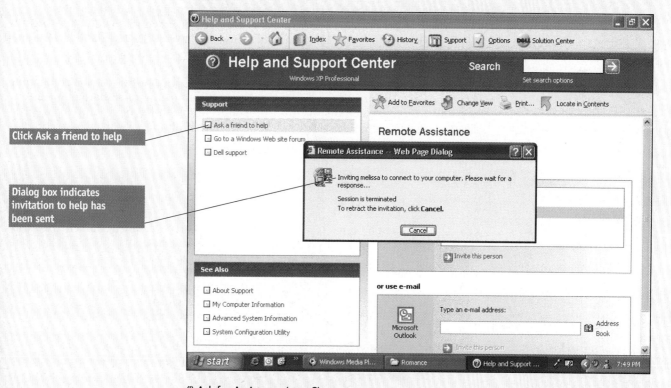

(i) Ask for Assistance (step 9)

FIGURE 19 Hands-on Exercise 5 (*continued*)

SUPPORT ONLINE

Microsoft provides extensive online support in a variety of formats. Start at the Windows XP home page (www.microsoft.com/windowsxp), then click the Support button to see what is available. You will be able to search the Microsoft Knowledge Base for detailed information on virtually any subject. You can also post questions and participate in threaded discussions in various newsgroups. Support is available for every Microsoft product.

All VBA procedures are created using the ***Visual Basic editor*** as shown in Figure 3. You may already be familiar with the editor, perhaps in conjunction with creating and/or editing macros in Word or Excel, or event procedures in Microsoft Access. Let's take a moment, however, to review its essential components.

The left side of the editor displays the ***Project Explorer***, which is similar in concept and appearance to the Windows Explorer, except that it displays the objects associated with the open document. If, for example, you are working in Excel, you will see the various sheets in a workbook, whereas in an Access database you will see forms and reports.

The VBA statements for the selected module (Module1 in Figure 3) appear in the code window in the right pane. The module, in turn, contains declarations and procedures that are separated by horizontal lines. There are two procedures, MsgBoxExamples and InputBoxExamples, each of which was explained previously. A ***comment*** (nonexecutable) statement has been added to each procedure and appears in green. It is the apostrophe at the beginning of the line, rather than the color, that denotes a comment.

The ***Declarations section*** appears at the beginning of the module and contains a single statement, ***Option Explicit***. This option requires every variable in a procedure to be explicitly defined (e.g., in a Dim statement) before it can be used elsewhere in the module. It is an important option and should appear in every module you write.

The remainder of the window should look reasonably familiar in that it is similar to any other Office application. The title bar appears at the top of the window and identifies the application (Microsoft Visual Basic) and the current document (VBA Examples.xls). The right side of the title bar contains the Minimize, Restore, and Close buttons. A menu bar appears under the title bar. Toolbars are displayed under the menu bar. Commands are executed by pulling down the appropriate menu, via buttons on the toolbar, or by keyboard shortcuts.

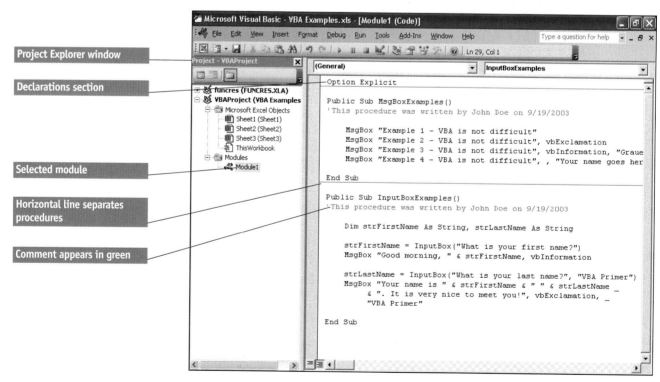

Project Explorer window

Declarations section

Selected module

Horizontal line separates procedures

Comment appears in green

FIGURE 3 The VBA Editor

Introduction to VBA

Objective   To create and test VBA procedures using the MsgBox and InputBox statements. Use Figure 4 as a guide in the exercise. You can do the exercise in any Office application.

Step 1a: **Start Microsoft Excel**

- We suggest you do the exercise in either Excel or Access (although you could use Word or PowerPoint just as easily). Go to step 1b for Access.

- Start **Microsoft Excel** and open a new workbook. Pull down the **File menu** and click the **Save command** (or click the **Save button** on the Standard toolbar) to display the Save As dialog box. Choose an appropriate drive and folder, then save the workbook as **VBA Examples**.

- Pull down the **Tools menu**, click the **Macro command**, then click the **Visual Basic Editor command** as shown in Figure 4a. Go to step 2.

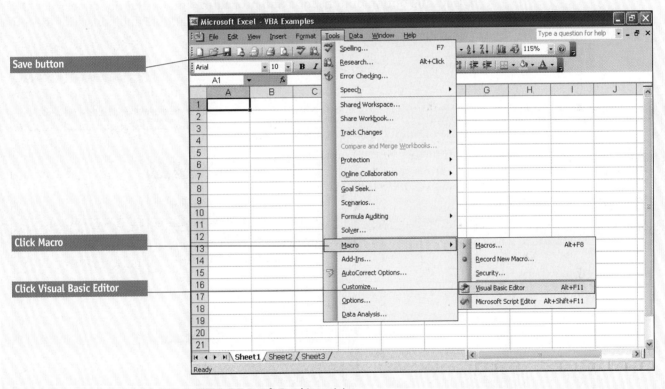

(a) Start Microsoft Excel (step 1a)

FIGURE 4   Hands-on Exercise 1

Step 1b: **Start Microsoft Access**

- Start **Microsoft Access** and choose the option to create a **Blank Access database**. Save the database as **VBA Examples**.

- Pull down the **Tools menu**, click the **Macro command**, then click the **Visual Basic Editor command**. (You can also use the **Alt+F11** keyboard shortcut to open the VBA editor without going through the Tools menu.)

Step 2: Insert a Module

- You should see a window similar to Figure 4b, but Module1 is not yet visible. Close the Properties window if it appears.

- If necessary, pull down the **View menu** and click **Project Explorer** to display the Project Explorer pane at the left of the window. Our figure shows Excel objects, but you will see the "same" window in Microsoft Access.

- Pull down the **Insert menu** and click **Module** to insert Module1 into the current project. The name of the module, Module1 in this example, appears in the Project Explorer pane.

- The Option Explicit statement may be entered automatically, but if not, click in the code window and type the statement **Option Explicit**.

- Pull down the **Insert menu** a second time, but this time select **Procedure** to display the Add Procedure dialog box in Figure 4b. Click in the **Name** text box and enter **MsgBoxExamples** as the name of the procedure. (Spaces are not allowed in a procedure name.)

- Click the option buttons for a **Sub procedure** and for **Public scope**. Click **OK**. The sub procedure should appear within the module and consist of the Sub and End Sub statements.

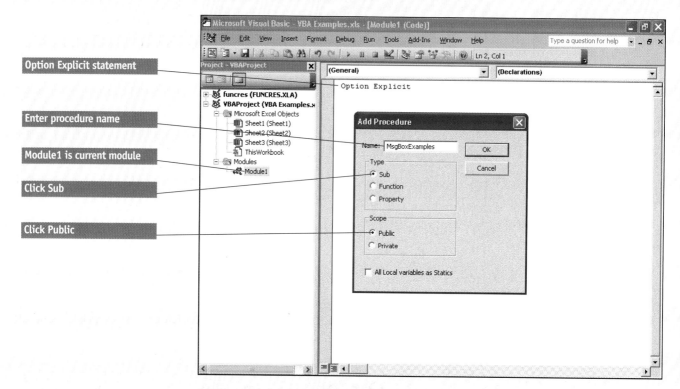

Option Explicit statement

Enter procedure name

Module1 is current module

Click Sub

Click Public

(b) Insert a Module (step 2)

FIGURE 4 Hands-on Exercise 1 (*continued*)

THE OPTION EXPLICIT STATEMENT

The Option Explicit statement is optional, but if it is used it must appear in a module before any procedures. The statement requires that all variables in the module be declared explicitly by the programmer (typically with a Dim, Public, or Private statement), as opposed to VBA making an implicit assumption about the variable. It is good programming practice and it should be used every time.

Step 3: The MsgBox Statement

- The insertion point (the flashing cursor) appears below the first statement. Press the **Tab key** to indent the next statement. (Indentation is not a VBA requirement, but is used to increase the readability of the statement.)

- Type the keyword **MsgBox**, then press the **space bar**. VBA responds with Quick Info that displays the syntax of the statement as shown in Figure 4c.

- Type a **quotation mark** to begin the literal, enter the text of your message, **This is my first VBA procedure**, then type the closing **quotation mark**.

- Click the **Run Sub button** on the Standard toolbar (or pull down the **Run menu** and click the **Run Sub command**) to execute the procedure.

- You should see a dialog box, containing the text you entered, within the Excel workbook (or other Office document) on which you are working.

- After you have read the message, click **OK** to return to the VBA editor.

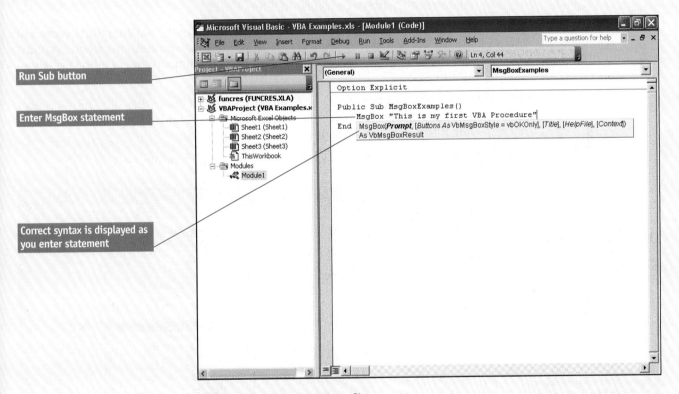

(c) The MsgBox Statement (step 3)

FIGURE 4 Hands-on Exercise 1 (*continued*)

QUICK INFO—HELP WITH VBA SYNTAX

Press the space bar after entering the name of a statement (e.g., MsgBox), and VBA responds with a Quick Info box that displays the syntax of the statement. You see the arguments in the statement and the order in which those arguments appear. Any argument in brackets is optional. If you do not see this information, pull down the Tools menu, click the Options command, then click the Editor tab. Check the box for Auto Quick Info and click OK.

Step 4: Complete the Procedure

- You should be back within the MsgBoxExamples procedure. If necessary, click at the end of the MsgBox statement, then press **Enter** to begin a new line. Type **MsgBox** and press the **space bar** to begin entering the statement.

- The syntax of the MsgBox statement will appear on the screen. Type a **quotation mark** to begin the message, type **Add an icon** as the text of this message, then type the closing **quotation mark**. Type a **comma**, then press the **space bar** to enter the next parameter.

- VBA automatically displays a list of appropriate parameters, in this case a series of intrinsic constants that define the icon or command button that is to appear in the statement.

- You can type the first several letters (e.g., **vbi**, for vbInformation), then press the **space bar**, or you can use the **down arrow** to select **vbInformation** and then press the **space bar**. Either way you should complete the second MsgBox statement as shown in Figure 4d. Press **Enter**.

- Enter the third MsgBox statement as shown in Figure 4d. Note the presence of the two consecutive commas to indicate that we omitted the second parameter within the MsgBox statement. Enter your name instead of John Doe where appropriate. Press **Enter**.

- Enter the fourth (and last) MsgBox statement following our figure. Select **vbExclamation** as the second parameter, type a **comma**, then enter the text of the title bar, as you did for the previous statement.

- Click the **Save button** to save the changes to the module.

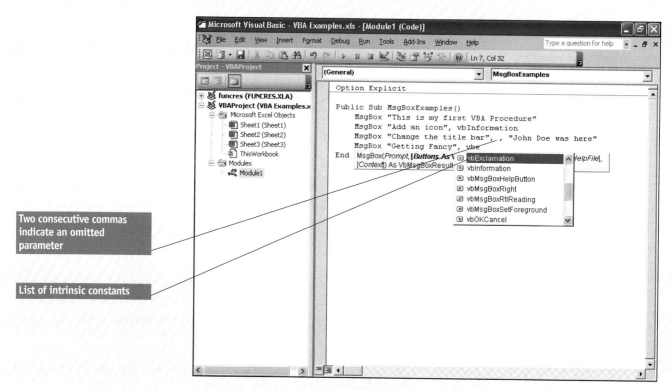

(d) Complete the Procedure (step 4)

FIGURE 4 Hands-on Exercise 1 (*continued*)

Step 5: Test the Procedure

- It's convenient if you can see the statements in the VBA procedure at the same time you see the output of those statements. Thus we suggest that you tile the VBA editor and the associated Office application.

- Minimize all applications except the VBA editor and the Office application (e.g., Excel).

- Right click the taskbar and click **Tile Windows Horizontally** to tile the windows as shown in Figure 4e. (It does not matter which window is on top. (If you see more than these two windows, minimize the other open window, then right click the taskbar and retile the windows.)

- Click anywhere in the VBA procedure, then click the **Run Sub button** on the Standard toolbar.

- The four messages will be displayed one after the other. Click **OK** after each message.

- Maximize the VBA window to continue working.

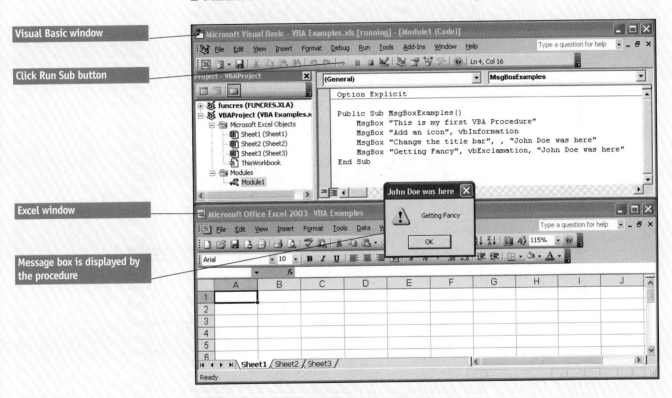

(e) Test the Procedure (step 5)

FIGURE 4   Hands-on Exercise 1 (*continued*)

HIDE THE WINDOWS TASKBAR

You can hide the Windows taskbar to gain additional space on the desktop. Right click any empty area of the taskbar to display a context-sensitive menu, click Properties to display the Taskbar properties dialog box, and if necessary click the Taskbar tab. Check the box to Auto Hide the taskbar, then click OK. The taskbar disappears from the screen but will reappear as you point to the bottom edge of the desktop.

Step 6:   Comments and Corrections

- All VBA procedures should be documented with the author's name, date, and other comments as necessary to explain the procedure. Click after the procedure header. Press the **Enter key** to leave a blank line.

- Press **Enter** a second time. Type an **apostrophe** to begin the comment, then enter a descriptive statement similar to Figure 4f. Press **Enter** when you have completed the comment. The line turns green to indicate it is a comment.

- The best time to experiment with debugging is when you know your procedure is correct. Go to the last MsgBox statement and delete the quotation mark in front of your name. Move to the end of the line and press **Enter**.

- You should see the error message in Figure 4f. Unfortunately, the message is not as explicit as it could be; VBA cannot tell that you left out a quotation mark, but it does detect an error in syntax.

- Click **OK** in response to the error. Click the **Undo button** twice, to restore the quotation mark, which in turn corrects the statement.

- Click the **Save button** to save the changes to the module.

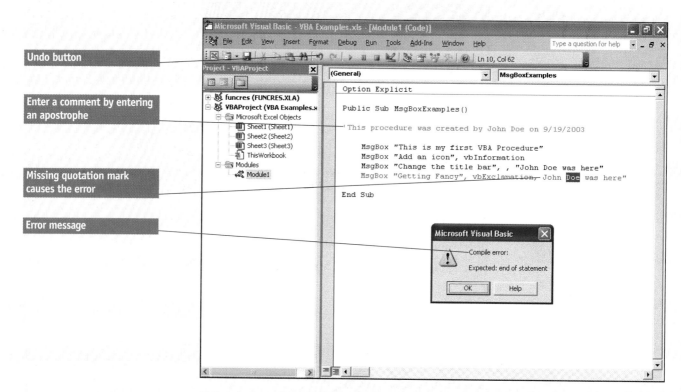

Undo button

Enter a comment by entering an apostrophe

Missing quotation mark causes the error

Error message

(f) Comments and Corrections (step 6)

FIGURE 4   Hands-on Exercise 1 (*continued*)

RED, GREEN, AND BLUE

Visual Basic for Applications uses different colors for different types of statements (or a portion of those statements). Any statement containing a syntax error appears in red. Comments appear in green. Keywords, such as Sub and End Sub, appear in blue.

Step 7: Create a Second Procedure

■ Pull down the **Insert menu** and click **Procedure** to display the Add Procedure dialog box. Enter **InputBoxExamples** as the name of the procedure. (Spaces are not allowed in a procedure name.)

■ Click the option buttons for a **Sub procedure** and for **Public scope**. Click **OK**. The new sub procedure will appear within the existing module below the existing MsgBoxExamples procedure.

■ Enter the statements in the procedure as they appear in Figure 4g. Be sure to type a space between the ampersand and the underscore in the second MsgBox statement. Click the **Save button** to save the procedure before testing it.

■ You can display the output of the procedure directly in the VBA window if you minimize the Excel window. Thus, **right click** the Excel button on the taskbar to display a context-sensitive menu, then click the **Minimize command**. There is no visible change on your monitor.

■ Click the **Run Sub button** to test the procedure. This time you see the Input box displayed on top of the VBA window because the Excel window has been minimized.

■ Enter your first name in response to the initial prompt, then click **OK**. Click **OK** when you see the message box that says "Hello".

■ Enter your last name in response to the second prompt and click **OK**. You should see a message box similar to the one in Figure 4g. Click **OK**.

■ Return to the VBA procedure to correct any mistakes that might occur. Save the module.

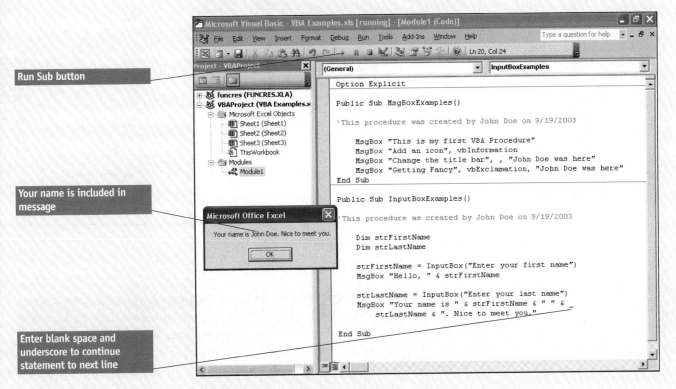

(g) Create a Second Procedure (step 7)

FIGURE 4 Hands-on Exercise 1 (*continued*)

Step 8: Create a Public Constant

- Click after the Options Explicit statement and press **Enter** to move to a new line. Type the statement to define the constant, **ApplicationTitle**, as shown in Figure 4h, and press **Enter**.

- Click anywhere in the MsgBoxExamples procedure, then change the third argument in the last MsgBox statement to ApplicationTitle. Make the four modifications in the InputBoxExamples procedure as shown in Figure 4h.

- Click anywhere in the InputBoxExamples procedure, then click the **Run Sub button** to test the procedure. The title bar of each dialog box will contain a descriptive title corresponding to the value of the ApplicationTitle constant.

- Change the value of the ApplicationTitle constant in the General Declarations section, then rerun the InputBoxExamples procedure. The title of every dialog box changes to reflect the new value.

- Save the procedure. Do you see the advantage of defining a title in the General Declarations section?

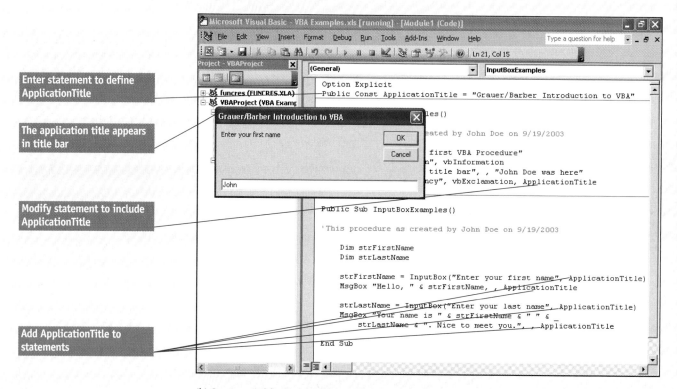

Enter statement to define ApplicationTitle

The application title appears in title bar

Modify statement to include ApplicationTitle

Add ApplicationTitle to statements

(h) Create a Public Constant (step 8)

FIGURE 4 Hands-on Exercise 1 (*continued*)

CONTINUING A VBA STATEMENT—THE & AND THE UNDERSCORE

A VBA statement can be continued from one line to the next by typing a space at the end of the line to be continued, typing the underscore character, then continuing on the next line. You may not, however, break a line in the middle of a literal (character string). Thus, you need to complete the character string with a closing quotation mark, add an ampersand (as the concatenation operator to display this string with the character string on the next line), then leave a space followed by the underscore to indicate continuation.

Step 9: Help with VBA

- You should be in the VBA editor. Pull down the **Help menu** and click the **Microsoft Visual Basic Help command** to open the Help pane.

- Type **Input Box function** in the Search box, then click the arrow to initiate the search. The results should include a hyperlink to InputBox function. Click the **hyperlink** to display the Help screen in Figure 4i.

- Maximize the Help window, then explore the information on the InputBox function to reinforce your knowledge of this statement.
  - ❏ Click the **Print button** to print this page for your instructor.
  - ❏ Click the link to **Example** within the Help window to see actual code.
  - ❏ Click the link to **See Also**, which displays information about the MsgBox statement.

- Close the Help window, but leave the task pane open. Click the **green** (back) **arrow** within the task pane to display the Table of Contents for Visual Basic Help, then explore the table of contents.
  - ❏ Click any closed book to open the book and "drill down" within the list of topics. The book remains open until you click the icon a second time to close it.
  - ❏ Click any question mark icon to display the associated help topic.

- Close the task pane. Pull down the **File menu** and click the **Close and Return to Microsoft Excel command** (or click the **Close button** on the VBA title bar) to close the VBA window and return to the application. Click **Yes** if asked whether to save the changes to Module1.

- You should be back in the Excel (or Access) application window. Close the application if you do not want to continue with the next exercise at this time.

- Congratulations. You have just completed your first VBA procedure. Remember to use Help any time you have a question.

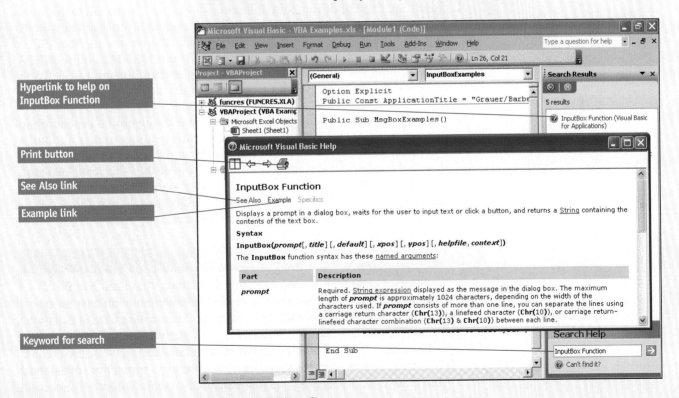

(i) Help with VBA (step 9)

FIGURE 4   Hands-on Exercise 1 (*continued*)

IF . . . THEN . . . ELSE STATEMENT

The ability to make decisions within a program, and then execute alternative sets of statements based on the results of those decisions, is crucial to any programming language. This is typically accomplished through an *If statement*, which evaluates a condition as either true or false, then branches accordingly. The If statement is not used in isolation, however, but is incorporated into a procedure to accomplish a specific task as shown in Figure 5a. This procedure contains two separate If statements, and the results are displayed in the message boxes shown in the remainder of the figure.

The InputBox statement associated with Figure 5b prompts the user for the name of his or her instructor, then it stores the answer in the variable strInstructorName. The subsequent If statement then compares the user's answer to the literal "Grauer". If the condition is true (i.e., Grauer was entered into the input box), then the message in Figure 5c is displayed. If, however, the user entered any other value, then the condition is evaluated as false, the MsgBox is not displayed, and processing continues with the next statement in the procedure.

The second If statement includes an optional *Else clause*. Again, the user is asked for a value, and the response is compared to the number 50. If the condition is true (i.e., the value of intUserStates equals 50), the message in Figure 5d is displayed to indicate that the response is correct. If, however, the condition is false (i.e., the user entered a number other than 50), the user sees the message in Figure 5e. Either way, true or false, processing continues with the next statement in the procedure. That's it—it's simple and it's powerful, and we will use the statement in the next hands-on exercise.

You can learn a good deal about VBA by looking at existing code and making inferences. Consider, for example, the difference between literals and numbers. *Literals* (also known as *character strings*) are stored differently from numbers, and this is manifested in the way that comparisons are entered into a VBA statement. Look closely at the condition that references a literal (strInstructorName = "Grauer") compared to the condition that includes a number (intUserStates = 50). The literal ("Grauer") is enclosed in quotation marks, whereas the number (50) is not. (The prefix used in front of each variable, "str" and "int", is a common VBA convention to indicate the variable type—a string and an integer, respectively. Both variables are declared in the Dim statements at the beginning of the procedure.)

Note, too, that indentation and spacing are used throughout a procedure to make it easier to read. This is for the convenience of the programmer and not a requirement for VBA. The If, Else, and End If keywords are aligned under one another, with the subsequent statements indented under the associated keyword. We also indent a continued statement, such as a MsgBox statement, which is typically coded over multiple lines. Blank lines can be added anywhere within a procedure to separate blocks of statements from one another.

THE MSGBOX FUNCTION—YES OR NO

A simple MsgBox statement merely displays information to the user. MsgBox can also be used as a function, however, to accept information from the user such as clicking a Yes or No button, then combined with an If statement to take different actions based on the user's input. In essence, you enclose the arguments of the MsgBox function in parentheses (similar to what is done with the InputBox function), then test for the user response using the intrinsic constants vbYes and vbNo. The statement, If MsgBox("Are you having fun?", vbYesNo)=vbYes asks the user a question, displays Yes and No command buttons, then tests to see if the user clicked the Yes button.

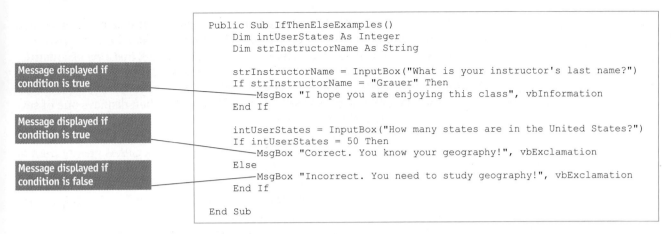

```
Public Sub IfThenElseExamples()
    Dim intUserStates As Integer
    Dim strInstructorName As String

    strInstructorName = InputBox("What is your instructor's last name?")
    If strInstructorName = "Grauer" Then
        MsgBox "I hope you are enjoying this class", vbInformation
    End If

    intUserStates = InputBox("How many states are in the United States?")
    If intUserStates = 50 Then
        MsgBox "Correct. You know your geography!", vbExclamation
    Else
        MsgBox "Incorrect. You need to study geography!", vbExclamation
    End If

End Sub
```

Message displayed if condition is true

Message displayed if condition is true

Message displayed if condition is false

(a) VBA Code

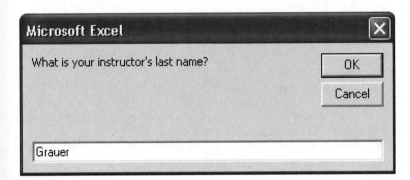

(b) InputBox Prompts for User Response

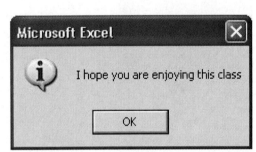

(c) Condition Is True

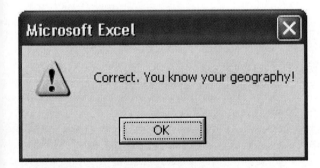

(d) Answer Is Correct (condition is true)

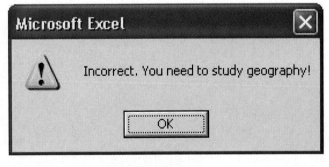

(e) Answer Is Wrong (condition is false)

FIGURE 5   The If Statement

CASE STATEMENT

The If statement is ideal for testing simple conditions and taking one of two actions. Although it can be extended to include additional actions by including one or more ElseIf clauses (If . . . Then . . . ElseIf . . . ElseIf . . .), this type of construction is often difficult to follow. Hence the **Case statement** is used when multiple branches are possible.

The procedure in Figure 6a accepts a student's GPA, then displays one of several messages, depending on the value of the GPA. The individual cases are evaluated in sequence. (The GPAs must be evaluated in descending order if the statement is to work correctly.) Thus, we check first to see if the GPA is greater than or equal to 3.9, then 3.75, then 3.5, and so on. If none of the cases is true, the statement following the Else clause is executed.

Note, too, the format of the comparison in that numbers (such as 3.9 or 3.75) are not enclosed in quotation marks because the associated variable (sngUserGPA) was declared as numeric. If, however, we had been evaluating a string variable (such as, strUserMajor), quotation marks would have been required around the literal values (e.g., Case Is = "Business", Case Is = "Liberal Arts", and so on.) The distinction between numeric and character (string) variables is important.

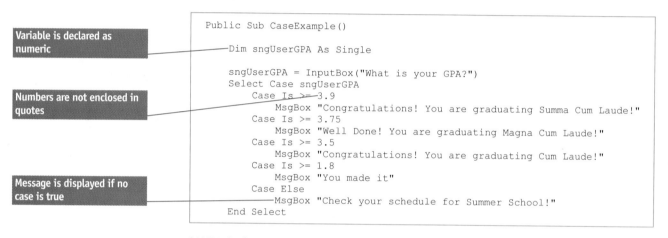

Variable is declared as numeric

Numbers are not enclosed in quotes

Message is displayed if no case is true

```
Public Sub CaseExample()

    Dim sngUserGPA As Single

    sngUserGPA = InputBox("What is your GPA?")
    Select Case sngUserGPA
        Case Is >= 3.9
            MsgBox "Congratulations! You are graduating Summa Cum Laude!"
        Case Is >= 3.75
            MsgBox "Well Done! You are graduating Magna Cum Laude!"
        Case Is >= 3.5
            MsgBox "Congratulations! You are graduating Cum Laude!"
        Case Is >= 1.8
            MsgBox "You made it"
        Case Else
            MsgBox "Check your schedule for Summer School!"
    End Select
```

(a) VBA Code

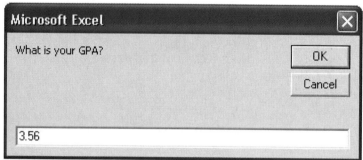

(b) Enter the GPA

(c) Third Option Is Selected

FIGURE 6   The Case Statement

CUSTOM TOOLBARS

A VBA procedure can be executed in several different ways. It can be run from the Visual Basic editor by pulling down the Run menu and clicking the Run Sub button on the Standard toolbar, or using the F5 function key. It can also be run from within the Office application (Word, Excel, or PowerPoint, but not Access), by pulling down the Tools menu, clicking the Macro command, then choosing the name of the macro that corresponds to the name of the procedure.

Perhaps the best way, however, is to create a ***custom toolbar*** that is displayed within the application as shown in Figure 7. (A custom menu can also be created that contains the same commands as the custom toolbar.) The toolbar has its own name (Bob's Toolbar), yet it functions identically to any other Office toolbar. You have your choice of displaying buttons only, text only, or both buttons and text. Our toolbar provides access to four commands, each corresponding to a procedure that was discussed earlier. Click the Case Example button, for example, and the associated procedure is executed, starting with the InputBox statement asking for the user's GPA.

A custom toolbar is created via the Toolbars command within the View menu. The new toolbar is initially big enough to hold only a single button, but you can add, move, and delete buttons following the same procedure as for any other Office toolbar. You can add any command at all to the toolbar; that is, you can add existing commands from within the Office application, or you can add commands that correspond to VBA procedures that you have created. Remember, too, that you can add more buttons to existing office toolbars.

Once the toolbar has been created, it is displayed or hidden just like any other Office toolbar. It can also be docked along any edge of the application window or left floating as shown in Figure 7. It's fun, it's easy, and as you may have guessed, it's time for the next hands-on exercise.

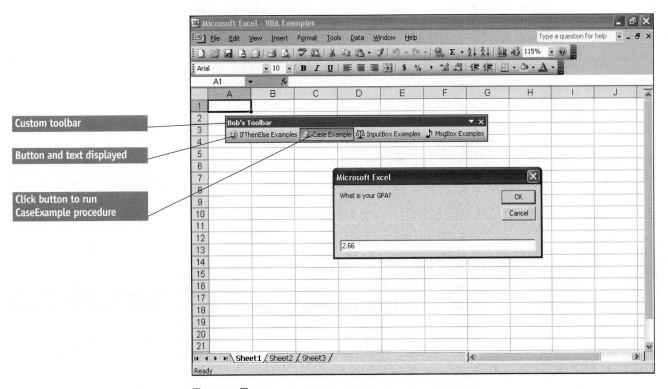

Custom toolbar

Button and text displayed

Click button to run CaseExample procedure

FIGURE 7   Custom Toolbars

2 Decision Making

Objective To create procedures with If . . . Then . . . Else and Case statements, then create a custom toolbar to execute those procedures. Use Figure 8 as a guide in the exercise.

Step 1: **Open the Office Document**

- Open the **VBA Examples workbook** or Access database from the previous exercise. The procedure differs slightly, depending on whether you are using Access or Excel.
  - ❑ In Access, you simply open the database.
  - ❑ In Excel you will be warned that the workbook contains a macro as shown in Figure 8a. Click the button to **Enable Macros**.

- Pull down the **Tools menu,** click the **Macro command,** then click the **Visual Basic Editor command.** You can also use the **Alt+F11** keyboard shortcut to open the VBA editor without going through the Tools menu.

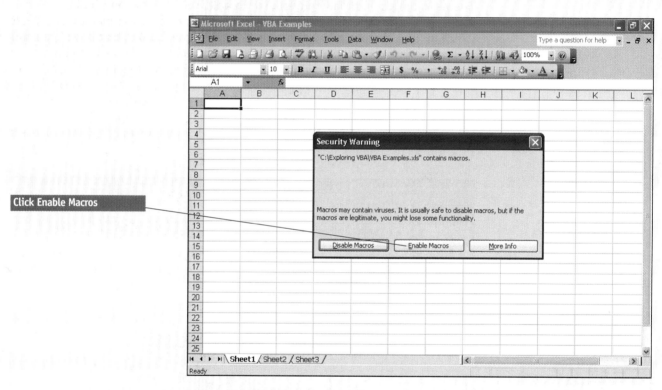

Click Enable Macros

(a) Open the Office Document (step 1)

FIGURE 8   Hands-on Exercise 2

MACRO SECURITY

A computer virus could take the form of an Excel macro; thus, Excel will warn you that a workbook contains a macro, provided the security option is set appropriately. Pull down the Tools menu, click the Options command, click the Security tab, and then set the Macro Security to either High or Medium. High security disables all macros except those from a trusted source. Medium security gives you the option to enable macros. Click the button only if you are sure the macro is from a trusted source.

Step 2: Insert a New Procedure

■ You should be in the Visual Basic editor as shown in Figure 8b. If necessary, double click **Module1** in the Explorer Window to open this module. Pull down the **Insert menu** and click the **Procedure command** to display the Add Procedure dialog box.

■ Click in the **Name** text box and enter **IfThenElseExamples** as the name of the procedure. Click the option buttons for a **Sub procedure** and for **Public scope**. Click **OK** to create the procedure.

■ The Sub procedure should appear within the module and consist of the Sub and End Sub statements as shown in Figure 8b.

■ Click within the newly created procedure, then click the **Procedure View button** at the bottom of the window. The display changes to show just the current procedure.

■ Click the **Save button** to save the module with the new procedure.

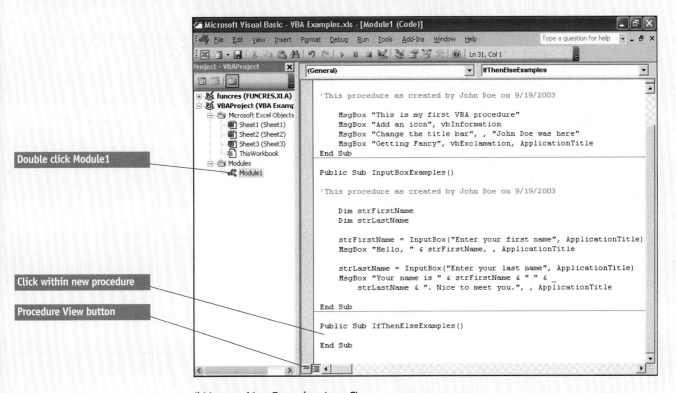

(b) Insert a New Procedure (step 2)

FIGURE 8 Hands-on Exercise 2 (*continued*)

PROCEDURE VIEW VERSUS FULL MODULE VIEW

The procedures within a module can be displayed individually, or alternatively, multiple procedures can be viewed simultaneously. To go from one view to the other, click the Procedure View button at the bottom of the window to display just the procedure you are working on, or click the Full Module View button to display multiple procedures. You can press Ctrl+PgDn and Ctrl+PgUp to move between procedures in either view.

Step 3: Create the If ... Then ... Else Procedure

■ Enter the IfThenElseExamples procedure as it appears in Figure 8c, but use your instructor's name instead of Bob's. Note the following:

□ The Dim statements at the beginning of the procedure are required to define the two variables that are used elsewhere in the procedure.

□ The syntax of the comparison is different for string variables versus numeric variables. String variables require quotation marks around the comparison value (e.g., strInstructorName = "Grauer"). Numeric variables (e.g., intUserStates = 50) do not.

□ Indentation and blank lines are used within a procedure to make the code easier to read, as distinct from a VBA requirement. Press the **Tab key** to indent one level to the right.

□ Comments can be added to a procedure at any time.

■ Save the procedure.

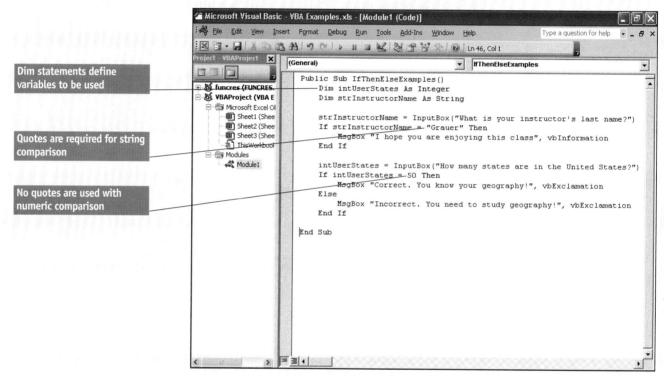

Dim statements define variables to be used

Quotes are required for string comparison

No quotes are used with numeric comparison

(c) Create the If ... Then ... Else Procedure (step 3)

FIGURE 8 Hands-on Exercise 2 (*continued*)

THE COMPLETE WORD TOOL

It's easy to misspell a variable name within a procedure, which is why the Complete Word tool is so useful. Type the first several characters in a variable name (such as "intU" or "strI" in the current procedure), then press Ctrl+Space. VBA will complete the variable name for you, provided that you have already entered a sufficient number of letters for a unique reference. Alternatively, it will display all of the elements that begin with the letters you have entered. Use the down arrow to scroll through the list until you find the item, then press the space bar to complete the entry.

Step 4: Test the Procedure

- The best way to test a procedure is to display its output directly in the VBA window (without having to switch back and forth between that and the application window). Thus, right click the Excel button on the taskbar to display a context-sensitive menu, then click the **Minimize command**.

- There is no visible change on your monitor. Click anywhere within the procedure, then click the **Run Sub button**. You should see the dialog box in Figure 8d.

- Enter your instructor's name, exactly as it was spelled within the VBA procedure. Click **OK**.

- You should see a second message box that hopes you are enjoying the class. This box will be displayed only if you spell the instructor's name correctly. Click **OK**.

- You should see a second input box that asks how many states are in the United States. Enter **50** and click **OK**. You should see a message indicating that you know your geography. Click **OK** to close the dialog box.

- Click the **Run Sub button** a second time, but enter a different set of values in response to the prompts. Misspell your instructor's name, and you will not see the associated message box.

- Enter any number other than 50, and you will be told to study geography.

- Continue to test the procedure until you are satisfied it works under all conditions. We cannot overemphasize the importance of thorough testing!

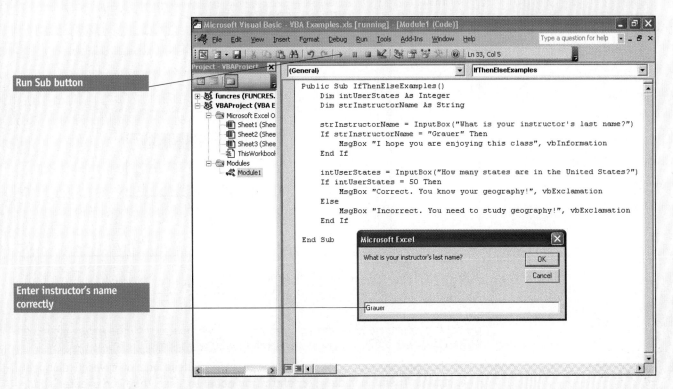

(d) Test the Procedure (step 4)

FIGURE 8   Hands-on Exercise 2 (*continued*)

Step 5: Create and Test the CaseExample Procedure

- Pull down the **Insert menu** and create a new procedure called **CaseExample**, then enter the statements exactly as they appear in Figure 8e. Note:
  - The variable sngUserGPA is declared to be a single-precision floating-point number (as distinct from the integer type that was used previously). A floating-point number is required in order to maintain a decimal point.
  - The GPA must be tested in descending order if the statement is to work correctly.
  - You may use any editing technique with which you are comfortable. You could, for example, enter the first case, copy it four times in the procedure, then modify the copied text as necessary.
  - The use of indentation and blank lines is for the convenience of the programmer and not a requirement of VBA.

- Click the **Run Sub button**, then test the procedure. Be sure to test it under all conditions; that is, you need to run it several times and enter a different GPA each time to be sure that all of the cases are working correctly.

- Save the procedure.

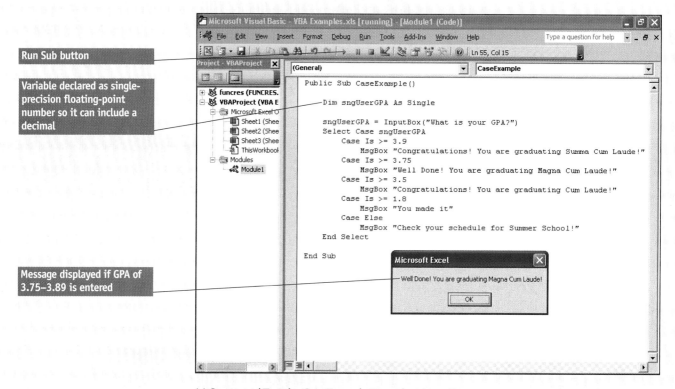

Run Sub button

Variable declared as single-precision floating-point number so it can include a decimal

Message displayed if GPA of 3.75–3.89 is entered

```
Public Sub CaseExample()

    Dim sngUserGPA As Single

    sngUserGPA = InputBox("What is your GPA?")
    Select Case sngUserGPA
        Case Is >= 3.9
            MsgBox "Congratulations! You are graduating Summa Cum Laude!"
        Case Is >= 3.75
            MsgBox "Well Done! You are graduating Magna Cum Laude!"
        Case Is >= 3.5
            MsgBox "Congratulations! You are graduating Cum Laude!"
        Case Is >= 1.8
            MsgBox "You made it"
        Case Else
            MsgBox "Check your schedule for Summer School!"
    End Select

End Sub
```

(e) Create and Test the CaseExample Procedure (step 5)

FIGURE 8   Hands-on Exercise 2 (*continued*)

RELATIONAL OPERATORS

The condition portion of an If or Case statement uses one of several relational operators. These include =, <, and > for equal to, less than, or greater than, respectively. You can also use >=, <=, or <> for greater than or equal to, less than or equal to, or not equal. This is basic, but very important, information if you are to code these statements correctly.

Step 6: **Create a Custom Toolbar**

- Click the **View Microsoft Excel** (or **Access**) **button** to display the associated application window. Pull down the **View menu**, click (or point to) the **Toolbars command**, then click **Customize** to display the Customize dialog box in Figure 8f. (Bob's toolbar is not yet visible.) Click the **Toolbars tab**.

- Click the **New button** to display the New Toolbar dialog box. Enter the name of your toolbar—e.g., **Bob's toolbar**—then click **OK** to create the toolbar and close the New Toolbar dialog box.

- Your toolbar should appear on the screen, but it does not yet contain any buttons. If necessary, click and drag the title bar of your toolbar to move the toolbar within the application window.

- Toggle the check box that appears next to your toolbar within the Customize dialog box on and off to display or hide your toolbar. Leave the box checked to display the toolbar and continue with this exercise.

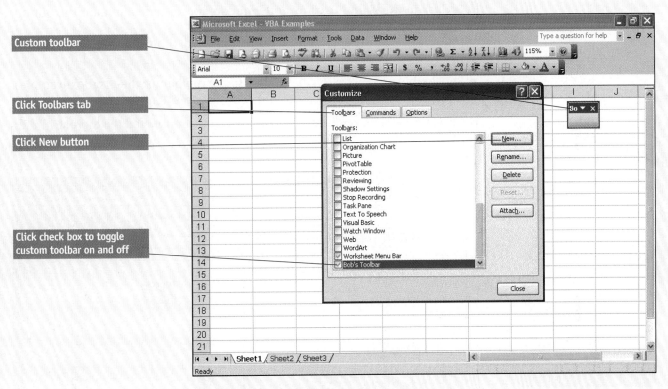

(f) Create a Custom Toolbar (step 6)

FIGURE 8 Hands-on Exercise 2 (*continued*)

FIXED VERSUS FLOATING TOOLBARS

A toolbar may be docked (fixed) along the edge of the application window, or it can be displayed as a floating toolbar anywhere within the window. You can switch back and forth by dragging the move handle of a docked toolbar to move the toolbar away from the edge. Conversely, you can drag the title bar of a floating toolbar to the edge of the window to dock the toolbar. You can also click and drag the border of a floating toolbar to change its size.

Step 7: **Add Buttons to the Toolbar**

- Click the **Commands tab** in the Customize dialog box, click the **down arrow** in the Categories list box, then scroll until you can select the **Macros category**. (If you are using Access and not Excel, you need to select the **File category**, then follow the steps as described in the boxed tip on the next page.)

- Click and drag the **Custom button** to your toolbar and release the mouse. A "happy face" button appears on the toolbar you just created. (You can remove a button from a toolbar by simply dragging the button from the toolbar.)

- Select the newly created button, then click the **Modify Selection command button** (or right click the button to display the context-sensitive menu) in Figure 8g. Change the button's properties as follows:
  - ❏ Click the **Assign Macro command** at the bottom of the menu to display the Assign Macro dialog box, then select the **IfThenElseExamples macro** (procedure) to assign it to the button. Click **OK**.
  - ❏ Click the **Modify Selection button** a second time.
  - ❏ Click in the **Name Textbox** and enter an appropriate name for the button, such as **IfThenElseExamples**.
  - ❏ Click the **Modify Selection button** a third time, then click **Text Only (Always)** to display text rather than an image.

- Repeat this procedure to add buttons to the toolbar for the MsgBoxExamples, InputBoxExamples, and CaseExample procedures that you created earlier.

- Close the Customize dialog box when you have completed the toolbar.

- Save the workbook.

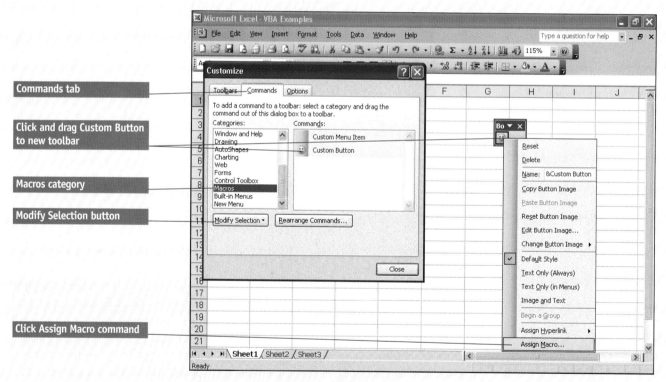

(g) Add Buttons to the Toolbar (step 7)

FIGURE 8 Hands-on Exercise 2 (*continued*)

Step 8: Test the Custom Toolbar

- Click any command on your toolbar as shown in Figure 8h. We clicked the **InputBoxExamples button**, which in turn executed the InputBoxExamples procedure that was created in the first exercise.

- Enter the appropriate information in any input boxes that are displayed. Click **OK**. Close your toolbar when you have completed testing it.

- If this is not your own machine, you should delete your toolbar as a courtesy to the next student. Pull down the **View menu**, click the **Toolbars command**, click **Customize** to display the Customize dialog box, then click the **Toolbars tab**. Select (highlight) the toolbar, then click the **Delete button** in the Customize dialog box. Click **OK** to delete the button. Close the dialog box.

- Exit Office if you do not want to continue with the next exercise.

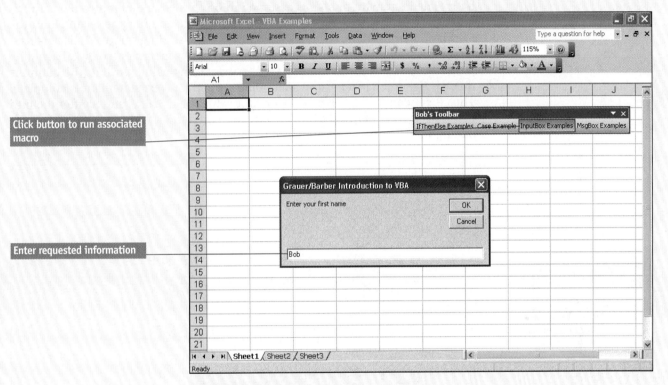

Click button to run associated macro

Enter requested information

(h) Test the Custom Toolbar (step 8)

FIGURE 8 Hands-on Exercise 2 (*continued*)

ACCESS IS DIFFERENT

The procedure to add buttons to a custom toolbar in Access is different from the procedure in Excel. Pull down the View menu, click the Toolbars command, then click the Customize command. Select the File category within the Customize dialog box, then click and drag the Custom command to the newly created toolbar. Select the command on the toolbar, then click the Modify Selection command button in the dialog box. Click Properties, click the On Action text box, then type the name of the procedure you want to run in the format, =procedurename(). Close the dialog boxes, then press Alt+F11 to return to the VBA editor. Change the keyword "Sub" that identifies the procedure to "Function". Return to the database window, then test the newly created toolbar.

FOR . . . NEXT STATEMENT

The ***For . . . Next statement*** executes all statements between the words For and Next a specified number of times, using a counter to keep track of the number of times the statements are executed. The statement, For intCounter = 1 to N, executes the statements within the loop N times.

The procedure in Figure 9 contains two For . . . Next statements that sum the numbers from 1 to 10, counting by 1 and 2, respectively. The Dim statements at the beginning of the procedure declare two variables, intSumofNumbers to hold the sum and intCounter to hold the value of the counter. The sum is initialized to zero immediately before the first loop. The statements in the loop are then executed 10 times, each time incrementing the sum by the value of the counter. The result (the sum of the numbers from 1 to 10) is displayed after the loop in Figure 9b.

The second For . . . Next statement increments the counter by 2 rather than by 1. (The increment or step is assumed to be 1 unless a different value is specified.) The sum of the numbers is reset to zero prior to entering the second loop, the loop is entered, and the counter is initialized to the starting value of 1. Each subsequent time through the loop, however, the counter is incremented by 2. Each time the value of the counter is compared to the ending value, until it (the counter) exceeds the ending value, at which point the For . . . Next statement is complete. Thus the second loop will be executed for values of 1, 3, 5, 7, and 9. After the fifth time through the loop, the counter is incremented to 11, which is greater than the ending value of 10, and the loop is terminated.

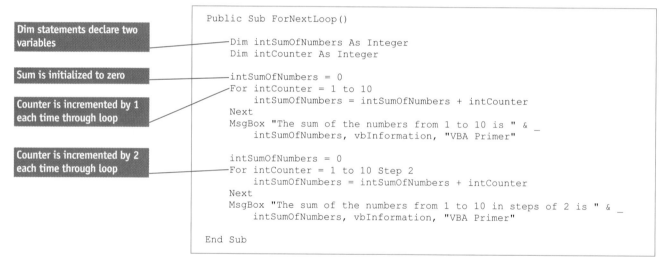

Dim statements declare two variables

Sum is initialized to zero

Counter is incremented by 1 each time through loop

Counter is incremented by 2 each time through loop

```
Public Sub ForNextLoop()

    Dim intSumOfNumbers As Integer
    Dim intCounter As Integer

    intSumOfNumbers = 0
    For intCounter = 1 to 10
        intSumOfNumbers = intSumOfNumbers + intCounter
    Next
    MsgBox "The sum of the numbers from 1 to 10 is " & _
        intSumOfNumbers, vbInformation, "VBA Primer"

    intSumOfNumbers = 0
    For intCounter = 1 to 10 Step 2
        intSumOfNumbers = intSumOfNumbers + intCounter
    Next
    MsgBox "The sum of the numbers from 1 to 10 in steps of 2 is " & _
        intSumOfNumbers, vbInformation, "VBA Primer"

End Sub
```

(a) VBA Code

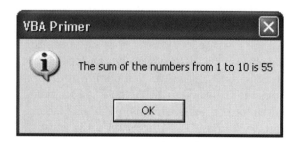

(b) In Increments of 1

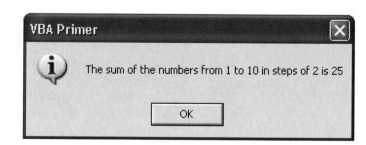

(c) In Increments of 2

FIGURE 9 For . . . Next Loops

DO LOOPS

The For . . . Next statement is ideal when you know in advance how many times you want to go through a loop. There are many instances, however, when the number of times through the loop is indeterminate. You could, for example, give a user multiple chances to enter a password or answer a question. This type of logic is implemented through a Do loop. You can repeat the loop as long as a condition is true (Do While), or until a condition becomes true (Do Until). The choice depends on how you want to state the condition.

Regardless of which keyword you choose, Do While or Do Until, two formats are available. The difference is subtle and depends on whether the keyword (While or Until) appears at the beginning or end of the loop. Our discussion will use the Do Until statement, but the Do While statement works in similar fashion.

Look closely at the procedure in Figure 10a, which contains two different loops. In the first example the Until condition appears at the end of the loop, which means the statements in the loop are executed, and then the condition is tested. This ensures that the statements in the loop will be executed at least once. The second loop, however, places the Until condition at the beginning of the loop, so that it (the condition) is tested prior to the loop being executed. Thus, if the condition is satisfied initially, the second loop will never be executed. In other words, there are two distinct statements **Do . . . Loop Until** and **Do Until . . . Loop**. The first statement executes the loop, then tests the condition. The second statement tests the condition, then enters the loop.

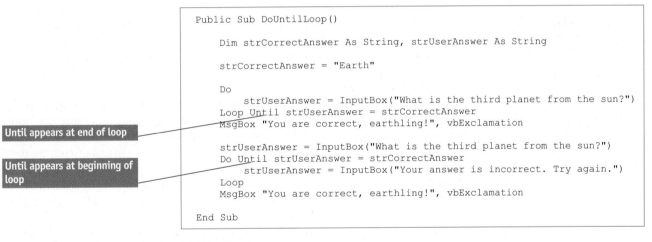

Until appears at end of loop

Until appears at beginning of loop

```
Public Sub DoUntilLoop()

    Dim strCorrectAnswer As String, strUserAnswer As String

    strCorrectAnswer = "Earth"

    Do
        strUserAnswer = InputBox("What is the third planet from the sun?")
    Loop Until strUserAnswer = strCorrectAnswer
    MsgBox "You are correct, earthling!", vbExclamation

    strUserAnswer = InputBox("What is the third planet from the sun?")
    Do Until strUserAnswer = strCorrectAnswer
        strUserAnswer = InputBox("Your answer is incorrect. Try again.")
    Loop
    MsgBox "You are correct, earthling!", vbExclamation

End Sub
```

(a) (VBA Code)

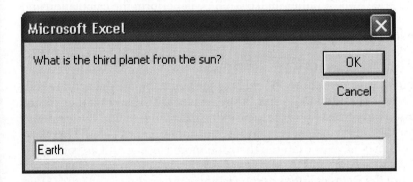

(b) Input the Answer

(c) Correct Response

FIGURE 10 Do Until Loops

(d) Wrong Answer Initially   (e) Second Chance

FIGURE 10   Do Until Loops (*continued*)

It's tricky, but stay with us. In the first example the user is asked the question within the loop, and the loop is executed repeatedly until the user gives the correct answer. In the second example the user is asked the question outside of the loop, and the loop is bypassed if the user answers it correctly. The latter is the preferred logic because it enables us to phrase the question differently, before and during the loop. Look carefully at the difference between the InputBox statements and see how the question changes within the second loop.

DEBUGGING

As you learn more about VBA and develop more powerful procedures, you are more likely to make mistakes. The process of finding and correcting errors within a procedure is known as *debugging* and it is an integral part of programming. Do not be discouraged if you make mistakes. Everyone does. The important thing is how quickly you are able to find and correct the errors that invariably occur. We begin our discussion of debugging by describing two types of errors, *compilation errors* and *execution* (or *run-time*) *errors*.

A compilation error is simply an error in VBA syntax. (Compilation is the process of translating a VBA procedure into machine language, and thus a compilation error occurs when the VBA editor is unable to convert a statement to machine language.) Compilation errors occur for many reasons, such as misspelling a keyword, omitting a comma, and so on. VBA recognizes the error before the procedure is run and displays the invalid statement in red together with an associated error message. The programmer corrects the error and then reruns the procedure.

Execution errors are caused by errors in logic and are more difficult to detect because they occur without any error message. VBA, or for that matter any other programming language, does what you tell it to do, which is not necessarily what you want it to do. If, for example, you were to compute the sales tax of an item by multiplying the price by 60% rather than 6%, VBA will perform the calculation and simply display the wrong answer. It is up to you to realize that the results of the procedure are incorrect, and you will need to examine its statements and correct the mistake.

So how do you detect an execution error? In essence, you must decide what the expected output of your procedure should be, then you compare the actual result of the procedure to the intended result. If the results are different, an error has occurred, and you have to examine the logic in the procedure to find the error. You may see the mistake immediately (e.g., using 60% rather than 6% in the previous example), or you may have to examine the code more closely. And as you might expect, VBA has a variety of tools to help you in the debugging process. These tools are accessed from the *Debug toolbar* or the *Debug menu* as shown in Figure 11 on the next page.

The procedure in Figure 11 is a simple For . . . Next loop to sum the integers from 1 to 10. The procedure is correct as written, but we have introduced several debugging techniques into the figure. The most basic technique is to step through the statements in the procedure one at a time to see the sequence in which the statements are executed. Click the **Step Into button** on the Debug toolbar to enter (step into) the procedure, then continue to click the button to move through the procedure. Each time you click the button, the statement that is about to be executed is highlighted.

Another useful technique is to display the values of selected variables as they change during execution. This is accomplished through the **Debug.Print statement** that displays the values in the **Immediate window**. The Debug.Print statement is placed within the For . . . Next loop so that you can see how the counter and the associated sum change during execution.

As the figure now stands, we have gone through the loop nine times, and the sum of the numbers from 1 to 9 is 45. The Step Into button is in effect so that the statement to be executed next is highlighted. You can see that we are back at the top of the loop, where the counter has been incremented to 10, and further, that we are about to increment the sum.

The **Locals window** is similar in concept except that it displays only the current values of all the variables within the procedure. Unlike the Immediate window, which requires the insertion of Debug.Print statements into a procedure to have meaning, the Locals window displays its values automatically, without any effort on the part of the programmer, other than opening the window. All three techniques can be used individually, or in conjunction with one another, as the situation demands.

We believe that the best time to practice debugging is when you know there are no errors in your procedure. As you may have guessed, it's time for the next hands-on exercise.

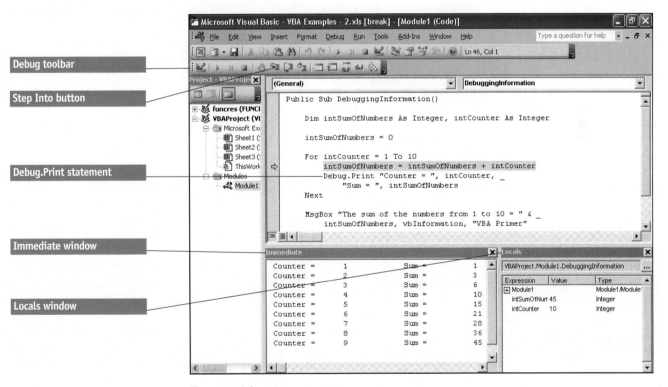

FIGURE 11 Debugging

3 Loops and Debugging

Objective To create a loop using the For . . . Next and Do Until statements; to open the Locals and Immediate windows and illustrate different techniques for debugging. Use Figure 12 as a guide in the exercise.

Step 1: **Insert a New Procedure**

- Open the **VBA Examples workbook** or the Access database from the previous exercise. Either way, pull down the **Tools menu**, click the **Macro command**, then click **Visual Basic editor** (or use the **Alt+F11** keyboard shortcut) to start the VBA editor.

- If necessary, double click **Module1** within the Project Explorer window to open this module. Pull down the **Insert menu** and click the **Procedure command** to display the Add Procedure dialog box.

- Click in the **Name** text box and enter **ForNextLoop** as the name of the procedure. Click the option buttons for a **Sub procedure** and for **Public scope**. Click **OK** to create the procedure.

- The Sub procedure should appear within the module and consist of the Sub and End Sub statements as shown in Figure 12a.

- Click the **Procedure View button** at the bottom of the window as shown in Figure 12a. The display changes to show just the current procedure, giving you more room in which to work.

- Save the module.

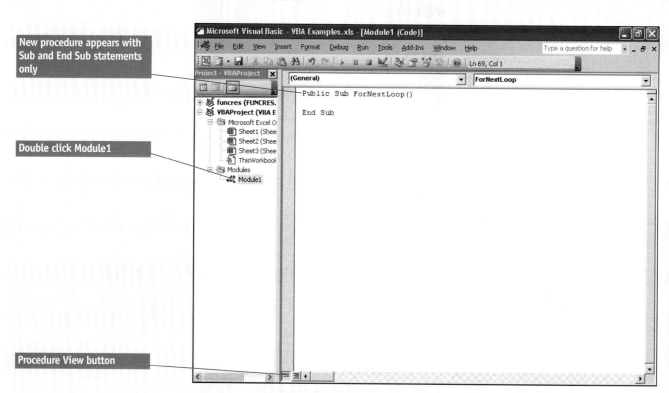

(a) Insert a New Procedure (step 1)

FIGURE 12 Hands-on Exercise 3

Step 2: **Test the For … Next Procedure**

- Enter the procedure exactly as it appears in Figure 12b. Note the following:
  - ❑ A comment is added at the beginning of the procedure to identify the author and the date.
  - ❑ Two variables are declared at the beginning of the procedure, one to hold the sum of the numbers and the other to serve as a counter.
  - ❑ The sum of the numbers is initialized to zero. The For … Next loop varies the counter from 1 to 10.
  - ❑ The statement within the For … Next loop increments the sum of the numbers by the current value of the counter. The equal sign is really a replacement operator; that is, replace the variable on the left (the sum of the numbers) by the expression on the right (the sum of the numbers plus the value of the counter.
  - ❑ Indentation and spacing within a procedure are for the convenience of the programmer and not a requirement of VBA. We align the For and Next statements at the beginning and end of a loop, then indent all statements within a loop.
  - ❑ The MsgBox statement displays the result and is continued over two lines as per the underscore at the end of the first line.
  - ❑ The ampersand concatenates (joins together) the text and the number within the message box.

- Click the **Save button** to save the module. Right click the **Excel button** on the Windows taskbar to display a context-sensitive menu, then click the **Minimize command**.

- Click the **Run Sub button** to test the procedure, which should display the MsgBox statement in Figure 12b. Correct any errors that may occur.

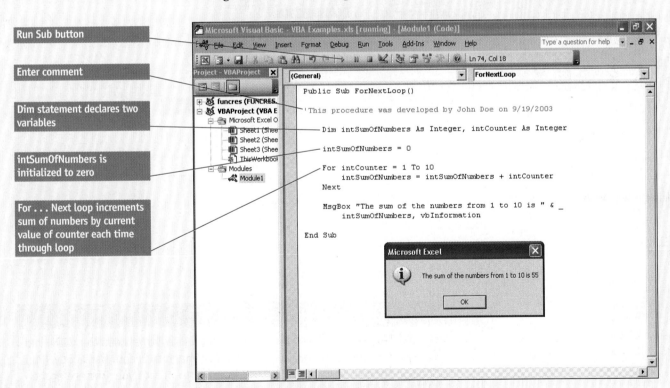

(b) Test the For … Next Procedure (step 2)

FIGURE 12 Hands-on Exercise 3 (*continued*)

Step 3: Compilation Errors

- The best time to practice debugging is when you know that the procedure is working properly. Accordingly, we will make some deliberate errors in our procedure to illustrate different debugging techniques.

- Pull down the **View menu**, click the **Toolbars command**, and (if necessary) toggle the Debug toolbar on, then dock it under the Standard toolbar.

- Click on the statement that initializes intSumOfNumbers to zero and delete the "s" at the end of the variable name. Click the **Run Sub button**.

- You will see the message in Figure 12c. Click **OK** to acknowledge the error, then click the **Undo button** to correct the error.

- The procedure header is highlighted, indicating that execution is temporarily suspended and that additional action is required from you to continue testing. Click the **Run Sub button** to retest the procedure.

- This time the procedure executes correctly and you see the MsgBox statement indicating that the sum of the numbers from 1 to 10 is 55. Click **OK**.

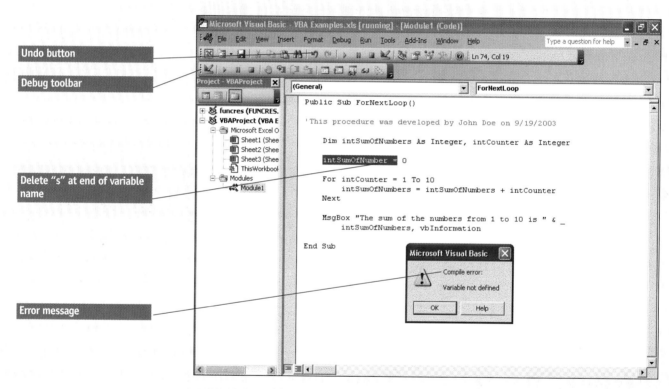

(c) Compilation Error (step 3)

FIGURE 12 Hands-on Exercise 3 (*continued*)

USE HELP AS NECESSARY

Pull down the Help menu at any time (or press the F1 key) to access the VBA Help facility to explore at your leisure. Use the Print command to create hard copy. (You can also copy the help text into a Word document to create your own reference manual.) The answers to virtually all of your questions are readily available if only you take the time to look.

Step 4: **Step through a Procedure**

- Pull down the **View menu** a second time and click the **Locals Window command** (or click the **Locals Window button** on the Debug toolbar).

- If necessary, click and drag the top border of the Locals window to size the window appropriately as shown in Figure 12d.

- Click anywhere within the procedure. Pull down the **Debug menu** and click the **Step Into command** (or click the **Step Into button** on the Debug toolbar). The first statement (the procedure header) is highlighted, indicating that you are about to enter the procedure.

- Click the **Step Into button** (or use the **F8** keyboard shortcut) to step into the procedure and advance to the next executable statement. The statement that initializes intSumOfNumbers to zero is highlighted, indicating that this statement is about to be executed.

- Continue to press the **F8 key** to step through the procedure. Each time you execute a statement, you can see the values of intSumOfNumbers and intCounter change within the Locals window. (You can click the **Step Out button** at any time to end the procedure.)

- Correct errors as they occur. Click the **Reset button** on the Standard or Debug toolbars at any time to begin executing the procedure from the beginning.

- Eventually you exit from the loop, and the sum of the numbers (from 1 to 10) is displayed within a message box.

- Click **OK** to close the message box. Press the **F8 key** a final time, then close the Locals window.

- Do you see how stepping through a procedure helps you to understand how it works?

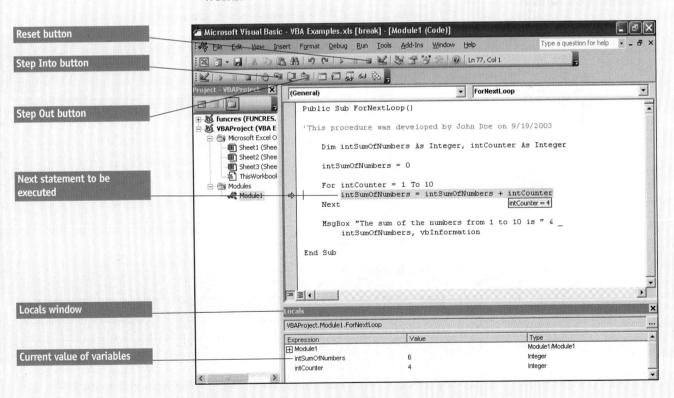

(d) Step through a Procedure (step 4)

FIGURE 12 Hands-on Exercise 3 (*continued*)

Step 5:   The Immediate Window

- You should be back in the VBA window. Click immediately to the left of the Next statement and press **Enter** to insert a blank line. Type the **Debug.Print** statement exactly as shown in Figure 12e. (Click **OK** if you see a message indicating that the procedure will be reset.)

- Pull down the **View menu** and click the **Immediate Window command** (or click the **Immediate Window button** on the Debug toolbar). The Immediate window should be empty, but if not, you can click and drag to select the contents, then press the **Del key** to clear the window.

- Click anywhere within the For . . . Next procedure, then click the **Run Sub button** to execute the procedure. You will see the familiar message box indicating that the sum of the numbers is 55. Click **OK**.

- You should see 10 lines within the Immediate window as shown in Figure 12e, corresponding to the values displayed by the Debug.Print statement as it was executed within the loop.

- Close the Immediate window. Do you see how displaying the intermediate results of a procedure helps you to understand how it works?

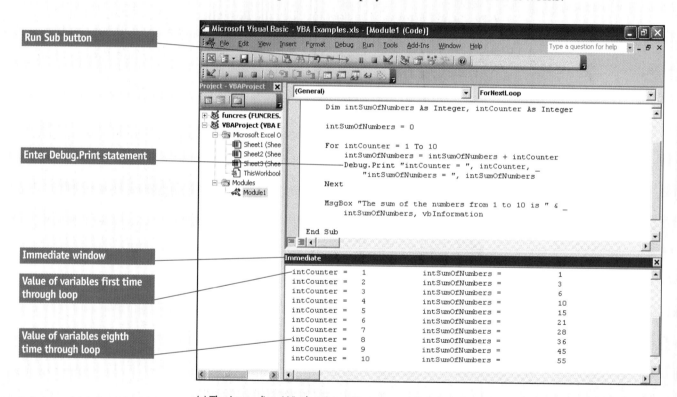

(e) The Immediate Window (step 5)

FIGURE 12   Hands-on Exercise 3 (continued)

INSTANT CALCULATOR

Use the Print method (action) in the Immediate window to use VBA as a calculator. Press Ctrl+G at any time to display the Immediate window. Click in the window, then type the statement Debug.Print, followed by your calculation, for example, Debug.Print 2+2, and press Enter. The answer is displayed on the next line in the Immediate window.

Step 6: A More General Procedure

- Modify the existing procedure to make it more general—for example, to sum the values from any starting value to any ending value:
  - ❏ Click at the end of the existing Dim statement to position the insertion point, press **Enter** to create a new line, then add the second **Dim statement** as shown in Figure 12f.
  - ❏ Click before the For statement, press **Enter** to create a blank line, press **Enter** a second time, then enter the two **InputBox statements** to ask the user for the beginning and ending values.
  - ❏ Modify the For statement to execute from **intStart** to **intEnd** rather than from 1 to 10.
  - ❏ Change the MsgBox statement to reflect the values of intStart and intEnd, and a customized title bar. Note the use of the ampersand and the underscore, to indicate concatenation and continuation, respectively.

- Click the **Save button** to save the module.

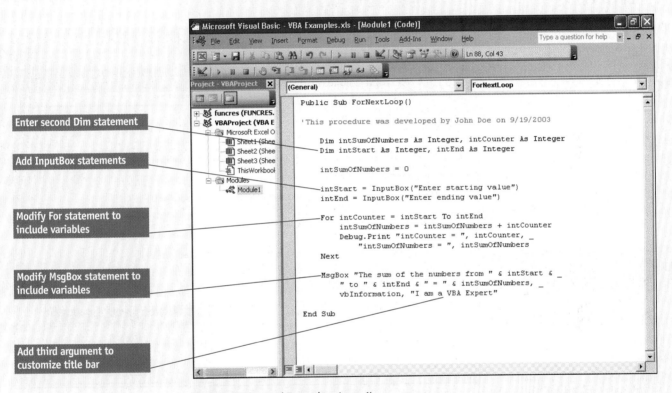

(f) A More General Procedure (step 6)

FIGURE 12 Hands-on Exercise 3 (*continued*)

USE WHAT YOU KNOW

Use the techniques acquired from other applications such as Microsoft Word to facilitate editing within the VBA window. Press the Ins key to toggle between the insert and overtype modes as you modify the statements within a VBA procedure. You can also cut, copy, and paste statements (or parts of statements) within a procedure and from one procedure to another. The Find and Replace commands are also useful.

Step 7: Test the Procedure

- Click the **Run Sub button** to test the procedure. You should be prompted for a beginning and an ending value. Enter any numbers you like, such as 10 and 20, respectively, to match the result in Figure 12g.

- The value displayed in the MsgBox statement should reflect the numbers you entered. For example, you will see a sum of 165 if you entered 10 and 20 as the starting and ending values.

- Look carefully at the message box that is displayed in Figure 12g. Its title bar displays the literal "I am a VBA expert", corresponding to the last argument in the MsgBox statement.

- Note, too, the spacing that appears within the message box, which includes spaces before and after each number. Look at your results and, if necessary, modify the MsgBox statement so that you have the same output. Click **OK**.

- Save the procedure.

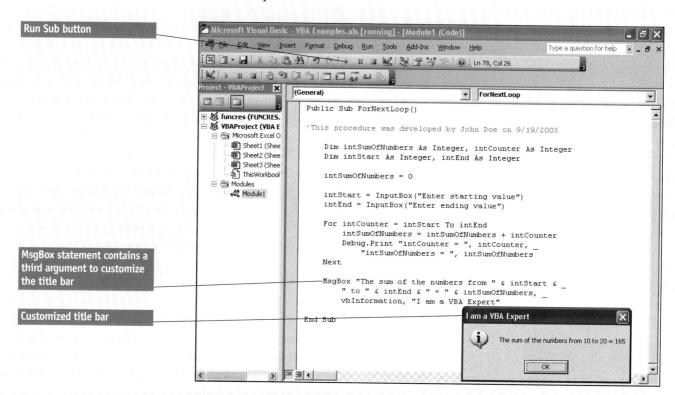

(g) Test the Procedure (step 7)

FIGURE 12   Hands-on Exercise 3 (*continued*)

CHANGE THE INCREMENT

The For . . . Next statement can be made more general by supplying an increment within the For statement. Try For intCount = 1 To 10 Step 2, or more generally, For intCount = intStart to intEnd Step intStepValue. "Step" is a Visual Basic keyword and must be entered that way. intCount, intEnd, and intStepValue are user-defined variables. The variables must be defined at the beginning of a procedure and can be initialized by requesting values from the user through the InputBox statement.

Step 8: Create a Do Until Loop

■ Pull down the **Insert menu** and click the **Procedure command** to insert a new procedure called **DoUntilLoop**. Enter the procedure as it appears in Figure 12h. Note the following:
  ❑ Two string variables are declared to hold the correct answer and the user's response, respectively.
  ❑ The variable strCorrectAnswer is set to "Earth", which is the correct answer for our question.
  ❑ The initial InputBox function prompts the user to enter his/her response to the question. A second InputBox function appears in the loop that is executed if and only if the user enters the wrong answer.
  ❑ The Until condition appears at the beginning of the loop, so that the loop is entered only if the user answers incorrectly. The loop executes repeatedly until the correct answer is supplied.
  ❑ A message to the user is displayed at the end of the procedure after the correct answer has been entered.

■ Click the **Run Sub button** to test the procedure. Enter the correct answer on your first attempt, and you will see that the loop is never entered.

■ Rerun the procedure, answer incorrectly, then note that a second input box appears, telling you that your answer was incorrect. Click **OK**.

■ Once again you are prompted for the answer. Enter **Earth**. Click **OK**. The procedure ends.

■ Save the procedure.

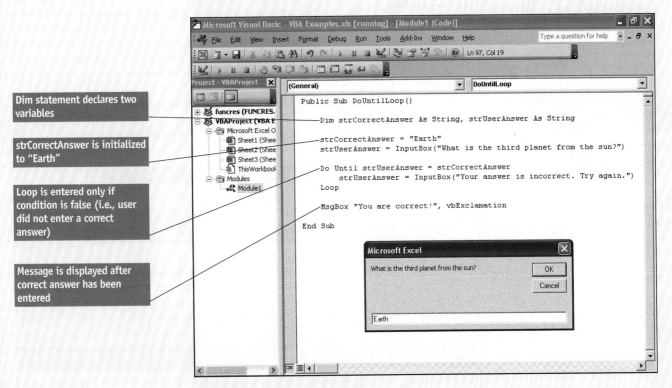

Dim statement declares two variables

strCorrectAnswer is initialized to "Earth"

Loop is entered only if condition is false (i.e., user did not enter a correct answer)

Message is displayed after correct answer has been entered

(h) Create a Do Until Loop (step 8)

FIGURE 12 Hands-on Exercise 3 (*continued*)

Step 9: A More Powerful Procedure

- Modify the procedure as shown in Figure 12i to include the statements to count and print the number of times the user takes to get the correct answer.
  - ❑ The variable intNumberOfAttempts is declared as an integer and is initialized to 1 after the user inputs his/her initial answer.
  - ❑ The Do loop is expanded to increment intNumberOfAttempts by 1 each time the loop is executed.
  - ❑ The MsgBox statement after the loop is expanded prints the number of attempts the user took to answer the question.

- Save the module, then click the **Run Sub button** to test the module. You should see a dialog box similar to the one in Figure 12i. Click **OK**. Do you see how this procedure improves on its predecessor?

- Pull down the **File menu** and click the **Print command** to display the Print dialog box. Click the option button to print the current module for your instructor. Click **OK**.

- Close the Debug toolbar. Exit Office if you do not want to continue with the next hands-on exercise at this time.

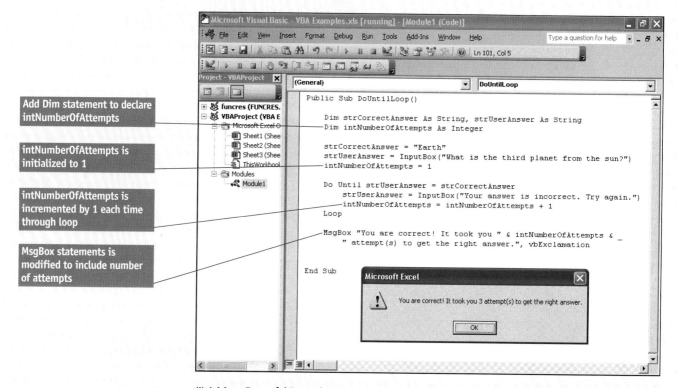

(i) A More Powerful Procedure (step 9)

FIGURE 12 Hands-on Exercise 3 (*continued*)

IT'S NOT EQUAL, BUT REPLACE

All programming languages use statements of the form N = N + 1, in which the equal sign does not mean equal in the literal sense; that is, N cannot equal N + 1. The equal sign is really a replacement operator. Thus, the expression on the right of the equal sign is evaluated, and that result replaces the value of the variable on the left. In other words, the statement N = N + 1 increments the value of N by 1.

Our approach thus far has focused on VBA as an independent entity that can be run without specific reference to the applications in Microsoft Office. We have covered several individual statements, explained how to use the VBA editor to create and run procedures, and how to debug those procedures, if necessary. We hope you have found the material to be interesting, but you may be asking yourself, "What does this have to do with Microsoft Office?" In other words, how can you use your knowledge of VBA to enhance your ability in Microsoft Excel or Access? The answer is to create *event procedures* that run automatically in response to events within an Office application.

VBA is different from traditional programming languages in that it is event-driven. An *event* is defined as any action that is recognized by an application such as Excel or Access. Opening or closing an Excel workbook or an Access database is an event. Selecting a worksheet within a workbook is also an event, as is clicking on a command button on an Access form. To use VBA within Microsoft Office, you decide which events are significant, and what is to happen when those events occur. Then you develop the appropriate event procedures.

Consider, for example, Figure 13, which displays the results of two event procedures in conjunction with opening and closing an Excel workbook. (If you are using Microsoft Access instead of Excel, you can skip this discussion and the associated exercise, and move to the parallel material for Access that appears after the next hands-on exercise.) The procedure associated with Figure 13a displays a message that appears automatically after the user executes the command to close the associated workbook. The procedure is almost trivial to write, and consists of a single MsgBox statement. The effect of the procedure is quite significant, however, as it reminds the user to back up his or her work after closing the workbook. Nor does it matter how the user closes the workbook—whether by pulling down the menu or using a keyboard shortcut—because the procedure runs automatically in response to the Close Workbook event, regardless of how that event occurs.

The dialog box in Figure 13b prompts the user for a password and appears automatically when the user opens the workbook. The logic here is more sophisticated in that the underlying procedure contains an InputBox statement to request the password, a Do Until loop that is executed until the user enters the correct password or exceeds the allotted number of attempts, then additional logic to display the worksheet or terminate the application if the user fails to enter the proper password. The procedure is not difficult, however, and it builds on the VBA statements that were covered earlier.

The next hands-on exercise has you create the two event procedures that are associated with Figure 13. As you do the exercise, you will gain additional experience with VBA and an appreciation for the potential event procedures within Microsoft Office.

HIDING AND UNHIDING A WORKSHEET

Look carefully at the workbooks in Figures 13a and 13b. Both figures reference the identical workbook, Financial Consultant, as can be seen from the title bar. Look at the worksheet tabs, however, and note that two worksheets are visible in Figure 13a, whereas the Calculations worksheet is hidden in Figure 13b. This was accomplished in the Open workbook procedure and was implemented to hide the calculations from the user until the correct password was entered.

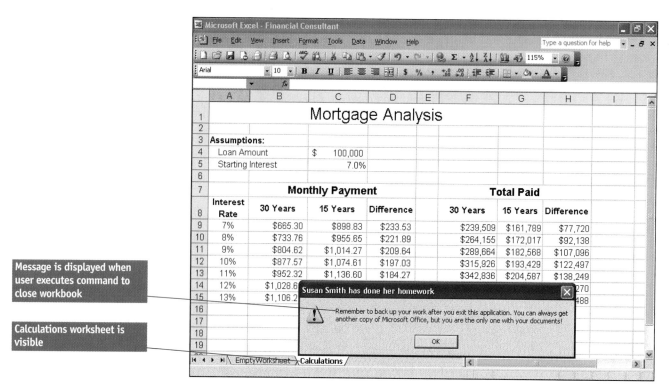

Message is displayed when user executes command to close workbook

Calculations worksheet is visible

(a) Message to the User (Close Workbook event)

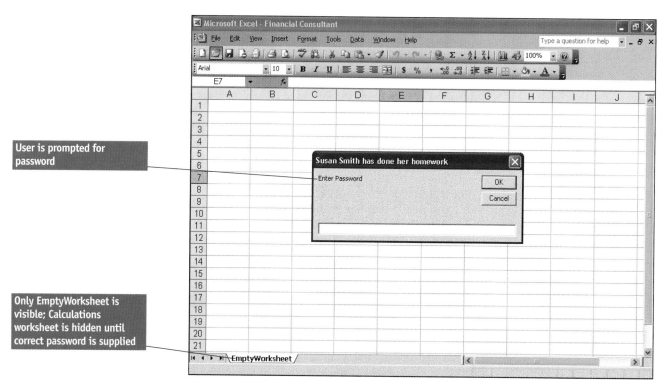

User is prompted for password

Only EmptyWorksheet is visible; Calculations worksheet is hidden until correct password is supplied

(b) Password Protection (Open Workbook event)

FIGURE 13 Event-Driven Programming

Event-Driven Programming (Microsoft Excel)

Objective To create an event procedure to implement password protection that is associated with opening an Excel workbook; to create a second event procedure that displays a message to the user upon closing the workbook. Use Figure 14 as a guide in the exercise.

Step 1: **Create the Close Workbook Procedure**

- Open the **VBA Examples workbook** you have used for the previous exercises and enable the macros. If you have been using Access rather than Excel, start Excel, open a new workbook, then save the workbook as **VBA Examples**.

- Pull down the **Tools menu**, click the **Macro command**, then click the **Visual Basic Editor command** (or use the **Alt+F11** keyboard shortcut).

- You should see the Project Explorer pane as shown in Figure 14a, but if not, pull down the **View menu** and click the **Project Explorer**. Double click **ThisWorkbook** to create a module for the workbook as a whole.

- Enter the **Option Explicit statement** if it is not there already, then press **Enter** to create a new line. Type the statement to declare the variable, **ApplicationTitle**, using your name instead of Susan Smith.

- Click the **down arrow** in the Object list box and select **Workbook**, then click the **down arrow** in the Procedure list box and select the **BeforeClose event** to create the associated procedure. (If you choose a different event by mistake, click and drag to select the associated statements, then press the **Del key** to delete the procedure.)

- Enter the comment and MsgBox statement as it appears in Figure 14a.

- Save the procedure.

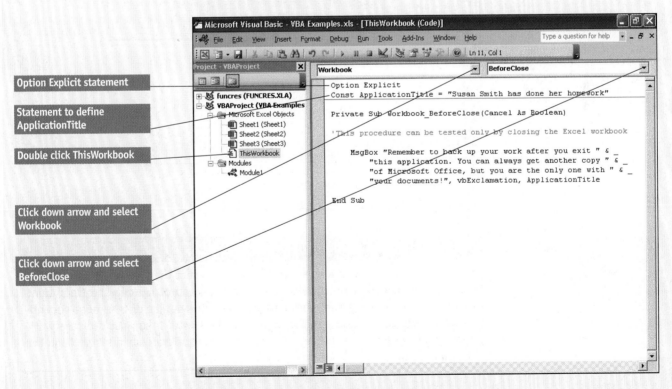

(a) Create the Close Workbook Procedure (step 1)

FIGURE 14 Hands-on Exercise 4

Step 2: Test the Close Workbook Procedure

- Click the **View Microsoft Excel button** on the Standard toolbar or on the Windows taskbar to view the Excel workbook. The workbook is not empty; that is, it does not contain any cell entries, but it does contain multiple VBA procedures.

- Pull down the **File menu** and click the **Close command**, which runs the procedure you just created and displays the dialog box in Figure 14b. Click **OK** after you have read the message, then click **Yes** if asked to save the workbook.

- Pull down the **File menu** and reopen the **VBA Examples workbook**, enabling the macros. Press **Alt+F11** to return to the VBA window to create an additional procedure.

- Double click **ThisWorkbook** from within the Project Explorer pane to return to the BeforeClose procedure and make the necessary corrections, if any.

- Save the procedure.

Message is displayed when you execute the Close command

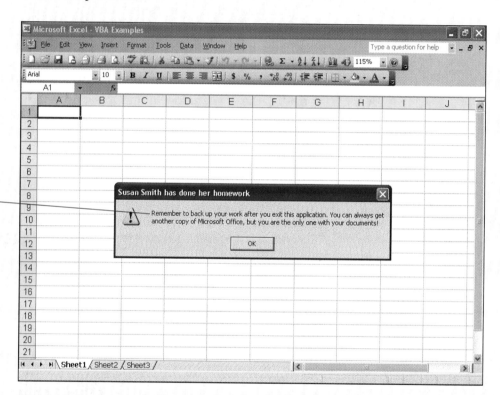

Susan Smith has done her homework

Remember to back up your work after you exit this application. You can always get another copy of Microsoft Office, but you are the only one with your documents!

OK

(b) Test the Close Workbook Procedure (step 2)

FIGURE 14 Hands-on Exercise 4 (*continued*)

THE MOST RECENTLY OPENED FILE LIST

One way to open a recently used workbook is to select the workbook directly from the File menu. Pull down the File menu, but instead of clicking the Open command, check to see if the workbook appears on the list of the most recently opened workbooks located at the bottom of the menu. If so, just click the workbook name, rather than having to make the appropriate selections through the Open dialog box.

Step 3: Start the Open Workbook Event Procedure

- Click within the Before Close procedure, then click the **Procedure View button** at the bottom of the Code window. Click the **down arrow** in the Procedure list box and select the **Open event** to create an event procedure.

- Enter the VBA statements as shown in Figure 14c. Note the following:
  - ❏ Three variables are required for this procedure—the correct password, the password entered by the user, and the number of attempts.
  - ❏ The user is prompted for the password, and the number of attempts is set to 1. The user is given two additional attempts, if necessary, to get the password correct. The loop is bypassed, however, if the user supplies the correct password on the first attempt.

- Minimize Excel. Save the procedure, then click the **Run Sub button** to test it. Try different combinations in your testing; that is, enter the correct password on the first, second, and third attempts. The password is case-sensitive.

- Correct errors as they occur. Click the **Reset button** at any time to begin executing the procedure from the beginning. Save the procedure.

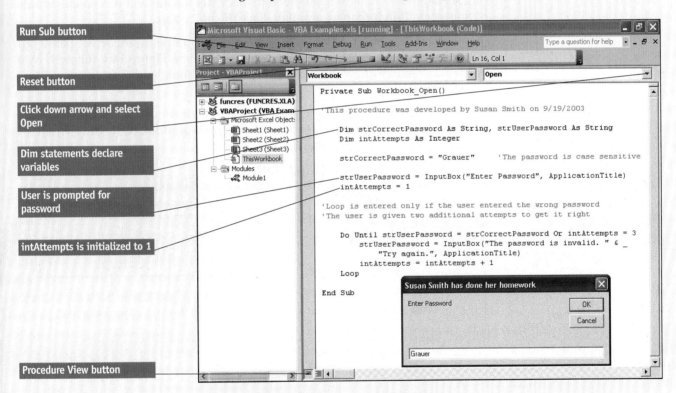

Run Sub button

Reset button

Click down arrow and select Open

Dim statements declare variables

User is prompted for password

intAttempts is initialized to 1

Procedure View button

(c) Start the Open Workbook Event Procedure (step 3)

FIGURE 14 Hands-on Exercise 4 *(continued)*

THE OBJECT AND PROCEDURE BOXES

The Object box at the top of the code window displays the selected object such as an Excel workbook, whereas the Procedure box displays the name of the events appropriate to that object. Events that already have procedures appear in bold. Clicking an event that is not bold creates the procedure header and End Sub statements for that event.

Step 4: Complete the Open Workbook Event Procedure

- Enter the remaining statements in the procedure as shown in Figure 14d. Note the following:
  - ❏ The If statement determines whether the user has entered the correct password and, if so, displays the appropriate message.
  - ❏ If, however, the user fails to supply the correct password, a different message is displayed, and the workbook will close due to the **Workbooks.Close statement** within the procedure.
  - ❏ As a precaution, put an apostrophe in front of the Workbooks.Close statement so that it is a comment, and thus it is not executed. Once you are sure that you can enter the correct password, you can remove the apostrophe and implement the password protection.

- Save the procedure, then click the **Run Sub button** to test it. Be sure that you can enter the correct password (**Grauer**), and that you realize the password is case-sensitive.

- Delete the apostrophe in front of the Workbooks.Close statement. The text of the statement changes from green to black to indicate that it is an executable statement rather than a comment. Save the procedure.

- Click the **Run Sub button** a second time, then enter an incorrect password three times in a row. You will see the dialog box in Figure 14d, followed by a message reminding you to back up your workbook, and then the workbook will close.

- The first message makes sense, the second does not make sense in this context. Thus, we need to modify the Close Workbook procedure when an incorrect password is entered.

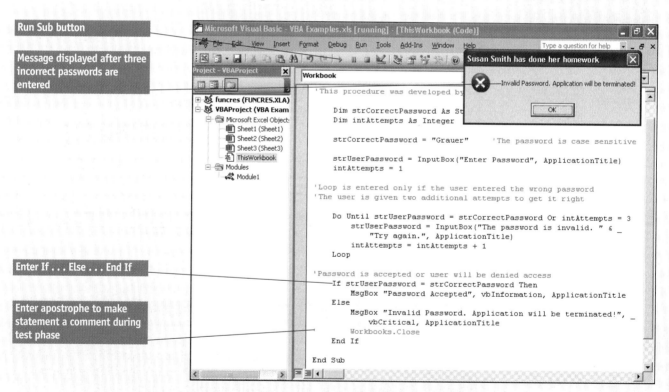

(d) Complete the Open Workbook Event Procedure (step 4)

FIGURE 14 Hands-on Exercise 4 (*continued*)

Step 5: Modify the Before Close Event Procedure

- Reopen the **VBA Examples workbook**. Click the button to **Enable Macros**.

- Enter the password, **Grauer** (the password is case-sensitive), press **Enter**, then click **OK** when the password has been accepted.

- Press **Alt+F11** to reopen the VBA editor, and (if necessary) double click **ThisWorkbook** within the list of Microsoft Excel objects.

- Click at the end of the line defining the ApplicationTitle constant, press **Enter**, then enter the statement to define the **binNormalExit** variable as shown in Figure 14e. (The statement appears initially below the line ending the General Declarations section, but moves above the line when you press Enter.)

- Modify the BeforeClose event procedure to include an If statement that tests the value of the binNormalExit variable as shown in Figure 14e. You must, however, set the value of this variable in the Open Workbook event procedure as described in step 6.

- Save the procedure.

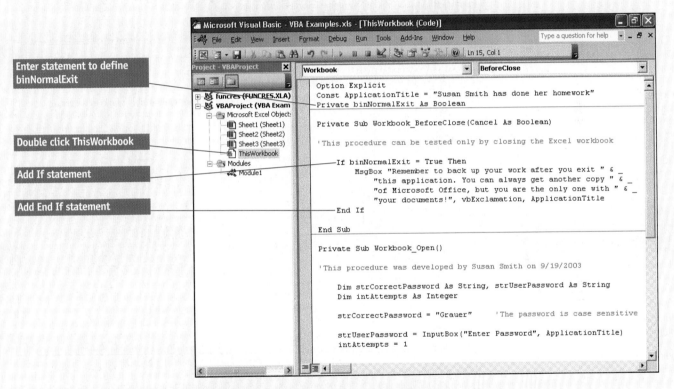

(e) Modify the Before Close Event Procedure (step 5)

FIGURE 14 Hands-on Exercise 4 (*continued*)

SETTING A SWITCH

The use of a switch (binNormalExit, in this example) to control an action within a procedure is a common programming technique. The switch is set to one of two values according to events that occur within the system, then the switch is subsequently tested and the appropriate action is taken. Here, the switch is set when the workbook is opened to indicate either a valid or invalid user. The switch is then tested prior to closing the workbook to determine whether to print the closing message.

Step 6: Modify the Open Workbook Event Procedure

- Scroll down to the Open Workbook event procedure, then modify the If statement to set the value of binNormalExit as shown in Figure 14f:
  - ❑ Take advantage of the Complete Word tool to enter the variable name. Type the first few letters, "**binN**", then press **Ctrl+Space**, and VBA will complete the variable name.
  - ❑ The indentation within the statement is not a requirement of VBA per se, but is used to make the code easier to read. Blank lines are also added for this purpose.
  - ❑ Comments appear throughout the procedure to explain its logic.
  - ❑ Save the modified procedure.

- Click the **Run Sub button**, then enter an incorrect password three times in a row. Once again, you will see the dialog box indicating an invalid password.

- Click **OK**. This time you will not see the message reminding you to back up your workbook. The workbook closes as before.

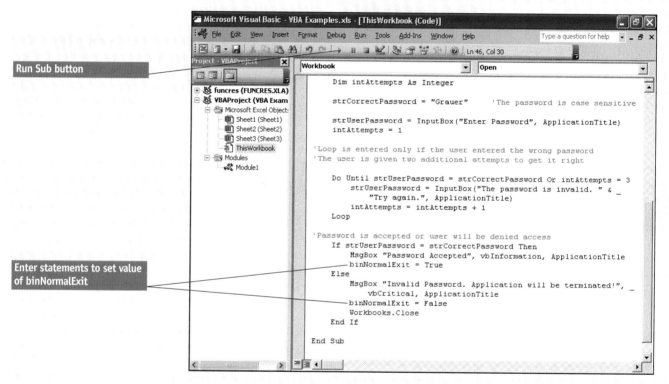

(f) Modify the Open Workbook Event Procedure (step 6)

FIGURE 14 Hands-on Exercise 4 (*continued*)

TEST UNDER ALL CONDITIONS

We cannot overemphasize the importance of thoroughly testing a procedure, and further, testing it under all conditions. VBA statements are powerful, but they are also complex, and a misplaced or omitted character can have dramatic consequences. Test every procedure completely at the time it is created, while the logic of the procedure is fresh in your mind.

Open a Second Workbook

- Reopen the **VBA Examples workbook**. Click the button to **Enable Macros**.

- Enter the password, **Grauer**, then press **Enter**. Click **OK** when you see the second dialog box telling you that the password has been accepted.

- Pull down the **File menu** and click the **Open command** (or click the **Open button** on the Standard toolbar) and open a second workbook. We opened a workbook called **Financial Consultant**, but it does not matter which workbook you open.

- Pull down the **Window menu**, click the **Arrange command**, click the **Horizontal option button**, and click **OK** to tile the workbooks as shown in Figure 14g. The title bars show the names of the open workbooks.

- Pull down the **Tools menu**, click **Macro**, then click **Visual Basic editor**.

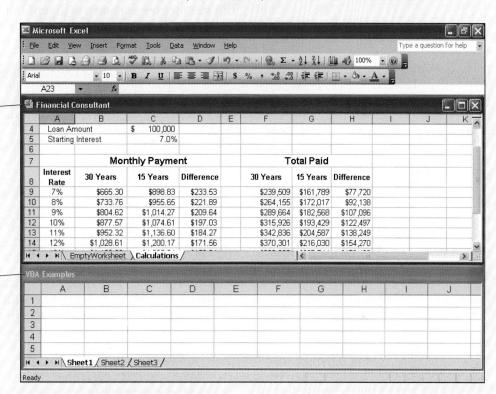

Financial Consultant workbook

VBA Examples workbook

(g) Open a Second Workbook (step 7)

FIGURE 14 Hands-on Exercise 4 (*continued*)

THE COMPARISON IS CASE-SENSITIVE

Any literal comparison (e.g., strInstructorName = "Grauer") is case-sensitive, so that the user has to enter the correct name and case for the condition to be true. A response of "GRAUER" or "grauer", while containing the correct name, will be evaluated as false because the case does not match. You can, however, use the UCase (uppercase) function to convert the user's response to uppercase, and test accordingly. In other words, UCase(strInstructorName) = "GRAUER" will be evaluated as true if the user enters "Grauer" in any combination of upper- or lowercase letters.

Step 8: **Copy the Procedure**

- You should be back in the Visual Basic editor as shown in Figure 14h. Copy the procedures associated with the Open and Close Workbook events from the VBA Examples workbook to the other workbook, Financial Consultant.
  - ❏ Double click **ThisWorkbook** within the list of Microsoft Excel objects under the VBA Examples workbook.
  - ❏ Click and drag to select the definition of the ApplicationTitle constant in the General Declarations section, the binNormalExit definition, plus the two procedures (to open and close the workbook) in their entirety.
  - ❏ Click the **Copy button** on the Standard toolbar.
  - ❏ If necessary, expand the Financial Consultant VBA Project, then double click **ThisWorkbook** with the list of Excel objects under the Financial Consultant workbook. Click underneath the **Option Explicit command**.
  - ❏ Click the **Paste button** on the Standard toolbar. The VBA code should be copied into this module as shown in Figure 14h.

- Click the **Save button** to save the module.

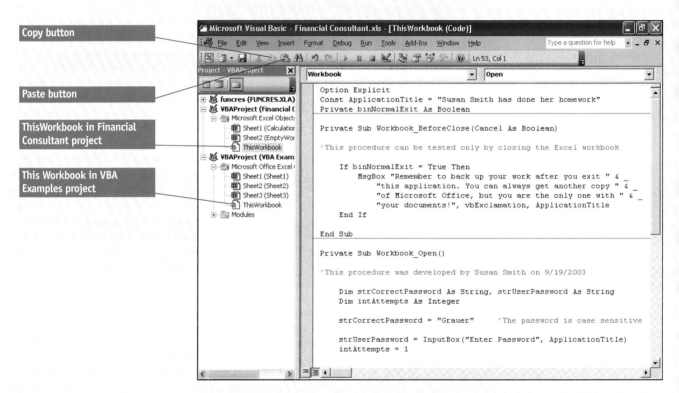

(h) Copy the Procedure (step 8)

FIGURE 14 Hands-on Exercise 4 (*continued*)

THE VISIBLE PROPERTY

The Calculations worksheet sheet should be hidden until the user enters the correct password. This is accomplished by setting the Visible property of the worksheet to false at the beginning of the Open Workbook event procedure, then setting it to true after the correct password has been entered. Click in the Open Workbook event procedure after the last Dim statement, press Enter, then enter the statement Sheet1.Visible = False to hide the Calculations worksheet. Scroll down in the procedure (below the MsgBox statement within the If statement that tests for the correct password), then enter the statement Sheet1.Visible = True followed by the statement Sheet1.Activate to select the worksheet.

Step 9: **Test the Procedure**

- Click the **View Microsoft Excel button** on the Standard toolbar within the VBA window (or click the **Excel button** on the Windows taskbar) to view the Excel workbook. Click in the window containing the Financial Consultant workbook (or whichever workbook you are using), then click the **Maximize button**.

- Pull down the **File menu** and click the **Close command**. (The dialog box in Figure 14i does not appear initially because the value of binNormalExit is not yet set; you have to open the workbook to set the switch.) Click **Yes** if asked whether to save the changes to the workbook.

- Pull down the **File menu** and reopen the workbook. Click the button to **Enable Macros**, then enter **Grauer** when prompted for the password. Click **OK** when the password has been accepted.

- Close this workbook, close the **VBA Examples workbook**, then pull down the **File menu** and click the **Exit command** to quit Excel.

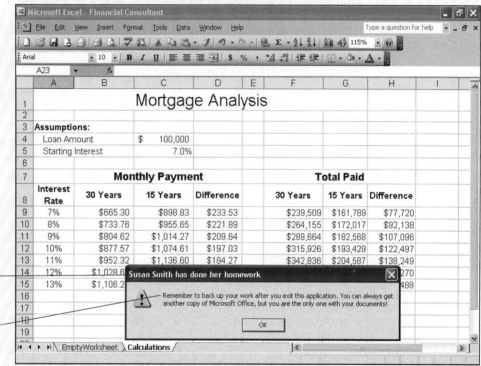

(i) Test the Procedure (step 9)

FIGURE 14 Hands-on Exercise 4 (*continued*)

SCREEN CAPTURE

Prove to your instructor that you have completed the hands-on exercise correctly by capturing a screen, then pasting the screen into a Word document. Do the exercise until you come to the screen that you want to capture, then press the PrintScreen key at the top of the keyboard. Click the Start button, start Word, and open a Word document, then pull down the Edit menu and click the Paste command to bring the captured screen into the Word document. Right click the screen within the Word document, click the Format Picture command, click the Layout tab, and select the Square layout. Click OK to close the dialog box. You can now move and size the screen within the document.

The same VBA procedure can be run from multiple applications in Microsoft Office, despite the fact that the applications are very different. The real power of VBA, however, is its ability to detect events that are unique to a specific application and to respond accordingly. An event is defined as any action that is recognized by an application. Opening or closing an Excel workbook or an Access database is an event. Selecting a worksheet within a workbook is also an event, as is clicking on a command button on an Access form. To use VBA within Microsoft Office, you decide which events are significant, and what is to happen when those events occur. Then you develop the appropriate *event procedures* that execute automatically when the event occurs.

Consider, for example, Figure 15, which displays the results of two event procedures in conjunction with opening and closing an Access database. (These are procedures similar to those we created in the preceding pages in conjunction with opening and closing an Excel workbook.) The procedure associated with Figure 15a displays a message that appears automatically after the user clicks the Switchboard button to exit the database. The procedure is almost trivial to write, and consists of a single MsgBox statement. The effect of the procedure is quite significant, however, as it reminds the user to back up his or her work. Indeed, you can never overemphasize the importance of adequate backup.

The dialog box in Figure 15b prompts the user for a password and appears automatically when the user opens the database. The logic here is more sophisticated in that the underlying procedure contains an InputBox statement to request the password, a Do Until loop that is executed until the user enters the correct password or exceeds the allotted number of attempts, then additional logic to display the switchboard or terminate the application if the user fails to enter the proper password. The procedure is not difficult, however, and it builds on the VBA statements that were covered earlier.

The next hands-on exercise has you create the event procedures that are associated with the database in Figure 15. The exercise references a switchboard, or user interface, that is created as a form within the database. The switchboard displays a menu that enables a nontechnical person to move easily from one object in the database (e.g., a form or report) to another.

The switchboard is created through a utility called the Switchboard Manager that prompts you for each item you want to add to the switchboard, and which action you want taken in conjunction with that menu item. You could do the exercise with any database, but we suggest you use the database we provide to access the switchboard that we created for you. The exercise begins, therefore, by having you download a data disk from our Web site.

EVENT-DRIVEN VERSUS TRADITIONAL PROGRAMMING

A traditional program is executed sequentially, beginning with the first line of code and continuing in order through the remainder of the program. It is the program, not the user, that determines the order in which the statements are executed. VBA, on the other hand, is event-driven, meaning that the order in which the procedures are executed depends on the events that occur. It is the user, rather than the program, that determines which events occur, and consequently which procedures are executed. Each application in Microsoft Office has a different set of objects and associated events that comprise the application's object model.

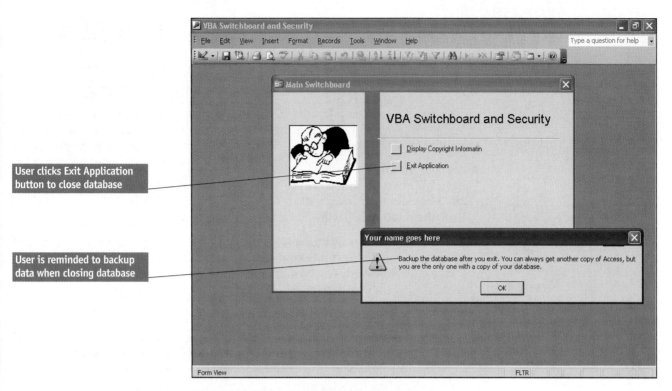

User clicks Exit Application button to close database

User is reminded to backup data when closing database

(a) Reminder to the User (Exit Application event)

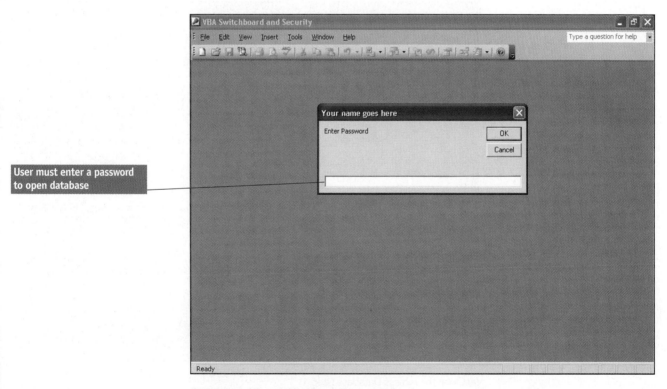

User must enter a password to open database

(b) Password Protection (Open Form event)

FIGURE 15   Event-Driven Programming (Microsoft Access)

Event-Driven Programming (Microsoft Access)

Objective To implement password protection for an Access database; to create a second event procedure that displays a message to the user upon closing the database. Use Figure 16 as a guide in the exercise.

Step 1: **Open the Access Database**

- You can do this exercise with any database, but we suggest you use the database we have provided. Go to **www.prenhall.com/grauer**, click the **Office 2003 book**, which takes you to the Office 2003 home page. Click the **Student Download tab** to go to the Student Download page.

- Scroll until you can click the link for **Getting Started with VBA**. You will see the File Download dialog box asking what you want to do. Click the **Save button** to display the Save As dialog box, then save the file on your desktop.

- Double click the file after it has been downloaded and follow the onscreen instructions to expand the self-extracting file that contains the database.

- Go to the newly created **Exploring VBA folder** and open the **VBA Switchboard and Security database**. Click the **Open button** when you see the security warning. You should see the Database window in Figure 16a.

- Pull down the **Tools menu**, click the **Macro command**, then click the **Visual Basic Editor command**. Maximize the VBA editor window.

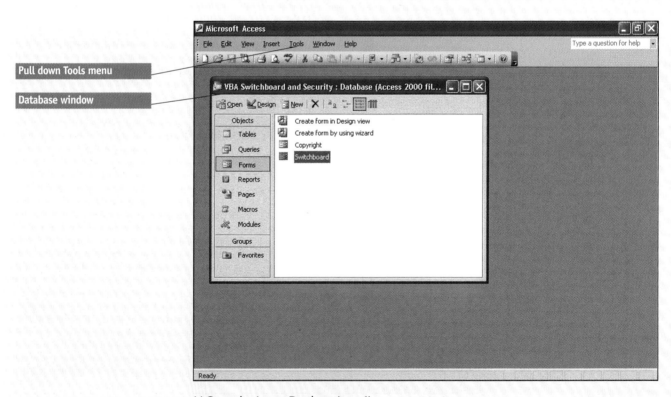

(a) Open the Access Database (step 1)

FIGURE 16 Hands-on Exercise 5

Step 2: Create the ExitDatabase Procedure

- Pull down the **Insert menu** and click **Module** to insert Module1. Complete the **General Declarations section** by adding the Option Explicit statement (if necessary) and the definition of the ApplicationTitle constant as shown in Figure 16b.

- Pull down the **Insert menu** and click **Procedure** to insert a new procedure called **ExitDatabase**. Click the option buttons for a **Sub procedure** and for **Public scope**. Click **OK**.

- Complete the ExitDatabase procedure by entering the **MsgBox** and **DoCmd.Quit** statements. The DoCmd.Quit statement will close Access, but it is entered initially as a comment by beginning the line with an apostrophe.

- Click anywhere in the procedure, then click the **Run Sub button** to test the procedure. Correct any errors that occur, then when the MsgBox displays correctly, **delete the apostrophe** in front of the DoCmd.Quit statement.

- Save the module. The next time you execute the procedure, you should see the message box you just created, and then Access will be terminated.

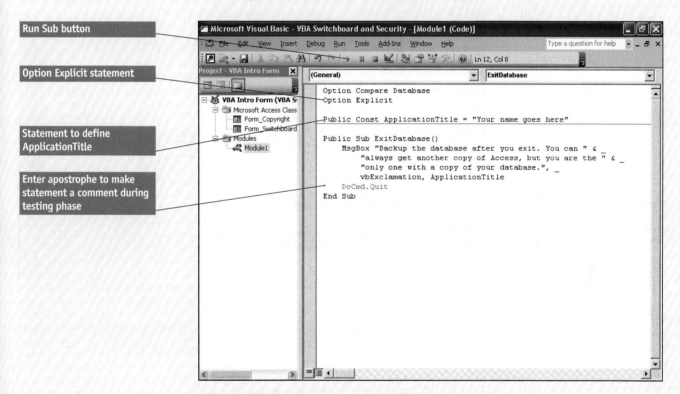

(b) Create the ExitDatabase Procedure (step 2)

FIGURE 16   Hands-on Exercise 5 (*continued*)

CREATE A PUBLIC CONSTANT

Give your application a customized look by adding your name or other identifying message to the title bar of the message and/or input boxes that you use. You can add the information individually to each statement, but it is easier to declare a public constant from within a general module. That way, you can change the value of the constant in one place and have the change reflected automatically throughout your application.

Step 3: Modify the Switchboard

- Click the **View Microsoft Access button** on the Standard toolbar within the VBA window to switch to the Database window (or use the **F11** keyboard shortcut).

- Pull down the **Tools menu**, click the **Database Utilities command**, then choose **Switchboard Manager** to display the Switchboard Manager dialog box in Figure 16c.

- Click the **Edit button** to edit the Main Switchboard and display the Edit Switchboard Page dialog box. Select the **&Exit Application command** and click its **Edit button** to display the Edit Switchboard Item dialog box.

- Change the command to **Run Code**. Enter **ExitDatabase** in the Function Name text box. Click **OK**, then close the two other dialog boxes.

- The switchboard has been modified so that clicking the Exit button will run the VBA procedure you just created.

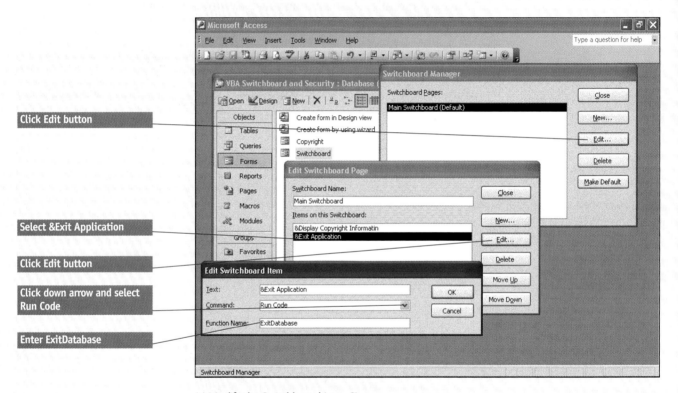

Click Edit button

Select &Exit Application

Click Edit button

Click down arrow and select Run Code

Enter ExitDatabase

(c) Modify the Switchboard (step 3)

FIGURE 16 Hands-on Exercise 5 (*continued*)

CREATE A KEYBOARD SHORTCUT

The & has special significance when used within the name of an Access object because it creates a keyboard shortcut to that object. Enter "&Exit Application", for example, and the letter E (the letter immediately after the ampersand) will be underlined and appear as "Exit Application" on the switchboard. From there, you can execute the item by clicking its button, or you can use the Alt+E keyboard shortcut (where "E" is the underlined letter in the menu option).

Step 4: Test the Switchboard

- If necessary, click the **Forms button** in the Database window. Double click the **Switchboard form** to open the switchboard as shown in Figure 16d. The switchboard contains two commands.

- Click the **Display Copyright Information command** to display a form that we use with all our databases. (You can open this form in Design view and modify the text to include your name, rather than ours. If you do, be sure to save the modified form, then close it.)

- Click the **Exit Application command** (or use the **Alt+E** keyboard shortcut). You should see the dialog box in Figure 16d, corresponding to the MsgBox statement you created earlier. Click **OK** to close the dialog box.

- Access itself will terminate because of the DoCmd.Quit statement within the ExitDatabase procedure. (If this does not happen, return to the VBA editor and remove the apostrophe in front of the DoCmd statement.)

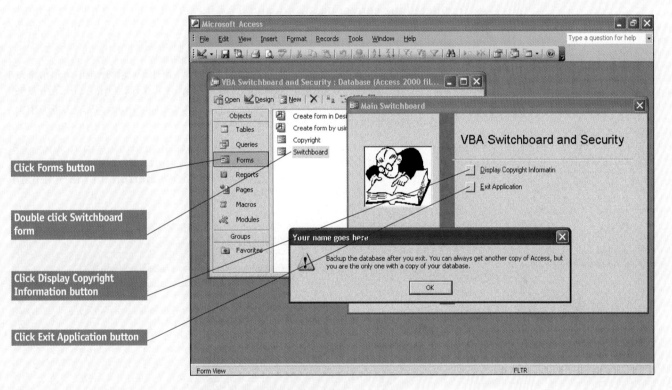

(d) Test the Switchboard (step 4)

FIGURE 16   Hands-on Exercise 5 (*continued*)

BACK UP IMPORTANT FILES

It's not a question of *if* it will happen, but *when*—hard disks die, files are lost, or viruses may infect a system. It has happened to us, and it will happen to you, but you can prepare for the inevitable by creating adequate backup before the problem occurs. The essence of a backup strategy is to decide which files to back up (your data), how often to do the backup (whenever it changes), and where to keep the backup (away from your computer). Do it!

Step 5: Complete the Open Form Event Procedure

- Start Access and reopen the **VBA Switchboard and Security database**. Press **Alt+F11** to start the VBA editor.

- Click the **plus sign** next to Microsoft Office Access Class objects, double click the module called **Form_Switchboard**, then look for the partially completed **Form_Open procedure** as shown in Figure 16e.

- The procedure was created automatically by the Switchboard Manager. You must, however, expand this procedure to include password protection. Note the following:
  - ❏ Three variables are required—the correct password, the password entered by the user, and the number of attempts.
  - ❏ The user is prompted for the password, and the number of attempts is set to 1. The user is given two additional attempts, if necessary, to get the correct password.
  - ❏ The If statement at the end of the loop determines whether the user has entered the correct password, and if so, it executes the original commands that are associated with the switchboard. If, however, the user fails to supply the correct password, an invalid password message is displayed and the **DoCmd.Quit** statement terminates the application.
  - ❏ We suggest you place an **apostrophe** in front of the statement initially so that it becomes a comment, and thus it is not executed. Once you are sure that you can enter the correct password, you can remove the apostrophe and implement the password protection.

- Save the procedure. You cannot test this procedure from within the VBA window; you must cause the event to happen (i.e., open the form) for the procedure to execute. Click the **View Microsoft Access button** on the Standard toolbar to return to the Database window.

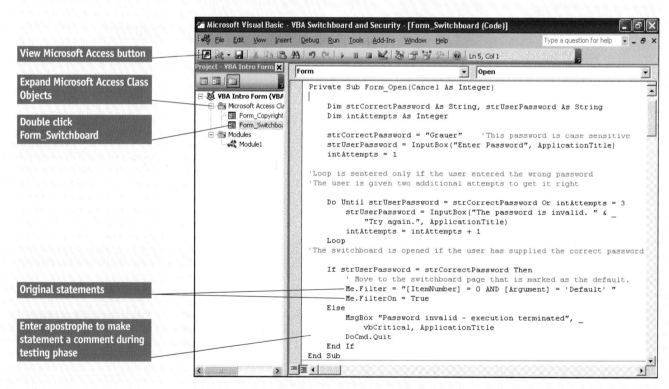

(e) Complete the Open Form Event Procedure (step 5)

FIGURE 16 Hands-on Exercise 5 (*continued*)

Step 6:   Test the Procedure

■ Close all open windows within the Access database except for the Database window. Click the **Forms button**, then double click the **Switchboard form**.

■ You should be prompted for the password as shown in Figure 16f. The password (in our procedure) is **Grauer**.

■ Test the procedure repeatedly to include all possibilities. Enter the correct password on the first, second, and third attempts to be sure that the procedure works as intended. Each time you enter the correct password, you will have to close the switchboard, then reopen it.

■ Test the procedure one final time, by failing to enter the correct password. You will see a message box indicating that the password is invalid and that execution will be terminated. Termination will not take place, however, because the DoCmd.Quit statement is currently entered as a comment.

■ Press **Alt+F11** to reopen the VBA editor. Open the **Microsoft Access Class Objects folder** and double click on **Form_Switchboard**. Delete the apostrophe in front of the DoCmd.Quit statement. The text of the statement changes from green to black to indicate that it is an executable statement. Save the procedure.

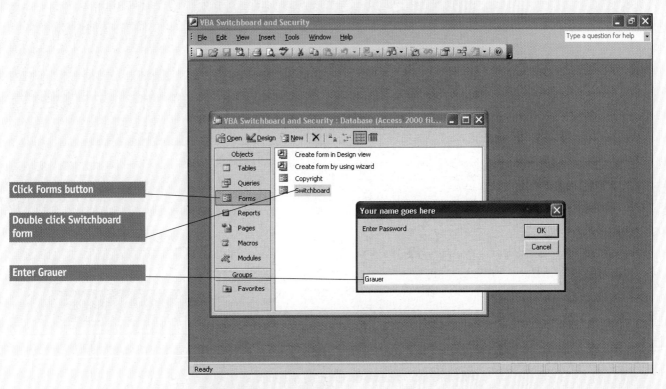

(f) Test the Procedure (step 6)

FIGURE 16   Hands-on Exercise 5 (*continued*)

TOGGLE COMMENTS ON AND OFF

Comments are used primarily to explain the purpose of VBA statements, but they can also be used to "comment out" code as distinct from deleting the statement altogether. Thus, you can add or remove the apostrophe in front of the statement, to toggle the comment on or off.

Step 7:   Change the Startup Properties

■ Click the **View Microsoft Access button** on the VBA Standard toolbar to return to the Database window.

■ Close all open windows except the Database window. Pull down the **Tools menu** and click **Startup** to display the Startup dialog box as shown in Figure 16g.

■ Click in the **Application Title** text box and enter the title of the application, **VBA Switchboard and Security** in this example.

■ Click the **drop-down arrow** in the Display Form/Page list box and select the **Switchboard form** as the form that will open automatically in conjunction with opening the database.

■ Clear the check box to display the Database window. Click **OK** to accept the settings and close the dialog box.

■ The next time you open the database, the switchboard should open automatically, which in turn triggers the Open Form event procedure that will prompt the user to enter a password.

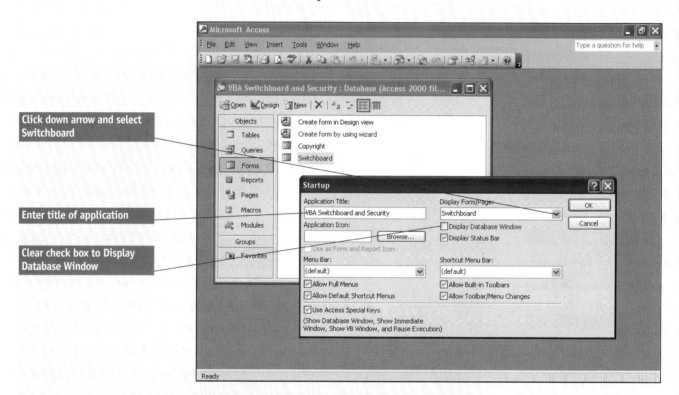

Click down arrow and select Switchboard

Enter title of application

Clear check box to Display Database Window

(g) Change the Startup Properties (step 7)

FIGURE 16   Hands-on Exercise 5 (*continued*)

HIDE THE DATABASE WINDOW

Use the Startup property to hide the Database window from the novice user. You avoid confusion and you may prevent the novice from accidentally deleting objects in the database. Of course, anyone with some knowledge of Access can restore the Database window by pulling down the Window menu, clicking the Unhide command, then selecting the Database window from the associated dialog box. Nevertheless, hiding the Database window is a good beginning.

Step 8: **Test the Database**

- Close the database, then reopen the database to test the procedures we have created in this exercise. The sequence of events is as follows:
  - ❏ The database is loaded and the switchboard is opened but is not yet visible. The Open Form procedure for the switchboard is executed, and you are prompted for the password as shown in Figure 16h.
  - ❏ The password is entered correctly and the switchboard is displayed. The Database window is hidden, however, because the Startup Properties have been modified.

- Click the **Exit Application command** (or use the **Alt+E** keyboard shortcut). You will see the message box reminding you to back up the system, after which the database is closed and Access is terminated.

- Reopen the database. This time, however, you are to enter the wrong password three times in a row. You should see a message indicating that the execution was terminated due to an invalid password.

- Testing is complete and you can go on to add the other objects to your Access database. Congratulations on a job well done.

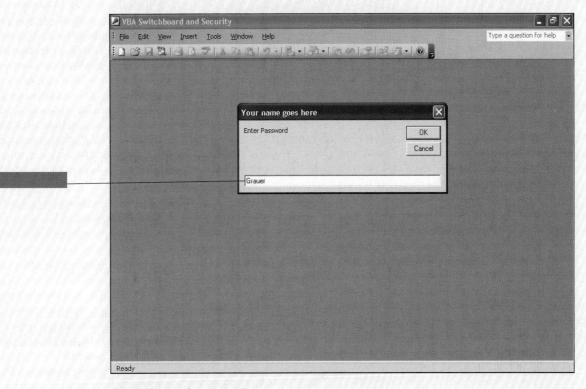

Enter password

(h) Test the Database (step 8)

FIGURE 16 Hands-on Exercise 5 (*continued*)

RESTORING HIDDEN MENUS AND TOOLBARS

You can use the Startup property to hide menus and/or toolbars from the user by clearing the respective check boxes. A word of caution, however—once the menus are hidden, it is difficult to get them back. Start Access, pull down the File menu, and click Open to display the Open dialog box, select the database to open, then press and hold the Shift key when you click the Open button. This powerful technique is not widely known.

SUMMARY

Visual Basic for Applications (VBA) is a powerful programming language that is accessible from all major applications in Microsoft Office XP. A VBA statement accomplishes a specific task such as displaying a message to the user or accepting input from the user. Statements are grouped into procedures, and procedures in turn are grouped into modules. Every procedure is classified as either private or public.

The MsgBox statement displays information to the user. It has one required argument, which is the message (or prompt) that is displayed to the user. The other two arguments—the icon that is to be displayed in the dialog box and the text of the title bar—are optional. The InputBox function displays a prompt to the user requesting information, then it stores that information (the value returned by the user) for use later in the procedure.

Every variable must be declared (defined) before it can be used. This is accomplished through the Dim (short for Dimension) statement that appears at the beginning of a procedure. The Dim statement indicates the name of the variable and its type (for example, whether it will hold a character string or an integer number), which in turn reserves the appropriate amount of memory for that variable.

The ability to make decisions within a procedure, then branch to alternative sets of statements is implemented through the If . . . Then . . . Else or Case statements. The Else clause is optional, but may be repeated multiple times within an If statement. The Case statement is preferable to an If statement with multiple Else clauses.

The For . . . Next statement (or For . . . Next loop as it is also called) executes all statements between the words For and Next a specified number of times, using a counter to keep track of the number of times the loop is executed. The Do . . . Loop Until and/or Do Until . . . Loop statements are used when the number of times through the loop is not known in advance.

VBA is different from traditional programming languages in that it is event-driven. An event is defined as any action that is recognized by an application, such as Excel or Access. Opening or closing an Excel workbook or an Access database is an event. Selecting a worksheet within a workbook is also an event, as is clicking on a command button on an Access form. To use VBA within Microsoft Office, you decide which events are significant, and what is to happen when those events occur. Then you develop the appropriate event procedures.

KEY TERMS

MULTIPLE CHOICE

1. Which of the following applications in Office XP has access to VBA?

   (a) Word
   (b) Excel
   (c) Access
   (d) All of the above

2. Which of the following is a valid name for a VBA variable?

   (a) Public
   (b) Private
   (c) strUserFirstName
   (d) int Count Of Attempts

3. Which of the following is true about an If statement?

   (a) It evaluates a condition as either true or false, then executes the statement(s) following the keyword "Then" if the condition is true
   (b) It must contain the keyword Else
   (c) It must contain one or more ElseIf statements
   (d) All of the above

4. Which of the following lists the items from smallest to largest?

   (a) Module, procedure, statement
   (b) Statement, module, procedure
   (c) Statement, procedure, module
   (d) Procedure, module, statement

5. Given the statement, MsgBox "Welcome to VBA", "Bob was here", which of the following is true?

   (a) "Welcome to VBA" will be displayed within the resulting message box
   (b) "Welcome to VBA" will appear on the title bar of the displayed dialog box
   (c) The two adjacent commas will cause a compilation error
   (d) An informational icon will be displayed with the message

6. Where are the VBA procedures associated with an Office document stored?

   (a) In the same folder, but in a separate file
   (b) In the Office document itself
   (c) In a special VBA folder on drive C
   (d) In a special VBA folder on the local area network

7. The Debug.Print statement is associated with the:

   (a) Locals window
   (b) Immediate window
   (c) Project Explorer
   (d) Debug toolbar

8. Which of the following is the proper sequence of arguments for the MsgBox statement?

   (a) Text for the title bar, prompt, button
   (b) Prompt, button, text for the title bar
   (c) Prompt, text for the title bar, button
   (d) Button, prompt, text for the title bar

9. Which of the following is a true statement about Do loops?

   (a) Placing the Until clause at the beginning of the loop tests the condition prior to executing any statements in the loop
   (b) Placing the Until clause at the end of the loop executes the statements in the loop, then it tests the condition
   (c) Both (a) and (b)
   (d) Neither (a) nor (b)

10. Given the statement, For intCount = 1 to 10 Step 3, how many times will the statements in the loop be executed (assuming that there are no statements in the loop to terminate the execution)?

    (a) 10
    (b) 4
    (c) 3
    (d) Impossible to determine

... continued

11. Which of the following is a *false* statement?

    (a) A dash at the end of a line indicates continuation

    (b) An ampersand indicates concatenation

    (c) An apostrophe at the beginning of a line signifies a comment

    (d) A pair of quotation marks denotes a character string

12. What is the effect of deleting the apostrophe that appears at the beginning of a VBA statement?

    (a) A compilation error will occur

    (b) The statement is converted to a comment

    (c) The color of the statement will change from black to green

    (d) The statement is made executable

13. Which of the following If statements will display the indicated message if the user enters a response other than "Grauer" (assuming that "Grauer" is the correct password)?

    (a) If strUserResponse <> "Grauer" Then MsgBox "Wrong password"

    (b) If strUserResponse = "Grauer" Then MsgBox "Wrong password"

    (c) If strUserResponse > "Grauer" Then MsgBox "Wrong password"

    (d) If strUserResponse < "Grauer" Then MsgBox "Wrong password"

14. Which of the following will execute the statements in the loop at least once?

    (a) Do . . . Loop Until

    (b) Do Until ..... Loop

    (c) Both (a) and (b)

    (d) Neither (a) nor (b)

15. The copy and paste commands can be used to:

    (a) Copy statements within a procedure

    (b) Copy statements from a procedure in one module to a procedure in another module within the same document

    (c) Copy statements from a module in an Excel workbook to a module in an Access database

    (d) All of the above

16. Which of the following is true about indented text in a VBA procedure?

    (a) The indented text is always executed first

    (b) The indented text is always executed last

    (c) The indented text is rendered a comment and is never executed

    (d) None of the above

17. Which statement will prompt the user to enter his or her name and store the result in a variable called strUser?

    (a) InputBox.strUser

    (b) strUser = MsgBox("Enter your name")

    (c) strUser = InputBox("Enter your name")

    (d) InputBox("Enter strUser")

18. Given that strUser is currently set to "George", the expression "Good morning, strName" will return:

    (a) Good morning, George

    (b) Good morning, strName

    (c) Good morning George

    (d) Good morning strName

ANSWERS

1. d	7. b	13. a
2. c	8. b	14. a
3. a	9. c	15. d
4. c	10. b	16. d
5. a	11. a	17. c
6. b	12. d	18. b

Index

MULTIPLE CHOICE

1. Which of the following is true regarding a dialog box?

   (a) Option buttons indicate mutually exclusive choices

   (b) Check boxes imply that multiple options may be selected

   (c) Both (a) and (b)

   (d) Neither (a) nor (b)

2. Which of the following is the first step in sizing a window?

   (a) Point to the title bar

   (b) Pull down the View menu to display the toolbar

   (c) Point to any corner or border

   (d) Pull down the View menu and change to large icons

3. Which of the following is the first step in moving a window?

   (a) Point to the title bar

   (b) Pull down the View menu to display the toolbar

   (c) Point to any corner or border

   (d) Pull down the View menu and change to large icons

4. Which button appears immediately after a window has been maximized?

   (a) The Close button

   (b) The Minimize button

   (c) The Maximize button

   (d) The Restore button

5. What happens to a window that has been minimized?

   (a) The window is still visible but it no longer has a Minimize button

   (b) The window shrinks to a button on the taskbar

   (c) The window is closed and the application is removed from memory

   (d) The window is still open but the application has been removed from memory

6. What is the significance of a faded (dimmed) command in a pull-down menu?

   (a) The command is not currently accessible

   (b) A dialog box appears if the command is selected

   (c) A Help window appears if the command is selected

   (d) There are no equivalent keystrokes for the particular command

7. The Recycle Bin enables you to restore a file that was deleted from

   (a) Drive A

   (b) Drive C

   (c) Both (a) and (b)

   (d) Neither (a) nor (b)

8. Which of the following was suggested as essential to a backup strategy?

   (a) Back up all program files at the end of every session

   (b) Store backup files at another location

   (c) Both (a) and (b)

   (d) Neither (a) nor (b)

9. A shortcut may be created for

   (a) An application or a document

   (b) A folder or a drive

   (c) Both (a) and (b)

   (d) Neither (a) nor (b)

10. What happens if you click the Folders button (on the Standard Buttons toolbar in the My Computer folder) twice in a row?

    (a) The left pane displays a task pane with commands for the selected object

    (b) The left pane displays a hierarchical view of the devices on your system

    (c) The left pane displays either a task pane or the hierarchical view depending on what was displayed prior to clicking the button initially

    (d) The left pane displays both the task pane and a hierarchical view

... continued

multiple choice

11. The Search Companion can

    (a) Locate all files containing a specified phrase
    (b) Restrict its search to a specified set of folders
    (c) Both (a) and (b)
    (d) Neither (a) nor (b)

12. Which views display miniature images of photographs within a folder?

    (a) Tiles view and Icons view
    (b) Thumbnails view and Filmstrip view
    (c) Details view and List view
    (d) All views display a miniature image

13. Which of the following statements is true?

    (a) A plus sign next to a folder indicates that its contents are hidden
    (b) A minus sign next to a folder indicates that its contents are hidden
    (c) A plus sign appears next to any folder that has been expanded
    (d) A minus sign appears next to any folder that has been collapsed

14. Ben and Jessica are both registered users on a Windows XP computer. Which of the following is a *false statement* regarding their personal folders?

    (a) Ben and Jessica each have a My Documents folder
    (b) Ben and Jessica each have a My Pictures folder that is stored within their respective My Documents folders
    (c) Ben can access files in Jessica's My Documents folder
    (d) Jessica cannot access files in Ben's My Documents folder

15. When is a file permanently deleted?

    (a) When you delete the file from Windows Explorer
    (b) When you empty the Recycle Bin
    (c) When you turn the computer off
    (d) All of the above

16. What happens if you (left) click and drag a file to another folder on the same drive?

    (a) The file is copied
    (b) The file is moved
    (c) The file is deleted
    (d) A shortcut menu is displayed

17. How do you shut down the computer?

    (a) Click the Start button, then click the Turn Off Computer command
    (b) Right click the Start button, then click the Turn Off Computer command
    (c) Click the End button, then click the Turn Off Computer command
    (d) Right click the End button, then click the Turn Off Computer command

18. Which of the following can be accomplished with Windows Messenger?

    (a) You can chat with up to three other people in the conversation window
    (b) You can place telephone calls (if you have a microphone and speaker) without paying long-distance charges
    (c) You can ask for remote assistance, which enables your contact to view your screen as you are working
    (d) All of the above

ANSWERS

1. c	7. b	13. a
2. c	8. b	14. c
3. a	9. c	15. b
4. d	10. c	16. b
5. b	11. c	17. a
6. a	12. b	18. d